Capital Budgeting

Custom Edition For Suffolk University

Neil Seitz | Mitch Ellison

Capital Budgeting: Custom Edition For Suffolk University

Neil Seitz | Mitch Ellison

Senior Project Development Manager:
Linda deStefano

Market Development Manager:
Heather Kramer

Senior Production/Manufacturing Manager:
Donna M. Brown

Production Editorial Manager:
Kim Fry

Sr. Rights Acquisition Account Manager:
Todd Osborne

For product information and technology assistance, contact us at
Cengage Learning Customer & Sales Support, 1-800-354-9706

For permission to use material from this text or product,
submit all requests online at **cengage.com/permissions**
Further permissions questions can be emailed to
permissionrequest@cengage.com

This book contains select works from existing Cengage Learning resources and was produced by Cengage Learning Custom Solutions for collegiate use. As such, those adopting and/or contributing to this work are responsible for editorial content accuracy, continuity and completeness.

ISBN-13: 978-1-305-00605-8

ISBN-10: 1-305-00605-4

Cengage Learning
5191 Natorp Boulevard
Mason, Ohio 45040
USA

Cengage Learning is a leading provider of customized learning solutions with office locations around the globe, including Singapore, the United Kingdom, Australia, Mexico, Brazil, and Japan. Locate your local office at:
international.cengage.com/region.

Cengage Learning products are represented in Canada by Nelson Education, Ltd.
For your lifelong learning solutions, visit **www.cengage.com/custom.**
Visit our corporate website at **www.cengage.com.**

Printed in the United States of America

Brief Contents

Strategy and Value

PART ONE

The financial decisions of the firm begin with the choice of a business strategy designed to create value. The strategy is then implemented by making investments—by committing resources to particular courses of action. The investment decisions are the primary source of risk, and risk must be considered in the investment selection process. Investments require money, so they also result in financing needs. Financing costs and, therefore, the return that must be earned on an investment depend on the types of investments, including the riskiness of those investments. The figure below summarizes those relationships. Chapters 1 through 4 focus on the first box, strategy and goals, with particular emphasis on how value is created and measured as well as how value is related to strategy. Chapter 1 provides a general overview of the financial decisions faced by the firm, as well as the linkage between values, strategy, and financial decisions. Chapter 2 deals with strategy in more detail because strategy is the basis for value. Chapter 3 introduces time value of money, the basis for understanding value. Chapter 4 applies time value principles to the valuation of companies and specific assets. These four chapters lay the foundation for capital investment choice, risk analysis, and financial structure choice.

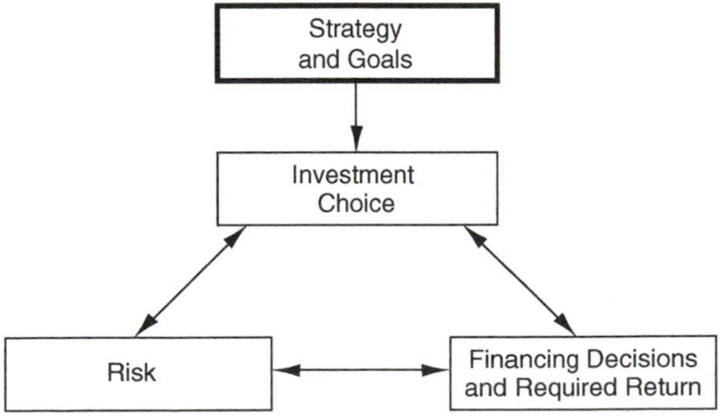

CHAPTER 1

Long-Term Investing and Financial Decisions

After completing this chapter you should be able to:

- Describe why capital budgeting and appropriate financing is important to the firm, to society, and to you personally in your career or private life.
- Discuss the merits of wealth maximization versus the other goals of the firm.
- Identify the different parties that benefit from optimal capital budgeting and financing decisions.
- Explain current business events in relation to the parties that benefit and the parties that may have lost in a particular event.
- Recognize and discuss the sources of competitive advantage.
- List and describe the importance of the steps involved in the capital investment process.
- Describe the variables important in planning the long-term financing of the firm.

Imagine yourself in the enviable, yet daunting, position of Lee Scott, President and Chief Executive of Wal-Mart. With over $200 billion in sales; operations in the United States, Latin America, Europe, and Asia; and more than 1,000,000 associates to manage he has a lot of responsibility. As a guidepost, he relies heavily on the principles and wisdom of Sam Walton, the founder of Wal-Mart. These principles include: treat all of your stakeholders with respect, always provide excellent service to the customer, and strive for excellence in everything that you attempt.

In serving the customer stakeholder, Wal-Mart does not charge what the "market would bear" but instead maintains a policy of pricing at 30 percent above cost and then religiously tries to bring cost down. Its consistent appearance on the *Fortune* list of "America's Most Admired Companies" is evidence of the importance placed on the employee and management stakeholders. The societal and government stakeholders benefit from the lower prices, the large number of people employed, the annual $2 billion in tax receipts, and the large donations to various charities. The merchandise and capital supplier stakeholders have seen tremendous rewards too. For example, a shareholder who purchased $10 in Wal-Mart stock in 1973 would see the value increase to over $8,000 thirty years later. To continue this service to the stakeholders, Wal-Mart annually commits billions to new store capital projects in the United States and internationally. In addition, it is increasing its international presence with the acquisition and "turning around" of lesser international players.

Lee Scott's role at Wal-Mart represents the types of decisions faced by all leaders. Every leader must (1) establish a vision, (2) accumulate resources to realize that vision, and (3) deploy resources to realize that vision. The vision is a general description of how the company will position itself to offer to customers something with value in excess of cost. Business leaders establish and seek realization of a vision because they believe that it will allow their company to compete effectively for customers and resources, both surviving and prospering in the long run. They believe that jumping from one seemingly attractive opportunity to the next without a clear vision as a compass is a formula for eventual failure. They seek a vision not as an alternative to profitability, but because they believe it is the surest route to profitability in the long run.

Finance is not a sideshow to the activities of leaders; it is an integral part of the action in the center ring. The vision itself must be justified in financial terms: Do the expected benefits exceed the cost of resources used? The fundamental resource that must be accumulated is money, because you can buy other resources if you are able to attract money from investors. Every use of resources must be thought of as an investment. To be judged attractive, an investment must typically meet three tests: (1) Does it contribute to the vision? (2) Will it provide enough benefits to satisfy the investors who furnished the money? (3) Is the investment at an acceptable level of risk? The two primary functions of financial management, *arranging funding* and help in *selecting investments* of those funds, are clearly central to the responsibilities of business leaders.

Financial management is not limited to the CEO or a few wizards in the back room. Whether you are an engineer, an advertising manager, or a human resource specialist, you will allocate resources, and thus make investment decisions, every day. Most managers participate at least occasionally in decisions about investments that require years to pay off fully. Many managers will someday participate in that watershed strategic investment decision that determines the success or failure of their company. To make those investments, the company must design financing that fits the investments and that meets the objectives of investors. As evidenced by Wal-Mart's expansion into Mexico, Great Britain, Germany, and Japan, the investment, financing, and sale of resulting products increasingly occurs in world markets. This book is about how to make those investment and financing decisions.

CENTRAL ROLE OF WEALTH MAXIMIZATION

The purpose of this book is to help current and prospective managers make better investment and financing decisions. If a choice is better, it must be better by some standard. Otherwise, one alternative is as good as the next. That standard is **wealth maximization.**

An action increases wealth if the benefits gained exceed the benefits expended. We will measure benefits primarily as money gained and given up. Money is a uniquely convenient benefit because we can exchange it for virtually any other product. To supplement the general focus on money, we will take a few side trips to deal with benefits that cannot be measured entirely in dollar values, such as healthy babies.

The wealth criterion is so general that it fits a vast range of decisions. In single-period business decisions, wealth is created if cash inflow exceeds cash outflow by more than we would have earned by investing our money somewhere else during that period. In Economics 101, this wealth creation was called **economic profit.** Figure 1-1 illustrates a typical calculation of economic profit. In multi-period decisions, the **present value** of an expected future cash flow is the amount that must be invested elsewhere, at the same risk, to generate the same expected cash flow. The **net present value** of an investment or course of action is the present value of all cash inflows, minus the present value of all cash outflows. Thus, net present value is the economic profit or wealth created by a multi-period investment. Companies develop strategies, goals, and visions so they will be in a position to create economic profit and wealth. Figure 1-2 uses a celebrity endorsement example to illustrate the calculation of a net present value.

Some considerations that immediately seem to create conflicts with the wealth maximization goal are actually ways to implement the wealth maximization goal. Business leaders develop and work toward visions as the most likely method of achieving long-term wealth creation, not as an alternative to wealth creation. When we discuss competitive advantage and strategy, these are again methods of creating wealth. Financing alternatives are also analyzed in the context of wealth creation.

Risk is inherent in most business decisions, and consideration of risk is part of the process of making wealth-maximizing choices. We are, after all, making decisions about future costs and benefits. We are seldom certain about future events. Investors require higher expected returns as compensation for taking on additional risk. If $60 invested in a bank account would grow to $100 in ten years, the present value of a **certain** $100 ten years from today would be $60. Suppose, on the other hand, there is a highly uncertain payoff in 10 years, which could be $0 or $200 with equal probability. The present value in this case might be as low as $30, or even less, depending on investor attitudes toward risk at that particular time. Risk and the appropriate management of this risk is

FIGURE 1-1 Calculating an Economic Profit

This figure shows the calculation of an economic profit for a company with $500,000 in assets, a risk level requiring a 10 percent cost of funds, revenues of $250,000, expenses of $120,000, and taxes of $45,000.

Revenues	$250,000
Expenses	$120,000
Taxable income	$130,000
Taxes	$45,000
After tax accounting income	$85,000
Requires return*	$50,000
Economic profit	$35,000

*Required return is the asset base of $500,000 times the risk weighted cost of funding of 10 percent.

Economic profit is a single period measure of wealth created because it includes not only the revenues and expense but also the risk and assets employed.

FIGURE 1-2 Calculating a Net Present Value

This figure shows the calculation of a net present value for a project. You can purchase the endorsement of a famous athlete for the next 3 years for $400,000. Your marketing department believes that this endorsement will increase sales by $500,000 per year for 3 years. Your variable costs (costs that vary directly with sales) are 20%, additional fixed costs are $75,000 per year, and taxes are 40%.

	Year 1	Year 2	Year 3
Additional revenues	$500,000	$500,000	$500,000
Variable expenses	$100,000	$100,000	$100,000
Fixed expenses	$75,000	$75,000	$75,000
Taxable income	$325,000	$325,000	$325,000
Taxes	$130,000	$130,000	$130,000
After tax accounting income	$195,000	$195,000	$195,000
Present value interest factor*	.9091	.8264	.7513
Present value	$177,275	$161,148	$146,504
Total present value of cash benefits	$484,926		
Cost of the endorsement	$400,000		
Net present value of this project	$84,926		

*Present value interest factor is the value of $1 received at the end of each year respectively using a 10% cost of funds.

Net present value is a multi-period measure of wealth created because it includes not only the revenues and expense but also considers the risk and level of assets employed. Much more will be said about this later in the book.

such an important consideration that we give it five chapters of explicit coverage in this book: Chapters 11 through 15.

The wealth standard applies equally well to the financing decisions of the firm. Financing arrangements that decrease tax liabilities or minimize transaction costs of financing can increase wealth by leaving more money available after providing investors their required return. A financing arrangement that more appropriately manages risk for the investors can decrease the return they require, and can therefore create wealth by leaving more money available after providing them with their required return.

WHO BENEFITS FROM WEALTH MAXIMIZATION?

Stakeholders are parties who share in the results of business or nonprofit organization activity. The corporation serves as a framework for bringing together the money or labor of numerous stakeholders to create products that meet the needs of other stakeholders who, in turn, provide revenue that is used to pay the stakeholders providing money and labor. We discuss the interests of these various stakeholders in relation to the wealth maximization objective.

Owners

Shareholder (owner) wealth maximization is the most common answer when we ask whose wealth is to be maximized. In fact, finance textbook authors routinely assume that shareholder wealth maximization is the dominant goal of the firm, if not the only goal. As an example of the importance of shareholders, the inside covers of many annual reports contain the words Maximizing Shareholder Wealth and graphs of the annual return on equity, or an economic profits calculation such as EVA[1] (economic value added).

Reasons cited for use of the shareholder wealth maximization goal include both the ethical standards and self-interests of managers. It is frequently argued that maximization of shareholder wealth is the professional responsibility of managers because they are legally the agents of the shareholders. Lawyers, real estate brokers, and stockbrokers are but a few of the professionals who are required by both law and standards of their profession to act on behalf of their principals, subject to other ethical constraints such as the requirement that they behave honestly and legally when dealing with others. Thus, a belief that you as a manager have ethical obligations toward the stockholders would not seem far-fetched.

The net present value of an investment is the amount by which the investment increases the current wealth of the shareholders. We would expect an increase in the value of the company's stock equal to the net present value when an unanticipated capital investment is announced, unless investors expect managers to use part of the investment's future cash flows for something that is not

---

[1] EVA, a registered trademark of Stern Steward Consulting, is a popular method or calculating economic profit or residual income. The actual mechanics of calculating an economic profit will be discussed in Chapter 2.

in the best interests of the shareholders. If competing projects are being considered, the combination that increases total net present value the most will maximize the wealth of the owners. If the present value of the benefits from an investment does not exceed the present value of the outlays, the owners would be better off to pass up the opportunity and invest their money outside the firm.[2]

Managers

Some observers base their analysis on the assumption that **management welfare maximization** is the dominant business goal. Belief in this goal follows from the assumption that managers, like everyone else, are interested in their own welfare. In perfect competition, managers must maximize wealth just to survive. But in the absence of perfect competition, managers have some leeway and may decide to act in their own self-interest. Stockholders are not privy to every decision made by managers, and attempts to closely monitor managers involve costs in terms of both time and money.

Managers have several interests that may conflict with those of shareholders. Managers are frequently accused of preferring size over profitability, partly because compensation is related to size, and therefore making some investments that cannot be justified in terms of shareholder wealth maximization. Managers may also be tempted to consume excessive perquisites, such as luxury offices and golden parachutes.[3] Finally, managers may have different attitudes toward risk.

Different attitudes toward risk are particularly difficult to deal with because they are often difficult to observe and can often be observed only well after irreversible results. One problem occurs when the personal wealth of a manager consists primarily of human capital and company stock, both of which are affected by the company's performance. Because many managers have all their eggs in one basket, they may be more risk-averse than shareholders. Another problem occurs when the wealth of managers is primarily in the form of options, so that they will gain large amounts if the company succeeds but will not share in the losses if the company fails. A contributing factor to massive losses in the savings and loan industry was a structure that allowed managers to share generously in the gains while transferring the losses to the taxpayers.

The conflicts between the goals of managers and stockholders create *agency* problems. An agency problem exists whenever one person (the agent) is employed to act on behalf of another person (the principal). The principal always faces the risk that the agent will be less than faithful. The principals in this case are the stockholders, and the agents are the managers. When Ralston-Purina invested heavily in the St. Louis Blues hockey team, for example, questions arose about whether this was a decision to maximize shareholder wealth or a decision based more on the interests of executives. When top management changed a

---

[2] For a detailed discussion of the relationship between value maximization and the welfare of shareholders, see Ezra Solomon, *The Theory of Financial Management* (New York: Columbia University Press, 1963).

[3] A **golden parachute** is an employment contract guaranteeing top executives large payments, often in the millions of dollars, if they are forced from their positions through a takeover by another company.

few years later, the hockey connection was severed as part of a general restructuring. When the risks of problems such as this exist, the principal either faces the cost of closely monitoring the agent or accepts less than would be expected if the agent were completely faithful. Managers can resolve these agency problems by accepting shareholder wealth maximization as an ethical obligation. Alternately, these agency problems may be resolved through close monitoring, compensation plans, or even capital structure decisions.

Monitoring of top executives is difficult and expensive, but compensation plans have proved to be a powerful tool for limiting these agency problems. Incentive pay systems, including bonuses and stock option plans, serve to tie the managers' wealth to the value of the common stock at over 90 percent of the large corporations in the United States. Even though the top executives of major corporations typically own only a small percentage of the corporation they lead, their interest in the corporation represents the great bulk of their personal wealth. They are motivated to protect and increase that wealth. In addition, managers who do not concentrate on the interests of the shareholders may risk being sued, fired, or pushed aside through hostile takeovers or as a result of a proxy fight. Thus, even managers who do not recognize a professional responsibility to the shareholders may spend most of their time trying to increase the wealth of the shareholders.

Conflicts between managers and shareholders do occasionally arise with regard to nonmonetary objectives and use of wealth created by wealth-maximizing decisions. These conflicts are the stuff of newspaper headlines or courtroom drama and are probably the reason why many corporations are more interested in prescribing a code of ethics or conduct for their employees today than they were in the past.[4] The fact that a conflict or choice may exist should not obscure the dominance of common interests. Both groups favor capital investments that maximize wealth, and both groups generally prefer to operate at an acceptable level of risk, even if they do not have identical views about risk. Thus, the objectives of increasing wealth and avoiding noncompensated or excessive risk dominate investment and financing decisions whether the goal is shareholder wealth maximization or management welfare maximization.[5]

Creditors

In general, the creditors' protection increases when wealth increases. There are, however, exceptions. An investment that increases risk may decrease the value of the creditors' claims, even if it increases the value of the firm. In these cases, which we discuss in more detail in Chapter 15, the wealth maximization criterion must be extended to consider not only total wealth but also the wealth of shareholders and creditors separately.

---

[4] It is important for the student to realize that the alternatives confronted in reality are not black and white. To facilitate understanding, we have added at least one ethics question or problem at the end of each chapter.

[5] For a discussion of the relationship between management and shareholder interests, see Michael C. Jensen and William A. Meckling, "Theory of the Firm: Managerial Behavior, Agency Costs, and the Ownership Structure," *Journal of Financial Economics* 3 (October 1976): 305–360.

Customers, Employees, and Suppliers

The shareholder wealth maximization standard does not leave customers and employees high and dry. You must attract customers and sell your products above cost if you are to increase wealth. Thus, the desire to maximize wealth motivates companies to strive for better products and more efficient production. The same desire drives companies to design compensation packages that will attract and motivate the employees who can contribute to quality and efficiency.

Competition is critical in aligning the interests of shareholders, customers, and employees. Competition keeps companies from overpricing products and underpaying employees and suppliers. Competition for high-quality employees pressures the company not only to pay wages but also to provide stable employment and a desirable work environment. Strong relationships with suppliers are increasingly seen as a source of competitive advantage by assuring a stable source of high-quality inputs, such as parts. Suppliers want more than just the price of their goods. They want clear product quality expectations and stable demand, which will allow them to invest in their own futures. This, in turn, assures the company a stable source of high-quality inputs. Other producers of products and other employers force companies seeking wealth maximization to jointly pursue product quality, efficiency, strong supplier relationships, and the attraction and retention of employees.

Problems sometimes arise when it is time to divvy up the wealth. Should it all go to the shareholders, or should it be divided among workers, suppliers, managers, and shareholders, for example? Before foreign competition reshaped the automobile industry, General Motors created a substantial pool of wealth. Stockholders, managers, and workers shared the wealth and earned more than they could have earned by taking their respective time and money elsewhere. Even today Edward Jones spends approximately 4 percent of its payroll on training with more than 140 hours on average for each employee.[6] The problem of dividing up wealth is not solved in this book, but it will not arise unless some wealth is created in the first place. A plan for sharing wealth gains is often a key part of management's plan to encourage wealth-maximizing behavior. Table 1-1 illustrates the basic conflict between the goals of other stakeholders and the shareholders of any company. Competitive bidding in the marketplace typically resolves this conflict.

Society

Society wealth maximization is sometimes cited as the ultimate goal of business activity. Fortunately, the benefits of an attractive capital investment often extend to broad segments of society. Consider, for example, an investment to improve the efficiency of a factory. Customers benefit when reduced production costs lead to increased price competition. Workers benefit because increases in wages over the years have followed from increases in productivity.[7] Overall economic

---

[6] *Fortune*, July 20, 2003.

[7] The benefit is not necessarily limited to the industry in which the improved efficiency occurred. Average wages in an economy tend to move with changes in the marginal productivity of labor in that economy.

TABLE 1-1 Conflict between the Interest of Shareholders and Other Stakeholders

This table shows the basic conflict between the goal of the owners or shareholders for dividends and/or stock appreciation and the goals of the other stakeholders.

STAKEHOLDER	IDEAL GOAL	RESULT	EFFECT ON INCOME OR WEALTH
Managers	High salary and perquisites	Lower income	Lower wealth
Creditors	Low risk, return of their money and interest	Lower income	Lower wealth
Customers	Low prices or many features	Lower income	Lower wealth
Employees	High salaries, job security	Lower income	Lower wealth
Suppliers	High prices and long relationships	Lower income	Lower wealth
Society	Good citizenship and taxes	Lower income	Lower wealth

This conflict is resolved in a free market economy by supply and demand. For example, one of the benefits of learning the material in this textbook is the ability to sell the application of this knowledge to employers or owners. Because the supply of managers with this ability is limited and the value to the owners is immense, the salary should reflect a sharing of this benefit with the price being the intersection of the supply and demand curves.

growth is enhanced because increased productivity frees up resources to be used in other areas of the economy. Finally, increased profitability enhances the tax revenues to support government services.

Conflicts between business and society in terms of wealth maximization arise in two areas. First, there are problems with nonpriced costs such as pollution and nonpriced benefits such as community stability. If mercury waste destroys commercial fishing in Lake Michigan, for example, the cost is widespread, but the polluting companies may not be charged for the damage. Second, there are questions about how wealth is to be allocated among members of society. For example, a company may choose an investment solely to reduce its taxes, the collection of which is one of society's tools for allocating wealth. In these cases, the investments that maximize the owners' wealth may not maximize society's wealth. These problems often arise from poorly thought-out government policies that inadvertently encourage companies to behave in ways not really desired by the public. If government policies in areas such as taxation and pollution are properly designed, the investments that maximize shareholder wealth will generally contribute to the wealth of society as well.[8]

A statement by John M. Henske, chairman of Olin Corporation, reflects one executive's recognition of a responsibility to consider the role of the business firm in society:

[8] There may be situations in which monitoring costs are so high that the societal wealth decreases caused by certain activities are less than the monitoring costs needed to modify companies' behavior. In these cases, there is a genuine conflict between corporate and societal wealth maximization.

TABLE 1-2 Distribution of Revenue among Stakeholders

This table illustrates the size of the financial flows to various stakeholders in three diverse companies in 2002 (using only revenues and expenses as a proxy for flows).

STAKEHOLDER	MICROSOFT	TARGET	SOUTHWEST AIRLINES
Revenue or inflow from the customer	100.0%	100.0%	100.0%
Outflow to the employees, suppliers, and management	59.4%	93.3%	91.3%
Taxes or outflows to the government	13.0%	2.1%	2.7%
Interest expense or outflows to the creditors	0.0%	1.2%	1.6%
Net income or potential outflow to the shareholders	27.6%	3.4%	4.4%

Based on data from each company's 2002 annual report.

> I believe that every corporation must serve several constituencies. Shareholders are certainly an important one. So are employees, so are customers. We have a responsibility to the communities in which we work, to the public who use and are exposed to our products, and to our suppliers, who have committed resources to supply us reliably. To my mind, the chief executive officer has the responsibility of serving all of these. [Olin Corporation 1986 Annual Report]

J. M. Smuckers, the makers of peanut butter, jellies, and other products, shows its support for society by offering its employees unlimited time off to volunteer in the community.[9] Table 1-2 shows the distribution of wealth, using revenue as a proxy, for Microsoft, Target Stores, and Southwest Airlines. This table is important because it reiterates the point that all wealth creation must begin with the sale of some service or product to the customer. After that, as you can see from the table, most of the revenue generated flows to suppliers of merchandise, labor, or talent.

Company Goals and Nonmonetary Considerations

Nonmonetary considerations are sometimes important, regardless of whether managers are focusing on the interests of owners or themselves. Some nonmonetary goals that appear to be used instead of wealth maximization are actually policy guidelines designed to implement the vision of the corporation. Requiring that investments support the company's vision is a tool for seeking wealth creation, not an alternative to wealth creation. As an example, consider the capital budgeting process at Xerox Corporation. Executives there have identified leadership in information management as their route to the creation of products with value in excess of cost. If Xerox managers want to be sure they have identified the investments that will maximize wealth, they must evaluate the fast-food business,

[9] Ibid.

the rubber tree plantation business, the movie production business, and so on prior to every capital budgeting decision. The search would take forever, cost unlimited amounts, and distract attention from the vision. Because the attempt to identify and evaluate every possible capital investment on and off the earth would paralyze the company, top executives must provide guidance as to where to search for attractive investment opportunities. Generally, top executives will direct the search to areas in which the company can enjoy an advantage in relation to competitors, because those are the areas in which attractive investments are most likely to be found. A goal of capturing 30 percent of the office typewriter market, for example, would tell managers to focus on finding attractive investments in the office typewriter businesses, in which Xerox is already a strong competitor.

As another example, goals stated in terms of accounting income may arise because management compensation is tied to accounting income and accounting income is reported to investors. A chief executive who hears on the evening news that the price of a competitor's stock fell following unfavorable earnings news may be hesitant to select investments that will temporarily hurt income, even if those investments have positive net present values. This overemphasis on short-term earnings was cited as the reason for Coca-Cola's decision in 2003 to break with the rest of the market and discontinue providing analysts with estimates or guidance concerning the next quarter's earnings. Chief executive Douglas Daft believed that this would force the market to take a closer look at Coca-Cola's strategic position and its competitive advantage rather than the next quarter's earnings. Trade-offs between accounting income and net present value of cash flows may sometimes be necessary, but these conflicts can be minimized. Income is important because investors use it to predict future cash flows. A history of honest communication with investors helps managers to decrease reliance on accounting income as a communication tool.

Some nonmonetary goals represent conflicts between interests of owners and managers. You may, for example, want to be chief executive of the largest company in the industry even if that does not mean maximizing wealth, as long as you can earn a "satisfactory" return for the owners. You may also be less willing to take risks than the diversified shareholders, even if wealth could be increased by adopting a more risky position. When other, nonmonetary goals are also important, capital budgeting involves trade-offs between nonmonetary goals and wealth maximization. It is the responsibility of management to be aware of the nonmonetary goals of the stakeholders and to decide which of those goals result in a management obligation.

Nonprofit Organizations

Nonprofit organizations such as hospitals and churches are also involved in capital investment decisions. Many so-called nonprofit organizations seek to maximize wealth just as if they were profit-seeking businesses. For example, many hospitals face such vigorous competition that wealth-maximizing decisions are necessary just to survive. In other cases, such as deciding whether to make a church building more energy efficient, the decision process is not significantly different from that in a profit-seeking company; the decision that creates the greatest wealth gives the organization the most resources to allocate to the pursuit of its mission.

When a nonprofit organization faces alternate ways of achieving its mission, the basic wealth maximization model also works. If either of two capital investments will achieve the mission, the one with the smallest present value of costs is desirable, leaving the maximum amount available for other purposes.

When competing investments lead to the achievement of different missions, it is more difficult to apply the wealth maximization principle. One approach is to use resources to maximize the wealth of the organization's constituency. This may be a useful guideline for an association of doctors, lawyers, or accountants, but charities have more difficulty identifying and measuring benefits. To use the wealth maximization criterion for a charity, you must be willing to assign relative values to various missions. However, decision makers are often unwilling to assign relative values to saving a starving child in the sub-Sahara and educating a minority student in the United States. If you are not willing to assign relative values to missions, minimization of the present value of outlays may help you find the most efficient way to achieve each mission and the amount of one mission that must be given up for a unit of another mission. The topic of capital budgeting in a nonprofit setting is discussed in greater detail in Chapter 23.

COMPETITIVE ADVANTAGE AND WEALTH CREATION

We know from Economics 101 that perfect competition has the following characteristics:

- There are no restrictions keeping producers from entering or exiting the market.
- No one producer or buyer is large enough to affect price through any action.
- All producers manufacture identical products.
- All producers have identical costs.
- Everyone is perfectly informed about what everyone else is doing.

We also know from Economics 101 that nobody can expect continued economic profit in these conditions because a price that allows an economic profit will attract new producers until the extra supply causes the price to fall. Where there are no opportunities to increase a firm's economic profit, there are no opportunities for wealth creation. Earlier we mentioned that competition helps solve conflicts between the goals of owners, managers, customers, and so on. Perfect competition solves these problems perfectly, but does so by assuring that the company will create no wealth. Most managers would prefer to create wealth and struggle with the agency problems that follow.

A company sets the stage for wealth creation by creating **competitive advantage,** which is the elimination of some of the conditions for perfect competition so that an economic profit is possible. When executives talk about vision and strategy, they are talking about the process of positioning themselves to achieve competitive advantage, therefore economic profit, and positive net present values. **Strategy** includes decisions as to what businesses we are in and how we intend to position our organization in relation to others in those businesses to gain competitive advantage. The investment decisions of successful companies create wealth by implementing their strategies.

Competitive advantage is typically achieved by product advantage or cost advantage. A **product advantage** exists if your product is differentiated from those of your competitors so that you are selling your product without matching their prices. A **cost advantage** exists when you can produce your product at a lower cost than your competitors so that you can earn an economic profit while matching their prices. Investments that create wealth are then aimed at giving the company lower costs or a superior product.[10]

The most successful companies coordinate financing decisions with their strategy. Financing arrangements that minimize the annual cash flows required by investors may, for example, increase the company's ability to withstand competitors' attempts to increase market share by reducing price. The company's ability to withstand such an attack may be sufficient to discourage the attack in the first place. Financing choices may also give the company a cost advantage by reducing the return that investors require.

OVERVIEW OF THE CAPITAL INVESTMENT PROCESS

A **capital investment** is defined as an outlay that is expected to result in benefits in the future. **Capital budgeting** is the process of selecting capital investments.

Capital investments can be physical, financial, or intangible. **Physical assets** such as factories and machinery are familiar capital investments, but computers, airplanes, and highways are also physical assets that qualify as capital investments. A **financial asset** is a claim against some other party for monetary payment; examples include savings accounts, bonds, and stock. Financial assets generally have value because money was used to acquire some other asset that will provide cash flows. **Intangible investments** are not physical in nature and do not serve as claims for payment by some other party but are expected to result in future benefits. Examples of intangible assets include a training program for marketing representatives, a membership drive for a symphony orchestra, and a franchise. For Wal-Mart to meet its expansion plans, investments will include both buildings and the outright purchase of other retailers outside the United States. The buildings are tangible assets, while the goodwill resulting from the purchases is an intangible investment because the purchases are expected to result in future benefits, even though they do not result directly in an identifiable asset.

The decision process is similar for all capital investments regardless of how those investments are classified. Because capital investments are so important to

[10] A recent article by Michael Porter and Mark Kramer discusses various ways corporations have used corporate philanthropy to gain or enhance a competitive advantage. Please see references at the end of the chapter.

FIGURE 1-3 Flow Chart of the Capital Investment Process
This flow chart represents the sequence of steps followed in a typical, well-organized capital investment process.

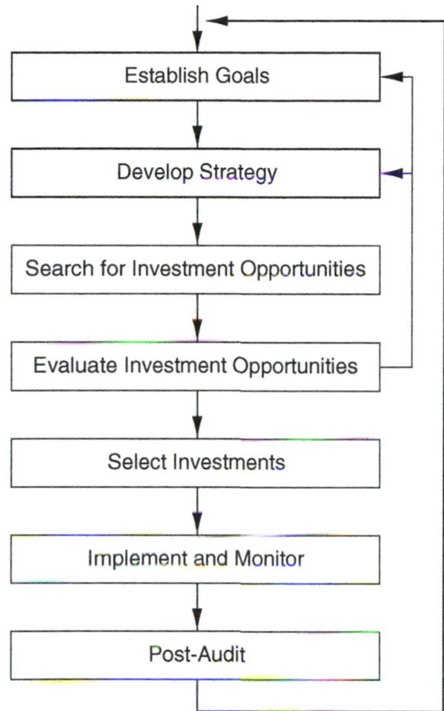

the success of the organization, most companies have formal policies guiding the decision process. Figure 1-3 illustrates the typical capital investment process, and a discussion of each step in that process follows.

Establish Goals

Wealth creation is generally the overall goal, but wealth creation is abstract. It is difficult to know if shareholder wealth was maximized, for example, because we do not know what share price would have been if we had taken other courses of action. Therefore, chief executives often translate the wealth goal into more concrete goals against which performance can be measured. When John F. McDonnell took over McDonnell-Douglas (now a subsidiary of Boeing), for example, he identified four standards by which progress would be measured: rate of return, size of government contracts, response by financial markets, and ranking among *Fortune*'s most admired corporations.[11] Ideally, these are the *attainable*

[11] *St. Louis Post-Dispatch* (May 8, 1988): E,1.

goals that managers believe will increase wealth the most. There may also be nonmonetary goals such as reduction of injuries, improved reading ability, or cleaner water. Monetary goals are dominant for businesses, while governmental and nonprofit organizations often focus on nonmonetary goals.

Develop Strategy

Strategy sets the general direction of the organization and provides the framework within which capital investment opportunities are sought. The goals and strategy of the corporation are typically combined in the vision. According to former General Electric chairman Jack Welch, the job of the boss is to "develop a vision" and then oversee a change in the set of shared values and beliefs that make up the organization's culture in order to accomplish it.[12] As discussed at the beginning of this chapter, the job of the boss is also to accumulate and allocate resources in support of that vision. Goals and strategy therefore set the framework for leading people, accumulating resources, and allocating resources.

The major focus of strategy is the generation of wealth through creation and use of competitive advantage. Strategic assessment often begins with an analysis of **opportunities** and **threats** in the environment, followed by an analysis of the company's **strengths** and **weaknesses.** From this analysis, general directions for development are chosen.

Strategy is the foundation of a successful capital budgeting system. Strategy is the framework in which resources are marshaled in pursuit of goals. Strategy also tells members of the organization where to search for profitable capital investments. Successful capital budgeting and wealth maximization are therefore dependent on sound strategy. Likewise, sound strategic planning will not lead to wealth creation unless strategy is implemented with the goal of maximizing wealth. Thus, sound strategic planning, sound capital budgeting, and sound financing plans are essential.

An example was Southwestern Bell Telephone's decision to focus on its core business after deregulation and to convert its trunk system to fiber-optic technology. This strategy, which required capital investments measured in the billions of dollars, gave Southwestern Bell a clearer signal and better ability to handle the rapidly growing data transmission business. The adoption of this strategy provided guidance to the capital budgeting process for years. It proved to be more successful than strategies followed by some other telephone companies, such as expansion into business unrelated to telecommunications.

A less successful strategy was Sony's decision to severely limit licensing of its Beta video-recorder format and keep most of the manufacturing investment opportunity to itself. Managers knew the beta format was technically better than the competing VHS format and therefore assumed that beta would win out in the marketplace. By refusing to license the beta format to other manufacturers,

---

[12] Jack Welch, "How Good a Manager?" *Business Week* (December 14, 1977), 92–94.

Sony would have competitive advantage and control over price; it would create the opportunity for large, highly profitable capital investments. Unfortunately, the strategy failed. VHS became the dominant format because it was freely licensed. After a long, expensive struggle, Sony was eventually forced to switch to VHS format production itself. Apple computer followed a similar strategy in protecting its operating system, and like Sony, lost the industry standard position to Microsoft, which did not sell computers and therefore was not tempted to restrict the use of its operating systems to one manufacturer.

Each strategic decision is in itself a general capital budgeting decision, in that it is based on estimates of wealth creation and other contributions to company goals that can be expected from later capital investments in pursuit of a particular strategy. Goal setting and strategy choice are interactive processes, as shown in Figure 1-3, because goals are often readjusted in response to information about feasibility gained in the strategic assessment process.

Search for Investment Opportunities

The identification of potential capital investments is a critical stage in the capital budgeting process. The remainder of the process can only assure that the best of the proposed investments are selected. Fortunately, companies that want to be successful in identifying capital investment opportunities can organize themselves for success. The first part of that organization is development of realistic goals, sound strategy, and appropriate rewards for successful managers. Then, specific attention must be devoted to the search process.

A corporate culture that encourages creativity must support the search for investment opportunities; otherwise, there will be no good proposals to evaluate. 3M Corporation has been widely recognized for encouraging creative thinking about new business opportunities. Results include such home-run new product investments as Scotchgard and Post-it Notes. For comparison, consider the (mercifully) anonymous quote from a manager of another company: "The trick to getting ahead here is to never make a mistake. Nobody would submit a capital request if there was any doubt that it would test out." This company languishes with an outmoded product line in a stagnant market.

A successful search process generally requires the commitment of resources. Research, product development, and consumer attitude surveys are all ways to identify investment opportunities. If the strategy involves acquisition of other companies, an acquisition group may be responsible for searching out and evaluating opportunities. These various approaches have in common the willingness to spend money on people to search for attractive capital investments.

Training in support of strategy is another example of organization for a successful search. Executives are increasingly realizing that training of employees is not a sideline activity for good years but an important part of strategy implementation. Managers at all levels must be aware of company goals and strategy if they are to search out the right types of capital investment opportunities. In addition, managers at all levels must have some skill in capital budgeting so that they can perform at least preliminary analysis of potential investments.

A successful search for investment opportunities will be carried out at all levels of the organization. Major capital investments that involve a *change in strategy* will probably be identified at a top management level. General Motors' decision to build the Saturn plant, for example, involved a new strategy as well as a capital investment of $5 billion.[13] This project was developed at the highest levels of the company. **Major investments in support of existing strategy** will typically be developed at a high level, such as the senior executive in charge of marketing or production. Examples include the introduction of a new cereal by General Mills and Chrysler's addition of a new factory to increase production of its minivan. **Smaller investments** are identified and given preliminary screening by the person in a position to perceive a need. Examples include thousands of decisions by industrial engineers to replace or modernize specific pieces of equipment, by supervisors to send employees to training programs, by marketing managers to run advertisements, and so on. Although these investments are smaller in scale, they are vitally important due to their cumulative effect. Because people are involved at all levels, efforts to encourage the search for attractive investments must reach people at all levels of the organization.

Evaluate Investment Opportunities

The ideal corporate culture will result in numerous capital investment proposals, each of which must be evaluated. The fundamental question is whether the present value of the cash benefits or savings to be generated by an investment exceed the present value of the outlays. Identifying these outlays and benefits is by no means a trivial exercise. In fact, survey respondents have identified project definition and cash flow estimation as the most difficult stage of the evaluation process,[14] and there is evidence that estimates are systematically biased.[15] Cash flow estimation requires sales forecasts, cost forecasts, engineering analyses, inflation estimates, tax estimates, and so on. Deciding which cash flows will be affected by a particular investment is a major challenge. Chapters 8 through 10 are devoted to the identification of cash flows. Chapters 11 through 15 deal with uncertainty surrounding cash flows.

Strategic considerations are often on an equal footing with cash flow analysis because investments that are not consistent with the corporation's strategy are not likely to create wealth. K-Mart's decision to enter building products and books with the development of Builder's Square and Waldenbooks subsidiaries may have made sense in terms of cash flow related to those new retail avenues. But the lack of emphasis K-Mart placed on maintaining its once dominant strategic competitive advantage in discount retailing allowed Wal-Mart to gain the more dominant position and consequently the cash flows for years to come.

---

[13] During the implementation stage, General Motors backed away from the strategy (a new strategic decision, in effect), scaling down the size of the investment and relying on less radical production methods.

[14] David F. Scott, Jr., and J. William Petty II, "Capital Budgeting Practices in Large American Firms," *The Financial Review* 19 (March 1984): 111–123.

[15] David I. Levine, "Do Corporate Executives Have Rational Expectations?" *Journal of Business* 66 (April 1993): 271–293.

Risk analysis is a standard part of the evaluation of most capital investments. We are estimating future events, and those estimates are almost always fraught with uncertainty. Total project risk is often analyzed by looking at the sources of uncertainty, then estimating the wealth effects of changes in those values. If sales levels are a key variable, for example, analysts may compute net present values using several different sales forecasts. Risk that cannot be diversified away is of particular importance and receives special attention. Results of changes in overall economic conditions are hard to diversify away, while factors related to a particular project, such as technological life or shifting customer tastes, can be diversified away when the company or its shareholders spread their money among a number of different projects. Managers must ultimately use this information to decide if the potential benefits are worth the risk. Chapters 11 through 15 deal with risk analysis and decision making with the goal of managing risk.

Other considerations come into play as well. Companies often lack sufficient resources to acquire all attractive investments and must make choices. An investment might have good cash flow characteristics but seriously reduce reported income for several years. Conflicts between accounting income and wealth creation would not occur in a world of perfect information, but these conflicts are sometimes important to managers. An investment may look good in isolation but have disastrous public relations consequences. Because of these and other considerations, the evaluation process commonly includes review by finance, production, engineering, marketing, legal, and public relations departments.

The information gained from the evaluation of scores of investment proposals feeds back into strategy development. If an area of emphasis identified in strategic planning cannot provide attractive investments, it may be necessary to revise the strategy.

Select Investments

The selection of investments is typically a multilevel process. A plant manager may, for example, have authority to approve individual capital investments of up to $100,000 in cost, *provided* that the investments meet the company's criteria and the sum of those investments is within the total budget limit. Capital investments endorsed by the plant manager, but beyond the plant manager's authority, may then go to a division vice president who can approve capital investments up to, say, $500,000, provided that they meet company standards and fall within an overall budget. Decisions on the largest investments are then made at the top management level.

Committees are commonly involved in the decision process. A capital budgeting committee may prioritize investment opportunities at the factory or division level. The largest investments may ultimately be chosen by a corporate capital budgeting committee, the executive committee, or the board of directors. The decision makers on these committees bring a wide range of interests, expertise, and communication skills to the table. Some are highly trained in the use and explanation of financial analysis tools, while others may have expertise in the areas of engineering, law, human resource management, marketing, and so on.

Some will focus primarily on the forecasted financial numbers, for example, while others are more interested in strategic issues or employee implications. The discussion can therefore be far-reaching, and the analysis required to support this discussion can be extensive. Higher-level executives will be very comfortable with the search for consensus among people with varied interests and different levels of understanding, while junior members of the corporation may be new to this type of decision process.

Not every company follows the process just outlined. The president of one multibillion-dollar, multidivision company insisted on personally signing off on *every* capital investment proposal. His average analysis time was under five minutes per proposal, and his approval rate approached 100 percent on all but the largest projects. Obtaining his signature was obviously a formality, with the real decisions on most proposals being made informally at other levels.

Unfortunately, capital budgeting is sometimes viewed as little more than an exercise in saying no. This view is understandable on the part of a manager who submitted proposals and received no feedback other than "request denied." Viewed in broader context, though, capital budgeting begins with encouraging people to search for investment opportunities and culminates with the selection of the investments that make the greatest contribution to company goals. Clear guidelines and reasonable feedback on how and why choices were made, along with some positive reinforcement for people whose proposals were not chosen, should contribute to a positive view of capital budgeting.

Implement and Monitor

The implementation and monitoring process begins once a capital investment has been approved. Capital investments are monitored during the actual period of acquisition or construction because deviations, either good or bad, should be recognized, taken into consideration, and dealt with. Cost overruns are the most common deviations during construction or acquisition and are dealt with by changing control procedures or taking another look at the attractiveness of the investment. Likewise, the capital investment should be monitored as it goes into operation to spot deviations and take corrective action.

Post-Audit

The post-audit is primarily a learning tool because it is carried out at the end of a capital investment's life or after the investment has matured to a stable level of activity and profitability. The post-audit includes an assessment of the actual performance of the investment and a comparison with forecasted performance. Reasons for deviation from anticipated performance are sought. Post-audits will allow you to identify the strengths and weaknesses of your capital budgeting systems. Some companies construct business case histories from post-audits and use those cases in their management education programs.

Monitoring and post-audit encourage managers to be accurate in the estimates used in their capital investment proposals and help counter the tendency to adjust the numbers to make proposed investments look better. Managers receiving proposals frequently express concern that the numbers have been adjusted to make the projects look good, and managers submitting proposals sometimes brag (privately) about adjusting the numbers to get the result they know they will need to sell the project. As an example, a regional telephone company sent back the year's capital budgeting requests with a note that a post-audit process was being introduced. Managers were given an opportunity to revise their proposals in light of a future post-audit. Hundreds of proposals were withdrawn and benefit estimates were scaled back for scores of others.

When conducting a post-audit, the distinction between a good *decision* and a good *outcome* must be kept in mind. An oil company may, for example, drill hundreds of exploratory wells knowing that only one out of ten will hit oil. Penalizing an engineer who chose one of the sites that turned out to be dry is counterproductive if the site met the required conditions for exploratory drilling at the time the well was drilled. Likewise, the treasurer who sinks all of the company's cash into the state lottery is not vindicated just because he chooses a winning number. The company may decide to change the decision process if the number of successful outcomes is smaller than expected, but in a world of uncertainty, some good decisions will result in bad outcomes, and vice versa.

The information garnered from a series of post-audits can result in a new look at goals and strategies. Consequently, the capital investment process is dynamic, with the entire process being continually reviewed and modified as new information becomes available. The fundamental objective of this dynamic process is the identification and selection of the capital investments that will make the greatest possible contribution to the firm's value and other goals.

OVERVIEW OF LONG-TERM FINANCING DECISIONS

A finance theory called the separation principle holds that investment and financing decisions of the firm can be dealt with separately. The principle is correct under perfect market conditions, in which wealth is unaffected by the ways in which the firm finances its activities. In the imperfection-loaded world of normal activity, financing choices matter, and the use of financing appropriate for your company's investments can increase wealth. Capital investments that meet customer needs cost-effectively can make you a big winner in the wealth creation race. Likewise, you can raise funds on favorable terms, and therefore increase wealth, if you meet the needs of investors. The importance of satisfying investors is why one chief financial officer at a large finance company described his group as "the other marketing department." It is their job to meet the needs of investors so that the company will have a continual supply of funds with which to take advantage of attractive investment opportunities.

The plan for long-term financing begins with the amount of money needed for attractive investment opportunities, both now and in the foreseeable future. The decisions about how much is needed, what it is needed for, and how to raise that money are interactive. The wealth impact of a capital investment is affected by the rate of return that must be paid to investors. The rate of return that must be paid depends on how much money is needed, risk, and how that money will be raised. The lower the rate of return that must be paid to investors, the greater the number of attractive investment opportunities the company will have. Because investment and financing decisions are interrelated, you need at least some familiarity with financing considerations even if your personal responsibility is only related to investment decisions.

Financing Choices

Financing sources are divided primarily between stock (equity) holders, who share in ownership of the residual after other claims have been paid, and creditors, who are promised a fixed return for the use of their money. The first choice, then, is the **debt-equity mix.**

The financing job is, however, much more complex than simply choosing a mix of debt and equity. **Maturity** of debt is one key issue. For companies, like individuals, the ability to carry debt is not determined by the absolute amount of debt but by the payments. From academics like Gordon Donaldson[16] to practitioners like conglomerate builder Meshulah Ricklis, the role of cash payments in the measurement of debt capacity has long been stressed. When considering maturity, the company must consider not only the minimum payment it must make but the maximum payment it is allowed to make. In other words, the company is concerned about its right to repay the loan early if it no longer needs that funding.

The **priority of each claim** is another important consideration. Some debt may be senior to other debt, meaning that the senior debt holders have a higher priority in the event of bankruptcy. Creditors may also be given liens against specific assets. We may, for example, give one creditor first claim against the office building and another creditor first claim against the inventory in the event of bankruptcy. Even when raising additional equity capital, the company faces a choice between selling common stock, which is the final residual claim, and preferred stock, which is typically assured dividends before anything is given to the common stockholders.

Source of financing is also given careful consideration. The company may sell debt in the public markets, typically through investment bankers, or it may prefer private borrowing, from banks, insurance companies, or pension funds, for example. Sale of additional stock involves similar choices. The company may seek a private placement in which stock is sold to one or a few investors. Alternately, the company may seek to sell the stock exclusively to employees or to distribute it as widely as possible to the public.

The range of financing choices becomes even broader when we realize that for every two alternatives, there is a hybrid choice in between. The distance between debt and common stock, for example, can be bridged by issuing convertible debt, which the lender can later exchange for common stock, or by issuing

---

[16] Gordon Donaldson, "New Framework for Corporate Debt Capacity," *Harvard Business Review* 40 (March–April 1962): 117–131.

preferred stock. Likewise, the company may issue warrants, which allow investors to acquire stock later, at a price fixed today.

Considerations in Financing

Cost is, of course, a principal consideration in financing choice. The lower the rate of return required by investors, the greater will be the net present value and wealth contribution of each capital investment. Cost is affected by a number of considerations. Because interest expense reduces taxes while stockholders must be paid from after-tax income, we would expect debt to be a cheaper source of funds. However, the tax advantage of debt is offset by several other costs. Large amounts of debt, for example, may increase the risk of bankruptcy or other problems that arise when companies cannot pay their creditors on time. Furthermore, the larger the amount of debt, the smaller is the probability that the company will have enough income before tax to take full advantage of the interest deduction from debt.

Agency costs are a particularly difficult and important category of costs that must be considered when choosing financing. Recall that agency problems occur whenever one person (the agent) is employed to act on behalf of another person (the principal). The principal either incurs the cost of monitoring the agent or accepts less than would be expected if the agent were completely faithful. An all-equity capital structure leaves the stockholders with the risk that managers will not always act in their interest. Because there is no requirement to repay stockholders, investors are concerned about the risk that managers will continually reinvest in projects that do not create wealth. Debt reduces this concern because debt must be repaid, forcing managers to return to the investors to justify new investment plans. Debt has its own agency costs, though. Managers might take more risks than the creditors anticipated, for example. The higher the level of debt, the greater is this risk. Specific asset pledges and repayment schedules help to decrease this risk, but these arrangements also have costs.

A good deal of the effort in designing a financing mix is aimed at minimizing these agency costs. A mix of senior debt, with first priority in bankruptcy, and junior debt that gets paid only after the senior debt is one example of a solution. The senior creditors are substantially relieved of monitoring cost, and the monitoring problem is concentrated in the hands of the junior creditors. The company might, for example, sell the senior debt to a broad group of investors while selling the junior debt to one or a few investors who are in a good position to monitor the company. Asset type obviously affects the monitoring problem as well. The use and maintenance of a hotel can be easily observed, for example, while the use of a research laboratory is much more difficult to monitor. Not surprisingly, investors will generally lend a high percentage of the cost of a hotel compared to what they will lend for a research program.

Beyond cost, the company is concerned about *availability* and *flexibility*. The financial markets as well as the company are subject to a wide variety of influences, and the company does not want to be in a position where it has excellent investment opportunities but cannot raise money. The company also wants to be able to change its financing by, for example, repaying debt before maturity.

Keeping a lower debt-to-equity ratio than creditors would accept is one way of assuring access to either the equity or credit markets at all times. Maintenance of numerous credit arrangements as well as international listing of the firm's stock keeps the company from being dependent on one market. Banking problems decreased the supply of bank loans in the early 1990s, for example, and companies that had relied exclusively on bank credit complained bitterly that they could no longer raise funds. Companies have sold stock to the public when they did not really need the money, just so they could establish a market for their stock in case of later need.

Strategy plays a role in financing choice. The strategy that is designed to create competitive advantage and guide the capital investment process also guides financing plans. If your strategy calls for gaining market share from strong competitors, for example, you may expect a period of low profitability that will be more than compensated by higher profitability later. You cannot commit yourself to large cash payments to investors in the low-profitability period. You can avoid this problem by using more equity and using long-term rather than short-term debt. You may also use convertible debt so that creditors will see an opportunity to participate in the success if you win. As another example, secrecy may be an element of your strategy, and you would then need to seek private financing to avoid publishing the intended use of the money. Thus, financing decisions support investment decisions not just by providing money but by supporting the strategy behind those decisions.

Obvious from this discussion of financing considerations is the point that it is impossible to completely divorce investment and financing decisions. Low-cost financing always makes investments more attractive. Stability of cash flows from the investment allows more fixed payments to creditors than would be possible with unstable cash flows. Some assets are more easily monitored than others, and creditors may be more willing to advance large amounts of money for those assets. Finally, some sources of financing, such as industrial revenue bonds and leases, are available only for a particular capital investment. For these reasons, capital investments and long-term financing decisions are both treated in this book. Financing decisions and their relationship to capital investment choice are covered in detail in Chapters 16 through 22.

THE CAPITAL INVESTMENT "CRISIS"

Capital investments are important to the economy for two reasons. In the short run, the business cycle is affected by the amount of demand for new capital investments. Current discussion of a capital investment "crisis," though, focuses on the long-run problem. Problems with *types of capital investments* being made in the United States was brought into focus with a study led by Michael E. Porter at Harvard University. He concludes that "the U.S. system of allocating investment capital both within and across companies is failing."[17] Porter summarizes a

---

[17] Michael E. Porter, "Capital Disadvantage: America's Failing Capital Investment System," *Harvard Business Review* (September–October 1992): 65–82.

research project involving eighteen separate studies, so it is not surprising that he finds multitudinous problems. Chief among these is an emphasis on actions that produce short-term results. Reduced investment in promising research and development is an example of how a company might increase short-term income, because R&D is treated as an expense in the accounting records, at the expense of long-term success. He blames this short-term focus on stockholders who rapidly churn diversified portfolios and focus on short-term income because they are unwilling to learn about the company or wait for long-term results. He also blames CEOs who reward managers primarily for short-term financial performance and who assemble diversified corporations with no understanding of what really goes on in the various divisions. He suggests numerous cures by both government and business, including changes in accounting rules, reduced restrictions on disclosure of "insider" information to significant long-term owners, changes in tax rules to encourage long-term investment in stock, and a management goal of maximizing long-term shareholder value rather than current stock price. He does not directly object to the wealth maximization criterion, but rather suggests that much current practice does not result in capital investment decisions that result in long-run wealth maximization.

Porter's view has considerable support, including the eighteen studies he summarizes. The general business press has been reporting on perceived national problems in the capital investment arena for years. As early as 1987, a Conference Board survey confirmed the existence of a general concern about excessive focus on short-term thinking that may reduce the international competitiveness of U.S. businesses in the years ahead. A favorite refrain of managers is that investors force them into a short-term focus.

Others have been quick to argue that managers are on thin ice when they blame investors for their myopia. Woolridge, for example, observed that only a small fraction of the value of the typical stock can be accounted for through anticipated dividends over the next few years,[18] and dividends are the only thing the company gives the shareholders in most cases. While an individual stockholder may sell shares to another investor, the only thing the stockholder is selling is a stream of future dividends. As a typical example of Woolridge's point, Southwest Airlines sold for $12.61 a share on February 14, 2003, and annual dividends were $.02 per share. Barring a major change in dividend policy, the dividends over the next five years accounted for less than 1 percent of the value of the stock. Therefore, investors were buying the stock primarily for cash flows expected to be paid out over the long term.

Stock prices do, of course, respond to news about company plans and profits, even though the news is not directly about cash flow. An increase in profits, a new patent, or new factory at Dow Chemical would likely lead to an expectation of increased future cash flows, and therefore to a change in the stock price. The primary job of a security analyst is to interpret the news about a company in terms of its impact on future cash flows and therefore value. The principles of

---

[18] J. Randall Woolridge, "Competitive Decline and Corporate Restructuring: Is a Myopic Stock Market to Blame?" *Journal of Applied Corporate Finance* (Spring 1988): 26–36.

stock value are developed in detail in Chapter 4, but in the meantime we should not misread changes in expected long-term cash flows based on current news as a short-term focus. Executives who believe there is excess reaction to transitory events may be seeing evidence that they have not done an adequate job of educating investors and security analysts about their strategy. In early 2003, as Home Depot and Lowe's were both undertaking rapid expansion plans, the market decreased both companies' stock price fearing that over capacity would damage both their profits. When asked about this, Robert Tillman, CEO of Lowe's, remarked that it was not Home Depot's market that Lowe's was after but instead the other 70 percent of the $100 billion home improvement market that was held by relatively small players. Woolridge is one of a number of researchers who have provided evidence that investors not only respond positively to capital expenditure announcements but also to research and development expenditure announcements, even though the R&D expenditures often push income down in the short term.[19] Announcements of large short-term earnings declines as a result of a change in accounting for retiree benefits did not lead to corresponding drops in stock prices, which would be expected if investors cannot see beyond current income. Porter himself observes that the U.S. capital budgeting system is more effective than that of Germany or Japan when it comes to providing funding for emerging high-tech industries that are expected to be the basis for future economic growth, even though current income is typically low or nonexistent.

The debate over the quality of current capital budgeting policies will go on for years, and we cannot afford to wait. Fortunately, we have more agreement about how to do it right than we have about whether people are doing it right. We address the capital budgeting "crisis" in this book by focusing on capital budgeting methods that increase the likelihood of selecting wealth-maximizing investments in both the short and long run, and on management policies that support those methods.

THE GLOBALIZATION OF INVESTMENTS AND FINANCING

International business was once defined primarily in terms of imports and exports, but managers increasingly view the entire planet as the bazaar in which to search for the best places to:

1. Acquire raw materials.
2. Acquire production equipment.
3. Acquire labor.
4. Acquire financing.
5. Sell the product.
6. Invest the profits.

It would be surprising if the same country turned out to be the best choice for all six activities. Reasons for choosing different countries for each activity include comparative advantages of a particular country such as lower labor costs

[19] Ibid.

or proximity to raw materials, diversification, differences in capital accumulation rates, differences in tax treatment, and differences in regulation. We discuss these considerations more fully in Chapter 2 because they are central to the strategic decisions of the firm.

Globalization of business leads to some special considerations for capital investment and financing decisions. Cash flow and reported income are both affected by exchange rates between the various currencies. Financing decisions are affected by tax laws, regulatory rules, and supply-demand relationships in each country. Additional risks experienced in global operations include unanticipated exchange rate risk movements, economic instability, and government instability. Because of the broad range of issues encountered in global business, we will return to global considerations in most chapters of this book.

A NOTE TO ENGINEERS

Many readers of this book are or have been engineering students rather than business students. The topics covered in this book are broader than those typically covered in an engineering economics textbook. This is necessary because your responsibilities are likely to be broader than those of the prior generation. Integrated decision making is a major focus of leading companies. You will be concerned about more than how to generate the desired production or even the cheapest way to achieve the desired production. You must also consider how manufacturing decisions affect company strategy, risk, ability to raise money from investors, and so forth. You will be promoted farther and faster if you are able to deal with all of the implications of your capital budgeting proposals.

SUMMARY

This book is about the investment and financing decisions of the firm. The goal pursued in these decisions is **wealth maximization.** An increase in wealth increases the amount that can be divided among the owners, managers, employees, suppliers, creditors, and society. For a single-period decision, wealth is created if cash inflow exceeds cash outflow by more than we would have earned if we had invested our money elsewhere. The amount of wealth creation is called **economic profit.** The **present value** of an expected future cash flow is the amount that must be invested elsewhere, at the same risk, to generate the same expected cash flow. For a multi-period decision, wealth creation is the **net present value,** which is the present value of cash inflows minus the present value of the outflows.

Shareholder wealth maximization is generally considered to be the goal of investment and financing. The interests of managers are similar to the interests of shareholders in most cases, and the interests of customers, employees, and society are also served in most cases by shareholder wealth maximization. In general, shareholder wealth maximization is achieved by choosing investments for which the present value of benefits exceeds the present value of outlays. This same selection procedure also works for nonprofit organizations when they are considering investments with monetary benefits.

Economic profit is not possible in perfect competition. Therefore, all wealth creation comes from competitive advantage, typically in the form of product advantage or cost advantage over competitors. Thus, the investment and financing actions of the firm have as their goal the generation of wealth by creating or exploiting competitive advantage.

Capital investments are key components of the plan for achieving wealth. A **capital investment** is an outlay that is expected to result in benefits in the future. **Capital budgeting** is the process of selecting capital investments. Capital investments include physical assets such as factories and airliners, but also include monetary assets such as securities and intangible investments such as advertising campaigns or celebrity endorsements.

The capital investment process consists of seven steps: establishment of goals, development of strategy, search for investment opportunities, evaluation of investment opportunities, selection of investments, implementation and monitoring, and post-audit. Careful management of each stage of this process leads to capital investments that make the maximum attainable contribution to shareholder wealth.

Financing choices begin with the amount of money needed and a decision about the proportions of debt and equity. Then managers look at specific characteristics of financing, such as maturity, priority of claims, and which particular investors will be approached. The company seeks the lowest possible cost of funds. This requires meeting investor needs, consideration of taxes, and dealing with agency costs as effectively as possible. Beyond cost, managers are concerned about availability, flexibility, and consistency with strategy.

For both the individual organization and the corporation as a whole, selection and financing of capital investments are key components of success. Much has been written about actual and potential problems caused by inappropriate methods. The objective of this book is to help people make capital investment and financing decisions that will maximize wealth.

QUESTIONS

1-1. Why is wealth maximization used as the guiding goal for financial decisions?

1-2. How is wealth generation measured for (a) a single-period decision, (b) a multi-period decision?

1-3. How can the wealth maximization criterion help a nonprofit organization in making capital investment decisions?

1-4. Define the terms **present value** and **net present value.**

1-5. Define the terms **capital investment** and **capital budgeting.**

1-6. List the seven steps in the capital budgeting process.

1-7. What are the main factors considered in deciding if a proposed capital investment is attractive to the company?

1-8. Who in the corporation is involved in the capital budgeting process?

1-9. Who makes the final decision on whether a proposed capital investment is to be made?

1-10. List the main categories of financing choices.

1-11. What is the primary consideration in choosing a financing method?

1-12. There is probably an abandoned retail store in your town. It was pointed out in the chapter that coming up with investment opportunities is often the most difficult, most critical, and most profitable element in creating wealth. You are now going to be given the chance to test your abilities in this area. Develop at least three different capital budgeting ideas (projects or businesses) that you believe might use this abandoned property and have a positive net present value.

1-13. For the above projects, what information or studies would you want to collect or perform before you approach the loan officer or investing public with your idea?

1-14. Recently Monsanto decided to split into two companies, one specializing in biotechnology and the other specializing in chemicals. They issued two different shares of stock to formalize the split. List the benefits of this action in terms of the financing variables discussed in the chapter. What are the disadvantages?

1-15. Several companies formed in the late 1990s by the purchase of other companies have since split back into two separate companies and issued stock in two new companies. As a result, the stock prices of the two separate companies typically reflects more total value than the stock of the combined company. Why?

1-16. The tax rates on capital gains from increases in asset values have recently been reduced. In respect to the parties that benefit from capital investment or wealth creation, explain why investment would decrease or increase as a result of the change in tax rates.

1-17. **(Ethical Considerations)** How would the following actions redistribute the size of the claims of parties discussed in the chapter (shareholders, creditors, employees, managers, suppliers, customers, government, and society)? Is this redistribution ethical in your opinion?

a. A large international automobile maker decides to move production from a plant in Germany to a plant in Alabama.

b. A large airline negotiates with the unions to take pay and benefit concessions to encourage the creditor to delay possible bankruptcy proceedings.

c. A large electronics firm reports a record loss due in part to the high cost of severance packages paid to terminated workers.

d. An astute company president terminates an overfunded pension plan and takes the excess to the company coffers.

e. A group of executives of a particular company line up an investment banker to float a debt issue to take the company private for a 20 percent equity stake for themselves. They suspect that the company is undervalued in the marketplace and they will reap tremendous benefits after this leveraged buyout.

f. SAS Institute offers childcare to its employees for $300 per month and a pianist in its cafeteria.

CASE PROBLEM

Night Baseball[20]

After the Chicago Cubs baseball team had sustained several years of operating losses in the early 1960s, William Schlensky, a minority stockholder, brought suit to force the Cubs management to equip Wrigley Field, where the home games were held, with lights so that games could be held at night. Baseball was first played at night in 1935, and Wrigley Field remained the only major league ballpark without lighting for night games.

Schlensky concluded that the Cubs' losses were directly attributed to inadequate attendance at home games and that if the directors maintained their refusal to equip Wrigley Field with lights, the Cubs would continue to sustain losses and the corporation's financial condition would continue to deteriorate. Schlensky argued that funds for the financing could be obtained readily through financing and that the cost of the installation would be recaptured quickly by increased revenues from growth in attendance.

Philip K. Wrigley was president and owner of approximately 80 percent of the stock of Chicago National League Ball Club, Inc., which operated Wrigley Field, concession sales during home games, and television and radio broadcasts of Cubs' home games, as well as leased the field for football games and other events. He opposed the installation of lights. He expressed his personal opinion that baseball is a daytime sport. Wrigley also noted his concern that the lighting and night traffic would cause deterioration of the residential neighborhood around the ballpark.

Schlensky alleged that the other corporate directors simply acquiesced in the policy set out by Wrigley and that they permitted him to dominate the board of directors even though they knew he was not motivated by the best interests of the corporation, but solely by his personal views.

The court observed that Schlensky did not show that increased revenue from night attendance would be sufficient to cure the corporate deficit; nor did he address possible increases in operating costs associated with night games.

Case Questions

1. What facts and arguments could Schlensky have provided to strengthen his case?
2. Do you see any tensions between a corporation's commitments to its community and to its shareholders?
3. Was Wrigley's insistence on playing baseball according to his personal perception of the game responsive to the interests of the corporation?
4. What, if any, are the responsibilities of the other directors if they disagree with Wrigley?

[20] Contributed by Ellen Harshman, St. Louis University.

SELECTED REFERENCES

Agrawal, Anup, and Ralph A. Walking. "Executive Careers and Compensation Surrounding Takeover Bids." *The Journal of Finance* 49 (July 1994): 985–1014.

Anstaett, Kurt W., Dennis P. McCrary, and Stephen T. Monahan, Jr. "Practical Debt Policy Considerations for Growth Companies: A Case Study Approach." *Journal of Applied Corporate Finance* 1 (Summer 1988): 71–78.

Baldwin, Carliss Y., and Kim B. Clark. "Capabilities and Capital Investment: New Perspective on Capital Budgeting." *Journal of Applied Corporate Finance* 5 (Summer 1992): 67–82.

Bernstein, Peter L. "Are Financial Markets the Problem or the Solution? A Reply to Michael Porter." *Journal of Applied Corporate Finance* 5 (Summer 1992): 17–22.

Bierman, Harold, Jr., and Seymour Smidt. *The Capital Budgeting Decision,* 8th ed. New York: Macmillan, 1993.

"Capital Budgeting." *Financial Management* 18 (Spring 1989): 10–17.

Chan, Su, John Kensinger, and John Martin. "The Market Rewards Promising R&D, and Punishes the Rest." *Journal of Applied Corporate Finance* 5 (Summer 1992): 59–66.

Comment, Robert, and Gregg A. Jarrell. "Corporate Focus and Stock Returns." *Journal of Financial Economics* 37 (January 1995): 67–87.

Dean, Joel. *Capital Budgeting.* New York: Columbia University Press, 1951.

Denis, David J., and Diane K. Denis. "Performance Changes Following Top Management Dismissals." *The Journal of Finance* 50 (September 1995): 1029–1057.

Donaldson, Gordon. "Voluntary Restructuring: The Case of General Mills." *Journal of Applied Corporate Finance* 4 (Fall 1991): 6–19.

Emerick, Dennis, and William White. "The Case for Private Placements: How Sophisticated Investors Add Value to Corporate Debt Issues." *Journal of Applied Corporate Finance* 5 (Fall 1992): 83–91.

Fama, Eugene F. "Agency Problems and the Theory of the Firm." *Journal of Political Economy* (April 1980): 288–307.

Froot, Kenneth, Andre Perold, and Jeremy Stein. "Shareholder Trading Practices and Corporate Investment Horizons." *Journal of Applied Corporate Finance* 5 (Summer 1992): 42–58.

Jensen, Michael C., and William A. Meckling. "Theory of the Firm: Managerial Behavior, Agency Costs, and the Ownership Structure." *Journal of Financial Economics* 3 (October 1976): 305–360.

Kester, W. Carl. "Governance, Contracting, and Investment Horizons: A Look at Japan and Germany." *Journal of Applied Corporate Finance* 5 (Summer 1992): 83–98.

Lessard, Donald R. "Global Competition and Corporate Finance in the 1990s." *Journal of Applied Corporate Finance* 3 (Winter 1991): 59–72.

Levine, David I. "Do Corporate Executives Have Rational Expectations?" *Journal of Business* 66 (April 1993): 271–293.

Lippert, Robert L., and William T. Moore. "Monitoring Versus Bonding: Shareholder Rights and Management Compensation." *Financial Management* 54 (Autumn 1995): 54–62.

May, Don O. "Do Managerial Motives Influence Firm Risk Reduction Strategies?" *The Journal of Finance* 50 (September 1996): 1291–1308.

Mehran, Hamid. "Executive Compensation Structure, Ownership, and Firm Performance." *Journal of Financial Economics* 38 (June 1995): 163–184.

Narayanan, M. P. "Form of Compensation and Managerial Decision Horizon." *Journal of Financial and Quantitative Analysis* 31 (December 1996): 467–491.

Park, Sangsoo, and Moon H. Song. "Employee Stock Ownership Plans, Firm Performance, and Monitoring by Outside Blockholders." *Financial Management* 24 (Winter 1995): 52–65.

Porter, Michael E. "Capital Choices: Changing the Way America Invests in Industry." *Journal of Applied Corporate Finance* 5 (Summer 1992): 4–16.

———. "Capital Disadvantage: America's Failing Capital Investment System." *Harvard Business Review* (September–October 1992): 65–82.

Porter, Michael E., and Mark R. Kramer. "The Competitive Advantage of Corporate Philanthropy." *Harvard Business Review* 80 (December 2002): 56–68.

Prueitt, George C., and Chan S. Park. "Monitoring Project Performance with Post-Audit Information: Cash Flow Control Charts." *The Engineering Economist* 36 (Summer 1991): 307–335.

Shapiro, Alan C. "International Capital Budgeting." *Midland Corporate Finance Journal* 1 (Spring 1983): 26–45.

Shleifer, Andrei, and Robert W. Vishny. "A Survey of Corporate Governance." *The Journal of Finance* 52 (June 1997): 737–783.

Smith, Michael P. "Shareholder Activism by Institutional Investors: Evidence from CalPERS." *The Journal of Finance* 51 (March 1996): 227–252.

Sridharan, Uma V. "CEO Influence and Executive Compensation." *The Financial Review* 31 (February 1996): 51–66.

Stewart, G. Bennett III. "Market Myths." *Journal of Applied Corporate Finance* 2, no. 3 (Fall 1989): 6–23.

Sullivan, G. William. "A New Paradigm for Engineering Economy." *The Engineering Economist* 36 (Spring 1991): 187–200.

Szewczyk, Samual H., George P. Tsetsekos, and Zaher Zantout. "The Valuation of Corporate R&D Expenditures: Evidence from Investment Opportunities and Free Cash Flow." *Financial Management* 25 (Spring 1996): 105–110.

Woolridge, J. Randall. "Competitive Decline and Corporate Restructuring: Is a Myopic Stock Market to Blame?" *Journal of Applied Corporate Finance* (Spring 1988): 26–36.

Zantout, Zaher, and George P. Tsetsekos. "The Wealth Effects of Announcements of R&D Expenditure Increases." *The Journal of Financial Research* 17 (Summer 1994): 205–216.

CHAPTER 3

Measuring Wealth: Time Value of Money

After completing this chapter you should be able to:

- Explain to somebody why you have to put future dollars on a common basis before you can add them. For example, can you add a dollar expected in year one and a dollar expected in year two to get a meaningful answer?
- Calculate the present dollar equivalent (present value) of a future amount.
- Compute the future dollar equivalent (future value) of a present amount.
- Define an **annuity** and find the present value or future value of an annuity.
- Recognize the numerous instances in which you come in contact with the pricing of future cash flows.
- Price future cash flows so that you know a bargain when you see it.
- Adjust for instances in which the interest is compounded more than once a year.
- Value cash flows that are received at various points in the year.
- Value perpetual cash flows.

For-profit education is now estimated to be in the billions of dollars worldwide. Sylvan Learning Systems, founded in 1979, now has over 700 franchised learning centers and a market capitalization of over $2 billion. To open one of these centers an entrepreneur must invest $34,000 to $42,000 for the franchise and another $76,000 to $137,000 in start-up costs. For this investment, the owner receives training and an exclusive right to use the Sylvan name and Sylvan programs designed to help grade school and high school students with reading, math, and study skills. In addition, several professional continuing education programs and testing services are being offered at these centers. Fees for these programs average \$30 to \$40 per hour or \$1,000 to \$3,000 per course. Instructors' wages for these educational services average 40 percent of the revenue charged for the service. The remainder of the revenue must cover the fixed costs with enough profit left to allow the entrepreneur an adequate return on his or her average \$140,000 investment. With investors demanding returns in the neighborhood of 12 percent, these entrepreneurs must determine if there is enough demand to justify the investment. The time value concepts developed in this chapter will help you to make these decisions.

These same time value concepts are invaluable for a myriad of planning purposes. Valuation of a potential acquisition is primarily an exercise in determining the present value of future cash flows. Amounts required for sinking fund and pension fund contributions depend on the rate at which money will grow over time if invested. Choice of financing methods also involves trade-offs between money now and money later. In the personal realm, retirement planning, house financing, and savings programs all involve trade-offs between money now and money later. The principles covered in this chapter are the key to making optimal choices in these and hundreds of other situations, as well as optimal capital budgeting decisions.

SINGLE AMOUNT PROBLEMS

The basis for all time value analysis is that a dollar invested today will grow to a greater amount in the future. The mathematical formula describing that growth is for finance what the laws of motion are for astronomy; it is the foundation for much of our understanding of how the financial world operates.

Every day individuals, businesses, and governments give up dollars with hopes of receiving more dollars in the future. How much more is determined by the forces of supply and demand in the market for particular funds. At the very least, one would expect to be compensated for forgoing present consumption and for any risk involved. This compensation is referred to as the cost of money or the cost of capital. For debt securities, this cost is referred to as interest, and for equity securities this cost is a required rate of return. How the market operates to determine the interest rate or required rate of return is discussed in the next chapter. For now we know there is a cost of money, and this dollar cost is determined by the size of the cash flow, the present value (PV) or future value (FV), the amount of time the money is invested (n), and the cost of the money in percentage terms (k). In this section we will illustrate how to solve all four types of single amount problems using formulas, tables, the typical financial calculator, and the Excel spreadsheet packages. We begin with a discussion of future value of single amount problems, then discuss rate of return problems, number of period problems, and conclude this section with present value of single amounts.

Future Value of a Single Amount

A simple savings account can be used to develop the future value principle. Suppose a savings account at Montgomery National Bank pays 10 percent interest, compounded annually. This means that at the end of each year, if there were no deposits or withdrawals during the year, the bank adds to the account 10 percent of the balance at the beginning of the year. Letting FV_n be the amount in the account at the end of n years, the growth of the account over a 2-year period can be summarized as follows:

$$FV_1 = \$100 + (.10 \times \$100) = \$100(1 + .10) = \$110$$

$$FV_2 = \$110 + (.10 \times \$110) = \$110(1 + .10) = \$100(1 + .10)^2 = \$121$$

This growth pattern can be generalized for any present value, any interest rate, and any number of periods:

$$FV_n = PV(1 + k)^n \qquad \textbf{(3-1)}$$

where

PV = the present value
n = the number of periods, and
k = the interest rate or rate of return per period

The mechanical problem of solving for $(1 + k)^n$ when n is large can be resolved by use of a financial calculator, a computer spreadsheet program such as Excel, or Table A-1 at the back of this book. Table A-1 contains values of $(1 + k)^n$ for numerous values of k and n.

Future value of a single amount example: One hundred dollars will be invested in the previously discussed savings account at Montgomery National Bank, and the deposit will be left to grow for 20 years at 10 percent annual interest. The problem can be stated as follows:

Formula solution: $FV_{20} = \$100(1 + .10)^{20}$

Table solution: By turning to Table A-1, going to the 20 period row, and then going across to the 10 percent column, $(1 + .10)^{20}$ is found to equal 6.7275. In 20 years, the \$100 deposit will grow to:[1]

$$FV_{20} = \$100 \times 6.7275 = \$672.75$$

[1]If you need a factor from one of the time value tables (A-1 through A-5) for an interest rate not shown in the table, you can find the approximate amount using the following linear interpolation formula:

$$F(k) = F(k_b) + [F(k_a) - F(k_b)][(k - k_b)/(k_a - k_b)]$$

where k is the interest rate for which a factor is desired, k_a is the interest rate immediately above k in the table, and k_b is the interest rate immediately below k in the table. $F(k_a)$ and $F(k_b)$ are the factors from the table for interest rates k_a and k_b respectively.

Suppose, for example, you want to find $(1 + .094)^{20}$ using Table A-1. Using interpolation, the value is approximately:

$$5.6044 + [6.7275 - 5.6044][(.094 - .09)/(.10 - .09)] = 6.0536$$

In other words, at 9.4 percent interest, \$100 would grow to approximately \$100 × 6.0536 = \$605.36

Calculator solution: Most financial calculators have five buttons that allow the user to find the solution to most financial problems. In this case you would enter \$100 (or minus \$100 depending on the make of the calculator) and press the PV button, enter 20 and press the N button, enter .10 and press the I/Y button, then press the compute button and then the FV button and the calculator will return the answer of \$672.75.

Spreadsheet example: To solve the above problem using Excel, you first click on the paste function icon on the formatting toolbar. This will bring up a listing of the function categories on the left and function names on the right. We are interested in the financial function named FV. Click financial on the left and then FV on the right. This will bring up the overlay where you will enter the rate as .10, the NPER as 20, and the PV as –100. When you press enter, \$672.75 will appear as the answer in the cell. The field PMT and TYPE should be left blank. Rounding the tables at four decimal places causes any slight difference from the table answer.

Rate of Return on a Single Amount

The rate of return earned on an investment can also be found using Equation 3-1.

Rate of return on a single amount example: An investment of \$1,000 today in a mutual fund offered by Troy Securities is expected to grow to \$4,661 in 20 years.

Table solution: To find the rate of return, we need to solve for k in the equation:

$$\$4{,}661 = \$1{,}000(1 + k)^{20}$$

Dividing both sides of the equation by \$1,000 yields:

$$4.661 = (1 + k)^{20}$$

The value of k can be found by using a calculator to take the 20th root of both sides of the equation or by going to the 20-year row in Table A-1 and looking for the number 4.661. This number is found at the 8-percent column, so the rate of return earned on the investment is 8 percent.

Calculator solution: In this case you would enter \$4,661 and press the FV button, enter 20 and press the N button, enter –\$1,000 and press the PV button, then press the compute button and then the I/Y button and the calculator will return the answer of 8 percent.

Spreadsheet example: In Excel, return to the listing of financial functions as described previously and select the RATE function. In the overlay, enter 20 as the NPER, –1000 as the PV, and 4661 as the FV. When you press enter, 8% will appear as the answer in the cell. The field PMT and TYPE should again be left blank. You must enter the PV as a negative number with no commas. In fact all dollar amounts should be entered without commas.

Equation 3-1 is written in terms of rates of return, but it applies to any situation in which growth occurs at a rate of k each period. At a 5 percent inflation rate, for example, the price of a building lot selling for $20,000 today will increase in 10 years to:

$$FV_{10} = \$20{,}000\ (1 + .05)^{10} = \$20{,}000 \times 1.6289 = \$32{,}578$$

Number of Periods for a Single Amount

The number of periods it takes an investment to grow to a specific amount can be found using Equation 3-1.

Number of periods for a single amount example: An investment of $1,000 today in a mutual fund offered by Troy Securities is expected to earn 8 percent in the future. How long will it take for this investment to grow to $4,661? (From the prior example we know the answer will be 20 years, but let's check this out.)

Table solution: To find the number of periods, we need to solve for k in the equation:

$$\$4{,}661 = \$1{,}000(1 + .08)^{n}$$

Dividing both sides of the equation by $1,000 yields:

$$4.661 = (1 + .08)^{n}$$

The value of n can be found by trial and error by raising 1.08 by increasing values for n, or by going to the 8 percent column in Table A-1 and looking for the number 4.661. This number is found at the 20 period row, so it takes 20 years for this $1,000 investment to grow to $4,661.

Calculator solution: In this case you would enter $4,661 and press the FV button, enter .08 and press the I/Y button, enter –$1,000 and press the PV button, then press the compute button and then the N button and the calculator will return the answer of 20 years.

Spreadsheet solution: In Excel return to the listing of financial functions as described previously and select the NPER function. In the overlay, enter .08 as the RATE, –1000 as the PV, and 4661 as the FV. When you press enter, 20 will appear as the answer in the cell. The field PMT and TYPE should again be left blank. Again, you must enter the PV as a negative number with no commas.

Present Value of a Single Amount

The amount we would be willing to pay now in exchange for a dollar at some future date would not exceed the amount we would need to invest today to have a dollar by that future date. The present value of a future amount can be found by rearranging the terms in Equation 3-1:

$$PV = FV_n/(1 + k)^n = FV_n[1/(1 + k)^n] \qquad \textbf{(3-2)}$$

In this context, k is the interest rate or rate of return that can be earned elsewhere. Table A-1 at the end of this book contains values of $(1 + k)^n$ for numerous combinations of k and n, while Table A-2 contains values of $1/(1 + k)^n$. A financial calculator or a spreadsheet program such as Excel can also be used.

Present value of a single amount example: Shares in a timber stand near Tuscaloosa cost $10,000 today, and will be worth an estimated $20,000 in 5 years. Other investments provide returns of 10 percent.

Formula solution: The present value of the $20,000 future amount is therefore:

$$PV_5 = \$20{,}000[1/(1 + .10)^5] = \$20{,}000 \times .6209 = \$12{,}418$$

In other words, $12,418 invested elsewhere at 10 percent would result in $20,000 in 5 years, so the present value of the timber stand is $12,418. The shares are therefore a bargain at $10,000.

Calculator solution: In this case you would enter $20,000 and press the FV button, enter .10 and press the I/Y button, enter 5 and press the N button, then press the compute button and then the PV button and the calculator will return the answer of –$12,418. The minus means that you must have an outflow of $12,418 today to equate with $20,000 in 5 years if you can earn 10 percent on investments of equal risk.

Spreadsheet example: In Excel, return to the listing of financial functions as described previously and select the NPER function. In the overlay, enter .08 as the RATE, 5 as the NPER, and 20000 as the FV. When you press enter, $12,418 will appear as the answer in the cell. The field PMT and TYPE should again be left blank. Again, you must enter the dollar amounts with no commas.

The relationships between rate of return, time, and present value are illustrated in Figure 3-1. The same relationship can be seen by scanning across rows

FIGURE 3-1 Relationship between Present Value, Rate of Return, and Time

These figures show the relationship between present value, future value, and rate of return. The two curves in each figure show the difference between the impacts of 5 percent and 10 percent rates of return.

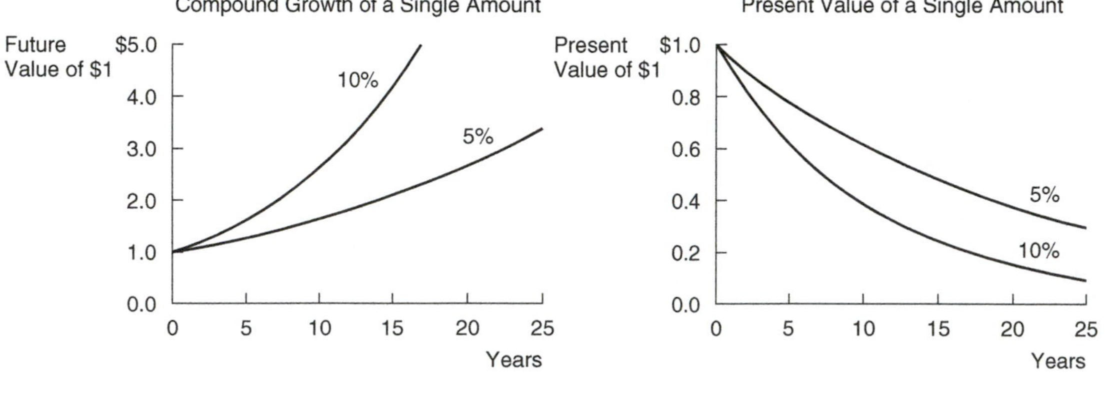

and down columns in Table A-2. The longer the time between present and future amounts, and the higher the required return, the smaller will be the present value of the future amount, and vice versa.

ANNUITY PROBLEMS

Annuity problems come in two types. Ordinary annuities have cash flows that occur at the end of the period and annuities due have cash flows that occur at the beginning of the period. Unless otherwise stated, please assume that we are talking about ordinary annuities. In this section we will discuss future value of annuity problems and then present value of annuity problems.

Future Value of an Annuity—Looking for the Future Value

As part of its capital investment planning, Normal Corporation wants to put away money each year to replace a major asset when it wears out. This is but one of hundreds of situations in which managers need to know the amount to which an **annuity**—a payment each period—will grow. These questions could be answered using Equation 3-1, but the process would be tedious. Future value of annuity formulas and tables are created to eliminate the tedium. A good financial calculator or a spreadsheet program like Excel can also be used to solve these problems quickly.

To develop the process for finding the future value of an annuity, consider what will happen if you deposit $1,000 in an account at Florence National Bank at the end of each year for 3 years, with the account paying 10 percent annual interest. Since payments are made at the end of the year, the first annual payment will have had 2 years to earn interest, the second annual payment will have had 1 year to earn interest, and the third payment will have earned no interest. The growth of each payment can be determined using Equation 3-1, and the individual future values can be summed to find the future value of the annuity, as illustrated in Table 3-1. Figure 3-2 illustrates the analysis from Table 3-1 in the form of a time line. The future value of this annuity can be rewritten as:

$$FVA_3 = \$1{,}000(1 + .10)^2 + \$1{,}000(1 + .10)^1 + \$1{,}000(1 + .10)^0 = \$3{,}310$$

TABLE 3-1 Future Value of an Annuity

This table illustrates the growth of $1,000 invested at the end of each year for 3 years at a 10 percent annual interest rate.

PAYMENT #	YEARS TO GROW	COMPOUND VALUE
1	2	$\$1{,}000(1 + .10)^2 = \$1{,}210$
2	1	$\$1{,}000(1 + .10)^1 = \$1{,}100$
3	0	$\$1{,}000(1 + .10)^0 = \$1{,}000$
TOTAL FUTURE VALUE		$3,310

FIGURE 3-2 Time Line Illustration of the Future Value of an Annuity
This figure illustrates the future value of an annuity of $1,000 a year for 3 years, at a 10 percent rate of return.

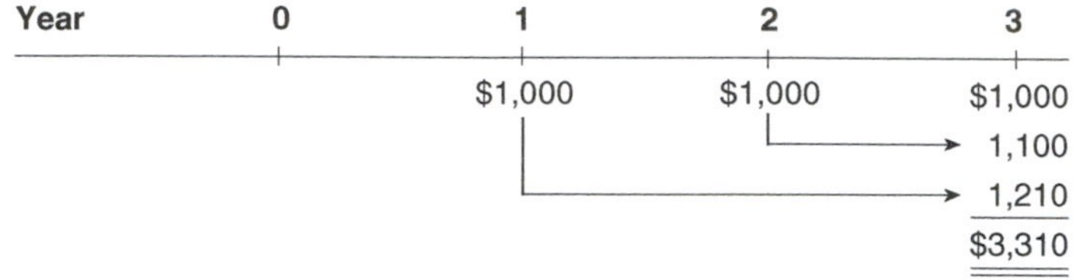

Extending this concept, the general formula for the future value of an annuity is:

$$FVA_n = \sum_{t=1}^{n} PMT_t(1 + k)^{n-t} \qquad \textbf{(3-3)}$$

where PMT_t is the payment at the end of period t. As previously defined, k and n are the rate of return and the number of periods. When the payment is the same each period, Equation 3-3 can be simplified with a little rearrangement of terms to:[2]

$$FVA_n = PMT \times [(1 + k)^n - 1]/k \qquad \textbf{(3-3a)}$$

$$FVA_n = PMT \times FVA1_{n,k} \qquad \textbf{(3-3b)}$$

where $FVA1_{n,k} = [(1 + k)^n - 1]/k$, the future value of an annuity of $1 at the end of each period for n periods, at a rate of return of k per period.

The annuity just described is a **level** or **uniform** annuity because the payment is the same each period. The term **annuity** without a qualifier is generally used to refer to a level annuity.

As with the other time value formulas, Equation 3-3 can be readily solved using a calculator, a computer program, or Table A-3 at the back of this book. To find the future value of an annuity, it is only necessary to find the future value of an annuity of $1 for the appropriate values of n and k in Table A-3, then multiply that factor by the amount of cash flow per year (PMT).

Future value of an annuity—looking for the future value example: You decide to deposit $1,000 in an Individual Retirement Account at the end of each year for

---

[2]First, substitute PMT for PMT_t in Equation 3-3. Then multiply both sides of Equation 3-3 by $(1 + k)$ and rearrange terms to give:

$$FVA_n(1 + k) = PMT \times \sum_{t=1}^{n} (1 + k)^t$$

Subtracting Equation 3-3 from this new equation gives $FVA_n \times k = PMT[(1 + k)^n - 1]$. Dividing both sides of this equation by k gives Equation 3-3a.

the remaining 40 years of your working life. The money can be invested at an interest rate of 10 percent a year. How much will you have at the end of 40 years?

Table solution: The $1,000 per year will then grow to:

$$FVA_{40} = \$1{,}000 FVA1_{n,k}$$
$$= \$1{,}000 \times 442.59 = \$442{,}590$$

The value 442.59 is found at the intersection of the 10-percent column and 40-year row in Table A-3.

Calculator solution: In this case you would enter –1,000 and press the PMT button, enter .10 and press the I/Y button, enter 40 and press the N button, then press the compute button and then the FV button and the calculator will return the answer of $442,590.

Spreadsheet solution: In an empty cell in Excel, return to the listing of financial functions as described previously and select the FV function. In this case you would enter .10 as the rate, 40 as the NPER, –1000 as the PMT, PV is left empty, and the type field is left empty or a 0 can be entered to signify end of the year payments. When you press enter, $442,592.56 will appear as the answer in the cell. Again, you must enter the payment dollar amounts as a negative with no commas to signify an outflow of cash. If the payments were at the beginning of the periods, you would enter all of the above data, but a 1 in the type field.

Future Value of an Annuity—Looking for the Payment

Future value of an annuity—looking for the payment example: Birmingham Corporation needs to replace a piece of equipment in 5 years, at an estimated cost of $1 million. The company wants to make equal payments into an investment account at the end of each year for 5 years to accumulate the $1 million. The invested funds will earn 10 percent interest annually. What annual payment (paid at the end of each year) is necessary?

Table solution: The annual payment can be found as follows:

$$FVA_5 = PMT \times FVA1_{5yrs,10\%}$$

Using the 10 percent, 5-year factor from Table A-3 and substituting $1,000,000 for FVA_5 gives the annual payment needed (PMT):

$$\$1{,}000{,}000 = PMT \times 6.1051$$
$$PMT = \$1{,}000{,}000/6.1051 = \$163{,}797.48$$

Calculator solution: In this case you would enter $1,000,000 and press the FV button, enter .10 and press the I/Y button, enter 5 and press the N button, then press the compute button and then the PMT button and the calculator will return the answer of –$163,797.48. The negative sign signifies an outflow of cash.

Spreadsheet example: In an empty cell in Excel, return to the listing of financial functions as described previously and select the PMT function. In this case you would enter .10 as the rate, 5 as the NPER, $1000000 as the FV, PV is left empty, and the type field is left empty or a 0 can be entered to signify end of the year payments. When you press enter –$163,797.48 will appear as the answer in the cell. The negative sign on the answer is used to signify an outflow of cash. If the payments were at the beginning of the periods, you would enter all of the above data, but a 1 in the type field.

Future Value of an Annuity—Looking for the Rate of Return

Future value of an annuity—looking for the rate of return example: You invested $1,000 in mutual fund shares at the end of each year for the last 10 years. Your shares are now worth $19,337. What effective rate of return did you earn?

Table solution: To find the effective rate of return, it is first necessary to solve Equation 3-3b for $FVA1_{10yrs,k}$:

$$\$19,337 = \$1,000FVA1_{10yrs,k}$$

$$FVA1_{10yrs,k} = \$19,337/\$1,000 = 19.337$$

In the 10-year row of Table A-3, the factor 19.337 is found at the 14 percent column, so the effective rate of return was 14 percent.

Calculator solution: In this case you would enter – $1,000 and press the PMT button, enter 10 and press the N button, enter 19337 and press the FV button, then press the compute button and then the I/Y button and the calculator will return the answer of 14 percent.

Spreadsheet example: There are two functions in Excel that will work for this problem. The RATE function will work only on problems with even and consistent cash flows or payments. The IRR functions will work for uneven cash flows and cash flows that skip years. To use the RATE function, go to an empty cell in Excel, then return to the listing of financial functions as described previously and select the RATE function. In this case you would enter 10 as the NPER, –1000 as the PMT, $19337 as the FV, PV is left empty, and the type field is left empty or a 0 can be entered to signify end of the year payments. When you press enter, 14 percent will appear as the answer in the cell. If the payments were at the beginning of the periods, you would enter all of the above data, but a 1 in the type field. To use the IRR function, you must first enter a 0 (your investment today), then 9 columns of –1000, and then 18337 ($19,337 the future value minus the last $1,000 payment). Then move to a free cell and use the formatting toolbar, pick the financial function IRR. In the overlay field labeled "values," go to the rightmost cell with the 0 in it and right-click the mouse and then drag the mouse across all eleven columns ending with the cell with the 18337; release and hit enter. The answer 14 percent will appear. This function works the same when years are skipped and for uneven amounts. In skipped years, you must enter a 0 in each year or column in which you do not receive or pay any money.

Annuities Due versus Ordinary Annuities

The annuities previously examined are called **ordinary annuities** or **annuities in arrears** because payment occurs at the end of each period. An **annuity due** or **annuity in advance** has payments at the beginning of each period. Payments for a $1,000, 3-year ordinary annuity and annuity due are as follows:

YEAR	0	1	2	3
Ordinary annuity		$1,000	$1,000	$1,000
Annuity due	$1,000	$1,000	$1,000	

Equation 3-3a and Table A-3 are used to find the future value at the end of year n when payments are made at the end of each year. If payments are to be made at the beginning of each year for n years, the future value of an annuity factor from Table A-3 must be multiplied by $(1 + k)$, or the right-hand sides of Equations 3-3a and 3-3b must be multiplied by $(1 + k)$ to recognize the extra interest earned by having the funds invested for one more year.[3] When using the Excel functions, you specify ordinary annuity or annuity due by entering a "0" for an ordinary annuity and a "1" for an annuity due in the TYPE field.

Annuity due example—looking for the future value: Athens Life Insurance Company will sell you a 20-year term policy for $500 at the beginning of each year. If you are still alive at the end of 20 years, you get nothing back. A whole life policy, on the other hand, requires a payment of $1,500 at the beginning of each year for 20 years. If you are still alive at the end of 20 years, you can cash in the policy for $40,000. You can earn 8 percent on investments of equal risk.

Table solution: To make a decision, you consider the amount you would have if you bought the term insurance and invested the other $1,000 at the beginning of each year in an alternate investment earning an 8 percent annual return. The amount you would have at the end of 20 years is:

$$\$1{,}000 \times 45.762 \times 1.08 = \$49{,}423$$

You would end up with more money if you bought the term policy and invested the extra money somewhere else.

Spreadsheet example: In an empty cell in Excel, return to the listing of financial functions as described previously and select the FV function. In this case you would enter .08 as the I/Y, 20 as the N, –1000 as the PMT, 1 in the type field,

[3]**Proof:** If payment is at the beginning of the period,

$$FVA_n = PMT_1(1+k)^n + PMT_2(1+k)^{n-1} + \ldots + PMT_n(1+k)^1$$
$$= \sum_{t=1}^{n} PMT_t + k)^{n-t+1} = (1+k)\left[\sum_{t=1}^{n} PMT_t(1+k)^{n-t}\right]$$

The bracketed portion is the right-hand side of Equation 3-3, which is $FVA1_{n,k}$ if $PMT_t = \$1$ for all t.

and the PV field is left empty. When you press enter, $49,422.92 will appear as the answer in the cell. The difference from the table answer is due to rounding in the table numbers. The computer automatically adjusts for the annuity due payment when you specify a "1" in the type field.

Present Value of an Annuity—Looking for the Present Value

Trade-offs between costs now and streams of benefits in the future are typical of capital budgeting. The purchase of a business or a share of stock also involves payment now in exchange for a series of cash benefits in the future. Present value of annuity concepts provide a convenient method of deciding if the stream of future cash benefits is worth the present cost.

To develop the present value of an annuity, consider an investment that will pay you $1,000 at the end of each year for 3 years. You could earn 10 percent a year if you invested your money elsewhere. The present value of each individual cash inflow can be found using Equation 3-2 and Table A-2, and the individual present values can then be added to find the value of the investment:

YEAR	CASH FLOW	PRESENT VALUE AT 10 PERCENT
1	$1,000	$\$1{,}000[1/(1+.10)^1] = \$1{,}000 \times .9091 = \$909.10$
2	$1,000	$\$1{,}000[1/(1+.10)^2] = \$1{,}000 \times .8264 = \$826.40$
3	$1,000	$\$1{,}000[1/(1+.10)^3] = \$1{,}000 \times .7513 = \$751.30$
TOTAL PRESENT VALUE		$2,486.80

If the market price of the investment is less than $2,486.80, it is attractive. This present value can also be illustrated in the form of a time line:

YEAR	0	1	2	3
		$1,000	$1,000	$1,000
	$909.10			
	826.40			
	751.30			
	$2,486.80			

This procedure could be used even if the investment was expected to generate cash flows over a period of 50 years, but the calculations would become tedious. The present value of annuity formulas and tables make calculations faster and easier. The present value of an annuity formula can be developed using the investment example just analyzed. The computation procedure for this problem can be rewritten:

$$PVA_3 = \$1{,}000/(1+.10) + \$1{,}000/(1+.10)^2 + \$1{,}000/(1+.10)^3$$

This procedure can be generalized as the present value of an annuity (PVA_n):

$$PVA_n = \sum_{t=1}^{n} PMT_t / (1 + k)^t \quad \textbf{(3-4)}$$

where PMT_t is the payment at the end of period t, k is the required return, and n is the number of periods. When the payment is the same each period, Equation 3-4 can be simplified with a little rearrangement of terms to:[4]

$$PVA_n = PMT \times [1 - 1/(1 + k)^n]/k \quad \textbf{(3-4a)}$$

$$PVA_n = PMT \times PVA1_{n,k} \quad \textbf{(3-4b)}$$

where $PVA1_{n,k} = [1 - 1/(1 + k)^n]/k$, the present value of an annuity of $1 at the end of each period for n periods at an interest rate of k per period.

As with other time value formulas, Equation 3-4 can be readily solved using a calculator, a computer spreadsheet program such as Excel, or Table A-4 at the back of this book. This table contains present values of annuities of $1 at the end of each period for various rates of return and numbers of periods. To find the present value of any annuity with equal payments, it is only necessary to find the present value of an annuity of $1 for the appropriate values of n and k in Table A-4 and multiply that factor by the amount of cash flow per period (PMT).

Present value of an annuity—looking for the present value example: A winner of the Super Lottery will receive $20 million, but the lucky winner should not expect a $20 million check. The winner receives an immediate payment of $1 million, then $1 million at the end of each year for 19 years. At a 10 percent discount rate, what is the present value of this prize?

Table solution: The present value of the payment is:

$$\text{Present value} = \$1{,}000{,}000 + \$1{,}000{,}000 PVA1_{19yrs,10\%}$$

$$= \$1{,}000{,}000 + \$1{,}000{,}000 \times 8.3649 = \$9{,}364{,}900$$

The present value interest factor of 8.3649 can be found in Table A-4 under the 10 percent column and across in the 19-year row (because there are 19 payments left). This table factor is multiplied by $1,000,000 and then added to the initial $1,000,000 installment paid at the beginning of the year.

Table solution—modified for the beginning of the year payments: The lottery winner in the previous example received $1 million immediately, plus $1 million

[4]First, recognize that $PVA_n = FVA_n/(1 + k)^n$. This equality can be verified by dividing the right-hand side of Equation 3-3 by $(1 + k)^n$ and rearranging terms to yield Equation 3-4. Substituting from Equation 3-3b for FVA_n gives:

$$PVA_n = \{PMT[(1 + k)^n - 1]/k\}/(1 + k)^n$$

Rearranging terms yields Equation 3-4a.

a year for 19 years. This is equivalent to $1 million at the *beginning* of each year for 20 years. Equation 3-4 and Table A-4 are for payment at the end of each period. If payments are at the beginning of each year (annuity due), it is only necessary to multiply the present value of the annuity or the right-hand side of Equation 3-4 by (1 + k).

$$\text{Present value} = \$1{,}000{,}000\text{PVA1}^{20\text{yrs},10\%} \times 1.10$$
$$= \$1{,}000{,}000 \times 8.5136 \times 1.10 = \$9{,}364{,}960$$

Spreadsheet solution: The present value of these winnings can be determined by using the Excel PV or NPV functions. The PV functions can be used only when there is a consistent and equal payment, while the NPV function can be used with equal or unequal year-end cash flows over time. Using the present value function you would enter .10 as the RATE, 20 as the NPER, –1000000 as the PMT, 1 in the type field, and the PV field is left empty. When you press enter $9,364,920.09 will appear as the answer in the cell. The difference from the table answer is due to rounding in the table numbers. To use the NPV function you must first enter 20 columns of –1000000. Move to an empty cell, call up the NPV function in the Rate field and enter .10, then in the VALUES field begin at the second column and right-click and drag the mouse across the remaining 19 columns. Press enter and the answer will come back $8,364,920.09. To this solution you add the initial column that contains the number 1000000 and the final answer is $9,364,920.09. In reality, the winner will pay about 40 percent of all winnings in taxes, so the present value of what she will get to keep is $5,618,940.

Present Value of an Annuity—Looking for the Payment

Present value of an annuity—looking for the payment example: A senator once used the purchase of a letter opener for $475,000 as an example of government waste. The letter opener, produced by AES Systems of Elk Grove, Illinois, was designed to save substantial amounts of labor for public utilities, insurance companies, and other organizations that receive large numbers of payment envelopes. Assuming a 10 percent required return, a 10-year life, and year-end cash flows, what annual expense reduction is needed to justify this letter opener? (We ignore taxes for simplicity.)

Table solution: The present value of the payment is:

$$\$475{,}000 = \text{PMT} \times \text{PVA1}^{10\text{yrs},10\%}$$
$$\$475{,}000 = \text{PMT} \times 6.1446$$
$$\text{PMT} = \$475{,}000/6.1446 = \$77{,}303.65$$

The present value interest factor of 6.1446 can be found in Table A-4 under the 10-percent column and across in the 10-year row. This table factor is divided into the $475,000 purchase price to arrive at the $77,303.65 answer.

Spreadsheet solution: Using the letter opener example from above, this problem can be solved with the Excel PMT function. Using the PMT function you would enter .10 as the RATE, 10 as the NPER, –475000 as the PV; the type field and the PV field are left empty. When you press enter, $77,304.06 will appear as the answer in the cell. The difference from the table answer is due to rounding in the table numbers. The investment would be profitable if it did the work of half a dozen people opening letters manually at an annual labor cost of greater than $12,884 each.

Present Value of an Annuity—Looking for the Rate of Return

Present value of an annuity—looking for the rate of return example: If Jacksonville Repair Service buys a new personal computer for $3,790.80, bookkeeping expense will be reduced by $1,000 a year for an estimated 5 years. What rate of return is Jacksonville earning on this computer investment?

Table solution: Equation 3-4b and Table A-4 can also be used to find the effective rate of return on an investment. The problem can be written as:

$$\$3{,}790.80 = \$1{,}000 \times PVA1^{5yrs,k}$$

$$PVA1^{5yrs,k} = \$3{,}790.80/\$1{,}000 = 3.7908$$

The present value of an annuity of $1 a year for 5 years is 3.7908. Going across the 5-year row of Table A-4, 3.7908 is found at the 10-percent column, so the effective rate of return is 10 percent. If Jacksonville Repair's cost of funds is less than 10 percent, the investment is attractive.

In more general terms, the effective rate of return is the discount rate that leads to a present value of benefits equal to the present value of costs. When the stream of cash flows is complex, it is often necessary to use trial and error to find the rate of return from the tables. Fortunately, some calculators and computer programs like Excel have built-in financial functions for solving these otherwise tedious problems.

Spreadsheet solution: In Excel, you could use the RATE function or the IRR function illustrated under the "Future Value of an Annuity—Rate of Return Problems" heading earlier in the chapter.

COMPLEX CASH FLOW PROBLEMS

The problems addressed thus far have been solved by using one equation and one table. Frequently, the equations and tables are used in combination to solve more complex cash flow problems. A complex cash flow is one where the cash flow amounts are not equal and consistent but instead either miss periods or change in amount.

Complex cash flow present value example: Oakland Chips, which has a 10 percent required return, is considering a new extractor. Because of anticipated start-up delays, cash flow will be $1,000 at the end of each year for years 4 through 20. What is the present value of this investment?

Table solution: We could find the present values of the 17 cash flows separately, then add them up. This would, however, be tedious. We can speed the analysis with the following calculation procedure:

$$\text{PV of \$1,000 a year for years 1 through 20} = \$1{,}000 \times 8.5136 = \$8{,}513.60$$

$$-\text{PV of \$1,000 a year for years 1 through 3} = \$1{,}000 \times 2.4869 = 2{,}486.90$$

$$= \text{PV of \$1,000 a year for years 4 through 20} \quad \$6{,}026.70$$

This same solution procedure can then be written as:

$$\text{PV} = \$1{,}000(8.5136 - 2.4869) = \$6{,}026.70$$

Spreadsheet solution: To solve this problem with the computer, you would set up the following spreadsheet:

	A	B	C	D	E	F	...	T
1								
2	Years	0	1	2	3	4	...	20
3	Cash inflows		0	0	0	1000	1000	1000
4	Present value	$6,026.71 = NPV(0.1,B3:T3) is the function to bring the future cash flows back to present						

Note that zeros need to be entered in the first three columns to tell the computer that the cash flow will not start until the end of the fourth year. After you press ENTER the computer will return the answer of $6,026.71.

Complex cash flow net present value example: Fairbanks Partners are considering the purchase of a small retail outlet. The outlet will cost $100,000, and $50,000 will be spent in the next year to make the outlet serviceable. After that, cash inflows will be $25,000 a year, and the outlet can be sold in 10 years for an estimated $80,000.

Table solutions: The cash flows are summarized as follows:

YEAR	0	1	2 THROUGH 10	10
Cash flow	–$100,000	–$50,000	$25,000 a year	$80,000

The firm can evaluate this investment by subtracting the present values of the outflows from the present values of the benefits to provide a **net present value.** At a 10 percent required return, the net present value is:

YEAR	CASH FLOW	PRESENT VALUE OF $1 FACTOR (10%)	PRESENT VALUE
0 (now)	-$100,000	1.0000	-$100,000
1	-50,000	.9091	-45,455
2–10	25,000	(6.1446 – .9091)	130,888
10	80,000	0.3855	30,840
		Net Present Value	$ 16,273

Since the net present value is positive in this case, the present value of the benefits is greater than the present value of the costs and the initial outlay. Thus, the investment is attractive.

Multiple inflows and outflows complex cash flow net present value example: Assume a rental property in Stockton can be purchased for $40,000. The property will generate cash flows of $8,000 at the end of each year for 7 years, before equipment replacement. A new $6,000 furnace will be needed at the end of 5 years, and the building will be worth an estimated $50,000 at the end of 7 years. If you can invest elsewhere at 10 percent, what is the net present value of this project?

The cash flows are as follows:

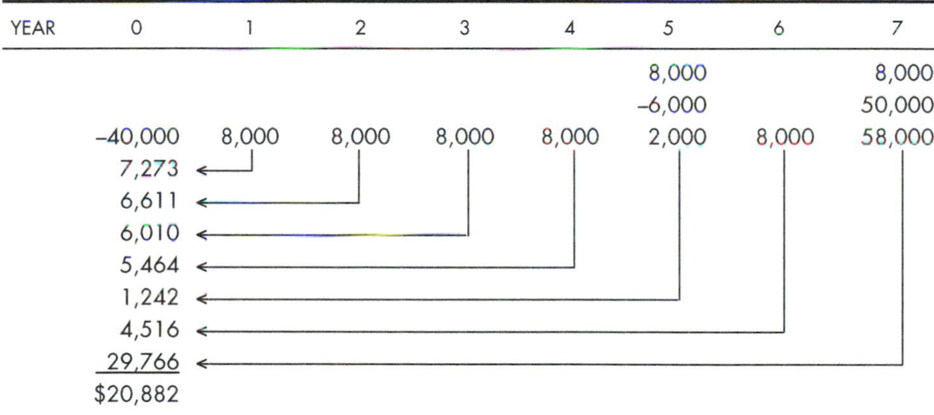

An alternate table solution form is as follows:

YEAR	CASH FLOW	PRESENT VALUE FACTOR	PRESENT VALUE
0	-40,000	1.0000	-40,000
1–7	8,000	4.8684	38,947
5	-6,000	0.6209	-3,725
7	50,000	0.5132	25,660
			$20,882

Spreadsheet solution: To solve this problem with the computer, you would set up the following spreadsheet:

	A	B	C	D	E	F	G	H	I
1									
2	Years	0	1	2	3	4	5	6	7
3	Purchase price	–40000							
4	Cash inflows		8000	8000	8000	8000	8000	8000	8000
5	Furnace replacement						–6000		
6	Salvage value								50000
7	Total cash flows	–40000	8000	8000	8000	8000	2000	8000	58000
8		= sum(b3..b6 is the formula to total the cash flows above. It should be							
9		copied across the spreadsheet							
10	Present value	\$60,880 = NPV(0.1,C7:17) is the function to bring the							
11		future cash flows back to present							
12	Net present value	\$20,880 = + B7 + B10 is the formula to calculate the net present value							

COMPOUNDING MORE THAN ONCE PER PERIOD

This chapter was introduced with an example in which a year's interest was added to a savings account at the end of each year. However, your bank probably adds interest earned on a monthly or even daily basis. Most bonds pay interest twice a year instead of once a year, and interest on the typical loan to an individual, whether a credit card loan or a mortgage loan, is charged on a monthly basis. Many capital investments provide benefits on a daily or weekly basis rather than in annual lump sums. This section covers the extensions needed to get accurate answers in these situations.

If a savings account pays 10 percent interest, with interest compounded annually, a \$100 deposit will grow to \$110 by the end of one year. If semiannual compounding is used, the account will pay 5 percent interest in each 6-month period. The amount in the account after one year will be:

$$\$100 \times (1.05)^2 = \$110.25$$

The account effectively grows at a rate of 10.25 percent a year rather than at 10 percent a year because of the semiannual compounding. The annual rate before considering the effect of compounding more than once per period (10 percent in this case) is called the **nominal** interest rate; in lending circles it is called the **annual percentage rate** (APR). The effective annual growth rate with compounding more than once per period considered (10.25 percent in this case) is called the **effective** interest rate.

The situation with compounding more than once per period can be generalized as follows:

$$FV_n = PV \times (1 + k'/q)^{nq} \quad \textbf{(3-5)}$$

where k′ is the nominal annual rate of return (10 percent in the previous example) and q is the number of times interest is compounded during the year.

The effective annual interest rate (k) with interest compounded q times a year is:[5]

$$k = (1 + k'/q)^q - 1 \quad \textbf{(3-6)}$$

Semiannual compounding example: Anchorage Service Workers Credit Union pays interest of 10 percent a year, compounded semiannually. If you deposit $100 today, what will be the balance in the account at the end of 3 years?

Formula solution:

$$FV_3 = \$100(1 + .10/2)^{3 \times 2} = \$134$$

The effective interest rate is:[6]

$$k = (1 + .10/2)^2 - 1 = 10.25\%$$

To find the present value or future value of a single amount with compounding more than once a period, Equation 3-1 or 3-2 can be used, with k being the effective interest rate. Alternately, these equations can be used with k′/q as the rate of return and qn as the number of periods.

Spreadsheet example: To solve the above problem using Excel, you first click on the paste function icon on the formatting toolbar. This will bring up a listing of the function categories on the left and function names on the right. For this problem, we are interested in the financial function named FV. Click financial on the left and then FV on the right. This will bring up the overlay where you will enter the rate as .10/2, the NPER as 3 * 6, and the PV as –100. When you press enter, $134.01 will appear as the answer in the cell. The field PMT and TYPE should be left blank. As was just illustrated, to adjust for multiple compounding of interest within a year in the spreadsheet, you simply fill the cells with the semiannual, quarterly, or monthly cash flow and adjust the interest rate within the function to a semiannual, quarterly, or monthly interest rate.

Quarterly compounding example: The present value of $10,000 to be received in 10 years at a nominal required return of 16 percent a year, compounded quarterly, is:

$$PV = \$10{,}000[1/(1 + .16/4)^{10 \times 4}] = \$10{,}000 \times .2083 = \$2{,}083$$

---

[5]For a discussion of the importance of recognizing the correct required return in these cases, see Philip A. Horvath, "A Pedagogic Note on Intra-Period Compounding and Discounting," *Financial Review* 20 (February 1985): 116–118.

[6]The bank that advertises the 10.25 percent effective interest rate will not make the same adjustment for loans. A 10 percent mortgage loan with monthly payments and monthly compounding of interest—the standard procedure for mortgage loans—has an effective interest rate of $(1 + .10/12)^{12} - 1 = 10.47$ percent, but a 10 percent rate will be advertised. In other words, financial institutions typically advertise k for their deposit accounts and k′ for their loan accounts, calling k the effective interest rate and k′ the annual percentage rate (APR).

Alternately, Equation 3-6 can be used to find the effective interest rate of $k = (1 + .16/4)^4 - 1 = 16.986\%$ and the value of k can then be used:

$$PV = \$10{,}000[1/(1 + .16986)^{10}] = \$2{,}083$$

Monthly compounding spreadsheet example: What is the present value of an 8 percent loan requiring a $460 monthly payment for the next 20 years? The PV function can be used to solve this problem. We would enter .08/12 in the RATE field, 20 * 12 in the NPER field, and –460 in the PMT field. The computer will return with an answer of $54,994.97. The .08/12 in the RATE field is the annual interest rate divided by 12 months in the year.

ALTERNATE PAYMENT PATTERNS

Payments often occur at some time during the year other than at year-end. It is easy to handle a payment received during the year because the future value of a single payment is found in the same way whether n is a whole number or a fraction. To see that this is true, consider a $100 deposit in a savings account that has semiannual compounding and pays 5 percent each 6-month period. If the money is left on deposit for 3.5 years, this is equivalent to a 7-year period at 5 percent a year. The amount in the account at the end of 3.5 years is:

$$FV_{3.5} = \$100(1 + .05)^7 = \$140.71$$

Note that the effective interest rate for this savings account is $k = (1 + .05)^2 - 1 = 10.25\%$, and that:

$$FV_{3.5} = \$100(1 + .1025)^{3.5} = \$140.71$$

Thus, the future value of this single payment could be found with Equation 3-1 even though n was not an integer.

To generalize this concept, we assume that money received any time during the year can be immediately invested as profitably as if it were received at the end of the year. This is probably a reasonable assumption in most cases, because there is nothing magical about year-end that causes superior investment opportunities to become available. Capital investments, for example, are made throughout the year. Stated formally, we *assume that the rate earned during any fraction (1/q) of a year is compounded q times a year.* Given this assumption, the future value of a single payment can be found with Equation 3-1 whether or not n is an integer.[7] It also follows from the justification for Equation 3-2 that the present value of a single payment can also be found with that equation whether or not n is an integer.

[7]**Proof:** The effective interest rate per fraction (1/q) of a year is $k_q = (1 + k)^{1/q} - 1$. Assume money is left to grow for $y + 1/q$ years at an interest rate of k_q per 1/q of a year. Then, $FV_{y+1/q} = PV(1 + k_q)^{yq+1} = PV(1 + k)^{y+1/q}$. Substituting n for y +1/q gives us Equation 3-1, with n being an integer or noninteger number.

Alternative compounding example: What is the present value of $1,000 to be received in 3.75 years, at an effective annual required return of 10 percent?

Formula solution:

$$PV = \$1,000/(1 + .10)^{3.75} = \$699.48$$

Calculator solution: In this case you would enter $1000 (or minus $1000 depending on the make of the calculator) and press the PV button, enter 3.75 and press the N button, enter .10 and press the I/Y button, then press the compute button and then the FV button and the calculator will return the answer of $699.48.

Spreadsheet solution: To solve the above problem using Excel, you first click on the paste function icon on the formatting toolbar. This will bring up a listing of the function categories on the left and function names on the right. We are interested in the financial function named PV. Click financial on the left and then PV on the right. This will bring up the overlay where you will enter the rate as .10, the NPER as 3.75, and the FV as 1000. When you press enter, $–699.48 will appear as the answer in the cell. The field PMT and TYPE should be left blank. The negative sign implies that you must invest this amount to receive the $1,000 in 3.75 years. Investments or expenditures of money are negative and receipts are positive.

For an annuity with payments 1/q of a year before year-end, the present value or future value is found using Equation 3-3a or 3-4a, and then multiplying by $(1 + k)^{1/q}$. At a 10 percent effective required return, for example, the present value of $100 received at the end of each year for 10 years is:

$$PVA_{10} = \$100PVA1_{10yrs,10\%} = \$100 \times 6.1446 = \$614.46$$

If payment is received at the end of the third quarter rather than at the end of each year, the present value is $\$614.46 \times (1 + .10)^{1/4} = \$629.28$.

Payments Spread Evenly across the Year

Many payment series are spread over the year, with a payment received at the end of each period of 1/q of a year. The effective interest rate per payment period is:[8]

$$k_q = (1 + k)^{1/q} - 1$$

[8]The effective interest rate per period of 1/q of a year is defined as the rate that, when compounded q times a year, gives the same growth rate of money as investing at a rate of k with compounding once a year:

$$(1 + kq)^q = (1 + k)$$

Rearranging terms gives $k_q = (1 + k)^{1/q} - 1$.

Present and future value of an annuity procedure can then be carried out as previously explained, recognizing that there are n × q (n times q) payment periods, a required return of k_q per payment period, and a payment each payment period 1/q times the total annual payment. If we receive $1,000 a year for 10 years, divided into equal daily payments, with an effective annual interest rate of 10 percent, Equation 3-4b can be used as follows to find the present value:

$$k_{365} = (1 + .10)^{1/365} - 1 = .000261158$$

$$PVA_{3650}\ \text{days} = (\$1{,}000/365)PVA1_{3650\text{days},.0261158\%} = \$6{,}446.07$$

Example: A management contract for Resorts International had the potential to pay $30 million a year for 10 years. We want to find the present value for year-end payments, midyear payments, and daily payments with a 10 percent required return. The patterns are illustrated graphically as follows. (Numbers in the figure are in $ thousands.)

YEAR	0		1		2		3		4		5 etc.
Year-end			30,000		30,000		30,000		30,000		30,000
Midyear		30,000		30,000		30,000		30,000		30,000	
Daily	---------------------------------82.19 per day for 10 years-----------------------------										

If the payments are received at year-end, the present value is:

$$PVA_{10} = \$30{,}000{,}000PVA1_{10\text{yrs},10\%} = \$30{,}000{,}000 \times 6.1446 = \$184{,}338{,}000$$

If payments are received at midyear, the present value is:

$$\begin{aligned} PVA_{10} &= \$30{,}000{,}000PVA1_{10\text{yrs},10\%}(1 + .10)^{1/2} \\ &= \$30{,}000{,}000(6.1446)(1 + .10)^{1/2} = \$193{,}335{,}325 \end{aligned}$$

If payments are spread evenly over the year on a daily basis, the interest rate per day is:

$$k_q = (1 + .10)^{1/365} - 1 = .0261158\%$$

The present value is:

$$PV = (\$30{,}000{,}000/365)PVA1_{3650\text{days},.0261158\%} = \$193{,}382{,}189$$

Note that treating daily cash flows as if they arrived at the end of the year would lead to an error of 4.68 percent in this example, but treating daily cash flows as if they were a midyear lump sum resulted in an error of only 0.02 percent. The similarity of the present value with daily cash flows and midyear lump-sum cash flows follows from the assumption that cash flows arriving anytime during the year can be immediately invested as profitably as if they were received at the end of the year. *To simplify calculations, many companies treat cash flows spread evenly across the year as if they arrive in a lump sum at midyear.*[9] Many of the problems in later chapters use the midyear assumption to approximate the daily cash flows that most businesses experience. It is important to remember that the cash flows are not received at midyear but are instead received daily. We use this shortcut only to approximate the value of daily cash flows without all the columns of work.

Using midyear to approximate daily cash flows example: Boeing Corporation spent a total of $100 million on its 7J7 jet design over a 3-year period before backing off. Assuming one-third of the $100 million is paid evenly over each year, we can use midyear payments to approximate these cash flows. Assuming the investment opportunity rate is 10 percent, what is the future value of the Boeing investment?

Formula solution: The compound cost of Boeing's investment at the end of 3 years was:

$$(\$100{,}000{,}000/3)(3.310)(1+.10)^{1/2} = \$115{,}718{,}576$$

In other words, Boeing would have had $115,718,576 by the end of 3 years if it had invested the money elsewhere at a 10 percent rate of return.

Spreadsheet solution: To solve this problem with the computer, you would set up the following spreadsheet:

	A	B	C	D	E
1	Excel Spreadsheet 3				
2	Interest rate		10%	10%	10%
3	Years	0	0.5	1.5	2.5
4	Cash inflows		33333333	33333333	33333333
5	Present value	= FV(C2,C3, –C4) is used to bring these cash flows to the future			
6		This is copied across the spreadsheet			
7			$34,960,295	$38,456,324	$42,301,956
8	Total present value	$115,718,575 = + C7 + D7 + E7 is used to add the future values			

[9]For additional discussion of intraperiod cash flows, see G. A. Fleisher, "Discounting an Intraperiod Cash Flow," *The Engineering Economist* 32 (Fall 1986): 56–58.

PRESENT VALUE OF A NO-GROWTH PERPETUITY

A perpetuity pays cash each period forever. A bank account is the simplest example: $1,000 left in a 10 percent bank account will earn $100 a year forever if the interest is withdrawn each year rather than reinvested. We can state the annual return on this bank account as an equation:

$$\text{PMT} = \text{PV} \times k \qquad \textbf{(3-7)}$$

where PV is the amount deposited in the account and k is the interest rate paid by the bank. To find the present value of a perpetual stream of constant cash flows, then, it is only necessary to rearrange terms:

$$\text{PV} = \text{PMT}/k \qquad \textbf{(3-7a)}$$

At a 10 percent required return, the value of $100 at the end of each year forever is:

$$\text{PV} = \$100/.10 = \$1{,}000$$

This makes sense; if $1,000 deposited in a savings account will earn interest of $100 a year forever, there is no reason to pay more than $1,000 for an investment that provides $100 a year forever.

Example: Preferred stock of Duke Power pays an annual dividend of $7.80, or 7.8 percent of the $100 par value. Interest rates in general had fallen by 2004, so investors could earn only 7.46 percent elsewhere in similar investments. Using Equation 3-7a, the present value was then:

$$\text{PV} = \$7.80/.0746 = \$104.56$$

If holders of Duke Power's preferred stock wanted to sell their shares in 2004, they could expect to find buyers at a $104.56 price, more than the $100 par value.

PRESENT VALUE OF A CONSTANT-GROWTH PERPETUITY

A special type of perpetual investment is the investment that provides a constantly growing stream of cash flows. If cash flows will grow at the percentage rate g and PMT_1 represents the cash flow expected at the end of the first period, the value of this perpetual investment is:[10]

$$\text{PV} = \text{PMT}_1/(k - g) \qquad \textbf{(3-8)}$$

---

[10]The present value of a constantly growing annuity with a life of n periods is:

$$\text{PV} = \text{PMT}_1/(1 + k)^1 + \text{PMT}_1(1 + g)/(1 + k)^{2'} - \text{PMT}_1(1 + g)^2/(1 + k)^3 + \ldots + \text{PMT}_1(1 + g)^{n-1}/(1 + k)^n \qquad \textbf{(A)}$$

Multiplying both sides of Equation A by $(1 + k)/(1 + g)$ and subtracting Equation A from this new equation yields:

$$\text{PV}[(1 + k)/(1 + g) - 1] = \text{PMT}_1/(1 + g) - [\text{PMT}_1(1 + g)^{n-1}/(1 + k)^n]$$

As the life, n, goes to infinity, the last bracketed expression goes to zero (as long as $k > g$). Rearranging the remaining terms gives Equation 3-8.

Equation 3-8 is called the **constant growth model.** Sometimes it is referred to as the Gordon Model, after the person who popularized it. To avoid misuse of this equation, several points should be stressed. First, note that PMT_1, not PMT_0, is used in the formula. PMT_1 is the payment at the end of the first period. If a payment is due immediately, that payment must be added to the present value found using Equation 3-8. Second, growth of payments must be *perpetual* at the rate of g for the formula to apply. Finally, the constant growth model is derived under the assumption that the growth rate, g, is less than the discount rate, k.

Example: Auburn Corporation's common stock is expected to pay dividends of $4 a share at the end of the first year. Thereafter, dividends are expected to grow at a rate of 5 percent a year forever. The required return is 10 percent. The present value of the dividends is:

$$PV = \$4/(.10 - .05) = \$80$$

If no future growth in dividends were anticipated, the present value would be:

$$\text{Present Value} = \$4/.10 = \$40$$

The formulas for finding present values of perpetuities are, of course, not limited to securities. A capital investment that allows the company to move into a new market, for example, may be perceived as having perpetual benefits, either constant or growing.[11] The present value of the perpetual stream of benefits should be compared to the present value of the cash outlays to decide if the venture is attractive.

SUMMARY

Time value of money concepts are the basic tools for evaluating capital investments. These concepts are also useful for dealing with a wide variety of business and personal financial decisions. The basis for all time value analysis is the concept of compound growth, which is captured in the future value of a single payment formula:

$$FV_n = PV(1 + k)^n \qquad \textbf{(3-1)}$$

where FV_n is the amount to which the present amount PV will grow if invested for n periods at a rate of k per period. The extensions of this formula to various patterns of payments are summarized in Table 3-2.

[11] In some of these cases, growth may be negative as the product declines in profitability. Suppose, for example, a product will generate cash flows of $100,000 the first year, with cash flows declining 5 percent a year thereafter. The present value at a 10 percent required return will be $V = \$100{,}000/[.10 - (-.05)] = \$666{,}667$.

TABLE 3-2 Time Value Formulas

These formulas serve as convenient tools for applying the basic compound value principles to a broad variety of problems.

DESCRIPTION OF PAYMENTS	VALUE FORMULA	EQUATION NUMBER
Future value (compound value) of a single payment	$FV_n = PV(1 + k)^n$	(3–1)
Present value of a single payment	$PV = FV_n[1/(1 + k)^n]$	(3–2)
Future value of an annuity[a]	$FVA_n = PMT \times FVA1_{n,k}$	(3–3b)
Present value of annuity[b]	$PVA_n = PMT \times PVA1_{n,k}$	(3–4b)
Present value of a perpetuity	$PV = PMT/k$	(3–7a)
Present value of an amount PMT_1 in period 1, thereafter growing at a rate of g per period	$PV = PMT_1/(k - g)$	(3–8)

[a] $\sum_{t=1}^{n} FVA1_{n,k} = (1 + k)^{n-t} = [(1 + k)^n - 1]/k$

[b] $\sum_{t=1}^{n} PVA1_{n,k} = 1/(1 + k)^t = [1 - 1/(1 + k)^n]/k$

When interest is compounded more than once a year, the *effective* annual interest rate is:

$$k = (1 + k'/q)^q - 1$$

where k′ is the *nominal* annual interest rate (the rate without compounding more than once a period) and q is the number of compounding periods per year.

QUESTIONS

3-1. List several personal decision problems for which you or other individuals might use the concepts in this chapter to help you make a decision.

3-2. Why is a dollar received in the future worth less than a dollar received today?

3-3. Define the terms (a) **annuity,** (b) **level annuity,** (c) **annuity due,** (d) **annuity in arrears,** (e) **ordinary annuity,** (f) **annuity in advance.**

3-4. Give an example of a business application for each of the formulas in Table 3-2.

3-5. Give an example of a situation in which you would know the cash flows involved and would want to find the effective rate of return.

3-6. A capital investment requires payment in anticipation of future returns. What are the conditions necessary for a capital investment to be attractive?

3-7. List several examples of investments that would be perpetuities.

3-8. Differentiate between the terms **nominal interest rate** and **effective interest rate.**

3-9. If interest rates on mortgages rise from 6 percent to 10 percent, what will happen (in general terms) to the present value of these mortgages to the savings and loan?

3-10. Suppose you want to retire when you have $1,000,000. If the interest rates paid by banks on individual retirement accounts (IRAs) rise from 4 percent to 8 percent, what will happen to the time it takes to reach your targeted retirement savings amount?

PROBLEMS

(**Note:** You may notice that taxes will affect the net benefits received in some of the following problems. Assume no taxes in working these problems. Taxes will be incorporated in later chapters.)

Single Amount Problems:

3-1. The Phoenix Growth Opportunity mutual fund claims to have provided an effective average annual return of 14 percent in recent years. If the fund continues to earn this rate of return, a $10,000 investment will grow to how much in 20 years?

3-2. If the inflation rate continues at 3 percent a year over the next 10 years, a college education that presently costs $14,000 will be expected to cost how much then?

3-3. You purchased a piece of land in Alberta 10 years ago for $20,000 and sold the land today for $74,144. What effective annual rate of return did you earn?

3-4. If you sold the piece of land described in problem 3 for $39,343, what effective annual rate of return would you have earned?

3-5. You currently are in a position where you can place $100,000 into a retirement account or a larger house. If you choose the retirement account, you can earn 8 percent. How long would it take for your $100,000 investment to grow to $1,000,000?

3-6. To replace a piece of machinery, Tuscon Cement will need $100,000 in 10 years. If funds can be invested at an effective return of 10 percent a year, how much must Tuscon Cement invest today to have $100,000 in 10 years?

3-7. A zero-coupon bond pays no interest and simply pays the principal amount at maturity. A 20-year, $1,000 principal amount, zero-coupon bond is currently priced at $258.40. What is the effective annual interest rate?

Multiple Amount Problems:

3-8. An investment will generate the following cash inflows.

At an effective annual required return of 8 percent, what is the present value of these cash flows?

YEAR	0	1	2	3
Cash Inflow	–	$20,000	$40,000	$60,000

3-9. You decide to invest $2,000 in an Individual Retirement Account at the end of each year for the next 40 years. You will have how much at the end of 40 years if you earn an effective annual return of 6 percent? 8 percent?

3-10. Suppose you decide to invest $2,000 in an Individual Retirement Account at the *beginning* of each year for 40 years. If an 8 percent return is earned, you will have how much at the end of 40 years?

3-11. Flagstaff Fabricating Company will need $100,000 for machinery replacement in 10 years. The treasurer wants to make equal payments at the end of each year into a fund for the purpose of accumulating this amount. If the fund can earn an effective annual return of 8 percent, how much must the company invest each year?

3-12. A $150,000 loan from First State Bank of Poplar Bluff carries an annual percentage rate of 12 percent. It will be paid off through equal year-end installments, including both principal and interest, over a 20-year period. What is the annual payment required?

3-13. What would be the monthly payment if the loan in the preceding problem were paid off in monthly installments, with an annual percentage rate of 12 percent and interest compounded monthly?

3-14. Second National Bank of Jonesboro pays a nominal interest rate of 12 percent on deposits. What is the effective interest rate if interest is compounded quarterly? monthly?

3-15. Batesville Manufacturing is considering a capital investment that will provide cash flows of $1,000 a year for 20 years. The payments are spread across the year in daily payments rather than being made at year-end. The effective annual required return is 12 percent. What is the present value of these benefits? What would be the present value of benefits if all cash flows occurred at midyear?

3-16. United Airlines plans to buy 34 airplanes for $120,000,000. Flight operations and ground costs are expected to be $7,000,000 per year and $4,000,000 per year respectively. United expects to sell 300,000 tickets and variable costs are expected to be 20 percent of revenue. With a 14 percent required rate of return, what annual revenue is needed to justify the purchase of the airplanes? (Assume a 20-year life and no salvage value for the airplane at the end of 20 years.)

3-17. You intend to place 10 percent of your salary in a mutual fund at the end of each year for 20 years. Your salary will be $40,000 the first year, and you anticipate average raises of 7 percent a year. If the fund earns an effective annual return of 12 percent, how much will you have at the end of 20 years?

3-18. You are considering the purchase of a rental property for $100,000, with a $20,000 down payment. Cash flows after loan payments will be as follows. The loan balance will be $70,000 at the end of 10 years. For what price must you sell the property at the end of 10 years to provide an effective annual return of 15 percent on your equity investment? (Assume year-end cash flows.)

YEAR	1	2	3	4	5	6	7–10
Cash flow	$2,000	$2,120	$2,240	$2,360	$2,480	$2,600	$2,720

3-19. Several salary surveys indicate that accountants who hold the Certified Public Accountant designation earn on the average $9,000 more than their noncertified counterparts. If this certification raises your average salary by $9,000 over your 40-year working life and money costs you 8 percent, how much is this certification worth today? (Assume year-end cash flows.)

3-20. You plan to retire in 40 years and can invest to earn 6 percent. You estimate that you will need $38,000 at the end of each year for an estimated 25 years after retirement, and you expect to earn 5 percent during those retirement years. How much do you need to set aside at the end of each year to accumulate the money necessary for your retirement? (Assume year-end cash flows.)

3-21. You have two options for the purchase of a new car. You can either receive a $3,000 discount off of the $25,000 price, or you can receive 1 percent financing for 5 years. Assume annual, year-end payments and an 8 percent cost of funds. Should you take the 1 percent financing or the $3,000 discount?

3-22. With a Coverdell Educational Savings Account individuals are allowed to place $2,000 per year into an "educational IRA" to be used for college tuition. How much will the average student have accumulated when she enters college after saving in one of these plans for 18 years and earning 8 percent on her investment?

3-23. Currently only 14 percent of the population smokes cigarettes. If smoking costs $10 per week or $1,120 per year, and this amount were saved and invested at the end of each year for 40 years at 8 percent, how much would the individual have accumulated at the end of 40 years?

3-24. In 2003 the national debt of the United States stood at approximately $5.7 trillion. If this debt is allowed to grow at a rate of 3 percent annually for 30 years, how much will be owed in 2028?

3-25. If a college education costs $80,000 and money can be invested to earn 8 percent, how much does the annual salary for a college graduate have to exceed that of a high school graduate for the college education to be financially feasible? (Assume a 40-year working life.)

3-26. Please complete an amortization table for a loan with the following characteristics: an interest rate of 8 percent, a life of 5 years, and an initial borrowing of $15,000. Assume that payments are made annually at the end of each year. Please use the following headings:

BEGINNING PRINCIPAL	PAYMENT	INTEREST	PRINCIPAL REDUCTION	ENDING PRINCIPAL

3-27. **(Applications)** It was reported in *The Wall Street Journal* that 307 companies out of 366 surveyed by Goldman Sachs & Company were using a discount rate of 8 percent or more to calculate their pension obligations. They were assuming that the funds in their plans would earn 8 percent or better even though the market rate at this time on long-term high-grade corporate bonds was roughly 7 percent. Several *Fortune* 100 companies were using a 9 percent rate. Assume for simplicity that you have $600,000,000 in your pension plan and have estimated your pension obligation to be $40,000,000 per year for the first 10 years and to be $60,000,000 per year for the next 40 years. Is your pension fund over- or underfunded at a 7 percent interest rate? an 8 percent interest rate? a 9 percent interest rate? (Assume year-end cash flows.)

3-28. **(Ethical considerations)** Please reread problem 3–27. Assume that you are the president of one of these companies, and you are using a 9 percent rate. As a result, you have a pension surplus and are contributing income to the income statement each year. In reality you have not "locked in" this 9 percent rate and will more likely "roll" into a 7 percent rate as current securities mature. This will cause your company to move into a position where an unfunded pension liability will exist, and income will be reduced to accrue pension expense each year. What is the ethical dilemma? Do you think that in the absence of the Securities and Exchange Commission's recommendation, companies would move to the lower rate? What would you do?

CASE PROBLEM

Retirement Planning Case

It is currently popular to talk about retiring earlier, dying rich, or dying poor. Three of the more important financial decisions you will make in your life include the type of house you live in, the kind of car you drive, and the number of children you have. Listed here is an income statement for the average two-income family with two children.

Pretax income	$95,000
Taxes	$25,000
After tax income	**$70,000**
Household expenses	53% of after tax income
House payment	depends on lifestyle
Car payment	depends on lifestyle
Children's college savings	to be calculated
Residual retirement savings	**after tax income less the four items above**

To test the impact that the housing and car decision have on the retirement, please run the following scenarios:

	ANT LIFESTYLE	MIDDLE OF THE ROAD LIFESTYLE	GRASSHOPPER LIFESTYLE
House	$100,000	$200,000	$300,000
Car	$30,000	$44,000	$56,000

- Your home is financed with a 30-year mortgage and you pay an after tax interest rate of 5 percent. You make annual year-end payments.
- Your cars are financed over 8 years, which coincidentally is also the life of your cars. Your after tax interest rate on these loans is 8 percent.
- College expenses today are $40,000 per child or $80,000 per family and are expected to grow at an annual rate of 4 percent per year for 20 years when the expenses will actually be paid for your child's education. You will set aside an equal amount of money at the end of each year into your children's college savings account. This account will earn an after-tax return of 10 percent until it is needed in 20 years.
- All leftover money is invested at the end of each year into a retirement account that earns a 7 percent return.
- You will work for 40 years, replace your car every 8 years, and your house will last for 70 years.

Assuming no increases in income please calculate the following for each lifestyle:

1. The residual retirement savings for the first 20 years while you are saving for your children's college and paying off the mortgage on your house.
2. The residual retirement savings for years 21 to 30 while you are paying off the mortgage, but you are no longer paying for the college education.
3. The residual retirement savings for years 31 to 40 when both college and the house are paid for.
4. Please calculate the yearly retirement income you may withdraw each year assuming that upon retirement in 40 years you shift the entire retirement account into a 6 percent annuity with an annual payout over 30 years. After 30 years of retirement you want to "die poor" with a balance of $0 in your retirement account.

APPENDIX 3-A

CONTINUOUS COMPOUNDING

For many capital investments, the cash flows come in continuously over the year rather than in a lump sum. While it is often assumed, for simplicity, that the cash flows occur once a year, a more precise approach is to actually recognize the continuous nature of the flows. Also, the values of cash flows that occur at frequent intervals, such as daily, can be closely approximated using continuous compounding.

FUTURE VALUE OF A SINGLE PAYMENT

Continuous compounding is the extreme special case of compounding more than once a period. Recall from Equation 3-5 that the compound growth formula with compounding more than once a period is:

$$FV_n = PV \times (1 + k'/q)^{nq} \tag{3-5}$$

where FV_n is the amount to which a present amount PV will grow in n periods if invested at a nominal interest rate of k′ per period, with interest compounded q times per period. If compounding was on a daily basis, q would be 365. If compounding was on a continual basis, q would be infinity. You can confirm with any elementary calculus text that:

$$\lim_{q\to\infty} (1 + k'/q)^{nq} = e^{k'n} \tag{3-A-1}$$

where e is the base of the system of natural or Napierian logarithms: 2.7183 … . The future value of a single payment with continuous compounding is therefore:

$$FV_n = PV \times e^{k'n} \tag{3-A-2}$$

Values of $e^{k'n}$ appear in Table A-5. With continuous compounding, the effective interest rate is:

$$k = e^{k'} - 1 \tag{3-A-3}$$

and

$$k' = \ln(1 + k) \tag{3-A-3a}$$

where ln(.) refers to the natural logarithm.

As an example, a 10 percent nominal interest rate with continuous compounding is an effective interest rate of $e^{.10} - 1 = 10.52$ percent. An investment of $1,000 at a 10 percent nominal interest rate with continuous compounding will grow in 5 years to:

$$FV_5 = \$1{,}000\ e^{.10 \times 5} = \$1{,}000 \times 1.6487 = \$1{,}648.70$$

Table A-5 was used to find $e^{.10 \times 5}$. These problems can also be solved with a pocket calculator that has a built-in function for finding e raised to any power. Computer programs like Excel also have built-in functions for this purpose.

To see the closeness of daily compounding to continuous compounding, note the amount to which $1,000 will grow with various compounding schemes if invested at 10 percent a year for 5 years:

	AMOUNT	DIFFERENCE FROM CONTINUOUS COMPOUNDING
Continuous compounding	$1,648.70	NA
Daily compounding	$1,648.60	$.10
Annual compounding	$1,610.50	38.20

Because of the similarity between daily and continuous compounding, continuous compounding often serves as a convenient approximation. Continuous compounding is also used in the development of theoretical models because the resulting integrals are easier to manipulate than the sums that result with discrete compounding.

PRESENT VALUE OF A SINGLE PAYMENT

The present value of a future payment with continuous compounding is found by rearranging terms in Equation 3-A-2:

$$PV = FV_n/e^{k'n} \tag{3-A-4}$$

Example: Your deferred compensation plan will pay you $1,000 in 5 years. The required return is a nominal 10 percent a year, with daily compounding. Continuous compounding is used as a convenient approximation:

$$PV = \$1{,}000/e^{.10 \times 5} = \$1{,}000/1.6487 = \$606.54$$

The value 1.6487 was found in Table A-5, at the 5-year row and 10-percent column; it could have been computed directly with a calculator.

FUTURE VALUE OF AN ANNUITY

The future value of a series of continuous payments, continuously compounded, can be stated as an extension of Equation 3-A-2 in the form of the integral:

$$FVA_n = \int_{t=0}^{n} a_t e^{k9t} dt \tag{3-A-5}$$

where a_t is the amount received instantaneously at time t. This integral is analogous to the future value of a discrete payment annuity in Equation 3-3. The future value of continuous flows can also be found by rewriting Equation 3-3a for the continuous case. The future value of an annuity of PMT/q at the end of each 1/q of a period for n periods can be written by substituting PMT/q for PMT, k′/q for k, and nq for n in Equation 3-3a:

$$FVA_n = (PMT/q)\ [(1 + k'/q)^{nq} - 1]/(k'/q)$$

Substituting into this equation for the value of $(1 + k'/q)^{nq}$ as q approaches infinity—see Equation 3-A-1—and rearranging terms yields:

$$FVA_n = PMT[e^{k'n} - 1]/k' \quad \textbf{(3-A-6)}$$

Example: You decide to invest $10,000 a year for 20 years in a bond mutual fund, with payments spread continuously over the year. The money is expected to earn an effective annual interest rate of 10.517 percent. With continuous compounding, k′ is therefore ln(1 + .10517) = 10 percent. The future value of the annuity is:

$$FVA_{20} = \$10{,}000[e^{.10 \times 20} - 1]/.10$$
$$= \$10{,}000[7.3891 - 1]/.10 = \$638{,}910$$

The value 7.3891 is the 20-year, 10 percent value from Table A-5.

PRESENT VALUE OF AN ANNUITY

The present value of a continuous stream, with interest continuously compounded, is commonly stated as an extension of Equation 3-A-4 in the form of the integral:

$$PVA_n = \int_{t=0}^{n} a_t/e^{k9t}, \quad \textbf{(3-A-7)}$$

where a_t is the amount received instantaneously at time t. The present value of a continuous stream of payments can also be found by rewriting Equation 3-4a for the continuous case, substituting PMT/q for PMT, k′/q for k, and nq for n:

$$PVA_n = (PMT/q)[1 - 1/(1 + k'/q)^{nq}]/(k'/q)$$

Substituting into this equation for the value of $(1 + k'/q)^{nq}$ as q approaches infinity—see Equation 3-A-1—and rearranging terms yields:

$$PVA_n = PMT[1 - 1/e^{k'n}]/k' \quad \textbf{(3-A-8)}$$

This formula can be applied with a calculator that has a function for raising e to a power, or by looking up $e^{k'n}$ in Table A-5 and then using the formula.

Example: Searcy Hat Company is considering a building expansion that will provide cash flows of $100,000 a year, arriving continuously over the years, for 20 years. At the end of the 20-year period, the investment can be sold for $200,000. The effective required return is 10.517 percent a year, and k′ is therefore ln(1 + .10517) = 10 percent. Using Table A-5, the present value of the benefits is:

$$PV = \$100{,}000[1 - 1/e^{.10 \times 20}]/.10 + \$200{,}000/e^{.10 \times 20}$$

$$= \$100{,}000[1 - 1/7.3891]/.10 + \$200{,}000/7.3891 = \$891{,}732$$

The value 7.3891 is from the intersection of the 20-year row and 10-percent column of Table A-5.

Continuous compounding is frequently used for theoretical analysis because it is easy to use for mathematical derivations. In practical application, continuous compounding is a convenient tool when cash flows occur continuously over the year or when very frequent compounding periods, such as daily compounding, are used.

PROBLEMS

3-A-1. A $1,000 investment will earn a return of 16 percent a year. How much will the investment grow to in 10 years if interest is compounded annually? quarterly? continuously?

3-A-2. Talladega National Bank is advertising that its savings accounts have continuous compounding for an effective annual interest rate of 12.75 percent. What is the nominal interest rate?

3-A-3. A payment of $1,000 is to be received in 20 years. What is the present value at a 12 percent return compounded annually? quarterly? continuously?

3-A-4. A sum of $10,000 is to be invested at the end of each year into an investment account that earns a return of 10 percent a year, compounded continuously. What is the *effective* interest rate? What will be the amount in the account at the end of 20 years?

3-A-5. Tempe Electric is considering a capital investment that will provide cash benefits of $20,000 a year for 10 years, with cash flows being continuous over the year. The required return is 14 percent, compounded continuously. What is the *effective* required return? What is the present value of the cash flows?

3-A-6. A capital investment will provide cash benefits of $100,000 a year for 20 years. The effective required return is 12 percent (k = 12 percent).

a. What is the present value if the cash flows are received at the end of each year?

b. What is the present value if the annual cash flows are divided into four equal payments, one at the end of each quarter?

c. What is the present value if the cash flows arrive continuously over the year?

SELECTED REFERENCES

Fleisher, G. A. "Discounting an Intraperiod Cash Flow." *The Engineering Economist* 32 (Fall 1986): 56–58.

Glasco, P. W., W. J. Landes, and A. F. Thompson. "Bank Discount, Coupon Equivalent, and Compound Yields." *Financial Management* 11 (Autumn 1982): 80–84.

Horvath, Philip A. "A Pedagogic Note on Intra-Period Compounding and Discounting." *Financial Review* 20 (February 1985): 116–118.

Linke, Charles M., and J. Kenton Zumwalt. "The Irrelevance of Compounding Frequency in Determining a Utility's Cost of Equity." *Financial Management* 16 (Autumn 1987): 65–69.

Capital Investment Choice

PART TWO

The integrity and value goals of the corporation are implemented by making investments—by committing resources to particular courses of action. These investments in turn determine the risk and financing needs of the corporation. The financing choices and risk in turn determine the required return, and help to determine which investments are desirable.

A successful strategy creates numerous investment opportunities. The company must find ways to identify those investments that will contribute to its wealth-creation goals. This part of the book develops the techniques used to evaluate capital investments and measure their contribution to the value of the firm. Chapter 5 focuses on net present value, the most widely recommended method of capital investment analysis. Chapter 6 compares net present value to several alternative evaluation methods. Chapter 7 moves beyond the question of whether or not an investment is attractive to the ranking of competing, attractive investments.

CHAPTER 5

Measuring Investment Value: You Can Trust NPV

After completing this chapter you should be able to:

- Calculate the net present value of a project with even or uneven cash flows.
- Value a perpetual no-growth project and value a perpetual project with growing cash flows.
- Measure the wealth created for the shareholders using net present value.
- Describe the relationship among market imperfections, economic profit, and net present value.
- Demonstrate that NPV measures the wealth created whether or not the company includes debt in its capital structure, and in the presence of corporate income taxes.
- Appreciate the role of management in practicing due diligence in estimating the cash flows and NPVs and in keeping the shareholders informed, so that the market price of the firm's stock will approximate the intrinsic value over time.
- Describe the difficulties faced by management when investors are not fully informed, so that the market price is substantially different from the intrinsic value.

Bill Gates, Saudi Prince Alwaleed Bin Talal, Boeing Inc., and Craig McCaw, who sold his cellular phone company, McCaw Cellular, to AT&T for billions of dollars, are now private partners in a new company called Teledesic. The objective of Teledesic is to blanket the earth with 288 low-level satellites that would form an information superhighway in the sky. Unlike with traditional phone lines, the user could transmit data or voice information from a moving car, the beach, or anywhere else in the world with the use of a small parabolic disk that sends the information to the nearest satellite to be relayed across the network of satellites until it reaches its intended destination. The cost of placing the satellites into orbit and building the initial system is estimated to be at least $9 billion. Gates and McCaw believe that this system will be so superior to existing line and cellular systems that they will attract a significant portion of the $140 billion that is spent on telecommunications services annually. The success of this venture depends on the ultimate ability of this system to attract enough customers to pay for the initial $9 billion investment. The focus of this chapter is on the frequently faced question of whether future benefits are worth the investment required.

Since Chapter 1, net present value (NPV) has been described as the present value of benefits, minus the present value of costs. It has also been claimed that NPV measures a project's contribution to wealth and is, therefore, *the* criterion for project desirability. In this chapter, we define net present value more rigorously and explore more fully its role as the investment selection criterion that leads to wealth maximization.

The focus of this chapter is on **absolute desirability:** considering this investment in isolation, are the benefits worth the outlay? If a proposed investment does not conflict with any other investments, the decision can be based on absolute desirability. There are, however, many types of conflicts between desirable investments, such as two investments that are different ways of doing the same thing, or desirable investments that exceed the amount of money available to invest. In these cases, investments must be chosen according to *relative* desirability. The techniques developed in this chapter are extended in Chapter 6 to measure relative desirability.

Except where indicated otherwise, we base the analysis in this chapter on the assumption that all costs and benefits are monetary and have been adjusted for tax implications. Taxes are introduced in Chapter 8, nonmonetary considerations are discussed in Chapter 24, and risk is dealt with in Chapters 11 through 15.

DEFINITION AND ILLUSTRATIONS OF NPV

An investment's **net present value** (NPV) is the sum of the present values of its expected benefits, minus the present values of all expected cash outlays. Benefits are generally in the form of cash flows. Let k be the rate of return that can be earned elsewhere if the money is not used for this investment. Letting I_0 be the initial outlay and CF_t be the cash flow at the end of period t, the net present value is:[1]

$$NPV = \frac{CF_1}{(1+k)^1} + \frac{CF_2}{(1+k)^2} + \cdots + \frac{CF_n}{(1+k)^n} - I_o$$

$$= \sum_{t=1}^{n} \frac{CF_t}{(1+k)^t} - I_o \qquad \textbf{(5-1)}$$

Recall that $CF_n/(1 + k)^n$ is the **present value** of amount CF_n; it is the amount that could be invested elsewhere today at rate of return k in order to have amount CF_n at the end of period n. The arbitrage pricing principle then requires that the value of an investment is the sum of the present values of all future cash flows. The difference between the value of future cash flows and the initial outlay needed to achieve those cash flows is the increase (or decrease) in wealth for the investor acquiring that investment. A company investing on behalf of the stockholders would create shareholder wealth increases equal to the NPV.

Year-end cash flows net present value example: If you invest \$1,500 today, you will receive \$1,000 at the end of each year for 2 years. If you could invest elsewhere to earn a 10 percent return, what is the net present value?

Table solution:

$$NPV = (\$1{,}000PVA1_{2yrs,10\%}) - \$1{,}500$$
$$= \$1{,}735.50 - \$1{,}500$$
$$= \underline{\$235.50}$$

Computer spreadsheet solution: Using Excel, you would set up the following spreadsheet:

	A		B		C		D
1	**Year-End Cash Flows Net Present Value**						
2	Discount rate		10.00%				
3	Year		0		1		2
4	Initial outlay	$	(1,500.00)				
5	Cash inflow			$	1,000.00	$	1,000.00
6	Total cash flow	$	(1,500.00)	$	1,000.00	$	1,000.00
7	Present value		$1,735.54	←			= NPV(B2,C6:D6)
8	Net present value		$235.54	←			= +B7+B6

[1] In the case in which the required return changes from period to period, the net present value formula is:

$$NPV = \sum_{t=1}^{n} CF_t / \prod_{i=1}^{t} (1 + k_i) - I_o$$

where

$$\prod_{i=1}^{t} (1 + k_i) = (1 + k_1)(1 + k_2) \cdots (1 + k_t)$$

Required return could vary by period because of anticipated changes in general interest rates or in the company's debt-equity mix over time.

You would be required to invest $1,735.50 elsewhere to receive $1,000 at the end of each year for 2 years. Thus, the future cash inflows have a *value* of $1,735.50. When you buy a stream of payments for less than its value, you create wealth. In this case, you create wealth of $235.50 by spending $1,500 to generate cash flows with a value of $1,735.50. Looking at the investment in a slightly different way, an entrepreneur who had identified this opportunity, but who had no capital, could raise $1,735.50 based on a promise to provide the investors with the future cash flows from the project and could pocket the $235.50 excess as her wealth increase.

Complex Cash Flows

Cash flows are typically not even over the life of a capital investment, and there may be outlays in more than one period. Equation 5-1 makes it clear that even cash flows are not required. Likewise, there is no requirement that all future cash flows be positive. Suppose an investment has the expected cash flows shown in Table 5-1. As shown in Table 5-1, we can still evaluate this project using Equation 5-1 because no restrictions are placed on the signs of the cash flows in that equation.

The wealth effect of the NPV may not be as obvious when there are additional outlays in future years, but it is still there. Suppose, for example, we wanted to put away enough money today to fund both present and future outflows for this investment in Table 5-1. An amount of $1,652.89 temporarily invested at 10 percent would provide $2,000 to cover the outlay at the end of year 2. Thus, the total investment that must be made today is:

$$\text{Total investment: } \$1{,}000 + \$2{,}000/1.10^2 = \$2{,}652.89$$

For that investment, we receive $1,000 at the end of year 1 and $3,000 at the end of year 3. The amount that must be invested elsewhere to acquire those same benefits is:

$$\text{Value of future inflows: } \$1{,}000/1.10 + \$3{,}000/1.10^3 = \$3{,}163.03$$

TABLE 5-1 Illustration of NPV for Uneven and Mixed Cash Flows

This table demonstrates that NPV still measures wealth impact when cash flows are uneven and when cash outflows are mixed between inflows.

TIME	CASH FLOW	PRESENT VALUE	
Now	−1,000		$−1,000.00
End of year 1	+1,000	$+1{,}000 \div 1.10^1 =$	909.09
End of year 2	−2,000	$-2{,}000 \div 1.10^2 =$	−1,652.89
End of year 3	+3,000	$+3{,}000 \div 1.10^3 =$	2,253.44
Net Present Value			$ 510.14

Thus, this investment allows us to buy the set of benefits for $510.14 less than it would cost to buy those same benefits elsewhere. The net present value still measures the wealth impact in the case of complex cash flows.

Perpetuities

Some investments are essentially perpetuities. Expansion into a new market area and acquisition of another company are examples of investments with no natural ends to their lives. When UPS spent $30 million on TV advertisements to publicize its new overnight letter service, for example, managers certainly expected to gain a permanent position in that market.

The net present value of a perpetuity with a constant annual cash flow is an application of Equation 3-8:

$$NPV = CF_1/(k - g) - I_o \quad \textbf{(5-2)}$$

where CF_1 is the expected cash flow at the end of the first year, and cash flows are expected to grow at a constant rate of g per year.[2]

Example: When Daimler-Benz paid $5.1 billion for Chrysler, perpetual cash flows were anticipated. Suppose the required return is 15 percent and Chrysler will generate $700 million at the end of each year. The net present value, in millions, is then:

$$NPV = \$700/(.15 - 0) - \$5{,}100 = \underline{\underline{-\$433}}$$

The investment is not attractive because it decreases wealth. If, however, cash flows are expected to grow at 4 percent a year, after beginning at $700 million at the end of the first year, the net present value, in millions, is positive, so the investment is attractive:

$$NPV = \$700/(0.15 - 0.04) - \$5{,}100 = \underline{\underline{\$1{,}264}}$$

Computer spreadsheet solution: Using Excel, you would set up the following spreadsheet:

	A	B	C	D	E	F	
1	Year-End Cash Flows Net Present Value with Perpetual Constant Growth						
2	Discount rate	15.00%					
3	Year	0	1	2	3	....	
4	Initial outlay	$ (5,100,000,000)					
5	Cash inflow		$ 700,000,000	$ 728,000,000	$ 757,120,000	$ 787,404,800	....
6	Total cash flow	$ (5,100,000,000)	$ 700,000,000	$ 728,000,000	$ 757,120,000	$ 787,404,800	....

[2] Recall from Chapter 3 that g must be less than k, and it is reasonable to expect g to be less than k.

	A	B	C	D	E	F
7	Present value	$ 6,363,636,364	←———	= NPV(.15,C6:IV6)		
8	Net present value $	1,263,636,364	←———	= +B7+B6		

Steps:
Lay out the initial outlay and first year.
Go to cell D5 and enter the formula +c5* 1.04 to grow at 4%.
Then copy the entry in cell D6 across the entire spreadsheet to column IV.

NET PRESENT VALUE AND WEALTH CREATION: PERFECT FINANCIAL MARKETS

We have talked about the NPV as the gain to an investor making a decision about the use of his or her money. If we are acting on behalf of that investor, the same decision rules hold. The impact of an investment on the investor's wealth depends on the characteristics of the choice, not the identity of the person making the decisions. We will see, though, that imperfect financial markets can change the optimal investment choice, particularly when we are making decisions on behalf of other investors. Because imperfect markets increase choices, difficult decisions arise with regard to both wealth-maximizing choices for the shareholders and implied ethical obligations to other stakeholders.

We will first examine the position of a stockholder in a firm that operates in perfect financial markets. Recall that in perfect financial markets there are no taxes, transaction costs, or other restrictions keeping buyers and sellers from entering or exiting the market; no one buyer or seller is large enough to affect price through any action; identical information is costlessly available to everyone, resulting in identical beliefs; and all participants are rational wealth maximizers.

We begin with a firm financed entirely with equity. Then we consider a firm funded with both debt and equity. Then we introduce financial market imperfections in the form of taxes and incomplete information. We will see that the net present value directly measures wealth in perfect markets and is robust with regard to the handling of imperfections.

All-Equity Financing

In these perfect market conditions, there is no difference between making the decision for ourselves and making it for our shareholders. In the case of all-equity financing, cash flow from an investment is also cash available to distribute to the shareholders or reinvest on their behalf. This is the simplest case, and we showed in the prior chapter that the wealth of the shareholders is increased by the net present value of the investment. We demonstrated in the prior chapter that the value of an investment opportunity was the same in perfect markets, whether the equity portion of its funding came from retention of earnings or the sale of new stock.

TABLE 5-2 Analysis of Berner Corporation Capital Investment

This table illustrates the computation and meaning of NPV when a company is financed entirely with equity.

YEAR:	0	1	2
Cash flow	(1,500.00)	1,200.00	800.00
Present value (12%)	(1,500.00)	1,071.43	637.75
Total present value	1,709.18		
Net present value	209.18		

Example: Berner Corporation is financed entirely with equity, and Berner's stockholders could earn a 12 percent return elsewhere. Berner is considering an investment that requires an initial outlay of $1,500 and generates the year-end cash inflows in Table 5-2.

If 12 percent is the rate shareholders could earn elsewhere, then they would be required to invest $1,709.18 elsewhere to buy the same benefits generated by this asset, so the benefits have a value of $1,709.18. The value of the benefit exceeds the required investment by $209.18, the amount by which the wealth of the shareholders is increased.

Debt-Equity Mix and NPV

When companies finance their investment with a combination of debt and equity, we refer to the average opportunity cost—the average rate of return investors could earn elsewhere—as the weighted average cost of capital. The weighted average cost of capital (WACC) is:

$$\text{WACC} = W_d K_d + (1 - W_d) K_e \quad \textbf{(5-3)}$$

where

W_d = debt as a percent of the present value of remaining future benefits from the investment

K_d = the rate of return creditors could expect elsewhere by taking the same risk they are taking when they lend to this company

K_e = the rate of return stockholders could expect elsewhere by taking the same risk they are taking when they invest in the stock of this company

Suppose Berner Corporation were to buy the prior asset but maintain debt equal to 50 percent of value. Further, suppose that stockholders could earn 14 percent elsewhere with the same risk they are taking by investing in this company, and bondholders could earn 10 percent elsewhere. For this company, the weighted average cost of capital is then:

$$\text{WACC} = .5 \times .10 + (1 - .5).14 = 12\%$$

TABLE 5-3 NPV to Stockholders with Debt

This table demonstrates that NPV also measures wealth creation for shareholders when debt is included in the financing and maintained at a constant percentage of the present value of future cash flows.

YEAR:	0	1	2
Cash flow from investment	(1,500.00)	1,200.00	800.00
P.V. of remaining cash flows (12%)	1,709.18	714.29	0.00
Debt (50% of P.V. of remaining cash flows)	854.59	357.14	0.00
Borrow (repay)	854.59	(497.45)	(357.14)
Cash flow from investment	(1,500.00)	1,200.00	800.00
Interest expense*		85.46	35.71
Borrow (repay)	854.59	(497.45)	(357.14)
Cash flow to (from) equity	(645.41)	617.09	407.15
PV (14%)	(645.41)	541.30	313.29
PV	854.59		
NPV	209.18		

*Debt outstanding at time zero is not repaid until the end of year 1, so first-year interest is .10 × $854.59 = $85.46, and second year interest is .10 × 357.14 = $35.71.

or

COMPONENT	COMPONENT COST	COMPONENT WEIGHT	WEIGHTED COST
Debt	.10	.50	.05
Equity	.14	.50	.07
Weighted average cost of capital			.12

Since Berner's cost of capital is still 12 percent in this example, the net present value is still $209.18, but are the shareholders still better off by $209.18? The key to answering the question is to analyze the cash flows to and from the shareholders, as is done in Table 5-3.

Remember that we assumed debt would remain at 50 percent of the *present value of future benefits,* with the WACC used as the discount rate to compute that present value. At time 0, the present value is $1,709.18, so the amount of debt is half of that amount, or $854.59, and the initial equity required is only $645.41 ($1,500 – $854.59). In later periods, debt must be reduced to half of the present value of remaining benefits, so part of the cash flow from the investment is used to repay debt as well as to make interest payments.

The cash flows to the shareholders are discounted at the return shareholders could have earned elsewhere by taking the same risk: 14 percent. The shareholders would have to invest $854.59 elsewhere to get the same expected cash flows, but they can buy these cash flows for $645.41 by joining the creditors in funding this investment. The wealth of the shareholders is increased by the difference of $209.18.

What can we conclude? The net present value computed using the weighted average cost of capital as the discount rate is the amount by which the wealth of the shareholders is increased if the company acquires the investment. This conclusion rests on the assumption that debt remains a constant percentage of the present value of future benefits. The net present value would still measure shareholder wealth creation if the debt ratio were determined in some other way, but the opportunity cost of debt and equity would probably change from period to period. It was also assumed that the financial markets were perfect. We will see that the net present value computed using the weighted average cost of capital still holds if taxes are introduced as a market imperfection.

INCOME TAXES, NPV, AND WEALTH CREATION

While taxation of business income causes a variety of annoying problems, including reductions in the *amount* of net present value, they do not change the *meaning* of the net present value. With or without taxes, and with or without debt, the net present value is the amount by which an investment increases the wealth of the shareholders.

We will avoid a lengthy discussion of taxes at this time, but there are two important tax considerations that must be recognized. Tax law does not allow a company to deduct the cost of acquiring an asset from its taxable income. Instead, tax law generally allows the company to recognize the wearing out of an asset as depreciation expense each year over the asset's life, so taxable income after the asset acquisition year is typically less than cash benefits. Tax laws specify the amount of depreciation expense that can be used each year to reduce taxable income. Second, interest expense is treated in the tax laws as an expense that reduces taxable income, while payments to stockholders and repayment of debt do not reduce taxable income.

To illustrate the unchanged meaning of net present value when taxes are introduced, assume that Berner now pays tax equal to 40 percent of income. The initial $1,500 purchase price of the asset does not reduce taxable income, but tax laws allow depreciation expense of $900 in year 1 and $600 in year 2. There are no tax consequences from the asset purchase at time zero, but later income taxes, in the absence of interest expense, are as follows:

$$\text{Year 1 tax: } (\$1{,}200 - \$900) \times .40 = \$120$$

$$\text{Year 2 tax: } (\$800 - \$600) \times .40 = \$80$$

After tax cash flows near the top of Table 5-4 reflect these tax implications.

The company still uses debt equal to 50 percent of the present value of remaining cash flows. The equity holders could still earn 14 percent (after corporate tax but before personal tax) by investing elsewhere at equal risk. Bondholders could earn 10 percent before personal tax by investing somewhere else at

TABLE 5-4 NPV to Stockholders with Debt and Taxes

This table demonstrates that the NPV also measures wealth creation for shareholders when debt is included in the financing and the company must pay income tax.

YEAR:	0	1	2
Cash flow from investment	($1,500.00)	$1,200.00	$800.00
–Tax		120.00	80.00
After tax cash flow from investment without interest expense	(1,500.00)	1,080.00	720.00
P.V. of remaining cash flows at WACC of 10%	1,576.86	654.55	0.00
Debt	788.43	327.28	0.00
Borrow (repay)	788.43	(461.15)	(327.28)
After tax cash flow from investment	(1,500.00)	1,080.00	720.00
Interest expense		(78.84)	(32.73)
Interest tax savings		31.54	13.09
Borrow (repay)	788.43	(461.15)	(327.28)
Cash flow to (from) equity	(711.57)	571.55	373.08
Present value (14%)	(711.57)	501.36	287.07
PV	788.43		
NPV	$76.86		

equal risk. A dollar of interest expense reduces taxes by $0.40, so the after tax cost of debt is:

$$K_d = .10(1 - .40) = 6\%$$

The weighted average cost of capital is then:

$$WACC = .50 \times .06 + (1 - .50) \times .14 = 10\%$$

or

COMPONENT	COMPONENT COST	COMPONENT WEIGHT	WEIGHTED COST
Debt	.06	.50	.03
Equity	.14	.50	.07
Weighted average cost of capital			.10

We continue in Table 5-4 to identify the cash flows to and from the shareholders. The first step is to compute the present value of future benefits using the 10 percent cost of capital as the discount rate. The next step is to determine the amount of debt each period, in order to maintain debt equal to 50 percent of the present value of future benefits. Cash flows to shareholders are then determined by subtracting debt repayment and interest expense from cash flows. The computation of cash flows to shareholders is the same as in Table 5-3, except that each dollar of income is taxed, and each dollar of interest expense reduces taxable income by one dollar.

The analysis of cash flows to and from shareholders yields a NPV of $76.86, so we know that the wealth of the shareholders is being increased by $76.86. This is lower than the NPV in the absence of taxes, because part of the benefits of the project was shared with the government.

As was true in the absence of taxes, we can also find the same NPV by computing the present values of after tax cash flows as they would be in the absence of interest expense, discounted at the weighted average cost of capital:

$$\text{NPV} = \$1{,}080/1.10^1 + \$720/1.10^2 - \$1{,}500 = \$76.86$$

This example again illustrates the following relationship.

Net present value of after tax cash flows from the investment, before considering the impact of financing choice, discounted at the weighted average cost of capital	=	Wealth gain to the shareholders, based on an analysis of the cash flows to and from the shareholders, considering the shareholders' opportunity cost

We will avoid delving further into taxes until later, and avoid delving into the details of weighted average cost of capital until later as well. For the time being, though, we can be comfortable knowing that if we are given some cash flows and a weighted average cost of capital, the net present value of those cash flows, using the weighted average cost of capital, is the amount by which the investment will increase the wealth of the shareholders.

ECONOMIC PROFIT AND NPV

Economic profit and net present value are closely linked strategically in that competitive advantage is needed for economic profit, and net present value can be thought of as economic profit for a multiyear decision. Therefore, positive net present values have competitive advantage as their foundation. It was mentioned in Chapter 4, and demonstrated for a perpetuity, that *net present value is the present value of economic profit.* The same relationship holds for other capital investments. To demonstrate this point, assume that the tax people were right in determining the depreciation of $900 the first year and $600 the second year that was used to determine taxable income for Table 5-4; the asset actually loses value at that rate. If we define profit as actual cash flow plus or minus any change in the value of the asset, then profit, as shown in Table 5-5, is $180 in year 1 and $120 in year 2. The normal profit is the 10 percent weighted average cost of capital applied to the value of the asset: $1,500 at the beginning of the

TABLE 5-5 Economic Profit and NPV

This table demonstrates that net present value is the present value of economic profit when the asset's life is limited.

YEAR:	1	2
After tax cash flow in the absence of interest expense	$1,080	$720
Depreciation	900	600
Profit (Cash flow – Loss of value)	180	120
Normal profit (10% of beginning value)	150	60
Economic profit	30	60
Present value (10% WACC)	27.27	49.59
NPV = $27.27 + $49.59 = $76.86		

first year and $1,500 – $900 = $600 at the beginning of the second year.[3] The present value of the economic profit exactly equals the NPV that was previously computed using both cash flows without interest expense and cash flows to and from stockholders.

The important point from Table 5-5 is the linkage between net present value and economic profit. We can say two things about economic profit:

NPV = Present value of benefits – Present value of cash outlays

NPV = Present value of economic profit

The relationship between economic profit and net present value is important because it highlights the role of competitive advantage in creating wealth. A competitive advantage is necessary to create an economic profit. A sustainable large competitive advantage can create a lot of wealth for investors. For example, due to switching cost and continued innovation, Microsoft has a very large and sustainable competitive advantage through its ownership of the Office Product. Every day analysts refine their estimates of the size and duration of this advantage to predict movement in Microsoft's share price.

[3]For the purpose of concluding that NPV is the present value of economic profit, we need not be overly concerned about whether the tax collector was right in determining depreciation amounts. Letting D_1 be the amount of actual loss in value in year one, the calculations in Table 5-5 can be written as the following formula:

$$NPV = (1{,}080 - D_1 - .10 \times 1{,}500)/1.10 + [720 - (1{,}500 - D_1) - .10(1{,}500 - D_1)]/1.10^2$$

Rearranging terms,

$$NPV = (1{,}080 - .10 \times 1{,}500)/1.10 + (720 - 1{,}500 - .10 \times 1{,}500)/1.10^2 - D_1/1.10 + 1.10\,D_1/1.10^2$$

D_1 cancels out of the formula. Therefore, the NPV does not depend on the amount of actual loss of value each year, as long as the total loss is $1,500; otherwise residual value would be part of the cash flow. A change in the amount the tax collector allows each year would matter, on the other hand, because it would change the timing of the tax reduction from depreciation.

UNCERTAINTY AND NPV

Our conclusions about the meaning of the net present value also hold in the face of risk. We assume here that all investments being considered are equally risky. (Measuring and adjusting for differences in risk will be dealt with in Part Three of this book.) To deal with risk, we define k_o a bit more precisely as the return available elsewhere on opportunities of equal risk to those of our company. This is, of course, not a radical redefinition. After all, k_o is the average return we must pay to investors, and investors generally require compensation if they are to take risks. Therefore, other companies with similar risks must provide investors with similar expected returns. We substitute expected cash flow at time t, $E(CF_t)$, for known cash flow at time t. By saying that other investments of equal risk have an expected return of k_o, we mean that the price of an alternate investment that provides a single expected amount $E(CF_t)$ at time t has a price of:

$$\text{Price of alternate investment} = E(CF_t)/(1 + k_o)^t$$

The net present value of an investment that provides expected cash flows in a number of future periods is then:

$$NPV = \sum_{t=1}^{n} \frac{E(CF_t)}{(1 + k_o)^t} - I_o \tag{5-4}$$

Net present value has the same general meaning in risk and certainty. The present value of an expected cash flow is the amount that could be invested elsewhere to generate the same expected cash flow.

UNINFORMED INVESTORS AND NPV

If investors are not well informed about future profitability of the company's existing assets and investment opportunities, the market value of the stock may be different from its **intrinsic value,** which is the value that would exist if all potential investors had the same information that was available to the person determining the intrinsic value. This problem was first discussed in Chapter 4, when valuation principles were being established. Difference between current market price and intrinsic value can cause otherwise attractive investments to actually decrease shareholder wealth and can, therefore, lead to the rejection of otherwise attractive investments. Poorly informed investors are a serious problem, which management must work to correct. Nevertheless, the net present value criterion can still be applied, with a modification.

A key point about the problem of investors being misinformed about the current value of the company is that the investors' mistaken view is temporary. Investors become informed over time as cash flows come in. Eventually, they will most likely be properly informed and share price will equal intrinsic value per share. Even if the share price is never properly adjusted, the bulk of the value will be in the benefit stream over a long time horizon, and all of the value will be in the benefit stream over an infinite time horizon. A reasonable approach is to measure the impact of a new investment on intrinsic value. For this purpose, we define the intrinsic net present value of a proposed capital investment:

$$NPV_I = IE_n(S_o/S_n) - IE_o \tag{5-7}$$

where

IE_n = intrinsic value of the equity with the proposed capital investment
IE_o = intrinsic value of the equity without the proposed capital investment
S_n = number of shares of stock if the new investment is made
S_o = number of shares of stock already outstanding

Example: Albers Corporation generates cash flow of $1 million a year for the shareholders, after reinvesting a sufficient portion of income to assure continuation at the current level of profitability. The company has 100,000 shares of stock outstanding. Cash flow per share is therefore $10. Stockholders could earn 10 percent elsewhere taking the same risk. The stockholders are misinformed, so they expect cash flow of only $8 a share.

	PER SHARE	TOTAL EQUITY
Intrinsic value	$10/.10 = $100	$100 × 100,000 = $10,000,000
Actual price	$8/.10 = $80	$80 × 100,000 = $8,000,000

The company has an opportunity to make a new investment that would require $2 million of additional equity. The present value of the cash inflows to equity would be $2.4 million, so the project is attractive. If investors were properly informed, the project would have a net present value of $400,000. Because investors are not informed, the total number of shares that will exist if the new investment is made is:

$$S_n = 100{,}000 + 2{,}000{,}000/80 = 125{,}000$$

Thus, the intrinsic net present value is:

$$NPV_I = \$12{,}400{,}000(100{,}000/125{,}000) - \$10{,}000{,}000 = \$80{,}000$$

The investment is unattractive because investors are not well informed, despite the fact that the investment would have created wealth of $400,000 for existing shareholders if investors were properly informed.

What about using retained earnings to fund the project and avoid the problem of selling stock below its intrinsic value? Bear in mind that a stockholder who receives dividends can use those dividends to buy more stock at the lower price, and a stockholder who wants cash will be forced to sell some stock at the lower price if dividends are not paid. Thus, the retention of earnings to fund new investments does not mitigate the problem of a stock price below the intrinsic value. What about funding the new project with debt to avoid using undervalued equity? This is sometimes done, but changes in the debt-equity mix involve a complex set of trade-offs that we discuss later in this book.

What is the best solution to the problem of misinformed investors? Work hard to ensure that your estimates of future benefits are correct. Then communicate honestly with the investors. Honesty might be viewed as its own reward, but in this case ethical behavior has more direct benefits in that it helps you establish a reputation for honesty. A reputation for honesty is an extremely useful tool for keeping investors informed so that the price does not diverge from the intrinsic value.

MIDYEAR NET PRESENT VALUE PROBLEM

Let's revisit the Sylvan Learning Centers' example used at the introduction to Chapter 3 and find the net present value of one of these centers. Let's assume the initial franchise fee is $40,000, after tax start-up costs are $105,000, revenues are $250,000 per year, variable expenses are 50 percent of revenues, and fixed expenses are $40,000 per year. For simplicity, we will assume that there are no taxes or depreciable assets (these are introduced in Chapter 8). All of the preceding cash flows are daily cash flows that are treated as midyear in calculating the net present value (for reasons explained in Chapter 3). In addition, you estimate that the business can be sold at the end of 3 years for $200,000. Looking at similar investments, you believe that a 12 percent required return is appropriate. What is the net present value of this project?

	A	B	C	D	E	F
1	**Year-End Cash Flows Net Present Value with Perpetual Constant Growth**					
2	Discount rate	12.00%				
3	Year	0	0.5	1.5	2.5	3
4	Acquisition Stage Cash Flows:					
5	Initial Franchise Fee	$ (40,000)				
6	After-tax Start Up Cost	$ (105,000)				
7	Total Acquisition Stage Cash Flow	$ (145,000)				
8						
9	Operating Stage Cash Flows					
10	Revenues		$ 250,000	$ 250,000	$ 250,000	
11	Variable Expenses		$ (125,000)	$ (125,000)	$ (125,000)	
12	Fixed Expenses		$ (40,000)	$ (40,000)	$ (40,000)	
13	Operating Stage Cash Flows		$ 85,000	$ 85,000	$ 85,000	
14						
15	Dispositions Stage Cash					$ 200,000
16						
17	Total cash flows from the project	$ (145,000)	$ 85,000	$ 85,000	$ 85,000	$ 200,000
18	Present value interest factor	1.0000	0.9449	0.8437	0.7533	0.7118
19	Present value	$ (145,000)	$ 80,317	$ 71,712	$ 64,029	$ 142,356
20	Net present value	$ 213,414				

Note: To calculate the present value interest factor in Excel, use the PV function.
Within the PV function enter the rate, click on the year for that column, then enter the –1 in the future value field.

The net present value for this project is $213,414. This example foreshadows the work we will do later in the book. In particular it is important to understand that most projects have an acquisition stage where most of the cash flows are negative, or outflows; an operating stage when many times the cash flows turn from negative to positive; and a disposition stage where the cash flows are again typically positive.

SUMMARY

Wealth creation is generally considered to be the goal of the firm. Net present value measures the amount by which a proposed investment will increase the wealth of the shareholders, assuming the cash flows from the investment are used for the benefit of the shareholders. Net present value is defined as:

$$= \sum_{t=1}^{n} \frac{CF_t}{(1+k)^t} - I_o$$

where CF_t is cash flow at time t, I_o is the initial investment, and k is the rate of return investors could earn elsewhere by taking the same risk. The net present value measures both the wealth creation of the shareholders and the ability of the shareholders to increase consumption today while holding consumption constant in all future periods. It can also be thought of as the economic profit for a project with a life longer than one period.

The net present value is a robust measure of investment desirability. Three different forms of computation result in precisely the same net present value as long as a constant ratio of debt to value is maintained:

NPV = present value of cash benefits, minus the present value of cash costs other than financing costs, discounted at the average cost of debt and equity funds

NPV = present value of cash flows to stockholders, minus present value of cash flows from stockholders, discounted at the stockholders' opportunity cost

NPV = present value of economic profits, discounted at the stockholders' opportunity cost

The validity of the net present value as the measure of wealth creation is easily demonstrated in the case of perfect financial markets. Fortunately, the net present value also measures wealth creation when there are taxes and when results are uncertain. A modification called the intrinsic net present value can even measure wealth creation from the shareholders' perspective when investors have biased expectations.

If our goal is to create wealth, and net present value measures the amount by which a capital investment creates wealth, it then follows that net present value is the key guideline for capital investment decisions. We will be applying net present value throughout the remainder of this book.

QUESTIONS

5-1. Explain in your own words the meaning of net present value.

5-2. How is the meaning of net present value changed when cash flows are uncertain?

5-3. How is the meaning of net present value changed when investors are not fully informed?

5-4. What conditions define a perfect financial market?

5-5. Explain the relationship between economic profit and net present value. Why is that relationship important?

5-6. Why is it in management's best interest to keep shareholders informed of the size and the nature of the capital projects accepted in a given year?

5-7. Why is it in management's best interest to have the market price equal the intrinsic price?

5-8. What may happen if the market price is greater than the intrinsic value?

5-9. It can be said that net present value measures three things. What are they?

5-10. Given the market's propensity to extrapolate the growth in the past into the future, is it better to excel in a slow-growth industry or to be middle-of-the-road in a rapid-growth industry? What dangers are involved with each situation?

5-11. Many firms have encouraged their employees to own stock in the company they work for. Using this chapter and what you have learned so far about wealth creation, how would you explain to the employee the importance of his job in increasing the stock price? Assume that this employee is an operations person meeting the customer.

5-12. **(Applications)** Pfizer Corporation announced a new capital investment program, and its stock price increased. Western Digital Corporation (a disk-drive maker) announced a new capital investment program, and its stock price decreased. How do you explain these opposing responses? What should a company that is considering a new capital investment conclude from this evidence?

5-13. **(Ethical Considerations)** There are several ways you might earn an economic profit, and therefore a positive net present value. For each of the methods discussed below, indicate whether it is ethical to earn a positive net present value in that way.

- **a.** Take advantage of economies of scale.
- **b.** Force competitors out of business by temporarily cutting your price until they go bankrupt.
- **c.** Charge more than cost for a lifesaving drug that you invented and patented.
- **d.** Develop a superior product.
- **e.** Develop a unique image through advertising.
- **f.** Acquire all of your competitors to create a monopoly.
- **g.** Meet with your competitors to agree on a common price.

PROBLEMS

(Assume no taxes unless taxes are specifically mentioned in the problem.)

5-1. Sealand Corporation is considering acquiring a newer, more modern machine. The machine, which requires an initial outlay of $3 million, will generate cash flows of $1 million at the end of each year for 5 years. Investors could earn 10 percent elsewhere in opportunities of equal risk. Compute the net present value and explain what it means to investors.

5-2. Compute the net present value for the asset in problem 1 if cash inflows are received at midyear.

5-3. Claremont Corporation is considering starting a new division. The required investment is $1 million. Cash inflows are expected to be $50,000 at the end of the first year and are expected to grow at 6 percent a year thereafter. At a required return of 10 percent, compute the net present value.

5-4. Conway Auto is considering a new business development program. Anticipated benefits are $100,000 in the first year, $200,000 in the second year, and $400,000 in the third year. Benefits will decline 10 percent a year after the third year, and will end after the tenth year. Assume these benefits are received at year-end. The effective required return is 10 percent. What is the present value of these benefits? If the development program requires an initial outlay of $500,000, what is the net present value?

5-5. Alborg Corporation is considering the introduction of a new product. The required investment is $1 million, and anticipated year-end cash flows are as follows:

YEAR	1	2	3	4
Cash flow	$300,000	$400,000	$500,000	$200,000

Compute the net present value using a 10 percent required return.

5-6. Find the net present value for the investment in problem 5 if cash inflows arrive at the end of the third quarter each year rather than at the end of the year.

5-7. A machine can be purchased today for $1 million. It will generate cash flows of $200,000 at the end of each year for 10 years. However, a $300,000 overhaul will be required at the end of year 5. At a 10 percent opportunity cost of money, compute the net present value of this investment.

5-8. A new factory at Arcata requires an initial outlay of $1 million. Of this $1 million, $400,000 must be paid immediately and $200,000 will be paid at the end of each year for the next 3 years. At the end of the 3-year construction period, the factory will go into service and will last for 10 years, after which it can be sold for a salvage value of $200,000. Sales will be $1 million during the first year of operation and will grow at a rate of

10 percent a year after that. Variable costs will be 50 percent of sales and fixed costs will be $300,000 a year. All costs are in cash. Assume cash flows occur at year-end. At a 10 percent required return, is the factory an attractive investment? If there are 1,000 shares outstanding, how much wealth per share has been created?

5-9. Alpha Corporation is considering a new $3 million capital investment that will generate cash flows of $1 million at the end of each year for 4 years. The company, which pays no taxes, finances its investments with debt equal to 40 percent of the present value of future cash flows. Lenders charge 6 percent and stockholders require a 16 percent return.

a. Compute the net present value of the capital investment using a weighted average cost of capital.

b. Compute the net present value of the cash flows to and from shareholders using the shareholders' required return.

5-10. Beta Corporation pays a 40 percent tax rate. A new $3 million investment will generate after tax cash flows of $1 million a year for 4 years if the company uses no debt. The company will, however, use debt equal to 60 percent of the present value of future cash flows. Pre-tax interest on debt is 10 percent, and stockholders require a 16 percent return on their investment.

a. Compute the net present value of the capital investment using a weighted average cost of capital.

b. Compute the net present value of the cash flows to and from shareholders using the shareholders' required return.

5-11. A $1 million capital investment will generate cash flows of $700,000 at the end of each year for 2 years, after which it will be worthless.

a. Compute the net present value using a 10 percent required return.

b. Assume depreciation of $600,000 the first year and $400,000 the second year, compute the economic profit for each year, and compute the present value of the economic profit.

5-12. Kerlagen Corporation's existing assets will provide cash flows for the stockholders of $1 million a year indefinitely, and stockholders require a 10 percent return. The company has 500,000 shares of stock outstanding, dividends are $2 per share per year, and the stock is currently selling for $20 a share. A new $100,000 capital investment will provide cash flows of $30,000 a year for 5 years, which will be paid out as additional dividends.

a. Compute the net present value. Is the investment attractive?

b. By how much will the investment increase the intrinsic net present value of the project?

5-13. For Kerlagen Corporation (problem 12), is the investment attractive if investors are not informed and the stock is selling for $12 a share? $18 a share?

5-14. An asset needed by La Jolla Corporation can be purchased for $100,000. Maintenance and other ownership expenses will be $20,000 at the end of each year for the asset's 10-year life. Alternately, the company can avoid the purchase price and ownership costs by leasing the asset for $45,000 at the end of each year for 10 years. If the required return is 10 percent, which alternative should the company use?

5-15. Nancy Geer is considering an MBA degree. She estimates that she will forgo after tax income of $9,600 a year (she will have a part-time job), during the two years it will take her to complete the degree, but her expenses will be $3,600 a year less than if she were working. Tuition will be $10,000 at the beginning of each year. She estimates that her income will be $4,800 a year higher, after tax, for her 40-year working life if she receives the MBA. She can borrow the money needed at an interest cost of 8 percent, after tax. Would you recommend that she pursue the MBA degree?

5-16. Suppose Geer (problem 15) will have income that is $4,000 higher the first year, and the difference will grow at 4 percent a year thereafter. What does this do to the attractiveness of the MBA degree?

5-17. If Texarkana Retread Tire Company purchases an automatic blender, material waste will be reduced by $10,000 in the first year. Because of inflation, the savings will increase 8 percent a year over the blender's 10-year life, after which the blender can then be sold as scrap for $20,000. Assume savings occur at year-end. At a 10 percent effective required return, what is the maximum price the company can afford to pay for the blender?

5-18. An investment being considered by Siloam Spring Water Distributing requires an initial outlay of $1 million and an additional outlay of $500,000 at the end of 5 years. The investment will provide returns of $200,000 a year for the first 5 years and $300,000 a year for the second five years. These cash inflows will be received at midyear. At the end of 10 years, the investment will be sold for a salvage value of $250,000. At a 10 percent effective required return, is this an attractive investment?

CASE PROBLEM

Midcity Center, Inc. (A)

The board of trustees meeting of Midcity Center, Inc., was called to order at 7:30 P.M. There was considerable interest in several proposals before the board, and the discussion promised to be lively.

Midcity Center, Inc., was located in a run-down part of an old industrial city. The center was a nonprofit corporation formed by a coalition of churches to serve the needs of inner-city poor. Services provided by the center included temporary quarters for the homeless, hot meals once a day for the indigent, and the General Store. The General Store carried free used clothing and free nonperishable foods for the poor. In addition, the center housed a store called the "Center Boutique," which sold donated items to help cover the center's costs.

Midcity Center was funded by annual pledges from the coalition churches. The center also had an endowment fund as a result of several substantial bequests. The endowment fund was controlled by the center's board of trustees, who had complete discretion with regard to investment policy. The board also had the authority to spend the entire endowment fund, but they had always maintained a strict policy of preserving the principal and spending only the income.

The endowment fund had a balance of $1.2 million, invested entirely in corporate bonds. The average interest rate on the bonds was 7 percent, but many of the bonds were selling at a discount due to rising interest rates since their purchase. Yields to maturity for bonds of this type were currently 10 percent.

The proposals before the board that evening involved the use of endowment principal. The center had been plagued by rising energy costs, with heating bills for the past year totaling $14,230. T. Haley, the board member who chaired the building committee, had brought in a consultant to conduct an energy survey. Two proposals arose from that survey.

One proposal involved sixty-eight storm windows at a cost of $230 each. This would decrease heat usage by 20 percent. Another proposal called for the acquisition of a new high-efficiency furnace for $27,630. This furnace would reduce the amount of fuel used for each unit of heat by 40 percent. Haley analyzed both proposals assuming a 10-year building life, and recommended both. Since the building budget included only $12,000 a year for improvements, this would mean dipping into the endowment. Several members objected strongly to spending the endowment principal, suggesting that this would start a trend leading to bankruptcy. One member suggested that borrowing money would be preferable and indicated that a local bank would charge 12 percent with the endowment assets as security. Another member said that the endowment should serve the poor, not the building, and took the opportunity to argue again for an allocation of $100,000 of endowment principal to develop a center for abused children.

After a long discussion, the president broke in. "I believe all positions have been clarified. May we have a motion so that we can vote?"

Case Questions

1. Using a 10 percent discount rate, compute the net present value of the storm window investment without a new furnace.
2. Using a 10 percent discount rate, compute the net present value of the furnace investment without new storm windows.
3. Using a 10 percent discount rate, compute the combined net present value from investing in both furnace and storm windows.
4. Is an investment in energy reduction more risky than an investment in corporate bonds?
5. What discount rate should be used to evaluate the energy savings project?
6. Which investments, if any, should the board accept?
7. If you recommended accepting one or both investments, how should these investments be financed?
8. Would you characterize the board's approach to capital investment decisions as guided by strategy or as reaction as proposals arise?
9. Comment on the capital investment policy of Midcity Center. How could that capital investment policy be improved?

APPENDIX 5-A

ENTREPRENEURS, WEALTH, AND CONSUMPTION

In the chapter we have addressed the net present value from the point of the wealth of equity investors who gain from attractive investments. Suppose, instead, that the investment opportunity has been discovered by an entrepreneur who has no personal capital. Inspection of Tables 5-2, 5-3, or 5-4 should make it clear that the present value of the future cash flows from an investment, discounted at the weighted average cost of capital, is the amount that could be raised from a combination of external equity investors and lenders by promising them all the future cash flows from the investment. If that present value exceeds the required outlay for the investment, the resulting net present value is the entrepreneur's wealth increase. In Table 5-4, for example, the entrepreneur could raise \$1,576.86, half from stockholders and half from creditors, in exchange for the future cash flows from the investment. Since only \$1,500 is actually required, the entrepreneur can pocket the remaining \$76.86 as her wealth increase.

The entrepreneur provides a convenient launching point for the observation that the net present value also measures the change in current consumption made possible by an investment, *for any given pattern of future consumption.* To show this to be true, start with a person who has some wealth and a capital investment opportunity, hereafter called the *wealth holder.* This wealth holder wants to increase present consumption without decreasing planned future consumption. The wealth holder has decided to spend amount C_t on consumption at time t and is considering an investment that will provide CF_t at time t.

The present value of a series of future cash flows is the amount of money that can be raised from a combination of creditors and equity investors, based on the promise to give them the future stream of cash flows. Thus, the amount of capital that can be raised *today* based on a promise to pay $CF_t - C_t$ at time t is:

$$\text{Capital raised today} = \frac{(CF_t - C_t)}{(1 + I_o)^t}$$

where k_o is the weighted average cost of capital: $W_d k_d + (1 - W_d)k_e$. If the capital investment will provide cash flow over n future periods, and the wealth holder wants to consume in each of those periods, the amount the wealth holder can consume at present (C_o) is:

$$C_o = \sum_{t=1}^{n}\left[\frac{CF_t - C_t}{(1 + I_o)^t}\right] + (W_o - I_o) \qquad \textbf{(5-5)}$$

where W_o is the wealth holder's beginning wealth and I_o the cost of the proposed capital investment. Rearranging terms gives Equation 5-6:

$$C_o = \left[\sum_{t=1}^{n}\frac{CF_t}{(1 + k_o)^t} - I_o\right] + \left[W_o - \sum_{t=1}^{n}\frac{C_t}{(1 + I_o)^t}\right] \qquad \textbf{(5-6)}$$

The first bracketed expression in Equation 5-5 is the net present value of the proposed investment. The second bracketed expression includes wealth and consumption that were not changed as a result of the investment. Thus, the net present value is the change in ability to consume now as a result of the investment. Instead of present consumption, the wealth holder may wish to maximize consumption in some future period t, while holding consumption constant in the present period and all other future periods. The change in the amount that can be consumed in that one future period increases by:

$$\text{Change in period t consumption} = \text{NPV}(1 + k_o)^t$$

Example: Assume the Berner Corporation investment opportunity in Table 5-4 was discovered by an entrepreneur whose personal wealth of $500 was invested in a combination of corporate stocks and bonds, providing an average return of 10 percent. The entrepreneur could use part of her own money for this investment, but to keep it simple we will assume she does not. She will consume $100 now and leave the remaining $400 invested at 10 percent so she can consume $240 at the end of the first year and $220 at the end of the second year, which will exhaust her wealth.[4] The entrepreneur raises $1,576.86, half in debt and half in equity. She uses $1,500 to acquire the project, and the entire future proceeds will be required to pay off the creditors and stockholders. The $76.86 difference between the amount raised based on a promise of all future benefits and the amount needed for the investment can be used by the entrepreneur to increase immediate consumption, while holding future consumption constant. Using Equation 5-4, the same conclusion is drawn:

$$\text{Co} = \frac{(\$1,080 - \$240)}{1.10^1} + \frac{(\$720 - \$220)}{1.10^2} + (\$500 - \$1,500) = \$176.86$$

Recall that the entrepreneur was going to consume $100 immediately, without the capital investment. Immediate consumption is increased by the amount of the NPV, with no change in future consumption. Alternately, the extra $76.86 could be invested at 10 percent to increase consumption in some future period by more than $76.86.

It is not surprising that the net present value, which measures the impact of an investment on shareholder wealth, also measures the impact of an investment on the ability of the shareholder who owns the company's investment opportunities to consume goods and services. This is simply another confirmation of the usefulness of net present value as a decision tool.

[4]The $400 grows 10 percent to $440 in one year, and $240 is then consumed, leaving $200. The $200 grows 10% to $220 at the end of the second year.

PROBLEMS

5-A-1. John Smith has $1 million invested at 10 percent return. Smith can either invest or borrow at the 10 percent rate. A new $200,000 investment opportunity has come up. The investment will provide cash flows of $60,000 a year for 5 years.

a. Compute the NPV of the new investment.

b. Smith intends to consume $100,000 at the end of each year forever. How much more can Smith consume today with the new investment?

5-A-2. Suppose Smith does not want to increase present consumption. Instead, Smith would like to increase consumption at the end of each year from $100,000 to some higher amount. By how much can Smith increase consumption at the end of each future year as a result of this investment?

SELECTED REFERENCES

Aucamp, Donald C., and Walter L. Eckardt, Jr. "A Sufficient Condition for a Unique Nonnegative Internal Rate of Return—Comment." *Journal of Financial and Quantitative Analysis* 11 (June 1976): 329–332.

Bailey, M. J. "Formal Criteria for Investment Decisions." *Journal of Political Economy* (October 1959).

Beaves, Robert G. "The Case for a Generalized Net Present Value Formula." *Engineering Economist* 38 (Winter 1993): 119–133.

Brigham, Eugene F., and Richard H. Pettway. "Capital Budgeting by Utilities." *Financial Management* 2 (Autumn 1973): 11–22.

Dearden, J. "The Case against ROI Control." *Harvard Business Review* (May–June 1969): 124–135.

Dorfman, Robert. "The Meaning of Internal Rates of Return." *Journal of Finance* 36 (December 1981): 1011–1021.

Durand, David. "Comprehensiveness in Capital Budgeting." *Financial Management* 10 (Winter 1981): 7–13.

Fama, Eugene F. "Organizational Forms and Investment Decisions." *Journal of Financial Economics* 14 (March 1985): 101–119.

Fisher, Irving. *The Theory of Interest.* New York: Macmillan, 1930.

Fogler, H. Russell. "Overkill in Capital Budgeting Technique?" *Financial Management* 1 (Spring 1972): 92–96.

Gitman, Lawrence J., and John R. Forrester, Jr. "A Survey of Capital Budgeting Techniques Used by Major U.S. Firms." *Financial Management* 6 (Fall 1977): 66–71.

Gurnami, G. "Capital Budgeting Theory and Practice." *Engineering Economist* 30 (Fall 1984).

Hastie, K. Larry. "One Businessman's View of Capital Budgeting." *Financial Management* 3 (Winter 1974): 36–44.

Hayes, R., and W. Abernathy. "Managing Our Way to Economic Decline." *Harvard Business Review* (July–August 1980): 67–77.

Hirshleifer, Jack. "On the Theory of Optimal Investment Decision." *Journal of Political Economy* (August 1958): 329–352.

Khan, Aman. "Capital Budgeting Practices in Large U.S. Cities." *Engineering Economist* 33 (Fall 1987): 1–12.

Klammer, Thomas P., and Michael C. Walker. "Capital Budgeting Questionnaires: A New Perspective." *Quarterly Journal of Business and Economics* 26 (Summer 1987): 87–95.

———. "The Continued Increase in the Use of Sophisticated Capital Budgeting Techniques." *California Management Review* 27 (Fall 1984): 137–148.

Lewellen, Wilbur G., Howard P. Lanswe, and John J. McConnell. "Payback Substitutes for Discounted Cash Flow." *Financial Management* 2 (Summer 1973): 17–23.

Martin, John D., Samuel H. Cox, and Richard D. MacMinn. *The Theory of Finance: Evidence and Applications.* Hinsdale, Ill.: Dryden Press, 1988.

McConnell, John, and C. Muscarella. "Corporate Capital Expenditure Decisions and the Market Value of the Firm." *Journal of Financial Economics* 14 (September 1985): 399–422.

Middlaugh, J. Kendall, II, and Scott S. Cowen. "Five Flaws in Evaluating Capital Expenditures." *Business Horizons* 30 (March–April 1987): 59–67.

Mukherjee, Tarun K., and David F. Scott, Jr. "The Capital Budgeting Process in Large Firms: An Analysis of Capital Budgeting Manuals." Paper presented at the Eastern Finance Association meeting, April 1987.

Narayanan, M. P. "Observability and the Payback Criterion." *Journal of Business* 58 (July 1985): 309–323.

Reimann, Bernard C. "Stock Price and Business Success: What Is the Relationship?" *Journal of Business Strategy* 8 (Summer 1987): 38–49.

Ross, Marc. "Capital Budgeting Practices of Twelve Large Manufacturers." *Financial Management* 15 (Winter 1986): 15–22.

Samuelson, Paul A. "Some Aspects of the Pure Theory of Capital." *Quarterly Journal of Economics* (May 1937): 469–496.

Schall, Lawrence D., Gary L. Sundem, and William R. Geijsbeek. "Survey and Analysis of Capital Budgeting Methods." *Journal of Finance* 33 (March 1978): 281–287.

Scott, David F., Jr., and J. William Petty III. "Capital Budgeting Practices in Large American Firms: A Retrospective Analysis and Synthesis." *Financial Review* 19 (March 1984): 111–125.

Sundem, Gary L. "Evaluating Capital Budgeting Models in Simulated Environments." *Journal of Finance* 30 (September 1975): 977–992.

Woods, John C., and Maury R. Randall. "The Net Present Value of Future Investment Opportunities: Its Impact on Shareholder Wealth and Implications for Capital Budgeting Theory." *Financial Management* 18 (Summer 1989): 85–92.

CHAPTER 6

Alternate Measures of Capital Investment Desirability

After completing this chapter you should be able to:

- Calculate and explain the meaning of:
  - Profitability index
  - Modified profitability index
  - Internal rate of return
  - Modified internal rate of return
  - Payback period
  - Present value payback
  - Accounting rate of return
- Explain the reinvestment rate assumption underlying the internal rate of return method and explain when this can be a problem.
- Recognize the causes and remedies for multiple internal rates of return.
- Describe why companies use multiple measures of capital investment desirability.

When Southwestern Bell Telephone Company (now renamed SBC) designed a new computerized capital investment analysis system called Finplan, capital budgeting managers knew that net present value was the best measure of capital investment desirability. Naturally, they designed the computerized analysis system to compute the net present value. They also designed the system to compute profitability index, internal rate of return, payback period, even accounting rate of return. Why would they use all of these other measures when they knew net present value was right?

They knew that capital budgeting decisions would be made by committees of finance people, engineers, marketing managers, and so on. In addition to different areas of primary responsibility, the participants would have different training and backgrounds. The capital budgeting managers knew that people might be persuaded to focus on net present value, but would still want to look at measures with which they might be more familiar. The capital budgeting managers also knew that each measure conveyed some information about the investment being considered.

Like the managers at SBC, you need to be familiar with all of these measures if you want to argue credibly for the capital investments that will maximize wealth. The objective of this chapter is to give you that familiarity. The definition and meaning of each of these measures is discussed in this chapter.

PROFITABILITY INDEX

The profitability index (PI) is the value increase per dollar invested. If an initial investment I_o will generate cash flows in future years, with cash flow in year t designated CF_t, the profitability index is:

$$PI = \left[\sum_{t=1}^{n} \frac{CF_t}{(1+k)^t}\right] / I_o \qquad \textbf{(6-1)}$$

This equation can also be written as:

$$PI = 1 + NPV/\text{Initial Investment}_o \qquad \textbf{(6-1a)}$$

As an example, a computer store requires an initial outlay of \$500,000 and is expected to generate cash flows of \$100,000 at the end of each year for 10 years. At a 10 percent required return and using Equation 6-1, the profitability index is:

$$PI = (\$100{,}000 \times 6.1446)/\$500{,}000 = 1.23$$

In other words, this investment will generate \$1.23 of present value for every dollar invested, and it will increase net present value by \$0.23 for every dollar invested.

If the net present value is positive, the profitability index will be greater than 1.00, and vice versa.[1] A profitability index greater than 1.00 means the investment is attractive.

There is a definition problem with the profitability index when investments are spread over several years rather than being made as a lump sum. The following investment, for example, requires a cash outlay now and again in 2 years. Is the investment amount just the first \$1,000, is it \$3,000, or is it some other number?

---

[1]Suppose cash flows for a capital investment are divided between *investment flows* and *other flows*. The present values of the two types of flows are PV_i and PV_o respectively. Net present value and profitability index are defined as follows:

$$NPV = PV_i - PV_o$$

$$PI = PV_i \div PV_o$$

It can be seen by inspection that whether the net present value is positive and whether the profitability index is greater than 1.0 both depend on whether PV_i is greater than PV_o.

YEAR	0	1	2	3	4
Cash flow	−1,000	500	−2,000	2,000	2,000

The question of whether to subtract the present value of a future outlay from the numerator or add it to the denominator does not matter as long as we are only concerned about whether the profitability index is greater than 1.0. If you want to compare projects using the profitability index, though, it is necessary to establish a standard rule for dealing with later cash outflows. The modified profitability index provides one such rule.

Modified Profitability Index

The modified profitability index[2] is based on the assumption that the initial commitment to a project should be in the denominator. The **initial commitment** to a project is the initial investment plus any amount that we would need to set aside today to provide funds for future outflows. The modified profitability index is then:

$$\text{Modified profitability index} = 1 + \frac{\text{Net present value}}{\text{Initial outlay} + \text{PV of future commitments}} \quad \textbf{(6-2)}$$

The initial commitment for the prior investment, assuming a 10 percent required return, is determined as follows:

YEAR	0	1	2	3	4
Cash flow	−$1,000	$1,500	−$2,000	$2,000	$2,000
		−$1,818 ←			
		−$1,318			
	−$1,198 ←				
Initial commitment	$2,198				

An amount of $1,818 must be invested at the 10 percent required return rate at the end of year 1 to provide the $2,000 needed at the end of year 2. A cash flow of $500 coming in at the end of year 1 can be used as part of the $1,818, so $1,318 must come from $1,198 invested at 10 percent now. Consequently, the total initial commitment is $2,198.

The net present value is:

$$\text{NPV} = -1{,}000 + 500/1.10 - 2{,}000/1.10^2 + 2{,}000/1.10^3 + 2{,}000/1.10^4 = \$670$$

[2]The modified profitability index was suggested at Bellcore.

If your only question is whether the benefits exceed the cost, the two profitability indexes give the same signal. Both will be greater than 1.0 when the net present value is positive, and vice versa. If you want to use the profitability index to discuss the degree of attractiveness, though, the two measures are substantially different. The profitability index and modified profitability index are:

Profitability index = 1 + $670/$1,000 = 1.67

Modified profitability index = 1 + $670/$2,198 = 1.30

Net present value of $0.67 is generated for each dollar initially invested in the project, but only $0.30 is generated for each dollar of initial commitment to the project. Because the two measures give substantially different results, it is obviously necessary to apply consistent rules for handling later cash outflows if you are going to compare investments using the profitability index.[3]

Although companies sometimes use the profitability index to measure relative attractiveness of investments, it is a poor tool for this purpose. Even if you use consistent rules for handling later cash outflows, the rules are arbitrary so there is no clear relationship between the profitability index and wealth creation. Second, the profitability index ignores project size and, therefore, ignores the amount of net present value generated. A $1.00 investment with a profitability index of 1.31 looks more attractive than a $1 million investment with a profitability index of 1.30, despite the fact that the "superior" project creates wealth of 31 cents while the "inferior" project creates wealth of $300,000.

While the profitability index is limited as a tool for measuring relative desirability, it is sometimes used as a measure of the margin for error and, therefore, as an indicator of risk. A profitability index of 1.3, for example, suggests that benefits are 30 percent greater than what is required to generate a net present value of $0 and just break even on the project. Thus, the profitability index gives an indication of how much benefits can fall below expectations before the project begins to destroy wealth.

Computer solution for profitability index: Using the data in the previous example you would set up a spreadsheet with the following information.

Profitability Index

YEARS:	0	1	2	3	4
Total cash flow	$ (1,000.00)	$ 500.00	$ (2,000.00)	$ 2,000.00	$ 2,000.00
Present value	$ 1,670.31				
Net present value	$ 670.31				
Profitability index	1.67				

[3]An additional method for calculating the profitability index where there are additional investments in later years is to divide the present value of net yearly cash inflows by the absolute value of the present value of net yearly cash outflows. Using this method would result in a profitability index of:

$$(500/1.10 + 2{,}000/1.10^3 + 2{,}000/1.10^4) \div (1{,}000 + 2{,}000/1.10^2) = 1.25$$

After entering the data rows years and total cash flow, use the NPV function to bring the year-end cash flows back to present at 10 percent. The net present value cell is calculated by netting the present value with the initial outlay. In the profitability index cell enter the formula = 1 + the cell containing the net present value / – (the cell containing the initial outlay). The negative sign converts the denominator to a positive number as needed in the calculation of profitability index.

Modified Profitability Index

YEARS:	0	1	2	3	4
Total cash flow	$ (1,000.00)	$ 500.00	$ (2,000.00)	$ 2,000.00	$ 2,000.00
Adjusted back one year		$ (1,818.18)			
Netted against the inflow		$ (1,318.18)			
Adjusted back one year	$ (1,198.35)				
Initial commitment	$ (2,198.35)				
Modified profitability index	1.30				

To calculate the modified profitability index, start at the right most negative number (in this case the –$2,000 in year 2). Then discount this amount back 1 year by entering the formula = the cell to be discounted / (1 + interest rate). This result is then netted against the cash inflow for that year. If the result is positive, and there are no additional yearly outflows between this year and year 0, stop because this is a self-financing project. If the result is negative, continue to discount back 1 year and net the result with the yearly cash flow. After discounting to year 0, add this result to the initial outlay to calculate the initial commitment. In the modified profitability index cell enter the following: = 1 + net present value cell / – (the initial commitment cell).

INTERNAL RATE OF RETURN

The internal rate of return is the rate of return earned on money committed to a capital investment[4] and is analogous to interest rates generally quoted in the financial marketplace. The effective annual interest rate that a bank promises on its savings accounts is the internal rate of return, and the annual percentage rate on a loan (APR) is similar to the internal rate of return.[5] The internal rate of return, then, states the profitability of an investment in terms that are generally familiar to managers, whether or not the managers have strong financial backgrounds.

The internal rate of return is formally defined as the discount rate that results in a net present value of zero. In other words, it is the level of k that would result in a net present value of zero in Equation 5-1. A **conventional capital investment** requires cash outlays before any cash inflows are received and has cumulative cash flows that change from negative to positive only once. A higher discount rate

[4]The term **internal** differentiates the return earned on funds tied up **in** an investment from required returns or returns that could be earned elsewhere.

[5]See footnote 6 in Chapter 3 for the difference between an effective interest rate and an annual percentage rate.

FIGURE 6-1 Net Present Value Profile

This figure shows the relationship between the net present value and the discount rate for a conventional capital investment. The internal rate of return is the discount rate, the value of k, that results in a net present value of $0.

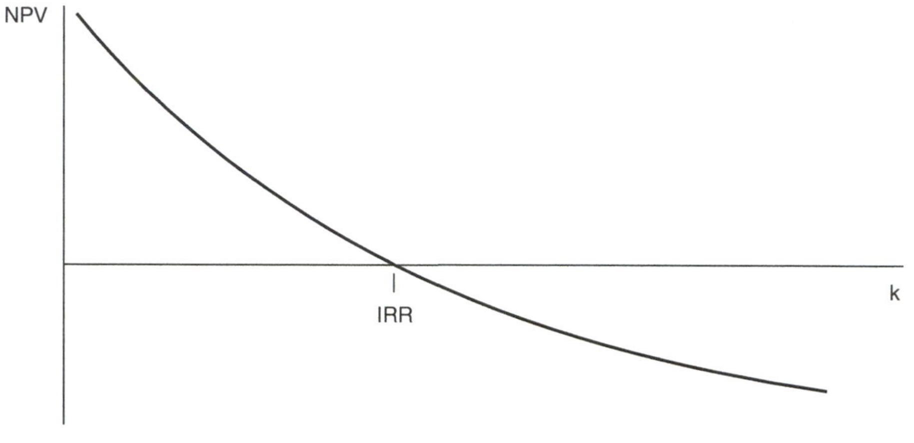

results in a smaller net present value for a conventional investment. This relationship is illustrated in the net present value profile in Figure 6-1. The internal rate of return is the discount rate at the point where the net present value profile line crosses the horizontal axis—the point at which the net present value is zero.

To find the internal rate of return for a *conventional* capital investment, it is only necessary to apply the present value equations from Chapter 3 or look up a factor in Table A-2 or A-4. Take, for example, the $300 million George Steinbrenner's Tampa-based American Ship Building was planning to spend on two cruise ships for the Hawaiian market. Suppose the ships generate cash flow of $35,237,700 at the end of each year over a 20-year life. Setting this up as a present value of an annuity problem, using Equation 3-4b, gives:

$$\text{Present value} = \text{PMT} \times \text{PVA1}_{n,k} \quad \textbf{(3-4b)}$$

Substituting in the known values gives:

$$\$300{,}000{,}000 = \$35{,}237{,}700 \times \text{PVAI}_{20yrs,k}$$

$$\text{PVAI}_{20yrs,k} = \$300{,}000{,}000/\$35{,}237{,}700 = 8.5136$$

Going to the 20-year row of Table A-4 and searching across that row, 8.5136 is found at the 10 percent column; the internal rate of return on this investment is 10 percent. A discount rate of 10 percent will cause the present value of benefits to equal the initial outlay and the net present value, therefore, to equal zero.

To solve this problem with the Excel spreadsheet software, first set up the following spreadsheet:

YEARS	0	1	2	3	4 ...	... 20
Total cash flow	$(300,000,000)	$35,237,000	$35,237,000	$35,237,000	$35,237,000	$35,237,000
Internal rate of return	10.00%					

After entering the year and cash flow data, locate the =IRR function overlay. In the overlay field values highlight the values from year 0 to year 20. After hitting enter, the computer will return 0.099996, or 10 percent for the answer. If the computer returns "NUM," then you forgot to enter the year 0 number as an outflow or negative number.

Uneven Cash Flows

Finding the internal rate of return is tedious if cash flows are uneven over the asset's life. The objective is still to find the point in Figure 6-1 where the net present value equals zero, but that point is generally found by trial and error. For a conventional capital investment, the net present value is first computed with an arbitrarily chosen discount rate. If the net present value is positive, the process is repeated with a higher required return, and vice versa, until the discount rate that results in a net present value of zero is found.

Example: Berkeley Development Partnership is considering the purchase of two lots for $264,050. The first lot will be sold for $100,000 at the end of the first year and the second lot will be sold for $200,000 at the end of the second year. Arbitrarily selecting a discount rate of 10 percent, the net present value (NPV) is found using the present value factors from Table A-2:

$$\text{NPV} = \$100{,}000 \times [1/1.10] + \$200{,}000 \times [1/1.10^2] - \$264{,}050$$

$$\text{NPV} = \$100{,}000 \times 0.9091 + \$200{,}000 \times 0.8264 - \$264{,}050 = -\$7{,}860$$

Since the net present value is negative, a lower discount rate must be tried. A discount rate of 8 percent is chosen, again arbitrarily:

$$\text{NPV} = \$100{,}000 \times [1/1.08] + \$200{,}000 \times [1/1.08^2] - \$264{,}050$$

$$\text{NPV} = \$100{,}000 \times 0.9259 + \$200{,}000 \times 0.08573 - \$264{,}050 = \$0$$

Using excel to solve uneven midyear cash flows: Using the numbers from the preceding example and assuming midyear cash flows instead of year-end cash flows, enter the boldface data in the following spreadsheet:

Discount rate	**10.00%**		
Years	**0**	**0.5**	**1.5**
Total cash flow	**$ (264,050)**	**$ 100,000**	**$ 200,000**
Present value	$ (264,050)	$ 95,346	$ 173,357
Net present value	$ 4,653		
After running the GOAL SEEK the solution will be as follows:			
Discount rate	11.69%		
Years	0	0.5	1.5
Total cash flow	$ (264,050)	$ 100,000	$ 200,000
Present value	$ (264,050)	$ 94,621	169,429
Net present value	$ 0		

In the present value row, in the year 0 column, call up the PV function overlay. Within this function enter the RATE by clicking on the cell containing 10%, the NPER by clicking on the year 0 field, skip the PMT field, and in the FV field enter a – sign then click on the total cash flow for year 0. When you hit enter, –$264,050 will appear. Repeat this process for each of the other years then use the Σ icon to sum the present values to get the net present value. After calculating the net present value, go to the TOOLS menu and then click on the GOAL SEEK item; this will pull up the fields SET CELL, TO VALUE, and BY CHANGING CELL. In the "set cell" field click on the net present value, in the "to value" field enter a zero, in the "by changing cell" field click on the cell containing the 10% discount rate. When you hit enter, the computer will go through numerous iterations to arrive at the answer 11.69%. This "goal seek" process is necessary because the prepackaged IRR function will not work for midyear cash flows.

Interpolation and Other Solution Methods

The internal rate of return in each of these examples was conveniently equal to a whole percentage that could be found in the tables. If the internal rate of return is between two of the interest rates in the tables, it can be found exactly by iterative use of Equations 3-2 and 3-4b to find the value of k that leads to a net present value of zero, or the internal rate of return can be estimated by linear interpolation.[6] Manual searches for the internal rate of return, with or without interpolation, are being replaced by use of computers and financial calculators. The reader is encouraged to read the owner's manual to the financial calculator. Specific instructions differ depending on the make and model of the calculator.

Use of the Internal Rate of Return

As a decision criterion for conventional capital investments, the internal rate of return gives the same accept-reject signals as the net present value and prof-

[6]The interpolation formula for the internal rate of return is:

$$IRR = k_b + (k_a - k_b)[NPV_b/(NPV_b - NPV_a)]$$

where b is the discount rate below the IRR and a is the discount rate above the IRR in the tables. NPV_a and NPV_b are the net present values at discount rates k_a and k_b respectively. By definition NPV_a will be negative and NPV_b will be positive.

itability index. If the internal rate of return is above the required return, the net present value will be positive, and the profitability index will be greater than 1.0. If the internal rate of return is below the required return, the net present value will be negative and the profitability index will be less than 1.0.

The internal rate of return does provide additional information. First, because the internal rate of return is stated in terms of a rate of return or interest rate, it is often easier to explain to people who lack formal training in finance. They are familiar with similar measures, such as the interest rates on their mortgages and bank accounts. Second, because a higher internal rate of return is more desirable, other things being equal,[7] the internal rate of return can be used as a ranking method when choosing between competing investments. Third, the internal rate of return may give an indication of risk; the farther it is above the required return, the greater is the margin for error.

Unfortunately, there are also problems associated with the internal rate of return. Like the profitability index, it ignores the size of the project and therefore does not give an indication of the amount of wealth created. It also ignores project life. As discussed in the following sections, projects may have more than one internal rate of return, and managers may make implicit reinvestment rate assumptions that are unrealistic. These problems can lead to conflicts between net present value and internal rate of return selection.

Reinvestment Rate Assumptions

Some observers fear that managers will mistakenly believe that the entire investment is earning the internal rate of return over its entire life when, in fact, only the *unrecovered* investment is earning that rate.[8]

Example: Two $10,000 investments generate the following cash flows:

		CASH BENEFITS	
INVESTMENT	INITIAL INVESTMENT	YEAR 1	YEAR 2
A	$10,000	$ 0	$14,400
B	$10,000	10,000	2,400

Each investment has a 20 percent internal rate of return and a 2-year life. If the company has a required return of less than 20 percent, both investments are equally attractive using the internal-rate-of-return criterion. But most of the capital from investment B is received back at the end of the first year, so only a small amount is left invested at 20 percent in the second year.

[7]Although the internal rate of return is often used as a ranking method, "other things being equal" is a strong requirement. Projects must have equal costs, equal lives, equal risk, and similar cash flow patterns, such as level annual cash flows, to satisfy this requirement.

[8]John J. Clark, Thomas J. Hindelang, and Robert E. Pritchard, *Capital Budgeting: Planning and Control of Capital Expenditures,* 2nd ed. (Englewood Cliffs, NJ: Prentice-Hall, 1984), 62–64.

Suppose this company's required return is 10 percent, and any cash inflows will be reinvested at the 10 percent rate. If investment B is chosen, the total value at the end of the second year will be:

$$\$10{,}000(1 + .10) + \$2{,}400 = \underline{\underline{\$13{,}400}}$$

compared to $14,400 with investment A. Thus, A gives more terminal value. The preference of A is also confirmed with the net present value:

$$NPV_A = \$14{,}400/(1 + .10)^2 - \$10{,}000 = \underline{\underline{\$1{,}901}}$$

$$NPV_B = \$10{,}000/(1 + .10) + \$2{,}400/(1 + .10)^2 - \$10{,}000 = \underline{\underline{\$1{,}074}}$$

As this example illustrates, the internal rate of return and net present value can give different measures of relative desirability. Since we have shown that the net present value measures the increase in wealth, a rule that leads to the choice of projects that does not maximize net present value is not desirable.

The internal rate of return incorrectly led to the conclusion that A and B were equally attractive because of an implied assumption about the reinvestment rate. When the internal rate of return is used, the implied assumption is that cash flows generated by the investment can be reinvested at the internal rate of return. When the net present value is used, the implied assumption is that funds can be reinvested at the company's required return. Since the required return is determined by investment opportunities available elsewhere, the net present value relies on a more reasonable implied assumption.

Multiple Internal Rates of Return

Despite the superiority of net present value, the internal rate of return is used by many companies. It is, therefore, important to understand the problem of multiple internal rates of return and implications for investment choice.

An investment requires outlays in anticipation of future benefits. Financing, on the other hand, provides benefits in exchange for future outlays. Some projects have characteristics of an investment over part of their lives and characteristics of a financing arrangement during other parts. These projects are unconventional investments, having *cumulative* cash flows that change between negative and positive more than once. These projects may have more than one internal rate of return, and they may have negative net present values even though they have internal rates of return above the required return. Consequently, special care is needed when the internal rate of return method is used to analyze mixed cash flow projects. The reasons for and implications of multiple internal rates of return are discussed in the following paragraphs. A simple method of checking for the possible existence of multiple internal rates of return is explained in Appendix 6-A.

As an example of multiple internal rates of return, consider projects F and G, which have the following cash flows.

YEAR	0	1	2
Cash Flow F	–100	275	–180
Cash Flow G	100	–275	180

To calculate the internal rate of return for investment F, set the net present value equal to $0 and solve for k:

$$NPV = -100 + 275/(1 + k) - 180/(1 + k)^2 = 0$$

Using the quadratic equation formula, k equals 7.4 percent and 67.6 percent;[9] either value of k will result in a net present value of zero.

The net present values for various interest rates are shown in Figure 6-2. For project G, which simply has all the cash flows reversed, the graph would be inverted and the internal rates of return would be the same.

[9]First, let NPV = 0 and let $R = 1/(1 + k)$. Then, rearranging terms:

$$-180R^2 + 275R - 100 = 0$$

Using the quadratic equation formula:

$$R = \frac{-275 + \sqrt{275^2 - 4(-180)(-100)}}{2(-180)}, \text{ so } R = .9311 \text{ and } R = .5966$$

Therefore, k equals .074 and .676.

FIGURE 6-2 Net Present Values for a Project with Mixed Cumulative Cash Flows

Net present value at various discount rates for an investment requiring an initial outlay of $100, providing a cash inflow of $275 at the end of the first year and then requiring an outflow of $180 at the end of the second year.

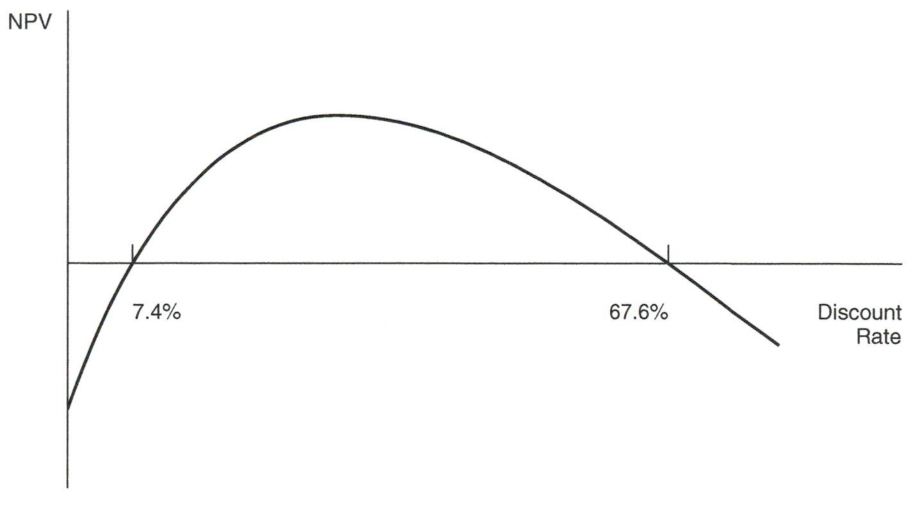

Assume our required return is 15 percent; we can raise money by paying a return of 15 percent and can invest excess funds at 15 percent. The net present values for the two projects are:

$$NPV_F = -100 + 275/1.15 - 180/1.15^2 = +\$3$$

$$NPV_G = +100 - 275/1.15 + 180/1.15^2 = -\$3$$

Based on the net present value, F is attractive while G is not. The internal rate of return, on the other hand, gives ambiguous signals because each project has internal rates of return above and below the required return.

The correctness of the net present value rule in the face of multiple internal rates of return can be demonstrated with investments F and G. Suppose an investor with a 15 percent opportunity cost of funds is considering these two assets and wants to consume as much as possible now for a given pattern of consumption in future periods. Current consumption with the two investments is as follows:

Investment F: $C_o = W_o - 100 + (275 - C_1)/1.15 - (180 - C_2)/1.15^2$
$= W_o + 3 - C_1/1.15 - C_2/1.15^2$

Investment G: $C_o = W_o + 100 - (275 - C_1)/1.15 + (180 - C_2)/1.15^2$
$= W_o - 3 - C_1/1.15 - C_2/1.15^2$

Neither Investment: $C_o = W_o - C_1/1.15 - C_2/1.15^2$

where C_t = consumption at time t and W_o = beginning wealth.

For any combination of C_1 and C_2, investment F increases present consumption by $3 and investment G decreases present consumption by $3. Therefore, anyone who preferred more wealth and consumption to less wealth and consumption would invest in F and reject G. As long as money can be raised or invested at the company's required return, the investment that maximizes net present value also allows the owners to maximize consumption.

Multiple Internal Rates of Return and Capital Rationing

Capital rationing is treated in Chapter 22. However, it is appropriate to comment briefly at this point on multiple internal rates of return and capital rationing. When a company is facing capital rationing, defined as having a fixed amount of money to invest and attractive investments in excess of the amount of money available, *the highest internal rate of return is the rate at which a capital base will grow if all cash flows from the project are invested in projects with the same internal rate of return.*[10] Thus, there is a potentially useful interpretation of the internal rate of return in the case of capital rationing, even if the investment has more than one internal rate of return.

---

[10]Robert Dorfman, "The Meaning of Internal Rates of Return," *Journal of Finance* 36 (December 1981): 1011–1021.

Modified Internal Rate of Return

Managers wanting to use the internal rate of return sometimes use a **modified internal rate of return** to develop a single internal-rate-of-return measure when a project has multiple internal rates of return. This involves two steps:

1. Compute the terminal value of all cash flows except the initial outlay.
2. Calculate by interpolation or other means the modified internal rate of return that sets the terminal value equal to the initial outlay (or present value of the outlays if there are more than one).

Modified internal rate of return example: San Jose Development is considering the purchase of three lots for $264,050. The first lot will be sold for $100,000 at the end of the first year, the second lot will be sold for $100,000 at the end of the second year, and the third will be sold for $100,000 at the end of the third year.

Formula solution—modified internal rate of return: The terminal cash flow is calculated by discounting to the end of the project all intermediate cash flows using the cost of capital as the discount rate. Stated differently, it is finding the future value of the cash inflows at the end or termination of the project life.

$$\text{Terminal value} = \$100{,}000 \times [1.10^2] + \$100{,}000 \times [1.10] + \$100{,}000$$

$$\text{Terminal value} = \$121{,}000 + \$110{,}000 + \$100{,}000 = \$331{,}000$$

$$\text{Initial outlay} \times (1 + \text{MIRR})^3 = \$331{,}000$$

By interpolation the MIRR = 7.8%

Computer spreadsheet solution—modified internal rate of return: This problem can be solved with Excel by setting up the following spreadsheet (enter only the boldface numbers):

Years:	0	1	2	3
Cash flow	**$ (264,050)**			
Cash flow		**$ 100,000**	$ 110,000	$ 121,000
Cash flow			**$100,000**	$ 110,000
Cash flow				**$100,000**
	$ (264,050)	0	0	$ 331,000
Modified internal rate of return	7.82%			

After stair-stepping the cash flows under years 1, 2 and 3, move to the right of the year 1 cash flow and enter the formula + the cell with the year 1 cash flow * (1 + discount rate). When you hit enter, the solution $110,000 will be returned.

Simply copy this formula across to the end of the project's life. Repeat this formula and copy for each of the other year's cash flows. Sum the terminal values. Back fill year 1 and 2 with zeros. Bring the -$264,050 initial outlay down. Go to the modified internal rate of return cell and call up the IRR function. In the values field, highlight the values from year 0 across the back filled zero and the terminal value sum. Hit enter and the answer 7.82% will be returned.

One of the purposes of calculating a modified internal rate of return is to give the analysts an unambiguous accept-reject signal when multiple internal rates of return are possible. Another advantage of the modified internal rate of return procedure is that it gives the user the most conservative estimate of the internal rate of return by using the company's cost of capital as the assumed reinvestment rate and financing rate. When a firm cannot generate projects that have returns greater than the firm's cost of capital it may return funds to the suppliers of capital. By definition, when a firm returns money to the debtors and shareholders (in the same proportions as were used to calculate the weighted average cost of capital), the firm earns the cost of capital. In other words, the modified internal rate of return calculates the internal rate of return on a project as if the cash flow coming off the project were returned to the suppliers of capital. This is a more conservative situation, but this measure does provide some information content in light of the fact that thousands of firms are announcing share repurchases each year.

Analysts using this method to compare projects will compute a terminal value as of the end of the life of the longest life project. When the modified internal rate of return is greater than the required return, the investment is attractive. However, the earlier cited problems with the internal rate of return as a ranking tool still exist. Most importantly, there is still no adjustment for project size and, therefore, amount of value contribution. Furthermore, the method does not work well for investments that have no initial outlay or for investments with the outlay spread over several years.

On the Dominance of Discounted Cash Flow

The capital investment evaluation methods discussed thus far are based on the use of discount rates to compare cash flows occurring at different times. These discounted cash flow methods, as they are commonly called, are recognized as the best methods for evaluating a capital investment because they base the investment decision on whether or not the investment will increase the owners' wealth. As long as the objective of the firm is the maximization of owners' wealth, investments that are not in competition with each other and will not change the company's risk should be accepted if they meet the acceptability criteria of the discounted cash flow evaluation methods. (The decision rules are extended to competing investments and risk differences in later chapters.) A survey conducted by Graham and Harvey[11] and published in 2001 show

[11]Please see the Graham and Harvey study listed in the selected reference section at the end of the chapter for additional detail on the current practice of capital budgeting.

approximately 75 percent of all firms answering the survey use net present value (74.9 percent) or internal rate of return (75.7 percent). The payback method discussed in the next section was still used in smaller firms and in firms lead by CEOs without MBAs or lead by CEOs over 59 years of age. By comparing these results to earlier studies we observe that previously discussed discounted cash flow methods continue to grow in acceptability.

The two remaining measures of capital investment desirability to be discussed in this chapter are the payback period and the accounting rate of return. These measures are sometimes referred to as primitive methods because they were developed before discounted cash flow concepts were widely understood and they do not recognize the timing of benefits. Today, these measures are more accurately viewed as supplementary information because many firms use them to supplement the information provided by discounted cash flow analysis. These measures are still used as the primary decision criteria for some firms, though.

PAYBACK PERIOD

The payback period is the number of years it takes to recover the initial investment. Stated more precisely, the **payback period** is the number of years until the cumulative cash benefit equals the money invested. For an investment that requires an initial outlay of $100,000 and provides cash benefits of $20,000 a year, the payback period is:

$$\text{Payback} = 100{,}000/20{,}000 = 5 \text{ years}$$

As another example, consider an investment that requires an initial outlay of $100,000 and provides the following cash benefits.

YEAR	CASH FLOW	CUMULATIVE CASH FLOW
1	$40,000	$ 40,000
2	30,000	70,000
3	25,000	95,000
4	20,000	115,000

As the cumulative flow column shows, all of the cash flows through the third year and part of the cash flows from the fourth year are required to recover the $100,000. Specifically, $5,000 of the cash flows from the fourth year are needed to reach $100,000. Since total cash flows for the fourth year are $20,000, one-fourth of these flows are needed. The payback period is therefore:[12]

$$\text{Payback} = 3 + (5{,}000/20{,}000) = 3\tfrac{1}{4} \text{ years}$$

[12]To be precise, we should note that the investment is recovered in 3¼ years only if cash flows are spread evenly over the year.

Payback was the principal capital budgeting criterion in practice for a number of years. Simplicity was one reason for its popularity. You can establish a minimum acceptable payback period, such as three or five years, and easily explain the rule to employees with no background in finance. This approach works fairly well if all investments have identical lives and are characterized by one initial outlay followed by level cash benefits over their lives. For a given project life and constant annual inflows, any payback standard corresponds with some discount rate. For example, a 5-year payback period, standard for investments with 10-year lives, is equivalent to a 15 percent required return.[13]

The payback period is also used as a risk measure. Managers often believe that the longer it takes to recover the original investment, the more chances there are for something to go wrong. When Intel committed itself to a mobile wireless personal computer technology called Centrino in 2002, one of the questions was certainly how long the technology would last before becoming obsolete. The payback period gives an indication of how long the technology must survive for the company to recover its costs. A high level of cash flow from a project is also important for *liquidity* purposes; a short payback indicates that the project makes a greater contribution per year, on average, toward cash flow needed for debt repayment and other purposes. Liquidity is often of particular importance for new companies.

Narayanan cites managers' concerns for their own reputations as another reason for using payback. Given two projects with identical net present values, managers would prefer a shorter payback because the public would become aware of their ability to find superior investments sooner, and the value of their human capital would increase.[14] The same argument applies to a manager who needs to establish credibility with investors so that additional funds can be raised.

The payback period has two important weaknesses. First, it ignores the timing of cash flows and the fact that a dollar received now is worth more than a dollar received later. With the payback measure, $10,000 in the first year and $50,000 in the second year is just as good as $50,000 in the first year and $10,000 in the second year. Furthermore, the payback measure ignores all cash flows after the payback period. A $100,000 project that provides cash flows of $20,000 a year will have the same payback whether it has a life of 5 years or 50 years. For these reasons, the payback is not recommended as a primary evaluation method, and its use for that purpose is declining.

The payback period is used today primarily as supplementary information. Some managers who relied on payback in earlier years will still want to look at the payback even if they rely primarily on net present value. Many capital investment decisions are made by committee, and members of the committee who are not familiar with discounted cash flow techniques may rely primarily on payback, while other members are focusing on net present value or internal rate of return.

---

[13]A 5-year payback period is equivalent to saying annual cash flow must be at least $20 per $100 of initial outlay. The internal rate of return, or implied discount rate, is found as follows.

$$\$100 = \$20 \times PVA1_{10yrs,k}$$

Using the internal rate of return solution procedure, k = 15.1 percent.

[14]M. P. Narayanan, "Observability and the Payback Criterion," *Journal of Business* 58 (July 1985): 309–323.

Present Value Payback (Discounted Payback)

The present value payback is the number of years it takes for the cumulative present value of cash flows to equal zero. For an investment that requires an initial outlay of $2,000 and generates cash benefits of $1,000 at the end of each year, the present value payback with a 10 percent required return is found by first computing the cumulative present value:

YEAR	CASH BENEFIT	PV FACTOR	PRESENT VALUE	CUMULATIVE PRESENT VALUE
1	$1,000	.9091	$909.10	$ 909.10
2	1,000	.8264	826.40	1,735.50
3	1,000	.7513	751.30	2,486.80

From this information, the cumulative present value will match the $2,000 outlay somewhere in the third year. Specifically, the amount of additional present value still needed at the end of year 2 is $2,000 – $1,735.50 = $264.50. The proportion of year 3's present value this represents is $264.50/$751.30 = .35, so the present value payback period is said to be 2.35 years. If risk increases with the passage of time, this investment would be less risky than an investment with a present value payback period of 3 years.

ACCOUNTING RATE OF RETURN

The accounting rate of return, also called the average rate of return or return on investment (ROI), differs from the evaluation techniques discussed thus far in that it focuses on accounting income rather than cash flow. The **accounting rate of return** is defined as the ratio of average accounting income to average investment. The average accounting income for this purpose may be simply income after tax, income before interest and tax (EBIT), or the after tax income that would be generated by the project if it did not result in more interest expense: EBIT × (1 – tax rate).

The after tax measure is generally preferred because income after tax is the income that provides benefits to the owners. After-tax income that would be generated in the absence of debt is often used because it allows the capital investment analyst to focus on the project without being sidetracked by a study of the company's debt policy. Thus, a widely used computation formula for the accounting rate of return is:

$$\text{Accounting Rate of Return} = \frac{\text{EBIT} \times (1 - \text{tax rate})}{(\text{Beginning value} + \text{Ending value})/2} \quad \textbf{(6-3)}$$

Example: The development of a new safety valve requires an investment of $1 million by San Diego Engineering. The product has an estimated technological life of 10 years and is expected to generate profits of $184,545 a year before interest and tax. The company's tax rate is 36 percent. The company estimates a value of $0 in 10 years, so the ending value of the fixed assets will be $0. The accounting rate of return is therefore:

$$\text{Accounting Rate of Return} = \frac{\$184,545(1 - .36)}{(\$1,000,000 + \$0)/2} = 23.6\%$$

To make an investment decision, the accounting rate of return is compared to a standard, such as the existing average accounting return on the company's assets, or to the company's target accounting return on investment. The investment proposal is accepted if the accounting rate of return is higher than the established standard.

There are a number of variations on the accounting-rate-of-return formula. Beginning assets are sometimes used instead of average assets, and average assets are sometimes found by averaging assets for each year or even each day rather than by using just beginning and ending assets. In some cases, total income over the investment's life, less the initial investment, is divided by the number of years to arrive at the average income. As previously mentioned, income may be measured before or after tax.

John F. McDonnell provides an example of the wide use of the accounting rate of return by managers. When he became chief executive officer of McDonnell-Douglas in 1988, he noted that the company was the leader in defense contract awards, but Lockheed, Rockwell, and General Dynamics earned higher rates of return.[15] Although he did not spell out a specific measure, he was apparently focusing on accounting numbers such as EBIT ÷ Total Assets, Net Income ÷ Total Assets, or Net Income ÷ Equity. A statement such as McDonnell's may send a message to managers, telling them that they should focus their attention on projects that will improve the company's income in relation to assets used. Managers would then use the accounting rate of return on assets as their capital investment decision guideline.

The accounting rate of return has three advantages that result in continued use despite some weaknesses. One advantage of the method is simplicity; the accounting rate of return is easy to calculate without worrying about things like present value formulas. If an investment is a perpetuity with constant annual income, depreciation is just sufficient to cover replacement, and there are no changes in working capital, then the accounting rate of return will often be approximately the same as the internal rate of return. The accounting rate of return is often used for the evaluation of new products and services by financial institutions, since the main assets of these institutions are generally financial instruments, and there is very little depreciation or working capital requirement. If development costs for the products are insignificant, these institutions can get the same accept/reject decision as the net present value, profitability index, or internal rate of return with less effort.

---

[15] *St. Louis Post-Dispatch* (May 8, 1988): E1.

A second advantage of the accounting rate of return is that it is consistent with the numerous management reward systems that focus on accounting return on investment. If you are going to be evaluated according to the income of your division in relation to assets used, you will prefer to select capital investments using the same criterion. Advanced methods of simultaneously considering net present value and accounting profitability are explained in Chapter 24, but using the accounting rate of return is the simplest way to consider accounting income. A better alternative, of course, is to change the way success is measured, so that wealth creation is recognized and rewarded.

A third advantage of the accounting rate of return is that it reflects the importance of accounting income for managers who are concerned about the income they report to their shareholders. Once again, managers can reduce reliance on accounting income by establishing credibility with investors.

The accounting rate of return suffers from three weaknesses. First, like the payback period, it does not recognize the importance of timing. Income in the tenth year counts the same as income in the first year. Second, the method also ignores asset life. A \$100,000 investment that generates income of \$20,000 a year will have the same accounting rate of return whether it has a life of 2 years or 20 years. Finally, the accounting rate of return method focuses on accounting income rather than on cash flow. The measures that use cash flow focus on the benefits actually received, while the accounting rate of return focuses on accounting reports given to shareholders and others.

While the accounting rate of return has declined in popularity as a principal criterion, it continues to be used as supplementary information. It also continues to be used as the primary criterion in some cases because of its ease of use, its consistency with many management reward systems, and its consistency with accounting information given to shareholders.

SUMMARY EXAMPLE

Clutter Corporation of Pasadena is considering the purchase of personal computers at a cost of \$3,600 each. The computers will reduce labor expense, thereby saving the company \$1,000 a year per computer. It is estimated that the computers will have a 5-year technological life and will have no value at the end of 5 years. Clutter Corporation has a 10 percent required return and is not subject to income tax. The net present value and profitability index are:

$$\text{Net Present Value} = \$1{,}000 \times PVA1_{5yrs,10\%} - \$3{,}600$$

$$= \$1{,}000 \times 3.7908 - \$3{,}600 = \underline{\underline{\$190.80}}$$

$$\text{Profitability Index} = \$3{,}790.80/\$3{,}600 = \underline{\underline{\$1.05}}$$

To find the internal rate of return, we solve for the discount rate, k, such that:

$$\$1{,}000 \times PVA1_{5yrs,k} = \$3{,}600 = 0$$

$$PVA1_{5yrs,k} = \$3{,}600/\$1{,}000 = 3.60$$

Going to the 5-year row of Table A-4, the value of 3.6048 is found at the 12 percent column, so the internal rate of return is approximately 12 percent (12.05 percent using a calculator or interpolating, if you want to be more accurate).

$$\text{The payback period is } \$3{,}600 \div \$1{,}000 = \underline{\underline{3.6 \text{ years}}}$$

The present value payback is found as follows:[16]

YEAR	CASH FLOW	PRESENT VALUE	CUMULATIVE PRESENT VALUE
1	$1,000	$909.10	$ 909.10
2	1,000	826.40	1,735.50
3	1,000	751.30	2,486.80
4	1,000	683.00	3,169.80
5	1,000	620.90	3,790.70

The present value payback period is therefore:

$$\text{Present value payback} = 4 + \frac{\$3,600 - \$3,169.80}{\$620.90} = \underline{\underline{4.7 \text{ years}}}$$

Assume that the purchase will increase earnings before interest and taxes by $500 a year and the company has a 36 percent income tax rate. The accounting rate of return is:

$$\text{Accounting rate of return} = \frac{\$500(1 - .36)}{(\$3,600 + 0)/2} = \underline{\underline{17.8\%}}$$

The three discounted cash flow techniques—net present value, profitability index, and internal rate of return—all give the same accept-reject signal. The net present value is $190.80, meaning the purchase of one of these computers will increase shareholder wealth by $190.80. The profitability index of 1.05 means that $1.05 of present value is created for each dollar invested, which may be interpreted as a fairly narrow margin for error. The internal rate of return is 12 percent, which is above the required return, so the investment is again confirmed to be attractive. Managers can compare 12 percent to the required return in gauging the profitability of this investment, and can use the difference between 12 percent and the 10 percent required return as another indicator of the margin for error.

The payback period of 3.6 means the first 3 years' cash flows and 60 percent of the fourth year's cash flows are needed just to recover the money invested. The present value payback of 4.7 means that the first four years' cash benefits and 70 percent of the present value of the fifth year's cash benefits are required

[16] The $.10 difference between cumulative present value and the present value computed using the present value of an annuity formula is a result of rounding in Tables A-2 and A-4.

to provide a 10 percent return. Once again, the difference between the 5-year life and the 4.7-year present value payback is a measure of the margin for error, and the margin for error is not extremely large.

The accounting rate of return gives an indication of the impact of the decision on accounting profitability. Managers can compare the 17.8 percent accounting rate of return to the company's existing return on assets to determine if this investment will improve or hurt return on assets. Suppose EBIT for existing assets is .283 percent, and the company's marginal tax rate is 36 percent, so after tax return is $.28 \times (1 - .36) = 18.1\%$. This investment will decrease return on assets as reported by the accountants.

With this information assembled, managers still have a decision to make. The net present value, profitability index, and internal rate of return tell them that the investment is attractive. However, the profitability index and present value payback tell them that the margin for error is narrow. (Risk analysis will be covered in detail later in this book.) The accounting rate of return tells them that the investment will decrease return on assets, as reported to the shareholders. If investors are fully informed and managers want to maximize shareholder wealth, the investment will be accepted. In practical decision making, managers may also consider their own risk and impacts on accounting profitability. Thus, managers may factor other considerations into the decision-making process. This is one reason major capital investment decisions are often made by a committee of executives rather than by following automatically from a decision rule, such as net present value.

CAPITAL BUDGETING PRACTICE

Surveys of corporate capital budgeting practices have been conducted extensively since 1959. Payback and accounting rate of return were the favored decision tools in the earlier surveys. Fewer than 30 percent of the companies surveyed in the earlier studies used discounted cash flow techniques at all. By 1977, 74 percent of the survey respondents in a study by Gitman and Forrester[17] indicated that the primary capital budgeting technique was a discounted cash flow method. By the time of Ferreira and Brooks's 1988 survey, over 75 percent of companies were relying on discounted cash flow methods.[18] The previously mentioned Graham and Harvey survey published in 2001 confirms a continued trend toward using discounted cash flow techniques of net present value, profitability index, and internal rate of return.[19] These same surveys make it clear, though,

[17]Lawrence J. Gitman and John R. Forrester, Jr., "A Survey of Capital Budgeting Techniques Used by Major U.S. Firms," *Financial Management* 6 (Fall 1977): 66–71.

[18]Eurico J. Ferreira and LeRoy Brooks, "Capital Budgeting: A Key Management Challenge," *Business* 38 (October–December 1988): 22–29.

[19]See, for example, Ravindra Kamath and Eugene Oberst, "Capital Budgeting Practices of Large Hospitals," *Engineering Economist* 37 (Spring 1992): 203–232; Thomas P. Klammer and Michael C. Walker, "The Continued Increase in the Use of Sophisticated Capital Budgeting Techniques," *California Management Review* 27 (Fall 1984): 137–148; Marc Ross, "Capital Budgeting Practices of Twelve Large Manufacturers," *Financial Management* 15 (Winter 1986): 15–22; Ferreira and Brooks, "Capital Budgeting"; A. Charlene Sullivan and Keith Smith, "Capital Budgeting Practices for U.S. Factory Automation Projects," Purdue University Working Paper #90-11-1 (November 1990); and R. H. Pike, "A Longitudinal Study of Capital Budgeting Practices," *Journal of Business, Finance and Accounting* 23 (1996): 79–92.

that companies compute a number of different measures of desirability. Other measures, such as payback and accounting rate of return, are more likely to be used as supplementary information than as the primary decision tool.

Internal rate of return continued to be at least as popular as net present value, despite its well-known limitations. Ease of explanation and provision of a simple ranking system are apparently powerful advantages to practitioners.

SUMMARY

The capital investment desirability measures in this chapter are best viewed as supplementary information to net present value because none of these methods directly measures the wealth created by an investment. Each does, however, provide some information. It is not unusual to compute each of these measures in addition to the net present value.

The **profitability index** is the ratio of the present value of benefits to investment amount. A profitability index of greater than 1.0 means the present value of net cash benefits exceeds the present value of investment, and the investment is desirable. It gives some indication of the margin for error. Unfortunately, it ignores project size and, therefore, total wealth creation. It also requires arbitrary rules for treatment of later cash outflows.

The **internal rate of return** is the rate of return earned on money committed to an investment. It is analogous to interest rates generally quoted in the financial marketplace. The internal rate of return is formally defined as the discount rate that results in a net present value of zero. For a conventional investment, an internal rate of return above the required return means the investment is desirable, and vice versa. The internal rate of return is limited as a rule of relative desirability in that it ignores both project size and project life: $1 invested at a particular internal rate of return for 1 year looks as good as $1 million invested for 10 years.

The **payback period** is simply the number of years it takes to recover the money originally invested. Payback ignores timing of cash flows and cash flows beyond the payback period, but it is simple to use and it also provides some information about liquidity and risk. The **present value payback** measures the number of years for cumulative present values of benefits to surpass outlays or, in other words, the number of years it takes for the cumulative net present value to surpass $0. The present value payback also gives some indication of risk in that it tells us how long the investment must perform as expected in order to earn our required return.

The **accounting rate of return,** also called the average rate of return or return on investment, is defined as the ratio of average income generated by the investment to the average book value of the investment. The accounting rate of return fails to consider cash flows or timing. It is used because it is consistent with the accounting data used for public reporting and incentive reward systems, and because of its simplicity.

TABLE 6-1 Selected Strengths and Weaknesses for the Alternate Measures of Capital Investment Desirability

Profitability index:
Strengths of the profitability index
- It measures the wealth created per dollar of initial outlay.
- It measures the margin of safety or margin for error.

Weaknesses of the profitability index
- Does not account for size differentials

Modified profitability index:
Strengths of the modified profitability index over the profitability index
- It tells you the up-front initial commitment needed to finish the project.
- You can use this to ask the regulators or financing bodies for rate hikes or commitments, or to raise the appropriate amount of money up front rather than at many points in the future which could be perceived as a negative signal and can be quite costly.

Weaknesses of the modified profitability index
- Does not account for size differentials

Internal rate of return:
Strengths of the internal rate of return
- Returns the solution in the form of a percentage

Weaknesses of the internal rate of return
- Assumes that new projects will come along in future years that will pay at least the internal rate of return (reinvestment rate assumption)
- Ignores the size of the project

Modified internal rate of return:
Strengths of the modified internal rate of return
- It eliminates the reinvestment rate assumption.
- Many companies are generating more cash than worthwhile projects. In this case, the MIRR may give a better indication of the return from the project.

Payback period:
Strengths of the payback method
- Is a measure of liquidity
- Can be used as a shortcut in industries where the product life is very short

Weaknesses of the payback method
- Does not use the time value of money
- Ignores all cash flows after the payback period
- Does not allow for differences in risk

Present value payback period:
Strengths of the present value payback method
- Adjusts for the time value of money
- Allows for differences in risk

QUESTIONS

6-1. Which capital investment analysis methods apply the discounted cash flow concepts discussed in Chapter 3?

6-2. What are the advantages of using discounted cash flow methods of capital investment evaluation?

6-3. If an investment has a positive net present value, it will also have a profitability index greater than 1.0 and an internal rate of return in excess of the required return. Likewise, an investment with a negative net present value will also have a profitability index less than 1.0 and an internal rate of return less than the required return. Since all three measures give the same accept-reject signal, why do companies bother to compute all three of these measures?

6-4. Explain in your own words the meaning of the profitability index, modified profitability index, and internal rate of return.

6-5. Explain in your own words the meaning of the payback period and accounting rate of return.

6-6. The internal rate of return is the most widely used measure of investment desirability in practice. Why might this measure be preferred by practitioners?

6-7. What supplementary information does the payback period provide if an investment has already been evaluated using one of the discounted cash flow methods?

6-8. What supplementary information does the accounting rate of return provide if an investment has already been evaluated using one of the discounted cash flow methods?

6-9. According to survey results, which methods of capital investment evaluation are increasing in popularity, and which are decreasing? Why?

6-10. What conditions can cause an investment to have more than one internal rate of return?

6-11. **(Applications)** Anheuser-Busch, like many other companies, uses the internal rate of return to evaluate proposed capital investments. The company has very substantial cash flows available for investment because its core beer business is profitable, but beer sales in the United States are not growing. Managers there are highly educated with regard to capital budgeting methods, so their choice of internal rate of return is a conscious one. Why might it be possible that Anheuser-Busch finds that internal rate of return provides satisfactory results?

6-12. **(Ethical Considerations)** You are working as the capital investment analyst, reporting to the manager of a division of a company that uses internal rate of return to justify capital investments. You have computed net present values for projects as well, because you know it is the correct tool. The boss must recommend one of two competing projects. You know that the project that maximizes internal rate of return has a substantially lower net present value because it is substantially smaller. You explain this to your boss, and he decides to recommend the project that maximizes IRR anyway. The stated goal of the company is shareholder wealth maximization. What are your alternatives in this situation? Recommend and justify one of these alternatives.

PROBLEMS

6-1. A quality-improvement investment at Los Angeles Leather requires an initial outlay of $100,000 and generates cash flows of $20,000 at the end of each year for 10 years. The required return is 10 percent. Find the net present value and profitability index. Is the investment desirable? Why?

6-2. Find the internal rate of return for the investment in problem 1. Is the investment desirable according to this criterion? Why?

6-3. Find the payback and present value payback for the investment described in problem 1. What do the payback calculations tell you?

6-4. For the investment in problem 1, assume that EBIT(1 – tax rate) is the same as cash flow and the investment is depreciated to $0 over its 10-year life. Compute the accounting rate of return. What does the accounting rate of return tell you?

6-5. A capital investment at San Francisco Marine Electric requires an initial outlay of $1 million, and will generate cash flows of $300,000 at the end of each year for 5 years. The required return is 10 percent. Find the net present value. Is the investment attractive?

6-6. For the investment in problem 5, EBIT(1 – tax rate) is the same as cash flow. If the asset will be worth $0 at the end of 5 years, what is the accounting rate of return?

6-7. The shop foreman at Santa Barbara Rig Service proposed a portable service unit requiring an initial outlay of $100,000 and providing the following year-end cash flows:

YEAR	1	2	3	4	5
Cash Flows	$30,000	-$50,000	$70,000	$60,000	$50,000

At a 10 percent required return, find the net present value. Is the investment desirable? Explain why this is desirable or undesirable assuming your audience is not trained in finance.

6-8. Compute the profitability index and modified profitability index for the investment in problem 7. Interpret these measures for a manager who is not trained in finance.

6-9. Find the internal rate of return and modified internal rate of return for the investment in problem 7. Interpret these measures for a manager who is not trained in finance.

6-10. Find the payback period and present value payback period for the investment in problem 7. Interpret these measures for a manager who is not trained in finance.

6-11. Assume that EBIT(1 – tax rate) is the same as cash flow for the investment in problem 7. The asset is being depreciated to zero over its 5-year life. Compute the accounting rate of return. Interpret this measure for a manager who is not trained in finance.

6-12. Find the profitability index for the investment in problem 7 if cash inflows arrive at midyear rather than at the end of the year.

6-13. San Jose Industries is considering a capital investment that requires an initial outlay of $100,000 and generates the year-end cash flows shown below. The required return is 12 percent. Compute the modified profitability index. Is the investment attractive?

YEAR	CASH FLOW	YEAR	CASH FLOW	YEAR	CASH FLOW
1	–$20,000	6	–$50,000	11	$35,000
2	–10,000	7	50,000	12	30,000
3	0	8	50,000	13	25,000
4	10,000	9	40,000	14	20,000
5	30,000	10	50,000	15	20,000

6–14. Davis Corporation is considering an investment that requires an initial outlay of $400,000 and will provide cash benefits of $100,000 at the end of each year over its 5-year life. In addition, the asset will have a salvage value of $200,000 at the end of its 5-year life. At a 10 percent required return, compute the net present value and profitability index.

6-15. Compute the internal rate of return for the investment in problem 14.

6-16. Claremont Corporation is considering starting a new division. The required investment is $1,000,000. Cash benefits are expected to be $50,000 at the end of the first year and are expected to grow at 6 percent a year thereafter. At a required return of 10 percent, compute the net present value and profitability index.

6-17. Compute the internal rate of return for the investment described in problem 16.

6-18. Chico Manufacturing must choose between two methods of producing a new product. The outlays and year-end benefits are as follows:

YEAR	METHOD A	METHOD B
0	–$1,000,000	–$2,000,000
1	200,000	800,000
2	250,000	600,000
3	300,000	500,000
4	350,000	400,000
5	400,000	400,000

Assuming the required return is 10 percent, compute the net present value and internal rate of return for each production method. Which production method should be used? Why?

6-19. Compute the modified internal rates of return for the two production methods described in problem 18. Does the modified internal rate of return help you to make a choice?

6-20. You are considering the purchase of a rental property for $100,000, with a $20,000 down payment. Cash flows after loan payments will be as follows.

YEAR	1	2	3	4	5	6	7–10
Cash flow	$2,000	$2,120	$2,240	$2,360	$2,480	$2,600	$2,720

The loan balance will be $70,000 at the end of 10 years. For what price must you sell the property at the end of 10 years to provide an effective annual return of 15 percent? (Assume year-end cash flows.)

CASE PROBLEM

Dash Buildings, Inc.

Ann Smith is the president of Dash Buildings, Inc. (DBI), a subsidiary of Dash, Inc., one of the new long-distance telephone companies that sprang up as a result of deregulation of long-distance telephone service in the United States. DBI is responsible for purchasing and managing real estate used by the various units of Dash. DBI acts like a private real estate investment firm—acquiring properties, managing those properties, and providing space to the other divisions of Dash. DBI occasionally rents space to other tenants when it acquires a building that has more space than is needed by Dash. DBI does not, however, purchase buildings for the express purpose of renting to non-Dash tenants.

DBI is a corporation rather than a department only for reasons of legal convenience. DBI acts like any other department within Dash. DBI does not raise its own funds but receives them from the corporate treasury.

When Smith first joined Dash as a property manager, internal rate of return was the primary tool for project analysis. This often forced DBI to acquire smaller, older, less efficient buildings. Her role on a task force leading the conversion to net present value was the source of recognition that led to her eventual promotion to president of DBI. Net present value analysis had allowed DBI to acquire newer, larger, and more modern buildings. This had led to a dramatic decrease in complaints about buildings and greater overall employee satisfaction.

Oversight of capital budgeting at Dash was the responsibility of the treasurer. The prior treasurer had allowed each operating unit to use its own capital investment analysis methods, with some choosing net present value, some choosing internal rate of return, and some even choosing accounting rate of return. The new treasurer, who comes from a background in investment banking, wants to standardize analysis so proposals can be compared from one unit to the other. While the treasurer has not issued a formal policy, it is clear that he is leaning toward internal rate of return.

DBI has been formally evaluated as a profit center, being credited with revenue equal to the estimated cost of renting space of the same type in the local market.

Smith and her employees receive bonuses based on the profit of DBI. Bonuses at DBI had been quite small in the early years, but rising rents along with some well-timed purchases at the bottom of a real estate depression made the division profitable enough to bring it up to the maximum allowable bonus. She is, therefore, able to concentrate on maximizing satisfaction, which she believes to be the source of any further career advancement. Smith is concerned that internal rate of return will force her to return to acquiring less desirable office space. Dissatisfaction and complaints about building quality could derail her career.

DBI is currently working on additional office space for Sun City. The alternatives in Sun City are typical of those in most other locations. An older building could be acquired for $7 million. Imputed rent savings from ownership would be $1.5 million the first year, and would then grow 3 percent a year. After deduction of operating cost and taxes from imputed rent savings, net cash flow would be $1 million the first year and would grow 3 percent a year thereafter. It is estimated that the after tax sale price at the end of the 10-year planning horizon required by Dash would be $5 million.

Alternately, DBI could construct a new building of the same size at a cost of $10.1 million. Because the space would be more luxurious, imputed rent savings would be $1.8 million and would be expected to grow 5 percent a year because of the excellent location of the building. After deduction of operating cost and taxes from imputed rent savings, net cash flow would be $1.1 million the first year and would grow 5 percent a year thereafter. It was estimated that the building would be worth $12 million after tax at the end of the 10-year planning horizon.

The after tax cash flow return available on other investments similar to the risk of the DBI division (real estate) is estimated to be 12 percent. The after tax cash flow return available on investments with risk similar to the other divisions of Dash (telecommunications) is 15 percent. Dash is not earning its opportunity cost of capital, and its stock price is low, so management is under pressure to improve profitability. Most units are not earning bonuses at all because of low profitability.

Questions

1. Compute the net present value, internal rate of return, profitability index, and payback period for each of the alternatives. For present value calculations, assume midyear cash flows except for initial outlay and terminal value.
2. Recommend the alternative that should be chosen.
3. Prepare a presentation to the treasurer explaining how the company would benefit from using net present value instead of internal rate of return.
4. Comment on the company's methods for evaluating and rewarding success. Does the reward structure encourage optimal capital investments in DBI and the rest of the company?
5. Would you recommend that the reward structure be changed in any way?

APPENDIX 6-A

TESTING FOR MULTIPLE INTERNAL RATES OF RETURN

When using internal rate of return, it is important to determine if the investment being considered has more than one internal rate of return. One way to achieve this is to prepare a graph similar to Figure 6-2 by computing the internal rate of return at discount rates from 0 percent to some fairly high rate such as 1,000 percent. This is, of course, tedious. Fortunately, this effort can be avoided in most cases with a few simple checks.

From Descartes's rule, we know that the number of internal rates of return cannot exceed the number of changes of signs in cash flows. If all cash flows are positive or all cash flows are negative, there can be no internal rate of return. For an initial outlay followed by a stream of cash inflows, there can be only one internal rate of return. Thus, cash flows must be mixed, with more than one sign change, for there to be multiple internal rates of return. Cash flows for project H appear below.

YEAR	0	1	2	3	4
Project H Cash Flows	−100	300	−800	1,800	−1,200

There are four changes of sign in the cash flows, so this sign test would suggest that as many as four internal rates of return are possible. Note that this simple counting of signs does not identify the actual number of internal rates of return; it only identifies an upper limit. Fortunately, that upper limit can frequently be reduced with an additional simple test.

The number of *positive, real* internal rates of return cannot exceed the number of changes in the signs of cumulative cash flows. Cumulative cash flows for investment H are as follows:

YEAR	0	1	2	3	4
Project H Cash Flows	−100	300	−800	1,800	−1,200
Cumulative Cash Flows	−100	200	−600	1,200	0

A move from either a positive or negative number to zero does not count as a sign change, so there are three sign changes in cumulative cash flows; there could be as many as three internal rates of return.

Fortunately, more powerful tests for multiple internal rates of return have been developed. One of the easier-to-use tests was developed by Pratt and Hammond as an extension of the simple cumulation test. This test will often improve on simple cumulations to confirm the existence of only one internal rate of return when simple sign changes or cumulative sign changes indicate the *possibility* of more than one rate. Pratt and Hammond's test consists of repeated cumulations, in which

TABLE 6A-1 Repeat Cumulation Test for Multiple Internal Rates of Return

Each stage of the cumulations is a cumulation of the numbers in the preceding row. The maximum possible number of real, positive internal rates of return is found by counting the number of sign changes going across the bottom row, around the corner, and up the right-hand side of the table of cumulative values.

YEAR:	0	1	2	3	4
Project H Cash Flows	–100	300	–800	1,800	–1,200
Cumulations					
Stage 1	–100	200	–600	1,200	0
Stage 2	–100	100	–500	700	700
Stage 3	–100	0	–500	200	900

the cumulative cash flows from one stage are cumulated to provide the cumulation in the next stage.[20] This is illustrated in Table 6-A1 for project H.

After each stage, the maximum possible number of real, positive internal rates of return is found by counting the number of sign changes going across the bottom row, around the corner, and up the right-hand side of the table of cumulative values. The sequence to be checked after stage two is –100, 100, –500, 700, 700, 0. This involves three sign changes, so the number of possible internal rates of return is still three. Going on to stage three, the sequence to be checked is –100, 0, –500, 200, 900, 700, 0. Remembering that movement to zero and back to the same sign does not constitute a sign change, there is only one sign change at stage three: from –500 to +200. Therefore, this investment has only one internal rate of return.

This cumulation process can be continued for any number of stages, with the minimum number of sign changes achieved at any stage being the maximum possible number of positive, real internal rates of return. There are also various extensions of this process as well as other processes for further narrowing the number of possible internal rates of return.[21]

[20]John W. Pratt and John S. Hammond III, "Evaluating and Comparing Projects: Simple Detection of False Alarms," *Journal of Finance* 34 (December 1979): 1231–1242.

[21]See Donald C. Aucamp and Walter L. Eckardt, Jr., "A Sufficient Condition for a Unique Nonnegative Internal Rate of Return—Comment," *Journal of Financial and Quantitative Analysis* 11 (June 1976): 329–332; Richard H. Bernard, "A More General Sufficient Condition for a Unique Nonnegative Internal Rate of Return," *Journal of Financial and Quantitative Analysis* 14 (June 1979): 337–341; Richard H. Bernard and Carl J. Norstrom, "A Further Note on Unrecovered Investment, Uniqueness of the Internal Rate of Return, and the Question of Project Acceptability," *Journal of Financial and Quantitative Analysis* 15 (June 1980); R. Capettini, R. A. Grimlund, and H. R. Toole, "Comment: The Unique Real Internal Rate of Return," *Journal of Financial and Quantitative Analysis* 14 (December 1979); Clovis De Faro, "A Sufficient Condition for a Unique Nonnegative Internal Rate of Return: Further Comments," *Journal of Financial and Quantitative Analysis* 13 (September 1978): 577–584; M. M. Hajdasinski, "A Complete Method for Separation of Internal Rates of Return," *Engineering Economist* 28 (Spring 1983); Anthony F. Herbst, "The Unique Real Internal Rate of Return: Caveat Emptor!," *Journal of Financial and Quantitative Analysis* 13 (June 1978); David Longbottom and Linda Wiper, "Necessary Conditions for the Existence of Multiple Rates in the Use of the Internal Rate of Return," *Journal of Business Finance and Accounting* (Winter 1978).

If the possibility of multiple internal rates of return cannot be eliminated through these various tests, then the net present values should be plotted as was done in Figure 6-2 in order to determine if there actually are multiple internal rates of return, to determine the internal rates of return, and to determine the net present values at various discount rates. This can be done without too much difficulty using software such as Excel. Of course, use of the net present value criterion avoids these problems entirely.

PROBLEMS

6-A-1. An investment being considered by Dover Corporation generates the following year-end cash flows. Is it possible that this investment has more than one internal rate of return?

YEAR	0	1	2	3	4	5
Cash Flow	–100	600	–1,000	1,000	–1,500	2,500

6-A-2. A capital investment at Newark Corporation has the following year-end cash flows. Given the Pratt and Hammond test, is it possible that this investment has more than one internal rate of return?

YEAR	0	1	2	3	4
Cash Flow	–1,000	3,000	-4,000	8,000	-6,000

6-A-3. Confirm your answer to problem A-2 by graphing the relationship between net present value and required return.

SELECTED REFERENCES

Aucamp, Donald C., and Walter L. Eckardt, Jr. "A Sufficient Condition for a Unique Nonnegative Internal Rate of Return—Comment." *Journal of Financial and Quantitative Analysis* 11 (June 1976): 329–332.

Bailey, M. J. "Formal Criteria for Investment Decisions." *Journal of Political Economy* (October 1959): 476–488.

Bernard, Richard H. "Base Selection for Modified Rates of Return and Its Irrelevance for Optimal Project Choice." *Engineering Economist* 35 (Fall 1989): 55–65.

———. "Income, Wealth Base and Rate of Return Implications of Alternative Project Evaluation Criteria." *Engineering Economist* 38 (Spring 1993): 165–176.

———. "A More General Sufficient Condition for a Unique Nonnegative Internal Rate of Return." *Journal of Financial and Quantitative Analysis* 14 (June 1979): 337–341.

Bernard, Richard H., and Carl J. Norstrom. "A Further Note on Unrecovered Investment, Uniqueness of the Internal Rate of Return, and the Question of Project Acceptability." *Journal of Financial and Quantitative Analysis* 15 (June 1980): 421–423.

Bierman, Harold. "Beyond Cash Flow ROI." *Journal of Applied Corporate Finance* 5, no. 4 (Winter 1988): 36–39.

Brick, Ivan E., and Daniel G. Weaver. "A Comparison of Capital Budgeting Techniques in Identifying Profitable Investments." *Financial Management* 13 (Winter 1984): 29–39.

Brigham, Eugene F., and Richard H. Pettway. "Capital Budgeting by Utilities." *Financial Management* 2 (Autumn 1973): 11–22.

Calderon-Rossell, Jorge R. "Is the ROI a Good Indicator of the IRR?" *Engineering Economist* 37 (Summer 1992): 315–340.

Capettini, R., R. A. Grimlund, and H. R. Toole. "Comment: The Unique Real Internal Rate of Return." *Journal of Financial and Quantitative Analysis* 14 (December 1979): 1091–1094.

Cook, Thomas J., and Ronald J. Rizzuto. "Capital Budgeting Practices for R&D: A Survey and Analysis of Business Week's R&D Scoreboard." *Engineering Economist* 34 (Summer 1989): 291–304.

Dearden, J. "The Case against ROI Control." *Harvard Business Review* (May–June 1969): 124–135.

De Faro, Clovis. "A Sufficient Condition for a Unique Nonnegative Internal Rate of Return: Further Comments." *Journal of Financial and Quantitative Analysis* 13 (September 1978): 577–584.

Doenges, R. Conrad. "The `Reinvestment Problem' in a Practical Perspective." *Financial Management* 1 (Spring 1977): 85–91.

Dorfman, Robert. "The Meaning of Internal Rates of Return." *Journal of Finance* 36 (December 1981): 1011–1021.

Durand, David. "Comprehensiveness in Capital Budgeting." *Financial Management* 10 (Winter 1981): 7–13.

Eschenbach, Ted G., and Alice Smith. "Sensitivity Analysis of EAC's Robustness." *Engineering Economist* 37 (Spring 1992): 263–276.

Fama, Eugene F. "Organizational Forms and Investment Decisions." *Journal of Financial Economics* 14 (March 1985): 101–119.

Ferreira, Eurico J., and LeRoy Brooks. "Capital Budgeting: A Key Management Challenge." *Business* 38 (October–December 1988): 22–29.

Fisher, Irving. *The Theory of Interest.* New York: Macmillan, 1930.

Fogler, H. Russell. "Overkill in Capital Budgeting Technique?" *Financial Management* 1 (Spring 1972): 92–96.

Gitman, Lawrence J., and John R. Forrester, Jr. "A Survey of Capital Budgeting Techniques Used by Major U.S. Firms." *Financial Management* 6 (Fall 1977): 66–71.

Graham, John R., and Campbell R. Harvey. "The Theory and Practice of Corporate Finance: Evidence From the Field." *Journal of Financial Economics* 60 (May/June 2001): 187–243.

Gurnami, G. "Capital Budgeting Theory and Practice," *Engineering Economist* 30 (Fall 1984).

Hajdasinski, Miroslaw M. "A Complete Method for Separation of Internal Rates of Return." *Engineering Economist* 28 (Spring 1983): 207–250.

———. "On Bounding the Internal Rates of Return of a Project." *Engineering Economist* 33 (Spring 1988): 235–270.

———. "The Payback Period as a Measure of Profitability and Liquidity." *Engineering Economist* 38 (Spring 1993): 177–191.

Hastie, K. Larry. "One Businessman's View of Capital Budgeting." *Financial Management* 3 (Winter 1974): 36–44.

Hayes, R., and W. Abernathy. "Managing Our Way to Economic Decline." *Harvard Business Review* (July–August 1980): 67–77.

Herbst, Anthony F. "A FORTRAN VI Procedure for Determining Return on Invested Capital." *Management Science* (February 20, 1974): 1022.

———. "The Unique Real Internal Rate of Return: Caveat Emptor!" *Journal of Financial and Quantitative Analysis* 13 (June 1978): 363–370.

Hirshleifer, Jack "On the Theory of Optimal Investment Decision." *Journal of Political Economy* (August 1958): 329–352.

Kamath, Ravindra, and Eugene Oberst. "Capital Budgeting Practices of Large Hospitals." *Engineering Economist* 37 (Spring 1992): 203–232.

Khan, Aman. "Capital Budgeting Practices in Large U.S. Cities." *Engineering Economist* 33 (Fall 1987): 1–12.

Klammer, Thomas P., and Michael C. Walker. "Capital Budgeting Questionnaires: A New Perspective." *Quarterly Journal of Business and Economics* 26 (Summer 1987): 87–95.

———. "The Continued Increase in the Use of Sophisticated Capital Budgeting Techniques." *California Management Review* 27 (Fall 1984): 137–148.

Lewellen, Wilbur G., Howard P. Lanswe, and John J. McConnell. "Payback Substitutes for Discounted Cash Flow." *Financial Management* 2 (Summer 1973): 17–23.

Longmore, Dear R. "The Persistence of the Payback Method: A Time-Adjusted Decision Rule Perspective." *Engineering Economist* 34 (Spring 1989): 185–194.

Luxhoj, James T., and Marilyn S. Jones. "A Framework for Replacement Modeling Assumptions." *Engineering Economist* 32 (Fall 1986): 39–49.

Martin, John D., Samuel H. Cox, and Richard D. MacMinn. *The Theory of Finance: Evidence and Applications.* Hinsdale, Ill.: Dryden Press, 1988.

McConnell, John, and C. Muscarella. "Corporate Capital Expenditure Decisions and the Market Value of the Firm." *Journal of Financial Economics* 14 (September 1985): 399–422.

Meal, H. C. "Putting Production Decisions Where They Belong." *Harvard Business Review* (March–April 1984).

Middlaugh, J. Kendall, II, and Scott S. Cowen. "Five Flaws in Evaluating Capital Expenditures." *Business Horizons* 30 (March–April 1987): 59–67.

Mukherjee, Tarun K., and David F. Scott, Jr. "The Capital Budgeting Process in Large Firms: An Analysis of Capital Budgeting Manuals." Paper presented at the Eastern Finance Association meeting, April 1987.

Narayanan, M. P. "Observability and the Payback Criterion." *Journal of Business* 58 (July 1985): 309–323.

Pike, Richard H. "Do Sophisticated Capital Budgeting Approaches Improve Investment Decision-Making Effectiveness?" *Engineering Economist* 34 (Winter 1989): 149–161.

———. "An Empirical Study of the Adoption of Sophisticated Capital Budgeting Practices and Decision-Making Effectiveness." *Accounting and Business Research* (Autumn 1988): 341–351.

Porter, Michael. "Capital Choices: Changing the Way America Invests in Industry." *Journal of Applied Corporate Finance* (1992): 4–16.

Pratt, John W., and John S. Hammond III. "Evaluating and Comparing Projects: Simple Detection of False Alarms." *The Journal of Finance* 34 (December 1979): 1231–1242.

Proctor, Michael D., and John R. Canada. "Past and Present Methods of Manufacturing Investment Evaluation: A Review of the Empirical and Theoretical Literature." *Engineering Economist* 38 (Fall 1992): 45–58.

Ramis, Francisco J., Gerald J. Thuesen, and Tina J. Barr. "A Dynamic Target-Wealth Criterion for Capital Investment Decisions." *Engineering Economist* 36 (Winter 1991): 107–126.

Reimann, Bernard C. "Stock Price and Business Success: What Is the Relationship?" *Journal of Business Strategy* 8 (Summer 1987): 38–49.

Robichek, Alexander A., and James C. Van Horne. "Abandonment Value and Capital Budgeting." *Journal of Finance* 22 (December 1967): 577–590.

Ross, Marc. "Capital Budgeting Practices of Twelve Large Manufacturers." *Financial Management* 15 (Winter 1986): 15–22.

Samuelson, Paul A. "Some Aspects of the Pure Theory of Capital." *Quarterly Journal of Economics* (May 1937): 469–496.

Schall, Lawrence D., Gary L. Sundem, and William R. Geijsbeek. "Survey and Analysis of Capital Budgeting Methods." *Journal of Finance* 33 (March 1978): 281–287.

Schull, David M. "Efficient Capital Project Selection through a Yield-Based Capital Budgeting Technique." *Engineering Economist* 38 (Fall 1992): 1–18.

Scott, David F., Jr., and J. William Petty III. "Capital Budgeting Practices in Large American Firms: A Retrospective Analysis and Synthesis." *Financial Review* 19 (March 1984): 111–125.

Stewart, G. Bennett, III. "Market Myths." *Journal of Applied Corporate Finance* 2, no. 3 (Fall 1989): 6–23.

Sullivan, A. Charlene, and Keith Smith. "Capital Budgeting Practices for U.S. Factory Automation Projects." Purdue University Working Paper #90-11-1 (November 1990).

Sundem, Gary L. "Evaluating Capital Budgeting Models in Simulated Environments." *Journal of Finance* 30 (September 1975): 977–992.

Wilner, Neil, Bruce Koch, and Thomas Klammer. "Justification of High Technology Capital Investment—An Empirical Study." *Engineering Economist* 37 (Summer 1992): 341–353.

CHAPTER 7

Ranking Mutually Exclusive Investments

After completing this chapter you should be able to:

- Identify mutually exclusive projects and know how to choose the better project.
- Demonstrate why net present value is superior to other methods in ranking mutually exclusive projects.
- Compare projects with different life spans or durations.
- Compute the equivalent annuity for different projects.
- Explain when and why the equivalent annuity method is used to compare projects with unequal lives.
- Determine the optimal abandonment time for a project.

After studying energy conservation decisions at numerous manufacturing firms, researcher Marc Ross developed the following composite profile:

> Bill Johnson is part of an energy-conservation team at a large plant of a basic-materials manufacturer. On the initiative of a vendor, he has identified an approach to cutting energy cost of a heater: advanced combustion controls, which would reduce excess air in the combustion zone.
>
> Bill looks into other approaches, such as total replacement of the heater or added heat exchangers (to capture heat from the stack gases to preheat the product). However, the projects overlap; he can advocate at most one.[1]

[1]Marc Ross, "Capital Budgeting Practices of Twelve Large Manufacturers," *Financial Management* 15 (Winter 1986): 15–22.

Like Bill Johnson, managers are often forced to choose between attractive investments, and various discounted cash flow measures sometimes give conflicting messages about which investment is best. What is Exxon to do, for example, if new supertankers have the highest net present values but smaller used tankers have higher internal rates of return? Acquiring both types of tankers is not the answer because the company can acquire enough of either type to carry all available oil. Some capital investments have more than one internal rate of return, and what should a company do about a capital investment that has internal rates of return of 2 percent and 200 percent? Choices between attractive investments must be made, and this chapter is devoted to capital investment choice when at least two alternatives are attractive.

Investments may compete because they are mutually exclusive or because the company faces capital rationing. Two investments are **mutually exclusive** if, like Exxon's tankers, there is a reason other than money that makes the selection of both infeasible. **Capital rationing** occurs when managers limit the total amount of money to be invested, so that they do not select all investments with positive net present values, even though the investments are not mutually exclusive. Mutually exclusive investments and investments with more than one internal rate of return are treated in this chapter, and capital rationing is treated in Chapter 22 as part of the section on financing decisions and capital investment analysis.

REASONS FOR MUTUALLY EXCLUSIVE INVESTMENTS

Mutually exclusive capital investments are often alternative ways to achieve the same result or alternate uses of a scarce resource other than money. When an airline is comparing the purchase of new and used airplanes, it is looking at two different ways to carry the same passengers. When Boeing was considering production of the 7J7 airplane, managers knew that airlines needing additional capacity could buy a used airplane for $12 million or a new, fuel-efficient 7J7 for $30 million.[2] Boeing's managers thought that the airlines would rank used airplane investments higher than 7J7 investments and, therefore, decided not to build the 7J7.

Why do we get conflicting rankings? Addressing the question in mechanical terms, there are three conditions that can lead to ranking differences with the three discounted cash flow measures:[3]

1. Differences in the timing of cash flows for competing investments.

   When Chrysler bought American Motors, it got a design (Jeep) it could sell immediately, while years would otherwise be spent developing a competing design. Chrysler also got older, less efficient factories with shorter lives and immediate production instead of new, efficient factories with longer lives.

[2]"Bright Smiles, Sweaty Palms," *Business Week* (February 1, 1986): 22–23.

[3]Reinvestment rate assumptions may also be an issue, if explicit assumptions of reinvestment rates different from the company's required return are used.

2. Differences in the sizes of competing investments.

   Choices among investments of different sizes are illustrated by George Steinbrenner's decision to enter the Hawaiian cruise market by building $150 million, 1,200-passenger ships. Prior to this decision, $100 million, 800-passenger ships had been considered.
3. Differences in the use of scarce resources other than money.

   The world is rich with examples of investments that are competing uses of scarce resources. Neiman-Marcus has more potential uses for floor space at its Union Square store than it has space available. Skilled personnel are another type of resource constraint, and airline manufacturers are often seen vying with each other for a supply of engineers that is fixed in the short run. Other companies are forced to limit growth because they cannot expand their management team fast enough to take advantage of all opportunities without losing control. When the owners of the Los Angeles Rams decided to move their football team to Saint Louis, they made a choice between competing uses of a scarce resource: an NFL football franchise.

Time is an essential element in many mutually exclusive investment situations. Suppose Neiman-Marcus wants to expand its Union Square store, but no adjacent space is available. Land must be found, a purchase must be negotiated, architectural plans must be drawn, permits must be obtained, construction must be carried out, and a buyer for the old store must be found. The marginal cost of the increased space may be so high that the project is abandoned. Even if the process is feasible, it may take years, and space must be rationed in the meantime.

These examples make it clear that mutually exclusive investments are not oddities but part of the daily life of anyone who deals with capital investment proposals.

REMINDER: NPV IS STILL BEST

Commerce Energy Service illustrates the problems faced in choosing among mutually exclusive investments and can be used to demonstrate the superiority of net present value as the tool for choosing among these investments. Commerce can provide electricity to an industrial park using coal, gas, or oil as fuel. The three competing investments are summarized in Table 7-1. Each investment has a 4-year life in that it will produce electricity for 4 years, even though coal does not generate cash flows in all years. (The coal investment will just break even during the last 2 years, but the operation must be continued to meet contract obligations.) Given Commerce's 10 percent required return, each of the three investments is desirable according to net present value, profitability index, and internal-rate-of-return criteria. But each investment is best according to one of the measures and worst according to one of the others.

TABLE 7-1 Illustration of Investment Desirability Ranking Conflicts

Initial outlays and year-end cash flows for the three fuel choices available to Commerce Energy are shown, along with net present value (NPV), profitability index (PI), and internal rate of return (IRR). The required return is 10 percent. Rankings depend on which of these three measures is used.

	CASH FLOWS							
YEAR:	0	1	2	3	4	NPV	PI	IRR
Investment								
Coal	−1,000	750	500	0	0	95.04	1.095	18%
Gas	−1,000	350	350	350	350	109.45	1.109	15%
Oil	-500	180	180	180	180	70.58	1.141	16%

These reasons for differences in rankings are illustrated for Commerce Energy Service in Table 7-1. Coal is superior to gas in terms of internal rate of return, but cash inflows from coal occur sooner, so the higher return is earned for a shorter time. Oil generates more cash flow per dollar invested than does gas, but the oil investment is smaller in size so its contribution to net present value is less.

In Chapter 5, we demonstrated that net present value measures the increase in wealth. We could just quit with that point, because we know that the choice that maximizes net present value maximizes wealth, so any other choice does not maximize wealth. Since you may come up against the use of alternate ranking schemes, though, it is worthwhile to explore the implications of these alternate rankings a bit more.

Reasons for conflicting rankings can be further illustrated by comparison of the net present value profiles for coal and gas, shown in Figure 7-1. This profile is constructed by calculating the net present value for each project at various required rates of return. As these profiles illustrate, the investment choice that provides the highest net present value depends on the required return. At very low discount rates the gas project is preferred to the coal project. The intersection of the two profiles, called Fisher's intersection due to exploration of its significance by Irving Fisher,[4] occurs at the discount rate of 11.45 percent. Coal is superior if the required return is above 11.45 percent, and gas is superior otherwise.[5] In this case, gas makes the greatest contribution to wealth because the required return is 10 percent.

[4]See Irving Fisher, *The Rate of Interest* (New York: Macmillan, 1907) and *The Theory of Interest* (New York: Macmillan, 1930).

[5]We can also note that when two investments are being considered, net present value and internal rate of return rankings agree if the required return is above Fisher's intersection, and disagree otherwise.

FIGURE 7-1 Net Present Value Profiles for Mutually Exclusive Investments

This figure shows the net present values for coal and gas investments from Table 7-1, at various discount rates. The intersection of the two lines, called Fisher's intersection, is at the discount rate that results in the same net present value for both investments.

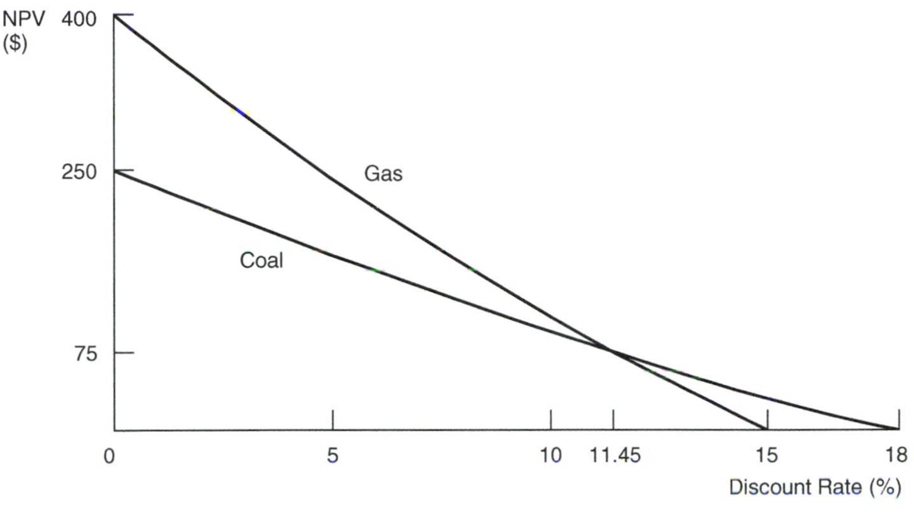

Suppose we are faced with the three alternatives in Table 7-1. Suppose further that we are making the decisions on behalf of an investor who can invest elsewhere at 10 percent and has $1,000 to invest, after setting aside the present value of the amount she wants to consume over the next 4 years. If this investor likes more money better than less, her objective with the $1,000 will be to end up with as much money as possible at the end of 4 years. Coal or gas will take all of her money, while oil will leave her with $500 to invest elsewhere at 10 percent. All cash inflows from the investment will be reinvested until the end of the 4-year period at 10 percent.

Her wealth at the end of the 4 years with each alternative is as follows:

Coal: $750(1.10)^3 + 500(1.10)^2 = \$1{,}603.25$

Gas: $350(1.10)^3 + 350(1.10)^2 + 350(1.10)^1 + 350 = \$1{,}624.35$

Oil: $500(1.10)^4 + 180(1.10)^3 + 180(1.10)^2 + 180(1.10)^1 + 180 = \$1{,}567.43$

Elsewhere (None): $1{,}000(1.10)^4 = \$1{,}464.10$

The project that maximized net present value also maximized terminal wealth. To be precise, the present value of the increase in terminal wealth, over the $1,464.10 from investing elsewhere, is the net present value:

	TERMINAL WEALTH (TW)	TERMINAL WEALTH GAIN (TW − 1,464.10)	PRESENT VALUE OF TERMINAL WEALTH GAIN
Coal	1,603.25	139.15	95.04
Gas	1,624.35	160.25	109.45
Oil	1,567.43	103.33	70.58

We set aside this investor's consumption plans and concentrated on terminal wealth. Of course, the investment that maximizes terminal wealth also maximizes current consumption potential if the investor wants to borrow against future cash flows at 10 percent interest rate. Once again, we see that the net present value is the correct ranking tool when choosing among mutually exclusive projects. Net present value gives the correct ranking for maximization of current share price, maximization of the investors' terminal wealth, and maximization of the investors' ability to consume at any one time, while holding consumption at other times constant. The example demonstrates that use of the other ranking methods (IRR and PI) leads to choices that do not maximize current wealth, future wealth, or consumption by investors.

Having recognized the superiority of the net present value ranking, it is useful to compare the information content of the various discounted cash flow measures. The net present value measures an investment's *total* contribution to shareholder wealth while the profitability index measures wealth creation *per dollar invested.* The profitability index has some limited use as a ranking tool in certain capital rationing situations, but in the absence of capital rationing, money committed to one investment is not diverted from other uses that would generate positive net present values. Therefore, total net present value creation, and not net present value creation per dollar invested, is the appropriate standard for choosing among mutually exclusive investments so as to maximize shareholder wealth.

The internal rate of return measures the rate of return on *unrecovered* investment. It gives no indication of the dollar *amount of investment* earnings that are returned or the *length of time* that return is earned. Consequently, the internal rate of return does not measure the size of the value contribution of an investment, even though it continues to be the most widely used discounted cash flow method in practice.

It is clear that net present value is the right way to choose, but application of the net present value can be complicated. In the remainder of this chapter, we will look at ways to apply the net present value rule to mutually exclusive capital investments with unequal lives, to mutually exclusive capital investments with costs and no direct benefits, to repair/replace decisions, and to abandonment decisions.

USING NPV WITH UNEQUAL LIVES

Unequal lives are a common problem in capital budgeting. The prospective choice of an airline between a Boeing 7J7 and a used airplane involved differences in life. A used airplane that cost $12 million might have a life of only 10 remaining years, while a new $30 million airplane might last 20 years. Thus, the 7J7 would provide both fuel economy and more years of usage. The question is whether the extra years of use and the fuel savings would be worth an extra $18 million of investment.

To deal with unequal lives, suppose that the coal investment in Table 7-1 has a life of only 2 years and that a new investment in electricity production can be made at that time. This is an important consideration. The goal is still to maximize net present value, but net present value must be measured over comparable periods. Assume that the industrial park will close after 4 years and none of the investments have salvage values if abandoned early. The oil and gas alternatives have equal lives, and we already know that the gas investment is preferred over the oil investment. The investments to consider are:

- Invest in coal, then invest in coal again at the end of 2 years.
- Invest in gas.

It would also be possible to consider sequences involving abandonment of an investment before the end of its life, but none of these capital investments happen to have positive net present values if abandoned early. Cash flows and net present values for the two sequences appear in Table 7-2.

In this example, the greatest net present value over the 4-year life of the industrial park is achieved by starting with coal and then repeating coal after 2 years. The preferability of this sequence is dependent on the particular set of assumptions about future opportunities. A change in the life of the constraining resource (industrial park), a change in future investment opportunities, or an opportunity to sell one of the investments before the end of its life could change

TABLE 7-2 Cash Flows with Alternate Investment Sequences

This table contains a cash flow and net present value analysis (at a 10 percent required return) for two possible investment sequences. The industrial park has a life of 4 years. The lives of investments end when cash flows stop, and none of the investments has salvage values if abandoned early.

YEAR:	0	1	2	3	4
I. Start with coal and then repeat coal					
Invest in coal	−1,000	750	500		
Invest in coal			−1,000	750	500
Total	−1,000	750	−500	750	500
Net present value =	$173.59				
II. Invest only in gas					
Invest in gas	−1,000	350	350	350	350
Net present value =	$109.45				

the sequence that has the highest net present value. Thus, the selection process is heavily dependent on assumptions about future opportunities. If the assumptions about future opportunities are correct, maximizing net present value over the life of the constraining resource (the industrial park's life) will maximize wealth.

Equivalent Annuity (EA)

Finding the investment sequence that maximizes net present value can be a difficult process when you can reuse a resource indefinitely. Suppose, for example, you were trying to choose between a new airplane that will last 21 years and a used airplane that will last 8 years, with an indefinite number of repetitions of either investment being feasible. A simple net-present-value ranking will not do because one investment provides service longer. You could evaluate the two alternatives by assuming that whichever investment was chosen initially would be repeated over the span of 168 years (8 × 21) that would be required to get a time horizon at which both assets would be reaching the ends of their lives simultaneously. This would, of course, be a bit tedious. The equivalent annuity, also referred to as the **annualized net present value,** is a useful tool for simplifying the analysis of problems of this type, as long as the projects being compared are of the same risk. The equivalent annuity is not an alternative to the net present value; it is a convenient way of selecting investments that will maximize net present value.

The **equivalent annuity** is the level annuity over the investment's life that has a present value equal to the investment's net present value. Expressed mathematically by rearranging terms in Equation 3-4b, the equivalent annuity (EA) is:

$$EA = NPV/PVA1_{n,k} \qquad \textbf{(7-1)}$$

The investment with the highest equivalent annuity will have the highest net present value of total cash flows if all competing investments are repeated to infinity or to a comparable time horizon at which the lives of all competing investments end.

Using the 10 percent required return, the equivalent annuities for coal and gas investments in Table 7-1, assuming coal can be repeated in 2 years, are:

$$EA_{coal} = \$95.04/PVA1_{2yrs,10\%} = \$95.04/1.7355 = \underline{\underline{\$54.76}}$$

$$EA_{gas} = \$109.45/PVA1_{4yrs,10\%} = \$109.45/3.1699 = \underline{\underline{\$34.53}}$$

The coal investment is superior to the gas investment using the equivalent annuity and will, therefore, be superior to the gas investment using net present value analysis with repeated investment out to any comparable time horizon.

To see the correspondence between the net present value and equivalent annuity ranking, note that the coal investment's equivalent annuity of $54.76, if continued for 4 years, is:

$$\$54.76\ PVA1_{4yrs,10\%} = \underline{\underline{\$173.59}}$$

This $173.59 is the same net present value found in Table 7-2 with the coal investment repeated after 2 years. If a capital investment is replaced with an identical investment at the end of its life forever, the net present value is:[6]

$$NPV_\infty = EA/k \tag{7-2}$$

The net present values for the coal and gas investments assuming repetition to infinity are:

$$NPV_{coal,\infty} = 54.76/.10 = \underline{\underline{\$547.60}}$$

$$NPV_{gas,\infty} = 34.53/.10 = \underline{\underline{\$345.30}}$$

Suppose the gas investment could be repeated indefinitely but the coal investment could not be repeated. If the coal investment were chosen, the company would have to switch to the gas investment after the end of the initial life of the coal investment. The value-maximizing choice would still be to start with the investment with the highest equivalent annuity and then switch to the investment with the second-highest equivalent annuity at the expiration of the first investment.[7]

Equivalent annuity—selection between mutually exclusive projects: You have been given the job of selecting the personal computers for your business. For simplicity assume that there are only two choices, Hi-Quality Computers brand and Lo-Quality Computers Brand. Hi-Quality models will last 4 years, cost $1,650 apiece, require yearly maintenance of $100 per machine, and will have an estimated salvage value of $75 at the end of the 4-year life. Because these machines run slightly faster than the other, we expect after tax labor cost savings of $750 per year. The Lo-Quality models will last 3 years, cost $1,000, require $150 in yearly maintenance, and will have a $10 salvage value at the end of the 3-year life. The Lo-Quality machines run slower than the other, so we expect

---

[6]Proof:

$$NPV_\infty = NPV + NPV/(1 + k)^n + NPV/(1+k)^{2n} + \ldots$$

$$= [NPV(1 + k)^n]/(1 + k)^n + [NPV(1 + k)^n]/(1 + k)^{2n} + [NPV(1 + k)^n]/(1 + k)^{3n} + \ldots$$

$$= [(1+ k)^n NPV]/[(1+ k)^n - 1]$$

By definition, $NPV = EA[1 - 1/(1 + k)^n]/k$. Substituting for NPV gives:

$$NPV_\infty = (EA/k)(1 + k)^n[1 - 1/(1 + k)^n]/[(1 + k)^n - 1] = EA/k$$

[7]Proof: Let NPV_A be the net present value from perpetual reinvestment in project A, let NPV_B be similarly defined, and let NPV_{AB} be the net present value from initial investment in A and then perpetual reinvestment in B after the initial n year life of A. EA_A and EA_B are the equivalent annuities of A and B respectively.

$$NPV_A = EA_A/k \text{ and } NPV_B = EA_B/k$$

$$NPV_{AB} = EA_A PVA1_{n.k} + [EA_B/k]/(1 + k)^n]$$

Subtracting NPV_B from both sides and rearranging terms yields:

$$NPV_{AB} - NPV_B = [EA_A - EA_B]\ PVA1_{n,k}$$

Since both bracketed expressions on the right-hand side are positive if $EA_A > EA_B$, it follows that starting with investment A and then switching to investment B will create more value than starting and staying with investment B.

after tax labor cost savings of only $725 per year. Using a 10 percent discount rate and assuming replication is possible, what is the better computer choice?

Computer solution—equivalent annuity selection between mutually exclusive projects: To solve this problem, you would set up the boldface fields in the following spreadsheet:

	A	B	C	D	E	F
1	Equivalent annuity—Selection between mutually exclusive projects					
2	Hi-Quality Computers:					
3	Year	0	1	2	3	4
4	**Initial outlay**	**$ (1,650.00)**				
5	**After tax labor savings**		**$ 750.00**	**$ 750.00**	**$ 750.00**	**$ 750.00**
6	**Maintenance cost**		**$ (100.00)**	**$ (100.00)**	**$ (100.00)**	**$ (100.00)**
7	**Salvage value**					**$ 75.00**
8	**Total cash flow**	**$ (1,650.00)**	**$ 650.00**	**$ 650.00**	**$ 650.00**	**$ 725.00**
9	Present value	$ 2,111.64				
10	Net present value	$ 461.64				
11	PVIF	3.1699				
12	Equivalent annuity	$ 145.63				
13	Lo-Quality Computers:					
14	Year	0	1	2	3	
15	**Initial outlay**	**$ (1,000.00)**				
16	**After tax labor savings**		**$ 725.00**	**$ 725.00**	**$ 725.00**	
17	**Maintenance cost**		**$ (150.00)**	**$ (150.00)**	**$ (150.00)**	
18	**Salvage value**				**$ 10.00**	
19	**Total cash flow**	**$ (1,000.00)**	**$ 575.00**	**$ 575.00**	**$ 585.00**	
20	Present value	$ 1,437.45				
21	Net present value	$ 437.45				
22	PVIF	$ 2.4869				
23	Equivalent annuity	$ 175.91				

After entering the data and totaling the cash flows, calculate the present value by bringing the total cash flows back to present by using the NPV function. Then net this with present value to get $461.64 as the net present value for the Hi-Quality machines and $437.45 for the Lo-Quality machines. Because the machines have different lives and we assume that comparable machines will be available at the end of each machine's useful life, we cannot say that the Hi-Quality machine is better. Instead, we must calculate the equivalent annuity before making our recommendation. To have the computer compute the PVIF (present value interest factor), use the PV function and enter the .10 in the rate field, the life of the project (in this case 4 for the Hi-Quality machines) in the NPER field, and a –1 in the payment field (the minus is necessary to keep the output in the correct sign). When you hit enter, a PVIF of 3.1699 will appear in the cell. In the equivalent annuity cell simply take the result in the net present value cell and divide it by the result in the PVIF cell to get the equivalent annuity of $145.63 for the Hi-Quality machines and $175.91 for the Lo-Quality machines. Therefore the Lo-Quality machines are the better selection. The equivalent annuity leads to the choice between two mutually exclusive investments that maximizes net present value and shareholder wealth when the investment can be repeated to a comparable time horizon, or at least one of the two investments can be repeated indefinitely. Several researchers, referenced at the end of the chapter, have pointed out that in reality the equivalent annuity method may have overly aggressive assumptions. They say that projects may have learning curves that lead to differences in the cost of investments, cash flows, and risk over time. Others may argue that if these imperfections influence both choices somewhat proportionally, then the equivalent annuity would still give the correct choice.

COST-ONLY ANALYSIS

Some mutually exclusive investments do not generate cash flows directly. An example is the choice of an air-conditioning system for a company's headquarters building. There was no need to spend time deciding if they should air condition the building. The question is simply which air-conditioning system has a series of costs with the lowest present value. If the lives of the two methods are equal, the one with the lower present value of costs should be chosen. If the lives are unequal and replacement will be needed to continue providing the service, each present value can be converted to an equivalent annuity, commonly referred to as the *equivalent annual charge* when used in this context.

Example: The Old Haven city government, with a 10 percent required return, is considering two alternative heating systems for city hall. Suppose the economy heating system will last 5 years and has costs with a present value of $100,000, while the deluxe heating system will last 7 years and has costs with a present value of $120,000. The equivalent annual charges (using the 5- and 7-year 10 percent present value factors from Table A-4) are:

HEATING METHOD	LIFE	PV OF COSTS	EQUIVALENT ANNUAL CHARGE
Economy	5 years	$100,000	$100,000/3.7908 = $26,380
Deluxe	7 years	120,000	$120,000/4.8684 = $24,649

The deluxe system has a lower equivalent annual charge and is therefore more desirable, assuming either alternative can be repeated indefinitely. The same conclusion could have been reached with more tedious calculations by assuming a 35-year time horizon with the deluxe heating system replaced four times and the economy system replaced six times.

REPAIR/REPLACEMENT DECISIONS

The choice between repairing and replacing a piece of equipment is effectively a choice between mutually exclusive investments. Many cities currently face choices between spending a few hundred million dollars to modernize their existing overburdened airports or building new airports for ten times the cost.

For the repair/replace decision, the cost of the old asset is the repair cost plus the forgone sale price or salvage value.[8] The equivalent annuity or equivalent annual charge can be used to account for uneven lives.

Example: You could sell your used automobile today for \$6,000, or you could have it extensively repaired at a cost of \$1,000 and use it for 5 more years, at which time it would be worth nothing. A new car could be purchased for \$10,000 and would last for 10 years, with no significant repairs and no salvage value. The cost of using the old car for 5 years is the forgone \$6,000 receipt from the sale plus the repair cost, for a total of \$7,000.

Using Equation 7-1 and a 10 percent required return, the equivalent annual charge over the 5-year period is:

$$\text{Equivalent annual charge (old car)} = \$7{,}000/3.7908 = \underline{\underline{\$1{,}846.58}}$$

The equivalent annual charge for the 10-year life of the new car is:

$$\text{Equivalent annual charge (new car)} = \$10{,}000/6.1446 = \underline{\underline{\$1{,}627.45}}$$

Since the equivalent annual charge is based on costs, not benefits, the lower number is desired, and the new car is preferred.

The correctness of the equivalent annuity solution can be confirmed by comparing the two alternatives using marginal cash flows over a 10-year horizon. To do this, assume that if the old car is kept, another old car will be bought for \$6,000 and repaired for \$1,000 at the end of 5 years.[9] The immediate \$3,000 marginal cash flow to buy a new car (the price of a new car minus the sale price of the old car, minus the avoided repair cost) allows us to avoid a \$7,000 expenditure to buy and repair a used car in 5 years. To summarize, the marginal cash flows for the new car are as shown in Table 7-3.

At a 10 percent required return, the net present value of the marginal cash investment to buy a new car is positive:

$$NPV = -3{,}000 + (\$7{,}000/1.1^5) = \$1{,}346$$

[8]We continue to ignore taxes or assume cash flows are on an after tax basis throughout this chapter. Recognition of taxes in the estimation of cash flows is taken up in Chapter 8.

[9]Using the proof in footnote 7, it can also be shown that buying a new car now is cheaper than repairing the old car and replacing it with a new car in 5 years. This conclusion is based on the assumption that a car will be needed indefinitely and identical cars will be available at identical prices in the future.

TABLE 7-3 Marginal Cash Flow Analysis of New Car Purchase

These calculations confirm that the equivalent annuity analysis of the cost-only car purchase decision leads to the same choice as net present value over time with repeat purchases.

YEAR:	0	5
Purchase new car	–$10,000	
Sell old car	6,000	
Avoided repair cost	1,000	
Total Initial Outlay	–$3,000	
Avoid purchase of used car		$6,000
Avoid repair of used car		1,000
Net benefit in Year 5		$7,000
Present Value		$4,346
Net Present Value	$1,346	

This $1,346 net present value is also the present value of the difference between the two equivalent annual charges over 10 years:

$$NPV = (1{,}846.58 - 1{,}627.45)6.1446 = \$1{,}346$$

This confirms the preferability of the new car, as determined using the equivalent annual charge.[10]

COMPLEX INVESTMENTS

The investments considered thus far were competing investments with only one constraining or scarce resource. A more complex situation would involve several scarce resources with each of a number of investments using different amounts of each scarce resource for different lengths of time. A factory, for example, may have limited assembly-line time, limited raw materials, and limited engineering time available, with each of a hundred competing products using these resources in different proportions. The objective in these cases is still to choose the feasible combination of investments that maximizes net present value, but finding that combination could require checking thousands or millions of combinations. Fortunately, tools like linear programming can be used to quickly find

[10]People will occasionally suggest that the cost of the new car is the purchase price minus the sale price of the old car, or $4,000, while the cost of keeping the old car is the $1,000 repair cost. This would give an answer consistent with net present value over a 10-year horizon if the old car would last for 10 years with a $1,000 repair every 5 years. It is an appropriate solution, but for a different problem.

the optimal combination of investments in these situations. Linear programming applications are discussed in Chapter 24.

ABANDONMENT DECISIONS

For many capital investments, the economic life is not fixed, and there are a number of different times at which the investment can be abandoned. Abandonment decisions are a form of mutually exclusive investment analysis because a choice between several streams of costs and benefits is required. Car rental companies such as Hertz and Avis have wrestled with this problem because a car could be kept in the rental fleet from a few days to a decade or more. Most rental car companies have opted to abandon (sell) their cars after a year or two, although some discount companies keep their cars longer.

If a project has no salvage value or other value that can be realized on abandonment, and it is not mutually exclusive with regard to other investments, it will generally be continued as long as it provides positive cash flows. If the investment has a value that can be realized on abandonment, you should abandon it at the point that maximizes net present value of all cash benefits, including abandonment value. Mathematically, the net present value with abandonment at the end of year d is:

$$NPV \sum_{t=1}^{d} CF_t/(1+k)^t - I_o + S_d/(1+k)^d \qquad \textbf{(7-3)}$$

where S_d is the salvage value at the end of year d. The net present value is computed in this way for values of d from one to the maximum possible life of the investment. The project life (d) that gives the highest net present value is the economic life of the investment.

Optimal abandonment example: Georgetown Corporation is considering a new hydraulic packer. The asset requires an initial outlay of $1,000 and then generates cash benefits at the end of each year for the next 3 years. The value that can be obtained on abandonment declines from $700 at the end of the first year to $50 at the end of the third year.

Table 7-4 shows an abandonment analysis. The net present value is computed on the assumption the investment is abandoned at the end of the first year. The computation is then repeated on the assumption of abandonment at the end of the second year and again for the assumption of abandonment at the end of the third year. A 10 percent required return was used for the analysis. The net present value, in this case, is maximized by abandonment at the end of the second year. It is sometimes suggested that a project should be abandoned when the present value of the future cash flows is less than the salvage value. The problem with this rule is that it ignores the future abandonment opportunities. This point can be illustrated with Table 7-4. At the end of the first year, the salvage

TABLE 7-4 Abandonment Analysis

Total net present value using a 10 percent required return is computed for each possible abandonment time. Net present value is maximized by abandonment at the end of year 2.

YEAR:	0	1	2	3
Cash flow	−$1,000	$500	$450	$300
Salvage value at the end of year d: (S_d)		700	350	50

ABANDON AFTER	NET PRESENT VALUE
1 year	$(500 + 700)/1.10 - 1{,}000 = 90.91$
2 years	$500/1.10 + (450 + 350)/1.10^2 - 1{,}000 = 115.70$
3 years	$500/1.10 + 450/1.10^2 + (300 + 50)/1.10^3 - 1{,}000 = 89.41$

value is $700 and the present value of the remaining cash flows is $450/1.10 + 300/1.10^2 = \$657$. This rule would lead to abandonment at the end of the first year, whereas the optimal abandonment time is at the end of the second year.

In the case of mutually exclusive investments with unequal lives, the use of the constraining resource after abandonment must be considered. If investment in an identical asset is assumed, the abandonment time that maximizes the equivalent annuity is optimal. For the three alternative abandonment times considered in Table 7-4, for example, the equivalent annuities are as follows:

ABANDONMENT YEAR (d)	NPV ÷ $PVA1_{d,10\%}$	= EQUIVALENT ANNUITY
1	90.91 ÷ .9091	= $100.00
2	115.70 ÷ 1.7355	= $ 66.67
3	89.41 ÷ 2.4869	= $ 35.95

Abandonment at the end of the first year gives the highest equivalent annuity. Therefore, abandonment at the end of the first year is optimal if abandonment frees up a constraining resource for reuse; net present value over time would be maximized by abandoning at the end of the first year and replacing the investment with an identical investment that is abandoned when it is 1 year old, and so on. If the constraining resource is not freed up by abandonment, the net-present-value rule identifies the end of the second year as the optimal abandonment time.

Spreadsheet solution to the optimal abandonment example: To solve the previous problem in an Excel spreadsheet you would set up the following table:

	A	B	C	D	E
1	Optimal abandonment problem on Excel				
2	If the asset is kept for 3 years:				
3	Year	0	1	2	3
4	Initial outlay	$(1,000.00)			
5	Cash inflows		$500.00	$ 450.00	$ 300.00
6	Salvage value				$ 50.00
7	Total cash flow	$ (1,000.00)	$ 500.00	$ 450.00	$ 350.00
8	Present value	$ 1,089.41			
9	**Net present value**	**$89.41**			
10	PVIF	2.4849			
11	**Equivalent annuity**	**$35.95**			
12	If the asset is kept for 2 years:				
13	Year	0	1	2	
14	Initial outlay	$(1,000.00)			
15	Cash inflows		$ 500.00	$ 450.00	
16	Salvage value			$ 350.00	
17	Total cash flow	$ (1,000.00)	$ 500.00	$ 800.00	
18	Present value	$ 1,115.70			
19	**Net present value**	**$ 115.70**			
20	PVIF	1.7355			
21	**Equivalent annuity**	**$ 66.67**			
22	If the asset is kept for 1 year:				
23	Year	0	1		
24	Initial outlay	$(1,000.00)			
25	Cash inflows		$ 500.00		
26	Salvage value		$ 700.00		
27	Total cash flow	$(1,000.00)	$1,200.00		
28	Present value	$ 1,090.91			
29	**Net present value**	**$90.91**			
30	PVIF	0.9091			
31	**Equivalent annuity**	**$ 100.00**			

It is easier to start with the longest life first, which in this case is to keep the asset for 3 years and then dispose of it for $50. After entering and then totaling the cash flows in years 1 to 3, you use the NPV function to bring the cash flows back to present at 10 percent. Then net the present value with the initial outlay to calculate the net present value. If the project cannot be replicated stop here, otherwise use the PV function to get the PVIF (present value interest factor). Within the PV function enter the .10 in the rate field, the life of the project (in this case 3) in the NPER field, and a –1 in the payment field (the minus is necessary to keep the output in the correct sign). When you hit enter, a PVIF of 2.4869 will appear in the cell. In the equivalent annuity cell simply take the result in the net present value cell and divide it by the result in the PVIF cell to get the equivalent annuity of $35.95.

Managers sometimes talk about the optimal replacement cycle rather than the optimal abandonment time. As an example, should San Jose Plastics replace injection pumps every 2 years or every 3 years? Reuse of a constraining resource is implied in these decisions, so a replacement cycle decision is really an abandonment time decision with a constraining resource.

Many readers may have identified the right to abandon as a "real option" that gives additional value to the project, and they are right. Later in the book, in Chapter 15, we will discuss the presence and valuation of "real options." For now, suffice it to say the right to abandon does have value that is considered in the net present value and equivalent annuity calculation. In capital-rationing situations, other abandonment rules are sometimes appropriate, and we will discuss these later, in Chapter 22. Abandonment opportunities can also be important in risk analysis, and the abandonment opportunity will be considered in that context in Chapter 12.

SUMMARY

In Chapter 6, we noted that the three discounted cash flow techniques—net present value, profitability index, and internal rate of return—are preferable to the payback period and accounting rate of return because they recognize the importance of the time value of money. While the three discounted cash flow measures give identical accept/reject signals for noncompeting investments, they often give conflicting rankings for mutually exclusive investments. The net present value is the amount by which the investment increases wealth. Thus, if the firm is not subject to capital rationing, ranking by net present value will lead to the choice between mutually exclusive investments that maximize wealth.

When mutually exclusive investments have unequal lives, the net-present-value ranking still leads to the choice that maximizes shareholder wealth, if the computation of net present value explicitly recognizes the difference in lives and possible later uses of the constraining resources. The equivalent annuity is not an alternative ranking method but simply a convenient way to develop the net-present-value ranking for mutually exclusive investments with unequal lives. The equivalent annuity formula is:

$$EA = NPV/PVA1_{n,k} \qquad \textbf{(7-4)}$$

The net present value and equivalent annuity concepts were extended to abandonment, replacement, and repair/replace decisions. These applications illustrate the robustness of the net-present-value rule.

Although many of the companies that rely on the internal rate of return for project selection will choose the same investments that would be chosen using net present value, they will not know if conflicting signals exist unless both the net present value and internal rate of return are computed. When both measures are computed and there is a conflict, the net-present-value signal is the one that should be used if the goal is to maximize shareholder wealth.

QUESTIONS

7-1. List some examples of conditions that could result in investments being mutually exclusive.

7-2. What is meant by the term **capital rationing?**

7-3. Why is it possible for an investment to have a higher net present value than a competing investment but still have a lower internal rate of return and profitability index than that competitor?

7-4. Define, in your own words, the equivalent annuity.

7-5. Give several examples of mutually exclusive investments that are not expected to increase revenues.

7-6. What is the criterion for selecting the optimal abandonment time?

7-7. What are the conditions in which the equivalent annuity gives a ranking the same as that achieved with the net present value?

7-8. Explain why the net present value is generally considered the superior measure for choosing between mutually exclusive investments.

7-9. Why is it not necessarily correct to sell a project when the salvage value is greater than the present value of cash inflows from future operations?

7-10. List five examples of resources other than money that can be constrained, and can, therefore, lead to mutually exclusive capital investments.

7-11. **(Applications)** On pages 198 and 203 of this chapter, two airplane alternatives were discussed: a $12 million used airplane that would last 10 years and a Boeing 7J7 that might last 20 years. In addition to direct equivalent annuity analysis, what strategic considerations might come into play in the choice between airplane types?

7-12. **(Ethical considerations)** Eli Lilly took on the challenge of reducing cash outflow by $1 billion over 3 years. The purpose was to make the company more lean and competitive. The company had never had a layoff up to that time. Is it ethically acceptable to make capital investments that will improve productivity but will also lead to layoffs in a company that has never laid off workers in the past?

PROBLEMS

(Continue to ignore taxes in analyzing these problems. The adjustment of cash flows for tax considerations will be taken up in Chapter 8.)

7-1. Initial costs, year-end cash flows, and desirability measures (net present value and internal rate of return) for mutually exclusive investments being considered by Stockton Corporation follow. The required return is 10 percent. Which investment should be chosen? Why?

YEAR	0	1	2	3	4	NP	IRR
P	−1,500	50	400	800	1,000	160	13.60%
Q	−1,800	1,200	600	400	50	121	14.55%

7-2. Initial costs and year-end cash flows for two mutually exclusive investments being considered by Stanford Partners follow. The required return is 10 percent. Which investment should be chosen? Why?

YEAR	0	1	2	3
R	-4,000	1,000	1,000	5,000
S	-5,000	5,000	1,000	1,000

7-3. Prepare a net present value profile for investments R and S from problem 2. Identify and interpret Fisher's intersection.

7-4. Santa Clara Corporation is considering investments T and U. Initial costs and year-end cash flows follow. Investment T has a life of 3 years and investment U has a life of 4 years. The limiting resource that caused the two investments to be mutually exclusive cannot be reused. The required return is 10 percent. Which investment should be chosen? Why?

YEAR	0	1	2	3	4
T	-50,000	25,000	25,000	25,000	
U	-65,000	25,000	25,000	25,000	25,000

7-5. For the mutually exclusive investments described in problem 4, which investment should be chosen if the constraining resource can be reused at the end of either investment's life? Why?

7-6. For the investment described in problem 4, assume that the constraining resource can be reused, but an investment similar to investment T will not be available when T expires. The constraining resource must be used for an investment similar to U at the end of the life of either T or U. Which investment should be chosen in this case? Why?

7-7. An office in Fort Collins uses 1,000 photocopies per working day, and there are 200 working days a year. The brand A copying machine costs $3,000 and will produce a total of 1 million copies before it wears out. The brand B machine costs $5,000 and will produce 2 million copies in its life. Maintenance and material costs are $.03 a copy with either machine, and neither machine will have any salvage value. The required return is 10 percent a year. Which machine should the company acquire? Why? (Assume year-end cash flows for simplicity.)

7-8. Which of the two copying machines described in problem 7 should the company choose if it uses 5,000 copies a day?

7-9. The board of directors at Boulder Corporation is considering two alternate ways of dealing with a deteriorated, demoralizing, and difficult-to-maintain office building. The existing building could be refurbished at a cost of $4 million, or a new building could be built at a cost of $6 million. The old building, even if refurbished, would not be as efficient as the new one, and energy costs would therefore be $200,000 a year higher. Either the new or the refurbished building would be used for 20 years. The salvage value for the new building would then be $1 million, while the salvage value for the old building would be $500,000. If the new building is acquired, the old building can be sold now for $250,000 in its present deteriorated condition. The required return for Boulder is 12 percent. Which alternative should be chosen? (Assume year-end cash flows for simplicity.)

7-10. Assume the old building described in problem 9 would only last 15 years if refurbished. The salvage value in 15 years would be $500,000. In this case, which building should be chosen?

7-11. A fast-food chain headquartered in Denver prefers to run stores for a few years and then sell them to franchise operators. The franchise operators pay an average fee of $100,000 a year per store above the cost of services provided. The company earns an average of $350,000 a year by operating a store itself. Sales prices, which depend on the time of sale, follow. The operating life of a store is 20 years. The company's required return is 14 percent, and it costs $1.5 million to build a store. The sale of a store does not free up any resource other than capital (the company is not operating under capital rationing) because it takes as much supervision for a franchise store as for a company-owned store. What is the optimum sale time? (Assume year-end cash flows for simplicity.)

YEAR	5	10	15	20
Sale price	$1,250,000	$1,000,000	$800,000	$50,000

7-12. For the stores described in problem 11, what would be the optimal sale time if the sale of one store freed up management time so that another store could be put in operation?

7-13. A taxi driver acquaintance drives a taxi 50,000 miles a year. A new cab costs $12,000. He can drive the cab 200,000 miles with the original engine and transmission. (It lasts longer than an ordinary car because he changes oil every 3,000 miles and because a taxi engine never gets cold, he explains.) Repair costs will average $.04 a mile for the first 200,000 miles. After 200,000 miles, he can sell the car for $200 or spend $2,000 for a rebuilt engine and transmission. With a new engine and transmission, the cab will then last another 200,000 miles with additional repair costs averaging $.08 a mile. The salvage value after 400,000 miles is approximately zero. His required return is 10 percent. Should he get a new cab every 200,000 miles or every 400,000 miles? (Assume year-end cash flows for simplicity.)

7-14. An asset being considered by Greeley Corporation has a 5-year life and a net present value of $100,000. At a 10 percent required return, what is the equivalent annuity?

7-15. Colorado Springs Technology must choose between two methods of producing a new product. The initial costs and year-end cash benefits are as follows:

YEAR	0	1	2	3	4	5
Method A	–$1,000,000	200,000	250,000	300,000	350,000	400,000
Method B	–$2,000,000	1,000,000	600,000	500,000	300,000	200,000

Assume all cash flows occur at year-end and the company's required return is 10 percent. Which production method should be used?

7-16. Storrs Corporation can sell an asset today for $1 million, or the asset can be kept for an additional 5 years and then scrapped for an estimated value of $200,000. If kept, the asset will generate cash flows of $200,000 at the end of each year for the next 5 years, exclusive of scrap value. The price will decline very rapidly, so the asset will not be sold until the fifth year if it is not sold immediately. At a 10 percent required return, should the asset be sold now or kept for another 5 years?

7-17. An asset costs $100,000 and will generate cash benefits of $30,000 at the end of each year for 5 years for Hartford Corporation. Salvage values are $50,000, $40,000, and $0 at the end of years 3, 4, and 5 respectively. The required return is 10 percent. Assuming that this asset can be replicated, when is the optimal time to abandon the investment?

7-18. An electric utility spends $1 billion on a new generating plant. Half of this $1 billion will be paid immediately and half will be paid at the end of 3 years, when the plant begins operation. The plant will then operate for 30 years. Fuel costs will be $100 million a year and other operating costs will be $50 million a year, both spread evenly over the year. Salvage value will be negligible. The utility has a 10 percent required return. What must be the annual charge to customers to cover all costs, including the purchase price of the plant? (Assume the revenues occur at midyear.)

7-19. New Haven Corporation is considering a new factory. Shutdown costs are expected to be extremely high at the end of the factory's life because by-products of the manufacturing process are highly toxic and difficult to dispose of. It will cost $1 billion to construct the factory, and the factory is expected to generate cash flows of $200 million at the end of each year for its 20-year life. Shutdown costs at the end of its life are then estimated to be $4 billion. The company has a 10 percent required return. Draw a net present value profile. Is this investment attractive?

7-20. An investment being considered by Danbury Corporation generates the following cash flows. It has two internal rates of return: 7 percent and 39 percent. The company has a required return of 10 percent. Draw a net present value profile. Should the company invest in this asset?

YEAR	0	1 THROUGH 19	20
Cash flow	–1,000	400 a year	–12,000

7-21. Fresno Corporation can sell an asset for $1 million or keep the asset for an additional 10 years and then sell it as scrap for $200,000. If kept, the asset will generate cash flows of $200,000 at the end of each year for the next 10 years, exclusive of scrap value. The sale price will decline very rapidly, so the asset will not be sold until the tenth year if it is not sold immediately. At a 14 percent required return, should the asset be sold now or kept for another 10 years?

7-22. For the asset in problem 21, suppose cash flows decline 10 percent each year. Should the asset be sold now or kept for another 10 years?

CASE PROBLEM

Zandts' Charter Sailboat

After spending over a decade of 12-hour workdays in successful management jobs, Barbara and Jim Zandt were in a comfortable financial position. But they had no time for themselves. Feeling a strong need to get away, the couple took a vacation on a charter sailboat out of St. Thomas in the Virgin Islands. By the end of the week, they decided this was where they wanted to spend their lives. For the next 2 years, they spent all of their vacation time in sailing courses and all of their spare time studying, both to enhance sailing skills and to understand the charter business.

The Zandts learned that most charter sailboats were owned by wealthy individuals who used the boats as tax-shelter investments, spending no more than two weeks a year on their boats. By joining several sailing clubs, advertising in a sailing magazine, and inquiring among their personal contacts, they found a physician who agreed to purchase a sailboat as an investment. The physician would bear all operating costs as the owner, while the Zandts would receive a percent of gross charter fees for their services as captain, crew, and manager.

The arrangement worked fine for 5 years, but the tax laws changed during that 5-year period. Typically, boats were kept in charter for 5 years, until the advantages of rapid depreciation had been used up. The owner would then trade for a new boat or pull the old boat out of charter service for personal use. Unfortunately, the new tax law eliminated investment tax credits and decreased the rate of depreciation. The physician wanted to sell the 5-year-old boat and did not want to replace it. Finding another investor seemed unlikely in the new tax environment. If they wanted to continue in this lifestyle, they would have to buy a boat themselves.

The Zandts faced several alternatives. They could buy the current 5-year-old boat from the physician for $50,000. It was due for refurbishing, which would cost $10,000. If they kept this boat for 5 years, it could be sold for approximately $25,000. If they kept this boat for 10 years, it could be sold for $15,000, but an overhaul after 5 years would cost $20,000.

Another alternative was to buy a new boat for $100,000. At the end of 5 years, the alternatives with the new boat would be the same as those with the existing boat. It could be sold for $50,000 or refurbished and kept for either 5 or 10 more years, with an overhaul when it was 10 years old if it were kept for 15 years.

A newer boat would attract more charter business and bring higher weekly fees. Barbara and Jim estimated that revenue per year during the first 5 years of a boat's life would be $50,000, but revenue would decline to $45,000 a year in the second 5 years and $40,000 a year in the third 5 years. The opposite would happen with operating expenses. Annual operating expenses would be $20,000 during the first 5 years, $25,000 during the second 5 years, and $30,000 during the third 5 years.

A new boat would be nice. The Zandts would have to spend less time on maintenance, and would have more time for pleasure. Also, it was fun to buy a new boat. On the other hand, their net worth was $200,000, and they were hesitant to sink half of it into one investment. A boat dealer had suggested that they could avoid the use of their capital by making a 25 percent down payment and borrowing the rest at a 12 percent annual interest rate. This, though, did not seem wise when they were only earning 10 percent on their own investments, which they guessed to be of similar risk to a boat. The dealer pointed out that the interest payments would be tax deductible, but the Zandts were in an income category that made taxes a negligible consideration.

Case Questions

1. List the alternatives to the Zandts.
2. Identify cash flows, net present value, and equivalent annuity for each alternative.
3. Discuss the risks that are inherent in each alternative.
4. Do the Zandts have a competitive advantage? Is there anything they can do to create or enhance a competitive advantage?
5. Which alternative would you recommend? Why?

SELECTED REFERENCES

Bacon, Peter W. "The Evaluation of Mutually Exclusive Investments." *Financial Management* 6 (Summer 1977): 55–58.

Brenner, Menachem, and Itzhak Venezia. "The Effects of Inflation and Taxes on Growth Investments and Replacement Policies." *Journal of Finance* 38 (December 1983): 1519–1528.

Brick, Ivan E., and Daniel G. Weaver. "A Comparison of Capital Budgeting Techniques in Identifying Profitable Investments." *Financial Management* 13 (Winter 1984): 29–39.

Capettini, Robert, and Howard Toole. "Designing Leveraged Leases: A Mixed Integer Linear Programming Approach." *Financial Management* 19 (Autumn 1981): 15–23.

Emery, Gary W. "Some Guidelines for Evaluating Capital Investment Alternatives with Unequal Lives." *Financial Management* 11 (Spring 1982): 14–19.

Fisher, Irving. *The Rate of Interest.* New York: Macmillan, 1907.

———. *The Theory of Interest.* New York: Macmillan, 1930.

Fogler, H. Russell. "Overkill in Capital Budgeting Technique?" *Financial Management* 1 (Spring 1972): 92–96.

Jones, Phillip C., James L. Zydiak, and Walace J. Hopp. "Generalized Imputed Salvage Values." *The Engineering Economist* 35 (Spring 1990): 214–229.

Luxhoj, James T., and Marilyn S. Jones. "A Framework for Replacement Modeling Assumptions." *The Engineering Economist* 32 (Fall 1986): 39–49.

Meal, H. C. "Putting Production Decisions Where They Belong." *Harvard Business Review* (March–April 1984): 102–110.

Meyer, Richard L., Scott Besley, and James R. Longstreet. "An Examination of Capital Budgeting Decision Alternatives for Mutually Exclusive Investments With Unequal Lives." *Journal of Business Finance & Accounting* 15 (Autumn 1988): 415–38.

Reimann, Bernard C. "Stock Price and Business Success: What Is the Relationship?" *Journal of Business Strategy* 8 (Summer 1987): 38–49.

Ristroph, John H. "Discount Rates for Mutually Exclusive Investments with Stationary Internal Rates of Return." *The Engineering Economist* 37 (Spring 1992): 233–49.

Robichek, Alexander A., and James C. Van Horne. "Abandonment Value and Capital Budgeting." *Journal of Finance* 22 (December 1967): 577–590.

Ross, Marc. "Capital Budgeting Practices of Twelve Large Manufacturers." *Financial Management* 15 (Winter 1986): 15–22.

Sachdeva, Kanwal S., and Lawrence J. Gitman, "Accounts Receivable Decisions in a Capital Budgeting Framework." *Financial Management* 10 (Winter 1981): 45–49.

Schrieves, Ronald E., and John M. Wachowicz, Jr. "Proper Risk Resolution in Replacement Chain Analysis." *The Engineering Economist* 34 (Winter 1989): 91–114.

Sundem, Gary L. "Evaluating Capital Budgeting Models in Simulated Environments." *Journal of Finance* 30 (September 1975): 977–992.

Sweeny, L. E. and Krishma Mantripragada. "Ranking Mutually Exclusive Investments: The Problem of Unequal Lives." *Journal of Business Finance & Accounting* 18 (June 1991): 609–619.

Estimating Cash Flows

PART THREE

In the previous three chapters we discussed investment choice first from a single project perspective and then concluded with a more realistic situation where multiple projects of unequal lines exist. In this section we take the book to a more realistic and practical level by introducing the reader to the difficult task of estimating the expected cash flows of a project. Chapter 8 focuses first on how to identify the relevant incremental cash flows from an investment, then expands the discussion with a detailed explanation of the construction of a projected cash flow statement for a typical project, and concludes with an introduction to some of the more common forecasting methods used in practice to estimate cash flows. Chapter 9 details the ramifications of taxes on cash flows. This chapter is important because of the significant and often increasing role that taxes (both domestic and international) play in influencing the size of the project's cash flow. In addition to the influence that taxes have on an international investment, Chapter 9 also introduces other unique concerns associated with estimating the cash flows for an international investment. Chapter 10 discusses the role of inflation in the estimation of cash flows for domestic investments. The chapter concludes with a discussion of the role that expected inflation in different countries has in the determination of future exchange rates and consequently the estimation of cash flows from a foreign investment to the parent company.

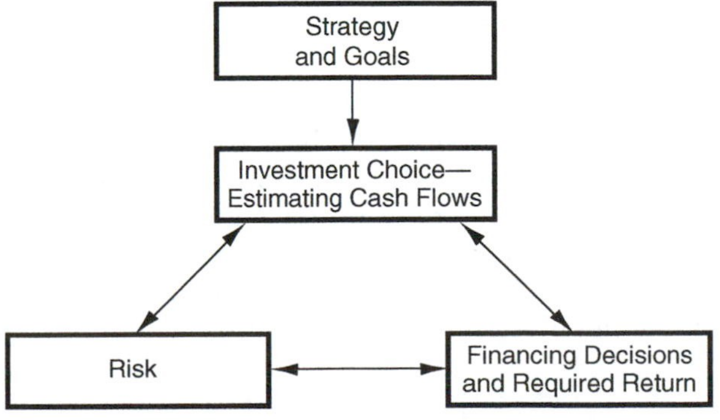

CHAPTER 8

Estimating Incremental Cash Flows

After completing this chapter, you should be able to:

- ➤ Differentiate between a relevant cash flow and an irrelevant cash flow.
- ➤ Discuss several hard-to-quantify benefits and costs associated with a capital investment.
- ➤ Understand the relevance or irrelevance of sunk cost, indirect cost, pure joint cost, and indirect benefits.
- ➤ Describe the steps involved in estimating cash flow and in putting together a cash flow statement.
- ➤ Construct a cash flow statement from an income statement by adjusting after tax income for depreciation and adjusting for balance sheet working capital items such as cash balances, accounts receivable, inventory, accounts payable, and accrued expenses.
- ➤ Estimate the incremental balance sheet impact resulting from a project in the form of land, buildings, and equipment and understand how these assets are depreciated, amortized, or depleted over time.
- ➤ Calculate the net present value of a project by identifying all incremental cash flows, adjusting for depreciation and taxes, and discounting back to the present.

After an extensive investment in research, Gillette developed a new shaving system, the MACH3, that provided a closer and smoother shave at a slightly higher production cost than the existing Sensor system. Special manufacturing equipment to produce the razors and blades would cost close to $800 million. To evaluate this replacement/new product decision, it was only necessary to identify and estimate the relevant cash flows and to make the investment if the net present value was positive.

In reality, identifying and estimating all relevant cash flows is easier said than done, though. In this example managers needed to decide how to treat the research investment and alternate use of the factory into which the new equipment would be placed. They needed to forecast production costs, working capital needs, and taxes. In addition, it was necessary to forecast sales and recognize sales of existing razor lines that would be lost when the new shaving system was introduced. Perhaps the most difficult problem was forecasting the number of years until some new development made these razors technologically obsolete. Gillette's problem is typical of the problems faced by a company when it attempts to estimate relevant cash flows for a capital investment.

This chapter begins with a discussion of relevant and irrelevant cash flows. Next, models are developed for the identification of relevant cash costs and benefits over the life cycle of a simple stand-alone investment. A comprehensive example illustrates the complete process, and the chapter concludes with a discussion of common forecasting techniques.

RELEVANT CASH FLOWS

A major part of capital budgeting is the separation of relevant from irrelevant cash flows. Considering a capital investment as a course of action, relevant and irrelevant cash flows can be defined as follows:

> A **relevant cash outflow** is the incremental cash outflow that will be caused by the course of action—a cash inflow that will be eliminated or an investment in assets and the respective claims by suppliers of capital that will be created.
>
> A **relevant cash benefit** is the incremental cash inflow that will be caused by the course of action—a cash outflow that will be avoided or a liquidation of assets and the claims by suppliers of capital that will be avoided.
>
> An **irrelevant cash flow** is a cash flow that will occur regardless of whether the proposed course of action is taken.[1]

Incremental or additional actual cash inflows and outflows, as well as cash inflows and outflows that are eliminated by the selection of a capital investment, are readily accepted as relevant cash flows. There are, however, several types of outlays and benefits that deserve special attention. These are discussed in the following paragraphs.

Sunk Costs

Sunk costs, which are expenditures that occurred prior to the time when the decision is being made, are a common source of confusion. Suppose, for example,

---

[1]Capital is defined as long-term financing, to include long-term debt, preferred stock, and common stock. The present value of future payments on certain leases also is included. Deferred taxes are generally excluded, even though they appear in the long-term liability section of the balance sheet, because they are not a source of cash but a means of reconciling accounting income with the cash flows used for capital budgeting.

that Nestlé has spent $1 million developing a new coffee flavor at its Maryville facility and must now decide whether to produce this flavor. Production of the new flavor will result in a net present value of $600,000 if the $1 million sunk cost is ignored. Recognizing the $1 million sunk cost leads to a net present value of negative $400,000. What should the company do? Consider that making the investment has the same value impact as selling the formula for $600,000; the company is $400,000 worse off than if it had never started the development, but $600,000 better off than if it simply forgot the whole thing. Managers may regret starting that particular development effort, but the sunk cost is not relevant for the decision about what to do with the results of that effort.

Indirect Costs

Indirect costs are also called joint costs, common costs, allocated costs, or overhead costs. These costs are shared by more than one activity, and it is often difficult to determine how these costs will be affected by changes in one particular activity. When Chrysler Corporation considers an expansion of the Fenton plant, for example, what will be the impact on home-office overhead? We may not know where a particular computer operator or accountant is going to be added, but we do know that there is a relationship between home-office expense and the total size of all operations. Failure to recognize potential increases in home-office costs will lead to overestimation of profitability. The allocations of these costs by cost accountants are often based on a requirement that all such costs be allocated somewhere, not on an estimate of an operation's marginal impact on costs. Thus, accounting allocations may not be useful. Statistical tools like regression analysis can often be used to estimate the relationship between total size and total overhead expense for the purpose of estimating the actual impact of an additional investment.

Pure Joint Costs

Pure joint costs are the extreme case of indirect costs. Pure joint costs are costs shared by two or more activities in such a way that changing the level of one activity while holding the other constant will not affect the costs at all. United Airlines, for example, hauls both people and express freight on passenger flights from Los Angeles to Chicago. Some costs are associated specifically with only one type of hauling; cabin attendants are not needed for freight, for example. But most of the costs are indeed pure joint costs. Attempts to allocate the pilot's salary between passengers and freight are of no help in decision making.

You can make wealth-maximizing decisions in the face of pure joint costs through a two-step decision process:

1. Compute the net present value of each capital investment using the best estimate of its impact on indirect costs. Consider the capital investment in step 2 only if it has a positive net present value solution in this step.

2. Compute the net present values for sets of capital investments that share costs, with all joint costs considered. Select a set of capital investments only if the total net present value from all of the investments in the set is positive when all joint costs and benefits are considered. This approach leads to value-maximizing capital investment decisions and avoids the problem of how to assign joint costs.

Example: UPS is considering adding seats to its airplane and utilizing these planes on Saturdays and Sundays since these are lighter days given that next-day packages will be delivered on Monday and can be moved over a two-day weekend.

Step 1: Estimating the net present value (NPV) of the parts

- NPV of the passenger service:
  Identify and estimate all the incremental costs associated with the addition of the seats and the extra flights. This would include labor to install the seats, the pilot's salary for the extra flight (if it would not otherwise be flown), gas, food, gate fees, and other expenses associated directly with the addition of passenger service. Expenses that would not be included are, for example, the president's salary, general corporate overhead, taxes, and other expenses that would not change as a result of instituting this new passenger service. A NPV would be calculated using the incremental revenues and expenses, and let's say it comes to $100 million.
- NPV of the freight service:
  Next, the freight service would estimate its incremental expenses the same way; assume that this solution is $250 million.

Step 2: Estimating the NPV of the whole operation including joint cost

Calculate the NPV of the entire UPS operation. Let's assume that this number is $300 million. As long as the whole operation including joint cost has a positive NPV (passengers and packages), then UPS would offer both services. If, on the other hand, both projects had positive NPVs but when combined and joint costs are included, the NPV for the entire operation becomes negative, then the operation should seek higher NPV projects, lower its joint cost, or shut down. In looking for another project to combine with packages, should another proposed project (of equal risk) have a higher combined NPV of $320 million, then this alternative is superior to the passenger alternative.

Indirect Benefits

Indirect benefits are the reverse of indirect costs. When BankAmerica attracts additional customers by offering a new checking account, an indirect benefit is that some of the new customers will sign up for the bank's credit cards. Profitable capital investments are sometimes rejected because indirect benefits are ignored. A set of capital investments is attractive if that set produces a positive net present value, even if no individual investment has a positive net present value when considered as a stand-alone project. Of course, a particular capital investment is attractive only if it adds to the net present value of the set.

Changes in Claims by Suppliers of Capital

If the firm finances projects by retaining the current earnings of the business, it is changing the claims of the suppliers of capital. Recall that the required return used in present value analysis is the return necessary to satisfy suppliers of capital. A $1,000 asset acquired by signing a note rather than by making a cash payment increases the amount of capital supplied by $1,000, and a satisfactory return must be earned on the $1,000. Likewise, owners' profits that are retained in the business instead of being paid as dividends must earn a return at least equal to what the owners could earn elsewhere. Thus, increases in obligations to suppliers of capital have the same decreasing effect on value as an increase in direct cash outflows. This claim is not quantified in dollar terms and subtracted from estimated cash benefits. Instead, this claim is considered in the discount rate used to calculate the net present value.

Interest Expense

Interest expense is another form of claim by suppliers of capital and, consequently, it is not included in the annual cash outlays of a capital investment. Interest expense is part of the cost of money that is used in determining the discount rate to use in computing net present value. A positive net present value means that the relevant cash benefits are more than enough to cover the relevant cash costs and pay the suppliers of capital their required returns. The actual cost of borrowed money, preferred equity, and common equity will be discussed and calculated in Chapter 16.

Opportunity Cost

The opportunity cost of a particular course of action is the cost of the next best action not taken. For example, for years Dole, Inc., owned many thousands of acres of prime real estate in Hawaii. The chosen course of action for this land was to grow pineapples. The opportunity cost for this action was the income that could be earned by converting this land to residential home sites, resort hotels, or some other commercial real estate purpose. In the late 1980s, management realized the opportunity cost associated with real-estate development was greater than the actual return realized from pineapple production and began to expand the real estate operation and exit the pineapple-growing business. In 1991, they attempted to split the company and put the food-processing business up for sale. This plan was later abandoned due to market and creditor reaction, and Dole is now both a food processor and a major land developer. It is important for management to recognize that the opportunity cost can surpass the profits from the existing business, and they may want to alter their strategy to increase the net present value of the company for the shareholders. Opportunity costs are harder to quantify than out-of-pocket costs, but they should not be ignored.

ESTIMATING CASH FLOWS FROM A PROJECT

Estimating the cash flows from a potential project is no small undertaking and it requires the help of engineers, cost analysts, marketing personnel, and others. We have broken down the process into the following steps:

Estimating the Income Statement

1. Estimate the relevant revenues and/or expenses you expect to receive from the project.
2. Assemble these revenues and expenses into a preliminary income statement making an appropriate calculation of the after tax income.

Estimating the Balance Sheet

3. Determine all of the balance sheet accounts that are impacted by the project.
4. Estimate the initial size of the investment in these balance sheet accounts. In particular, estimate the incremental investment in fixed assets, such as buildings and equipment, and in working capital items, such as cash balances, accounts receivable, inventory, accounts payable, and accrued expenses.
5. Determine size and growth of these accounts after the project is operational.

Roll the Income Statement and Balance Sheet into a Cash Flow Statement

6. Calculate the depreciation charge flowing from the fixed assets on the balance sheet to the income statement.
7. Estimate the life of the project.
8. Determine the terminal values for fixed assets and the disposition values of working capital (net of taxes).
9. Roll all of this information together into a projected cash flow statement.

Making the Decision

10. Calculate the net present value of the project using the appropriate discount rate.[2]
11. Make the appropriate accept or reject decision.

ESTIMATING THE INCOME STATEMENT

Definition of Corporate Income

In simple terms, the income of a business is the revenue, minus the expenses. The main sources of revenue for most businesses are the sales of goods and services. Also included in revenue is investment income such as interest, rent, and

[2]Determination of the appropriate discount rate given the risk for the project is discussed in the risk section of this book, Chapters 11 to 15.

so on. Companies may also receive revenue in the form of payments under licensing agreements or royalties for the use of their inventions or other creations. To arrive at ordinary income, expenses are subtracted from revenue. A typical income statement may look as follows:

+ Revenues
– Cost of goods sold
– Selling and administrative expenses
– Bad debt expense
– Wages, salaries, and employee benefits
– Repairs
– Rent expense
– Property taxes and other non income taxes paid
– Interest expense
– Depreciation expense (recognition of wearing out of fixed assets)
– Lease payment
= Taxable income
– Income tax
= After tax income

Incremental revenues are recorded as positive numbers because they are assumed to be cash inflows, and expenses are recorded as negative numbers because they require cash payment and are therefore cash outflows.

Accrual Concepts of Income

Most businesses and all publicly traded corporations keep their books on an accrual rather than a cash basis. A cash basis recognizes income and expenses during the period in which the payment is received or made. Under accrual accounting, revenue and expense are recognized in the period in which they constructively occur, whether or not payment occurs during that period. For example, an accrual-basis taxpayer will generally recognize revenue from a sale when title is passed, even if payment is not actually received for months.

With the accrual method, some expenditures are deemed costs in the period in which they occur, and other expenditures are deemed to be asset acquisitions. When goods are purchased or produced, the cost of purchase or production is considered to be an investment in inventory assets, not an expense. The cost of inventory is recognized as an expense when the inventory is sold. When an asset like a building or piece of machinery is acquired, the purchase itself is the acquisition of an asset, not an expense. The wearing out of the asset is recognized as a series of depreciation expenses over the life of the asset.

Example: To illustrate the determination of accrual income consider the activities of Georgetown Corporation summarized in Table 8-1. The company bought \$100 worth of raw material in 2004, and paid for the material in 2005. The company also paid workers \$200 in 2004 for work done in 2004, turning the raw materials into finished goods. The company sold these finished goods on credit for \$500 in 2006 and received payment in 2007.

TABLE 8-1 Comparison of Accrual Income and Cash Flow Using Accrual Accounting

This table illustrates the timing of accrual income recognition, and the difference between timing of cash flows and income, resulting from accrual accounting principles.

YEAR:	2004	2005	2006	2007
Sell products on credit			$500	
Receive payments for credit sales				$500
Buy raw materials on credit	$100			
Pay for raw materials bought on credit		$100		
Recognize the material as an expense			–$100	
Use and pay for labor	$200			
Recognize the labor as an expense			–$200	
Taxable income—cash flow accounting	–$200	–$100	0	$500
Taxable income—accrual accounting	0	0	$200[a]	0

[a]$500 sale price minus the $100 of raw material and $200 of production labor that were recorded as part of the value of the inventory.

In addition to illustrating the difference between cash flow accounting and accrual accounting in measuring taxable income, the example in Table 8-1 also demonstrates the importance of adjusting the typical accrual-based income statement to a cash flow statement before making the capital budgeting decision. Timing of benefits is important, and there is often little relationship between the timing of income and the timing of cash flows. Had Georgetown Corporation acquired production equipment in 2009 and recognized depreciation expense on that equipment, the differences between timing of cash flow and timing of income would have been even more pronounced.

ESTIMATING THE BALANCE SHEET

Most projects have an acquisition stage, an operating stage, and a disposition stage, and throughout these phases these projects affect both the balance sheet and the income statement. During the acquisition stage land is purchased, buildings are built, machines are installed, employees are trained, inventory is accumulated, and advertising is spent. The building, land, machines, and inventory are all first placed on the balance sheet as assets. As time passes, these buildings and machines are written off by recognizing yearly depreciation expense on the income statement. Training and advertising are recognized as expenses at the time these activities occur, resulting in a tax savings to the extent of the marginal tax rate of the organization.

In the first few days of operation, operating cash is needed to pay bills or transact business, credit is extended to customers, inventory is sold and replaced, credit is granted by suppliers, and employees perform services for which they are not yet paid. The extension of credit to the customers is recorded on the balance sheet as accounts receivable. The inventory purchased is placed into inventory on the balance sheet, while the inventory sold is recorded as a cost of goods sold expense on the income statement. The credit granted by the suppliers is recorded as an accounts payable on the balance sheet. The credit extended by the employees is recorded as an accrued expense on the balance sheet.

If all goes well in the first few years of operation, cash balances, inventory balances, and customers' accounts receivable balances will increase as sales increase and the firm grows. All of these increases will cause more cash to be tied up in working capital. As an offset, credit balances owed to suppliers (accounts payable) and employees (accrued expenses) will also increase and offset some of the working capital needs.

Table 8-2 summarizes the proper timing and treatment of many of the relevant balance sheet items for a typical project. As you can see, most assets begin

TABLE 8-2 Treatment and Timing of the Typical Balance Sheet and Income Statement Items for a Typical Project

ITEM	TREATMENT	TIMING
Buildings	A	Year 0 (and later if additional investment)
Equipment	A	Year 0 (and later if additional investment)
Land	C	Year 0 (and later if additional investment)
Initial training	B	Year 0 (additional expense recognized as cash expense)
Initial advertising	B	Year 0 (additional expense recognized as cash expense)
Cash balances	C	Year 0 (changes recognized yearly)
Accounts receivable	C	Year 0 (changes recognized yearly)
Inventory	C	Year 0 (changes recognized yearly)
Accounts payable	C	Year 0 (changes recognized yearly)
Revenues	D	Year 1, 2, 3, 4 until disposition
Cash expenses	D	Year 1, 2, 3, 4 until disposition

TYPES OF TREATMENTS

A—Begins as a balance sheet item and flows to income statement as a depreciation expense as the asset's economic or physical life expires (book depreciation) or due to the passage of time (tax depreciation). They are added directly to the cash flow statement as an investment in the time period in which the assets are paid for. Depreciation expense is deducted to calculate income tax but then added back to avoid double counting of the investment's impact on cash flows.

B—Starts as an investment of cash and is immediately expensed as a time 0 expense, thereby increasing the initial outlay. Since these expenses are tax deductible (and this tax saving will be assumed to be realized in time 0) the investment is not dollar for dollar but instead 60 cents on the dollar when the firm is in the 40 percent tax bracket.

C—Begins as a balance sheet item and continues as such over the life of the project. Any additional investment (or decrease in investment) is added (or subtracted) in the year of investment.

D—Flows straight to the income statement in the calculation of income. Any credit sale is handled as an account receivable and any credit purchase is handled as an account payable.

on the balance sheet and then flow through to the income statement over the life of the project.

ROLLING THE INCOME STATEMENT AND BALANCE SHEET INTO A CASH FLOW STATEMENT

So far, we have introduced an accrual-based income statement and discussed the timing and treatment of the typical accounts on the balance sheet that result from a project. In this section, we will integrate the two by taking each account and illustrating the process by which it flows to the income statement and the adjustments that are necessary to construct a cash flow statement.

Accounts Receivable

Credit sales are an example of an item that is recognized as a revenue at the time of sale using the accrual basis of accounting but as a change in the accounts receivable balance on the cash flow statement. In the normal course of business, we extend credit to our customers for collection at some later date. As some customers pay, others are receiving credit. The net effect is that credit is extended at the beginning of the project's life (year 0) and as sales grow, more credit is extended. These credit balances are not liquidated until the disposition stage of the project's life.

Since taxes are calculated based on the accrual accounting definition of revenue for most businesses, we typically include all incremental sales or revenues in the projected income statement and then adjust for the extension of credit as a line item in the cash flow statement.

The easiest way to measure the incremental extension of credit in a period is to look at the change in the accounts receivable balance for a given period. If the accounts receivable balances are increasing, then sales are being recognized in the income statement but cash is not being received. In reverse fashion, if accounts receivable balances are decreasing, then more cash is being received than is shown in the revenue numbers.

Example: Houston Corporation began operations on January 1, year 1, and expects the following sales and cash expenses:

	YEAR 0	YEAR 1	YEAR 2	YEAR 3
Sales		$50,000	$100,000	$150,000
Cash expenses		$20,000	$40,000	$60,000

Present experience, in related lines of business, has shown that credit sales will probably average 73 days outstanding. In addition, Houston Corporation expects to lose $3,000 upon liquidation of the credit balances at the end of the project's life (year 3). The income statement for Houston would look like this:

	YEAR 0	YEAR 1	YEAR 2	YEAR 3
Sales		$50,000	$100,000	$150,000
Cash expenses		$20,000	$40,000	$60,000
Taxable income		$30,000	$60,000	$90,000
Taxes at 40%		$12,000	$24,000	$36,000
After tax income		$18,000	$36,000	$54,000

The balance sheet would look like this:

	YEAR 0	YEAR 1	YEAR 2	YEAR 3
Accounts receivable	$10,000	$20,000	$30,000	$0

The accounts receivable balances are simply 73/365 times $50,000 for year 0, 73/365 times $100,000 for year 1, 73/365 times $150,000 for year 2, and $0 to reflect the liquidation of these accounts at the end of year 3. The $10,000 initial extension of credit is placed in year 0 because the credit is extended to the first customer on day one of the project's life (in theory, no money will be received until the 73rd day if everybody takes the credit terms). Since this outlay is closer to the beginning of the year than to the end of the year, we place the cash flow as a year 0 number. The $20,000 at the end of year 1 assumes that sales begin to average $100,000 starting on day one of year 2. This is a simplifying assumption made on the part of the authors.

The cash flow statement for Houston would look like this:

	YEAR 0	YEAR 1	YEAR 2	YEAR 3
Sales		$50,000	$100,000	$150,000
Cash expenses		($20,000)	($40,000)	($60,000)
Taxable income		$30,000	$60,000	$90,000
Taxes at 40%		($12,000)	($24,000)	($36,000)
After tax income		$18,000	$36,000	$54,000
Change in working capital				
Accounts receivable	($10,000)	($10,000)	($10,000)	($0)
Disposition-stage cash flow				
Accounts receivable (net of tax)				$28,200
Net cash flow	($10,000)	$8,000	$26,000	$82,200

Although $36,000 in after tax income is realized in year 2, the amount must be adjusted for the $10,000 increase in accounts receivable. As a result, the cash flow for year 2 is only $26,000. The disposition-stage cash flow for accounts receivable was calculated by taking the $30,000 balance and subtracting the $3,000 loss and then adding back the $1,200 tax savings from the loss (40 percent of $3,000).

Inventory

When Wal-Mart opens a new Super-Center, often the $10,000,000 worth of inventory inside the store is worth more than the land, building, and shelving combined. Add this to all the inventory at the supporting warehouses, and the cash invested in inventory accumulates to balances that are quite meaningful in a typical net present value analysis. For example, Wal-Mart showed a $25 billion inventory balance on its January 2003 balance sheet. Inventory balances come in two forms: items that are sold to customers, and parts inventory necessary to support physical assets. Regardless of the form, as inventory is sold or used, it must be replaced, and as the businesses grow, the investment in inventory usually grows also.

As with accounts receivable balances, the inventory investment is usually made in advance of a store's opening or the placing of an asset into service. This investment is commonly recorded as a year 0 (the first day of the project) investment. As the operation expands, additional inventory will be necessary to support the larger operation.

Over time, inventory can suffer holding losses due to obsolescence, theft, destruction, or many other reasons. These holding losses, if material, should be estimated and deducted from estimated benefits (revenues) of the project. Under current tax law, these losses are fully tax deductible.

Inventory Example: Dallas Corporation began operations on January 1, year 1, and expects the following sales and cash expenses:

	YEAR 0	YEAR 1	YEAR 2	YEAR 3
Sales		$50,000	$100,000	$150,000
Cash expenses		$20,000	$40,000	$60,000

Present experience indicates that inventory levels will be maintained at 25 percent of sales. In addition, Dallas Corporation expects to lose $1,000 annually in shrinkage and $5,000 upon liquidation at the end of the project's life (year 3). The income statement for Dallas would look like this:

	YEAR 0	YEAR 1	YEAR 2	YEAR 3
Sales		$50,000	$100,000	$150,000
Cash expenses		$20,000	$40,000	$60,000
Inventory shrinkage		$ 1,000	$1,000	$1,000
Taxable income		$29,000	$59,000	$89,000
Taxes at 40%		$11,600	$23,600	$35,600
After tax income		$17,400	$35,400	$ 53,400

The $1,000 shrinkage is subtracted as a normal cost of doing business in the calculation of taxable income.

The balance sheet would look like this:

	YEAR 0	YEAR 1	YEAR 2	YEAR 3
Inventory	$12,500	$25,000	$37,500	$0

The inventory balance is simply 25 percent times: $50,000 for year 0, $100,000 for year 1, $150,000 for year 2, and $0 to reflect the liquidation of these accounts at the end of year 3. The $12,500 is a year 0 cash flow because inventory must be present on day one of the project's life. Since this is closer to year 0 than to the end of the year, we place the cash flow as a year 0 number. The $25,000 at the end of year 1 is based on the same logic explained in the accounts receivable section earlier in the chapter.

The cash flow statement for Dallas would look like this:

	YEAR 0	YEAR 1	YEAR 2	YEAR 3
Sales		$50,000	$100,000	$150,000
Cash expenses		($20,000)	($40,000)	($60,000)
Inventory shrinkage		($1,000)	($1,000)	($1,000)
Taxable income		$29,000	$59,000	$89,000
Taxes at 40%		($11,600)	($23,600)	($35,600)
After tax income		$17,400	$35,400	$53,400
Change in working capital				
Inventory	($12,500)	($12,500)	($12,500)	($0)
Disposition-stage cash flow				
Inventory (net of tax)				$34,500
Net cash flow	($12,500)	$4,900	$22,900	$87,900

The $1,000 in shrinkage is a negative cash flow because missing inventory has to be replaced to maintain inventory levels at 25 percent of sales. The original investment in inventory and additions in later years are recorded as negative cash flows. The cash proceeds realized from the final sale are recorded as positive cash flow at the end of the project's life.

In the disposition year of the project, the inventory will be liquidated. It is usually assumed that the original purchase price will not be realized and some liquidation loss will be experienced on the final sale. In this case the $34,500 was calculated by taking the $37,500 balance and subtracting the $5,000 loss and then adding back the $2,000 tax savings from the loss (40 percent of $5,000).

Prepaid Expenses

Prepaid expenses are expenses that are paid before the period of their use. Suppose, for example, an insurance premium covering the next 2 years is paid in advance on January 1, year 1. Half of the payment is recognized as an expense in year 1, and half is recognized as an expense in year 2. On the year 1 balance sheet, the amount applicable to year 2 is an asset called prepaid expense. In the disposition year, prepaid expenses are usually projected to be fully recovered with no associated losses.

Cash Balances

Most, but not all, new projects will involve the need for some cash balance to transact business. For example, McDonald's adds a new outlet and on the first day that the doors open for business, the establishment must have enough cash in the register to make change for the level of purchases projected for the day. For simplicity's sake, we assume that the initial cash balance needed to operate through the first year is needed at the beginning of the project and would therefore be a year 0 cash flow. As the business grows in outlets or as sales increase in dollars, cash balance increases must be estimated.

Example: Ted's Ice Cream Shoppe will open for business on January 1, year 1, and will need $10,000 in operating cash to support $200,000 in sales. Sales are expected to increase to $350,000 in year 2 and the cash balance is expected to grow to $17,500. In year 2 sales are expected to stay at the $350,000 level and all cash is recovered in the disposition year.

Cash flows would be projected as follows:

	YEAR 0	YEAR 1	YEAR 2	DISPOSITION YEAR
Cash investment needed	($10,000)	($7,500)	0	$17,500

The bracketed (or negative) cash flows signify the money is being invested or used by the project. In the disposition year the $17,500 is recovered and is consequently shown as a positive number. Even though sales probably grew gradually over year 2, we assume that the $7,500 was needed at the beginning of that year and was projected as an end of year 1 cash flow. When the midyear convention is used to approximate daily cash flows, it is common to also use midyear as the interval for the increased investment in cash.

Accounts Payable and Accrued Expenses

Accounts payable result when an asset is acquired on credit and payment for the assets follows. When inventory is purchased on credit, the inventory itself is treated as an asset, and the amount owed is treated as an account payable.

Wages and many other expenses are not paid on a daily basis. These expenses are often recognized for accrual income purposes in the period in which they are incurred, even if they are actually paid for with cash in a different period. When these expenses are recorded but not paid, an accrued expense is shown on the balance sheet until payment is made. As with accounts payable, this delaying of the payment is considered a source of cash or a positive number in calculating the estimated after tax cash flow on the projected cash flow statement. Using the previously mentioned Wal-Mart example, most of its $25 billion investment in inventory is financed by suppliers who have extended $17 billion in credit. This credit from suppliers shows up on Wal-Mart's balance sheet as accounts payable.

Land

When a project requires the purchase of land, a building, and equipment as a package, then proper accounting requires that a portion of the purchase price be allocated to the land, a portion to the building, and a portion to the equipment based on appraised market values of each as if they were independently purchased. One reason for this is that land cannot be depreciated under IRS rules. Although it may seem unfair not to allow for the recovery of the investment in land over the life of the project, in the eyes of the tax code, land does not wear out and therefore it is not entitled to recovery.

The initial investment in land is recorded as a negative cash flow in year 0 and the recovery of the purchase price in the disposition year is recorded as a positive cash flow. If the recovery price is less than the original purchase price, the resulting loss is fully tax deductible. Should the land be sold for more than its purchase price, the excess is taxable as a gain. For corporations, there are no special capital gain or loss treatments, and both gains and losses are taxed at ordinary rates.[3]

It is important not to confuse land which cannot be depreciated with land improvements that are written off over their useful or economic life. For example, a parking lot is a land replacement that might be depreciated over a 25-year life or more.

Buildings

In the tax code, there are only two categories of investments in buildings—either residential buildings or nonresidential buildings. Residential buildings include houses that contain home offices as well as living quarters, apartment buildings, duplexes, and any place considered to be a private residence. Nonresidential buildings include office buildings, shopping centers, factories, and anything else not considered residential property.

The acquisition of either residential property or nonresidential property is recorded as negative cash flow at year 0 (the year they are placed into service). The wearing out of the building is recognized through an annual depreciation expense which is fully tax deductible on the income statement each year.

The specific depreciation rates allowed by the IRS differ depending on whether the investment is residential property or nonresidential property. Under current tax law, residential property is depreciated over 27.5 years using a mid-month convention, and commercial real estate is depreciated over 39 years also using a mid-month convention.

---

[3]Taxes and tax rates are discussed in Chapter 9.

Residential property example: An apartment building costing $1 million is placed into service on March 5, year 1. It is sold on September 25, year 8. What is the depreciation expense allowed for year 1, year 2, and the disposition year? Depreciation expense for year 1 is:

9.5/12 months times $1 million times 1/27.5 years

or (9.5/12)(1,000,000)(1/27.5) = $28,788

Depreciation expense for year 2 is:

12/12 months times $1 million times 1/27.5 years

or (12/12)(1,000,000)(1/27.5) = $36,364

Depreciation expense for the disposition year or year 8 is:

8.5/12 months times $1 million times 1/27.5 years

or (8.5/12)(1,000,000)(1/27.5) = $25,758

The 9.5 months used in year 1 are calculated by first going to the middle of the month, in this case March, counting March as one-half of a month, and then counting the remaining months in the year (April, May, and so on). In the disposition year, 8.5 months is used and computed by counting the months preceding the month of sale (January, February, and so on) and adding one-half of a month for the month of disposition or September. Naturally, any full year between the acquisition year and the disposition year would be allowed a full twelve months of depreciation.

Commercial property example: An office complex costing $1 million is placed into service on March 31, year 1. It is sold on September 1, year 8. What is the depreciation expense allowed for year 1, year 2, and the disposition year? Depreciation expense for year 1 is:

9.5/12 months times $1 million times 1/39 years

or (9.5/12)(1,000,000)(1/39) = $20,299

Depreciation expense for year 2 is:

12/12 months times $1 million times 1/39 years

or (12/12)(1,000,000)(1/39) = $25,641

Depreciation expense for the disposition year or year 8 is:

8.5/12 months times $1 million times 1/39 years

or (8.5/12)(1,000,000)(1/39) = $18,162

As before, the 9.5 months used in year 1 are calculated by first going to the middle of the month, in this case March, counting March as one half of a month, and then counting the remaining months in the year (April, May, and so on). Again, 8.5 months is used in the disposition year by counting the months preceding the month of sale (January, February, and so on) and adding one-half of a month for the month of disposition or September. Naturally, any full year between the acquisition year and the disposition year would be allowed a full twelve months of depreciation.

Equipment

Investment in a fixed asset such as a vehicle, equipment, and so on is recognized on the balance sheet at the purchase price plus any delivery fees, setup expenses, testing expenses, and other expenses associated with placing the asset into service. The wearing out of the asset is recognized through an annual depreciation expense.

The specific depreciation rates allowed by the IRS depend on the type of asset that is placed into service. Table 8-3 is a listing of the six classes of assets recognized by the IRS. The sampling of assets listed in the table is taken from the Internal Revenue Code. The actual listing in the Internal Revenue Code consists of page after page of assets for each category. As with all tax items, the reader is referred to a good tax book, tax counsel, or the code to clarify situations not specifically dealt with in the table. Another useful yet cumbersome resource is the web page http://www.IRS.gov.

TABLE 8-3 Asset Life Categories under the Accelerated Cost Recovery System

This table lists the six asset life categories recognized under the Accelerated Cost Recovery System as modified by the Tax Reform Act of 1986, along with samples of assets assigned to each category.

LIFE CATEGORY	SAMPLE ASSETS
3 year	Tractor units for over-the-road trucks, and special tools such as dies and jigs used in some specific types of manufacturing
5 year	Automobiles, taxis, light trucks, buses, over-the-road trailers, computers and peripherals, typewriters, copiers, other data-handling equipment, general construction equipment, and telephone company computer-based central office switching equipment, any property used in research and experimentation
7 year	Office furniture, many types of production equipment (some specific types of production equipment are assigned 5-, 10-, and 15-year categories), airplanes used by commercial airlines, agricultural equipment, and assets that have not been assigned by law to other categories
10 year	Vessels, barges, and single purpose agricultural or horticultural structure
15 year	Improvements to land like scrubs, fences, and roads; oil and gas pipelines, electric utility nuclear and combustion, turbine power plants; municipal wastewater treatment plants
20 year	Telephone company distribution plant, and electric and gas utility transmission and distribution plant

Once the asset has been located and the tax life determined, then Table 8-4 is used to determine the allowable depreciation rate. No adjustment for midyear or mid-month is necessary because a midyear convention is built into the rates in the table.

Year 1 in Table 8-4 is the year in which the asset was placed in service. An asset is considered to be placed in service when it is *available* for use, even if it has not actually been used full time.

Example: A laser copier costing $10,000 is placed into service on March 31, year 1. It is sold on September 1, year 6. What is the depreciation expense allowed for year 1, year 2, and the disposition year?

The first step is to determine the tax life of the copier. By referring to Table 8-3, copiers are found to have a 5-year tax life. Using the rates in Table 8-4 for 5-year property, the depreciation expense is calculated as follows:

TABLE 8-4 Depreciation Rates Using the Modified Accelerated Cost Recovery System

This table gives the depreciation rates as a percentage of original basis for assets in each life category eligible for declining balance depreciation. Year 1 is the year in which the asset is placed in service. The midyear convention is assumed.

YEAR	3 YEAR	5 YEAR	7 YEAR	10 YEAR	15 YEAR	20 YEAR
1	33.33%	20.00%	14.29%	10.00%	5.00%	3.75%
2	44.44	32.00	24.49	18.00	9.50	7.22
3	14.82	19.20	17.49	14.40	8.56	6.68
4	7.41	11.52	12.49	11.52	7.71	6.18
5		11.52	8.93	9.22	6.94	5.72
6		5.76	8.93	7.37	6.24	5.29
7			8.93	6.55	5.90	4.89
8			4.45	6.55	5.90	4.52
9				6.55	5.90	4.46
10				6.55	5.90	4.46
11				3.29	5.90	4.46
12					5.90	4.46
13					5.90	4.46
14					5.90	4.46
15					5.90	4.46
16					2.95	4.46
17						4.46
18						4.46
19						4.46
20						4.46
21						2.23

Depreciation expense for year 1 is:

$$.2000 \text{ times } \$10{,}000$$

or

$$(.2000)(10{,}000) = \$2{,}000$$

Depreciation expense for year 2 is:

$$.3200 \text{ times } \$10{,}000$$

or

$$(.3200)(10{,}000) = \$3{,}200$$

Depreciation expense for the disposition year or year 6 is:

$$.0576 \text{ times } \$10{,}000$$

or

$$(.0576)(10{,}000) = \$576$$

Careful inspection of Table 8-4 shows that the depreciation term exceeds the tax life by 1 year. For the copier, it is depreciated in year 6 even though it has a 5-year tax life. The midyear convention is what caused the term to exceed the tax life. In constructing the tables, the IRS reduces the first year's rate to assume that on average, assets will be placed into service throughout the year and will average one-half of a full year's depreciation. Notice that in each case the second (or first full) year's depreciation exceeds the first (or half) year's depreciation rate.

Adjusting Cash Flows for Depreciation

Depreciation is a common noncash expense included in the projected income statement. The accounting definition of depreciation is the systematic writing off or expensing of a physical asset over the shorter of its economic or useful life. The acquisition of the physical asset involves the use of cash but the expensing of the asset over its life is a noncash item.

Where you choose to adjust for depreciation in the cash flow statement is a personal choice. Table 8-5 illustrates the two typical treatments for depreciation in practice. The first and more common method is to deduct depreciation in arriving at taxable income, calculate taxable income, and then add the full depreciation amount back to get after tax cash flow. A second method is to leave depreciation out of the income calculation and add back depreciation (net of taxes) to the after tax income number to get after tax cash flow. Either method is acceptable and both will yield the same after tax cash flow.

Timing of Acquisition Stage Cash Flows

Up until now we have assumed that all land, buildings, and equipment have been placed into service on one day, and we have called that first day of the first year "year 0." Many acquisition outlays do not typically occur all on one day. A major capital investment may be put together over a period of several years, and additional investment may be required after a capital investment is first placed in service. In addition, working capital may continue to increase through the growth of inventory and accounts receivable, particularly if sales grow. As a prac-

TABLE 8-5 Two Common Treatments of Depreciation Used to Project After Tax Cash Flows

Method 1

+ Increases in sales revenue
– Increases in (+ decreases in) operating expenses before interest and depreciation
= Earnings before interest, depreciation, and taxes (EBDT)
– Depreciation
= Earnings before tax (EBT)
– Income tax (tax rate × Earnings before tax)
= Net income
+ Depreciation
= Net after tax cash flow (outlay)

Method 2

+ Increases in sales revenue
– Increases in (+ decreases in) operating expenses excluding depreciation
= Earnings before depreciation and taxes (EBDT)
– Income tax (tax rate × EBDT)
= Net income before depreciation
+ Depreciation expense net of taxes [depreciation × marginal tax rate]
= Net after tax cash flow (outlay)

tical matter, capital investments for which almost all of the relevant initial cash outlays occur over a period of a few months are frequently treated as if all the initial costs occurred at one time. When the investment is spread over several years, the net present value can be accurately computed by discounting all future cash costs and benefits, including future investment, to the date when investment first occurs. Some managers prefer to compute the net present value as of the date an asset was placed in service. To do this, they compute the **future value** of outlays prior to the date the asset is placed in service.

Example: A capital investment being considered by Evanston Technology requires a \$1,000 after tax cash outlay at the end of each year for 3 years, with use to begin at the start of the fourth year. The asset will then generate after tax cash inflows of \$1,000 at the end of each year for 5 years, and the company has a 10 percent required return. The future value of the investment outlay as of the date the asset is placed in service would be:

$$\$1{,}000 \times 1.1^2 + \$1{,}000 \times 1.1 + \$1{,}000 = \$3{,}310$$

If \$1,000 had been invested somewhere else at the end of each year for 3 years, it would have grown to \$3,310.

The net present value, as of the date the asset is placed in service, is:

$$NPV = \$1,000 \times PVA1_{5\ yrs.,\ 10\%} - \$3,310$$
$$= \$1,000 \times 3.7908 - \$3,310 = \$480.80$$

The net present value as of the date the asset is placed in service gives the same accept/reject signal as the net present value as of the date the first outlay occurred.[4]

Computer spreadsheet example: You are thinking of starting an ice cream stand to keep your family members employed and to bring in a little extra income. You have looked at comparable businesses in neighboring communities and have gathered the following data and estimates concerning the investment, revenues, and cost. You will start the business on May 21, 2004, and invest $100,000 in a commercial building and an additional $60,000 in equipment with a tax life of 3 years. Because you will extend credit to all of your customers, you estimate that you will have forty-two days of sales in accounts receivable. You believe that first-year sales will be $82,000 and second-year sales will be $112,000; after that, you expect sales to increase at an annual rate of 7 percent. Operating cash cost will be $43,000 in year 1, $58,000 in year 2, and will increase at 5 percent per year after that. Your tax rate is 40 percent and you estimate a required rate of return of 10 percent. At the end of 5 years you expect to collect all of your accounts receivables, sell the building for $60,000, and sell the equipment for $25,000. What is the net present value of this business.

Computer solution for acquisition stage cash flows: The acquisition stage cash flows for this example are given in the following spreadsheet:

Assumptions

YEAR:	0	1	2	3	4	5
Depreciation on 3 year equipment		33.33%	44.44%	14.82%	7.41%	
Depreciation rate building		1.60%	2.56%	2.56%	2.56%	
Growth rates for revenues		$ 82,000	$ 112,000	7.00%	7.00%	7.00%
Cost of goods sold		$ (43,000)	$ (58,000)	5.00%	5.00%	5.00%
Tax rate		40.00%				
Required rate of return		12.00%				
Accounts receivable balance	$ (9,436)	$ (12,888)	$ (13,790)	$ (14,755)	$ (15,788)	$0

Acquisition stage cash flow

YEAR:	0	1	2	3	4	5
Building	$ (100,000)					
3 year equipment	$ (60,000)					
Initial investment in accounts receivable	$ (9,436)					
Total acquisition stage cash flow	$ (169,436)					

[4]See, for example, Norbert L. Enrich, *Marketing and Sales Forecasting: A Quantitative Approach,* rev. ed. (Melbourne, Fla.: Krieger Publishing, 1979); Donald L. Hurwood, *Sales Forecasting* (New York: The Conference Board, 1978), and *Sales Forecasting: Timesaving and Profit-Making Strategies That Work* (Glenview, Ill.: Scott Foresman, 1978).

The spreadsheet starts with an assumptions section. In this section you want to lay out your assumptions so that you can communicate these to others later when you present your results and so that you can flex these assumptions to judge the risk of this project. Also in this section, you want to include items that are necessary in calculating cash flows but do not fit neatly into one of the three parts of the spreadsheet, for example the depreciation rates. The depreciation rates for the equipment come straight from Table 8-4. The first year's 1.6 percent depreciation rate for the building is 7.5/12 times 1/39. The 7.5 is one-half the month for May and 7 months for June, July, and the remaining 5 months in the year. It is multiplied by 1 divided by 39 because this is a commercial building. The 2.56 percent rate is simply 1 divided by 39 to represent a full year's depreciation. The fifth year's depreciation is 11.5 divided by 12 times 1 divided by 39 to represent the selling of the building on December 31 of year 5. The calculation of the accounts receivable balance of $-9,436 for year 0 is minus 42 days/365 days times the first year's sales of $82,000. The year 1 balance is –42/365 times $112,000. This is repeated for the remaining years. The initial investment under the acquisition stage cash flow is calculated by bringing down the initial balance of $-9,436. The additional investment in accounts receivable needed in later years will be dealt with in the next section when we estimate the operating stage cash flows.

Operating Stage Cash Flows and Net Working Capital

For brevity in reporting, companies sometimes report a net working capital requirement as one line in the analysis. When this is done, net working capital is calculated by adding all of the individual current assets accounts (cash, accounts receivable, inventory, and prepaid expenses) requiring incremental or additional investment and then subtracting all of the current liability accounts (accounts payable, and accrued expenses) that typically supply funds.

Computer solution for operating stage cash flows net of additional working capital investment: The operating stage cash flows net of additional working capital investment for the example started in the prior section are given in the following spreadsheet:

Operating stage cash flow

YEAR:	0	1	2	3	4	5
Revenue		$ 82,000	$ 112,000	$ 119,840	$ 128,229	$ 137,205
Cost of good sold		$ (43,000)	$ (58,000)	$ (60,610)	$ (63,337)	$ (66,188)
Depreciation exp building		$ (1,603)	$ (2,564)	$ (2,564)	$ (2,564)	$ (2,457)
Depreciation 3 year equip		$ (19,998)	$ (26,664)	$ (8,892)	$ (4,446)	$ —
Taxable income		$ 17,399	$ 24,772	$ 47,774	$ 57,881	$ 68,560
Taxes		$ (6,960)	$ (9,909)	$ (19,110)	$ (23,152)	$ (27,424)
After tax income		$ 10,440	$ 14,863	$ 28,664	$ 34,729	$ 41,136
Add back depreciation		$ 21,601	$ 29,228	$ 11,456	$ 7,010	$ 2,457
Cash flow from operations		$ 32,040	$ 44,091	$ 40,120	$ 41,739	$ 43,593

YEAR:	0	1	2	3	4	5
Additional investment in accounts receivable		$ (3,452)	$ (902)	$ (965)	$ (1,033)	$ 15,788
Operating stage cash flow net of working capital		$ 28,588	$43,189	$39,155	$ 40,706	$ 59,381

This section begins with the given sales for the first 2 years. For years 3 and beyond, you simply multiply the cell for the prior year by (1 plus the cell containing the assumed growth rates). The operating cost sales are completed in the same manner as the sales fields. Take the depreciation rate for each year and multiply it by the cost of the building to calculate depreciation expense for the building. Equipment depreciation is calculated in the same manner. All three of these costs are reflected as negative numbers or cash outflows. Totaling the cost and revenues will give you the taxable income. Taxes are calculated by multiplying the taxable income field by minus the tax rate field. The minus is necessary to reflect the fact that taxes on a positive income are a cash outflow to the government. Then net the taxes and taxable income together to get the after tax income. After adding back the depreciation expense taken in the spreadsheet for the building and equipment, this gives you the operating stage cash flow. The additional investment in working capital is calculated by taking the cell containing the $-12,888 accounts receivable balance and subtracting the field containing the $-9,436. The operating stage cash flow of $32,040 is added to the negative $3,452 additional investment in accounts receivable to get the operating stage cash flows net of additional working capital requirements of $28,588 for year 1.

Disposition Stage Cash Flows

Cash flows at the time of termination are an important part of the analysis of a capital investment. This importance grows as you use a shorter life for the project. Oftentimes the disposition proceeds can make or break the net present value for a project.

Computer solution for disposition stage cash flows net of additional working capital investment: The disposition stage cash flows net of additional working capital investment for the example started in the prior section are given in the following spreadsheet:

Disposition stage cash flow

	BUILDING	EQUIPMENT	TOTAL
Original purchase price	$100,000	$ 60,000	
Depreciation taken	$ (11,752)	$(60,000)	
Remaining basis	$ 88,248	0	

	BUILDING		EQUIPMENT			TOTAL
Selling price	$ 60,000		$ 25,000			
Remaining basis	$ 88,248		0			
Gain or (loss)	$ (28,248)		$ 25,000			
Gain or (loss)	$ (28,248)		$ 25,000			
Tax rate on gain or losses	$ 40.00%		40.00%			
Tax on gain or refund on loss	$ 11,299		$(10,000)			
Selling price	$ 60,000		$ 25,000			
Tax on gain or refund on loss	$ 11,299		$(10,000)			$ 86,299
Net proceeds from disposition	$ 71,299		$ 15,000			$ 86,299
Summary of the prior three spreadsheet totals:						
Total acquisition stage cash flow	$(169,436)					
Operating stage cash flow net of working capital		$28,588	$ 43,189	$39,155	$40,706	$ 59,381
Net proceeds from disposition						$ 86,299
Total cash flows	$(169,436)	$28,588	$ 43,189	$39,155	$40,706	$145,680
Present value	$ 209,359					
Net present value	$ 39,924					

To calculate the cash proceeds from the sale of fixed assets we must first find the remaining basis by subtracting the depreciation taken from the original purchase price. Taxable gain is calculated by subtracting the remaining basis from the selling price. If the remaining basis is higher than the selling price, a tax-deductible loss is incurred that will reduce taxes. This amount net of taxes should be added to the selling price to get net proceeds from disposition. If the selling price is greater than the remaining basis, then a taxable gain will result. Taxes are calculated on this gain using ordinary income tax rates for corporations. Individuals, partnerships, and subchapter S corporations are allowed to use capital gains rates that are discussed in the next chapter. To get net proceeds from the sale, simply subtract the taxes due from the selling price. In this case the net proceeds from the building are $71,299, which is the $60,000 cash from the sale plus $11,299 tax refund or savings from selling this asset at a loss. The equipment proceeds are $15,000, which consist of the $25,000 cash received from the sale less the $10,000 in taxes owed on the gain. In total, $86,299 in cash was raised net of taxes at the end of the fifth year. When combined with the net inflows (after working capital additions) during the operations stage, these totals are brought back to present and netted against the total outflow during the acquisition stage. Doing this produces a net present value for this project of $39,924.

Table 8-6 illustrates the proper format for calculating the net proceeds from both the sale of fixed assets and for working capital. The Indiana Legal Eagles example that follows illustrates a few more of the complexities you may deal with in realistically estimating the cash flows from an expansion project.

TABLE 8-6 Spreadsheet for Calculating the Cash Flow from Disposition for Fixed Assets and for Working Capital

Proceeds from the sale of fixed assets
Original purchase price
– Depreciation taken
= Remaining basis
Selling price
– Remaining basis
= Taxable gain or (loss)
Taxable gain or (loss)
× Tax rate
= Tax on gain or loss
Selling price
+ Tax on loss or – tax on gain
= Net proceeds from disposition
Proceeds from the sale of working capital
Liquidation value
– Accumulated value
= Taxable gain or (loss)
Taxable gain or (loss)
× Tax rate
= Tax on gain or loss
Liquidation value
+ Tax on loss or – Tax rate
= Net proceeds from disposition

INDIANA LEGAL EAGLES: A COMPREHENSIVE EXAMPLE

A successful Indianapolis law firm, Indiana Legal Eagles, was considering the opening of a legal clinic in the Fort Wayne area. Approximately $10,000 had already been spent on a feasibility study. The firm was taxed as a corporation, with a marginal tax rate of 34 percent. Land for the building would be acquired on January 1, 2005, at a cost of $200,000. A building would be built on the site at a cost of $500,000, including architects' fees and building permits. Of this building cost, $100,000 would be paid at the beginning of 2005, when construction started, and the remainder would be paid on January 1, 2006, when construction was completed. Office equipment (word processors and so on) and office furniture would be acquired and paid for around the end of 2005, at a cost of $50,000 for each of the two categories. The building and other assets would be considered placed in service on January 1, 2006. Various forms and other supplies would result in a total inventory need of $4,000. Prepaid expenses—insurance and so on—would initially be $3,000 as of January 1, 2006. At the time operations began, ac-

TABLE 8-7 Acquisition Cash Flows for a Legal Clinic

Summary of cash flows to begin operation of a legal clinic, recognizing the approximate timing of cash flows.

EXPENSES		
	START OF YEAR 2005	END OF YEAR 2005 START OF 2006
Promotional costs		(30,000)
Recruiting and training		(20,000)
= Total expenses		(50,000)
Tax savings from expenses		17,000
Net expenses		(33,000)
WORKING CAPITAL		
Increase in supplies inventory		(4,000)
Increase in prepaid expenses		(3,000)
Increase in accounts payable		1,000
Increased accrued expenses		1,000
Net increase in working capital		(5,000)
CAPITAL OUTLAYS		
Land	($200,000)	
Building	(100,000)	$ (400,000)
Equipment and furniture		
Purchase price		(100,000)
Delivery and installation		0
= Net Capital Outlays	$(300,000)	$ (500,000)
RELEVANT CASH OUTLAYS	$(300,000)	$ (538,000

Note: Outflows or investments of cash are in parentheses, and inflows of cash are not.

counts payable and accrued wages would total $1,000 each. Recruiting of new personnel to staff the business would cost an estimated $10,000. Personnel would be trained at the home office during the last couple of months of 2005 and would receive wages of $10,000 during that time. A promotion campaign to launch the clinic would cost an estimated $30,000. These promotional expenditures would occur in late 2005 and early 2006. The land and fixtures would be paid for from funds currently available, while the building would be financed with a 20-year, 9 percent term loan. Considering other expansion opportunities available, and the fact that both their equity capital and borrowing capacity was limited, the owners required a 10 percent after tax return on all new investments. The cash flows associated with acquisition of the investment are summarized in Table 8-7.

The cash flows in Table 8-7 have been grouped into two time periods, in keeping with normal conventions, rather than being separated by exact day for payment of each item. If the net present value is to be computed as of the beginning of year 2005, the present value of relevant acquisition outlays is \$300,000 + (\$538,000/1.10) = \$789,091. If the net present value is to be computed as of the end of 2005 and beginning of 2006, the value of acquisition outlays is (\$300,000 × 1.10) + \$538,000 = \$868,000.

Note, again, that financing methods and interest expenses do not affect the cash flow estimates. The requirement that the assets generate a rate of return sufficient to satisfy all suppliers of capital is captured in the required return or discount rate used in computing present values. The computation of that required rate, based on a study of the financing sources available, is taken up in Chapter 16.

Estimating Cash Flows from Operations

Having calculated the acquisition-stage cash flows, the next step is the construction of an income statement. Legal Eagles' new Fort Wayne legal clinic is expected to generate the following revenues and cash operating expenses over a 20-year planning horizon:

	YEAR 2006	THEREAFTER
Revenues	\$300,000	\$700,000
Wages	220,000	420,000
Other cash operating expenses	100,000	120,000

Additional working capital investments:

- Accounts receivable are expected to increase each period by 5 percent of the increase in sales.
- Supplies inventories are expected to be maintained at 3 percent of sales in addition to the initial \$4,000 investment.
- Prepaid expenses are expected to be 2 percent of sales in addition to the \$3,000 initial investment.
- Accounts payable are expected to be 4 percent of wages and other cash operating expenses for that period in addition to the initial \$1,000 investment.
- Accrued expenses are expected to be 1 percent of wages and other cash operating expenses for that period in addition to the initial \$1,000 investment.
- Equipment will be depreciated using the rates in Table 8-4.

Based on this information, the relevant cash flows through 2008 are shown in Table 8-8 (pages 250–251). The only changes in cash flows after 2008 result from the changing depreciation rates on the building and equipment.

For this law firm, the benefit is increased revenue but part of the increased revenue is offset by increased cash operating expenses. For other investments, the benefit could be decreased cash operating expenses, with no increase in revenue. As mentioned earlier, the differences between dates of recognition of revenue or expense and dates of payment or receipt are captured in the change in net working capital. Collections that lag behind sales mean, for example, that cash inflow from sales is less than sales, and the increase in net working capital is the measure of how much less. Remember also that interest expense was not deducted in arriving at net income because the cost of money is captured in the discount rate used for capital investment analysis.

In this law clinic example, each year is given a single column, as if each type of cash flow occurs at the same time or is spread across the year in the same pattern. This is a common-enough assumption in practice, but it is not an essential assumption. Suppose, for example, that sales are expected to be at the $300,000 per year rate immediately in 2006. The working capital commitment will occur very early in the year as January revenue will not be collected until mid-February, and so on. The other cash flows, on the other hand, would be spread through the year. These cash flow patterns can be handled more accurately by creating two or more columns for 2006—one for beginning relevant costs and benefits and another for cost and benefits spread continuously over the year—and additional columns for significant cash cost or benefits occurring at other times during the year. Alternatively, the working capital requirement occurring in the first month or two can be treated as part of the initial outlay.

An Alternative Operating Stage Cash Flow Format. Some analysts prefer a format for estimating cash flows that focuses more directly on cash impacts, rather than following a financial statement format. This format, and its application to 2007 for the previous law clinic example, is illustrated below.

ALTERNATIVE CASH FLOW STATEMENT

	YEAR 2007
Revenue	$700,000
Wages	(420,000)
Other operating expenses, except depreciation	(120,000)
Earnings before depreciation and tax (EBDT)	160,000
Income tax (.34 × EBDT)	(54,400)
Operating cash benefit	105,600
Depreciation tax savings (.34 × depreciation)	13,962
Increase in accounts receivable	(20,000)
Increase in supplies inventory	(12,000)
Increase in prepaid expenses	(8,000)
Increase in accounts payable	8,800
Increase in accrued expenses	2,000
NET RELEVANT CASH FLOW	$ 90,362

Note: This format is simply another way to organize the information, and it leads to the same estimate of net relevant cash flows.

TABLE 8-8 Operating Cash Costs and Benefits for the Legal Clinic

Revenues, wages, and cash operating expenses were given. Balances in accounts receivable, supplies inventory, prepaid expenses, accounts payable, and accrued expenses are 5%, 3%, 2%, 4%, and 1% respectively. The building is depreciated over 39 years as is allowed by the IRS. Equipment is depreciated using the rates in Table 8-4.

INCOME STATEMENT

YEAR:	2006	2007	2008	2009
Revenue	$300,000	$700,000	$700,000	
Wages	($220,000)	($420,000)	($420,000)	
Other Operating Expenses	($100,000)	($120,000)	($120,000)	
Depreciation Expense				
Depreciation, Building	($12,286)	($12,821)	($12,821)	
Depreciation, Office Equipment	($10,000)	($16,000)	($9,600)	
Depreciation, Office Furniture	($7,145)	($12,245)	($8,745)	
Total Depreciation	($29,431)	($41,066)	($31,166)	
Earnings before Taxes	($49,431)	$118,934	$128,834	
Income Taxes at 34%	$16,807	($40,438)	($43,804)	
Net Income	($32,624)	$78,496	$85,030	

BALANCE SHEET

YEAR:	2006	2007	2008	2009
Accounts Receivable Balance	$0	$15,000	$35,000	$35,000
Supplies Inventory Balance	$4,000	$13,000	$25,000	$25,000
Prepaid Expenses Balance	$3,000	$9,000	$17,000	$17,000
Accounts Payable Balance	($1,000)	($13,800)	($22,600)	($22,600)
Accrued Expenses Balance	($1,000)	($4,200)	($6,400)	($6,400)
Net Working Capital Balance	$5,000	$19,000	$48,000	$48,000

Estimating Disposition Stage Cash Flows

Continuing with the legal clinic example, assume that this project has an estimated life of 20 years. After 20 years, the remaining basis for the land would still be the original cost of $200,000 because no depreciation can be taken on land. The remaining basis for the building would be the $500,000 original cost less depreciation taken of $275,876 to leave a remaining basis of $224,124. Furniture and equipment would be fully depreciated and would therefore have a remaining basis of $0. Management estimates that the furniture and equipment would be worthless in 20 years while the building and land could be sold for $500,000 with $200,000 allocated to the land and $300,000 allocated to the building based

TABLE 8-8 (*Continued*)

CASH FLOW STATEMENT

YEAR:	2006	2007	2008	2009
Revenue	$300,000	$700,000	$700,000	
Wages	($220,000)	($420,000)	($420,000)	
Other Operating Expenses	($100,000)	($120,000)	($120,000)	
Depreciation Expense				
Depreciation, Building	($12,286)	($12,821)	($12,821)	
Depreciation, Office Equipment	($10,000)	($16,000)	($9,600)	
Depreciation, Office Furniture	($7,145)	($12,245)	($8,745)	
Total Depreciation	($29,431)	($41,066)	($31,166)	
Earnings before Taxes	($49,431)	$118,934	$128,834	
Income Taxes at 34%	$16,807	($40,438)	($43,804)	
Net Income	($32,624)	$78,496	$85,030	
Add Back Depreciation	$29,431	$41,066	$31,166	
Increase in Accounts Receivable	($15,000)	($20,000)	$0	
Increase in Supplies Inventory	($9,000)	($12,000)	$0	
Increase in Prepaid Expenses	($6,000)	($8,000)	$0	
Increase in Accounts Payable	$12,800	$8,800	$0	
Increase in Accrued Expenses	$3,200	$2,200	$0	
After Tax Cash Flow	($17,193)	$90,562	$116,196	

Supporting Calculations

2006 depreciation on the building = (11.5 months/12 months) times 1/39 times $500,000 = $12,286

2007 depreciation on the building = (12 months/12 months) times 1/39 times $500,000 = $12,821

2006 increase in accounts receivable = 5 percent times $300,000 = $15,000

2007 increase in accounts receivable = 5 percent times $400,000 = $20,000

2006 increase in accounts payable = 4 percent times $320,000 = $12,800

2007 increase in accounts payable = 4 percent times $220,000 = $8,800

Note: Again, inflows of cash are denoted as positive (non-bracketed) numbers and outflows of cash are negative or bracketed numbers.

on appraised values. The gain on the sale of the building is taxed at the 34 percent rate. Working capital accounts are projected to be $35,000 for accounts receivable, $25,000 in supplies inventory, $17,000 in prepaid expenses, $22,600 in accounts payable, and $6,400 in accrued expenses in 20 years. The receivables would be collected, but management estimates a loss of $4,000 on supplies inventory. The prepaid expenses would terminate in the last year and the accounts payable and accrued liabilities would be paid at face value. Disposition-stage cash flows are shown in Table 8-9.

TABLE 8-9 Disposition Stage Cash Flows for the Law Clinic

Land with a cost of $200,000 and a building with remaining basis of $224,124 are sold for $200,000 and $300,000, respectively. Current assets are $77,000, and a loss of $4,000 is experienced on the liquidation of supplies inventory. Current liabilities are $29,000. Sale of assets and liquidation occurs at year-end 2025.

LIQUIDATION OF FIXED ASSETS

	BUILDING	LAND	EQUIPMENT
Original purchase price	$500,000	$200,000	$100,000
Depreciation taken	$255,876	$0	$100,000
Remaining basis	$244,124	$200,000	$0
Selling price	$300,000	$200,000	$0
Less remaining basis	$244,124	$200,000	$0
Gain or (loss)	$55,876	$0	$0
Gain or (loss)	$55,876	$0	$0
Tax rate on gain or (loss)	34%		
Tax on (gain) or loss	($18,998)	$0	$0
Selling price	$300,000	$200,000	$0
Tax on (gain) or loss	($18,998)	$0	$0
Cash proceeds	$281,002	$200,000	$0

LIQUIDATION OF WORKING CAPITAL ITEMS

	RECEIVABLES	INVENTORY	PREPAID	PAYABLES	ACCRUED EXPENSES
Liquidation value	$35,000	$21,000	$17,000	$22,600	$6,400
Accumulated value	$35,000	$25,000	$17,000	$22,600	$6,400
Gain or (loss)	$0	($4,000)	$0	$0	$0
Gain or (loss)	$0	($4,000)	$0	$0	$0
Tax rate on gain or (loss)	34%	34%	34%	34%	34%
Tax on (gain) or loss	$0	$1,360	$0	$0	$0
Liquidation value	$35,000	$21,000	$17,000	$22,600	$6,400
Tax on (gain) or loss	$0	$1,360	$0	$0	$0
Cash proceeds	$35,000	$22,360	$17,000	($22,600)	($6,400)

Given the initial outlays in Table 8-7, the annual cash benefits in Table 8-8 (extended to cover the remaining years of operation), and the terminal cash flows in Table 8-9, the only remaining task is to compute the net present value of these flows to determine if the investment is attractive.

Tables 8-7 through 8-9 are summaries that result from substantial volumes of analysis. For example, detailed construction cost estimates were probably used for the initial cost estimates, and detailed market forecasts were probably used to estimate revenue. Table 8-10 is a further summary of all relevant cash costs and benefits from Tables 8-7 through 8-9. As shown in the present value analysis, the

TABLE 8-10 Capital Investment Analysis of the Legal Clinic

This table summarizes the cash flow analysis for the Indianapolis legal clinic. Present value analysis is based on a 10% required return and the assumption that operating cash flows occur at mid year.

YEAR:	BEG. 2005	END 2005 BEG. 2006	2006	2007	2008	2009	2010	2011	2012	2013	2014 TO 2025	END 2025
Revenue			$300,000	$700,000	$700,000	$700,000	$700,000	$700,000	$700,000	$700,000	$700,000	
Expenses												
Cash Expenses in the Acquisition Stage		($50,000)										
Cash Expenses												
Wages			($220,000)	($420,000)	($420,000)	($420,000)	($420,000)	($420,000)	($420,000)	($420,000)	($420,000)	
Other Operating Expenses			($100,000)	($120,000)	($120,000)	($120,000)	($120,000)	($120,000)	($120,000)	($120,000)	($120,000)	
Depreciation Expense												
Depreciation—Building			($12,286)	($12,821)	($12,821)	($12,821)	($12,821)	($12,821)	($12,821)	($12,821)	($12,821)	
Depreciation—Office Equipment			($10,000)	($16,000)	($9,600)	($5,760)	($5,760)	($2,880)	($0)	($0)	($0)	$0
Depreciation—Office Furniture			($7,145)	($12,245)	($8,745)	($6,245)	($4,465)	($4,465)	($4,465)	($4,225)	($0)	$0
Total Depreciation			($29,431)	($41,066)	($31,166)	($24,826)	($23,046)	($20,166)	($17,286)	($15,046)	($12,821)	$0
Earnings before Taxes		($50,000)	($49,431)	$118,934	$128,834	$135,174	$136,954	$139,834	$142,714	$144,954	$147,179	$0
Income Taxes at 34%		$17,000	$16,807	($40,438)	($43,804)	($46,959)	($46,564)	($47,544)	($48,523)	($49,285)	($50,041)	$0
Net Income		($33,000)	($32,624)	$78,496	$85,030	($89,215)	$90,390	$92,290	$94,191	$95,670	$97,138	$0
Add Back												
Depreciation Expenses		$0	$29,431	$41,066	$31,166	$24,826	$23,046	$20,166	$17,286	$17,046	$12,821	
Investment in Fixed Assets (Tables 8-7 to 8-9)	($300,000)	($500,000)	$0	$0	$0	$0	$0	$0	$0	$0	$0	$481,002
Investment in Working Capital (Tables 8-7 to 8-9)	$ 0	($5,000)	($14,000)	($29,000)	$0	$0	$0	$0	$0	$0	$0	45,360
After Tax Cash Flow	($300,000)	($538,000)	($17,193)	$90,562	$116,196	$114,041	$113,436	$112,456	$111,477	$110,716	$109,959	$526,362
PV Factor	1.000	0.9091	0.8668	0.7880	0.7164	0.6512	0.5920	0.5382	0.4893	0.4448	3.0307	0.1351
Present Value	($300,000)	($489,096)	($14,903)	$71,363	$83,243	$74,263	$67,154	$60,524	$54,546	$49,246	$333,253	$71,112
Net Present Value	$60,705											

investment is attractive when evaluated at the 10 percent required return. For the net present value computation, it was assumed that operating cash flows occurred at midyear.

FORECASTING SALES, OPERATING COST, AND WORKING CAPITAL NEEDS

The analysis thus far has been based on the assumption that revenue and expense streams have been determined, that collection patterns for accounts receivable have been estimated, and so on, and that the job at hand is the conversion of this information into relevant cash flows. Developing the projections that provide the basis for cash flow identification is obviously a major part of the capital investment analysis problem. Engineers, market researchers, cost accountants, human resource specialists, economists, and regulatory environment analysts are all involved in projecting information that is used in the estimation of costs and benefits. The capital investment analyst has the job of bringing together information from numerous sources to prepare a single profitability analysis.

While the provision of expertise in each of the areas that might provide input to the profitability analysis of a capital investment is obviously beyond the scope of this or any other single book, it is useful to review the basic tools that are widely used in preparing forecasts.

Forecasting Sales

If a capital investment is expected to result in increased revenues, sales forecasts are an integral part of the capital budgeting process. Sales forecasting is a specialty field of its own, and there are many excellent books on the topic. Some of the more widely used sales forecasting methods are discussed in the following paragraphs.

Trend Analysis. Trend analysis consists of the study of past revenue growth to predict future revenue. Typically, past growth is fitted to a standard trend pattern such as one of those in Figure 8-1. The dangers from mistaking the trend shape are illustrated by a series of bankruptcies in the Florida condominium market in the 1976–1980 period, the massive bankruptcies among Texas savings and loans in the 1980s and the billions in stock value lost in the Internet bubble of the late 1990s. In all of these cases, a growth curve like (c) in Figure 8-1 was mistaken for a curve like (b). As a result, loans to fund construction exceeded future demand for buildings, or in the Internet example sales were predicted to increase at astronomical rates for very long periods of time.

Example: Chrysler Corporation was considering the addition of pickup truck capacity in 1987, because pickup trucks had become increasingly popular as personal-use vehicles. Compact pickup truck sales grew at an annual rate of 44 percent from 1980 through 1986, while automobile sales grew at 4 percent a

FIGURE 8-1 Common Trend Patterns

This figure shows four types of sales trends wisely observed in practice; k, a, and b are the constants defining a particular trend.

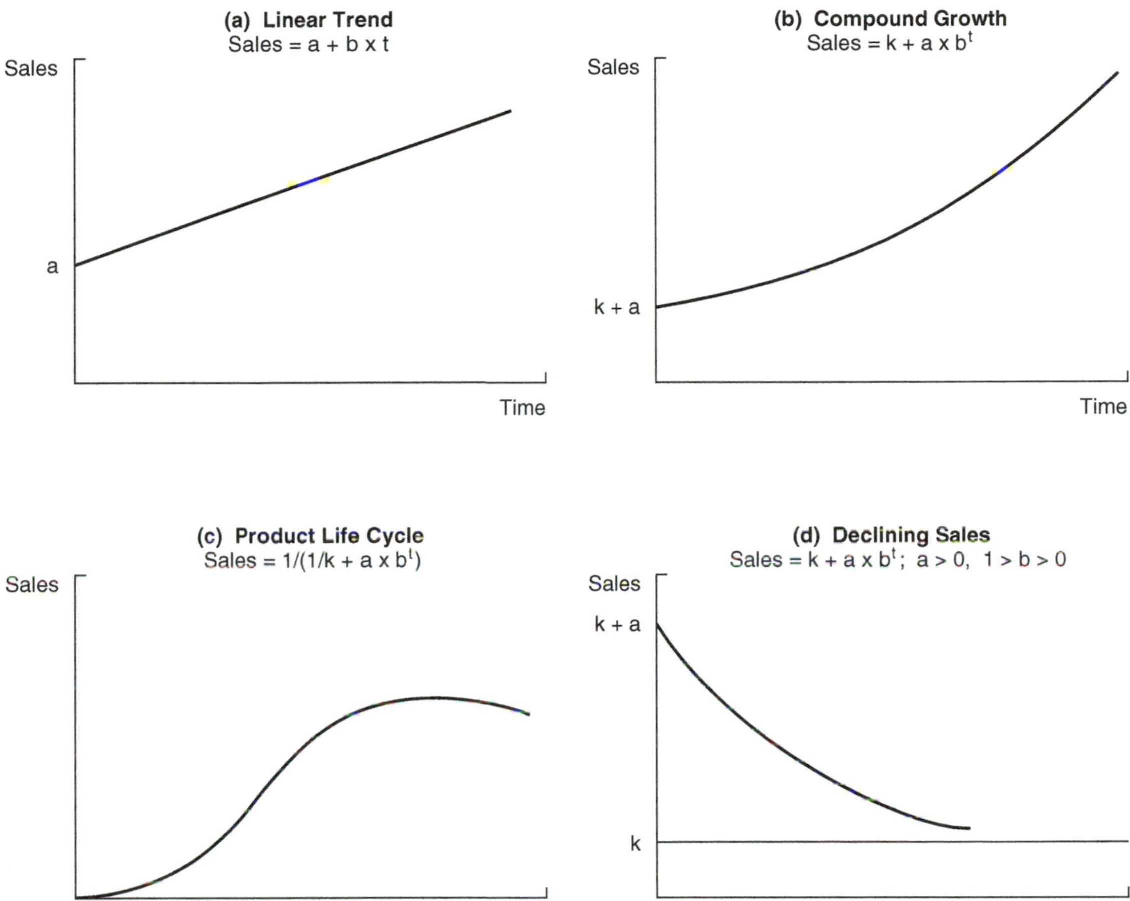

year. Compact pickup truck sales in the United States for the past 20 years are shown as the dots in Figure 8-2. Naturally, it is difficult to fit the growth precisely to any curve because of other events affecting sales. Line I is based on the assumption of compound growth, while line II is based on the assumption that sale of pickup trucks for personal use will follow the product life-cycle curve, with converts to pickup trucks slacking off and some drivers returning to automobiles. The resulting sales forecasts are radically different, depending on which assumption is made, so it is imperative that Chrysler gain additional information to help in identifying the type of growth trend that is occurring.

FIGURE 8-2 Sales of Pickup Trucks in the United States
The dots represent historical sales. Line I is based on the assumption of compound growth, while line II is based on the assumption that sale of pickup trucks for personal use will follow the product life-cycle curve.

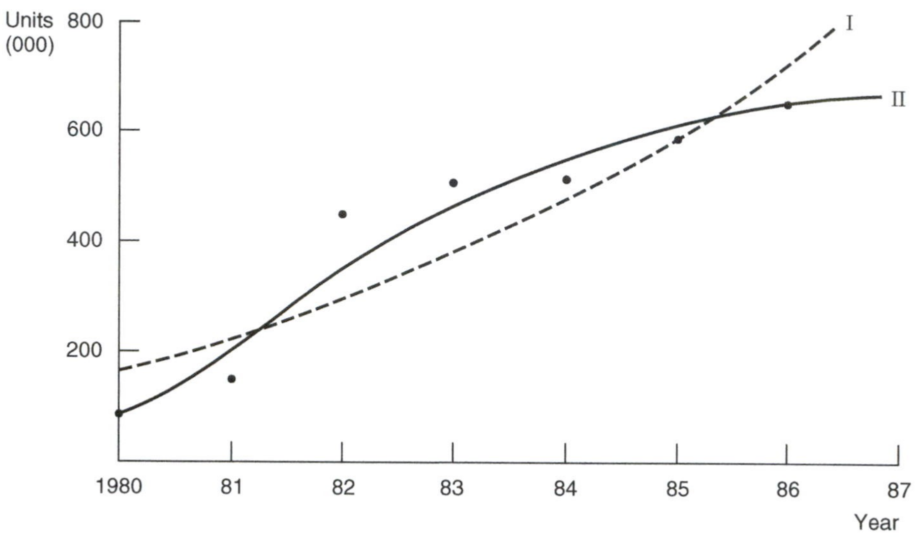

Study of Potential Purchasers. Potential customers can be studied in several ways. Chrysler Corporation may, for example, conduct surveys to determine how many automobile drivers expect to buy a truck, how many truck drivers intend to buy another truck, and so forth. Studies of the characteristics of truck buyers may give an indication of the maximum possible number of truck drivers. This information could be combined with analysis of recent trends to forecast truck sales.

Test marketing is another way to predict consumer response, although this may be difficult for pickup trucks. Nestlé can sell a new coffee flavor in several test markets to find out how many people will buy the product. Test markets also provide the opportunity to test different approaches to pricing, packaging, advertising, and so forth. This allows managers to choose the marketing mix that generates the greatest net present value.

Derived Demand. Demand for some products is derived from other activities, often beyond the control of the manufacturer. Sales by United States Steel, for example, are affected by automobile production, construction, and the general growth of the economy. Housing demand is affected by the overall health of the economy and the costs of mortgage money as well as the rate of family formation. Demand for John Deere farm equipment depends on the health of the farm economy. For products of this type, the emphasis is on forecasting the factors from which demand is derived and studying the relationship between demand and those factors. Professional economists are often useful in these cases.

Other Revenue Forecasting Methods. There are numerous other specialized revenue forecasting methods. Studies of demographic trends are the key to forecasting school enrollment and nursing home demand. Government budgets are used to predict demand for military equipment and roads. Panels of experts are sometimes assembled when other specific forecasting methods cannot be used.

Forecasting Costs

Capital investments that generate revenue generally result in increased costs as well. Other capital investments are acquired with the expectation of reducing costs. Some companies can forecast costs with considerable accuracy. If Kitchenaid develops a new dishwasher, for example, production managers will be able to estimate production costs accurately based on their long experience in production of similar products, supported by a good cost accounting system. In other cases, cost forecasts are extremely difficult, as evidenced by Union Electric's spending $2.4 billion on a nuclear power plant, when the original forecast was for an expenditure of $1.05 billion. With errors of this magnitude, efforts to improve the accuracy of cost forecasts are worthwhile.

Engineers and production managers often develop cost estimates for specific tasks or operation of specific machinery. Costs will include energy, repairs, labor, and so on. Personnel specialists can provide estimates of future costs per hour of labor. Purchasing agents can estimate costs of materials and components that must be purchased in order to produce a product. Marketing managers can prepare budgets for marketing and distribution.

In most cases, costs can be divided between fixed and variable portions. Variable costs depend on the level of output while fixed costs do not change over wide ranges of output. Once we decide to offer a flight from New York to Paris, for example, 90 percent of the costs are fixed. Variable costs include meals, commissions to travel agents, very small increases in fuel costs, and so on. At the other extreme, a small construction contractor may find that 90 percent of costs are variable, primarily in the form of material and labor. Cost accountants help by estimating fixed costs and by estimating variable costs per unit of output.

Fixed costs are only fixed over some specific time period and over some range of output. A factory can always be closed, so factory overhead is not fixed forever. Furthermore, demand in excess of factory capacity may lead to construction of a new factory, and additional fixed overhead. The new financial reporting system Pacific Resources, Inc., of Honolulu, acquired for $800,000, will not be made obsolete by the addition of one more small business unit, but with enough expansion the system will become inadequate, requiring replacement.

Example: Managers at Chrysler Corporation can estimate raw material, labor, and other direct production costs per pickup truck with considerable accuracy. The company can also estimate the fixed costs of having a factory open. Estimation of administration overhead is more difficult, though. Figure 8-3 shows the relationship between sales and administrative expense for Chrysler Corporation in recent years. This relationship can be used to forecast the administrative cost

FIGURE 8-3 Administrative Costs at Chrysler Corporation
This figure shows the relationship between sales revenue and administrative costs over time at Chrysler Corporation.

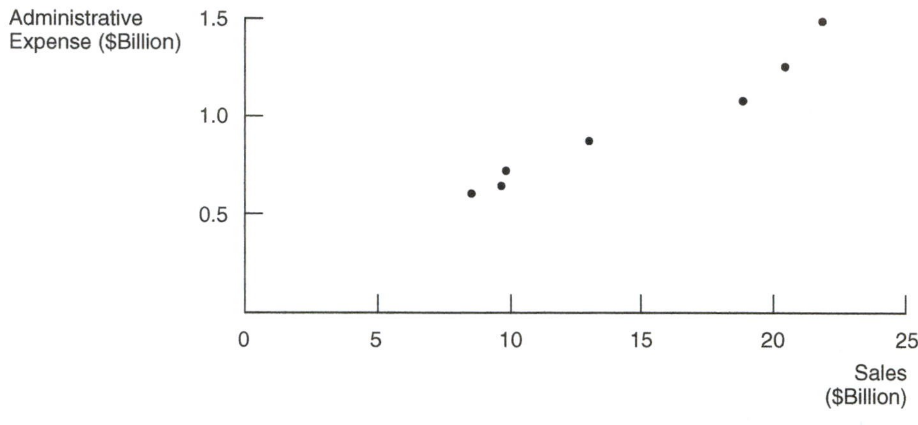

impact of an increase in sales. Using regression analysis on these numbers, for example, we estimate the following relationship between sales and administrative/marketing costs:

$$\text{Admin. \& marketing costs} = \$139 \text{ million} + .05 \times \text{Sales}$$

Given this relationship, we might expect administrative and marketing costs to increase by 5 percent of the sales increase.

Forecasting Working Capital Needs

Working capital investments are an important and frequently overlooked part of the relevant cash outlays required for a capital investment. Increased working capital requirements come from transaction cash needs, accounts receivable, inventory, and prepaid expenses. These needs are somewhat offset by increases in accounts payable and accrued expenses; the required increase in net working capital is a relevant cash cost. Inventory managers and credit managers can often be relied upon to generate estimates of needs in these important categories. Alternately, relationships between levels of these categories of assets and the level of sales can be studied for the same or similar products in past periods, in a manner similar to what was done with sales and administrative costs in Figure 8-3. Studies of past relationships or the terms of purchase for specific needed inputs can be used to estimate prepaid expenses, accounts payable, and accrued expenses.

Identification of relevant cash flows and computation of net present values are the culmination of the process of study and consultation with people in many fields of responsibility. The quality of the final decisions can be no better than the quality of the information that is generated from various sources within the business in the process of analyzing a proposed investment. The need to integrate information from many sources in the decision process is one reason degree requirements in business schools include courses in a broad range of topics, not just a narrow specialty.

SUMMARY

Capital investment analysis is based on relevant cash flows rather than accounting income or other measures of profitability. Cash flow is used because, unlike income, it is what is actually available to spend or reinvest. Cash flow analysis provides the necessary basis for choosing between benefits at different times.

For purposes of capital investment analysis, relevant cash flows are defined as follows:

- A relevant cash outflow is a cash outflow that will be caused by the course of action, a cash inflow that will be eliminated, or an increase in claims by suppliers of capital that will be created.
- A relevant cash benefit is a cash inflow that will be caused by the course of action, a cash outflow that will be avoided, or claims by suppliers of capital that will be avoided.
- An irrelevant cash flow is a cash flow that will occur whether or not the proposed course of action is taken.

Following are the major types of relevant cash costs and benefits at the beginning of an asset's life.

Capital Costs: Purchase and installation price of fixed assets, plus costs of licenses and patents.

Expenses: Training, advertising, legal, and other expenses associated with start-up, less the income tax savings resulting from these expenses.

Working Capital: Increases in current assets required at or near the beginning of a new activity, less current liabilities (accounts payable and accrued expenses) generated at or near the beginning of the activity.

Estimating the cash flows from a potential project is no small undertaking and it requires the help of engineers, cost analysts, marketing personnel, and others. We have broken the process into the following steps:

Estimating the Income Statement

1. Estimate the relevant revenues and/or expenses you expect to receive from the project.
2. Assemble these revenues and expenses into a preliminary income statement making an appropriate calculation of the after tax income.

Estimating the Balance Sheet

3. Determine all of the balance sheet accounts that are impacted by the project.
4. Estimate the initial size of the investment in these balance sheet accounts. In particular, estimate the incremental investment in fixed assets, such as

buildings and equipment, and working capital items, such as cash balances, accounts receivable, and inventory.

5. Determine size and growth of these accounts after the project is operational.

Rolling the Income Statement and Balance Sheet into a Cash Flow Statement

6. Calculate the depreciation charge flowing from the fixed assets into the balance sheet each year.
7. Estimate the life of the project.
8. Determine the terminal values for fixed assets and the disposition values of working capital (net of taxes).
9. Roll all of this information together into a projected cash flow statement.

Making the Decision

10. Calculate the net present value of the project using the appropriate discount rate.[5]
11. Make the appropriate accept or reject decision.

The forecasting of relevant costs and benefits frequently involves the expertise of many people inside and outside the business. The forecasting of benefits often starts with sales forecasts, which may be based on market research, economic analysis, and so on. The projection of costs may use the skills of cost accountants, engineers, production managers, and regulatory environment analysts as well as financial analysts. Thus, the capital budgeting process brings together the expertise of people throughout the business to identify and evaluate all of the relevant costs and benefits of a capital investment. The quality of the final decisions will depend on the quality of the information generated from these various sources.

QUESTIONS

8-1. Define, in your own words, the meaning of the phrases **relevant cash cost** and **relevant cash benefit.**

8-2. Why is an increase in working capital considered a relevant cash cost?

8-3. For a movie producer, give an example of sunk costs that might exist when the release of a new picture is being considered.

8-4. An airline is considering a new promotional campaign to attract college students by offering them the right to fly stand-by at low prices when seats are not otherwise filled. List several examples of relevant and irrelevant costs from the airline's point of view.

8-5. A shirt manufacturer is considering the addition of a line of neckties. Give examples of joint costs that might be encountered. How should these joint costs be considered in the decision process?

[5]Determination of the appropriate discount rate given the risk for the project is discussed in the risk section of the book, Chapters 11 to 15.

8-6. Why is interest expense not treated as a relevant cash cost in the capital budgeting process?

8-7. A broadcasting company is considering offering a new 24-hour sports news service. Who in the company may be involved in estimating the relevant costs and benefits?

8-8. In which of the following three categories would the following cash flows belong? (It is possible for a cash flow to go in more than one category.)
Categories: Initial Outlay, Yearly Cash Flows, Disposition Cash Flows

- **a.** The cost of training existing workers to use a new piece of equipment
- **b.** The incremental revenue generated from the project
- **c.** The proceeds of a "going out of business" sale
- **d.** The freight on the new piece of equipment
- **e.** The difference in the sale price of the old equipment and the trade-in allowed on the old equipment
- **f.** The cost of advertising the grand opening of the new business
- **g.** The cost of adding an indoor playground to the neighborhood McDonald's

8-9. (**Applications**) There has been an explosion in the popularity of rotisserie cooked chicken. Even country singer Kenny Rogers recognized the enthusiasm and opened his own chain of chicken outlets. Please list five initial outlay cash flows, three variable operating cash flows, three fixed operating cash flows, and three disposition cash flows. Note if cash flows are positive (inflows) or negative (outflows).

8-10. (**Applications**) Wal-Mart Corporation has announced its intention to expand its movement into groceries through the construction of Super Wal-Marts. In many cities, they are replacing the existing Wal-Mart discounted hard goods store with a much larger Super Wal-Mart that sells discount groceries, meats, produce, and an expanded line of hard goods carried in the traditional store. For this situation, list three sunk costs, three indirect costs, and three indirect benefits.

PROBLEMS

8-1. Fort Wayne Corporation expects the following revenues, cash expenses, and depreciation charges as a result of its recent opening of an affiliated store in Lansing:

YEAR	1	2	3	4	5
Revenues	$16,000	$20,000	$38,000	$48,000	$35,000
Cash Expenses	$8,000	$5,000	$14,000	$19,000	$19,000
Depreciation	$3,000	$4,000	$3,000	$3,000	$3,000

Fort Wayne is in the 40 percent tax bracket. Please compute the after tax cash flows from this investment in the Lansing store.

8-2. Right before opening the Lansing store discussed in problem 1, you have discovered that Fort Wayne forgot to budget 10 percent of revenues as a cash balance, 20 percent of cash expenses as an inventory balance, and 10 percent of cash expenses as an accounts payable balance. All of these balances would be needed at the beginning of each year and are estimated from the year-end annual estimates of revenues and cash expenses given earlier. Please recalculate the cash flows for the Lansing store investment.

8-3. Payson Corporation purchased a copying machine for $15,600 and placed it into service on January 1, year 1. This machine is expected to last for 5 years, during which it will produce approximately 200,000 copies each year. Copies will sell for an average of 6 cents each. Material, labor, and other variable costs will be approximately 3 cents a copy. Working capital needs will be negligible, as copying with this machine will be almost all on a cash basis and current liabilities will offset the supplies inventory need. The copier will be disposed of at the end of 5 years for $0. Please calculate the net present value of this copy machine investment using a 40 percent tax rate and a 10 percent cost of capital.

8-4. A new investment in inventory being considered by Quincy Corporation requires an initial outlay of $100,000 on January 1, year 1. The inventory is expected to be liquidated at the end of 5 years for $80,000. At a 40 percent income tax rate and a 10 percent required return, is the investment attractive?

This investment is expected to generate the following additional revenues and expenses:

YEAR	1	2	3	4	5
Revenues	$6,000	$10,000	$28,000	$38,000	$25,000
Expenses	$3,000	$5,000	$14,000	$19,000	$19,000
Liquidation loss					$20,000

8-5. You may have observed the increased popularity of "fashionable" pool halls. These pool halls are nothing like their often violent and smoke-filled predecessors. These establishments target an upscale clientele who like to meet for pool rather than dancing or some other activity. Assume that you build one of these establishments and spend $500,000 for the building and $100,000 for equipment (tax life of 5 years) and place it into service on January 1. The pool hall will bring in $10,000 per week in revenue and cost $4,300 per week in cash expenses. Assume a 50-week year. The building will be sold for $400,000 at the end of the fifth year, and the equipment will be sold for $10,000 at the end of the fifth year. No other cash flows will occur during the 5 years of operation. What is the net present value at a 15 percent interest rate?

8-6. Muncie Manufacturing is increasing its collection period by 25 days in hopes of attracting additional sales. Muncie currently has annual sales of

$500,000. They expect revenues to increase by $25,000 per year and expenses to increase by $10,000 per year. Muncie believes that an additional $3,000 will go uncollected each year as a result of this change in policy. This $3,000 loss will have to be replaced each year to keep the accounts receivable balance at the increased 25-day level. They project that they will be able to collect 90 percent of the outstanding balance at the end of year 4 (after replacement). Using a 4-year life, a 40 percent tax rate, and a 10 percent required return, is the investment attractive?

8-7. Myles Corporation is considering a new computer that can be purchased for $14,800. Delivery will cost $300 and setup will cost $500. What is the initial depreciable cost of the computer machine?

8-8. Terre Haute Cola Distribution can purchase a new executive airplane for $2,300,000. Delivery will cost $10,000 and fitting out after delivery will cost $130,000. The plane has a tax life of 5 years and the plane will be depreciated using the MACRS tables introduced in the chapter. The airplane will be used to transport its executives and it will physically last for 10 years (even though it was depreciated over 5 years). At the end of 10 years the plane will have no salvage value. Wages, repairs, fuel, and so on to operate the airplane are expected to total $250,000 a year. The airplane is expected to save 4,000 hours of management time a year. The managers involved receive salary and benefits that average $115 an hour. The company has a 40 percent tax rate and a 12 percent required return. Is the airplane an attractive investment?

8-9. A new broad-spectrum blood analyzer will allow Lafayette Clinic to earn additional test fees of $30,000 a year for the analyzer's estimated 8-year technical life. The analyzer will cost $100,000, including delivery and installation, and will have a 7-year depreciation life. There is space available in the laboratory that has no other use, and the laboratory technician can do the tests in about the same time it presently takes to send out the samples. The technician earns $20 an hour and will spend 5 percent of his time using this machine. It will be necessary to send the technician to a school to operate the new machine. The school costs $1,000, and a temporary replacement must be hired for the period at a cost of $1,200. The clinic has a 40 percent tax rate and a 12 percent required return. Is the analyzer attractive? (Assume January 1 installation.)

8-10. South Bend Building Services needs to replace a worn-out floor-stripping machine. A machine similar to the one being replaced costs $3,000. A new type of machine would cost $4,000, but would be more efficient to operate, reducing labor expense by $500 a year. Unfortunately, the new machine also requires some special maintenance tools that would cost $100 per machine. The tools are specific to the machine and will be depreciated over the 7-year tax life of the machine. The company has nineteen additional stripping machines that must be replaced within the next year. Either the old-style or the new-style machine will be placed in service January 1 and will last for 9 years, with no salvage value. Either machine will be depreciated using the depreciation rates discussed in the chapter. At a 40 percent tax rate, and a 10 percent required return, which machine should the company acquire? (Assume a 7-year tax life for the machine and the tools.)

8-11. Tom Yeager, a college student, is presently working 16 hours a week (50 weeks a year) at a menial job paying the minimum wage. He can get a job making deliveries for a pizza company in Ames at a $2 increase in his hourly wage, but he must have his own car. A used Chevette is for sale for $3,600. Insurance, gasoline, and maintenance would cost $1,000 a year. Tom would use the car only for business so that he could treat the car as a capital investment for tax purposes. Tom would place the car in service on December 31, 2004, and would use the car for this purpose through the end of 2007, at which time it would have an estimated market value of $1,000. Tom is in a 15 percent tax bracket and could otherwise invest at a rate of 10 percent after tax. Should Tom keep his current job or deliver pizzas?

8-12. Campus Dry-Cleaning has an on-campus location with 10 years to go on the lease. An existing dry-cleaning machine will last for the 10-year duration of the lease, at which time it will be worn out and worthless. A new machine will be more efficient and allow the company to handle a broader range of fabrics. As a result, the new machine will increase revenues by $1,500 a year and decrease operating costs other than depreciation by $600 a year. The old machine, which is fully depreciated, could be sold for $6,000 today. The new machine will cost $20,000. The lease is not renewable, and the new machine is expected to have a salvage value of $5,000 in 10 years. Campus Dry-Cleaning is in a 34 percent tax bracket and the required return on new investments is 10 percent. Should Campus Dry-Cleaning acquire the new machine?

8-13. For the new dry-cleaning machine in problem 12, redo the analysis assuming the lease can be renewed indefinitely and the new machine will last 15 years with no salvage value at the end of 15 years.

8-14. Central Telephone Company is considering the addition of a new type of call-waiting service for its customers. The service can be offered with present hardware, but new software must be purchased at a cost of $1 million. The software will be placed in service January 1, 1993, and depreciated over the estimated 5-year life of the equipment, using the straight-line method. Monthly fees for the service will be $2 initially and will increase 5 percent a year thereafter. An estimated 10,000 customers will sign up for the service in the first year, with the number increasing at 4 percent a year thereafter. The advertising expense for the service will be $100,000 at the time of introduction and $5,000 a month thereafter. The only variable cost will be bad debt expense, equal to 1 percent of revenue. The only significant working capital item is accounts receivable, and the average collection period will be 73 days. Because of uncertainty about developing technology, management wants to assume that the service will not be offered after the 5-year life of the existing hardware. The telephone company has a 12 percent required return. Is the call-waiting service an attractive offering?

8-15. Cedar Falls Menswear is considering the addition of a line of shirts and ties. After tax cash outlays and after tax benefits each year for the 10-year planning horizon are shown below. The required return is 10 percent, and no salvage values are anticipated. Should the company invest in either or both lines?

	SHIRTS	TIES	SHIRTS & TIES
Initial outlay	$5,000,000	$1,000,000	$5,900,000
Annual after tax revenue	6,000,000	800,000	7,000,000
Annual after tax outlays	5,000,000	700,000	5,800,000
Annual net cash flow	$1,000,000	$100,000	$1,200,000

8-16. (**Applications**) Several years ago Sears realized that it could not compete with the local Wal-Mart by carrying the same merchandise and advertising the same low price. By their very nature, most Sears stores were located as anchors to malls and as such paid higher rents than the standalone Wal-Marts. A corporate decision was made to differentiate the product offering at Sears from the product offering at the typical Wal-Mart. Assume that restocking the typical Sears store had the following cost (in thousands):

- $1,000 in losses on the sale of discontinued merchandise (year 0)
- $50 in additional advertising to introduce the new stores (year 0)
- $30 in training to sell the new higher-margin merchandise (year 0)
- $2,000 in additional inventory of higher-margin merchandise (years 1–5)
- $3,000 in additional sales (years 1–5)
- $1,500 in additional cost of merchandise sold (years 1–5)
- $200 in additional loss of inventory due to obsolescence or other reasons (years 1–5)
- $750 in additional loss from the liquidation sale (at the end of year 5)

Using a 5-year time horizon and a 12 percent cost of capital, what is the net present value of this strategic shift?

8-17. (**Applications**) One of Dell Computers' major competitive advantages is the production system that allows them to produce a computer to order for each customer per individual specifications. A side benefit of this system is the ability of Dell to hold substantially fewer dollars in parts and finished goods inventories than competitors like Compaq Computers that produce models and then sell these at retail stores. There is a new production system proposal that would cost $100,000,000 immediately and would yield the following reductions in inventory balances:

- Inventory reduction at the end of year 1—$20,000,000
- Inventory reduction at the end of year 2—$95,000,000

- Inventory reduction at the end of year 3—$15,000,000
- Thereafter—$0

Assume that 60 percent of the new system could be written off as a 5-year asset for tax purposes. Using a 10 percent cost of capital, calculate the net present value of this project.

8-18. Mason James Corporation expects to install a $100,000 machine in 2004 and another $120,000 machine in 2007. The first machine has a 5-year tax life and the second machine has a 7-year tax life. What is the total expected depreciation expense for these two machines in 2009?

CASE PROBLEM

Walton Medical Laboratory

Margaret Walton spent 10 years working in the laboratory at City Hospital. During that time, she advanced to the position of director of the laboratory and completed an MBA degree. She felt that opportunities for further advancement at the hospital were limited and was looking for a new challenge. She took a course in entrepreneurship and was fascinated by the idea of starting her own business. Walton decided that she would open an independent laboratory to provide medical tests for independent medical practices. She believed that she could help physicians reduce both their capital requirements and administrative chores, as well as provide more accurate testing.

Walton began assembling information. She discovered a piece of land available near a number of independent medical practices. The land could be purchased for $100,000, and a suitable building would cost approximately $400,000. The building would have a useful life of approximately 40 years. Laboratory equipment would cost $1 million. The equipment would have a life of 7 years for tax purposes, but would actually last 10 years. Although the business could continue indefinitely, Walton wanted to do the analysis based on the assumption of a life similar to that of the laboratory equipment: 10 years.

In addition to fixed assets, working capital such as cash, supplies, receivables, and payables would be needed. Walton wanted to maintain a minimum cash balance of $20,000. She estimated that $100,000 of supplies would be needed initially, and accounts receivable would rise to $20,000 within a month of starting the business. She estimated initial accounts payable at $40,000. She estimated that the cash, supplies, receivables, and payables categories would double at the end of the first year and would not increase thereafter.

Walton predicted revenue of $600,000 during the first year and $1,200,000 each year thereafter. She estimated that labor expenses, including a salary for her equal to what she was now earning, of $300,000 in the first year and $480,000 each year thereafter. She estimated a supplies expense of $120,000 in the first year and $190,000 each year thereafter. She estimated overhead expense, other than depreciation, of $100,000 a year.

Looking ahead, Walton estimated that the equipment would have a negligible value in 10 years, while the building would have lost one-fourth of its value and the land would still be worth $100,000. She guessed that supplies inventory could be sold for half its cost, and other working capital items would be settled at their book values.

Walton turned her attention to financing. She had limited capital of her own and would need to seek outside investors. She had heard enough horror stories about problems that occurred when companies could not make payments on debts, and she wanted to avoid those troubles. Thus, she wanted to try to arrange all equity financing, and use a bank line of credit only for temporary needs. Walton decided on a plan involving ten wealthy investors, preferably senior retired physicians who would then serve on the board of directors. She would fund the project by creating eleven shares—one share free to herself as a founder's share and one share to each of the investors. Each investor would then invest 10 percent of the capital requirements.

Walton tentatively discussed the project with several senior retired physicians to see what would be required. They viewed this as an investment of moderate risk and indicated that they would want a 12 percent after tax return from an investment of this type. While several investors encouraged her to continue, they were naturally unwilling to make a commitment without a proposal and a thorough financial analysis. Walton began to develop a profitability analysis and a proposal. She had to choose between the corporate tax form and an S form. She estimated that most investors would be in 28 percent tax brackets. All funds not needed internally would be paid out to the shareholders. She thought she could be ready to start by the first of the year, so assets would be considered placed in service in January.

Case Questions

1. Identify all cash flows on the assumption the business is taxed at a 28 percent tax rate.
2. Prepare a net present value analysis.
3. Does this investment provide a satisfactory rate of return to investors?
4. Is it fair and reasonable for Walton to get one-eleventh of the company without putting up equity capital of her own?

SELECTED REFERENCES

Ang, James S., Jess H. Chua, and Ronald Sellers. "Generating Cash Flow Estimates: An Actual Study Using the Delphi Technique." *Financial Management* 8 (Spring 1979): 64–67.

Barnett, F. William. "Four Steps to Forecast Total Market Demand." *Harvard Business Review* 88 (July–August 1988): 28–30+.

Brown, Keith C. "A Note on the Apparent Bias of Net Revenue Estimates for Capital Investment Projects." *The Journal of Finance* 29 (September 1974): 1215–1216.

Brunton, Nancy M. "Evaluation of Overhead Allocation." *Management Accounting* 70 (July 1988): 22–26.

D'Attilio David F. "Net Working Capital Forecasting at Dupont." *Journal of Business Forecasting Methods and Systems* 11 (Spring 1992): 11–23.

Dhavale, Deleep G. "Overhead and CIMS: Indirect Costs Take on Greater Importance and Require New Accounting Methods." *Industrial Engineering* 20 (July 1988): 41–43.

Enrich, Norbert L. *Marketing and Sales Forecasting: A Quantitative Approach,* rev. ed. Melbourne, Fla.: Krieger Publishing, 1979.

Howe, Keith M. "Does Inflationary Change Affect Capital Asset Life?" *Financial Management* 16 (Summer 1987): 63–67.

Hurwood, Donald L. *Sales Forecasting.* New York: The Conference Board, 1978.

Kroll, Yoram. "On the Differences between Accrual Accounting Figures and Cash Flows: The Case of Working Capital." *Financial Management* 14 (Spring 1985): 75–82.

McLean, Lawrence B., and A. William Worthman. "Methodology Aids Forecasting with Limited Information." *Industrial Engineering* 20 (February 1988): 18–23.

Pan, Judy, Donald R. Nichols, and O. Maurice Joy. "Sales Forecasting Practices of Large U.S. Industrial Firms." *Financial Management* 6 (Fall 1977): 72–77.

Schall, Lawrence D. "Taxes, Inflation, and Corporate Financial Policy." *The Journal of Finance* 39 (March 1984): 105–126.

Seitz, Neil E. *Business Forecasting: Concepts and Microcomputer Applications.* Englewood Cliffs, N.J.: Prentice-Hall, 1984.

Statman, Meir, and Tyzoon T. Tyebjee. "Optimistic Capital Budgeting Forecasts." *Financial Management* 14 (Autumn 1985): 27–33.

Winkler, Daniel T. "The Cost of Trade Credit: A Net Present Value Perspective." *Journal of Business and Economic Studies* 3 (Winter 1995, Spring 1996): 53–64.

CHAPTER 9

Taxes and Foreign Investments

After completing this chapter you should be able to:

- Understand the adjustments that need to be made for corporate taxes at the capital acquisition stage, the operating or asset usage stage, and the disposal stage.
- Describe the difference between accrual book basis accounting and accrual tax basis accounting.
- Grasp the meaning of the terms: **capital gains, depreciation, Modified Accelerated Cost Recovery System, Alternative Minimum Tax, loss carry-back, loss carry-forward,** and **S corporation.**
- Ascertain the depreciation method or combination of depreciation methods that result in the highest net present value given the firm's projected income.
- Explain the dividend exclusion rule as it applies to dividends paid between corporations.
- Understand the different tax treatments for proprietorships, partnerships, S corporations, and regular corporations as they relate to the capital budgeting decision.
- Evaluate the impact that many additional business taxes have on the capital budgeting decision such as state income tax, local income tax, excise taxes, social security taxes, unemployment compensation tax, and others.
- Show that net present value is still the optimal decision criterion even when taxes are introduced.
- Understand the proper tax treatment when an asset is replaced and there is a trade-in allowance involved.
- Describe the important factors that need to be considered in evaluating an international capital investment.
- Understand the cash flow implications of international capital budgeting projects.

It's not how much money you make that's important. It's how much you keep. Although we do not know who said this, this appears to be the predominate tax strategy in business today. It could be General Electric building one of the best tax teams in the country to manage the taxes of its worldwide operations; Tyco International conducting a reverse merger to change its corporate headquarters to Bermuda and save upwards of $600,000,000 per year in taxes; Marriott International, the hotel chain, investing in coal-treatment machinery for the tax credits associated with the energy favored investments; or Pitney Bowes investing in aircraft to turn around and lease to major airlines for the depreciation charges and consequent tax savings. All of these are examples of corporations attempting to keep more of their cash flows by giving less to the taxing authorities. A recent study by Martin Sullivan, a tax economist, has the taxes paid (as a percentage of income) by U.S. multinationals falling from 49.6 percent in 1983 to 22.2 percent in 1999. Half of the decrease is due to the Reagan-era tax reductions, which lowered the corporate rate to roughly 35 percent. The other half, he believes, is due to the shifting of income from countries with higher taxes to countries with lower taxes.[1]

Because so much wealth can accrue to the shareholder by legally reducing the tax burden on a company's cash flows, management's attention is frequently drawn from managing the business to managing tax liabilities. For U.S.-based multinationals, Uncle Sam (the U.S. government) is a major participant in their business, with the legal taxing authority to receive over a third of the typical large company's income in the form of taxes. Uncle Sam is also picky about when and how his share is calculated and paid. The federal income tax laws and accompanying Internal Revenue Service Regulations, for example, covered over 12,000 pages before being expanded by "tax simplification." If you always meant to read Shakespeare and never found the time, bear in mind that his complete works are one-fortieth of that length. The volume of laws and regulations pales, though, when compared to the additional 40,000 pages of administrative and court rulings that are used to determine tax implications of specific actions. In addition, state and local governments have their own tax laws.

In the meantime, the voluminous tax laws and regulations must be considered in estimating capital investment cash flows; otherwise, you may overestimate or underestimate cash flows by 100 percent or more. Equally important, a knowledge of taxes allows you to take advantage of opportunities to reduce taxes and, thereby, increase the profitability of capital investments. Businesses often employ tax experts because the average manager cannot keep up with the massive and ever-changing tax code. However, managers involved in domestic and international capital investment decisions must understand at least the general principles that will allow them to estimate the tax implications of their decisions and work toward reduction of taxes.

Fortunately, the massive volumes of tax laws and regulations are mostly applications of some general principles to specific situations. These principles have remained steady over time, even though details of the tax code have changed

---

[1]From an article in the March 31, 2003, *Business Week* entitled "The Corporate Tax Game—Special Report."

frequently. The focus of this chapter is on the application of general principles of taxation to capital budgeting, with current laws as an illustration.

The income tax is the basis of the tax system in the United States and the major tax affecting capital budgeting.[2] Following an overview of the general principles of income taxation, we trace the implications of income taxes over the life cycle of a capital investment, from acquisition to disposition. Businesses are assumed to be ordinary corporations in this discussion unless otherwise noted. Some differences for businesses not taxed as corporations are covered later in this chapter.[3]

ACCRUAL BOOK BASIS INCOME VERSUS ACCRUAL TAX BASIS INCOME

Income was defined in the last chapter as revenues less expenses. The meaning is the same here except that the timing and recognition of revenues and expenses for tax purposes may be different than the definition and timing of revenues and expenses for accrual accounting book purposes. The tax law defines what is recognized as revenues and expenses for tax purposes and, for the most part, this is the same as what is recognized for accrual accounting purposes. The difference lies in the timing and amounts to be recognized. For example, corporations typically want to show a higher level of income to their shareholders than to the IRS. They can do this by electing to use straight-line depreciation to depreciate their fixed assets for book purposes and by using the much more rapid Modified Accelerated Cost Recovery System (MACRS), discussed in Chapter 8, for calculating their taxable income. Using different book basis rules to calculate a higher income for the shareholder and tax basis rules to show a lower income to the IRS is known as tax avoidance rather than tax evasion. Knowing the difference between the two is critical. Tax avoidance is typically smart management because you can defer taxes until future years and pay them in cheaper dollars. Tax evasion is illegal and typically carries a federal prison sentence (if convicted).

Example: To illustrate the difference between accrual book basis income and accrual tax basis income, consider the activities of Merrill Corporation summarized in Table 9-1. The company bought a \$100 machine in 2004 that had a 3-year tax life but a 10-year economic life. Revenues were \$500 each year and cash expenses were \$300 each year. The company uses the MACRS rates discussed in Chapter 8 to depreciate for tax purposes and the straight-line method[4]

[2]Other taxes include property tax, social security tax, and excise taxes. These taxes must also be considered in that they affect cash flows. Many of the non-income taxes are levied by state and local governments and vary by jurisdiction.

[3]The reader who wants a more in-depth understanding of tax issues can start by acquiring one of the many detailed tax guides such as the *Federal Tax Course,* published annually by Commerce Clearing House.

[4]The straight-line method involves taking the acquisition cost and subtracting the expected disposal value and dividing the difference by the expected life of the asset. Sometimes this number is divided by 2 to adjust to a midyear convention. In this case, the \$100 acquisition cost less the salvage value of \$0 leaves a difference of \$100. Dividing this by 10 we arrive at a yearly depreciation of \$10.

TABLE 9-1 Comparison of Accrual Book Basis Accounting and Accrual Tax Basis Accounting

This table illustrates the differences in net income, the balance sheet, and the cash flow statement using accrual tax basis accounting and accrual book basis accounting.

INCOME STATEMENT (USING ACCRUAL TAX BASIS ACCOUNTING)

YEAR	2005	2006	2007	2008
Revenue	$500	$500	$500	$500
Cash expenses	(300)	(300)	(300)	(300)
Depreciation expense (MACRS)	(33)	(45)	(15)	(7)
Taxable income	167	155	185	193
Taxes	(67)	(62)	(74)	(77)
Net income	100	93	111	116

BALANCE SHEET (USING ACCRUAL TAX BASIS ACCOUNTING)

YEAR	2005	2006	2007	2008
Deferred taxes payable	$0	$0	$0	$0

CASH FLOW STATEMENT (USING ACCRUAL TAX BASIS ACCOUNTING)

YEAR	2005	2006	2007	2008
Revenue	$500	$500	$500	$500
Cash expenses	(300)	(300)	(300)	(300)
Depreciation expense (MACRS)	(33)	(45)	(15)	(7)
Taxable income	167	155	185	193
Taxes	(67)	(62)	(74)	(77)
Net income	100	93	111	116
Add back depreciation	33	45	15	7
Add (sub.) changes in deferred taxes	0	0	0	0
Cash flow	133	138	126	123

for accounting purposes. The asset is placed into service on January 1, 2005, and Merrill is in the 40 percent marginal tax bracket.

The example in Table 9-1 demonstrates the differences to the income statement, the balance sheet—specifically the deferred taxes payable account, and cash flow statement that result under tax basis accounting versus accrual book basis accounting. In this example Merrill reported a higher income to the owners than to the Internal Revenue Service in the first 3 years because depreciation

TABLE 9-1 Comparison of Accrual Book Basis Accounting and Accrual Tax Basis Accounting (*Continued*)

INCOME STATEMENT (USING ACCRUAL BOOK BASIS ACCOUNTING)

YEAR	2005	2006	2007	2008
Revenue	$500	$500	$500	$500
Cash expenses	(300)	(300)	(300)	(300)
Depreciation expense	(10)	(10)	(10)	(10)
Taxable income	190	190	190	190
Taxes	(76)	(76)	(76)	(76)
Net income	114	114	114	114

BALANCE SHEET (USING ACCRUAL BOOK BASIS ACCOUNTING)

YEAR	2005	2006	2007	2008
Change in deferred taxes	$9	$14	$2	$(1)
Deferred taxes payable	9	23	25	24

CASH FLOW STATEMENT (USING ACCRUAL BOOK BASIS ACCOUNTING)

YEAR	2005	2006	2007	2008
Revenue	$500	$500	$500	$500
Cash expenses	(300)	(300)	(300)	(300)
Depreciation expense	(10)	(10)	(10)	(10)
Taxable income	190	190	190	190
Taxes	(76)	(76)	(76)	(76)
Net income	114	114	114	114
Add back depreciation	10	10	10	10
Add (sub.) changes in deferred taxes	9	14	2	(1)
Cash flow	133	138	126	123

expense for accrual accounting purposes is not the same for tax accounting purposes.[5] These differences in income do not imply dishonesty. The accelerated depreciation rates presently used by the Internal Revenue Service are for the purpose of encouraging investment, not for the purpose of recognizing the

[5]Companies may also use different inventory valuation methods, warranty methods, pension methods, and receivable methods for tax and book accounting.

actual rates at which assets wear out. The income tax expense on the book basis income statement is approximately the tax that would have been paid if the income reported to the owners was also reported to the Internal Revenue Service. This difference between the tax expense reported to owners and the tax actually paid is treated as a deferred tax liability on the balance sheet. The taxes being avoided through accelerated depreciation will be paid later when tax depreciation is lower than accounting book depreciation. In this example this reversal begins in 2008 when MACRS depreciation is $7 and straight-line depreciation is $10.

The differences between book basis accounting and tax basis accounting are adjusted in the construction of the cash flow statement. When book basis accounting is used to construct the income statement, an adjustment for any increase or decrease in deferred taxes must be made in the cash flow statement. This annual increase or decrease in deferred taxes will be roughly the difference in the taxes owed using tax basis accounting and the taxes owed using book basis accounting.

CORPORATE TAX RATES

Corporate Rates on Ordinary Income

Ordinary income is income derived from the ordinary course of business. Taking revenues and subtracting expenses would calculate ordinary income. For Wal-Mart, ordinary income would be the sale of the merchandise less the cost of the merchandise, employee cost, insurance, and all other necessary or ordinary business expenses. Tax rates on ordinary income for corporations rise rapidly until they plateau at approximately $18,000,000 in taxable income. Beyond this amount, corporate ordinary income is taxed at a flat 35 percent. The particular tax rates and plateau amounts change periodically, but the principle has remained the same for many years. For the problems at the end of the chapter we assume a 40 percent tax rate. This assumption is based on a 35 percent federal income tax rate and an average state income tax rate of roughly 5 percent.

Capital or 1231, 1245, and 1250 Gains and Losses

Sometimes corporations invest in the stock or the financial instruments of other corporations for reasons besides control. When these financial instruments are sold, the gain or loss is treated as a capital gain or loss or 1231 gain or loss. To be 1231 the asset is typically not bought or sold in the ordinary course of business. For example, Wal-Mart parking some excess cash in Citibank preferred stock for 18 months would qualify for 1231 treatment.

1245 gains (and losses) occur when *depreciable assets other than real estate* are sold for more (or less) than the remaining basis.[6] 1250 gains (and losses) occur when *real estate* assets are sold for more (or less) than the remaining basis.

---

[6]Remember from Chapter 8 that the remaining basis is the initial cost of the asset less depreciation taken to date.

For the typical corporation (identified in the tax code as a "C" corporation) there is presently no difference in the tax rate on capital gains, 1245 gains, 1250 gains, or ordinary income. Therefore all four types of income are taxed at the same rate, roughly 35 percent. There is currently, and will probably always be, talk of reinstating lower rates on corporate 1245 and 1250 gains and losses to encourage businesses to invest in these hard assets. The actual calculation of these gains was explained in detail in the prior chapter in a section on asset disposal.

For partnerships, individuals, and "S" corporations, there are special rates, depreciation recapture, and gain calculations that apply. Since we are dealing with corporations in this text, we refer you to a tax book or sound tax counsel for these specific cases. In the following paragraphs, we illustrate the application of federal income tax laws over the life cycle of a capital investment, from acquisition through use and eventual disposal.

TAXES APPLYING TO CAPITAL INVESTMENT ACQUISITION

Capital outlays may be in the form of fixed assets such as land, buildings, machinery, airplanes, and furniture; short-term assets such as inventory; or expenses such as advertising campaigns and research. Many capital outlays, such as the introduction of a new product, are combinations of a variety of smaller investments. The tax implications of a capital outlay at the time of acquisition depend on the type of investment being acquired; they are discussed in the following sections.

Outlays Treated as Investments

Capital outlays involving the acquisition of actual assets—land, building, machinery, inventory, securities, and so on—are generally not treated as expenses for tax purposes. The same treatment is applied for certain intangible assets, such as licenses, patent rights, and purchased goodwill. Most of these assets are used up or wear out over time, and the use or wearing out is recognized as a depreciation or amortization expense that reduces taxes. The acquisition cost itself, though, is simply viewed as a change from one type of asset to another, such as from cash to fixed assets, and has no immediate tax implications.

Overhauls. An overhaul extends the life of an existing asset. The overhaul is treated as a capital expenditure for tax purposes and depreciated accordingly. A repair, on the other hand, is treated as an expense for tax purposes.

Investment Tax Credits. Governments periodically introduce investment tax credit programs to spur investment. An investment tax credit reduces the company's tax liability by some percent of the cost of the capital investment. The investment tax credit has come and gone several times in the United States. It was repealed again in 1986.

TABLE 9-2 Cash Outlay for the Additional Gainesville Discount Drug Center to Begin Operations

This example reflects the various cash outlays at the time of acquisition and the tax savings associated with acquisition, which arise from those items categorized as expenses for tax purposes.

Land	$ (250,000)
Building	(1,000,000)
Fixtures	(200,000)
Inventory	(1,000,000)
Advertising & training	(100,000)
Tax savings	$ (34,000)
Total cash flow	$ (2,516,000)

Outlays Treated as Expenses

Some capital investments are treated in the tax code as expenses that reduce taxable income in the period of expenditure even if benefits are anticipated over several years. Training programs and advertising expenses fall in this category, as do many research and development expenses. For example, an established retail store that is starting a new department spends $12,000 on training and $18,000 on advertising. If the company faces a marginal tax rate of 34 percent, these costs will result in a tax savings of ($12,000 + $18,000).34 = $10,200, and the after tax expenditure will be $19,800.

Example: Taxes and cash flows associated with the opening of an additional outlet of Gainesville Discount Drug are summarized in Table 9-2. The land will cost $250,000, the building will cost $1 million, fixtures will cost $200,000, and inventory will cost $1 million. Advertising and training prior to opening will cost $100,000. The company's marginal tax rate is 34 percent. The only expenditures with an immediate tax implication are the advertising and training,[7] which reduce taxes by .34 × $100,000 = $34,000.

Outlays That Must Be Amortized Over Sixty Months

When a business first starts, the original costs of establishing the business, such as legal fees, cost of permits, registration, advertising, and training, are capitalized as organizational cost. The IRS then allows the business to amortize or write these off against income equally over the first 60 months of operation.

[7]If the store is placed in service at or near the end of the company's tax year, depreciation tax savings may occur almost immediately, further reducing the net outlay. These depreciation benefits are discussed in association with tax treatment of ongoing operations.

TAXES APPLYING TO THE OPERATING STAGE

During the operating stage years of a capital project, income tax is affected. Tax rules are similar whether income is being taxed as corporate income or the income of the owner, but there are differences. The treatment of income under corporate tax rules is treated here. Differences in tax treatment when income is taxed as the income of the owner are discussed later in this chapter.

The accrual tax basis approach to measuring taxable income was explained earlier in this chapter and applies to taxation during the operating stage of the capital project. If the investment results in increased revenue, the taxable income from the investment each period is the increase in revenue, minus any increase in expenses. Some capital investments result in no new revenue but result in a net decrease in expenses. The reduction of expenses also increases taxable income, in most cases.

Depreciation

Depreciation is a particularly important expense for capital investment analysis. It was introduced in the prior chapter but we will review depreciation in greater detail here as it applies to taxes. Assets that wear out over time and are not bought or sold in the normal course of business are depreciated. Depreciation is a process of recognizing this wearing out, and the resultant loss of value, as an expense each period. This expense reduces taxable income. Depreciation has been a part of the tax law since 1913, with each type of asset assigned a life and then depreciated over that life using one of several approved formulas. Depreciation rates for most assets are currently governed by the Modified Accelerated Cost Recovery System that was introduced and discussed in Chapter 8.

Example: Continuing with the Gainesville Discount Drug Center example developed in the prior section, that same store can be used to summarize taxation during the operating stage of an asset's useful life. Assume the store was placed in service January 1, 2004, and sales were $1 million in 2004. The cost of goods sold was $700,000 and other expenses, excluding depreciation, were $100,000. The building is a 39-year asset, and the fixtures are 7-year assets. Depreciation on the building and fixtures for 2004 was therefore:

$$\text{Building: } \$1{,}000{,}000(11.5/12)(1/39) = \$24{,}572$$

$$\text{Fixtures: } \$200{,}000 \times .1429 = 28{,}580$$

Earnings before tax from operations for 2004 were therefore:

Sales	$1,000,000
Cost of goods sold	700,000
Operating expenses	100,000
Depreciation—Building	24,572
Depreciation—Fixtures	28,580
Earnings before tax	$ 146,848

If the company was taxed at 34 percent, the income tax owed would be $.34 \times 146{,}848 = \$49{,}928$.

Note from Table 9-2 that advertising and training expenses of $100,000 reduced taxes by $34,000 at opening time. The advertising and training expenses would affect either 2003 or 2004 taxes, depending on the year in which the expenditures occurred. Taxes associated with acquisition and taxes over the operating life are separated for convenience of discussion, not necessarily because the taxes occur in different years. It is, for example, possible that the $49,928 tax liability for the first year of operations and the $34,000 tax savings from start-up expenditures both occur in the same tax year, meaning the *net* tax for the first year is $49,928 – $34,000 = $15,928.

Other Depreciation Rules. Assets acquired prior to the enactment of each new tax law continue to be depreciated under the rules in effect at the time of acquisition. The tax code also specifies alternate depreciation rules that result in slower depreciation. These rules, which may be used if the company desires, are required in certain situations, such as when an asset is used outside the country for more than half of the year. For depreciation under these other rules, see a specialized tax guide, such as the *Federal Tax Course,* published annually by Commerce Clearing House.

Choosing a Depreciation Method

When there is a choice between depreciation methods, you will prefer the method that maximizes the present value of depreciation tax savings. If the tax rate is expected to be the same each year, MACRS depreciation will be preferred over straight line because the MACRS method provides the depreciation tax savings sooner. If the tax rate is expected to increase in the future, the depreciation methods should be compared on a present value basis.

Example: Jacksonville Machine Tool will acquire a special cutting die for $10,000 on January 1, 2004. The die will have a 3-year life for tax purposes. The company's marginal tax rate is expected to be 15 percent in 2004 and 2005, but is expected to be 34 percent in later years. Depreciation amounts and their present values are shown in Table 9-3. The company's required return is 10 percent. Tax payments are treated as year-end payments for simplicity. Because the tax rate will be higher in later years, the present value of depreciation tax savings is maximized in this case by choosing the straight-line method.

In this example, it is $321 better (in present value terms $1,878 – $1,557 = $321) for Jacksonville Machine Tool to use straight-line depreciation than the quicker MACRS depreciation. This is due to the fact that in the first 2 years Jacksonville will have a lower tax rate than in the later 2 years.

Alternate Minimum Tax

The alternate minimum tax (AMT) is a special aspect of the Tax Reform Act of 1986. Essentially, the AMT law requires corporations to compute two incomes:

TABLE 9-3 Analysis of Straight-Line and MACRS Depreciation

Present values of depreciation tax savings for a $10,000 asset are computed using both straight-line and MACRS depreciation. The company's tax rate is expected to be 15 percent in the first 2 years and 34 percent in the second 2 years. Required return is 10 percent.

YEAR	STRAIGHT-LINE DEPRECIATION	TAX SAVINGS	PRESENT VALUE FACTOR	PRESENT VALUE
2004	(1/6)10,000 = 1,667	1,667(.15) = 250	.9091	$ 227
2005	(1/3)10,000 = 3,333	3,333(.15) = 500	.8264	413
2006	(1/3)10,000 = 3,333	3,333(.34) = 1,133	.7513	851
2007	(1/6)10,000 = 1,667	1,667(.34) = 567	.6830	387
Present value of depreciation tax savings:				$1,878

YEAR	MACRS ACCELERATED DEPRECIATION	TAX SAVINGS	PRESENT VALUE FACTOR	PRESENT VALUE
2004	(.3333)10,000 = 3,333	3,333(.15) = 500	.9091	$ 455
2005	(.4444)10,000 = 4,444	4,444(.15) = 667	.8264	551
2006	(.1482)10,000 = 1,482	1,482(.34) = 504	.7513	379
2007	(.0741)10,000 = 741	741(.34) = 252	.6830	172
Present value of depreciation tax savings:				$1,557

regular income and alternate minimum income. A corporation earning over $18,333,333 is taxed at the higher rate of:

- 35 percent of regular income, or
- 20 percent of alternate minimum income

The alternate minimum income is computed by adding certain items, called **tax preferences or adjustments,** to regular income. There are over a dozen preference or adjustment items, but the ones of particular interest for capital investment are:[8]

- Excess of accelerated cost recovery depreciation over the Alternative Depreciation System (ADS)
- Seventy-five percent of the excess of adjusted current earnings (book income) over alternative minimum tax income.

[8]Others include difference between accelerated cost recovery depreciation and straight-line depreciation for real estate, excess of expensed R&D over R&D if amortization is used, deferred income under completed-contract method of accounting for long-term contracts, excess of percentage depletion over the adjusted basis of the property, net corporate capital gains not otherwise included, tax-exempt interest, profit deferred by using the installment method of accounting, untaxed appreciation on charitable contributions, and excess of financial institution bad-debt deduction over that allowed under experience method.

The Alternative Depreciation System is less accelerated than regular (MACRS) depreciation and is based on the actual estimated useful life of the assets. This ADS applies only to assets with a 3-, 5-, 7-, or 10-year MACRS life.

The alternate minimum tax provides a good example of how companies modify plans to minimize taxes. Many leasing plans are motivated by the alternate minimum tax. W. H. Sparrow, treasurer of CSX Corporation, estimates that the company saves $1,000 a year in taxes for every boxcar it leases instead of purchases. A statement by Mr. Nevitt of Bank Ameri-lease further highlights the importance of this type of planning to American business: "We're normally slack this time of year, but because of leasing volume to avoid the new tax act, six of our leasing specialists have had to cancel their ski vacations."[9]

Operating Loss Carry-Back and Carry-Forward

If a company experiences negative ordinary income some year, the loss can be carried back 2 years and then carried forward for up to 20 years or just carried forward for 20 years to offset taxable income.

Example: The ordinary income and taxes on that income for Atlanta Southern Corporation follow. The company paid income tax in the first 3 years, using a 15 percent tax rate. Then, the company had negative ordinary income of $100,000 in 2007. The company first used $30,000 of the 2007 loss to offset 2005 income. Next, it used $20,000 to offset 2006 income. As a result, the company qualified for a refund of the tax paid in those 2 years: $7,500. The total ordinary income for those 2 years was $50,000, so $50,000 of the 2007 loss remains unused. That amount can be carried forward for a maximum of 20 years and subtracted from ordinary income for future years, until it is used up, to reduce tax liabilities in those years.

YEAR	2004	2005	2006	2007
Taxable ordinary income	$20,000	$30,000	$20,000	-$100,000
Income tax	3,000	4,500	3,000	-10,500

TAXES APPLYING TO THE DISPOSITION STAGE

The final stage in the life cycle of a capital investment is the liquidation or sale of assets. Like every other stage in the life cycle, taxes are an important part of the picture and must be taken into account. Taxes differ somewhat between disposition under corporate taxation and disposition if the business income is treated as personal income of the owners, partners, and S corporation shareholders. Corporate taxation is treated here, and personal taxation is covered later.

Capital Gains and Losses

The major types of capital gains and losses are summarized in Table 9-4.

[9]Berton, "Surprise Loophole."

TABLE 9-4 Types of Gains and Losses

This table summarizes the categories of capital gains and losses under current tax law.

GAINS	LOSSES
CAPITAL OR 1231 GAINS	CAPITAL OR 1231 LOSSES
Excess of sale price over cost for nondepreciable assets not regularly bought or sold in the course of business, such as stock, bonds, and land	Amount by which sale prices of these same assets fall below cost
1250 GAINS	1250 LOSSES
Excess of sale price over remaining basis for real estate	Amount by which the sale price falls below cost for real estate used in the business
1245 GAINS	1245 LOSSES
Excess of sale price over original basis for depreciable assets other than real estate used in the business	Amount by which the sale price falls below cost for depreciable assets other than real estate used in the business

For individuals, there is a $3,000 annual capital loss allowance. For corporations, capital or 1231 losses must first be subtracted from capital or 1231 gains. 1250 losses must be matched first against 1250 gains and then any remainder is matched against capital or 1231 gains or losses. And 1245 losses are treated the same way. In the end everything is rolled into a 1231 capital gain or loss category, which is taxed presently at the same rates as ordinary income. If capital losses exceed capital gains in any year, the excess must be carried back 3 years to offset past capital gains. If there are not enough prior capital gains in the prior 3 years, the excess capital loss can be carried forward for a maximum of 5 years.[10]

Example: Boca Raton Development placed a copier (a 5-year asset) in service in 2004, with an original basis of $100,000. The asset was then sold for $90,000 at the beginning of 2006. Common stock of another corporation that had been purchased for $50,000 was sold for $30,000 in 2006, and the company had no other gains or losses on the sale of assets. The tax implications are as follows:

COPIER		COMMON STOCK	
Original basis for copier	$100,000	Sale price	$30,000
–$2004 depreciation	20,000	Purchase price	50,000
–$2005 depreciation	32,000	Capital loss	$20,000
= Remaining basis	$ 48,000		
1245 gain ($90,000 – $48,000)	$ 42,000		

[10]When an asset is traded in a like-kind exchange rather than being sold at the end of its life, no taxable gains or losses are created.

The capital loss on the stock sale, \$20,000[11] can be used to offset the 1245 gain on the copier sale. Because capital losses can eventually be offset against 1245 gains, the company must pay regular income tax on \$22,000 of additional income.

Trade-Ins

When an asset is traded in on a like-kind new asset rather than being sold and no additional debt is involved in the trade-in, no immediate tax consequences occur. The basis of the new asset is the remaining basis (original cost – depreciation) of the asset traded in, plus the additional amount paid.

Example: Athens Corporation bought a machine several years ago for \$100,000. Since then, the company has claimed \$56,270 of MACRS depreciation expense. The machine is now traded in on a new model. The new model was priced at \$170,000, but the dealer will give a trade-in allowance of \$60,000. The basis for the new machine is determined as follows:

Payment in addition to trade-in = 170,000 – 60,000 =	\$110,000
+ Remaining basis for trade-in = 100,000 – 56,270 =	\$ 43,730
= Basis for the new machine	\$153,730

If the new machine has a 7-year life for tax purposes, application of the MACRS depreciation rates in the prior chapter gives acquisition-year depreciation of:

$$.1429 \times \$153{,}730 = \$21{,}968$$

REPLACEMENT DECISIONS IN THE PRESENCE OF TAXES

Replacement decisions must be treated carefully because of their unique cash-flow implications. Replacement decisions fall in three general categories:

a. Replacement of a worn-out asset that has a sale value
b. Replacement of a worn-out asset that has a trade-in value different from the sale value
c. Replacement of a usable asset with another asset

Decisions in category (a) present no new problems. If an asset can no longer be used, but can be sold, that sale price is available whether or not a new asset is acquired, and therefore does not meet the definition of a relevant cash flow. Categories (b) and (c) are discussed in the following sections.

---

[11]The Revenue Reconciliation Act of 1993 allowed for the exclusion of 50 percent of the gain on the sale of stock of certain "qualified small business stock." This stock must be issued after August 10, 1993, and at the time of issuance the corporation cannot be larger than \$50,000,000 in gross assets. There are many additional requirements that must be met to qualify for this treatment.

Replacement with a Trade-In Value Different from the Sale Value

In some cases, though, there is an opportunity to trade in the asset for a higher value than would be available with a simple sale. The difference between the trade-in value and the sale value, adjusted for tax implications, would be a reduction in the relevant cost of the new asset.

Example: Quincy Excavation has a worn-out, fully depreciated back-hoe that can be sold for scrap at a price of $1,000. Alternately, a dealer will allow a $1,200 trade-in on the cost of a new $20,000 back-hoe. The new back-hoe will have a physical life of 10 years, but will be depreciated on a straight-line basis (using a midyear convention) over a 5-year period for tax purposes. It will generate earnings before depreciation and tax of $5,000 a year, and will have an estimated salvage value of $0. Straight-line tax depreciation is used for simplicity of illustration. The new back-hoe will be placed in service December 31, 2004, so an immediate depreciation tax savings would occur. Quincy Excavation's marginal income tax rate is 34 percent. The relevant cash flows are shown in Table 9-5.

TABLE 9-5 Relevant Cash Flows for a Back-hoe Purchase

A back-hoe can be purchased for $20,000. The old, fully depreciated back-hoe can be sold outright for $1,000 or traded in for a trade-in allowance of $1,200. A back-hoe will generate earnings before depreciation and tax of $5,000 and the company is in a 34 percent tax bracket.

YEAR	2004	2005–2008	2009	2010–2013
Earnings before dep. and tax	0	$5,000	$5,000	$5,000
–Depreciation[a]	1,880	3,760	1,880	
= Earnings before tax	–1,880	1,240	3,120	5,000
– Income tax payments		422	1,061	1,700
+ Income tax savings	639			
Net income	–1,241	818	2,059	3,300
+ Depreciation	1,880	3,760	1,880	
Cash flow	639	4,578	3,939	3,300
Purchase price	$20,000			
Less trade-in allowance	1,200			
Net cost	18,800			
Plus forgone sale of old[b]	660			
Net acquisition outlay[c]	19,460			
Net relevant cash flow	–$18,821	$4,578	$3,939	$3,300

[a] Basis for depreciation is $18,800 paid, plus the remaining basis of the asset traded in ($0 in this case).

[b] $1,000 – (.34 × $1,000).

[c] Although all 2004 cash flows are shown in one column, this does not imply that all 2004 cash flows occur at the same time. The acquisition flows will generally precede operating cash flows, and those timing differences must be taken into account in the present value calculations.

Replacement of One Usable Asset with a New Asset

Replacement of a usable asset with a new asset can present complications, particularly if the new asset has a life different from the remaining life of the existing usable asset. The trick in solving these problems is not in identifying marginal cash costs, but in deciding which alternatives should be assigned which costs. Errors often occur when the sale price of the old asset is deducted from the cost of the new asset, rather than being treated as an opportunity cost of using the old asset. The principles of cost assignment for those problems were developed in Chapter 7. The following example extends that analysis by treating the tax implications in such settings.

Example: Muncie Corporation has an old, fully depreciated machine that can be sold for $7,500 or repaired at a cost of $500 and used another 3 years, after which it will be worthless. Operating costs will be $1,000 a year. The relevant cash costs and net present value (at a 10 percent required return assuming year-end cash flows) to use this machine for 3 years are shown in Table 9-6. Muncie is in the 34 percent tax bracket.

As an alternative, Muncie Corporation can buy a new machine for $10,000. The entire cost of the new machine will be recognized as an expense in the year of acquisition as allowed under current tax law for very small businesses (and to

TABLE 9-6 Analysis of a Repair Option for Muncie Corporation

A fully depreciated asset can be sold today for $7,500 or repaired for $500 and used for 3 years, after which it will be worthless. Operating costs will be $1,000 each year. The required return is 10 percent.

YEAR	0	1–3
Operating expense		$1,000
Tax savings from operating expense		340
Net operating expense		660
Forgone sale price	$7,500	
Less tax on sale	2,550	
Forgone net proceeds from sale	4,950	
Repair cost	500	
Tax savings from repair	170	
Net repair cost	330	
Relevant cash costs	$5,280	$ 660
Present value factor	1.0000	2.4869
Present value	5,280	1,641

Total present value = $6,921

simplify the illustration). The new machine will last for 12 years, will cost $900 a year to operate, and will have no salvage value at the end of 12 years. The relevant cash flows and net present value are as follows:

YEAR	0	1–12
Operating cost		$900
Tax savings		306
Net operating cost		594
Cost of the new machine	$10,000	
Tax savings from purchase	3,400	
Net cost to purchase	6,600	
Relevant cash costs	$6,600	$594
Present value factor	1.0000	6.8137
Present value	6,600	4,047
Total present value = $10,647		

The present values of the net costs for the repair and replacement alternatives are $6,921 and $10,647 respectively. We assume for this example that the benefits are the same, and we are simply considering two ways of achieving those benefits. We also assume that services of these types will be needed in the future so that the repaired item can be replaced with a new machine (or another similar used machine) at the end of its 3-year life. With these assumptions, the equivalent annuity can be used to find an annual cost of providing whatever service these machine alternatives provide:

Alternative	PV of net costs ÷ $PVA1_{n,10\%}$ = Equivalent annual cost
Repair	6,921 ÷ 2.4869 = $2,783
Replace	10,647 ÷ 6.8137 = $1,563

Assuming a long-term need for the service of the asset, the replacement alternative is more attractive than the repair alternative because, if it were repeated on a continual basis, it would result in a lower present value of total cost.

As a rule we replace an asset when the net present value to the firm of continuing with the present asset is less than the net present value to the firm of acquiring and using the new asset. The existing asset can have value but it is replaced if this value is less than the value added by the new asset. In the previous example the equivalent cost of running the old asset was $2,783 while the equivalent cost of the replacement was $1,563. The present value of the firm is increased by the replacement of the old asset.

To see the importance of proper cost and benefit allocation, suppose we had subtracted the sales price of the old asset from the cost of the new asset. The equivalent annuities for the repair and replacement alternatives would then be:

Repair	$[330 + (660 \times 2.4869)]/2.4869 = \$793$
Replace	$[(10{,}000 - 7{,}500).66 + (594 \times 6.8137)]/6.8137 = \$836$

We would erroneously choose the repair over the replacement alternative even though its annual cost is almost twice as high when properly evaluated. A way to look at this problem that leads to the right assignment of relevant costs is to assume that the old machine was not owned now, but could be bought for $7,500. This is not economically different from the use of a machine that could be sold for $7,500.

CORPORATE INCOME AND TAXATION OF OWNERS

A corporation is a separate entity for tax purposes and pays taxes on its income as previously discussed. The owners are not taxed on their shares of the company's income and cannot deduct their shares of the company's losses from their taxable income. Owners are only required to recognize the dividends they receive as taxable income.

An exception to the above rule, known as the **dividend exclusion rule,** occurs when one corporation holds the stock of another corporation. Under this rule a corporation holding less than a 20 percent share of another corporation can exclude from income 70 percent of the dividend income received. Corporations holding 20 to 79 percent of another corporation's stock can exclude 80 percent of the dividend income received. If the company has 80 percent or more ownership, 100 percent is excluded from the receiving corporation's taxable income.

The owners of a business that is earning profits and retaining most of the profits to finance further growth would generally prefer that the business be taxed as a corporation because owners are not required to pay personal taxes on any of the income that is retained by the company. If the company is paying all its profits to the shareholders in the form of dividends, double taxation occurs; corporate income tax is paid on the income, then the remainder is taxed again as dividend income of the owners.[12] In this situation, the owners would prefer a form that caused the income to be taxed only once. In addition, the owners of a corporation that suffers losses cannot deduct those losses from their other income and might, therefore, prefer a form of organization that allows them to take advantage of the company's losses. The organization forms discussed in the following paragraphs avoid corporate tax by requiring the owners to be taxed on all of the businesses' income, but also allow the owners to deduct the losses of the businesses from their personal income from other sources.

---

[12]The Jobs and Growth Tax Relief Reconciliation Act of 2003 reduced the dividend tax to 5 percent or 15 percent for stock held for 60 days surrounding key dividend dates for qualifying dividends. Even with this lower double taxation, it is still double taxation.

BUSINESSES NOT TAXED AS CORPORATIONS

Several business forms that avoid corporate income tax are discussed in this section. Following this, the tax rules for income treated as personal income of the owners are outlined. Then, considerations leading to a choice of tax form are discussed.

Other Organizational Forms of Business

Proprietorship. If you decide to go into business and will be the sole owner of the business, the proprietorship form of organization can be used. The business is not recognized as a separate entity for tax or other legal purposes. The profits or losses of the business are simply treated as your personal income or losses as owner, and taxed accordingly.

Ordinary Partnership. The ordinary partnership form of business is similar to the proprietorship, except that the business has more than one owner. The owners do not apply for a corporate charter, which would give the business legal status as a separate entity. For tax purposes, the income and losses of the business are divided equally or by some other formula agreed to by the owners. The owners then pay tax on their shares of the business income (or have their taxable income reduced by the amount of their share of the losses), regardless of whether any income is actually distributed to them. The partnership form is attractive for a business that is expected to suffer losses in its early years.

Limited Partnership. A disadvantage of the ordinary partnership is that partners are fully liable for claims against the business in the event of its failure. In a limited partnership, certain investors, designated limited partners, put up money but take no part in running the business. In the event of default, these limited partners are not liable to creditors, and cannot lose more than their original investment. However, the limited partners are still able to deduct their share of the losses of the business up to their share of gains from other businesses. Because the IRS considers limited partnerships passive investments, investors must offset passive losses against passive gains. Real estate ventures and other businesses commonly referred to as "tax shelters" are generally set up as limited partnerships, with the general partner being a corporation.[13]

S Corporations. An S corporation has a charter from the state, like any other corporation, but is treated like a partnership for income tax purposes. This arrangement allows owners of a business to enjoy the benefits of limited personal liability offered by a corporation while enjoying the tax benefits of a partnership. An S corporation can have no more than seventy-five shareholders, so this form is generally limited to relatively small businesses. Many businesses are

[13]In the Tax Reform Act of 1986, the losses from many partnerships are classified as "passive losses." These losses can be used only to offset income from similar activities.

started as S corporations so that early losses can be used to reduce the taxable income of investors holding the stock, and then converted to regular "C" corporation tax status when they become profitable.

TAXATION OF PERSONAL INCOME

Personal tax rules are important for both investment and financing decisions of businesses. Partnership, proprietorship, and S corporate income is taxed at personal tax rates. Furthermore, the tax status of investors is important if you are planning the financing mix for a regular C corporation. The major components of taxable income for an individual (or household paying tax as a unit) are shown in Table 9-7.

Like corporations, individuals face a progressive tax structure, with the tax *rate* rising as income rises. Current tax laws have an initial 10 percent rate that increases to 15, 25, 28, 33 percent and tops out at 35 percent on income over approximately $300,000. The actual tax brackets applicable for each percentage have been adjusted for inflation yearly since 1988 and are scheduled to change at different intervals through 2010. After 2010 all of the existing legislation concerning the reduction in rates from the 2001 levels is scheduled to expire if not extended or modified by Congress.

Taxation of Gains and Losses on Sale of Assets. Gains or losses on the sale of assets are treated slightly differently for individuals than for corporations. Gains on the sale of depreciable assets held for more than 12 months are subject to the recapture of MACRS depreciation. Losses are not subject to recapture. Most of these gains and losses receive capital gains treatment. The maximum capital gains tax rate for individuals is currently 15 percent. But this is scheduled

TABLE 9-7 Calculation of Personal Taxable Income

This table summarizes the components of taxable personal income under current tax law.

Wages
+ Interest and dividend income
± Taxpayer's share of profit or loss from a partnership or proprietorship
+ Other categories of income such as rents and royalties
= Gross income
– Qualified deductions
= Adjusted gross income
– Personal exemptions
– Itemized deductions[a] or standard deduction, whichever is greater
= TAXABLE INCOME

[a]Primarily interest expense for a home mortgage, charitable contributions, medical expenses beyond some percent of income, and some taxes paid to state and local governments.

to revert back to 20 percent in 2009. Capital losses can be used to offset capital gains. Any net capital loss, after netting against capital gains, can be deducted from ordinary income up to a maximum of $3,000 per year. Any remaining amount can be carried forward indefinitely.

STATE AND LOCAL INCOME TAXES

Many state and municipal governments levy income taxes in addition to the federal income tax. These taxes are hardly trivial, as evidenced by the $325 million in tax concessions Toyota negotiated in developing plans for an automobile factory in Kentucky. State and local income taxes are generally a percentage of income taxable for federal tax purposes. State and local taxes other than sales tax are deducted in arriving at taxable income for federal taxes, so the *effective* state and local income tax rate is the state and local income tax rate multiplied by (1 – federal tax rate).

NON-INCOME TAXES

Businesses are subject to a number of taxes besides income tax. Property taxes levied by state and local governments must often be considered when evaluating capital investments, as must excise taxes (taxes based on amount sold), extraction taxes levied on mineral removal, and personnel-related taxes such as social security, unemployment, and workmen's compensation. These taxes vary by state and locality as well as by type of business, so generalization is difficult. If one is moving into a new locale or type of business, information about local and industry-specific taxes must be obtained. This frequently means turning to tax experts in the area.

CHOICE OF TAX FORM

Organizational form, like depreciation methods, can be chosen to minimize the present value of taxes. Taxes are computed for both a corporate and a personal tax form, and then the form with the lower present value of taxes is chosen.

Example: C. Jones is starting a new business on January 1, 2004. His income from other sources is such that Jones's marginal tax rate is 28 percent. Jones has a choice between setting up the business as an ordinary C corporation or an S corporation. Jones, who will be the sole stockholder, plans to plow all profits back into this business for the foreseeable future. Income before tax and taxes paid using the S form and corporate form are in Table 9-8. Year-end cash flows are assumed, and the required return is 10 percent.

In this example, the benefit of being able to use the 2004 loss to reduce personal income tax is more than offset by the higher tax rate that Jones must pay on later income; the present value of taxes is lower using the corporation tax form.

TABLE 9-8 Corporate and Personal Income Tax Example

This table is a present value comparison of taxes that would be paid on the income from a business if taxed as corporate income and if taxed as personal income.

PERSONAL TAX—S CORPORATION

YEAR	2004	2005	2006	2007	2008
Income before tax	−50,000	0	30,000	40,000	80,000
Personal income tax on income	−14,000	0	8,400	11,200	22,400
Present value factor	.9091	.8264	.7513	.6830	.6209
Present value	−12,727	0	6,311	7,650	13,908

Total present value of income tax = $15,142

CORPORATE TAX—C CORPORATION

YEAR	2004	2005	2006	2007	2008
Income before tax	−50,000	0	30,000	40,000	80,000
Tax loss carry-forward	—	—	30,000	20,000	—
Taxable income	—	—	—	20,000	80,000
Income tax paid	—	—	—	3,000	15,450
Present value factor				.6830	.6209
Present value				$2,049	$9,593

Total present value of income tax = $11,642

Another alternative is available though. Jones could start the company as an S corporation and convert to regular C corporation tax in 2006. Using this approach, the taxes would be as follows:

YEAR	2004	2005	2006	2007	2008
Income before tax	−50,000	0	30,000	40,000	80,000
Personal income tax	−14,000				
Corporate income tax			4,500	6,000	15,450
Present value factor	−.9091	.8264	.7513	.6830	.6209
Present value	−12,727	0	3,381	4,098	9,593

Total present value = $4,345

Using present value analysis, the best choice in this example is to start out as an S corporation and then switch to regular C corporate tax form by 2006.

TIMING OF TAX PAYMENTS

The exact timing of tax payments is sometimes important for present value analysis. Corporations are required to make estimated tax payments on the 15th day of the fourth, sixth, ninth, and twelfth months of their fiscal year (April 15, June 15, September 15, and December 15 for calendar-year payers). These payments must generally be equal in size and total the lesser of 100 percent of the prior year's taxes or 100 percent of the current year's taxes.

Individuals paying tax on a calendar-year basis must make estimated tax payments on April 15, June 15, September 15 of the current year, and then January 15 of the following year. These payments, combined with any additional income tax withheld from wages, must generally be equal and must generally total 90 percent of the tax liability for the year or 100 percent of the prior year's tax liability, with the balance due April 15 of the following year. For individuals earning over $150,000, the floor is raised to 110 percent of the prior year's taxes.

Tax payments and benefits are sometimes delayed because of disputes with the Internal Revenue Service. It took Herb Alpert and Lani Hall 10 years, for example, to get a court ruling in their favor for the depreciation schedule for their Hyatt Hotel near the Los Angeles Airport.[14]

FOREIGN CAPITAL INVESTMENT

Tax rates differ markedly from country to country, and businesses sometimes operate multinationals to take advantage of tax rate differences. Some countries give tax incentives to attract business, and companies may be able to allocate income among countries by changing the price at which goods they produce in one country are sold to a division in another country: for example, engines built in Mexico and imported to the United States for assembly into cars. In addition, import duties are avoided by producing in the country in which the goods are to be sold. By constructing a Honda plant in Marysville, Ohio, Honda avoided shipping costs, import duties, as well as decreasing its exchange rate risk and improving its public image with U.S. consumers. It was estimated by a tax study group, for example, that over a third of the jobs in Puerto Rico were accounted for by companies moving there to get breaks on their federal taxes.

Taxes and International Investment Analysis

Corporations doing business in more than one country typically pay tax in each country. Taxation by the U.S. government of multinational corporation income is treated first, followed by taxation by foreign countries.

---

[14] *Wall Street Journal* (April 1, 1987): 1.

Taxation by the U.S. Government. If foreign activities of a U.S. corporation are carried out through a division that is not separately incorporated, all income is taxed as U.S. income, just as if it were earned in the United States. Foreign subsidiaries are frequently used for this reason. The U.S. corporation is then simply a stockholder—possibly the only stockholder—of a foreign corporation. Income is taxed in the United States only when it is paid to the U.S. parent in the form of dividends. Unlike income received by a corporation from another domestic corporation, dividends from the foreign subsidiary are not eligible for dividend exclusion and are fully taxable income.[15]

Taxation by Foreign Countries. It is more difficult to summarize taxation by foreign countries. Virtually all countries tax income of foreign companies operating in their country. But methods of measuring income and methods of deciding what income was earned in what country vary widely. Developed countries charge higher tax rates while less developed countries often charge lower tax rates to encourage business. Property tax, sales tax, and so on, are also common. Value added tax is common in Europe. The value added tax is similar to a sales tax, except that it is applied to the increase in value rather than total value. If you buy bicycle parts for a total cost of $50 and sell the finished bicycle for $120, you pay a value added tax on $70.

Coordination of Taxes between Countries. When a U.S. corporation pays income tax to a foreign government, its U.S. tax on that income is reduced by the amount paid to the foreign government. Suppose, for example, that a corporation earns $1 million in Malaysia and pays Malaysian income tax of $300,000. The company's U.S. tax on that income would be $340,000. But U.S. tax is reduced by the $300,000 paid to Malaysia, so only $40,000 is paid to the U.S. government. Similar provisions apply to dividends received from foreign subsidiaries, but property taxes, sales taxes, and so on, are not offset. The United States has treaties with many countries governing the amount of tax collected from corporations by each country.

Estimating Cash Flows from International Capital Investments

The estimation of cash flows from international capital investments is not essentially different from that of domestic investments. In both cases, we are looking for increases in revenue, expense, and balance sheet accounts. Additional considerations faced when computing the cash-flow effects of international capital investments include exchange rate changes and restrictions on capital flows. We will consider both of these aspects of international investment analysis in the following paragraphs.

---

[15]In some cases, the domestic corporation will be required to pay tax on unrepatriated income of the subsidiary. This results from rules designed to discourage use of foreign subsidiaries solely to avoid tax.

Exchange Rates and International Cash-Flow Analysis

A U.S. corporation must evaluate capital investments in terms of their ultimate ability to generate cash flows for stockholders in the United States, and exchange rates are a key factor in that evaluation. Once cash flows from a foreign business are forecasted in the currency of the foreign country, they can be converted to U.S. dollars based on the expected exchange rate. Assume that the South Korean won is valued at $0.001237. Thus, 1 billion won would be converted to 1 billion times .001237 or $1,237,000. Unfortunately, exchange rates are highly volatile, and it is extremely difficult to predict future exchange rates. Thus, prediction of the dollar value of future cash flows is difficult. Methods of analyzing and dealing with exchange rate risk are treated in the next chapter.

Repatriation and International Cash-Flow Analysis

The analysis is sometimes confused by uncertainty as to whether cash flows for a capital investment will be reinvested in the foreign country or repatriated. As long as there are no restrictions on cash flows, though, analysis of a capital investment does not depend on the country in which earnings from that investment will be used. A new investment in Italy will be equally attractive whether funded by dollars that could be converted to lira or lira that could be converted to dollars.

Example: American International Motors (AIM) is an American corporation that specializes in automobile dealerships in foreign countries. AIM is considering a Cadillac dealership in Riyadh, Saudi Arabia, to be incorporated as a wholly owned subsidiary. The dealership will require a capital outlay of 17.5 million riyal. The current exchange rate is $0.2667 per riyal, and the riyal is expected to increase in value 5 percent a year against the dollar. Sales are expected to be 37.5 million riyal a year, and cash flow after Saudi tax is expected to be 15 percent of sales. This cash flow will be paid to the U.S. parent corporation as year-end dividends, and then taxed at the 34 percent tax rate. Management wants to use a 5-year planning horizon and a 15 percent required return. It is assumed that the after tax salvage value, after all taxes, will be $3 million. The present value analysis of this investment appears in Table 9-9.

Suppose AIM anticipates starting another dealership in Jidda within a few years. Cash flows from the Riyadh dealership could be used to fund the Jidda dealership, but that possibility does not affect the attractiveness of the Riyadh dealership. The analysis of the Jidda dealership is the same whether based on riyal that could be converted to dollars or dollars that will be converted to riyal.

The picture is more complicated when there are restrictions on repatriation of profits. These restrictions may be absolute or may be in the form of taxes to discourage repatriation. In these cases, the attractiveness of investments still depends on cash flows for the company's stockholders, given these restrictions. An absolute, permanent restriction on repatriation makes a foreign investment worthless. In the case of taxes or temporary restrictions, cash flow going into a country must be evaluated in light of the expected cash flows back out of that

TABLE 9-9 Present Value Analysis of Riyadh Automobile Dealership

This table shows the present value analysis of an automobile dealership in Riyadh, assuming a 5 percent annual increase in the value of the riyal (numbers are in thousands).

RIYAL VALUE	2004 $0.2667	2005 $0.2800	2006 $0.2940	2007 $0.3087	2008 $0.3242	2009 $0.3404
Sales (riyal)	37,500	37,500	37,500	37,500	37,500	
Outlay (riyal)	17,500					
Riyal flow	(17,500)	5,625	5,625	5,625	5,625	5,625
Dollar flow	($4,667)	$1,575	$1,654	$1,737	$1,823	$1,915
U.S. tax		536	562	590	620	651
Salvage						3,000
U.S. flow	($4,667)	$1,040	$1,092	$1,146	$1,204	$4,264
P.V. factor (15%)	1.0000	0.8696	0.7561	0.6575	0.5718	0.4972
Present value	($4,667)	$ 904	$ 825	$ 753	$ 688	$2,120
NPV = $624						

country. This may force investments to be interrelated when they would otherwise be independent.

Example: Suppose that Saudi Arabia places restrictions on capital flows such that funds cannot be taken out of the country before 2004. The Riyadh dealership would then be evaluated based on the present value of cash flows in 2004. To complete this analysis, it is necessary to make an assumption about rates of return that can be earned when cash flows from the dealership are reinvested in Saudi Arabia. Suppose the opportunity rate is expected to average 6 percent. The net present value is then determined as follows.

2004 riyal = 5,625FVA1$_{5yrs,6\%}$ =	31,709 riyal
2004 value of riyal	× .3403
2004 dollars	$10,790
–U.S. tax (.34 × 10,790)	3,669
+Salvage value	3,000
Total 2004 dollar flow	$10,121
Present value at 15%	5,032
–Original outlay	4,667
Net present value	$ 365

The temporary restriction on repatriation is not sufficient to make this investment unattractive, but it does cut the net present value almost in half.

SUMMARY

This chapter is a distillation of thousands of pages of laws, regulations, and rulings that focus on the main tax principles affecting capital investments.

At the time a capital investment is made, the investment itself is generally not treated as an expense for tax purposes. This rule holds for both long-term physical assets and working capital. It also holds for intangibles, such as patent rights. The only items that can generally be treated as expenses are things normally recognized as ongoing expenses of a business, such as advertising and training.

During the use life of a capital investment, increases in sales or other revenues are typically the major sources of increased taxable income. Expenses that reduce taxable income include materials, labor, overhead costs, interest, rent, and depreciation. Depreciation is a recognition of the wearing out of an asset and is computed based on guidelines provided by the Internal Revenue Service.

When an asset used in a business is sold at its cost—remaining basis for depreciable assets—the sale generally has no tax implications. When an asset used in a business is sold for more than its remaining basis, the gain is generally an increase in taxable income. If an asset is sold for less than the remaining basis, the loss is a decrease in taxable income.

Companies face many opportunities to control their tax expense. Based on expected income patterns, they can choose between MACRS accelerated and straight-line depreciation. They can choose between being taxed as corporations or having income treated as if it were income of the owners. They can also control the timing of asset sales, and therefore the year in which gains or losses are recognized. The loss carry-back and carry-forward is another of the provisions that can be used in planning. International diversification is another tool used for tax management. Generally this involves recognizing expenses in high tax jurisdiction and profits in low tax jurisdictions. The general objective of a value-maximizing business is to choose the set of tax treatments that maximizes net present value.

Replacement decisions require special care in the identification of relevant cash flows. When an asset is actually worn out, the potential salvage value is not a relevant cost because the asset will be sold regardless. If replacement of a used but usable asset is being considered, the forgone sale price of that asset is a relevant cost of its use.

International capital investments are evaluated in the same general way as domestic capital investments. The primary difference is that the ultimate measure of cash flow is the cash flow that can be repatriated to the home country, in the currency of that home country. The equity residual cash-flow method (discussed in Chapter 4) can be used to evaluate foreign investments because it provides a relatively easy way to deal with the variety of tax differences and exchange rate changes that affect foreign investments.

QUESTIONS

9-1. What are the major additions to the income of a business?

9-2. What are the major expenses that serve to reduce the income of a business?

9-3. Summarize the main tax considerations at the time an asset is acquired.

9-4. What are the tax implications if working capital is liquidated at cost? below cost? above cost?

9-5. If a piece of machinery is sold for more or less than its remaining basis, what are the tax implications?

9-6. Briefly explain the loss carry-back and carry-forward provisions. What types of businesses are helped by these provisions?

9-7. If a corporation pays 40 percent income tax as a corporation, what portion of its income is treated as income of the owners? How could this double taxation of income be avoided?

9-8. Under what conditions would it be preferable to avoid taxation as a corporation and have the income of a business considered income of the owners?

9-9. What are some of the main types of taxes, other than income taxes, that are levied on businesses?

9-10. Under what conditions is the trade-in value of an existing asset relevant in the analysis of a new asset?

PROBLEMS

9-1. Macon Corporation spent $30,000 on training and advertising expenses as part of its development of the new business activity. Dixon Corporation did not spend any money on training and advertising related to its new business activity. Both Macon and Dixon earned $60,000 before training and advertising expenses and both are in the 40 percent tax bracket. What are Macon's taxable income, net income, and cash flow? What are Dixon's taxable income, net income, and cash flow? How much did the $30,000 in training and advertising actually cost Macon in terms of cash flow?

9-2. Pocatello Corporation had sales of $100,000. The cost of goods sold was $60,000, administrative expenses were $20,000, and depreciation was $10,000. What were Pocatello's taxable income, net income, and cash flow?

9-3. Lewiston Corporation placed a $100,000 piece of equipment in service on January 1, 2004. This equipment has a 5-year life for tax purposes. The company's marginal income tax rate is 40 percent. By how much will depreciation reduce 2004 income tax?

9-4. Albion Corporation is taxed on the accrual basis. The company buys inventory for $100 in 2004 and pays for the inventory in 2005. The company spends $50 on advertising in 2005, which results in the sale of the inventory for $200. The inventory is sold on credit, and payment is actually received in 2006. What is the taxable income from these actions in each year?

9-5. Charleston Corporation has a choice between using 5-year MACRS depreciation or straight-line depreciation at the rate of $200,000 per year for the acquisition of a new $1,000,000 computer system. The system will be placed in service in 2004. Charleston expects the marginal tax rates shown below. Using a 10 percent required return, which depreciation method should be chosen?

YEAR	2004	2005	2006	2007	2008	2009
Marginal tax rate	15%	15%	40%	40%	40%	40%

9-6. Fairmont Stores began operations on January 1, 2004 (assets are considered to be placed in service on that date). The store cost $1 million, fixtures cost $200,000 (with a 7-year tax life) and the land cost $200,000, all paid for in 2003. Inventory was acquired on credit terms in 2003 at a cost of $500,000, with payment actually made in 2004. During 2004, additional inventory of $300,000 was acquired, with $200,000 of that inventory actually paid for in 2004. Sales in 2004 were $1 million, with $900,000 of payment actually received; the balance was still due on charge accounts. There was $200,000 worth of inventory still on hand at the end of 2004. Fairmont experienced labor, utility, maintenance, advertising, and insurance expenses totaling $100,000 in 2004, with 90 percent of these expenses paid during the year and the balance still owed. The company is to be taxed as a corporation. Please prepare the 2004 year-end abbreviated balance sheet, income statement, and cash flow statement for Fairmont using accrual tax basis accounting. (Hint: The value of inventory sold during the year equals beginning inventory, plus purchases, minus ending inventory.)

9-7. Sales for Fairmont (problem 6) increase to $1.2 million in 2005, with cost of goods sold being the same percentage of sales as before. Other operating expenses, except depreciation, remain at $100,000. Accounts payable for inventory was $120,000, ending inventory was $220,000, $100,000 in accounts payable for operating expenses, and inventory purchases were $149,000. Please prepare the 2005 year-end abbreviated balance sheet, income statement, and cash flow statement for Fairmont using accrual tax basis accounting.

9-8. In early 2006, Fairmont (problem 6) decided that it needed all new fixtures. Two of the old fixtures were sold for $60,000. What are the tax implications of this sale?

9-9. Suppose the fixtures in problem 8 had been sold for $250,000. What would be the tax implications of the sale?

9-10. Urbana Cleaning Service, Inc., a C corporation, bought its own building for $200,000 on January 1, 2004. Urbana sold the building on January 1, 2007, a year in which Urbana was in the 40 percent marginal tax bracket.

What would be the tax implications if the building was sold for $100,000? $150,000? $250,000?

9-11. Carbondale Corporation places a $100,000, 5-year piece of equipment into service on December 31, 2004. The asset was sold for $20,000 on January 1, 2008, a year in which Carbondale was in the 40 percent marginal tax bracket. What are the tax implications of this sale?

9-12. Interstate Airlines started business in 2004. Taxable income in 2004 through 2008 is shown below, before adjusting for loss carry-back and carry-forward. Determine the income tax that would be paid by Interstate in each year using a 40 percent tax rate.

YEAR	2004	2005	2006	2007	2008
Taxable income	−100,000	−20,000	50,000	100,000	200,000

9-13. Suppose Interstate (problem 12) was organized as an S corporation with stock held by individuals in 28 percent tax brackets.

a. Compute the tax implications each year for the stockholders.

b. Suppose, further, that the company did not intend to pay out any dividends in the foreseeable future. Should it change from S to regular corporate status during this 5-year period? If so, when?

9-14. DeKalb-Normal Corporation received taxable income of $100,000 from its operations in 2004. In addition, the company received dividends of $40,000 from an investment in the stock of another corporation. Compute DeKalb-Normal's income tax liability for 2004. (Assume 50 percent ownership and a 40 percent tax bracket.)

9-15. Peoria Industries, Inc., has income of $100,000 a year. The company is in a state that applies a 5 percent tax to all corporate income over $25,000 and pays state income tax accordingly. What is Peoria's total federal income tax for the year? What is Peoria's marginal income tax rate?

9-16. The average holder of Peoria Industries stock (problem 15) is in a 33 percent combined federal and state income tax bracket and holds stock in a number of other companies. Peoria pays out all of its after tax income in the form of dividends. What is the total of federal and state income tax, both corporate and personal, on Peoria's income? What could Peoria do to reduce this tax burden?

9-17. A farmer near Bloomington owns a combine and uses it to provide harvesting service to other farmers. He receives revenue of $40,000 a year, plus the avoidance of $2,000 in fees he would have to pay someone else to harvest his wheat if he did not own the machine. Fuel and repairs are $10,000 a year and the farmer does not have another profitable use for the time he spends harvesting wheat. Unfortunately, the existing combine is worn out and fully depreciated. It can be sold for its $1,000 spare parts value, but a dealer will allow $5,000 as a trade-in allowance on a new $100,000 combine. The new combine will last for an estimated 10 years, after which it will have a negligible salvage value. The farmer is in a 28 percent tax bracket and requires 10 percent after tax return on investments. Is the new combine an attractive investment? (Assume January 1 installation.)

9-18. Campus Dry-cleaning has an on-campus location with 10 years to go on the lease. An existing dry-cleaning machine will last for the 10-year duration of the lease, at which time it will be worn out and worthless. A new machine will be more efficient and allow the company to handle a broader range of fabrics. As a result, the new machine will increase revenues by $1,500 a year and decrease operating costs other than depreciation by $600 a year. The old machine, which is fully depreciated, could be sold for $6,000 today. The new machine will cost $20,000. The lease is not renewable and the new machine is expected to have a salvage value of $5,000 in 10 years. Campus Dry-cleaning is in a 34 percent tax bracket and the required return on new investments is 10 percent. Should Campus Dry-cleaning acquire the new machine?

9-19. For the new dry-cleaning machine in problem 18, redo the analysis assuming the lease can be renewed indefinitely and the new machine will last 15 years with no salvage value at the end of 15 years.

9-20. A rental house in Iowa City can be purchased for $40,000, with closing to occur on January 1, 2004. Closing costs will be $2,000, half of which will be treated as expenses and half of which will be treated as capital investments. The house can be rented for $450 a month. Insurance, maintenance, and so on, are expected to average $100 a month. The house will be held for 5 years and is not expected to increase or decrease in value. Is this an attractive investment for an investor in a 33 percent tax bracket who wants to earn a 10 percent after tax return?

9-21. For the rental house in problem 20, assume the investor will use $6,000 of his own money and borrow the remaining $36,000 at a 12 percent annual interest rate. The loan has a 30-year maturity and calls for payments of $370.30 at the end of each month. Is the investment attractive if the investor wants to earn a 15 percent return on his equity investment?

9-22. A capital investment costs 1 million New Zealand dollars today and will generate cash flow of 2 million New Zealand dollars in 5 years. The New Zealand dollar is presently worth U.S. $0.5772. Assuming the U.S. company making this investment has a 10 percent cost of capital and does not hedge the exchange rate risk, what is the net present value for each of the following prices of the New Zealand dollar in 5 years?

a. $0.5772
b. $0.75
c. $0.40

9-23. An investment in the United States will cost $1 million and will generate after tax cash flows of $500,000 at the end of each year for 3 years, after deducting income tax of $100,000 a year. By investing in a foreign country, taxes can be cut in half. The cost of capital is 10 percent and exchange rate risk will not be hedged. The value of a unit of the foreign currency in the spot market is $0.50. What is the minimum average value of the foreign currency over the next 3 years that will make the foreign investment more profitable than the domestic alternative?

9-24. At the present time, 7.8 Hong Kong dollars are worth one U.S. dollar. An asset costs 1 million Hong Kong dollars. What is the cost in U.S. dollars?

9-25. The Philippine peso is currently worth $0.04871. A capital investment costs 1 million pesos and provides 2 million pesos at the end of 5 years. If the exchange rate does not change, what is the internal rate of return for a U.S. company acquiring this asset? If the peso declines to .04 by the end of 5 years, what is the internal rate of return for a U.S. company acquiring this asset?

9-26. **(Ethical Considerations)** Section 162(m) of the Revenue Reconciliation Act of 1993 sets a $1 million limit on the deductibility of compensation paid to the chief executive officer and the next four highest-paid managers. This tax does not apply to commissions based on performance, bonuses paid for attaining performance goals approved by the shareholders, and payments to a qualified retirement plan.

a. Assume that there is a competitive market for executives, and that the average compensation package is in excess of $1 million. In terms of wealth, will this provision in the tax law create wealth or shift wealth among the stakeholders? Explain.

b. As a result of this provision, many corporations are placing performance measures in their proxy statements so that bonuses are "performance based" and, thus, exempt from the new provision. Assuming that the performance measures are set at levels at or below current performance, is it ethical for the corporation to include these performance measures in the proxy statements?

c. Is this an ethical role for government or should this be the responsibility of outside directors on the board of directors? Explain.

CASE PROBLEM

B and F Computer Repair (A)

Jane Burns and Carl Foster started a computer store several years ago. The first couple of years were excellent, but then they began to feel the pressure of increasing competition; volume and profit margins plummeted. After paying themselves $20,000 salaries each, they were just breaking even.

Burns and Foster noticed, though, that the computer repair business was not nearly as competitive. Most retailers wanted to sell computers and considered repair an annoyance. Burns and Foster considered leaving the retail business and starting a repair business. They would handle the management and marketing, hiring technicians to do the repairing, primarily on-sight. There were several technical schools offering training in computer repair, so they did not anticipate difficulty in finding trained technicians.

Burns and Foster hired a consultant to help them prepare forecasts and a feasibility study. The consultant charged $3,000 for a study that provided most of the numbers they would need for their final decision.

The test equipment and inventory for each technician would cost approximately $15,000 and $7,000, respectively. The technicians would be required to own their own vehicles. An office and small repair shop space could be rented in an industrial area for $1,000 a month, including rent and utilities. Special inventory and special test equipment at that location would cost $20,000 and $15,000 respectively. This special inventory and test equipment would have a 5-year tax life and could support up to two dozen technicians. Technicians could be hired for $2,000 a month, including fringe benefits and social security tax. The company could bill $50 per hour for a technician's time and could probably bill 30 hours per week per technician. Parts sales would be $20 per hour of billed time and the cost of parts sold would average 60 percent of sale price. Average collection period on revenues would be fifty-five days. Prepaid expenses would be 5 percent of revenue. Inventory would be purchased for cash. Accounts payable and accrued expenses would be 4 percent of revenue. Cash balances will be $10,000.

Burns and Foster expected to hire four technicians immediately, four more at the end of the first full year of operation, eight at the end of the second year, and four more at the end of the third year. They did not expect demand to grow beyond those twenty technicians.

The lease on the store ended December 31, so they could use that as their closing date, starting the new business on January 1. This would give them the next several months to start contacting businesses to sell the repair service, and to start hiring technicians. They could run the repair business out of the retail store until the end of the year and be fully operational by January 1. Repair revenue during the transition period would probably cover marginal costs for the period.

One area of concern was the loss they would suffer in closing the old store. Inventory valued at $135,000 would be sold at a going-out-of-business sale for no more than $100,000. Fixtures in the store had a remaining book value of $20,000 for accounting purposes and $12,000 for tax purposes. These fixtures would be worthless and would be written off. In addition, closing the old store would force them to repay their only debt—a $50,000 bank loan secured by the inventory.

Burns and Foster wanted to use a 15 percent required return and a 10-year time horizon with no salvage value for fixed assets to evaluate the investment. They did not want to assume a perpetual life in such a volatile field. The business would be set up as a subchapter S corporation. Burns and Foster were both in 28 percent tax brackets due to other family income.

Case Questions

1. What is the significance of the loss on closing the old store?
2. Identify all relevant cash flows.
3. Compute the net present value.
4. What are some of the things that could go wrong in this business?
5. Should Burns and Foster switch from retail sales to computer repair?

SELECTED REFERENCES

Amoako-Adu, Ben, and M. Rashid. "Corporate Tax Cut and Capital Budgeting." *The Engineering Economist* 35 (Winter 1990): 115–128.

Ang, James. "Tax Asymmetries and the Optimal Investment Decision of the Firm." *The Engineering Economist* 32 (Winter 1987): 135–161.

Ben-Horim, Moshe, Shalom Hochman, and Oded Palmon. "The Impact of the 1986 Tax Reform Act on Corporate Financial Policy." *Financial Management* 16 (Autumn 1987): 29–35.

Caks, John. "Sense and Nonsense about Depreciation." *Financial Management* 10 (Autumn 1981): 80–86.

Cooper, Ian, and Julian R. Franks. "The Interaction of Financial and Investment Decisions When the Firm Has Unused Tax Credits." *Journal of Finance* 38 (May 1983): 571–583.

Crutchley, Claire, Enyang Guo, and Robert S. Hansen. "Stockholder Benefits from Japanese-U.S. Joint Ventures." *Financial Management* 20 (Winter 1991): 22–30.

Dammon, Robert M., and Lemma W. Senbet. "The Effect of Taxes and Depreciation on Corporate Investment and Financial Leverage." *Journal of Finance* 43 (June 1988): 357–373.

Emery, Douglas R., Wilbur G. Lewellen, and David C. Mauer. "Tax-Timing Options, Leverage, and the Choice of Corporate Form." *The Journal of Financial Research* 11 (Summer 1988): 99–110.

Gordon, Roger H. "Can Capital Income Taxes Survive in Open Economies?" *Journal of Finance* 47 (July 1992): 1159–1180.

Graham, Edward M., and Paul R. Krugman. *Foreign Direct Investment in the United States.* Washington, D.C.: Institute for International Economics, 1991.

Heaton, Hal. "On the Bias of the Corporate Tax against High-Risk Projects." *Journal of Financial and Quantitative Analysis* 22 (September 1987): 365–371.

Hodder, James E. "Evaluation of Manufacturing Investments: A Comparison of U.S. and Japanese Practices." *Financial Management* 15 (Spring 1986): 17–24.

Hoffman, Michael J. R., and Bart P. Hartman. "Recent Changes in Tax Law and the Uncertainties in Capital Budgeting Decisions." *Business Horizons* 30 (January–February 1987): 12–19.

John, Kose, Lemma W. Senbet, and Anant K. Sundaram. "Cross-Border Liability of Multinational Enterprises, Border Taxes, and Capital Structure." *Financial Management* 20 (Winter 1991): 54–67.

Kim, Ji Soo, Il Geon Yoo, and Ju Chull Park. "Valuation of Income Producing Assets with Income Tax Consideration." *The Engineering Economist* 35 (Spring 1990): 173–190.

Malony, Kevin J., and Thomas I. Selling. "Simplifying Tax Simplification: An Analysis of Its Impact on the Profitability of Capital Investment." *Financial Management* 14 (Summer 1985): 33–42.

McCarty, Daniel E., and William R. McDaniel. "A Note on Expensing Versus Depreciating under the Accelerated Cost Recovery System: Comment." *Financial Management* 12 (Summer 1983): 37–39.

Oblak, David J., and Roy J. Helm, Jr. "A Survey and Analysis of Capital Budgeting Methods Used by Multinationals." *Financial Management* 9 (Winter 1980): 37–41.

Porcano, Thomas M. "Factors Affecting the Foreign Direct Investment Decision of Firms from and into Major Industrialized Countries." *Multinational Business Review* 1 (Fall 1993): 26–36.

Pruitt, Stephen W., and Lawrence J. Gitman. "Capital Budgeting and the Fortune 500." *Financial Management* 16 (Spring 1987): 46–51.

Remer, Donald S., and Yong Ho Song. "Depreciation and Tax Policies in the Seven Countries with the Highest Direct Investment from the U.S." *The Engineering Economist* 38 (Spring 1993): 193–208.

Shapiro, Alan C. "Capital Budgeting for the Multinational Corporation." *Financial Management* 7 (Spring 1978): 7–16.

Stanley, Marjorie T., and Stanley B. Block. "A Survey of Multinational Capital Budgeting." *Financial Review* 19 (March 1984): 36–54.

Stultz, R. M. "A Model of International Asset Pricing." *Journal of Financial Economics* 9 (December 1981): 383–406.

CHAPTER 10

Inflation and Capital Investment Analysis

After completing this chapter you should be able to:

- ➤ Describe why inflation and price changes in general are important to capital budgeting.
- ➤ Calculate the constant dollar equivalent price for a stream of cash flows.
- ➤ Recognize the difference between nominal and real interest rates and be able to adjust from one to the other.
- ➤ Identify the influence that inflation has on inventory values.
- ➤ Explain how inflation impacts taxes, debt repayment, and overall economic risk to possibly change shareholders' wealth.
- ➤ List and describe some of the gauges used to measure inflation.
- ➤ Describe how the equivalent annuity technique can be used to choose between mutually exclusive investments in an inflationary environment.
- ➤ Understand the influence that different inflation rates in other countries may have on the cash flows from a foreign subsidiary to the parent company.

The history of Butte, Montana, is closely linked with the copper ore that underlies the area. Prices of copper, like many other commodities, fluctuate with inflation rates and exchange rates. As a result, Butte has experienced numerous booms, followed by busts. The latest nadir of the cycle hit in the mid-1980s. Low inflation rates and a strong dollar drove the price of copper below the cost of bringing it out of the ground. Anaconda Minerals, a major local employer, had closed its last mine by 1986 and was getting out of copper.

By 1988, the dollar had weakened and copper had recovered from $0.60 to $1.10 a pound. Anaconda's mine was reopened by a new owner, who had originally purchased the mine to sell off the scrap equipment. Butte began another cycle of its copper-related history. Civic leaders of Butte also began restructuring the economy to become less dependent on price changes.[1]

Butte and Anaconda are not alone in finding the success of their investments strongly affected by changing prices. They are also not alone in their efforts to predict the impacts of price changes and decrease the sensitivity of their investments to price movements. The issues discussed in this chapter are of interest to most managers who are involved in capital budgeting. In fact, one of Dell Computer's competitive advantages is its ability to pass price decreases to the consumer more quickly. They do this by holding as little as three days supply of computer parts inventory and very little finished product inventory. Other computer makers have finished goods in stores and warehouses that must be sold (without suffering a loss in profits) before the cost decrease from parts suppliers are passed on to the consumer. This chapter begins with explanations of inflation terminology, including price indexes, current prices, constant dollar prices, nominal return, and real return. Then, the impact of inflation on income and cash flow is discussed. Finally, capital budgeting in the face of inflation is discussed.

INFLATION DEFINED

Inflation is defined as an increase in average prices. Inflation is generally expressed as a percent; if average prices increase from $100 to $106 over the course of a year, the inflation rate is 6 percent. Inflation is often measured using the consumer price index (CPI), which is the price of a "market basket" of goods and services purchased by a typical consumer, stated as a percent of the price at some base period. Numerous other indexes are also used, including the producers' price index and Gross National Product deflator.

Sometimes 1983 is used as a base period for the CPI, and the CPI of 177.1 at the end of 2001 meant that the price of the "market basket" was then 177.1 percent of (1.771 times) the average price in 1983. The consumer price index was 179.9 at the end of 2002. The inflation **rate** for 2002 was therefore $(179.9 - 177.1) \div 177.1 = 1.58$ percent.

Inflation rates have varied sharply from year to year and from country to country. During the early 1930s, the United States and many other countries actually suffered deflation, with average prices declining. Less than a decade later, inflation in Germany was so high that workers demanded pay for the morning's work at noon so that they could spend the money before its value was eroded by the afternoon's inflation. The inflation history of the United States appears in Figure 10-1.

[1]*Business Week* (July 16, 1988).

FIGURE 10-1 Inflation History of the United States
Both inflation rates and levels of the consumer price index appear. These illustrate the instability of inflation rates as well as the long-term effects on prices.

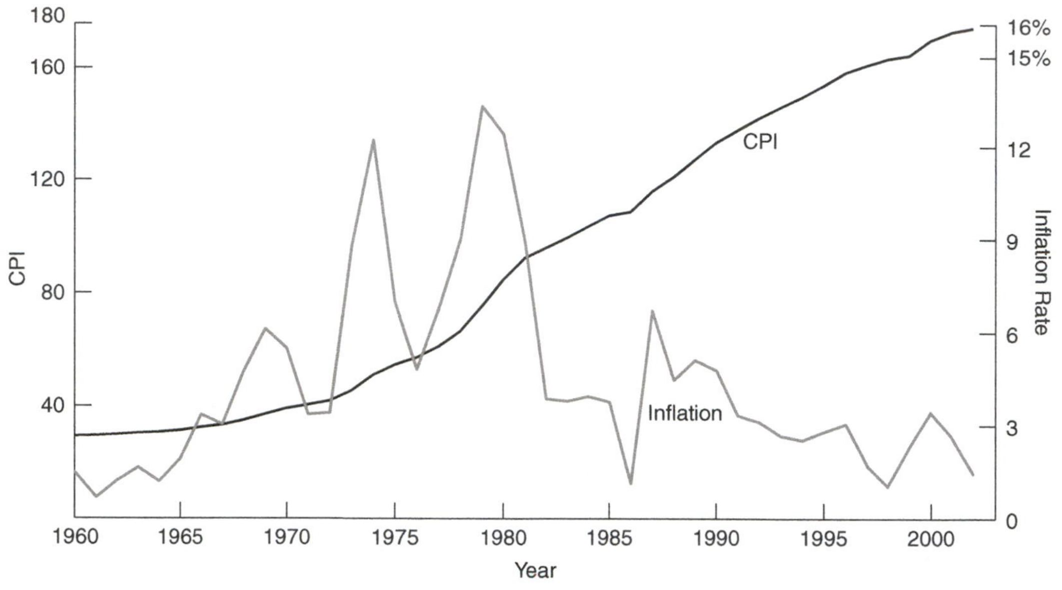

Inflation is, of course, the rate of change in average prices. As the earlier copper and Dell examples illustrated, prices do not all change at the same rate or in the same direction. The price of ethylene rose faster than the inflation rate in 1987 because of insufficient production capacity. The drought of 1988 caused beef prices to fall during the summer, as farmers culled their herds, and then rise during the winter, as fewer cattle came to market. Walter F. Williams, chairman of Bethlehem Steel Corp., was expecting increased profits in 1988, even though tonnage sales were expected to decline. One reason for optimism was an anticipated increase in the price of steel, relative to the prices of other goods.

CURRENT AND CONSTANT DOLLAR PRICES

The **current price** is the price at which an item could be purchased today. The **constant dollar price** is the current price adjusted to buying power at some base time. The constant dollar price, expressed in base year b buying power, is:

$$\text{Constant dollar price} = \frac{\text{Current price}_t}{PI_t \div PI_b} \qquad \textbf{(10-1)}$$

where PI_t is the price index in year t and PI_b is the price index in year b.

Example: In 1977, Ralston-Purina purchased the floriculture assets of Stratford of Texas for $35 million plus a $10 million, 10-year noninterest-bearing note. The consumer price index in 1977 was 61.1, in relation to the 1983 base of 100. By 1987, the consumer price index was 116.0. The value of the 1987 payment, expressed in 1977 purchasing power, was:

$$\frac{\$10,000,000}{116.0 \div 61.1} = \underline{\underline{\$5,267,241}}$$

The inflation from 1977 to 1987 reduced the constant dollar cost substantially for Ralston-Purina.

Example: The Dow-Jones Industrial Average (DJIA), a closely followed stock price index, increased from 995 in 1966 to 8,342 in late 2002, while the consumer price index increased from 32.4 in 1966 to 179.9 in late 2002. The 2002 level of the DJIA, expressed in 1966 dollars, was:

$$\text{2002 DJIA (in constant 1966 dollars)} = 8,342 \div (179.9 \div 32.4) = 1,502$$

In buying-power terms, the DJIA actually increased almost 600 points over the 36-year period. Dividends provided additional return so that investors gained even more over the 36-year period. A history of the DJIA, in current and constant (1974) dollars, appears in Figure 10-2. Failure to consider inflation gives a misleading picture of the profitability of common stock investments.

Constant and current dollar concepts are also used to forecast future cash flows generated by capital investments. Cash outlays and benefits are often forecasted in constant dollars, and then adjusted to estimate current dollars for future periods.

Example: In 2003, Lawrence Electronics was considering an expansion of its repair shop, to be placed in service on January 1, 2004. Revenue forecasts have been prepared without considering inflation and are, therefore, stated in 2003 dollars. The revenue forecasts reflect a 5 percent growth in the number of repairs. Assuming the consumer price index averaged 144.1 for 2003, managers expect inflation to average 4 percent a year. Constant (2003) dollar cash flow projections follow, along with projections of the consumer price index. These are used to estimate current dollar revenue for future periods. For example, the expected CPI for 2005 is $144.1(1.04)^2 = 155.9$, and the current dollar revenue forecast for 2005 is:

$$\text{2005 Current dollar revenue} = \$105,000(155.9 \div 144.1) = \underline{\underline{\$113,598}}$$

YEAR	2004	2005	2006	2007
Revenue in 2003 dollars	$100,000	$105,000	$110,250	$115,763
Consumer price index	149.9	155.9	162.1	168.6
Current dollar revenue	$104,000	$113,598	$124,022	$135,445

Using only 4 years and a fairly modest inflation rate of 4 percent, revenue forecasts would be substantially underestimated if inflation were ignored.

FIGURE 10-2 Current and Constant Dollar Stock Prices
This figure shows the Dow-Jones Industrial Average in current dollars and constant (1974) dollars.

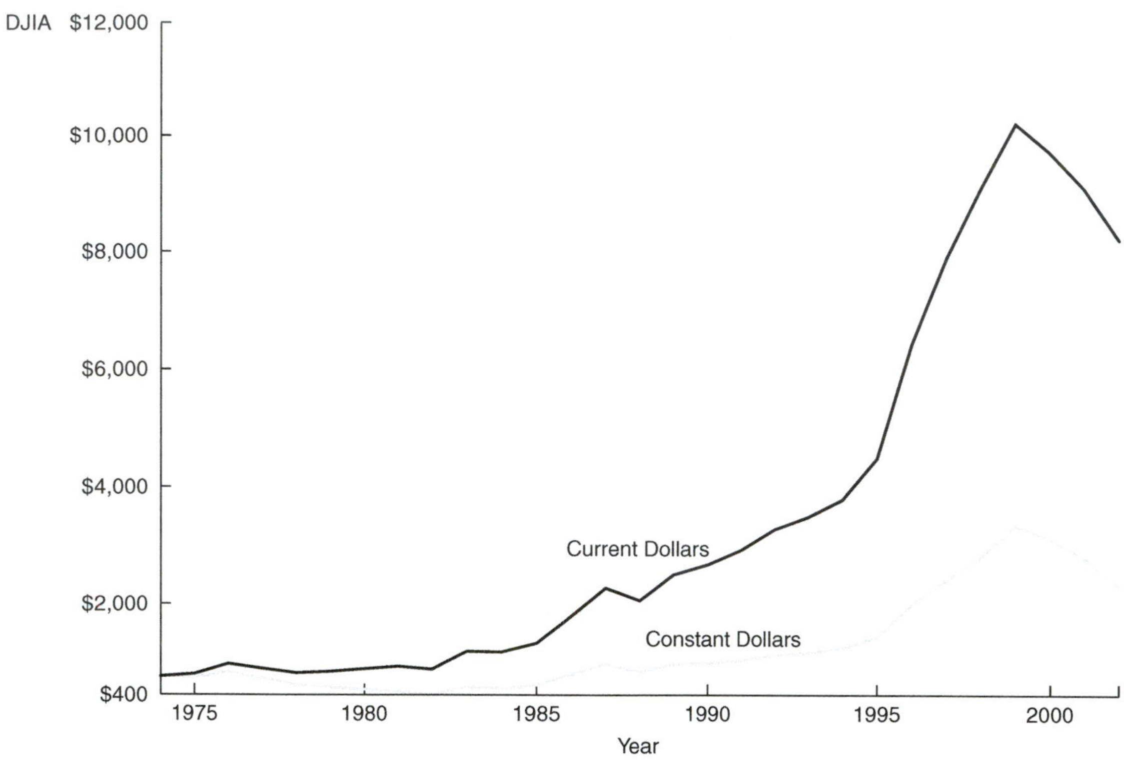

REAL AND NOMINAL INTEREST RATES

Interest rates and required returns in general rise when the inflation rate is expected to be high. The explanation of the increase in interest rates lies in the concept of real and nominal interest rates. The **nominal** interest rate is based on dollar interest paid or expected, and represents a percentage increase in dollars. The **real** interest rate is the percentage increase in buying power achieved when considering the interest rate and inflation. Suppose, for example, a 1-year treasury bill pays interest of 12 percent. If you invest $1,000 today, you will have $1,120 in 1 year. If prices increase 5 percent over the year, goods that cost $1.00 at the beginning of the year will cost $1.05 at the end. You could have used the $1,000 to buy 1,000 units at the beginning of the year. You can use the $1,120 to buy $1,120/$1.05 = 1,066.67 units at the end of the year. Your purchasing power has, therefore, increased (1,066.67 – 1,000)/1,000 = 6.67 percent. In other words, the real interest rate was 6.67 percent. The real interest rate (R_{real}) can be computed with a simple formula:[2]

$$R_{real} = \frac{1 + R_{nom}}{1 + Inf} - 1 \qquad \textbf{(10-2)}$$

where R_{nom} is the nominal interest rate and *Inf* is the inflation rate. Applying this formula to the example in the previous paragraph, the real interest rate is:

$$R_{real} = \frac{1 + .12}{1 + .05} - 1 = 6.67 \text{ percent}$$

Example: Alabama Power issued new 10 percent bonds in 2003. With an inflation rate of around 3 percent at the time, the real interest rate was:

$$R_{real} = \frac{1 + .10}{1 + .03} - 1 = 6.80 \text{ percent}$$

It is important to differentiate between expected and realized real rates. The **expected** real interest rate or rate of return is computed using the expected nominal rate and the expected inflation rate. The **realized** real rate is based on the nominal rate that has already been earned and the inflation that has already occurred.

Some economic theories are based on the assumption that the real interest rate will be stable, with the nominal rate adjusting to reflect inflation. The idea behind this theory is that both borrowers and lenders will base their negotiations on the real (buying power) impact of their loan contracts. In practice, nominal interest rates do respond strongly to increases in expected inflation, although the correlation between expected inflation and nominal interest rates is not perfect. Uncertainty is one reason the relationship is not perfect. Loan contracts are drawn in light of *expected* inflation, while actual inflation may be substantially different. Furthermore, inflation does not affect all prices equally, and economic activity is affected by inflation. Therefore, risks to both borrowers and lenders increase. Consequently, supply and demand for credit change, with resulting changes in real interest rates. However, real rates, both expected and realized, fluctuate much less than nominal interest rates, as shown in Figure 10-3.

When a business raises money for the purpose of making a capital investment, the return required by investors reflects the inflation expected by those investors. If inflation is ignored in forecasting the benefits from the investment, there will often be substantial errors in the estimates of benefits.

Expected inflation is even more important when the company is considering foreign capital investment because differences in inflation rates between the

---

[2]The real interest rate is sometimes defined as $R_{nom} - Inf$. This gives a close approximation to the true real interest rate because Equation 10-2 can be rearranged to give:

$$R_{nom} = R_{real} + Inf + R_{real}Inf$$

$R_{real}Inf$ is small if inflation rates are modest—for a real interest rate of 6.67 percent and an inflation rate of 5 percent, $R_{real}Inf = .0033$. Ignoring this small term and rearranging the remaining terms gives:

$$R_{real} - R_{nom} - Inf$$

FIGURE 10-3 Real and Nominal Interest Rates

This figure shows interest rate history in the United States, based on U.S. Treasury bill interest rates. These rates are adjusted using the consumer price index to give realized real interest rates.

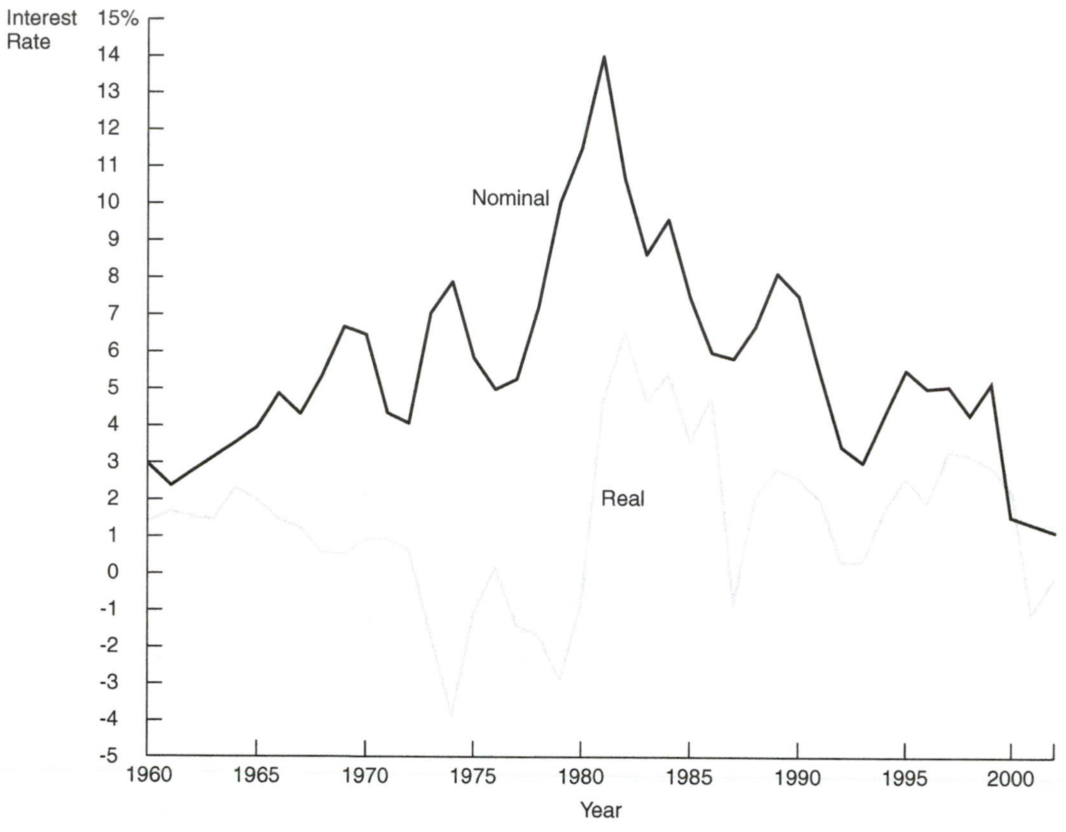

parent and subsidiary country will impact the exchange rate used to compute the cash flow to the parent. In this next section, we will first examine domestic inflation and then conclude with a discussion of the impacts of inflation on exchange rates and consequently cash flow to the parent.

INFLATION AND INCOME

The relationship between inflation and income is important because reported income matters to investors, because taxes are based on income, and because income statements are often used to develop cash flow estimates. Unfortunately, inflation does not affect income in a simple, direct way. Some prices change by more or less than inflation. Some costs, such as depreciation and interest, are fixed when the asset is acquired, and do not respond to inflation. Some prices tend to lead overall inflation, and some price changes tend to lag behind inflation. Methods of valuing inventory are particularly important in determining the impact of inflation on income.

Inventory Valuation. New Deal stereo store can be used to illustrate the accounting treatment of inventory. New Deal started carrying the RX2 DVD player in December 2004. Purchases and sales of the RX2 during the first 3 months were as follows:

MONTH		DEC 04	JAN 05	FEB 06
Purchases	Units	1	1	
	Price	$100	$120	
Sales	Units	1		
	Price			$130

What was the profit on the February sale? With **first in, first out** (FIFO) accounting, the cost of goods sold is the price of the oldest unit of inventory: $100. With **last in, first out** (LIFO) accounting, the cost is the price of the most recently purchased unit: $120. Profits and value of remaining inventory with FIFO and LIFO are as follows:

	FIFO	LIFO
Sales	$130	$130
Cost of goods sold	100	100
Earnings before tax	30	10
Value of remaining inventory	$120	$100

With either LIFO or FIFO, inflation will increase profit because the cost of goods sold represents a past cost of inventory, not the current cost. FIFO uses an older inventory cost, so the increase will be more pronounced with FIFO. LIFO is generally used for tax purposes because it results in lower reported income, and is often used for public reporting because it is believed to more accurately reflect actual profitability.

Example: For a broader look at inflation and income, consider Topeka Corporation in Table 10-1. There was no inflation in year 1, and inflation is expected to be 10 percent a year thereafter. Topeka sells one unit a year. The sale price will be $1,000 in year 1, and will increase at the general inflation rate each year thereafter. The company keeps two units in stock, and buys a replacement immediately when a unit is sold. The purchase price increases at the inflation rate, and the company uses LIFO inventory accounting. Therefore, the cost of goods sold is the previous year's purchase price. Labor is $200 a year, and increases proportionally with inflation. Depreciation is $100 a year, and is not affected by inflation.

The delay between purchase and sale of inventory is exaggerated in this example to simplify the analysis and highlight the impacts of inflation. The delay between purchase and sale of a unit of inventory is much less than a year for

TABLE 10-1 Financial Statements for Topeka Corporation

There is no inflation in year 1, and inflation is 10 percent in each year thereafter. LIFO inventory valuation is used, and inventory is purchased one year before sale.

YEAR	1	2	3	4
Sales	$1,000	$1,100	$1,210	$1,331
Cost of goods sold	600	600	660	726
Labor	200	220	242	266
Depreciation	100	100	100	100
Earnings before tax	100	180	208	239
Tax	34	61	71	81
Net income	$ 66	$ 119	$ 137	$ 158

most companies, so inventory valuation does not affect income as dramatically as in this example. However, the direction of change in income is the same as in this example.

While individual companies may experience leads or lags in prices of inputs purchased or output sold, net leads and lags for companies as a group are likely to be small. One company's fixed cost through a long-term contract is often another company's fixed revenue. Furthermore, net leads and lags across all sectors of the economy will be zero; a net lag across the economy would mean a lower inflation rate, for example.

If a company experiences no leads or lags in prices of inputs or outputs, and experiences no changes in volume of output, the effect of inflation is likely to be a growth in income from existing assets that is greater than the inflation rate. Inventory valuation methods increase income, and depreciation expense does not increase with inflation after the asset is acquired.

Accountants have attempted to adjust for the impact of inflation by producing income statements using replacement costs instead of historical costs to compute depreciation and the cost of goods sold. Table 10-2 shows the 1977 return on equity using historical and replacement cost for some sample companies. The inflation rate was approximately 7 percent in 1977. These numbers clearly illustrate the potentially large magnitude of the impact of inflation, although it should be noted that these are mostly capital-intensive companies for which the impact of inflation on income is greater than average.

Even if inflation increases a company's income, the company is not necessarily better off. First, the increase in income depends on unit sales volume remaining at least constant. High rates of inflation can cause disturbance to the economic system and, therefore, lead to decreased sales volume. Additionally, increased income does not necessarily mean increased cash flow. Replacement inventory must be purchased at ever-higher costs, for example. Finally, inflation causes discount rates to increase and, therefore, decreases the present value of

TABLE 10-2 Return on Equity Using Historical and Replacement Cost

Returns on equity using historical and replacement cost are shown for 1977, a year in which the inflation rate was 7 percent.

	HISTORICAL	REPLACEMENT
Alcoa	10.9%	14.6%
Ashland Oil	19.3	9.5
Consolidated Edison	11.7	4.3
General Telephone and Electric	15.0	6.8
Georgia-Pacific	17.1	9.6
Lockheed	25.1	9.3
Missouri Pacific Corporation	23.7	2.4
Procter & Gamble	17.6	10.2
Tenneco	15.0	7.3
Teledyne	29.2	18.1

Source: Forbes (June 12, 1978).

future benefits. We look at cash flow impacts of inflation in the next section and then look at the impact of inflation on value.

INFLATION AND CASH FLOW

For a given capital investment, cash flows resulting from inflation follow primarily from income changes and working capital changes. These effects can be illustrated by continuing with the previous example of Topeka Corporation from Table 10-1. The company purchases inventory on 1-year credit terms and sells its product on 1-year credit terms. The annual cash flows are shown in Table 10-3. Inventory value represents one original unit at $600, plus one unit bought at the current price. Accounts payable represent the one unit of inventory bought at current prices, and accounts receivable represent the sale price of one unit. Net cash flow is then net income plus depreciation, minus the increase in working capital.

The Topeka Corporation example illustrates the main cash flow issues with regard to inflation and existing capital investments. Net income will generally be expected to increase. However, cash flow may either increase or decrease, depending on how working capital for the particular company is affected. This depends, in turn, on inventory turnover and credit terms for both sales and purchases. Of course, some or all of the working capital may be recovered at the end of the asset's life, but a dollar in the future is less valuable than a dollar today.

The cash flow analysis was performed for existing capital investments. If the outlay for a capital investment is spread over several years, and the price is not contractually determined, the outlay will probably be affected by inflation.

TABLE 10-3 Topeka Corporation Cash Flow Analysis

The company uses LIFO inventory valuation and maintains two units of inventory, with a new unit acquired immediately when a unit is sold. Both purchase and sale are on 1-year credit terms.

YEAR	1	2	3	4
Sales	$1,000	$1,100	$1,210	$1,331
Cost of goods sold	600	600	660	726
Labor	200	220	242	266
Depreciation	100	100	100	100
Earnings before tax	100	180	208	239
Tax	34	61	71	81
Net income	$ 66	$ 119	$ 137	$ 158
+ Depreciation	100	100	100	100
Inventory	1,200	1,260	1,326	1,399
Accounts receivable	1,000	1,100	1,210	1,331
Accounts payable	600	660	726	799
Net working capital	1,600	1,700	1,810	1,931
– Change in net working capital	0	100	110	121
= Net cash flow	$ 166	$ 119	$ 127	$ 137

Furthermore, the analysis focused on a single capital investment. If an asset is to be replaced at the end of its life, the replacement cost will be higher because of inflation and will, therefore, further reduce cash flows to owners.

DOES INFLATION INCREASE SHAREHOLDER WEALTH?

The relationship between inflation and shareholder wealth has been studied extensively, with ambiguous results.[3] Reasons for ambiguous results can be understood by reference to Table 10-3. Assuming that the required return increases with an increase in inflation, it is necessary that cash flows increase by enough to provide the same net present value using a higher discount rate. Given constant unit sales, the cash flows may or may not increase, depending on working capital effects. Furthermore, a company is an ongoing concern and must replace assets as they wear out. The higher replacement costs mean that more earnings must be retained in the business to maintain the existing asset level, and the cash flow to owners is reduced.

Taxes. Taxes are an important issue in determining the value of a company in an inflationary environment. As illustrated in Table 10-3, taxes often rise during inflation periods, even if cash flows decline. Both cost of goods sold and depreci-

[3]See the selected references at the end of this chapter for a listing of many of these studies.

ation expenses are based on historical cost, not replacement cost. Therefore, the expense allowed for tax purposes is not sufficient to cover the cash flow for replacement.

Debt. Interest rates for many long-term loans are fixed when the loans are first arranged. Thus, interest expense is a fixed cost once an asset is acquired. If inflation increases unexpectedly after an asset is acquired, and market interest rates rise accordingly, the value of existing debt declines. Shareholders potentially gain at the expense of creditors. Whether this gain is sufficient to offset negative impacts of inflation depends on the characteristics of the particular company.

Economic Distortion. Inflation often leads to economic distortion, with growth slowed for the entire economy or growth increasing in some sectors while decreasing in others. At a minimum, increased inflation results in increased uncertainty. As a result, unit sales may increase or decrease for a particular business when inflation increases. These changes also affect cash flows.

From a review of these various factors, we can draw the firm conclusion that inflation may increase or decrease the value of a particular company. The characteristics of the particular company, as well as overall economic conditions, are important in predicting whether the value of a particular company will increase or decrease. Empirical studies during recent periods of high inflation suggest that, on average, the value of common stock has declined with increases in inflation rates. This does not mean that the values of all companies decline or that all capital investments become less attractive. The impact of inflation must be considered separately for each proposed investment.

RECOGNIZING INFLATION IN CAPITAL BUDGETING

To properly deal with inflation, you must recognize expected inflation in the projection of future cash flows and use a discount rate that reflects investors' expectations of future inflation. When your company raises money for the purpose of making a capital investment, the returns required by investors are stated in terms of nominal rates of return. The required returns are affected by interest rates in the financial markets and, therefore, reflect investors' expectations of inflation. Thus the required return should be applied to the actual cash flows expected, not the cash flows adjusted to base period buying power. The required return itself includes the adjustment for buying power loss.

Example: Wichita Corporation purchases an automatic pressure valve for $10,000 on December 31, 2003. The valve has a 5-year tax life and 5-year actual life. The asset will reduce labor expense by $2,800 a year at mid-2003 prices, and labor expense is expected to increase 4 percent a year due to inflation. The required return is 10 percent, which reflects investors' expectations of inflation. Ignoring inflation, the net present value from the investment would be as shown in Table 10-4.

The investment is unattractive because the net present value is negative. But if inflation is recognized in forecasting labor savings, the picture changes. In Table 10-5,

TABLE 10-4 Net Present Value Analysis Ignoring Inflation

Net present value analysis for a $10,000 automatic pressure valve with a 5-year life that will reduce labor expense by $2,800 a year. The required return is 10 percent and the annual cash flows are treated as if they occur at year-end.

YEAR	2003	2004	2005	2006	2007	2008
Labor savings		$2,800	$2,800	$2,800	$2,800	$2,800
Depreciation	($2,000)	(3,200)	(1,920)	(1,152)	(1,152)	(576)
Change in earnings before tax	(2,000)	(400)	880	1,648	1,648	2,224
Change in tax	680	136	(299)	(560)	(560)	(756)
Change in net income	(1,320)	(264)	581	1,088	1,088	1,468
+ Depreciation	2,000	3,200	1,920	1,152	1,152	576
– Initial outlay	(10,000)					
Net cash flow	(9,320)	2,936	2,501	2,240	2,240	2,044
P.V. factor	1.0000	0.9091	0.8264	0.7513	0.6830	0.6209
Present value	($9,320)	$2,669	$2,067	$1,683	$1,530	$1,269
Net Present Value	($102)					

TABLE 10-5 Net Present Value Recognizing Inflation

Net present value analysis of the automatic pressure valve analyzed in Table 10.4, recognizing that the $2,800 labor savings are at mid-2003 prices and inflation of wages is expected to be 4 percent a year.

YEAR	2003	2004	2005	2006	2007	2008
Labor savings		$2,912	$3,028	$3,150	$3,276	$3,407
Depreciation	($2,000)	(3,200)	(1,920)	(1,152)	(1,152)	(576)
Change in earnings before tax	(2,000)	(288)	1,108	1,998	2,124	2,831
Change in tax	680	98	(377)	(679)	(722)	(962)
Change in net income	(1,320)	(190)	731	1,319	1,402	1,869
+ Depreciation	2,000	3,200	1,920	1,152	1,152	576
– Initial outlay	(10,000)					
Net cash flow	(9,320)	3,010	2,651	2,471	2,554	2,445
P.V. factor	1.0000	0.9091	0.8264	0.7513	0.6830	0.6209
Present value	($9,320)	$2,736	$2,191	$1,856	$1,744	$1,518
Net present Value	$725					

expected labor savings are increased by 4 percent each year because the same hours of labor being saved would cost more each year in the future.

This investment is attractive when the impact of inflation on future benefits is properly recognized. A profitable investment would be erroneously rejected if inflation were ignored in the analysis.

The astute reader might ask what would happen to the net present value if the discount rate and the cash flows are not adjusted for inflation. Well we are glad you asked. In Table 10-6 we use a company that sells 10,000 units per year at $15 per unit. Each unit cost $5 and an additional annual cash expense of $20,000 is needed. We invest in a $60,000 building and equipment worth $30,000. Inventory is held at 20 percent of sales and is replenished at this level at the beginning of the year. Looking a Table 10.6 you will find that without inflation and using a 3 percent real rate, a net present value of $77,171 is achieved.

TABLE 10-6 Net Present Value Using a 3% Real Rate (no adjustment for inflation)

Sales in units		10,000	10,000	10,000
Selling price per unit without inflation		$ 15.00	$ 15.00	15.00
Cost per unit without inflation		$ 5.00	$ 5.00	$ 5.00
Working capital balance	$ (30,000)	$ (30,000)	$ (30,000)	$ —
	0	1	2	3
Building	$ (60,000)			
Equipment	$ (30,000)			
Working capital	$ (30,000)	$ —	$ —	$ 30,000
Acquisition stage cash flows	$(120,000)	$ —	$ —	$ 30,000
Revenues		$150,000	$150,000	$150,000
Cost of units sold		$ (50,000)	$ (50,000)	$ (50,000)
Expenses		$ (20,000)	$ (20,000)	$ (20,000)
Depreciation on building		$ (20,000)	$ (20,000)	$ (20,000)
Depreciation on equipment		$ (10,000)	$ (10,000)	$ (10,000)
Taxable income		$ 50,000	$ 50,000	$ 50,000
Taxes		$ (20,000)	$ (20,000)	$ (20,000)
After tax income		$ 30,000	$ 30,000	$ 30,000
Add back depreciation		$ 30,000	$ 30,000	$ 30,000
Operating stage cash flows		$ 60,000	$ 60,000	$ 60,000
Disposition stage cash flows				0
Total cash flows	$(120,000)	$ 60,000	$ 60,000	$ 90,000
Present value at 3% nominal rate	$ 197,171			
Net present value	$ 77,171			

TABLE 10-7 Net Present Value Using an 8.15% Nominal Rate (5% inflation)

Sales in units		10,000	10,000	10,000
Selling price per unit without inflation		$15.00	$ 15.75	$ 16.54
Cost per unit without inflation		$5.00	$5.25	$ 5.51
Working capital balance	$ (30,000)	$ (31,500)	$ (33,075)	$ —
	0	1	2	3
Building	$ (60,000)			
Equipment	$ (30,000)			
Working capital	$ (30,000)	$ (1,500)	$ (1,575)	$ 33,075
Acquisition stage cash flows	$(120,000)	$ (1,500)	$ (1.575)	$ 33,075
Revenues		$150,000	$157,500	$165,375
Cost of units sold		$ (50,000)	$ (52,500)	$ (55,125)
Expenses		$ (20,000)	$ (21,000)	$ (22,050)
Depreciation on building		$ (20,000)	$ (20,000)	$ (20,000)
Depreciation on equipment		$ (10,000)	$ (10,000)	$ (10,000)
Taxable income		$ 50,000	$ 54,000	$ 58,200
Taxes		$ (20,000)	$ (21,600)	$ (23,280)
After tax income		$ 30,000	$ 32,400	$ 34,920
Add back depreciation		$ 30,000	$ 30,000	$ 30,000
Operating stage cash flows		$ 60,000	$ 62,400	$ 64,920
Disposition stage cash flows				0
Total cash flows	$(120,000)	$ 58,500	$ 60,825	$ 97,995
Present value at 3% nominal rate	$ 183,563			
Net present value	$ 63,563			

Reworking this same information and allowing sales and cost to increase at 5 percent, we calculate a new net present value in Table 10-7. Depreciation cannot increase because the taxing authorities will not allow us to depreciate more than we have invested. The working capital investment will have to increase because inventory is more expensive. Taxes increase because we have a higher net income. Lastly, we will need to increase the discount rate from 3 percent to 8.15 percent to reflect 5 percent inflation ($1.031 \times 1.05 - 1 = 8.15\%$). Using 8.15 percent as the discount rate we find that the net present value decreases to $63,563, which is close to the $77,171 solution without inflation but not exactly the same. The difference lies in the treatment of depreciation, working capital, and the increases in taxes that are brought about by inflation. Because these are real factors that must be dealt with in reality, it is better to work the analysis with inflation and use the nominal rates than to ignore inflation and use real rates.

INFLATION AND CASH FLOW PROJECTION

To project cash flows in light of inflation, you must forecast the inflation rate and estimate the impact of inflation on each component of cash flows. Forecasting the inflation rate is an economic problem well beyond the scope of this book. There are many economic forecasting services that forecast the inflation rate, and methods of forecasting inflation are covered in economics texts.[4] It must be said, though, that accurate forecasts are hard to come by. The following quote from *Forbes* illustrates the problem.

> Monetarist economists and their followers in business and Wall Street have the public half crazy with fears of runaway inflation. Look at how fast the money supply is growing, they say, look how the Fed keeps pushing up interest rates.
>
> *Forbes*, whose approach to economics is eclectic rather than doctrinaire, says: "Yes, inflation is higher than it should be but it will slow down in the second half—along with the economy . . . the U.S. is not heading into 8 percent inflation, whatever the money supply figures seem to show."[5]

This forecast was published in July 1978, and inflation for the second half of 1978 was at almost exactly an 8 percent rate, followed by an unprecedented 13 percent rate in 1979! Inflation rates are directly affected by policies of the central banking system, which are, in turn, responses to economic conditions, political pressures, demographics, and international events. Predicting these various factors and the responses of the central banking system is extremely difficult. A so-called naive forecast, based on average inflation rates in the past, may be as accurate as the results of sophisticated models.

Once you have acquired an inflation rate forecast, you must estimate the impacts of inflation on various components of cash flow. The relationships between various cash flows and inflation can be summarized as follows:

Unaffected. Some cash flows are totally unaffected by inflation. Depreciation tax shields, for example, are determined by the cost of the asset and the depreciation rules in effect at the time of acquisition, and are unaffected by later inflation. Likewise, a long-term fuel contract, a labor contract, or the purchase of a commodity in the forward markets may lock in the present price, thereby making other components of cash flow independent of inflation.

Partially affected. Some benefits and costs may increase with inflation, but at a rate less than the inflation rate. Wages in many industries, for example, tend to rise at or above the inflation rate when the inflation rate is low to moderate, but rise at less than the inflation rate when inflation rates are high.

Fully affected. The prices of many consumer products, for example, can be expected to increase at approximately the inflation rate. Material costs can often be expected to respond in a similar way.

---

[4]See, for example, Geoffrey H. Moore, *Business Cycles, Inflation, and Forecasting*, 2nd ed. (Cambridge, Mass.: Ballinger Publishing Co., 1983).

[5] "Why Monetarists Are Wrong," *Forbes* (July 10, 1978): 103.

Leads and lags. Another important aspect of estimating the impact of inflation is the recognition of leads and lags. Some revenues and expenses may increase by the same percentage as inflation, but not at the same time. Public utility rates, for example, tend to move with the inflation rate, but with lags of six months to a year as the utility companies must apply to public utility commissions for permission to raise their rates.

INFLATION AND THE EQUIVALENT ANNUITY

The value of the equivalent annuity as a ranking tool for mutually exclusive investments with unequal lives was demonstrated in Chapter 7. The equivalent annuity can be used in inflationary environments if inflation over the long term is recognized in the computations. Recall that the equivalent annuity can be defined as the annual cash flow in perpetuity that would have a net present value the same as the net present value of the investment in question if that investment were repeated at the end of its life in perpetuity. Looked at from the other direction, the equivalent annuity can be defined as the present value with perpetual repetition, multiplied by the required return, k.

We assume, for the following analysis, that a constant inflation rate of *Inf* will occur. Assume the net present value of an investment has been computed with inflation recognized, as was done in Table 10-5, and NPV is used to signify that net present value. Now, place our decision maker at the end of the project's life. If the project is to be repeated, all costs and benefits will have risen, and the new net present value will be $NPV(1 + Inf)^n$ where n is the life of the investment. The equivalent annuity (EA) with perpetual repetition is then:[6]

$$EA = [NPV + NPV(1 + Inf)^n/(1 + k)^n + NPV(1 + Inf)^{2n}/(1 + k)^{2n} + \cdots]k \quad \textbf{(10-3)}$$

which can be simplified, with a little rearrangement of terms, to:

$$EA = NPV\{1 + 1/[(1 + k_{real})^n - 1]\}k \quad \textbf{(10-4)}$$

where k_{real} is the required return in real terms:[7] $k_{real} = (1 + k)/(1 + Inf) - 1$. The equivalent annuity for the investment in Table 10.5 is therefore:

$$EA = 725\{1 + 1/[(1 + .05769)^5 - 1]\}.10 = \$296$$

[6]If this statement is not intuitively appealing, go to Table 10-5 and assume a repeat with the capital investment now costing $10,000(1 + .10)^5 = \$16,105.10$ and all other costs and benefits likewise adjusted for expected inflation. The net present value will work out to be $\$1,130(1.10)^5 = \$1,820$.

[7]To begin, $(1 + Inf)^n/(1 + k)^n = 1/[(1 + k)^n/(1 + Inf)^n] = 1/(1 + k_{real})^n$. Consequently, equation 10-3 can be rewritten:

$$EA = [NPV + NPV/(1 + K_{real})^n + NPV/(1 = k_{real})^{2n} + NPV/(1 + k_{real})^{3n} + \cdots]k$$

From the value of a perpetuity formula, this can be rewritten:

$$EA = \{NPV + NPV/[(1 + k_{real})^n - 1]\}k = NPV\{1 + 1/[(1 + k_{real})^n - 1]\}k$$

Thus, in an inflationary environment, the equivalent annuity adjusted for inflation can be used for choosing between mutually exclusive investments in the same manner the equivalent annuity was used in the absence of inflation.

INFLATION, EXCHANGE RATES, AND INTERNATIONAL CAPITAL PROJECTS

Earlier in the chapter we illustrated the relationship between expected inflation and nominal interest rates. In this section we will explore the relationship between prices, inflation, interest rates, and the existing and expected exchange rates between countries. Portions of this material were introduced in Chapter 4 to illustrate the role of arbitrage in setting the value of a currency. This material is repeated here for completeness in the discussion of the influence that inflation has on expected exchange rates and consequently expected cash flows.

Exchange rates have fluctuated over wide ranges in recent years, as Figure 10-4 illustrates, and four theories are used to explain these movements: purchasing power parity theory, capital market equilibrium theory, expectation theory, and interest rate parity theory. Purchasing power parity is discussed first.

Purchasing Power Parity Theory

Purchasing power parity theory states that equilibrium exchange rates between two countries will result in identical goods selling at identical prices. If a hotel room rents for 22,484 yen in Tokyo and \$154 in Seattle, the purchasing power parity price of the yen is \$.00685 so that 22,484 yen can be exchanged for \$154. If the inflation rate over the course of a year is .5 percent in Japan and 3 percent in the United States, prices of hotel rooms will increase to 22,596 yen and \$158.62 respectively. For purchasing power parity to hold, the value of a yen will increase to \$158.62/22,596 = \$.00702. The inflation rates summarized in Table 10-8 would lead us to expect large fluctuations in exchange rates, and as expected, large fluctuations have occurred.

If purchasing power parity theory holds, the movements of exchange rates can be reduced to a simple formula:

$$Er_t = Er_{t-1}(1 + INF_D)/(1 + INF_F) \qquad \textbf{(10-5)}$$

where ER_t is the exchange rate at the end of period t expressed as the price of one unit of the foreign currency, INF_D is the domestic inflation rate for the period, and INF_F is the inflation rate in the foreign country for the period. We can confirm this formula by finding the end-of-period value of the yen for the previous example:

$$Er_t = .00685(1 + .03)/(1 + .005) = .00702$$

Purchasing power parity theory does not always hold in practice though. Differences in interest rates and perceived safety between countries can increase

FIGURE 10-4 Exchange Rate Movements

This figure shows the history of exchange rates between the U.S. dollar and three other currencies: the West German mark, the Japanese yen, and the Italian lira. This history illustrates the variability of exchange rates in recent years. The exchange value of the mark is expressed in U.S. dollars, while the values of the other two currencies are stated in U.S. pennies. The table ends with 1999 because the mark and lira were merged into the euro.

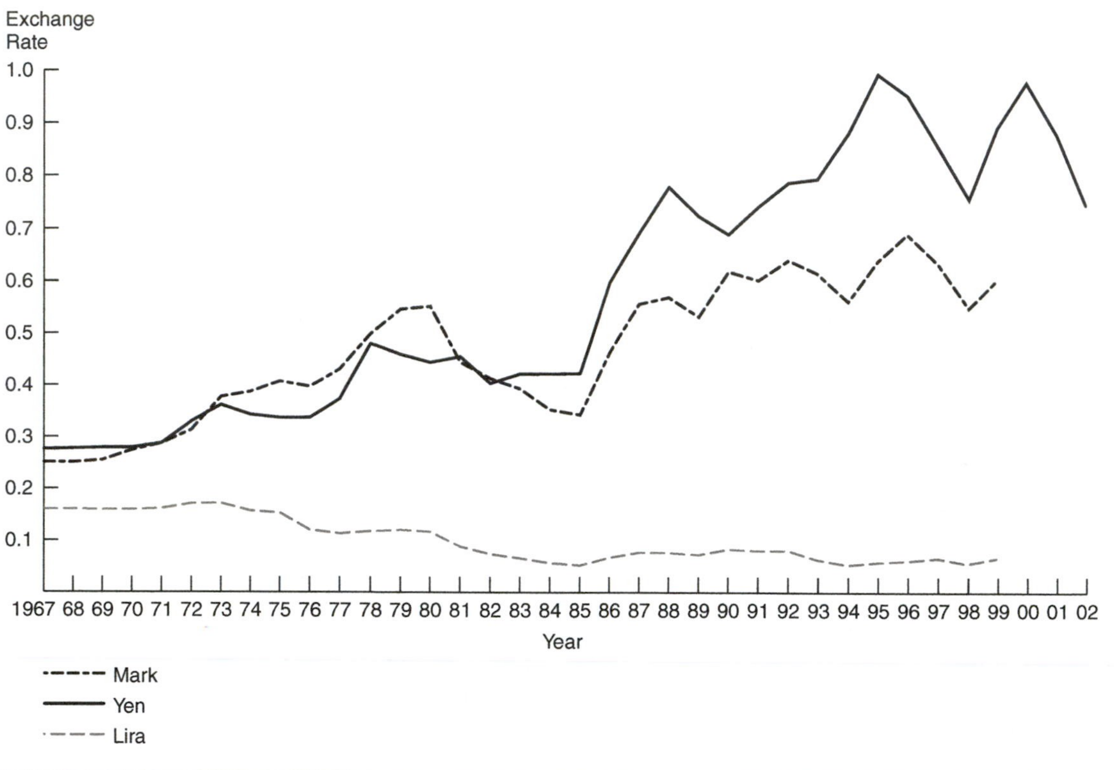

demand for one currency and decrease demand for the other. Market forces are not strong enough to ensure rapid movement to equilibrium. Japanese will not rush to Seattle for vacation to take advantage of the price disparity in hotel rooms, for example. Nevertheless, movements in exchange rates over the long run are strongly influenced by differences in inflation rates.[8]

[8]For additional reading, see Richard Roll, "Violations of the 'Law of One Price' and Their Implications for Differentially Denominated Assets," in *International Finance and Trade,* ed. M. Sarnat and G. Szego (Cambridge, Mass.: Ballinger Press, 1979); and Rita Maldonado and Anthony Saunders, "Foreign Exchange Futures and the Law of One Price," *Financial Management* 12 (Spring 1983): 19–23.

TABLE 10-8 Inflation Rates in Sample Countries

	UNITED STATES	CANADA	JAPAN	FRANCE	GERMANY	ITALY	UNITED KINGDOM
1980	13.5%	10.1%	7.9%	13.5%	5.2%	21.3%	17.9%
1981	10.3%	12.5%	4.7%	13.3%	6.5%	19.3%	12.0%
1982	6.2%	10.9%	2.8%	12.1%	5.2%	16.3%	8.5%
1983	3.2%	5.8%	1.8%	9.4%	3.4%	14.9%	4.6%
1984	4.3%	4.4%	2.3%	7.7%	2.4%	10.6%	5.0%
1985	3.6%	3.9%	2.0%	5.8%	2.0%	8.6%	6.0%
1986	1.9%	4.1%	0.7%	2.5%	–0.1%	6.1%	3.4%
1987	3.6%	4.4%	0.1%	3.3%	0.2%	4.6%	4.2%
1988	4.1%	4.1%	0.8%	2.7%	1.3%	5.0%	4.9%
1989	4.8%	5.0%	2.2%	3.6%	2.7%	6.6%	7.8%
1990	5.4%	4.8%	3.1%	3.3%	2.7%	6.1%	9.5%
1991	4.2%	5.6%	3.2%	3.0%	3.5%	6.3%	5.9%
1992	3.0%	1.5%	2.0%	2.9%	4.1%	5.4%	4.2%

Capital Market Equilibrium Theory

A general theory of interest rates, called the **Fisher Effect,**[9] suggests that interest rates in any country will adjust to inflation so that the real rate—the increase in buying power—remains constant. The idea behind the Fisher Effect is that investors and borrowers will compute the cost and benefit of interest in terms of purchasing power effect rather than nominal dollar effect. The specific formula for the real interest rate is:

$$R_{real} = (1 + R_{Nom})/(1 + INF) - 1 \quad \textbf{(10-6)}$$

where R_{Real} is the real interest rate, which is the percent increase in buying power after adjusting interest for inflation. R_{Nom} is the nominal interest rate, which is the interest rate actually paid, and INF is the inflation rate. International capital market equilibrium theory—the international version of the Fisher Effect—states that real interest rates will be the same in all countries and that nominal rate differences will reflect differences in expected inflation. Unfortunately, the Fisher Effect does not hold very well in domestic markets or international markets. Both supply and demand of credit are affected by increased inflation. And the changes in supply and demand may lead to different real interest rates in different countries. In the United States, for example, real

[9]Irving Fisher, *The Theory of Interest* (New York: Macmillan, 1930).

interest rates were negative during the high-inflation years in the 1970s. Nevertheless, nominal interest rates are strongly correlated with inflation rates.[10]

Expectation Theory

Expectation theory says that forward exchange rates are unbiased estimates of future spot rates. This is an efficient market theory in that contracts for future exchange involve no investment, and are therefore expected to provide zero return on average. The argument that someone would receive a positive return for risk-bearing is mitigated by the fact that each party to the contract may be using it to hedge other positions, and there may be no party identified as accepting risk for another party.

Expectation theory holds well in practice,[11] so you will not make money *on average* by speculating on future exchange rates. Likewise, you will not decrease expected return by hedging against exchange rate changes. This is important because it means you can hedge to eliminate exchange rate risk without sacrificing expected return. Specific hedging techniques typically involve options or option-type contracts, so further discussion of hedging is delayed until Chapter 15 when pricing of options is explained.

Interest Rate Parity Theory

Interest rate parity theory, which predicts a specific relationship between spot exchange rates, forward exchange rates, and interest rates, follows from the no-arbitrage-profit principle that is central to so much finance theory. Investors will always search for opportunities to make a risk-free investment at a superior rate of return. Suppose interest rates on risk-free government securities are higher in the United States than in Japan. You can convert yen into dollars, and buy the dollar-denominated securities. You can make this a risk-free investment by also entering into a futures contract to repurchase yen at the maturity date for the dollar-denominated security. The futures contract makes this a risk-free investment. If the investment provides a return above the domestic risk-free rate, numerous investors will join you in seeking to take advantage of the opportunity and will drive the return back into equilibrium. For the foreign investment to provide the same return as the domestic investment, the relationship between interest rates and exchange rates must be as follows:

$$R_{foreign} = (ER_{Spot}/ER_{Forward})(1 + R_{Domestic}) - 1 \qquad \textbf{(10-7)}$$

[10]For additional reading, see Fisher Black, "International Capital Market Equilibrium with Investment Barriers," *Journal of Financial Economics* 1 (December 1974): 337–352; R. M. Stultz, "A Model of International Asset Pricing," *Journal of Financial Economics* 9 (December 1981): 383–406; and Alex Kane, Leonard Rosenthal, and Greta Ljung, "Tests of the Fisher Hypothesis with International Data: Theory and Evidence," *Journal of Finance* 38 (May 1983): 539–551.

[11]See, for example, Bradford Cornell, "Spot Rates, Forward Rates and Exchange Market Efficiency," *Journal of Financial Economics* 5 (1977): 55–65; and R. M. Levich, "Tests of Forecasting Models and Market Efficiency in the International Money Market," in *The Economics of Exchange Rates: Selected Studies*, ed. A. Frenkel and H. G. Johnson (Reading, Mass.: Addison-Wesley, 1978).

where $R_{Foreign}$ and $R_{Domestic}$ are the foreign and domestic nominal risk-free interest rates, respectively. ER_{Spot} and $ER_{Forward}$ are the spot and forward exchange rates, respectively. The exchange rate is expressed as the price of the foreign currency in terms of the domestic currency.

To illustrate the use of Equation 10-7, we return to the yen which was experiencing an inflation rate of .5 percent while the dollar inflation rate was 3 percent. Assume the spot exchange rate is $.00685 per yen, and the 1-year forward contract rate is $.00702 per yen. The risk-free interest rate in dollar-denominated securities is 5.5 percent. The equilibrium interest rate in yen-denominated securities is therefore:

$$R_{foreign} = (.00685/.00702)(1 + .055) - 1 = 2.94\%$$

There are powerful forces at work to enforce interest rate parity. You can make deposits in a Japanese bank in any one of a number of currencies, with all of these deposits being virtually risk-free with regard to interest and principal payments. At the same bank, you can exchange one currency for another and enter into a futures contract. Given the Bank of Japan's .5 percent interest rate, it is easy to take advantage of any violation of interest rate parity theory, and investors will respond quickly to these money-making opportunities, bidding rates back into equilibrium.[12]

Interest rate parity theory can be used to understand how a government can temporarily drive exchange rates out of purchasing power equilibrium. Suppose the exchange and interest rates between Japan and the United States are in equilibrium as previously defined. The spot and 1-year forward exchange rates are $.00685 and $.00702 respectively. The interest rate is 2.94 percent in Japan, and the U.S. federal reserve bank decreases the money supply, driving interest rates up to 8 percent. The Japanese government, on the other hand, commits itself to a monetary policy that will maintain the 2.94 percent interest rate. Investors view these disturbances as temporary, so the future contract exchange rate does not change. For interest rate parity to hold, it is necessary for the spot rate to change as follows:

$$2.94 = (ER_{Spot}/.00702)(1 + .08) - 1; \; ER_{Spot} = .006691$$

The increase in interest rates in the United States drives the relative value of the yen down and the relative value of the dollar up. This change violates purchasing power parity, but it can be maintained at least temporarily through a high interest rate policy. Relationships between exchange rates and U.S. interest rates are summarized in Figure 10-5.

[12]For additional discussion, see T. Agmon and S. Bronfield, "The International Mobility of Short-Term Covered Arbitrage Capital," *Journal of Business Finance and Accounting* 2 (Summer 1975): 269–278; J. A. Frenkel and R. M. Levich, "Covered Interest Arbitrage: Unexploited Profits?" *Journal of Political Economy* 83 (April 1975): 325–338; F. X. Browne, "Departures from Interest Rate Parity: Further Evidence," *Journal of Banking and Finance* 7 (June 1983): 253–272; and Ian H. Giddy, "An Integrated Theory of Exchange Rate Equilibrium," *Journal of Financial and Quantitative Analysis* 11 (December 1976): 883–892.

FIGURE 10-5 Exchange Rates and Interest Rates
The exchange rate is the trade-weighted average of the exchange rate of the dollar against foreign currencies, with 100 being the January 1997 base value. The interest rate is the real (inflation-adjusted) interest rate on 10-year Treasury bonds.

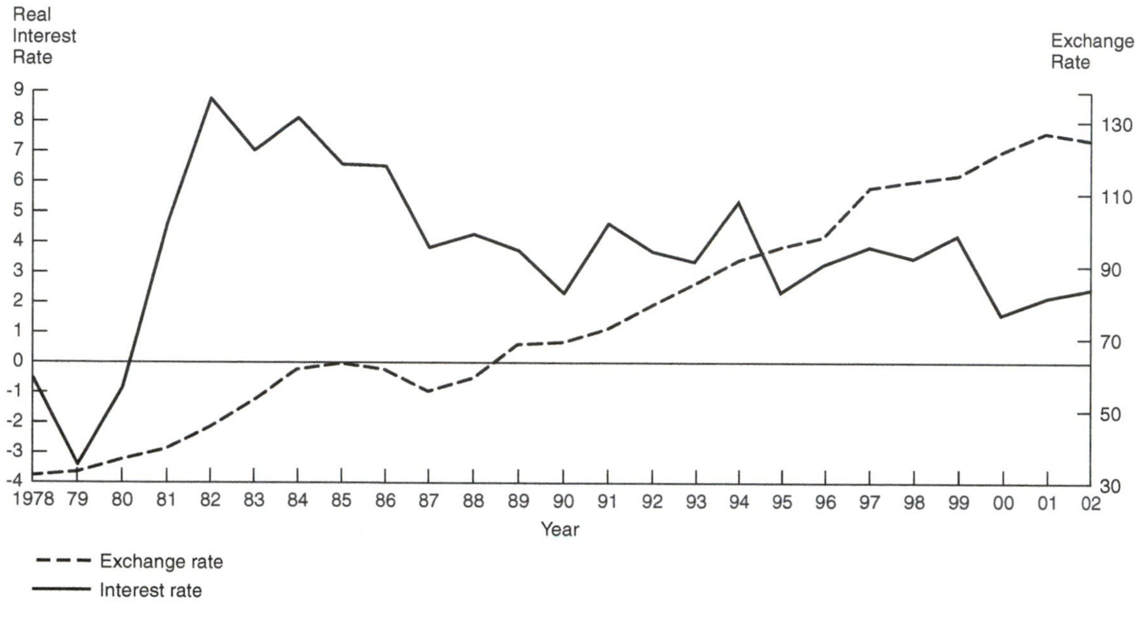

In summary, we know from observations that inflation rates are the primary determinants of exchange rate changes over the long run, but there are numerous disturbances to the purchasing power parity relationships. For example, the banking crisis in Indonesia, Thailand, and Japan in 1998 caused concern about Asian stability and there was a rush to the U.S. dollar as a safe-haven currency, temporarily driving up the value of the dollar. We also know that exchange rates are sensitive to monetary policy, because monetary policy affects interest rates. Thus, theory and observations tell us that we can expect sharp fluctuations in exchange rates. Fortunately, evidence supporting expectation theory also tells us that companies can use hedging to decrease exchange rate risk without decreasing expected return.

SUMMARY

Inflation is defined as an increase in average prices. The inflation **rate** is the percentage change in a **price index,** which is the price of some representative market basket as a percent of its price in a specified base period. The **current price** is the price at which an item could be purchased today. The **constant dollar price** is the current price adjusted to buying power at some base time. The constant dollar price, expressed in year b buying power, is:

$$\text{Constant dollar price} = \text{Current price}_t \div (PI_t \div PI_b) \qquad \textbf{(10-1)}$$

where PI_t is the price index in year t and PI_b is the price index in year b.

The **nominal** interest rate is the interest actually paid. The **real** interest rate is the percentage increase in buying power achieved when considering the interest rate and inflation. The formula for the real interest rate or rate of return (R_{real}) is:

$$R_{real} = (1 + R_{nom})/(1 + Inf) - 1 \qquad \textbf{(10-2)}$$

where R_{nom} is the nominal interest rate and *Inf* is the inflation rate.

Inflation often increases income more than proportionally. Some costs, like depreciation and interest, are fixed. In addition, inventory accounting procedures mean that the cost of goods sold lags behind inflation. Cash flows are another matter, though. The cost of an existing asset is not affected by subsequent inflation, but working capital needs often rise with inflation, so net cash flow may actually decrease with increased inflation, even though income increases. Whether a particular company gains or loses with an increase in inflation depends on a number of complicated considerations, including the state of the economy, the extent to which the inflation was anticipated through interest rates, and the extent to which prices for that company's inputs and outputs lead or lag inflation.

Inflation can dramatically affect the attractiveness of specific capital investments. The inflation rate expected by investors affects required return in the financial marketplace and is, therefore, incorporated in the required return. Failing to consider the impact of inflation in estimating cash flows can lead to serious errors, either overestimation or underestimation of cash flows. Therefore, ignoring inflation can lead to the acceptance of unprofitable investments and the rejection of profitable investments.

There is no simple relationship between inflation and cash flows for specific investments. Some cash flows are unaffected, some are partially affected, and some are fully affected by inflation. Net cash flows may even be negatively affected by inflation, particularly when the impact of taxes and replacement costs is considered. Furthermore, some cash flow effects occur at the same time as inflation while others lead or lag inflation. Because of these complications, it is necessary to study each component of cash flow independently to determine the impact of inflation on that component. A complete cash flow projection considering inflation must be based on summaries of the impact of inflation on the individual components of cash flow. We know from observations that inflation rates are the primary determinants of exchange rate changes over the long run, but there are numerous disturbances to the purchasing power parity relationships. We also know that exchange rates are sensitive to monetary policy, because monetary policy affects interest rates. Thus, theory and observations tell us that we can expect sharp fluctuations in exchange rates. These same theories and observations can sometimes allow us to predict the long-run direction of the exchange rate. Without some estimate of the direction of the exchange rate, it is difficult to estimate the after-translation cash flows to the parent company and, consequently, the net present value of the foreign project.

QUESTIONS

10-1. Define the terms **inflation** and **consumer price index.**

10-2. Suppose the consumer price index is 345.3 on a certain date, using 1983 as the base year. What does this mean?

10-3. Explain the difference between **current** and **constant dollar** price.

10-4. Explain the meaning of the terms **real** and **nominal** interest rate.

10-5. What factors may cause income to increase more than proportionally with an increase in inflation?

10-6. What factors may cause cash flow from a capital investment to decrease with an increase in inflation even if income increases?

10-7. Why is it *not* necessary to adjust the required return for expected inflation when evaluating capital investments in an inflationary environment?

10-8. Give examples of cash flows that are

a. Unaffected by inflation
b. Partially affected by inflation
c. Fully affected by inflation

10-9. Give examples of cash flows that lead and lag inflation.

10-10. **(Applications)** Peru's annual inflation rate for 1990 was 7,650 percent, an all-time high for this country. In 1991 the annual rate dropped back to approximately 140 percent. In September 1993, the annual rate was at approximately 20 percent, the lowest in 17 years. Given the high rate in 1990, is it possible to make a long-term capital investment in this environment? Given the scenario above, if you were to make a capital investment, what are the characteristics that would be most important to you? Address financing, pricing, cost of inputs, and any other factors.

10-11. **(Ethical considerations)** Recently a large regulated utility which supplied natural gas to residential customers filed for bankruptcy because managers had incorrectly predicted a large increase in the price of natural gas and a large decrease in price occurred. Prior to bankruptcy, they had locked in suppliers to very long contracts, thinking the price would move up. At the time of the filing, this company was still viable but decided to file early to keep from draining the resources of the company.

a. Is it ethical to use bankruptcy in this manner?
b. Who benefited and who lost?

Can you think of other business or personal situations that might result in a rash of bankruptcy filings if rapid inflation or deflation occurs?

10-12. Describe each of the following theories. Indicate the extent to which each theory holds in practice.

a. Purchasing power parity theory
b. Capital market equilibrium theory
c. Expectation theory
d. Interest rate parity theory

PROBLEMS

10-1. A capital investment generates cost savings of $1,000 in 2003. Assuming these costs increase with inflation, and the inflation rate is 4 percent, what will be the cost savings in 2013?

10-2. The consumer price index was 158.6 at the end of 1996 and 153.9 at the end of 1995. What was the inflation rate for 1996?

10-3. The consumer price index was 161.3 at the end of 1997. At a 3 percent inflation rate, what would be the consumer price index at the end of 1998? At the end of 2007?

10-4. The consumer price index was 161.3 at the end of 1997, measured against a base year of 1983. A portable television that sold for $99 in 1967, when the consumer price index was 33.3, could be purchased for $89 at the end of 1997. Restate the 1997 price in 1967 dollars. Comment on the rate of inflation in the price of portable televisions.

10-5. The consumer price index averaged 59.2 in 1977 and 160.6 in 1997. For an asset that cost $100,000 in 1997, express the price in 1977 dollars. For an asset that cost $100,000 in 1977, express the price in 1997 dollars.

10-6. The interest rate on Treasury bills was 5.07 percent in 1997. If the inflation rate for 1997 was 1.70 percent, what was the real interest rate for 1997?

10-7. Emporia Supply Corporation began stocking the new Superaid in January 2003. One unit was purchased in January for $100, one unit was purchased in February for $110, and one unit was sold in March for $120. What was the profit on this sale if the company used FIFO accounting? LIFO accounting?

10-8. Kansas City Corporation began operation on December 31, 2003. The company bought two units of inventory initially for $1,000 each. The company will sell one unit of inventory each year for $2,000 in 2003 dollars and immediately replace that unit. Depreciation will be $400 a year, and labor expenses will be $500 a year in the absence of inflation. Sale price and inventory purchase price will rise with inflation. Depreciation will remain fixed and labor expense will lag one year behind inflation due to labor contracts. The company's tax rate is 34 percent. Assume the inflation rate will be 0 percent in 2004 and 10 percent a year thereafter. Using FIFO, show net income for 2004, 2005, 2006, and 2007.

10-9. For Kansas City Corporation in problem 8, inventory is purchased for cash and sold for cash. Show the annual cash flows for 2004, 2005, 2006, and 2007.

10-10. For Kansas City Corporation in problem 8, assume inventory is sold for cash, but purchased on 1-year credit terms. Show the cash flow each year for 2004 through 2007.

10-11. Pittsburg Corporation has sales of $100,000 a year, and the sale price will increase with inflation. Inventory valuation is such that the effective cost of goods sold is the purchase price three months prior to sale. Depreciation is fixed, and other operating costs increase proportionately with inflation. The company sells on terms of net 30 and buys inventory on terms of net 60. All other purchases are for cash. Shown below is a financial statement for the first year of operation, with no inflation. Show the income for the following year, with a 10 percent inflation rate.

Sales	$100,000
Cost of goods sold	80,000
Depreciation	5,000
Other operating expenses	10,000
Earnings before tax	5,000
Tax	1,700
Net income	$ 3,300

10-12. For Pittsburg Corporation in the previous problem, goods are sold for cash. Inventory will be $50,000 with no inflation and $51,000 with 10 percent inflation. Accounts payable will be $30,000 with no inflation and $33,000 with 10 percent inflation. Show the cash flow with and without inflation.

10-13. Richmond Corporation can buy a new asset with a 5-year depreciation life for $10,000 at the end of 2003. The asset will reduce material waste by $3,000 a year, in mid-2003 prices. The inflation rate is expected to average 4 percent a year, and the cost of materials is expected to increase at the inflation rate. Materials are purchased for cash within a few days of their actual use, so there is no significant lag of cost behind inflation. The asset is expected to have a 6-year operating life. The required return is 10 percent and the company is in a 34 percent tax bracket. Compute the net present value for this investment.

10-14. A capital investment of $100,000 at the end of 2003 will be required if Frankfort Corporation is to introduce a new product. The capital investment will have a 10-year operating life and a 5-year life for tax purposes. In addition, inventory must be purchased for $50,000 at the end of 2003. The inventory will be sold for cash 1 year after purchase for $100,000 in 2003 prices, and replaced immediately. Other operating costs (excluding depreciation) will be $20,000 a year in 2003 prices. The product is expected to have a 10-year market life, and inflation is expected to be 6 percent a year over the next 10 years. Inventory cost, sale price, and operating costs are expected to increase at the inflation rate. The required return is 12 percent, and the tax rate is 34 percent. Is the investment attractive?

10-15. Investment A has a 5-year life and a net present value, considering inflation, of $100,000. Investment B has a 10-year life and a net present value, considering inflation, of $150,000. The required return is 16 percent, and the inflation rate is 6.48 percent. Investments A and B both use the same scarce resource. Both investments A and B can be repeated at the end of their life. Which investment do you recommend?

10-16. In problem 5-17, an investment in an MBA degree was evaluated. Rework the analysis for a 3 percent inflation of wages after the MBA is completed.

10-17. The Japanese yen is currently priced at $.00685. Suppose an apartment that would rent for $2,000 a month in New York is renting for 260,000 yen in Tokyo. Does this relationship violate purchasing power parity theory? Are there any market forces that would bring the prices in line?

10-18. The Russian ruble is currently priced at $.1598. A dress that would sell for $120 in Chicago is in a store in Moscow. What price for the dress would be consistent with purchasing power parity theory?

10-19. The value of country A's currency is $.50 on January 1 and $.60 on January 1 of the following year. Inflation over the period was 10 percent in the United States and 30 percent in country A. Is the change in currency value consistent with purchasing power parity theory?

10-20. Suppose the rate on 1-year U.S. Treasury securities is 12 percent and the inflation rate for the year is 9 percent. Is this consistent with the Fisher Effect if 3 percent is viewed as the equilibrium real interest rate?

10-21. The 1-year risk-free interest rates in countries A and B are 10 percent and 15 percent respectively. The anticipated inflation rates for countries A and B are 8 percent and 12 percent respectively. Are these relationships consistent with international capital market equilibrium?

10-22. The spot rate and 6-month forward rate for the Japanese yen are 146.25 yen per dollar and 142.41 yen per dollar respectively. The interest rate per 6-month period is 2.75 percent in the United States and .25 percent in Japan. Are these relationships consistent with interest rate parity theory?

SELECTED REFERENCES

Adler, Michael, and Bernard Dumas. "Exposure to Currency Risk: Definition and Measurement." *Financial Management* 13 (Summer 1984): 41–50.

Bailey, Andrew D., Jr., and Daniel L. Jensen. "General Price Level Adjustments in the Capital Budgeting Decision." *Financial Management* 6 (Spring 1977): 26–31.

Bernard, Victor L. "Unanticipated Inflation and the Value of the Firm." *Journal of Financial Economics* 15 (March 1986): 285–321.

Bjerksund, Petter, and Steiner Ekern. "Managing Investment Opportunities under Price Uncertainty: From 'Last Chance' to 'Wait and See' Strategies." *Financial Management* 19 (Autumn 1990): 65–83.

Brenner, Menachem, and Seymour Schmidt. "Asset Characteristics and Systematic Risk." *Financial Management* 7 (Winter 1978): 33–39.

Browne, F. X. "Departures from Interest Rate Parity: Further Evidence." *Journal of Banking and Finance* 7 (June 1983): 253–272.

Chang, Eric C., and J. Michael Pinegar. "Risk and Inflation." *Journal of Financial and Quantitative Analysis* 22 (March 1987): 89–99.

Chang, Rosita P., and S. Ghon Rhee. "Does the Stock Market React to Announcements of the Producer Price Index?" *Financial Review* 21 (February 1986): 125–134.

Chen, Andrew H., and James A. Boness. "Effects of Uncertain Inflation on the Investment and Financing Decisions of a Firm." *Journal of Finance* 30 (May 1975): 53–63.

Cooley, Philip L., Rodney L. Roenfeldt, and It-Keong Chew. "Capital Budgeting Procedures under Inflation." *Financial Management* 4 (Winter 1975): 18–27.

Ezzell, John R., and William A. Kelly, Jr. "An APV Analysis of Capital Budgeting under Inflation." *Financial Management* 13 (Autumn 1984): 49–54.

Fama, Eugene F. "Stock Returns, Real Activity, Inflation and Money." *American Economic Review* 71 (September 1981): 545–565.

Fama, Eugene F., and G. William Schwert. "Asset Returns and Inflation." *Journal of Financial Economics* 5 (November 1977): 115–146.

Feldstein, Martin A. "Inflation and the Stock Market." *American Economic Review* 70 (December 1980): 839–847.

Findlay, Chapman M., et al. "Capital Budgeting Procedures under Inflation: Cooley, Roenfeldt, and Chew vs. Findlay and Frankle." *Financial Management* 5 (Autumn 1976): 83–90.

Fisher, Irving. *The Theory of Interest.* New York: Macmillan, 1930.

Hasbrouck, Joel. "Stock Returns, Inflation, and Economic Activity: The Survey Evidence." *Journal of Finance* 39 (December 1984): 1293–1310.

Hochman, Shalom, and Oded Palmon. "The Irrelevance of Capital Structure for the Impact of Inflation on Investment." *Journal of Finance* 38 (June 1983): 785–794.

Kane, Alex, Leonard Rosenthal, and Greta Ljung. "Tests of the Fisher Hypothesis with International Data: Theory and Evidence." *Journal of Finance* 38 (May 1983): 539–551.

Kim, Moon. "Inflationary Effects in the Capital Investment Process: An Empirical Examination." *Journal of Finance* 34 (September 1979): 941–950.

Lease, Ronald C., John J. McConnell, and James S. Schallheim. "Realized Returns and the Default and Prepayment Experience of Financial Leasing Contracts." *Financial Management* 19 (Summer 1990): 11–20.

Metha, Dileep R., Michael D. Curley, and Hung-Gay Fung. "Inflation, Cost of Capital, and Capital Budgeting Procedures." *Financial Management* 13 (Winter 1984): 48–54.

Moore, Geoffrey H. *Business Cycles, Inflation, and Forecasting,* 2nd ed. Cambridge, Mass.: Ballinger Publishing Co., 1983.

Nelson, Charles R. "Inflation and Capital Budgeting." *Journal of Finance* 31 (June 1976): 923–931.

Pindyck, Robert S. "Risk, Inflation, and the Stock Market." *American Economic Review* 74 (June 1984): 335–351.

Rappaport, Alfred, and Robert A. Taggart, Jr. "Evaluation of Capital Expenditure Proposals under Inflation." *Financial Management* 11 (Spring 1982): 5–13.

Roll, Richard. "Violations of the `Law of One Price' and Their Implications for Differentially Denominated Assets," in *International Finance and Trade,* ed. M. Sarnat and G. Szego. Cambridge, Mass.: Ballinger Press, 1979.

Schwert, William G. "The Adjustment of Stock Prices to Information about Inflation." *Journal of Finance* 36 (March 1981): 15–29.

Soldofsky, Robert M., and D. F. Max. "Stock and Bonds as Inflation Hedges." *Michigan State University Business Topics* 26 (Spring 1978): 17–24.

Van Horne, James C. "A Note on Biases in Capital Budgeting Introduced by Inflation." *Journal of Financial and Quantitative Analysis* 8 (January 1971): 653–658.

Walter, James E. "Investment Planning under Variable Price Change." *Financial Management* 1 (Winter 1972): 36–50.

Williams, R. "Forecasting Inflation and Interest Rates." *Business Economics* 14 (January 1979): 57–60.

CASE PROBLEM

MidCity Center (B)

The MidCity Center (A) case appears in Chapter 5. In that case, the board was considering two energy conservation proposals.

One member of the board pointed out that the assumption of no fuel price increase was unrealistic. She suggested that a 5 percent increase in fuel price each year was a conservative estimate. Another member objected, noting that fuel prices had actually declined in recent years.

Assuming a 5 percent inflation rate, answer the following questions.

Case Questions

1. Using a 10 percent discount rate, compute the net present value of the storm window investment with and without a new furnace.
2. Using a 10 percent discount rate, compute the net present value of the furnace investment with and without storm windows.
3. Which investments, if any, should the board accept?

CASE PROBLEM

B and F Computer Repair (B)

B and F Computer Repair (A) appears at the end of Chapter 9. In that case, Burns and Foster did not consider the impact of inflation.

Burns attended a seminar on the economic outlook, and one of the speakers talked about the possibility of an increase in inflation. Burns suggested to Foster that they should consider the possible impact of inflation before making a decision. After considerable discussion, they made the following set of assumptions.

1. There would be no inflation in the first year, and inflation would be 5 percent a year thereafter.
2. The number of hours and parts would not be affected by inflation.
3. Hourly charges and the sale price of parts would both change proportionally with inflation.
4. Labor expense increases would lag 6 months behind inflation.
5. Because of LIFO inventory valuation, the average accounting cost of a part

would be the purchase price 3 months earlier.

6. Because of LIFO accounting, three-fourths of inventory would be valued at original cost while one-fourth would reflect approximately the current price.
7. Other costs would rise with inflation.
8. Because of the anticipated inflation, a 20 percent required return should be used in evaluating the investment.

Case Questions

1. Prepare income statements for each year.
2. Identify the changes in working capital for each year.
3. Identify cash flow for each year.
4. Compute the net present value with inflation considered.
5. Should Burns and Foster enter the computer repair business?

MACHINE TOOL CORPORATION (A)

Machine Tool Corporation was searching for ways to increase productivity and decrease costs. The company began to look at the use of robots. One possible use of robots was in gear hobbing. A gear-hobbing machining center consisted of four machines operated individually by semiskilled human operators. Two sets of machines operated in the shop. Depending upon production requirements, either the four-spindle hobbing machine and shaving machine (low volume) or the eight-spindle hobbing machine and shaving machine was used. Major operator functions involved loading gear blanks, cutting gear profiles, stacking semi-finished parts, and trimming the gears on the shaving machine. The cleaning and inspection operations, subsequent to shaving, were also done manually.

The existing workstation could be modified so that a single robot could perform all loading and unloading operations. Stacking the parts on incoming and outgoing trays, inspection, and overall supervision of the workstation could then be done by one operator, instead of the four operators required for the previous setup. The operator who remained would then be responsible for

1. programming and starting the robot,
2. arranging parts on the incoming tray,
3. periodic inspection of the finished parts,
4. unloading finished parts and stacking on the outgoing tray, and
5. general maintenance of the work center.

Special tools, to support the operation, were designed and the best robot for the use was identified. The layout of the modified workstation and specifications of robots available in the market were taken into consideration in identifying the best robot. Using the technical specifications of this robot, a time study was conducted and the cycle time for the operation was determined (88.1 seconds). From the cycle time, the production capacity of the robotized plant was determined. The production capacity of the human-operated work center was 800 units per day; for the robotized plant, the production capacity would be 1,315 units per day.

Economic Feasibility Study

Once the technical feasibility study was completed, an economic analysis from the company's perspective was performed to justify the investment (robot). To simplify the analysis, the following assumptions were made:

1. The company is unable to meet the demand due to low production capacity of the human-operated work center. The additional capacity, due to robot installation, can be sold without any difficulty.
2. The life period of the robot installation is ten years, with a salvage value of $10,000.
3. The interest rate is 12 percent per year.

TABLE IIIA-1 Initial Expenditure Due to Robot Installation

COST DESCRIPTION	AMOUNT ($)
Cost of robot (base)	$ 80,000
Special holders and tools	3,000
Installation cost	
Rearrangement cost	1,280
Installation cost	1,500
Feedback & interface devices	5,000
Feasibility study	300
Rearrangement cost	
Conveyor cost	4,362
Fence	670
Feeders & trays	2,000
Special tooling cost	
Grippers	4,000
Special arbor & fixtures	2,000
Control locks & safety	5,000
Total Expenditure	$109,112

4. All retraining costs are borne by the company.
5. The displaced employees, permanently unemployed, are not compensated by the company.
6. The effect of inflation can be ignored.
7. Working capital is not affected.
8. The company's required return is 25 percent.

Changes in the cash flow of the company due to robotization were estimated by identifying various costs and savings involved. The relevant costs and savings are described briefly.

1. Robot and accessories cost—includes cost of the robot, special tools, test equipment, etc.
2. Installation cost—labor and materials for the site, floor and foundation preparations, utilities and interface devices between the robot and fixtures.
3. Rearrangement cost—labor and material cost for the installation of the safety fence, conveyors, etc.
4. Special tooling costs—including costs of special end-of-arm devices and changes in the fixture design, clamps, limit switches, sensors, etc.
5. Indirect labor costs—repair and maintenance costs.
6. Operating supplies cost—annual cost of utilities and services used by the robot and the support equipment.
7. Maintenance supplies cost.
8. Launching costs—work stoppage due to installation costs.

TABLE IIIA-2 Changes in the Annual Cash Flow of the Company

DESCRIPTION OF THE CASH FLOW	AMOUNT ($/YEAR)
Maintenance and service labor cost for the robot work center	$ 6,000
Operating supplies	3,000
Training cost of the technician ($3,000 is distributed over 10 years using the 12 percent interest rate)	530
Tax and insurance (2.5%)	2,721
Increase in pay due to job upgrading of technician	5,000
Other miscellaneous costs	1,000
Total variable cost/year	$18,251
Savings due to labor displacement (20,000/year/displacement)	$60,000

9. Taxes and insurance.
10. Savings through reduced scrap, increased productivity, and other credits.
11. Savings in direct labor.

Case Questions

1. Identify after tax cash flows for the investment.
2. Find the net present value.
3. Find the internal rate of return.
4. Is the investment attractive from the company's perspective?
5. A 10-year life was assumed. What is the minimum life needed for the investment to be attractive?

MACHINE TOOL CORPORATION (B)

The economic analysis was expanded to include cost and revenue changes in the government's cash flow and to determine if it was still economically desirable to install the robot.

Robot installation would lead to the unemployment of three workers. This would cause changes in the cash flows to and from the government. Most changes were due to tax losses; additional costs were due to unemployment compensation, welfare, etc. If the employees were relocated to different jobs, tax revenues would be altered due to change in income. Increased profit from selling additional capacity, however, increases tax revenue to the government. These cash flows were not considered in the conventional economic analysis.

The following changed the cash flow of the government:

Federal corporate tax
State corporate tax
City and corporate franchise tax
Tangible property tax
Sales tax (due to increased sales)
Federal individual tax
State and city individual tax
Social security paid by the employees
Social security paid by the employer
Payroll tax
Unemployment compensation paid by the government
Welfare
Other miscellaneous taxes and expenditures

Taxes were computed from tax tables and forms provided by the various tax agencies (since local and state taxes vary widely, the final outcome can be significantly influenced). In this case study, taxes were calculated on the basis of the tax laws of the state of Ohio.

When determining changes in the cash flow of government, two different cases were examined:

Case 1: Displaced workers are permanently unemployed.
Case 2: Displaced workers are relocated.

Case 1. The displaced workers depend on unemployment compensation and welfare from the government. This change in their status alters the cash flow of the government. Various taxes paid by the employees stop. Also, some taxes paid by the employer stop. Government's expenses at the same time increase.

The increased productivity and labor savings, on the other hand, increase the company's profit. This profit, in turn, generates tax revenues to the government. The investment (robot) also increases the GNP.

Table IIIB-1 shows the additional revenues received by the government as the result of robotization. These were generated from the taxes from increased employer's savings and sales. The various costs to the government as the result of

TABLE IIIB-1 Changes in the Revenues of the Government

ITEM	AMOUNT ($/YEAR)
Federal corporation tax	18,930.84
State corporation tax	1,509.75
City tax	823.08
Corporate franchise tax (CFT)	5,864.88
Tangible property tax (TPT)	507.96
Sales tax	256.53
Indirect gain due to productivity and other sources	1,394.65
Total Revenue/Year	$29,287.69

TABLE IIIB-2 Cash Flow Lost by the Government Due to the Robot

ITEM	AMOUNT ($/YEAR)
Federal individual income tax (20.7% of company's profit)	$ 4,143.00
State income tax	549.33
City income tax	400.00
Social Security paid by the employee (SS1)(7%)	1,400.00
Payroll tax paid by the employer	1,240.00
Social Security paid by the employer (SS1)(7%)	1,400.00
Unemployment compensation paid by the government to the unemployed	7,000.00
Other governmental cost (10% of the above)	1,613.23
Total cost/year/employee	$17,745.56
Total cost/yr. = $17,745 × 3 workers = $53,235	

worker displacement are shown in Table IIIB-2. These costs were mainly due to losses in tax revenue, expenses on unemployment compensation, and welfare.

Case 2. In this case, it was assumed that the workers can be transferred to a different location in the company without retraining, since the new jobs require the same levels of skills. It was also assumed that the three workers, once relocated, will earn the same salary.

Impact of Robot Installation on GNP

Gross national product (GNP) is the yardstick of an economy's performance. It is the measure of overall annual flow of goods and services in the economy and consists of three major components.

1. Personal consumption expenditure (65% of GNP)
2. Government expenditure on goods and services (18% of GNP)
3. Gross private domestic investment (17% of GNP)

In the present case study, the personal consumption expenditure of each displaced worker was expected to change depending on his new income. If the worker remained unemployed, the reduction in personal consumption expenditure would be:

$$[1 - (7{,}000/20{,}000)] \times 100 = 65$$

where \$7,000 is the unemployment compensation and \$20,000 is the original income. This is approximately 3.95×10^{-11} of the GNP (as of April 1984 the GNP was \$3,541.6 billion). Since in this case study, three workers were displaced, the GNP was lowered by 11.85×10^{-11} percent. However, the increase in GNP due to investment (investment on robot installation was \$109,112) was 31.06×10^{-11} percent. It appears that in this case, there is a net increase in GNP. If we assume the total displacement nationwide of three million workers by robots by the year 1990, the net change in GNP will be a decrease of approximately 2 percent. If the worker is relocated instead of being unemployed, the change in the GNP is mainly due to the investment.

Case Questions

1. Assuming displaced workers are permanently unemployed, is the new investment attractive from the perspective of the government?
2. Assuming displaced workers are relocated, is the new investment attractive from the perspective of the government?
3. How should conflicts between government and company interests be dealt with in the company's decision-making process?

MACHINE TOOL CORPORATION (C)

Managers at Machine Tool Corporation want to consider the possibility of inflation in analyzing the robot investment. A 5 percent annual increase in all costs is assumed for this purpose. Assume that the company's required return already reflected anticipated inflation.

Case Questions

1. Identify the annual after tax cash flows to the company considering inflation.
2. Compute the net present value.

Risk and Investment Choice

PART FOUR

In the previous chapters, risk considerations were eliminated with the assumption that all of the company's investments were riskless or at least in the same risk class. In this part of the book, risk differences are incorporated into the analysis. General insights into decision making under risk are discussed in Chapter 11. Methods of recognizing risk from the perspective of an isolated investment are treated in Chapter 12. Method of recognizing risk from the perspective of the top management of the company, including diversification issues, are dealt with in Chapter 13. In Chapter 14, the mean-variance capital asset pricing model is used to consider risk from the perspective of a fully diversified shareholder. In Chapter 15, arbitrage pricing theory and the option pricing model are used as additional methods of considering risk from the perspectives of shareholders and the other affected parties. These chapters cover methods of measuring risk, methods of reducing or controlling risk, and methods of choosing investments in the face of risk. Upon completing these chapters, you will have an understanding of the general principles of risk analysis as well as a good kit of tools for risk analysis.

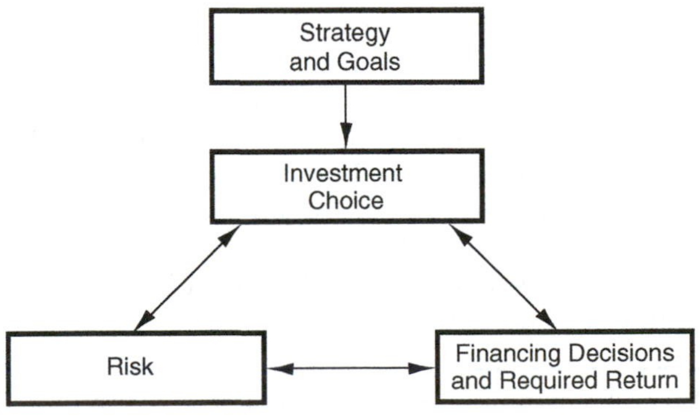

CHAPTER 11

Introduction to Risk Analysis

After completing this chapter, you should be able to:

- Apply basic probability rules to determine the probability of an outcome or range of outcomes.
- Describe the various ways of measuring risk.
- Describe and compute each summary measure of a central tendency including expected value, median, mode, and geometric mean.
- Calculate and understand the various measures of dispersion such as variance, standard deviation, coefficient of variation, and semivariance.
- Determine and explain the meaning of a risk-return indifference curve.
- Explain the implication of the statement that someone is an expected utility maximizer.
- Understand the importance of each of the five risk perspectives introduced in this chapter and developed in this section of the book.

Jim Burke, CEO of Johnson and Johnson, told the story of one of his earlier experiences in risk taking. He suggested that the company start a new products division, and was hired to head the fledgling unit. One of his first products was a chest rub for children. Unfortunately, the product was a complete failure.

Burke was called to the office of General Robert Wood Johnson, then chairman of the board. "Are you the one who just cost us all that money?" the General asked. Burke confirmed his guilt, while wondering if he was about to be fired. The General said, "Well, I just want to congratulate you. If you are making mistakes, that means you are making decisions and taking risks. And we won't grow unless we take risks."[1]

[1]John Steinbreder, "Taking Chances at J & J," *Fortune* (June 6, 1988): 60.

Risk is inherent in most long-term decisions, especially capital budgeting decisions. Both costs and benefits must be predicted for periods from a few years to a few decades in the future. Customers, suppliers, competitors, and governments all affect future cash flows, as do weather conditions and the activities of businesses, consumers, and nations having no direct dealings with the company. Businesses that fail to consider the risks to which they expose themselves will not be around long. On the other hand, like the proverbial turtle, you cannot make progress without sticking your neck out. Appropriate methods of dealing with risk are, therefore, essential for successful capital budgeting.

The objective of this chapter is to develop a foundation for capital budgeting in the face of risk. One characteristic of a risky investment is that there is more than one possible outcome. We developed the net present value as a way to compare cash flows occurring at different times, and we must also develop desirability measures that allow us to evaluate an investment characterized by a range of possible cash flows. Our first tasks are to define and measure risk. Then, we need to develop an understanding of how people respond to risk. Thus, we begin this chapter with some definitions, and then turn our attention to measurement tools used in the face of risk. The definitions and measurement tools provide the background for understanding utility theory, which is the next topic. Utility theory summarizes much of our understanding about how people decide when faced with risk. Since risk measures and investment choices are affected by our choices of the person(s) whose welfare is being maximized, this chapter ends with a discussion of whose perspective to use in decision making. The topics covered in this chapter provide the foundation for the various approaches to risky investment choice discussed in Chapters 12 through 15.

SOME DEFINITIONS

Terminology is important, in that many long-standing debates boil down to nothing more than the combatants using the same word to mean two different things. A brief overview of some widely used terminology may help to avoid such problems.

Risk. **Risk** is used in common language to mean exposure to the chance of an injury or loss. In finance, the term risk is used in general to refer to the chance of the loss of money. Risk may also refer to the chance of getting back less than was expected, less than the rate of return on a sure thing such as a Treasury bill, or less than would have been received from some other risky investment.

Probability. The probability of an occurrence is the likelihood of that event, expressed as a ratio. It is the expected relative frequency of the event when the number of observations is very large. If you flip a coin, for example, the probability of a head is 1/2; if the coin is flipped many times, we would expect heads half of the time. If a die is rolled, the probability of an even number less than six is 1/3 (a 2 or a 4 will satisfy these criteria, and there are six possible, equally likely, outcomes).

Risk vs. Uncertainty. Risk is sometimes used to identify only the situation in which the probabilities of all outcomes are known. When the term is used in this way, **uncertainty** is used to identify situations in which the probabilities of outcomes are not known. This is an unfortunate terminology choice for two reasons. First, the term risk is used in everyday conversation to refer to any situation involving the possibility of an undesired outcome, whether or not probabilities are known. Second, there is hardly ever a real-world environment other than the casino in which probabilities are known. Real-world decision making involves a continuum, with one end reflecting a high degree of confidence in probability estimates and the other end reflecting a low degree of confidence. In this book, we will use both risk and uncertainty in the more general sense, to cover situations in which the outcomes are not known with certainty, whether or not probabilities are known.

Probability Distribution. A probability distribution is a set of all possible occurrences and their associated probabilities. A **discrete** probability distribution has a finite number of possible occurrences, such as the two possible occurrences with the flip of a coin. Some probability distributions are **continuous** and, therefore, cover an infinite number of possible occurrences. The probability distribution of return on assets for General Electric is infinite; for example, for any two rates of return on assets, it is possible to have a rate between those two. Continuous distributions are generally defined by a mathematical function, and we generally talk about the probability of an occurrence within a particular range rather than the probability of any single occurrence.

Subjective vs. Objective Probability. Objective probability is probability that can be measured or otherwise computed. If we have determined that a pair of dice is fair, for example, we can objectively determine the probability of a total score of seven on any roll. Subjective probability is an estimate based on someone's opinion. The probability that Nike's jogging shoe sales will increase 5 percent or more next year is a subjective probability. While the estimate of the jogging shoe sales growth may be based on extensive analytical work, it depends on the analyst's judgment concerning which information is important in arriving at a probability estimate.[2]

Variation vs. Event Risk. In common language, risk is often associated with the chance of a specific undesired event. Risk of ruin, such as the risk of bankruptcy or public humiliation, is one such event risk in business. The possible failure of Monsanto's genetically engineered corn to pass Environmental Protection Agency tests could be another event risk. By way of comparison, a range of possible levels of jogging shoe sales rather than one known sales level is an example of variation risk. This latter type of risk is often described in terms of some measure of the variability of future cash flows, such as the standard deviation of the probability distribution, which is discussed later in this chapter.

[2]The most famous subjective estimate may be that of Murray Wiedenbaum, then chairman of the Council of Economic Advisors. In what David Stockman described as "the belly slap heard round the world," Wiedenbaum justified his pessimistic economic forecast by touching his midsection and saying "it comes from here."

Diversifiable vs. Nondiversifiable Risk. Diversifiable risk is risk that can be eliminated by combining one investment with other investments. Nondiversifiable risk, also referred to as systematic risk or portfolio risk, relates to factors that tend to affect all investments and consequently cannot be reduced by combining investments in portfolios. We can diversify away the risk that Nike's jogging shoes will be unpopular by buying stock in all running shoe companies. We can diversify away the risk of jogging shoes declining in favor of other recreation goods by buying the stocks of a broad range of recreation companies. A general downturn in the economy will, however, affect the sales of virtually all companies, and that risk cannot be diversified away. Nondiversifiable risk can generally be avoided only by investing in risk-free investments, which generally means accepting a lower expected return.

PROBABILITY RULES

Basic probability rules involving multiple events are often used in the analysis of risk. The most frequently used rules are discussed in this section.

Mutually Exclusive Events

Events are mutually exclusive if the occurrence of one eliminates any possibility of the occurrence of the other(s). Suppose developers in the downtown area and two suburbs of St. Louis are competing to have their sites chosen for a new baseball stadium. These are mutually exclusive choices because the team cannot simultaneously play at two stadiums. The probability of an occurrence from a set of mutually exclusive events is simply the sum of the probabilities of the individual events in the set. Suppose there is a .5 probability the stadium will be built in the northern suburb site and a .25 probability the southern suburb site will be approved. The probability of a suburban site being chosen is:

$$P(\text{Suburban}) = P(\text{North}) + P(\text{South}) = .50 + .25 = .75$$

where $P(\cdot)$ is the probability of the event(s) within parentheses. P(North), for example, is the probability of the northern site being chosen.

Independent Events

Two events are independent if the probability of one event is not affected by the outcome of the other event. The probability that Texaco's new well in the Bourbon field will produce oil is not affected by results from its well in the Arctic field. Let P(A) be the probability of event A and P(B) be the probability of event B. Since probabilities must sum to 1.0, the probability of A not occurring is $[1 - P(A)]$ and the probability of B not occurring is $[1 - P(B)]$. The probability of both A and B occurring is:

$$P(A \cap B) = P(A)P(B) \tag{11-1}$$

where $\cap$ means intersection in set theory terminology, so $P(A \cap B)$ is the probability of both A and B occurring.

There are four possible combinations of outcomes, and their probabilities are as follows:

	Event B occurs	Event B does not occur
Event A occurs	P(A)P(B)	P(A)[1 – P(B)]
Event A does not occur	[1 – P(A)]P(B)	[1 – P(A)][1 – P(B)]

Example: For Texaco, the probability that the Arctic well will be successful is .7, and the probability that the Bourbon well will be successful is .4. The projects are independent, so the probabilities of the possible combinations of outcomes are as follows:

	Bourbon is successful	Bourbon is unsuccessful
Arctic is successful	.7 × .4 = .28	.7 × .6 = .42
Arctic is unsuccessful	.3 × .4 = .12	.3 × .6 = .18

Each of the four combinations is mutually exclusive; a well cannot both succeed and fail. Therefore, the probability that one or more well will be successful can be found by adding probabilities:

$$P(\text{at least one well succeeds}) = .28 + .42 + .12 = \underline{\underline{.82}}$$

The probability of at least one investment succeeding can also be found as follows:

$$P(\text{at least one investment succeeds}) = 1 - P(\text{both fail}) = 1 - .18 = \underline{\underline{.82}}$$

Dependent Events

Suppose that the probability of B depends on whether or not A occurs. B is then dependent on A, and the rules of conditional probability must be applied. The probability that both A and B will occur is then:

$$P(A \cap B) = P(B|A)P(A) \tag{11-2}$$

where $P(B|A)$ is the probability of B occurring, given that A has occurred.

This basic conditional probability rule can be extended to chains of events in which the probability of an event depends on the occurrence of two or more previous events. If event C is dependent on events A *and* B, the formula is:

$$P(A \cap B \cap C) = P(C|A \cap B)P(A \cap B) \quad \textbf{(11-3)}$$

where $P(A \cap B \cap C)$ is the probability of A, B, and C all occurring, and $P(C|A \cap B)$ is the probability of C occurring, given that A and B have occurred.

Example: Suppose the northern suburb of St. Louis will put a bond issue on the ballot to fund a new stadium. There is a .8 probability that the bond issue will pass. The probability that the northern site will be approved depends on whether the bond issue passes, as follows:

1. If the bond issue passes, the probability of the northern site being selected is .6.
2. If the bond issue fails, the probability of the northern site being selected is .3.

The probabilities for the various possible outcomes are as follows:

	North selected	**North rejected**
Bond issue passes	.8 × .6 = .48	.8 × .4 = .32
Bond issue fails	.2 × .3 = .06	.2 × .7 = .14

Because each of the combinations is mutually exclusive, we can find the probability that the northern site will be selected:

$$P(\text{North selected}) = .48 + .06 = \underline{\underline{.54}}$$

These various probability rules will be applied in the following chapters when analyzing capital investments under conditions of risk.

MEASURING RISK

Risk is complex and many-faceted. While there have long been attempts to reduce risk to concrete measures, we are not yet to the point where any one measure adequately describes risk in every situation. Various risk measures are discussed in the following paragraphs, and each risk measure has its own information content. Managers often look at more than one risk measure as they describe risk, eliminate or control risk, and make investment decisions in the face of risk.

The simplest risk analysis is *descriptive* and *subjective*. Things that might go wrong are identified, and the decision makers are left to their own judgment as to the importance of these things in terms of either likelihood of occurrence or severity of consequences. The most basic risk analysis, then, may simply involve statements such as "we might be overly optimistic about the rate of demand growth" or "competitors may cut their prices too."

Sensitivity Analysis

Sensitivity analysis is a method of quantifying uncertainty without having to estimate probabilities. You simply estimate the consequences of different levels of one or more variables that affect the investment. You can, for example, assess the importance of a slower-than-anticipated growth rate in sales of 3M's new paper fastener by computing the net present value at various growth rates. Break-even analysis is one of the tools that has been useful in this regard, not just to measure risk but to consider approaches that can improve the profitability-risk trade-off. Despite the development of more sophisticated approaches, sensitivity analysis and break-even analysis continue to be useful tools and are discussed in more detail in Chapter 12.

Event Probability

A limitation of sensitivity analysis is that it shows us profitability at different levels of some variable, but tells us nothing about the likelihood of each level occurring. Thus, the next step is to assign probabilities to various outcomes. In a simple analysis, probability assessment may be attempted for only one or a few possible events. The statement that "there is a one-out-of-ten probability of bankruptcy if this strategy is followed" is a simple event probability assessment. At the other extreme, probabilities may be attached to each of a large number of possible events.

Beyond event probability, risk is often measured using summary statistics for the probability distribution of outcomes, such as the expected value and variance. These measures are covered in the next section.

SUMMARY MEASURES OF PROBABILITY DISTRIBUTIONS

If each possible amount of annual cash flow from Hewlett-Packard's factory investment is considered an event, the number of outcomes may be measured in the billions. Stating each possible outcome and its probability would be overwhelming. Some way to summarize the probability distribution of outcomes is needed. Distributions are frequently summarized with measures of central tendency and dispersion. Discussion of these measures follows. Capital investment decisions are often made using a measure of the central tendency as the index of desirability and a dispersion measure as the index of risk.

Measures of Central Tendency

The most widely used measures of central tendency are the expected value, the median, the mode, and the geometric mean. Each of these gives some indication of the likely result of an action.

Expected Value

The expected value is also called the arithmetic mean or simply the mean of the probability distribution. For a probability distribution with n possible outcomes, the expected value, E(X), is defined as follows:

$$E(X) = \sum_{i=1}^{n} p_i X_i \tag{11-4}$$

where p_i is the probability of amount X_i occurring. Suppose, for example, Alcoa is considering a capital investment with the following probability distribution of net present values:

NPV	100	200	300	400	500
Probability	.1	.2	.4	.2	.1

The expected net present value is:

$$E(NPV) = (.1 \times 100) + (.2 \times 200) + (.4 \times 300) + (.2 \times 400) + (.1 \times 500) = \underline{\underline{\$300}}$$

If Alcoa could repeat the investment an infinite number of times, the expected net present value of $300 is the expected average net present value per investment.

Median

There is an equal probability of an outcome greater or less than the median value. The median for the Alcoa example is $300; there is a .3 probability of a lower net present value and a .3 probability of a higher net present value.

Mode

The mode is the outcome with the highest probability. In the Alcoa example, the mode is $300 because the highest probability (.4) is associated with $300.

The mean, median, and mode are equal in this particular example, because the probability distribution is symmetrical; the probability of outcomes in any given range above the mean equals the probability of outcomes in that same

FIGURE 11-1 Nonsymmetrical Probability Distributions of Net Present Value
This figure illustrates the location of the expected value, median, and mode for nonsymmetrical distributions. The area under the curve between any two values, as a proportion of the total area under the curve, represents the probability of an outcome within that range.

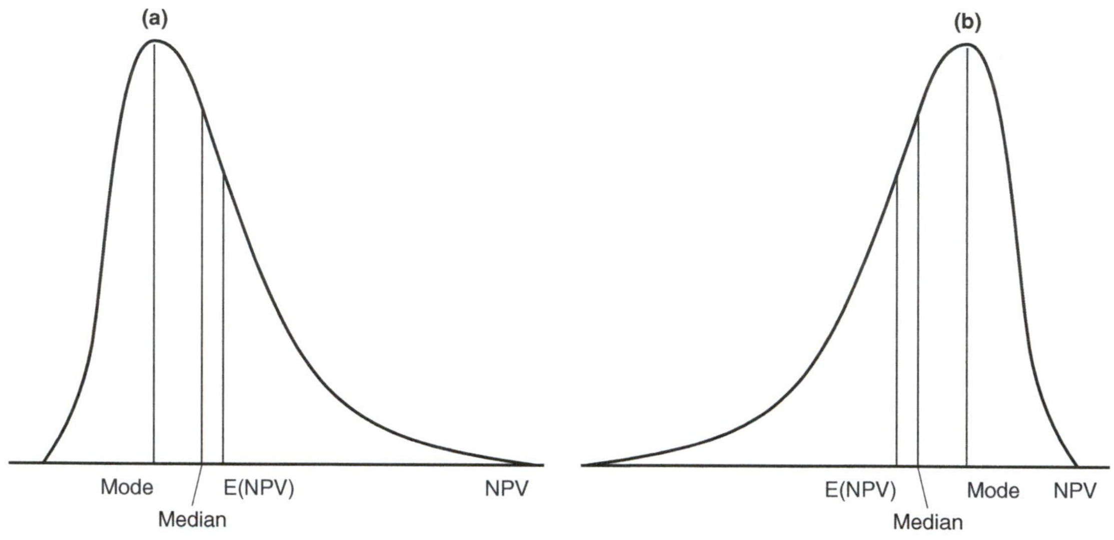

range below the mean. The probability of a NPV $200 above the mean equals the probability of a NPV $200 below the mean, for example.

Nonsymmetrical distributions typically have one tail that is longer than the other. In Figure 11-1, distribution (a) has a longer right tail meaning that a net present value much higher than the expected value is more likely than a net present value much lower than the expected value. The situation is opposite for distribution (b). Distribution (a) is said to be *skewed* to the right, and distribution (b) is said to be skewed to the left. Note the relative locations of the mode, median, and expected NPV for each distribution. A simple illustration, for a distribution skewed to the right, helps to demonstrate the relationships of the mean, median, and mode for skewed distributions:

NPV	100	200	300	400	500
Probability	.40	.20	.20	.15	.05

$$\text{Expected NPV} = .4 \times 100 + .2 \times 200 + .2 \times 300 + .15 \times 400 + .05 \times 500 = 225$$

The median is 200 because the probability of an outcome above 200 equals the probability of an outcome below 200.

The mode is 100, because the probability of 100 is greater than the probability of any other outcome.

Note that the median is higher than the mode and the expected value is higher than the median. This is because the mode is not affected by anything but the outcome with the highest probability, and the median is not affected by the exact shape of the tail. If the probabilities of 400 and 500 were exchanged, for example, the median and mode would not be affected, but the expected net present value would increase.

Geometric Mean

In finance, the geometric mean is associated with rates of return and represents the expected long-run growth rate of money, given repeated investments with the same probability distribution of returns. The formula for the geometric mean return, GM, is:

$$GM = (1 + R_1)^{P_1}(1 + R_2)^{P_2}(1 + R_3)^{P_3} \ldots (1 + R_n)^{P_n} \quad \textbf{(11-5)}$$

where

R_1 through R_n are the possible rates of return for any one period, defined as

(Ending value − Beginning value + cash flow during the period) ÷ Beginning value

P_1 through P_n are the associated probabilities

Example: An investment at Omaha Packing has the following probability distribution of annual rates of return:

Return	−.6	0	.2	.3	.5
Probability	.1	.2	.4	.2	.1

The expected return is:

$$E(R) = .1 \times (-.6) + .2 \times 0 - .4 \times .2 + .2 \times .3 + .1 \times .5 = \underline{\underline{.13}}$$

The geometric mean return is:

$$GM = (1 - .6)^{.1}(1 + 0)^{.2}(1 + .2)^{.4}(1 + .3)^{.2}(1 + .5)^{.1} = 1.077$$

In other words, wealth committed to this investment can be expected to grow at an annual rate of 7.7 percent over the long term.

The expected return for the previous example is 13 percent, but because of variability, the long-term growth rate of wealth is only 7.7 percent. This illustrates one disadvantage of variability. The long-term growth rate from a sure thing with an expected return of 13 percent is greater than the long-run growth rate from an investment with a 13 percent expected return and variability around that expected return. If the decrease in long-term growth were the only reason for disliking variability, the geometric mean might serve as a single measure of desirability combining risk and return. But variability has disadvantages in the short run as well as in the long run. Therefore, expected value is widely used as the central tendency measure, along with one of the following measures of dispersion.

MEASURES OF DISPERSION

Dispersion measures are summary statistics of the way possible outcomes are spread around some measure of central tendency, generally the expected value. The simplest approach is to describe the distribution in terms of ranges. For more sophistication, the most widely used measures are the variance and its square root, the standard deviation.

Ranges

Ranges provide a simple, practical, and easily understood way to describe a probability distribution. The probability of an outcome within a particular range can be determined by simply adding the probabilities of all outcomes within that range. For example, a project has the possible net present values shown below. There is a .60 probability of a positive net present value and a .15 probability of a negative net present value. The decision maker can use this range information to make a decision as to whether the expected benefit is worth the risk.

NPV	–\$200	–\$100	\$0	\$100	\$200	\$300	\$400
Probability	.05	.10	.25	.25	.20	.10	.05

Variance and Standard Deviation

When there are a number of possible outcomes, each with an associated probability, the **variance** is:

$$\sigma_X^2 = \sum_{i=1}^{n} p_i[X_i - E(X)]^2 \tag{11-6}$$

where p_i is the probability of value X_i and $E(X)$ is the expected value of X, as defined in Equation 11-4. The **standard deviation** is simply the square root of the variance.

Example: In Table 11-1, variance and standard deviation are illustrated with the Alcoa investment that was used to illustrate expected return, median, and mode.

The standard deviation, in particular, is a widely used measure of risk. It is preferred over the variance because it is expressed in the same units as the original problem, such as dollars, rather than in squared dollars, and is therefore

TABLE 11-1 Probability Distribution of Net Present Values for a Sample Alcoa Investment

The investment has five possible net present values, with probabilities as indicated. Expected net present value, variance, and standard deviation are computed from this information.

Net Present Value	100	200	300	400	500
Probability	.1	.2	.4	.2	.1

$E(NPV) = .1 \times 100 + .2 \times 200 + .4 \times 300 + .2 \times 400 + .1 \times 500 = \underline{\underline{\$300}}$

$\sigma_{npv}^2 = .1(100-300)^2 + .2(200-300)^2 + .4(300-300)^2 + .2(400-300)^2 + .1(500-300)^2$

$= 12{,}000$

$\sigma_{npv} = \sqrt{12{,}000} = \underline{\underline{110}}$

FIGURE 11-2 The Normal Curve

The area under the curve between any two values, as a proportion of the total area under the curve, represents the probability of an outcome within that range.

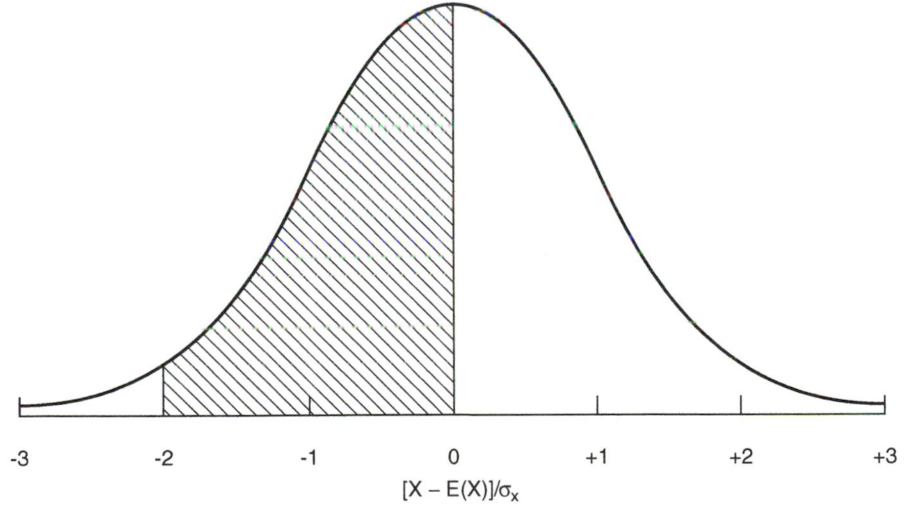

easier to interpret. The standard deviation can combine hundreds of possible outcomes and probabilities in a single risk statistic. The standard deviation is helpful in stating probabilities of occurrences within various ranges, particularly if the probabilities of outcomes are approximately normally distributed, as illustrated in Figure 11-2.

The normal distribution was first recognized by scientists in the eighteenth century, who observed an amazing degree of regularity in the distribution of errors of measurement. Nature and people have produced many things that are normally distributed. For example, the distributions of intelligence quotients and machined part diameters are approximately normal. Even when samples are drawn from a non-normal distribution, the distribution of sample means tends toward normality as the sample size becomes large. If events can be categorized according to success or failure, the probability distribution of the number of successes approaches normality as the number of trials becomes large.[3]

We cannot always count on normality, though. One characteristic of a normal distribution is that it is symmetrical; an outcome more than 20 percent below the mean equals the probability of an outcome more than 20 percent above the mean, for example. If return from a portfolio each year is drawn from a symmetrical distribution, the probability distribution of terminal wealth will not be symmetrical. Suppose, for example, return each year is +80 percent or –80 percent, each with a .5 probability. This is a symmetrical distribution with an expected value of 0 percent. The four equally likely outcomes over a 2-year period, with a beginning investment of $100, are:

YEAR 1	YEAR 2	TERMINAL WEALTH
+80%	+80%	324
+80%	–80%	36
–80%	+80%	36
–80%	–80%	4

This expected terminal wealth is $100, but the probability distribution is clearly not symmetrical around that expected value. Since symmetry can be destroyed in this way, and normal distributions are symmetrical, normality can be destroyed. Therefore, it is wise to check for normality rather than assuming its existence. Tests are explained in any elementary statistics book.

The normal distribution table in Appendix B can be used to find the probability of an outcome within any range if the expected value and standard deviation are known. Appendix B contains the probability of an occurrence between the expected value and the specified number of standard deviations on *one* side of the expected value. For example, the value for 2.00 in Appendix B is the shaded area in Figure 11-2, as a percent of the total area under the curve; it is the probability of an outcome being between the expected value and two standard deviations on one side of the expected value. Since the normal distribution is symmetrical, doubling the probability from the table gives the probability of an outcome within a certain distance above or below the expected value. To find the probability of being more than some specified number of standard deviations to one side of the expected value, simply find the probability of being between the mean and that value, then subtract that probability from .50. A similar procedure is used to find a value within a range, such as between 1.5 and 2.0 standard deviations below the mean.

[3]If there are n trials and the probability of success on any one trial is p, the expected value and variance are $E(V) = np$ and $\sigma_{npv}^2 = np(1 - p)$.

Example: The probability distribution of net present values[4] for an investment at Lexington Corporation is normally distributed with an expected value of \$300 and a standard deviation of \$110. We want to find the probability of a net present value less than \$150. To do this, we complete the following steps:

1. Note that (\$150 – \$300)/110 = –1.36, so \$150 is 1.36 standard deviations below the mean. The probability of a net present value between \$150 and \$300 is the probability associated with 1.36 in Appendix B: .4131.
2. The probability of a net present value between \$150 and \$300 is .4131.
3. The probability of a net present value less than \$150 is .5000 – .4131 = .0869. A graphical summary of the solution follows, with P representing probability within a range.

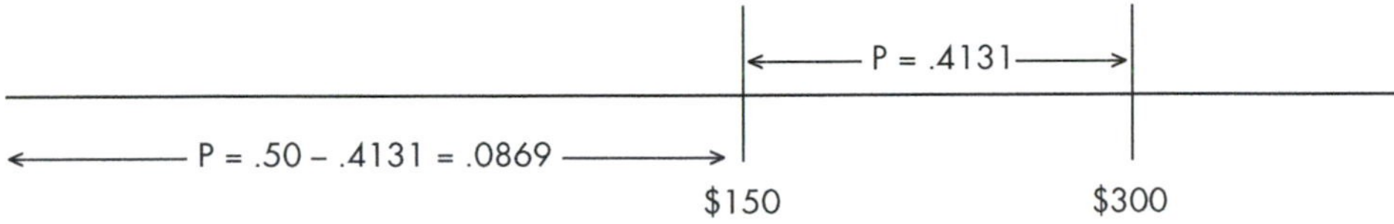

Example: With an expected net present value of \$300 and a standard deviation of \$110, managers at Lexington Corporation want to know the probability of a net present value between \$150 and \$250. A graphical summary of the solution follows this paragraph. First we find the probability of being between each of these values and \$300, using Appendix B:

$$(\$150 - \$300)/110 = -1.36;\ P(150 < NPV < 300) = .4131$$

$$(\$250 - \$300)/110 = -0.45;\ P(250 < NPV < 300) = .1736$$

The probability of a value between \$150 and \$250 is then:

$$P(150 < NPV < 250) = P(150 < NPV < 300) - P(250 < NPV < 300) = .4131 - .1736 = \underline{\underline{.2395}}$$

P = .4131
P = .4131 – .1736 = .2395
P = .1736
\$150
\$250
\$300

[4]In a strict sense, an investment has only one net present value, which is the amount by which the value of the probability distribution of future benefits exceeds the value of the probability distribution of outlays. Thus, net present value is the change in wealth when an investment is selected. Subsequent changes in wealth as uncertainty is resolved are not changes in the net present value. While it is true in this sense that an investment has only one net present value, a commonly used approach to risk analysis is to compute a net present value for each possible outcome. The probability of a negative net present value has meaning, for example, in that it is the probability that the subsequent cash flows will not be sufficient to provide investors a fair rate of return that compensates for risks taken.

The variance and standard deviation allow a description of risk in one statistic, and can be converted to statements of probability with regard to various ranges.

Coefficient of Variation

One problem with the variance and standard deviation is that they are not adjusted for scale. Using the standard deviation, an investment with an expected net present value of $1 million and a standard deviation of $11,000 would be viewed as more risky than an investment with an expected net present value of $1,000 and a standard deviation of $10,000.

The coefficient of variation restates the standard deviation in relation to the scale of the project. The formula for the coefficient of variation (CV) is:

$$CV = \sigma_X/E(X) \tag{11-7}$$

For an investment with an expected net present value of $300 and a standard deviation of $110, the coefficient of variation is:

$$CV = 110/300 = .367$$

Using the coefficient of variation, this investment would be viewed as less risky than an investment with an expected net present value of $100 and a standard deviation of $50; the latter investment would have a coefficient of variation of .50.

Semivariance

Another problem with the standard deviation is that it treats outcomes above and below the expected value in the same way. This is not likely to cause difficulty with a **symmetrical** distribution, such as that illustrated in Figure 11-2, for which the probability of being a certain amount above the expected value is the same as the probability of being that amount below. But problems arise if distributions are nonsymmetrical, such as those illustrated in Figures 11-1(a) and 11-1(b). The expected value and standard deviation are the same for each distribution, but the risk characteristics are quite different. There is a significant probability of large losses in the case of 11-1(b), but not in the case of 11-1(a).

The semivariance can be used to compare risk between projects when the probability distributions are skewed. The semivariance is computed in the same manner as the variance, except that only outcomes below the expected value are considered in its calculation. For the investment analyzed in Table 11-1, the semivariance is:

$$\text{Semivariance} = .1(100-300)^2 + .2(200-300)^2 = 6{,}000$$

The **semi-standard deviation** is the square root of the semivariance:

$$\text{Semi-standard deviation} = \sqrt{6{,}000} = \underline{\underline{77.46}}$$

To make the semivariance and variance comparable in scale, the semivariance can be adjusted by doubling; it will then equal the variance if the distribution is symmetrical. The adjusted semi-standard deviation is the square root of the doubled semivariance. For the investment in Table 11-1, the adjusted semi-standard deviation is:

$$\text{Adjusted semi-standard deviation} = \sqrt{2 \times 6,000} = 110$$

The adjusted semi-standard deviation will be the same as the standard deviation if the probability distribution is symmetrical, greater than the standard deviation if the distribution is skewed to the left, and less than the standard deviation if the distribution is skewed to the right. Any of these measures can also be divided by the expected value to convert them to coefficients adjusted for project size, as was done with the coefficient of variation.

ALTERNATE PROFITABILITY MEASURE AND RISK

With the exception of the geometric mean return, the risk measures discussed in this chapter are stated in terms of risk related to net present value. All of the same risk statistics can be computed in relation to the internal rate of return, payback, equivalent annuity, or most other measures that might be used for capital investment evaluation. It should be noted, though, that the limitations of specific desirability measures come along as unwanted baggage when these measures are carried into the risk analysis arena. A higher internal rate of return or shorter payback is not always better, for example, as illustrated with the following example.

Example: A capital investment at Bowling Green Corporation requires an outlay of $100 and will generate cash flows of $20 a year forever, if successful. Another possible outcome is a $125 inflow at the end of the first year, and nothing thereafter. Given a 10 percent required return, the two net present values and internal rates of return are:

OUTCOME	SUCCESS	ALTERNATE
Cash flow per year	$20	$125
Number of years cash flow is received	∞	1
Present value of inflow	$200	$113.64
Net present value	$100	$13.64
Internal rate of return	20%	25%

In this example, the higher internal rate of return is associated with a less desirable outcome, in net present value terms. Likewise, the less desirable outcome has a shorter payback period. Therefore, decisions based on the probability distribution of internal rate of return or payback period may lead to erroneous capital investment decisions.

TABLE 11-2 Production Methods for Manufacturing Disk Drives

PRODUCTION METHOD	MANUAL	SEMI-AUTOMATED	FULLY AUTOMATED
Expected net present value	$300,000	$400,000	$500,000
σ_{npv}	300,000	400,000	700,000
Coefficient of variation	1.00	1.00	1.40
Adjusted semi–standard deviation	300,000	350,000	700,000
P(NPV < 0)	.1587	.1271	.2389

COMPREHENSIVE EXAMPLE

Suppose you are a production manager for Treac, a manufacturer of disk drives. Three production methods available to meet increased demand are summarized in Table 11-2.

If there were no risk, you would choose the fully automated method because it has the highest net present value. However, the standard deviation suggests that you can increase the net present value only by increasing risk. The coefficient of variation, on the other hand, adjusts the standard deviation for project scale and suggests the semiautomated method is not more risky than manual production. Skewness is recognized with the adjusted semi-standard deviation, which is lowest as a ratio to NPV for semiautomated production.

You would prefer the semiautomated method over the manual method because it has a higher expected net present value and lower risk. Whether you would be willing to accept the higher risk of the fully automated method in exchange for higher expected net present value is a more difficult question, depending on your own preferences. If you will face a post-audit, for example, you may want to choose the semiautomated method to minimize the probability of negative net present value. Your stockholders' and superiors' preferences will depend on their utility functions, which brings us to our next topic.

UTILITY THEORY—PERSPECTIVE ON RISK TAKING

Utility theory is basic to much study of economic decision making. Utility is often referred to in economics as a measure of the degree of satisfaction received. In our analysis of decision making under uncertainty, we only need to define utility as an index to measure the relative desirability of monetary payoffs of varying degrees of uncertainty.

Use of utility theory in valuing risky alternatives was suggested by Daniel Bernoulli in 1738,[5] following his demonstration of the futility of using expected

---

[5]D. Bernoulli, "Specimen Theoriae Novae de Mensura Sortis" (St. Petersburg, 1738). English translation: *Econometrica* (1954): 23–36.

value as a guiding rule for evaluating gambles.[6] Bernoulli suggested that people choose between risky alternatives so as to maximize expected utility. Expected utility, E(U), is defined as:

$$E(U) = p_1U(X_1) + p_2U(X_2) + p_3U(X_3) + \cdot\cdot\cdot \qquad \textbf{(11-8)}$$

where p_1 is the probability of outcome 1, X_1 is the payment received if outcome 1 occurs, and $U(X_1)$ is an index that reflects the relative attractiveness of payment X_1 in relation to other possible payments. Widespread use of expected utility concepts followed rigorous development of the theory by Von Neumann and Morgenstern[7] and a pioneering application in finance by Markowitz.[8]

The reason for the use of expected utility is that choices consistent with expected utility maximization can be shown to be rational, while other choices are not rational. Rationality is not a very restrictive standard. The essential characteristic of rational choice is that if A is preferred over B and B is preferred over C, then A must be preferred over C; if rational people prefer Ford over Chevrolet and prefer Chevrolet over Chrysler, they will prefer Ford over Chrysler. This essential characteristic also implies that rational decision makers who are indifferent between A and B, and also indifferent between B and C, will be indifferent between A and C. A rational decision maker will be able to rank alternatives in this way whether A, B, and C are certain payments or gambles.

As a second characteristic, rational decision makers will not be fooled by method of presentation; a rational decision maker will be indifferent between a .25 probability of receiving $10 and a .5 probability of winning a free play in a coin-flip game that pays $10 if the coin comes up heads and $0 if it comes up tails.

To begin exploring the meaning of the expected utility criterion, take M. Clark, a rational decision maker who is considering a gamble that pays $5 or nothing, with the probability of a $5 payoff being h. The gamble can be shown graphically as follows, with p representing event probability.

p = h ———— $5
p = 1 – h ———— $0

Suppose we present Clark with numerous choices, each involving a certain $3 or the gamble with a different value of h. We find that Clark chooses the gamble whenever h is greater than .85 and chooses the certain $3 whenever h is less than .85. Clark is indifferent between a certain $3 and the gamble with h of .85.

---

[6]This demonstration, called the St. Petersburg paradox, involves a game in which a coin is flipped until it comes up heads. The payoff is $\$2^n$ where n is the number of flips until a head occurs. The expected value is:

$$E(V) = \$2(1/2) + \$4(1/4) + \$8(1/8) + \ldots = \infty$$

The expected value rule leads to the ludicrous conclusion that even the richest person would trade all of his or her wealth for a gamble with the probability of a payoff in excess of $16 being 1/16.

[7]John Von Neumann and Oskar Morgenstern, *Theory of Games and Economic Behavior,* 2nd ed. (Princeton, N.J.: Princeton University Press, 1947).

[8]Harry Markowitz, "Portfolio Selection," *Journal of Finance* 7 (March 1952): 77–91.

FIGURE 11-3 Indifference Curve for M. Clark

For each dollar amount, this curve shows the value of h such that the investor would be indifferent between the certain amount and a probability h of receiving $5 (with a probability 1 – h of receiving $0).

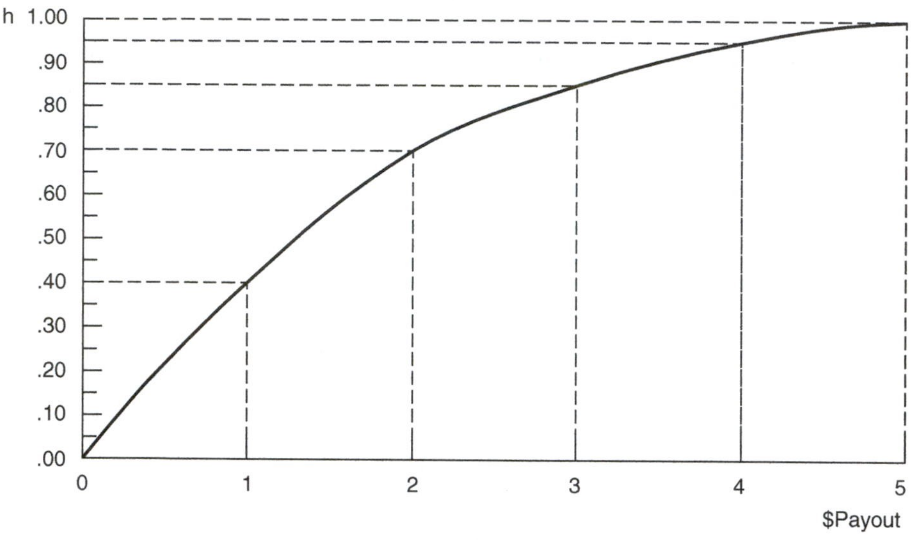

By repeating the questioning of Clark for other certain amounts, we can find Clark's indifference level of h for each certain amount between $0 and $5. The results of the questioning of Clark appear in Figure 11-3.

What happens if we decide to use the values of h as indexes of relative desirability? Let H be the total amount of h from a set of payments and E(H) be the expected H from a gamble involving various possible payments. Suppose we want to know how Clark will respond to gamble A, which has a payment of $2 or $4, with probabilities of .4 and .6 respectively:

p = .6 —— $4

p = .4 —— $2

The expected value of H for this gamble, using the h values for $2 and $4 from Figure 11-3, is:

$$E(H) = .4(.7) + .6(.95) = .85$$

Since .85 is the value of h associated with a certain $3, Clark will be indifferent between a certain $3 and gamble A, if Clark wishes to maximize E(H).

We see the choice that results from deciding so as to maximize E(H), but is that the right choice? Based on Clark's previously stated preferences, we can demonstrate that the choice that resulted from using E(H) as the guideline is rational, while any other choice is irrational. To show this, we first note that Clark previously expressed the following indifferences:

CERTAIN AMOUNT	GAMBLE TOWARD WHICH DECISION MAKER WAS INDIFFERENT
$2	.7 probability of $5 and .3 probability of $0
$4	.95 probability of $5 and .05 probability of $0

Given these indifferences and our definition of rational choice, these gambles can be substituted into gamble A in place of the certain payoffs of $2 and $4, without changing the desirability of gamble A. Therefore, a gamble that is equally attractive to gamble A is as follows:

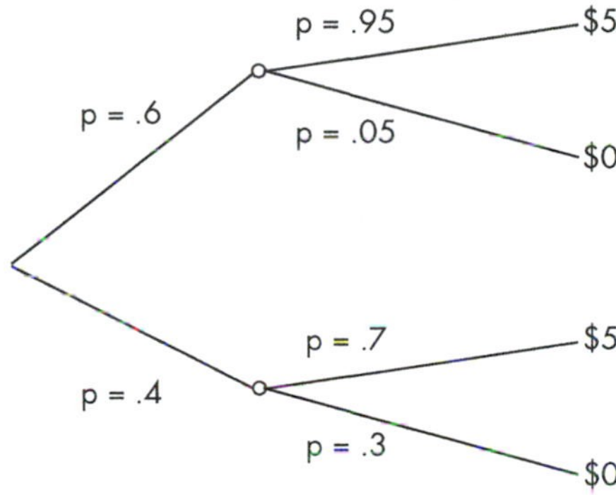

Rather than having a .6 probability of a $4 payoff, this gamble has a .6 probability of receiving another gamble that is of equal value to a certain $4 payoff for the decision maker, and so on. For this new gamble, the payouts and probabilities can be summarized as follows:

$$\text{Probability of receiving } \$5 = .6(.95) + .4(.7) = .85$$

$$\text{Probability of receiving } \$0 = .15$$

In other words, Clark will be indifferent between gamble A and a gamble that is as desirable as a certain $3. Concluding that gamble A was either more or less desirable than a certain $3 would be inconsistent with E(H) maximization. Concluding that gamble A was either more or less desirable than a certain $3 would also be inconsistent with stated preferences and, therefore, irrational.

The previous example demonstrates that the decisions based on E(H) are consistent with rational behavior, while decisions inconsistent with E(H) maximization are inconsistent with rational behavior. But what has this to do with maximization of expected utility? Recall that utility was defined as an index of the worths of monetary payoffs of varying degrees of uncertainty. Thus, the values of h meet the definition of a utility function.

Utility, like temperature, is only a relative measure. We can assign any arbitrary utility numbers to the freezing and melting points of water and then describe all other degrees of warmth in relation to those two points. Likewise, we can assign any arbitrary utility values to \$0 and \$5, then define the utilities of other payouts in relation to those two points. Mathematically, this is equivalent to saying that our decision maker's choices are consistent with any utility function for which utility, U, is:

$$U = a + bh \tag{11-9}$$

where *a* and *b* are constants. Letting $a = 0$ and $b = 1$ is equivalent to making the utility of \$0 equal to 0.0 and the utility of \$5 equal to 1.0 for Clark. The utility of any payout is then the value of h associated with that payout, and Figure 11-3 then represents the decision maker's utility function. Rational choice among risky alternatives is identical to choice that maximizes expected utility.

To further clarify the meaning of expected utility, the decision maker's beginning position must be specified. In the previous examples, we were implicitly assuming Clark started with wealth of \$0 and was choosing between certain and uncertain additions to wealth. Now suppose Clark has \$3. A gamble will either increase wealth by \$1, with a probability of .7, or decrease wealth by \$1, with a probability of .3. The utility of \$3 of wealth is .85, while the expected utility of the gamble is:

$$E(U) = .3U(\$2) + .7U(\$4) = .3(.7) + .7(.95) = .875$$

The gamble is attractive because expected utility is increased, by .025.

This same gamble could have been evaluated using marginal utility. In the case of a loss, wealth is decreased to \$2, and the change in total utility is $.70 - .85 = -.15$. In the case of a win, total wealth increases to \$4, and total utility increases by $.95 - .85 = .10$. The expected increase in total utility is:

$$E(\text{increase in total utility}) = .3(-.15) + .7(.10) = .025$$

From this example, we note that the desirability of a gamble depends on the decision maker's beginning wealth level. Depending on the shapes of their utility functions, decision makers may become more or less willing to accept gambles as their wealth increases.

Types of Utility Functions

Figure 11-4 includes three types of utility curves. Curve A shows declining marginal utility, the type illustrated in the previous example. Each additional dollar of wealth provides less utility than the previous dollar. As illustrated in the previous example, you will be **risk-averse** if you have this type of marginal utility curve. You will need payoffs with expected values sufficiently in excess of cost if you are to be induced to take risks. Line B is a utility curve for which each new

FIGURE 11-4 Utility of Wealth Curve

Curve A is the total utility curve for a risk-averse decision maker. Line B is the total utility curve for a risk-neutral decision maker, and Curve C is the total utility curve for a risk-seeker.

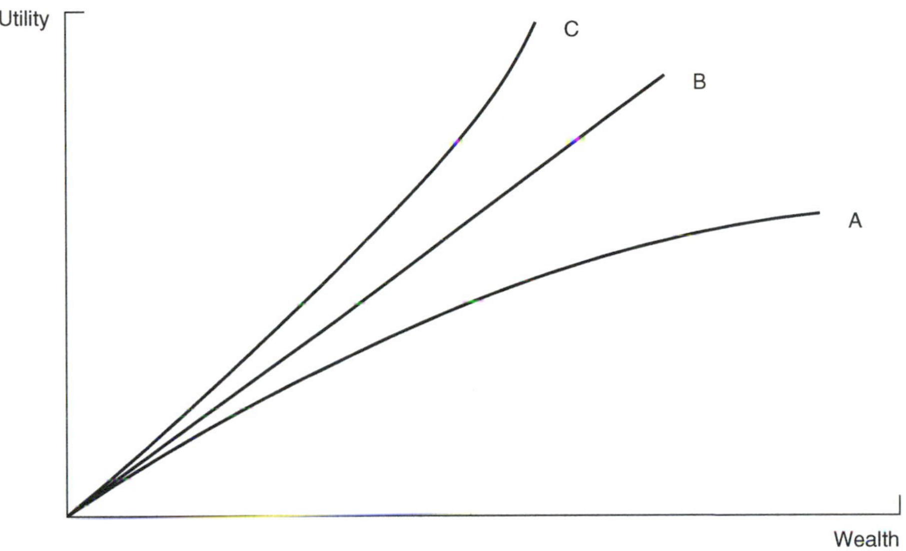

dollar of wealth has a utility equal to the utility of the last dollar. The decision maker with this curve would be **risk-neutral.** This decision maker will be indifferent about a gamble with an expected value equal to its cost, and will accept all gambles for which expected value exceeds cost, no matter how small the excess or how great the risk. Curve C is one for which the marginal utility of each new dollar is higher than the marginal utility of the previous dollar. This person is a **risk-seeker,** and would be willing to accept some gambles for which the expected value is less than the cost; this person may be found in casinos.

Evidence suggests that most decision makers are risk-averse and will, therefore, gamble only when expected value exceeds cost by a sufficient amount. People regularly buy insurance, for example, even though the expected payout is the insurance premium *minus* the insurer's administrative costs and profits. Bonds considered risky must pay higher interest rates to compensate investors for risk. Expected returns from common stock portfolios are higher than those for U.S. government bonds, because investors will take risks only if they can improve their expected returns.

Not everyone requires compensation to accept risk though. We have observed many people buying lottery tickets or gambling at casinos, thereby giving up expected return to get risk. We have also observed people simultaneously buying insurance and lottery tickets, both paying to reduce risk and paying to obtain risk. Gambling may be explained by utility curves with increasing marginal utility of wealth. Simultaneous purchase of lottery tickets and insurance policies may be explained by utility functions that reflect increasing marginal utility in one range and decreasing marginal utility in another.[9]

Using Utility Theory

In theory, we could question people about their preferences among various gambles and use this information to map their utility of wealth functions. This information could then be used to choose the risk-return trade-off they would prefer. This has been done, but as a practical matter it is not done frequently. Measurement of utility functions in this manner is extremely time-consuming and the utility functions appear to change frequently.

Furthermore, there is the question of whose utility function to use for business decisions. Should we measure the utility function of the project manager, the chief executive officer, or the owner? If we want to use the owner's utility function, which owner should we use when the stock is held by thousands of people?

There is another important reason for not measuring managers' utility functions. Managers generally want to make the major decisions of the organization based on input from analysts rather than giving input to analysts who then make the major decisions. Once the manager's utility function is measured and the manager expresses his or her beliefs with regard to payoffs and probabilities, the analyst can make the optimal decision based on the input from the manager. This process is exactly the opposite of that desired by most managers.

Why spend all of this time on utility theory if utility functions are seldom measured? Recall the no-arbitrage profit principle, which says that two assets with identical payoff characteristics must sell at identical prices in an efficient market. The expected utility criterion is analogous in that it is simply a result of the assumption that decision makers will act rationally and will, therefore, attach identical values to sets of payoffs toward which they have expressed indifference. Thus, expected utility theory is simply the theory of rational choice. Expected utility theory is the basis for many models for the analysis of investments under risk, such as the mean-variance capital asset pricing model. An understanding of utility theory is, therefore, essential for the understanding of financial decision making under conditions of risk. We will apply utility theory in later chapters, most directly in Chapters 14 and 15, to develop specific rules for capital budgeting in the face of risk.

CHOICE OF A RISK PERSPECTIVE

Regardless of the risk measure used, there are five general alternatives with regard to a perspective from which to view risk. Risk can be viewed from the perspective of:

---

[9]This explanation was first suggested by Friedman and Savage. See Milton Friedman and L. J. Savage, "The Utility Analysis of Choices Involving Risk," *Journal of Political Economy* (1948):279–304.

1. A *single investment* in isolation
2. An investment's contribution to the riskiness of a *portfolio of the company's assets*
3. An investment's contribution to the riskiness of the *portfolio of a shareholder*
4. An investment's contribution to the riskiness of the various *contingent claims* against the company
5. An investment's contribution to the riskiness of the *overall economy*

There are reasons for considering each perspective, and as a result, the risk of an investment is often considered from more than one perspective. Reasons for considering each perspective are outlined in the following paragraphs.

Single-Project Perspective. A manager responsible for a single project will probably be evaluated in terms of that project's *outcome,* not the nature of the probability distribution when the decision was made. Therefore, that manager will be concerned about the project's total risk, not its contribution to the company's risk. Furthermore, many managers are far removed from the executive suite, and do not have information about how other segments of the company are expected to respond to various economic conditions. Additionally, the dynamics of corporate decision making often mitigate in favor of the single-project view of risk. Final approval or recommendation is often made by a capital budgeting committee whose members are top-level managers with other full-time duties and varying levels of financial training. Investment proposals are generally reviewed one at a time so it is difficult to consider, in other than general terms, how they will fit together in a portfolio. Methods of single-project risk analysis are covered in Chapter 12.

Company Portfolio Perspective. Top managers are responsible for the overall performance of the company, and their compensation is generally tied to overall company performance. They will almost certainly care about the company's overall risk. In other words, top managers will view the company as a portfolio of capital investments, and they will be interested in how a particular investment contributes to the riskiness of that portfolio. Recognition of risk from the company perspective is covered in Chapter 13.

Shareholder Portfolio Perspective. Shareholder wealth maximization is a commonly cited goal of the firm. Acquisition of an asset by a company adds that asset to the shareholders' portfolios of assets. From the viewpoint of the shareholders, the important risk is that risk which cannot be diversified away. If investors have well-diversified portfolios, the only risk that cannot be diversified away is sensitivity to factors affecting returns on all investments. The general approach to recognizing risk from the shareholder perspective is to adjust required return for nondiversifiable risk. These adjustments are developed in Chapters 14 and 15.

Contingent Claims Perspective. Shareholders, creditors, and managers all have claims against the company which are contingent on future events. Bondholders, for example, will receive principal and interest payments only if the company can earn enough money to make the payments. A change in riskiness of capital investments can change the value of various claims against the company, even if it does not change the total value of the company. Option pricing models are used in Chapter 15 to measure the impact of risk on the relative values of claims against the company. These changes in relative values can be important for capital investment decision making.

Total Economy Perspective. Government policy makers may be interested in looking at the riskiness of the overall economy, and may want to encourage or discourage particular types of capital investments based on considerations of impact on the country's economy. A diversified shareholder's returns are closely correlated with the overall health of the economy in the long run, so the contribution of a capital investment to the riskiness of the shareholder's portfolio is similar to the contribution to the riskiness of the overall economy. The relationship is not perfect because of externalities, taxes, insurance, and government programs like crop and flood insurance. Nevertheless, the relationship is close enough that an understanding of the shareholder portfolio perspective is useful for thinking about a total economy perspective.

Numerous parties are involved in the typical capital investment decision, from the project's proponent to the capital budgeting committee and chief executive. In addition, capital investments frequently affect the welfare of workers and investors who do not participate in the decisions. Consequently, risk analysis frequently includes analysis from several different perspectives. Thus, the risk analysis methods discussed in Chapters 12 through 15 are often complementary rather than competing.

SUMMARY

This chapter focused on the general principles underlying the consideration of risk in the analysis of capital investments. Methods of defining risk are often quite helpful in decision making. Risk analysis may consist of qualitative statements about uncertainties, sensitivity analyses, statements about the probability of some failure, or summaries of the probability distribution of outcomes. Expected value is the most common measure of the central tendency of a distribution of possible outcomes. The most widely used dispersion measures are the variance, standard deviation, coefficient of variation, and semivariance. Methods will be developed in the following chapters for using these risk measures when analyzing capital investments.

Utility theory forms the basis of much of our understanding of decision making under risk. The fundamental assumption needed to justify the use of utility theory in evaluating risky alternatives is that decision makers are rational. It is generally believed that most decision makers have declining marginal utility of wealth functions and are therefore risk-averse; they will accept risk only if compensated with a sufficient increase in expected return.

QUESTIONS

11-1. Is risk a common or rare problem in capital budgeting? Explain.

11-2. Define the following terms: (a) risk, (b) probability, (c) probability distribution, (d) subjective probability, (e) objective probability, (f) risk-averse, (g) diversifiable risk, (h) nondiversifiable risk.

11-3. Explain the strengths and weaknesses of the variance and standard deviation as risk measures.

11-4. What weakness of the standard deviation is overcome through the use of the coefficient of variation?

11-5. What weakness of the standard deviation is overcome through the use of the semivariance?

11-6. Is it believed that the marginal utility of wealth for most decision makers increases or decreases with each additional dollar of wealth?

11-7. What types of utility curves (increasing, decreasing, or constant marginal utility of wealth) are generally associated with each of the following attitudes toward risk: (a) risk-averse, (b) risk-neutral, (c) risk-seeking?

11-8. Why are the utility functions of individuals not measured frequently in the process of risk analysis?

11-9. What are the justifications for viewing risk from the perspective of:

- **a.** Contribution to the riskiness of a shareholder's diversified portfolio?
- **b.** Contribution to the risk of the company's portfolio of assets?
- **c.** A single project in isolation (total project risk)?

11-10. (**Ethical considerations**) Many research labs of major corporations are cutting back on their expenditures on "pure" or "basic" research. Instead they have shifted the expenditures to product development. These managers believe in funding only research that shows promise of generating a profit. An example of "pure" or "basic" research is the Supercollider project that attempts to answer the question "What happens when atoms collide?" NEC has made the corporate decision to continue to invest in pure research regardless of how remote the probability of a profitable return.

- **a.** List several ethical arguments for NEC's continued investment in "pure" or "basic" research.
- **b.** List several ethical arguments for the more popular policy to discontinue funding for "pure" or "basic" research.

PROBLEMS

11-1. A die is fair in that there is an equal probability of it landing on each of its six sides. If a value of 1, 2, or 3 appears on the face of the die, the player receives \$50. If a 4 appears, the player receives \$150. If a 5 or

6 appears, the player receives $300. What is the expected value from a single roll? Would a risk-averse investor be willing to pay the expected value for the opportunity to play?

11-2. When an exploratory oil well is drilled, there is a .1 probability of finding oil. If two exploratory wells are drilled in different parts of the country, what is the probability that (a) oil will be found in both wells, (b) oil will be found in neither well, (c) oil will be found in one well?

11-3. If oil is found in an exploratory well, there is a .5 probability that the field will prove commercially viable. If the probability of finding oil in an exploratory well is .1, what is the probability that oil will be found in the exploratory well *and* the field will prove to be commercially viable?

11-4. If competitors do not respond to a new product, there is a .9 probability of a positive net present value. If competitors do respond, there is a .4 probability of a positive net present value. There is a .8 probability that competitors will respond. What is the probability of a positive net present value?

11-5. Possible net present values and associated probabilities for a new investment are as follows. What is the probability of a positive net present value?

NPV	−100	−50	0	50	100	200
Probability	.10	.10	.20	.20	.30	.10

11-6. For the investment in problem 5, what is the (a) expected value, (b) median, (c) mode?

11-7. An investment costs $100 today and has a 1-year life. There is a .5 probability of receiving $120 at the end of the year and a .5 probability of receiving $90 (in other words, a return of +20 percent −10 percent). What is the geometric mean return?

11-8. The net present values and associated probabilities for an investment, designated investment H, follow. Compute the expected value for the probability distribution.

NPV	0	200	400	600	800	1,000	1,200	1,400
Probability	.05	.1	.1	.2	.25	.15	.1	.05

11-9. Compute the variance and standard deviation for the probability distribution for investment H in problem 8.

11-10. Compute the coefficient of variation for the probability distribution for investment H in problem 8.

11-11. Compute the semivariance for the probability distribution for investment H in problem 8.

11-12. Compute the adjusted semi-standard deviation and the coefficient of adjusted semi-standard deviation for investment H in problem 8. Is the distribution skewed to the left or to the right?

11-13. Investment J has the probability distribution of net present values cited below. Is this investment preferable to investment H discussed in problem 8?

NPV	0	200	500	800	1,000
Probability	.1	.1	.6	.1	.1

11-14. The possible net present values for investment K are normally distributed with a mean of $100,000 and a standard deviation of $50,000. What is the probability of a negative net present value? a net present value above $150,000?

11-15. The expected net present value for investment L is $180,000 and the standard deviation is $100,000. The probability distribution is normal. What is the probability of a negative net present value? If we are primarily concerned about the risk of a negative net present value, which investment is riskier, K (in problem 14) or L?

11-16. D. Morton has been asked to choose between certain payments and gambles, with a probability h of receiving $10 (and a probability of 1-h of receiving $0). Morton's indifference values of h for various certain amounts are as follows:

Certain Amount	0	1	2	3	4	5	6	7	8	9	10
h	0	.289	.458	.578	.671	.744	.812	.867	.916	.960	1

Morton has starting wealth of $0. Morton is asked to choose between a certain $5 and a gamble. The gamble has a .5 probability of a $6 payoff and a .5 probability of a $4 payoff. Morton chooses the gamble. Is this rational?

11-17. Morton (problem 16), whose preferences were revealed above, has starting wealth of $0. Morton is offered a gamble with a .7 probability of a $7 payoff and a .3 probability of a $2 payoff. Morton will be indifferent between the gamble and what certain payment?

11-18. Morton (problem 16), whose preferences were revealed above, has beginning wealth of $5. A gamble involves a .5 probability of losing $1 and a .5 probability of gaining $2. In other words, the probabilities of ending wealth of $4 and $7 are each .5. If Morton is rational, will the gamble be chosen?

11-19. K. Nielsen makes decisions so as to maximize expected utility and has a utility function that is approximately as shown below over the relevant range:

$$\text{Total utility} = W - .0000001W^2$$

where W represents total wealth. Nielsen has $100,000 of total wealth and has the opportunity to spend that wealth on a gamble with a .5 probability of receiving nothing and a .5 probability of receiving $225,000. Would Nielsen be willing to take the gamble? Would Nielsen be willing to pay $1 million (if Nielsen had $1 million) in exchange for a gamble with a .5 probability of $2.25 million and a .5 probability of $0?

11-20. An expected utility-maximizing decision maker with $1 of wealth is indifferent between keeping a dollar or taking a gamble with a .5 probability of receiving $5 and a .5 probability of receiving nothing. For convenience, we can assign utility of 0.0 to $0 and 1.0 to $1. What is the utility of $5? Is this person risk-averse, risk-neutral, or risk-seeking?

11-21. **(Applications)** Several studies have reported that the historical rate of return in the stock market, as measured by an index like the Standard and Poor's 500, has averaged 15 percent per year from 1981 to 1997. The standard deviation of these annual returns during this same period was 12 percent. Assume that the past is indicative of the future and that the returns are distributed normally. What is the probability that the return in the stock market would have been minus 15 percent or lower in both 2001 and 2002?

SELECTED REFERENCES

Bernoulli, D. "Specimen Theoriae Novae de Mensura Sortis." St. Petersburg, 1738. English translation: *Econometrica* (1954): 23–36.

Carlson, Phillip G. "An Argument for 'Generalized' Mean-Coefficient of Variation Analysis: Comment." *Financial Management* 10 (Autumn 1981): 87–88.

Chow, Edward H., Wayne Y. Lee, and Michael E. Solt. "The Economic Exposure of U.S. Multinational Firms." *Journal of Financial Research* 20 (Summer 1997): 191–210.

Crum, R. L., and F. G. J. Derfinderen. *Capital Budgeting under Condition of Uncertainty*. Boston: Martinus Nijhoff, 1981.

Crum, Roy L., Dan J. Laughhunn, and John W. Payne. "Risk-Seeking Behavior and Its Implications for Financial Models." *Financial Management* 10 (Winter 1981): 20–27.

Forham, David R., and S. Brooks Marshall. "Tools for Dealing with Uncertainty." *Management Accounting* 79 (September 1997): 38–43.

Harris, Milton, and Artur Raviv. "The Capital Budgeting Process, Incentives, and Information." *Journal of Finance* 51 (September 1996): 1139–1174.

Ho, Simon S. M., and Richard H. Pike. "Organizational Characteristics Influencing the Use of Risk Analysis in Strategic Capital Investments." *The Engineering Economist* 43 (Spring 1998): 247–268.

Latané, Henry A., and Donald L. Tuttle. "Criteria for Portfolio Building." *Journal of Finance* 22 (September 1967): 359–373.

Lintner, John. "The Valuation of Risk Assets and Selection of Risky Investments in Stock Portfolios and Capital Budgets." *Review of Economics and Statistics* (February 1965): 13–37.

Markowitz, Harry M. "Investment for the Long Run: New Evidence for an Old Rule." *Journal of Finance* 31 (December 1976): 1273–1286.

———. "Portfolio Selection." *Journal of Finance* 7 (March 1952): 77–91.

May, Don O. "Do Managerial Motives Influence Firm Risk Reduction Strategies?" *Journal of Finance* 50 (September 1996): 1291–1308.

Morgan, George Emir. "Risk Aversion in the Approximate and in the Exact Forms." *Engineering Economist* 37 (Winter 1992): 137–144.

Morrin, Roger A., and A. Fernandez Suarez. "Risk Aversion Revisited." *Journal of Finance* 38 (September 1983): 1201–1216.

Sharpe, William F. "Capital Asset Prices: A Theory of Market Equilibrium under Conditions of Risk." *Journal of Finance* 19 (September 1964): 425–442.

Swalm, Peter O. "Utility Theory—Insights into Risk Taking." *Harvard Business Review* (November–December 1966): 123–136.

Thakor, Anjan V. "Game Theory in Finance." *Financial Management* 20 (Spring 1991): 71–94.

Von Neumann, John, and Oskar Morgenstern. *Theory of Games and Economic Behavior,* 2nd ed. Princeton, N.J.: Princeton University Press, 1947.

CHAPTER 12

Single Investment Risk Analysis

After completing this chapter you should be able to:

- Explain why it is important to look at risk exposure from the perspective of a single project.
- Conduct a simple sensitivity analysis and understand the results.
- Grasp the role that earnings break-even point and net present value break-even play as indicators of risk.
- Calculate a break-even point and know how changes in fixed cost, variable cost, and selling price influence the break-even point.
- Calculate the expected value and describe what it means.
- Discern between perfectly correlated, uncorrelated, and perfectly negatively correlated cash flows.
- Describe how simulation works.
- Diagram a decision tree and calculate the resulting probabilities.
- Understand some of the ways probability estimates are developed in practice.
- Explain some of the ways in which risk is managed.
- List several ways in which projects are selected when risky cash flows are involved.

Recognition Equipment of Irving, Texas, is a good example of the small high-technology companies that have accounted for much recent growth in the economy of the United States. With their small size and entrepreneurial spirit, these companies can respond rapidly to a dynamic marketplace.

Managers at Recognition Equipment knew the importance of flexibility. They also knew the importance of achieving cost-effective production through automation. Unfortunately, a capital investment in automated production equipment could tie up large amounts of capital and could, therefore, sharply reduce future flexibility. Inability to respond to sudden changes in markets or technology could mean missed opportunities, or worse. Managers assessed the risks to the company that were associated with various alternatives and sought ways to achieve their productivity goals while limiting their risk exposure. They settled on a strategy involving used automation equipment.[1]

Managers at Recognition Equipment are typical in that assessing and dealing with risk are important aspects of their capital budgeting programs. A complete evaluation of a proposed capital investment requires that risk be considered from the perspectives of numerous parties: the manager proposing the investment, the senior executives, the shareholders, and others affected by the company's actions. The assessment of risk often begins with **single investment risk** analysis, an examination of the investment's total risk as a stand-alone unit. There are five reasons for starting with single investment risk analysis:

1. The manager proposing a capital investment in a large organization often lacks comprehensive information about the company and its plans that would be needed to measure the investment's contribution to the risk profile of the company.
2. The manager proposing a capital investment is likely to be evaluated on the performance of that investment. In such cases, the proposing manager is concerned about total project risk, not contribution to the risk of the total company or its shareholders.
3. Single investment risk analysis is useful in developing ways to eliminate or decrease risk without proportional decreases in expected return.
4. Analysis of single investment risk often serves as the basis for understanding the investment's contribution to the company's risk, the shareholder's risk, and so forth.
5. Capital investments in many organizations are considered one at a time by a capital budgeting committee. The members seldom have the time or the background to fully consider interactions with all other investments being held or considered by the company or its shareholders.

This chapter begins with a survey of single investment risk measurement methods: sensitivity analysis, break-even analysis, and probability-based methods, including simulation and decision trees. These tools are used to help managers develop a clear picture of the risks to which they are exposed. A variety of tools are discussed because no one tool fits every situation. Sensitivity analysis and break-even analysis are simple to use and the results are easy to explain, but the simplicity is gained at the expense of an understanding of the probabilities of the various outcomes. Simulation and decision trees provide more insight into probabilities, but are more difficult (therefore more expensive and time consuming) to use. An extensive simulation study would probably be appropriate for the evaluation of a proposed second canal across Central America, but we would not go beyond simple sensitivity analysis for the choice between copy

[1]Ward Chartier and Mike Moline, "Selective Automation Can Be Profitable in a Small Factory," *Industrial Engineering* 20 (April 1988): 28–34.

machines at a neighborhood real estate office. Consequently, each risk-measurement tool has its place.

Once you have measured risk, you can begin to think of ways to control risk, decreasing or even eliminating some sources of uncertainty. Finally, you must decide if the expected profitability justifies the risks involved. Following the discussion of risk measurement methods, we will consider methods of controlling risk and capital investment choice in the face of risk.

SENSITIVITY ANALYSIS

The first question that arises in discussing the risk of an investment is often "what can go wrong?" followed by "what are the critical variables?" Both of these questions can be answered through sensitivity analysis. **Sensitivity analysis** is the computation of present value or other profitability measures for multiple values of at least one variable that will affect the investment. Suppose, for example, a capital investment is affected by sales volume and salvage value. Net present value would be computed for numerous combinations of sales volumes and salvage values.

Example: Rediform Concrete is considering a $5 million capital investment for a factory to manufacture formed concrete products, such as patio stones, mobile home stairs, and lawn decorations. The proposed factory will generate annual sales between $2 million and $5 million. After tax fixed costs are $500,000 and after tax variable costs are 50 percent of sales. Annual after tax cash flow is determined as follows:

$$\text{After tax cash flow} = (.5 \times \text{Sales}) - \$500{,}000$$

The expected life is 5 years, and the salvage value depends on land prices at the end of 5 years. The factory would be built on Palmetto Road, near the Sunshine Expressway. Depending on how a new freeway exit is located, the salvage value could be as low as $1 million or as high as $3 million. To consider the risks involved, managers compute the net present value for various combinations of sales and salvage value, as illustrated in Table 12-1. For example, using

TABLE 12-1 Sensitivity Analysis of the Rediform Concrete Factory

Net present values of the proposed formed concrete factory, letting revenue and salvage value vary. The net present values were computed using Excel.

	A	B	C	D	E	F	G	H
1				Sales ($000)				
2	Salvage							
3	Value	2,000	2,500	3,000	3,500	4,000	4,500	5,000
4	($000)							
5								
6	1,000	−2,484	−1,536	−588	359	1,307	2,255	3,202
7	3,000	−1,242	−294	654	1,601	2,549	3,497	4,444

Rediform's 10 percent required return, the net present value with sales of \$3.5 million and salvage value of \$1 million is:

$$NPV = [(.5 \times 3{,}500{,}000) - 500{,}000]PVA1_{5yrs,10\%} + 1{,}000{,}000/1.10^5 - 5{,}000{,}000$$
$$= \underline{\underline{\$359{,}000}}$$

The critical variables are often seen more easily with graphical sensitivity analysis. Figure 12-1 summarizes the information from Table 12-1 in graphical form.

It is relatively easy to carry out sensitivity analysis. Computer programs like Excel and Lotus 1-2-3 have built-in functions for performing sensitivity analysis

FIGURE 12-1 Sensitivity Analysis of the Rediform Concrete Fctory

This graph shows the sensitivity of net present value to sales and salvage value, drawn from the results from Table 12-1 and produced by Lotus 1-2-3.

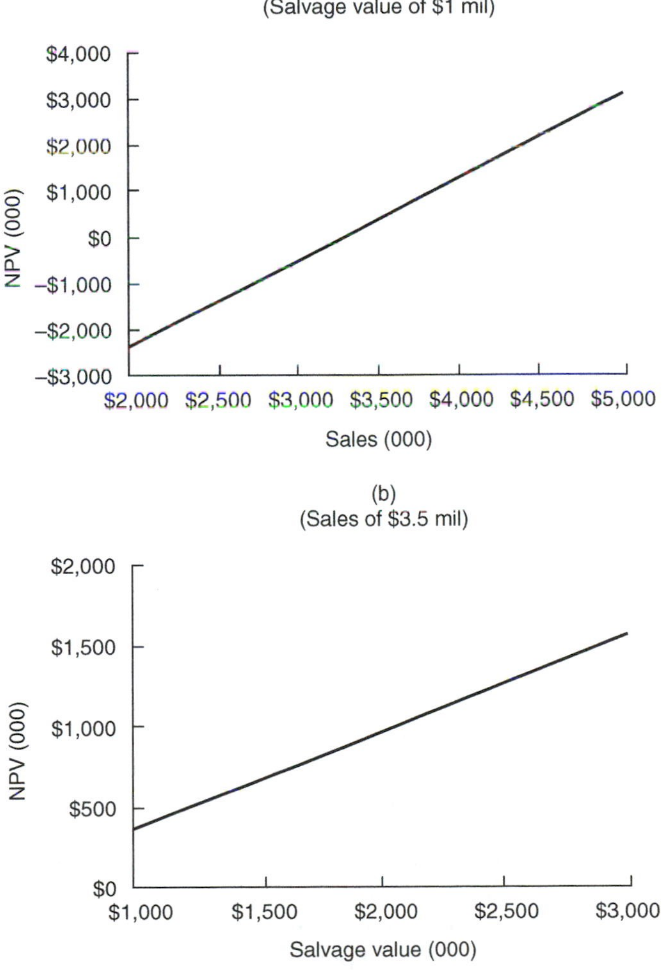

on one specified factor or two specified factors with both allowed to vary simultaneously. If sensitivity analysis is done using one of these spreadsheet programs, graphs such as those in Figure 12-1 can be readily produced with a few more keystrokes.

As illustrated in Table 12-1 and Figure 12-1, sensitivity analysis gives managers an easily understood picture of possible outcomes. Variables that serve as three primary drivers of success or failure can be identified, as can the levels of those variables needed for project success. Managers may attempt to objectively determine the probability of each outcome or to use their own subjective assessments of the probability of each outcome. Frequently, managers rely on their own judgment to decide if the risk is acceptable, without explicitly using probability. Managers may also decide to take risk-reduction actions, such as choosing another site or leasing rather than purchasing the land, to reduce uncertainty about the salvage value.

BREAK-EVEN ANALYSIS

Sensitivity analysis is helpful in identifying key variables, and sales are often one of those key variables. Earnings or cash flow break-even analysis focuses on the relationship between sales and profitability or cash flow. NPV break-even extends cash flow break-even and looks at the relationship between sales, cash flow, required return, and net present value.

To understand break-even we need to remember that in this analysis each cost is viewed as either a variable or a fixed cost. A variable cost is one that changes in total amount as the level of unit sales change but is usually assumed to stay constant in per-unit amount or percentage of sales. For example, a variable cost for Wendy's Hamburgers would be the "beef" they talk about in their commercials. As Wendy's sells one more hamburger at 99 cents they incur the cost of one more patty of beef at 10 cents. As Wendy's sells more hamburgers the total amount spent on hamburger patties will increase. This cost stays constant in per-unit amount or percentage of hamburger sales because as Wendy's sells more hamburgers, 10 cents per hamburger sold or roughly 10 percent of the sales price is spent on this variable cost, hamburger patties.

Fixed costs are costs that remain constant in total dollars as the sales level in units changes but decrease in per-unit amount as the volume increases within some range. The salary of the manager of a business would be an example of a fixed cost. To extend the Wendy's example, assume that a manager is paid $40,000 per year excluding any bonus. If Wendy's has the capacity to sell between 0 and 500,000 hamburgers under this manager's supervision then the total dollar management cost of selling 160,000 hamburgers is $40,000, or $40,000/160,000 or 25 cents per hamburger. At 500,000 hamburgers the total dollar management cost is still $40,000 (thus the name **fixed**), or $40,000/500,000 or 8 cents per hamburger. It is not coincidental that the fixed cost per unit is lowest when the business is using the asset (the manager in this case) at its capacity. This is one of the reasons break-even analysis is a good measure of the risk of a single project. Depending on where you expect sales to be and the variation in the level of sales, break-even analysis determines the sales level necessary to cross over from negative earnings to positive earnings or, in other words, break even.

The earnings or cash flow **break-even point** is the level of sales necessary to produce a profit or cash flow of $0. The break-even point in quantity sold (BEP_q) is:

$$BEP_q = \text{Fixed cost}/(\text{Price} - \text{Variable cost per unit}) \quad \textbf{(12-1)}$$

The break-even point in dollar sales ($BEP_\$$) is:

$$BEP_\$ = \text{Fixed cost}/(1 - \text{Variable cost as a percent of dollar sales}) \quad \textbf{(12-2)}$$

The formulas for earnings and cash-flow break-even point are the same, but the numbers plugged into these formulas may be different. In particular, accounting fixed costs may be different from cash fixed costs. Depreciation is an accounting cost affecting the earnings break-even point, but is not a cash outlay and therefore does not affect the accounting break-even point.

Example: Variable costs for Rediform Concrete are 50 percent of sales, and fixed cash costs are \$500,000. In unit terms, the price per cubic yard is \$40 and variable costs are \$20. The cash flow break-even points in terms of quantity sold and dollar sales are:

$$BEP_q = \$500{,}000/(40 - 20) = \underline{\underline{25{,}000}} \text{ cubic yards}$$

$$BEP_\$ = \$500{,}000/(1 - .5) = \underline{\underline{\$1{,}000{,}000}} \text{ sales}$$

To extend the analysis and calculate an NPV break-even, recall that annual cash flow for Rediform is (.5 × Sales) – \$500,000, the required return is 10 percent, and salvage value could be as low as \$1 million or as high as \$3 million. Break-even sales levels in terms of net present value are as follows:

Salvage value of \$1 million:

$$NPV = [(.5 \times \text{Sales}) - 500{,}000]PVA1_{5yrs,10\%} + 1{,}000{,}000/1.10^5 - 5{,}000{,}000 = 0$$

$$\text{Sales} = \underline{\underline{\$3{,}306{,}000}}$$

Salvage value of \$3 million:

$$NPV = [(.5 \times \text{Sales}) - 500{,}000]PVA1_{5yrs,10\%} + 3{,}000{,}000/1.10^5 - 5{,}000{,}000 = 0$$

$$\text{Sales} = \underline{\underline{\$2{,}655{,}000}}$$

The cash flow break-even tells us the level of sales necessary to earn \$0 in cash flow, a number that is useful in predicting our ability to meet future cash obligations. The earnings break-even point gives us the sales level necessary to report an income of \$0. This may be of interest if, for example, debt covenants result in some loss of control if the company does not earn a profit. In general, though, the NPV break-even point is the most interesting break-even point for capital budgeting purposes. It tells us the sales level above which wealth is created for the shareholders.

Managers occasionally want to know the break-even sales level in terms of earning a risk-free return. This would indicate the sales level below which we would have been better off leaving the money in some risk-free asset such as Treasury bills. For a risk-free rate of 6 percent after tax, the sales level that just provides the risk-free return with a $3 million salvage value is found as follows:

$$\text{NPV} = [(.5 \times \text{Sales}) - 500{,}000]\text{PVA}_{5\text{yrs},6\%} + 3{,}000{,}000/1.06^5 - 5{,}000{,}000 = 0$$

$$\text{Sales} = \underline{\underline{\$2{,}310{,}000}}$$

Break-even analysis is often presented graphically. Since the horizontal axis in Figure 12-1(a) is sales, Figure 12-1(a) is a graphical presentation of break-even analysis.

A limitation of sensitivity analysis, including break-even analysis, is that it generally shows the relationship between profitability and only one or two variables while holding all other variables constant. A table of net present values for ten levels of each of six factors would have 1 million entries, for example, and a graphical presentation would be virtually impossible. Thus, sensitivity analysis is useful for identifying one or two key drivers and measuring sensitivity to those factors *in isolation,* or for considering a limited number of scenarios. Probability-related methods are often more time-consuming to use, but give an improved *overall* understanding of risk, particularly when the project is subject to numerous sources of uncertainty.

RISK ANALYSIS METHODS BASED ON PROBABILITY

In Table 12-1, the net present value for the formed concrete plant could be between –$2,484,000 and +$4,444,000. The next question likely to be asked by managers is: "What is the probability of each outcome?" This question may be answered by computing the parameters of the probability distribution of net present value—expected net present value, standard deviation, and so on—or it could be answered by computing the probabilities of specific events. We first deal with methods of computing the expected net present value and standard deviation based on the probability distributions of future cash flows. Next, we look at Monte Carlo simulation, a process for combining large amounts of information in the form of a probability distribution of outcomes. Finally, we look at decision trees, a tool for computing the probabilities of specific outcomes when some decisions can be delayed until more information is available.

Expected Present Value

If expected cash flows for each future year are known, the expected present value of those flows is simply:

$$E(PV) = E(CF_0) + E(CF_1)/(1+k)^1 + E(CF_2)/(1+k)^2 + \cdot\cdot\cdot \qquad \textbf{(12-3)}$$

where $E(CF_t)$ is expected cash flow at time t, and k is the required return. This formula is valid whether cash flows are perfectly correlated, partially correlated, or uncorrelated from year to year.[2] Unfortunately, a similar rule does not hold for the internal rate of return.[3]

The standard deviation of the present value of a series of cash flows depends on correlation between year-to-year cash flows. Cash flows are correlated from period to period if the probability distribution of cash flow for one period is related to actual cash flows in prior periods. We begin by looking at the two extremes, perfect correlation and no correlation at all, and then look at ways to deal with the more typical case of partial correlation.

Standard Deviation of the Present Value of Perfectly Correlated Cash Flows

Cash flows are perfectly correlated from period to period if cash flows after the first period are completely determined by cash flows in the first period. In other words, all uncertainty about future cash flows is eliminated when the first cash flow occurs. If cash flows are perfectly correlated from year to year, the standard deviation of the present value of those flows, σ_{PV}, is:[4]

$$\sigma_{PV} = \sum_{t=1}^{n} \sigma_{CF_t}/(1+k)^t \qquad \textbf{(12-4)}$$

where σ_{CFt} is the standard deviation of the probability distribution of cash flows for year t, and k is the required return.

[2]We should note that when the life of an asset is uncertain, use of the expected life—the expected value from the probability distribution of life—will result in an inaccurate estimate of net present value. When life is uncertain, the net present value should be based on expected cash flow for each year, with the probability of the investment still operating in that year being used in the computation of expected cash flow.

[3]For methods of estimating the standard deviation of the probability distribution of internal rate of return under some conditions, see William Fairley and Henry D. Jacoby, "Investment Analysis Using the Probability Distribution of the Internal Rate of Return," *Management Science* 21 (August 1975): 1428–1437. But recall the limitations of this measure discussed in Chapter 11.

[4]Equation 12-4 follows directly from basic rules of statistics. The standard deviation of the sum of n perfectly correlated variables is

$$\sigma_{sum} = \sqrt{\sum_{t=1}^{n}\sum_{j=1}^{n} \sigma_{t,j}} = \sqrt{\sum_{t=1}^{n}\sum_{j=1}^{n} \sigma_t\sigma_j} = \sqrt{\left(\sum_{t=1}^{n} \sigma_{t,j}\right)^2} = \sum_{t-1}^{n} \sigma_t$$

Where $\sigma_{t,j}$ is covariance between variables t and j (variance when t = j), and σ_t is the standard deviation of variable t. The expression following the first = sign is the standard statistical formula for the variance of the sum of any series of variables. The expression following the second = sign reflects the facts that $r_{t,j}\sigma_t\sigma_j = \sigma_{t,j}$ where $r_{t,j}$ is the correlation coefficient between variables t and j (all $r_{t,j}$s are 1.0 for perfectly correlated numbers). The expressions following the third and fourth = signs are each mathematically equivalent to the prior expression. Since the standard deviation of any variable multiplied by a constant is that constant multiplied by the standard deviation of the variable, $\sigma_{CFt}/(1+k)^t$ can be substituted for each σ_t to give the standard deviation of present value.

TABLE 12-2 Rediform Concrete: Possible Annual Sales Levels and Cash Flows

Sales	2,000	2,500	3,000	3,500	4,000	4,500	5,000
Cash flow	500	750	1,000	1,250	1,500	1,750	2,000
Probability	.05	.10	.20	.30	.20	.10	.05

Standard Deviation of the Present Value of Uncorrelated Cash Flows

If cash flows are uncorrelated, the cash flows in any one year are independent of the cash flows in previous years. At the end of the first year, for example, we would not be able to use knowledge of actual cash flows for the first year to revise our estimates of cash flows for the second year. If a series of cash flows are uncorrelated, the formula for the standard deviation of the present value of those flows is:[5]

$$\sigma_{PV} = \sqrt{\sum_{t=1}^{n} (\sigma CF_t)^2/(1+k)^{2t}}$$

Example: Possible annual sales levels and cash flows for Rediform Concrete's proposed new factory are shown in Table 12-2 (in thousands).

Expected annual cash flow and standard deviation of annual cash flow are as follows. The numbers are in \$ thousands.

$$\begin{aligned} E(CF) &= .05(500) + .10(750) + .20(1{,}000) + .30(1{,}250) + .20(1{,}500) \\ &\quad + .10(1{,}750) + .05(2{,}000) \\ &= \underline{\underline{\$1{,}250}} \end{aligned}$$

$$\begin{aligned} \sigma_{CF} &= [.05(500 - 1{,}250)^2 + .10(750 - 1{,}250)^2 + .20(1{,}000 - 1{,}250)^2 \\ &\quad + .30(1{,}250 - 1{,}250)^2 + .20(1{,}500 - 1{,}250)^2 + .10(1{,}750 - 1{,}250)^2 \\ &\quad + .05(2{,}000 - 1{,}250)^2]^{1/2} \\ &= \underline{\underline{\$362}} \end{aligned}$$

If cash flows are perfectly correlated from year to year, the standard deviation of the present value of annual cash flows in thousands is:

$$\sigma_{PV} = \$362 PVA1_{5yrs,10\%} = \$1{,}372$$

If cash flows are uncorrelated, on the other hand, the standard deviation of the present value of annual cash flows in thousands is:

[5]This follows from the standard statistical property that the variance of the sum of a series of independent variables equals the sum of the variances.

$$\sigma_{PV} = \sqrt{362^2/1.1^2 + 362^2/1.1^4 + 362^2/1.1^6 + 362^2/1.1^8 + 362^2/1.1^{10}} = \underline{\underline{\$619}}$$

Suppose salvage value will be either $1 million or $3 million, with probabilities of .4 and .6 respectively. The expected salvage value and the standard deviation of the salvage value in thousands are:

$$E(\text{salvage value}) = .4(\$1{,}000) + .6(\$3{,}000) = \$2{,}200$$

$$\sigma_{\text{Salvage}} = \sqrt{.4(1{,}000 - 2{,}200)^2 + .6(3{,}000 - 2{,}200)^2} = \underline{\underline{\$980}}$$

The expected present value of the salvage value and the standard deviation of the present value of the salvage value in thousands are then:

$$E(\text{PV of salvage}) = \$2{,}200/1.10^5 = \underline{\underline{\$1{,}366}}$$

$$\sigma_{\text{PV of salvage}} = \$980/1.10^5 = \underline{\underline{\$609}}$$

The salvage value is uncorrelated with the annual operating cash flows, so we can apply the basic statistical rule that the variance of the sum of independent events equals the sum of the variances. Since the initial outlay is known, we can compute the expected net present value and the standard deviation of net present value under both the assumptions of no correlation from year to year and perfect correlation from year to year (in thousands):

$$E(NPV) = 1{,}250PVA1_{5yrs,10\%} + 2{,}200/1.1^5 - 5{,}000 = \underline{\underline{\$1{,}105}}$$

Perfect correlation from year to year:

$$\sigma_{NPV} = \sqrt{1{,}372^2 + 609^2} = \underline{\underline{\$1{,}501}}$$

Uncorrelated from year to year:

$$\sigma_{NPV} = \sqrt{619^2 + 609^2} = \underline{\underline{\$868}}$$

Perfect correlation and complete lack of correlation are extreme positions that we rarely see in practice. Partial correlation is much more common, with there being some relationship between cash flows in one year and cash flows in the following year. If sales are less than expected during the first year, for example, forecasts for the second year will probably be scaled down as well, but knowledge of sales in the first year will not eliminate all uncertainty about future sales.

The analysis of the two extremes is useful in the case of partial correlation. If cash flows are partially correlated, the standard deviation of net present value is somewhere between the two extremes, between $868,000 and $1,501,000 for the Rediform example. Judgment can be used, estimating a standard deviation close to $868,000 if correlation is believed to be low, and close to $1,501,000 if correlation is believed to be high. Alternately, various authors have contributed analytical methods of computing the standard deviation of net present value in particular situations involving partial correlation.[6]

Once expected net present value and standard deviation have been computed, managers can use the information in decision making, either applying judgment or developing policy guidelines for acceptable trade-offs between profitability and risk. We discuss decision making after explaining simulation and decision tree analysis, which are additional tools for studying the probability distribution of profitability.

Simulation

A **simulation model** is a model of a system that can be manipulated to learn how the real system would react in various situations. Some models are physical, such as the small-scale models of boat hulls that are tested in tanks to predict how the actual boats will perform. Most models, though, are constructed as a series of mathematical equations.

Like the man who had written prose all his life without knowing it, many people have used simulation models without knowing it. If you have ever set up a pro-forma financial statement in Excel and then changed sales or accounts receivable turnover to see how profit and cash flow were affected, you have constructed a simulation model and performed a simulation experiment on that model.

As a simple example of a simulation model, consider the Rediform Concrete factory again. The capital investment can be described as a series of equations, as illustrated in Table 12-3.

[6]Frederick Hillier, "The Derivation of Probabilistic Information for the Evaluation of Risky Investments," *Management Science* 9 (April 1963): 443–457; Frederick Hillier, *The Evaluation of Risky Interrelated Investments* (New York: American Elsevier Publishing Company, 1969); Roger Bey and J. Clay Singleton, "Autocorrelated Cash Flows and the Selection of Capital Assets," *Decision Sciences* 9 (October 1978): 640–657.

TABLE 12-3 The Rediform Concrete Factory Described as a Mathematical Model

The Rediform Concrete factory is described as a simple mathematical model. The first five equations are simply input variables, while the last two equations explain how these variables interact in generating a net present value.

Cost = \$5,000,000
Sales = \$3,000,000
Variable Cost Ratio = .5
Fixed Cost = \$500,000
Salvage Value = \$3,000,000
Cash Flow = Sales(1 – Variable Cost Ratio) – Fixed Cost
Net Present Value[a] = Cash Flow × $PVA1_{5yrs,10\%}$ + Salvage Value/1.1^5 – Cost

[a]The present value of an annuity formula would generally be entered directrly into the computer: $PVAl_{life}$,10% = $(1 - 1/1.10^{life})/.10$.

This model can easily be entered into a computer using Excel or any number of other software packages. The simulation experiment then consists of changing the input values in the first five equations to determine the impacts of various combinations of these input variables on net present value. Suppose, for example, you are uncertain about sales level, salvage value, and the variable cost ratio. You can construct a table of net present values as was done in Table 12-1 for uncertain sales and salvage values. The computer simply speeds up what would otherwise be some very tedious calculations.

If you are beginning to suspect that there is little difference between simulation analysis and simple sensitivity analysis, you are right. The difference is primarily one of scale. A simulation model, being a set of equations programmed into a computer, can describe a much more complex situation and can be used to examine the impacts of numerous variables changing in conjunction with one another. Monte Carlo simulation differs, though, in that probability is incorporated directly in the simulation model.

Monte Carlo Simulation

Monte Carlo simulation is a simulation technique that has been used for nearly four decades in capital investment analysis. The technique draws its name from the use of values that are randomly drawn, but with probability of each draw controlled to approximate the actual probability of occurrence.

To explain how Monte Carlo simulation works, consider the Rediform Concrete factory capital investment described in Table 12-3. Assume management is uncertain about sales, salvage value, and the variable cost ratio. Possible values of each variable are shown in Table 12-4 (in $ thousands), with probabilities in parentheses.

To perform a Monte Carlo simulation for this problem, we could set up three roulette wheels, one for each of the variables about which we are uncertain. These are illustrated in Figure 12-2. Take the variable cost ratio wheel, for example. One-fourth of that wheel represents a variable cost ratio of .4, one-half of the wheel represents a ratio of .5, and one-fourth of the wheel represents a ratio of .6, to correspond with the probability distribution of variable costs. When the

TABLE 12-4 Outcomes and Probabilities for Rediform Concrete

Sales and salvage value are in $ thousands, and variable costs are cash. Probabilities are in parentheses.

Sales	2,000	2,500	3,000	3,500	4,000	4,500	5,000
Probability	(.05)	(.10)	(.20)	(.30)	(.20)	(.10)	(.05)
Salvage value	1,000	3,000					
Probability	(.40)	(.60)					
Variable cost ratio	.40	.50	.60				
Probability	(.25)	(.50)	(.25)				

FIGURE 12-2 Simple Monte Carlo Simulation for Rediform Concrete (in $ thousands)

A simple Monte Carlo simulation model to incorporate probability distributions with regard to sales, salvage value, and the variable cost ratio in the analysis of a capital investment.

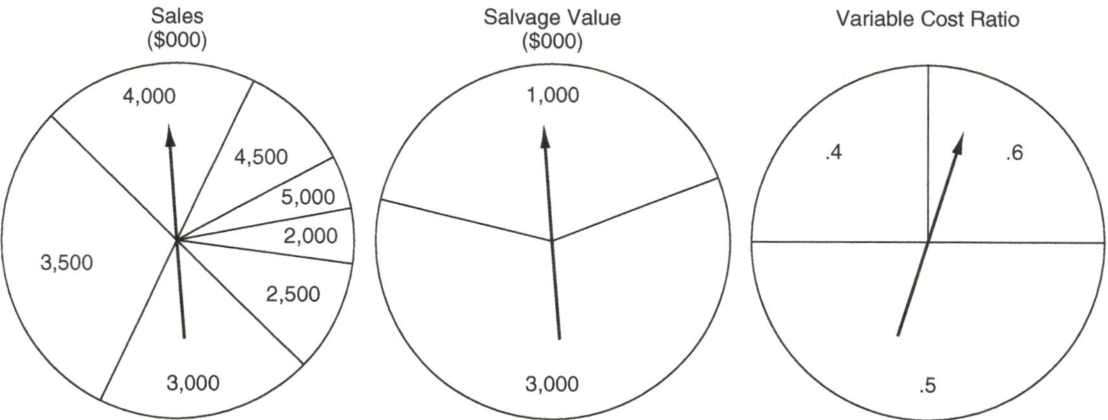

Cost = $5,000,000

Sales =

Salvage value =

Variable cost ratio =

Fixed cost = $500,000

Cash flow = Sales (1 − Variable cost ratio) − Fixed cost

$$\text{Net present value} = \text{Cash flow} \times \text{PVA1}_{5\text{yr.},\,10\%} + \frac{\text{Salvage value}}{1.1^5} - \text{Cost}$$

wheel is spun, the probability of it stopping on a particular variable cost ratio is the same as the actual probability of that ratio occurring. Each of the wheels is spun once, to provide values for sales, salvage value, and the variable cost ratio. Based on these three values, a net present value is computed. The three wheels are each spun again, and a new net present value is computed based on the new sales, salvage value, and variable cost ratio. This procedure is repeated several hundred times, with each repetition referred to as an **iteration.**

After a large number of iterations, the proportion of iterations that result in a particular net present value (or range of net present values) approximately equals the probability of that net present value (or range) occurring. One thousand iterations of the above model were carried out, and the results are summarized in Figure 12-3. Those results can be used for the same types of risk-return decision making used with probability distributions of net present value obtained in other ways.

FIGURE 12-3 Results of Monte Carlo Simulation Analysis of the Rediform Concrete Factory (in $ thousands)

A summary of the results from 1,000 iterations of the simulation model shown in Figure 12.2. Dollar amounts are in thousands.

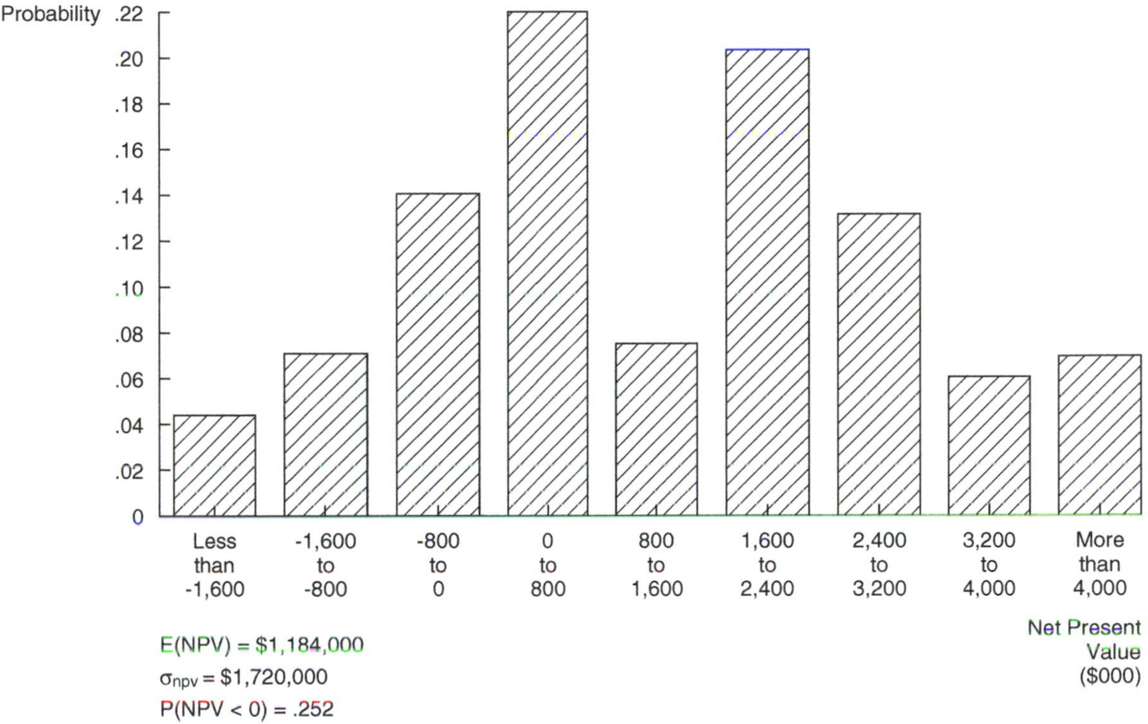

The Monte Carlo simulation gives managers a more detailed view of risk than the earlier-discussed probability methods. In addition to expected net present value and standard deviation, managers get a graphical picture of the probability distribution of net present value and the probability of a negative net present value. This more detailed picture of risk is often helpful in making capital investment decisions.

Naturally, it would be a bit tedious to go through a thousand iterations of even this simple model, and it would be much more tedious to perform numerous iterations on a complex model. This is where the computer comes in. The iterations reported in Figure 12-3 were actually carried out on a personal computer using a Basic language program, and could have been carried out using Excel. A random-number generator was used instead of roulette wheels.[7] The random-number generator used for this purpose generates a random number between 0 and 1, with all values being equally likely. For example, the variable cost ratio is assigned as follows:

[7]Random-number tables can also be used for this purpose.

VALUE OF RANDOM NUMBER	LESS THAN .25	.25 THROUGH .75	OVER .75
Variable cost ratio	.40	.50	.60

New random numbers were chosen for both sales and life so that the three variables were treated as uncorrelated items.

Some commercially available financial planning model packages, such as *Interactive Financial Planning System,* have built-in capabilities for performing Monte Carlo simulation. Using one of these packages basically involves two steps. First, a model is written as a series of equations, as was done in Table 12-3. Second, information about the nature of the probability distribution is provided for each input variable about which there is uncertainty. Given this information, the program then takes over and carries out the Monte Carlo simulation on its own.

Probability Distribution Shapes. For the example, it was assumed that the variables could have only a limited number of values; that is, sales could be \$2 million or \$2.5 million, but not \$2.3 million. This was done for simplicity in the illustration, but is not necessary. Virtually any probability distribution shape can be accommodated. Random-number generators are available for a number of widely used probability distribution shapes, and any distribution can be approximated by a set of discrete values with probabilities assigned.

Dealing with Correlation. In the example, we assumed no correlation between variables about which we were uncertain. If two variables are perfectly correlated, one is treated as a random variable, and the other is simply made a function of the random variable. One way to handle partial correlation is to specify a relationship with random coefficients. Suppose, for example, that sales are partially correlated from year to year. The relationship may be stated in a simple formula such as:

$$\text{Sales}_t = a + b \cdot \text{Sales}_{t-1}$$

where Sales_t = sales for the year t, and a and b are random variables, with a probability distribution and "roulette wheels" established for each. Simple regression might be used to develop estimates of a and b by studying the pattern of sales growth and sales in the past. The regression analysis will provide confidence ranges for a and b that can be used in developing information about the probability distributions of those variables.

Disadvantages of Simulation. Simulation analysis overcomes the limitations of many of the other risk analysis methods discussed in this chapter, but simulation has its disadvantages too. Data for a simulation model can be expensive to construct because probability distribution estimates must be developed for a number of variables, then a model must be constructed, programmed into the computer, and verified. This can cost many thousands of dollars in the time of skilled people, and it can delay decision making.

Critics also point out that Monte Carlo simulation does not separate out the nondiversifiable risk that is of primary concern to investors. This is true of Monte Carlo simulation as well as the other techniques discussed in this chapter, but as discussed in Chapter 11, many decision makers are personally concerned about total risk. Thus, they want to consider total risk as well as risk to diversified investors. Monte Carlo simulation can be supplemented with the analysis methods discussed in Chapters 13 through 15 that do focus on diversification and investor perspectives. In fact, Monte Carlo simulation can be used to generate inputs for some of those methods. Finally, Monte Carlo simulation shares with the other techniques discussed in the chapter the lack of a firm decision rule. Managers must still use their own judgment in deciding if the combination of benefits and risk summarized through the Monte Carlo simulation is attractive.

Decision Trees

Decision trees are particularly helpful when dealing with sequential decisions, such as the Boeing 7J7 project, in which $100 million was spent on preliminary development for a fuel-efficient airliner prior to a decision to commit $3 billion to go ahead with production. A sequential decision might also involve an opportunity to expand or abandon a factory depending on sales during the first year.

Example: Rediform can be used to explain decision tree analysis. Recall that annual cash flow for Rediform Concrete was (.5 × Sales) – $500,000. The salvage value at the end of the 5-year life would be either $1 million or $3 million. We extend the problem by adding the following assumptions:

1. Sales will be either $2 million or $4 million a year, with probabilities of .3 and .7, respectively.
2. Whatever sales occur in the first year will also occur in later years.
3. The factory can be sold for $3.5 million at the end of the first year.
4. There is a .4 probability of a $1 million salvage value at the end of year 5, and a .6 probability of a $3 million salvage value at that time.

The problem facing management is summarized in Figure 12-4. A square with lines branching out is a decision node, with each line representing an alternative; the square labeled A represents the original decision point: to build or not to build? A circle with lines branching out is an outcome node; given the decision that took us to that node, each branch represents a possible outcome. Arrival at node B occurs only if the factory is built, and the lines branching out from that node represent possible sales. Numbers in parentheses are probabilities, given arrival at that node, so there is a .3 probability that sales will be $2 million a year and a .7 probability that sales will be $4 million a year. The square labeled C is the decision node at the end of the first year if sales are $2 million. Management has a choice between receiving the $3.5 million salvage value or continuing for 4 more years and accepting an uncertain salvage value. The square labeled D is the decision node if sales are $4 million. The choice at point D is between the $3.5 million salvage value or continuing for 4 more years and accepting an uncertain salvage value.

Decision tree problems are solved by starting at the right-hand side and working backward, choosing the optimal decision at each decision node.[8] At decision

[8]We classify decision trees as a risk analysis tool because they are primarily used in risk settings, but they can actually be used to analyze sequential decision problems with no uncertainties involved.

FIGURE 12-4 Decision Tree Analysis of the Rediform Concrete Factory

The squares represent decision nodes and the circles represent outcome nodes. The numbers in parentheses are probabilities. This figure represents a factory investment with sales to be either $2 million or $4 million a year, and with an opportunity to abandon for $3.5 million after one year. Dollar amounts are in thousands.

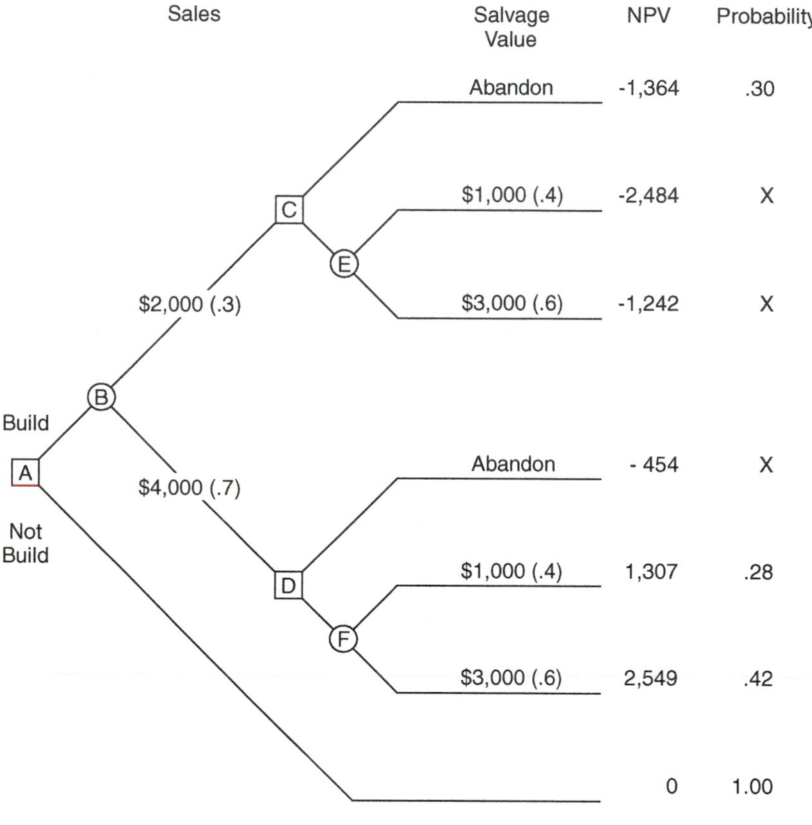

node C, the company faces a choice between $3.5 million in abandonment value and sales of $2 million a year for 4 years, with an uncertain abandonment value in 5 years. The expected net present value from continuing is:

$$E(NPV_{Continue}) = .4(-2{,}484) + .6(-1{,}242) = -\underline{\underline{\$1{,}739}}$$

If sales turn out to be $2 million, management will abandon the factory at the end of the first year. An X is placed in the probability columns for the outcomes resulting from continuance, to show that the continuance path will not be taken.

The analysis is continued in a similar way for sales of $4 million. It is clear that the investment would not be abandoned in this case since net present value with either salvage value at the end of the fifth year is higher than net present value with abandonment.

Given the decisions that will be made at the end of the first year, there are only three possible net present value outcomes for the investment. The expected net present value is therefore:

$$E(NPV) = .3(-1{,}364) + .28(1{,}307) + .42(2{,}549) = \underline{\$1{,}027}$$

Of course, the decision not to build results in a certain net present value of $0. Standard deviation, coefficient of variation, and so forth can also be computed from the probability distribution, and a graph similar to Figure 12-3 can be prepared. The internal rate of return can also be computed for each possible path, and the probability distribution of internal rates of return can be analyzed in the same manner.

Decision tree analysis, like other risk measurement methods, does not tell the managers which choice they should make. This tool does, however, give a clearer picture of the possible consequences of the decisions faced by the managers at Rediform. They can use this information to consider ways to control risk or to decide if the potential benefits are worth the risk.

For the illustration of decision tree analysis, we reduced the number of possible sales levels to two, from seven used in the simulation analysis. This was done only for simplicity of presentation. We could have used seven different sales levels by having seven branches instead of two at outcome node B. Computer programs are available for analyzing large, complex decision trees.

Decision trees can be combined with Monte Carlo simulation. We might, for example, conduct simulation studies given arrival at decision nodes C and D, to help managers decide what they would do at those points. Once decision rules at all later nodes are determined, a Monte Carlo simulation can be run for the entire proposed investment, incorporating the decision rules established for each decision node after the initial investment decision. Figure 12-5 shows the results of a simulation study of the Rediform factory assuming the probability distributions in Table 12-3. Results in this figure differ from Figure 12-3 in that managers have decided they will abandon the investment for $3.5 million at the end of the first year if

1. sales are $2 million;
2. sales are $2.5 million and the variable cost ratio is .5 or .6; or
3. sales are $3.0 million and the variable cost ratio is .6.

Monte Carlo simulation combined with decision tree analysis gives us a more specific view of risk and profitability than either tool used in isolation. Managers can now consider ways to reduce risk and reach their own decision as to whether the expected profitability is worth the risk.

Discount Rates and Risk Analysis

It is frequently argued that the appropriate discount rate for computing the probability distribution of net present value is the after tax risk-free rate. The reason for this position can be summarized with a simple example. The investment

FIGURE 12-5 Monte Carlo Simulation Combined with Decision Tree Analysis for Rediform (in $ thousands)

This figure extends the simulation result from Figure 12.3 to assume management will abandon the factory for $3.5 million at the end of the first year if

1. sales are $2 million;
2. sales are $2.5 million and the variable cost ratio is .5 or .6; or
3. sales are $3 million and the variable cost ratio is .6.

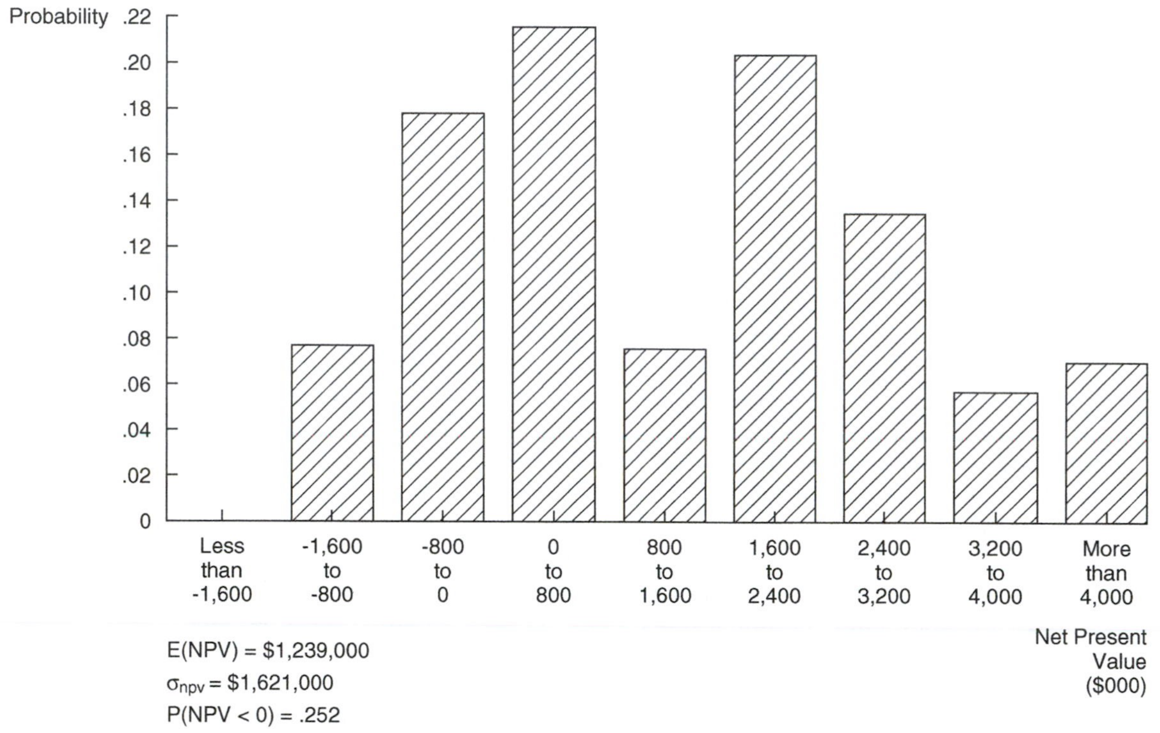

used for this example is affected by the level of sales. Net present values for each sales level using 6 percent, 9 percent, and 12 percent required returns are as follows:

OUTCOME	LOW SALES	MEDIUM SALES	HIGH SALES
NPV at 6%	$1,000	$2,000	$3,000
NPV at 9%	−500	500	1,500
NPV at 12%	−1,500	−500	500

At a 6 percent discount rate, there is no possibility the project will be unsuccessful. Assuming each outcome is equally likely, the probability of failure is 1/3 with a 9 percent discount rate and 2/3 with a 12 percent discount rate. Thus, the measured risk is affected by the discount rate, which is itself often affected by risk. It is often argued that the only way to compare the risk of investments is to use the after tax risk-free rate as the discount rate for the risk analysis.[9]

Nevertheless, managers gain important insights from risk analysis carried out using higher discount rates, particularly the company's cost of capital. We will argue in subsequent chapters that the cost of capital for a project is primarily the return necessary to compensate investors for the use of their money and for the acceptance of nondiversifiable risk, which typically accounts for only a small portion of total project risk. If managers want to know the probability that the returns from a capital investment will not be high enough to compensate investors for risks taken, a probability distribution of net present values using the appropriate cost of capital answers the question. If the objective is to determine the probability that a return less than the risk-free rate will be earned, then a probability distribution of net present values based on the risk-free rate will answer the question. Other questions could lead to other discount rates.

Developing Probability Estimates for Risk Analysis

The risk analysis methods simply start with probability information for input variables and work forward to probability distributions of outcomes. Finding the probability information about inputs is a major part of the task. The three primary ways of developing these probability estimates are study of historical data, experimentation, and judgment.

History. If you want to know variance of temperature or stock prices, you can compute the historical variance. If you want to estimate the probability of a recession in any future year you might look to the percent of years in which there were recessions in the past. When we run a regression analysis on past relationships between variables, we receive information about the variance of the probability distribution of each regression coefficient. These variances can be used as the variances in a Monte Carlo simulation model. To estimate a probability distribution from historical observations, it is necessary that the probability distribution has remained stable for a sufficient number of periods, and will remain stable in the future. These requirements do limit the use of the historical approach. However, history is often useful in estimating probabilities.

Experiments. Test markets and pilot production facilities are common types of experiments that lead to information about probabilities. If Procter & Gamble test-markets its new laundry soap in six cities, the test market results can be used to estimate the probability distribution of sales for the general market. Procter & Gamble may divide the test market into cells and vary the packaging or price slightly in each cell. Not only does the company end up with expected results and risk information, but it ends up with information about how the nature of the offering affects those characteristics.

---

[9]This point is discussed in more detail in Wilbur G. Lewellen and Michael S. Long, "Simulation Versus Single-Value Estimates in Capital Expenditure Analysis," *Decision Science* 3 (October 1972): 19–33.

Judgment. Knowledgeable people are often queried with regard to their estimates. This approach is particularly popular for forecasting future technology. For example, a knowledgeable person may be asked for the expected number of years until half the population has high-resolution television. A probability distribution can be estimated based on this information. There is an extensive literature on eliciting subjective probability estimates, and the method is widely used in certain fields.[10]

Choice of Risk Analysis Method

Each risk analysis method has advantages and disadvantages, as summarized in Table 12-5. There is no one measure that is right for all situations. The job of the professional is to choose the right measure for the right situation, whether it is a quick sensitivity analysis for a project of moderate size and risk or a decision tree approach that is often used when analyzing new international markets characterized by opportunities to enter small and expand later.

[10]See, for example, Irwin Kabus, "You Can Bank on Uncertainty," *Harvard Business Review* (May–June 1976): 95–105; Rakesh Kumar Sarin, "Elicitation of Subjective Probabilities in the Context of Decision Making," *Decision Sciences* 9 (January 1978): 37–48; and James S. Ang, Jess H. Chua, and Ronald Sellers, "Generating Cash Flow Estimates: An Actual Study Using the Delphi Method," *Financial Management* (Spring 1979): 64–67.

TABLE 12-5 Advantages and Disadvantages of Risk Analysis Tools

	ADVANTAGES	DISADVANTAGES
Sensitivity analysis and break-even analysis	Simple to compute and explain Does not require probability estimates Brings focus to one or two key drivers	No probability estimates of outcomes Limited ability to consider interactions between drivers Difficult to handle sequential decisions
Scenario analysis	Simple to explain Does not require probability estimates Allows consideration of multiple drivers, and their interactions Can accommodate sequential decisions	No probability estimates of outcomes Limits consideration to a few outcomes defined by scenarios
Monte Carlo simulation	Provides results in probability terms Considers multiple sources of uncertainty Can model sequential decision making	Expensive and time consuming Must input extensive probability estimates Limited ability to handle interactions between drivers Depends on a simulation model that is not transparent to the decision maker
Decision trees	Provides results in probability terms Not only accommodates, but focuses on sequential decision making	Requires probability estimates as inputs Can be time consuming to construct, depending on the complexity of the situation

MANAGING RISK

In addition to measuring risk, there are important opportunities to change the desirability of proposed investments by changing their risk-return characteristics. You may succeed in reducing risk without a commensurate decrease in expected benefits. You may even use tools like decision tree analysis to develop strategies that increase expected benefits while decreasing risk. On a less ambitious but still important scale, you may reduce the risk of a project so that managers are willing to take the personal risks associated with sponsoring it.[11] Some methods of controlling risk are discussed in the following paragraphs.

Fixed Cost and Variable Cost Changes

One of the more common ways to affect the risk of an investment is to change the mix of fixed costs and variable costs. Ford Motor Company, for example, made only $1.2 billion in 1979. By restructuring to create a lower break-even point, Ford earned $3 billion on the same volume in 1986.[12] Buying components as needed instead of manufacturing them makes the entire cost of those components variable, whereas manufacturing the components requires fixed costs. The net effect of a decision to outsource may be higher costs under normal conditions, but the absence of fixed costs during a slowdown will reduce risk.

Example: When computer companies like Hewlett-Packard first developed laser printers, they had a choice between designing printers from scratch or modifying existing personal copiers. Suppose cash outlays required for the two alternatives were as shown in Table 12-6 (we ignore taxes for simplicity). Assume further that the computer company had a 10 percent required return, the investment was expected to have a life of 5 years, the printers could be sold for $2,000 each, and the salvage value for the production facilities would be negligible. The net present value break-even points for the two alternatives are as follows.

[11]Risk reduction of this last type is generally not thought of as contributing to shareholder wealth, but shareholder wealth will be improved if managers are persuaded to accept wealth-creating investments they would have otherwise rejected.

[12]"Ford Continues to Outearn GM and Chrysler Combined," *Business Month* (June 1987): 10.

TABLE 12-6 Cash Outlays for Two Alternatives at Hewlett Packard

	MODIFY COPIER	DESIGN FROM SCRATCH
Design cost	$10,000,000	$20,000,000
Cost to convert factory	20,000,000	30,000,000
Fixed annual production cost	500,000	1,000,000
Fixed administrative and marketing cost	1,000,000	1,000,000
Variable production cost per unit	1,000	800
Variable administration and marketing cost per unit	200	200

Modified copier:

$$\text{NPV} = -30{,}000{,}000 + \text{PVA1}_{5\text{years},10\%}[Q(2{,}000 - 1{,}000 - 200) - 1{,}500{,}000] = 0$$

$$Q = 11{,}767 \text{ printers a year}$$

Design from scratch:

$$\text{NPV} = -50{,}000{,}000 + \text{PVA1}_{5\text{years},10\%}[Q(2{,}000 - 800 - 200) - 2{,}000{,}000] = 0$$

$$Q = 15{,}190 \text{ printers a year}$$

We note that design from scratch increases the NPV break-even point by 30 percent, increases the initial investment by two-thirds, and increases annual fixed costs by 33 percent. Furthermore, demand must be greater than 28,880 units a year—2.5 times the modified copier break-even point—before net present value is higher with design from scratch.[13] The break-even analysis tells us that the modified design approach is less risky, unless managers are certain that sales will be greater than 28,880 units a year. Managers must still rely on their judgment to decide which combination of expected benefits and risk is preferred. The decision was to reduce risk by taking advantage of existing copier designs.

Fixed and variable cost trade-offs occur in areas other than production. Banks, for example, commonly borrow on shorter terms than they lend, hoping to reduce their cost of funds in that way. But they also accept the risk that the interest rate they are paying may go above the rate charged on existing loans. Thus, they accept costs that vary, although the variance is not caused by changes in the volume of business. When considering a new loan product, the risk/return characteristics of the capital investment can be affected significantly by the funding decision. Likewise, farmers have a choice between taking a chance on market prices of their products at harvest time or locking in the price at planting time with a futures contract. A 3-year wage contract with the United Autoworkers Union makes Ford's costs more predictable than a 1-year contract, and so on.

Pricing Strategy

For many companies, pricing strategy is an important aspect of risk management. A lower price increases potential demand, but also increases the break-even point. This is one reason companies introducing new technology first bring out their models at a high price and then reduce the price after a few months. If it turns out that the product only meets a few specialized needs, those with the specialized needs are probably willing to pay the higher price,

[13]The net present value equations for the modified copier and design from scratch are set equal to each other and solved for Q:

$$-30{,}000{,}000 + \text{PVA1}_{5\text{years},10\%}[Q(2{,}000 - 1{,}000 - 200) - 1{,}500{,}000]$$
$$= -50{,}000{,}000 + \text{PVA1}_{5\text{years},10\%}[Q(2{,}000 - 800 - 200) - 2{,}000{,}000];\ Q = \underline{28{,}880}$$

and getting the higher price on some units decreases the break-even point. Sensitivity analysis and simulation are again helpful in evaluating the risks of various pricing alternatives.

Example: If demand for laser printers had turned out to be limited to a few specialized uses, those with the specialized needs would probably be willing to pay the higher price, and the higher price would decrease the break-even point. Suppose the computer company developing the laser printer decided to use a modified copier and chose the following pricing strategy:

YEAR	1	2	3–5
Unit price	$4,000	$3,000	$2,000

Managers believed that this price pattern would level out demand, and unit sales would be held constant through the price reduction. The net present value break-even point in annual sales would then be found as follows:

$$NPV = -30{,}000{,}000 + PVA1_{5yrs,10\%} \times 1{,}500{,}000 + Q[(4{,}000 - 1{,}200)/1.1 + (3{,}000 - 1{,}200)/1.1^2 + (2{,}000 - 1{,}200)/1.1^3 + (2{,}000 - 1{,}200)/1.1^4 + (2{,}000 - 1{,}200)/1.1^5] = 0$$

$$Q = 6{,}286 \text{ printers a year}$$

This pricing strategy decreases risk by reducing the break-even quantity by 47 percent.

Sequential Investment

In many situations, there is a choice between starting large or starting small and then expanding if demand is sufficient. Economies of scale are such that the total cost of achieving a particular capacity level will generally be lower with a single, large investment than with smaller, sequential investments. But the risk is also greater. Decision tree analysis or simulation analysis for each alternative provides information about the risk/return characteristics of each option.

Extent of Analysis

Additional study and experimentation, such as General Electric's $1 million expenditure for a pilot plant for its Ultem plastic, can decrease uncertainty. For many capital investments, a decision must be made as to how much analysis to do. This is itself a risk/return decision, because additional study can often improve predictability. Additional test marketing and testing of production technology in small-scale facilities are ways to reduce risk, but the direct cost and the opportunity cost from delayed action can be considerable. The analysis is similar to that for sequential investment. Decision trees are one way to evaluate the potential benefit of additional study. By deciding how they would respond to both positive and negative information, managers can often decide if the information is worth the cost.

Financial Leverage

We have discussed the mix of fixed and variable operating costs. Financial leverage is another way to affect risk. Financial leverage refers to the use of fixed cost financing: debt, preferred stock, and leasing. The use of financial leverage increases the return on equity if an investment is successful, but it also creates another set of fixed costs that must be met even in times of difficulty. Typically, companies that otherwise face high risks use less financial leverage, and vice versa. Financial leverage is covered in detail in Part Four of this book.

Diversification

Diversification is the reduction of risk by combining assets in portfolios. When investments are combined in a portfolio, the investments generally will not all respond in the same way to all changes in the environment. Therefore, the risk of the portfolio is often less than the sum of the risks of the assets in that portfolio. Diversification is the main topic of the next chapter.

PROJECT SELECTION UNDER RISK

Once all of the investments and risk/return alternatives have been identified and measured, you must still make a decision. There are five primary ways to incorporate risk in the decision process: judgment, adjustment of required return, certainty equivalents, a payback period requirement, and arbitrage valuation.[14]

Judgment

When judgment is used, managers consider the information about the risk and return characteristics of an investment and then make an accept/reject decision without formally defined selection standards. Decisions are often made by vote of a capital budgeting committee, an executive committee, or a board of directors. If judgmental decision making seems haphazard, consider how most of us make the most important personal decisions of our lives. Few of us select a career or a spouse by starting with a predefined selection formula and then running each alternative through that formula to look for the highest score; we collect information and apply judgment instead.

---

[14]Miller points out that because there are more bad opportunities than good ones, there is a bias toward overestimating the attractiveness of risky projects. So whatever method is used, it is important to control for this bias. See Edward Miller, "The Cutoff Benefit-Cost Ratio Should Exceed One." *The Engineering Economist* 46 #4 (2001): 312–319.

Required Return Adjustment

Many companies use higher required returns for more risky investments. Some companies make judgmental adjustments to the required return based on how risky a particular investment appears to be. Other companies use different required returns for capital investments in different divisions, based on the perceived risk of each division.

Many companies adjust the required return for the type of investment being considered, as follows:

> **Cost reduction** investments are given the lowest required return because costs and benefits are fairly predictable.
>
> **Volume expansion projects in existing product lines** are treated as intermediate risk investments. Cash flow forecasts depend on product demand forecasts, but the company does have experience with the product line. A required return intermediate between low and high risk projects is used.
>
> **New product lines** are considered the highest risk projects, and are assigned the highest required return. Cash flow forecasts depend on product demand forecasts in an area in which management has no prior experience.

The problem with assigning required return in this way is that the distinction between diversifiable and nondiversifiable risk is not recognized. Most of the extra risk associated with a new product line results from the company's lack of experience. Much of Armco's loss in insurance business—over half a billion dollars—can probably be attributed to Armco's lack of experience in insurance, a risk that can be readily diversified away by shareholders. Current finance theory suggests that required return should be adjusted only for risks that cannot be readily diversified away by the shareholders. Formal procedures for adjusting the required return in response to risk are explained in Chapters 14 and 15.

Certainty Equivalents

Another approach to risky capital investment decision making is to convert uncertain future cash flows to certainty equivalents. As generally used in capital budgeting, a **certainty equivalent** is defined as a certain dollar amount at time t which, if discounted to the present at the risk-free rate, is the amount you would be willing to pay today in exchange for the uncertain cash flow that will occur at time t. Suppose, for example, a capital investment will generate cash flows in year 5 with an expected value of $1,000 and a standard deviation of $500. The risk-free rate is 6 percent, and the company uses a 10 percent required return for investments with this level of risk. The certainty equivalent (CE) that would lead to the same present value as that computed using the risk-adjusted discount rate can be found as follows:

$$\frac{1,000}{(1+.10)^5} = \frac{CE_t}{(1+.05)^5}$$

$$\text{Solving, } CE_5 = \$1,000(1.05/1.10)^5 = \underline{\$792}$$

We can generalize from this example to say that the certainty equivalent (CE_t) gives the same net present value as the risk-adjusted discount rate if:

$$CE_t = E(CF_t)[(1 + r_f)/(1 + k)]^t \quad \textbf{(12-6)}$$

where r_f is the risk-free rate, $E(CF_t)$ is expected cash flow at time t, and k is the risk-adjusted required return. Some authors argue in favor of the certainty equivalent approach because the risk-adjusted discount rate method implicitly assumes a specific certainty-equivalent factor: $[(1 + r_f)/(1 + k)]^t$. They argue that it is better to use an explicit certainty-equivalent factor that can be specified for each period, according to the risk of that period's cash flows.[15]

A problem with certainty equivalents is the question of whose certainty equivalent to use. If we can instruct managers to consider only shareholder interest, there are some ways to compute certainty equivalents, and these are discussed in Chapter 15. If a decision maker wants to consider total project risk, though, the certainty equivalent is relevant only if it is a certainty equivalent that will be accepted by the decision maker. The decision maker must be willing to make numerous hypothetical choices so that certainty equivalent values can be based on this person's preference function.

The problem of mapping preference functions quickly explodes in complexity. If the decision maker is indifferent between an immediate payment from the probability distribution described in the previous example and an immediate payment of \$800, does it follow that the decision maker is indifferent between a payment from the probability distribution in 10 years or a certain \$800 in 10 years? There is reason to believe that the general answer is *no,* because the decision maker cannot develop an optimal pattern of consumption over time when future wealth is not known. Therefore, development of the utility function mapping needed to find the certainty equivalent would be extremely time consuming.

Payback Period Requirement

Some companies use net present value analysis as a project profitability criterion, but use payback period as a risk control criterion. If an investment is considered more risky, a shorter payback period is required for its acceptance, even if the net present value is positive. This approach is based on the assumption that risk is primarily related to the period of time until benefits are received. Recognition Equipment, discussed in the opening paragraphs of this chapter, used the payback criterion as part of its planning to control risk.

The longer we have to wait for payment, the greater is our uncertainty about economic conditions and other variables that change over time. Therefore, there is some relationship between risk and time until benefits are received. The shortened payback requirements are frequently used, for example, by companies investing in politically unstable countries. However, risk is related to things

[15]See, for example, Harold Bierman, Jr., and Seymour Schmidt, *The Capital Budgeting Decision,* 7th ed. (New York: Macmillan Publishing Co., 1988).

other than passage of time in most cases, and control of payback period is therefore an incomplete method of controlling risk exposure.

Arbitrage Valuation

Arbitrage valuation is based on the principle that two identical streams of expected cash flows, with identical risk characteristics, will have identical values. A publicly traded security portfolio that will provide the same expected cash flows and risks as the capital investment under consideration is constructed. A capital investment is desirable if it costs less than this substitute portfolio. Arbitrage methods in general are covered in Chapter 15. The mean-variance capital asset pricing model is a widely used application of the arbitrage concept, and is covered in Chapter 14.

Choosing How to Choose

In considering these project selection methods in the face of risk, it is helpful to distinguish between policies and decision support systems. For the hundreds or thousands of small capital-budgeting decisions faced each year, senior managers must establish policies that allow middle- and lower-level managers to make the right decisions without extensive project-by-project inputs from top management. A positive net present value requirement based on a risk-adjusted required return is often used for these purposes, sometimes supplemented with a payback requirement. Although the rules are often arbitrary, top managers can control risk exposure through policy without having to examine each individual investment proposal.

For the major investments in which senior managers are involved, decision support systems are needed. A decision support system must provide information about proposed investments, and *may* also include predetermined decision rules. If certainty equivalents or discount rates adjusted for total project risk are used, the decision support system includes some specific decision rules based on the manager's prior preference statements. If judgment is used as the decision method, the decision support system does not include predetermined decision rules; in comparing alternatives, the manager decides which combination of benefits and risks is more attractive. While some predetermined criteria may be used, managers have shown a preference for using judgment in the final decision process. This is why capital budgeting committees exist.

Risk Analysis of International Investments

Risk analysis is more extensive for international investments than for domestic investments. Risks encountered include project risk, political risk, and exchange rate risk.

Project risk is the same fundamental risk faced in domestic capital investments. We may experience technical difficulties with the product or production process, competitors may enter and force prices down, or customers may simply reject the product. Economic changes, climate changes, and so forth may affect the profitability of the project. While these are the same risks faced in domestic business, they are often heightened in the international arena. Because managers are less familiar with the environment in the foreign country, they have more difficulty in predicting outcomes. For a Cadillac dealership in Saudi Arabia, project risks include an economic decline due to falling oil prices and a strong preference for Mercedes instead of Cadillacs.

Political risk refers to political events that might be unfavorable to the investment. These range from increased taxation or controls on repatriating earnings to political upheaval and outright expropriation of assets. The stability and dependability of the government is a major consideration in risk analysis. A Persian Gulf war and an anti-Arab foreign policy tilt in Washington could completely wipe out the investment. Models have been developed for the prediction of government stability and there are services that monitor government stability.[16]

Exchange rate risk adds a new dimension to risk. The exchange rate between two currencies is the number of units of one currency that must be given in exchange for a unit of another. As an illustration, the Thai baht was \$0.0391 early in 1993 and \$0.0233 early in 2003. Suppose Emerson Corporation made an investment of \$1 million in 1993 with the expectation of receiving 100 million baht in 2003, and did not anticipate a change in the exchange rate. The expected and actual U.S. dollars would be as follows.

$$\text{Expected amount} = 100{,}000{,}000 \times .0391 = \$3{,}910{,}000$$

$$\text{Actual amount} = 100{,}000{,}000 \times .0233 = \$2{,}330{,}000$$

If Emerson had a 10 percent cost of capital, the anticipated and actual net present value were:

$$\text{Anticipated NPV} = \$3{,}910{,}000/(1+.10)^{10} - \$1{,}000{,}000 = \$507{,}474$$

$$\text{Realized NPV} = \$2{,}330{,}000/(1+.10)^{10} - \$1{,}000{,}000 = -\$101{,}684$$

The loss of value of the baht took Emerson from an anticipated NPV of over \$500,000 to a negative NPV of over \$100,000. In other periods, companies have lost money because the U.S. dollar lost value. This further illustrates the importance of exchange rate risk. Chapter 9 introduced exchange rates, this chapter mentions the risk exposure, and Chapter 15 discusses some of the ways exchange rate risk can be managed with the use of futures, swaps, and options.

Stanley and Block surveyed the largest multinational firms in the United States, and provided us with important insights concerning capital budgeting

[16]For additional discussion of political risk, see Pravin Banker, "You're the Best Judge of Foreign Risks," *Harvard Business Review* 61 (March–April 1983): 157–165.

practices for multinational investments.[17] One finding was that risk analysis is of critical importance in multinational capital budgeting, and 62 percent of the respondents used some risk adjustment technique. Over half used a different risk analysis method for foreign investments than for domestic investments. Respondents were evenly divided in their choices between discount rate adjustment and cash flow adjustment.

SUMMARY

This chapter focused on risk analysis from the total project perspective. In this chapter we covered methods of defining risk, methods of controlling risk, and investment decision making in the face of risk. Methods of defining risk were divided between those depending on probability and those not depending on probability.

Sensitivity analysis, including break-even analysis, is the primary method of defining risk without using probability. The objective in probability-related analysis is to develop a description of the probability distribution of profitability. Simulation and decision tree analysis are popular tools for this purpose.

Risk management is another important part of the problem. Managers have available to them numerous actions that can change the risk/return characteristics of an investment, possibly making it more desirable. Alternatives available to management include changing the fixed cost/variable cost mix, selection of the amount of study before the decision, making the investment commitment in stages, choice of pricing strategy, choice of financial leverage, and diversification.

Decision making under risk: once all the analysis is completed, someone has to make a decision, considering both risk and profitability. For small projects, predetermined standards such as risk-adjusted required returns and shortened payback periods are used. For large investments, certainty equivalents are possible, but many companies rely on judgment rather than predetermined rules.

Risk analysis of foreign investments begins with analysis of project risk, which is the same risk faced with domestic investments. Political risk is an additional risk and refers to various political events that might be unfavorable to the investment. Exchange rate risk adds another dimension to risk analysis in that it increases uncertainty with regard to the number of dollars the company will finally end up with. Some ways to manage exchange rate risk are discussed in Chapter 15.

The methods covered in this chapter focus primarily on total investment risk. Total risk is certainly important to managers making the investment decision, and total risk analysis is an important information source for risk management. However, risks viewed from the perspectives of the company's asset portfolio and an investor's investment portfolio are at least equally important. Risk analysis from these perspectives is covered in Chapters 13 through 15.

[17]Marjorie T. Stanley and Stanley B. Block, "A Survey of Multinational Capital Budgeting," *Financial Review* 19 (March 1984): 36–54.

QUESTIONS

12-1. As a tool for risk analysis, what are the advantages and disadvantages of sensitivity analysis?

12-2. One reason for numerous risk analysis techniques is that each one fits different types of problems. What are the characteristics for which each of the following techniques would be appropriate? What are the disadvantages of these methods?

a. Decision trees

b. Monte Carlo simulation

12-3. What is the difference between sensitivity analysis and simulation without probability?

12-4. List several examples of cash flows that would

a. be highly correlated from period to period.

b. have little or no correlation from period to period.

12-5. What are the restrictions in a Monte Carlo simulation with regard to the probability distribution characteristics that can be included?

12-6. Can a Monte Carlo simulation handle correlation between variables? Explain.

12-7. What are the guidelines for choice of a discount rate to use in simulation and the other risk analysis methods discussed in this chapter?

12-8. How can probability estimates for the input variables to a risk analysis be developed?

12-9. Discuss the methods available to alter the risk/return characteristics of a capital investment.

12-10. What methods do companies use to make capital investment decisions after risk analysis has been completed?

12-11. **(Ethical Considerations)** You are a management consultant in the middle of what has turned out to be a rather long-term engagement. You have just uncovered the following facts:

- Charris, the founder of a successful plastics company, sold the company to his banker, Rassie, 5 years ago for $250,000 but retained a substantial portion of the company's stock with a book value of $2,500,000. He has since died and left the stock to his widow who has very little business knowledge. The widow has hired an attorney to represent her.
- For a number of years, Rassie and his managers have been diverting money from the company mainly by starting and investing in negative net present value projects that are actually hobbies for Rassie.
- The local accounting firm audit fails to call attention to the diversion of funds into these hobbies and simply reports that the core plastics firm is unprofitable.
- After years of mismanagement, the firm is reporting a loss and the shares held by the widow have a book value of $300,000. Checks drawn on the plastics firm's account have paid for Rassie's condominiums, luxury cars, and a horse-breeding ranch which is in his mother's name.

- The widow, thinking the plastics firm is unprofitable, is persuaded on the advice of her attorney to sell her shares in the firm to Rassie for pennies on the dollar.
- Rassie puts the plastics business up for sale and a competitor pays $10,000,000 for the assets of the plastics firm.
- Rassie pockets most of this gain but also spreads $2 million around to the senior executives who participated in the diversion of funds.
- The business is operated by the new owners and is generating $500,000 a month in income. Given the facts above, clearly Rassie benefited at the widow's expense.
  - **a.** Was there an ethical violation from the viewpoint of the local CPA firm?
  - **b.** Was there an ethical violation from the viewpoint of the lawyer representing the widow?
  - **c.** Assume there is a 15 percent chance that the local CPA firm will admit to its mistake and a 25 percent chance that the lawyer will admit to his mistake. If either of these two parties comes forward, Rassie will probably have to return the $10,000,000 to the widow as well as go to jail for the diversion of funds. From Rassie's point of view, what is the expected value of the $10,000,000 payoff?

12-12. **(Applications)** Blockbuster Video has been extremely profitable in the past. Suppose you were considering opening a video store in your town.

- **a.** Describe the process you would go through to evaluate the risk of such a store.
- **b.** Describe how you would go about collecting the data needed for your analysis.
- **c.** Using your own numbers, calculate a break-even and be prepared to explain how you arrived at your numbers. Illustrate another method besides break-even to analyze the proposal.
- **d.** What are the two most important variables, under your control, to the success of a video store?

PROBLEMS

12-1. Athens Development Corporation is considering a new product that will be sensitive to both economic conditions and competitor response. The product manager has decided to focus on three equally likely economic conditions: weak economy, normal economy, and strong economy. Competitors either will or will not respond with a competitive product, and competitor response is unlikely unless economic conditions turn out to be strong. Annual cash flows for each of these conditions appear below. The product has a 5-year life and will require an initial cash outlay of $100,000. The cost of capital is 10 percent. Should Athens invest in this product? Explain.

COMPETITOR RESPONSE	WEAK ECONOMY	NORMAL ECONOMY	STRONG ECONOMY
Yes	$10,000	$20,000	$30,000
No	20,000	30,000	40,000

12-2. Define a weak economy as no growth, a normal economy as 3 percent growth, and a strong economy as 6 percent growth. Prepare a graphical sensitivity analysis for the new product investment in problem 1.

12-3. Denver Doughnuts is considering a new store location. For accounting purposes, fixed operating costs for a store are $23,500 a year, and variable costs are 40 percent of sales. Compute the break-even sales level for a store location.

a. If average revenue per customer is $1.40, how many customers must be served each hour to break even in earnings? (The stores are open twenty-four hours a day, 365 days a year.)

b. If the price (only) is raised 10 percent, what will be the new earnings break-even point?

12-4. For Denver Doughnuts (problem 3), fixed cash outlays are $18,750 a year at each location, and variable cash outlays are 40 percent of sales. A store requires an initial outlay of $60,000, and the company uses a 14 percent required return. Because of changing neighborhood characteristics, the company does its analysis based on a 10-year store life. Since the locations are leased, the terminal value is minimal. Ignore taxes for simplicity.

a. What annual sales volume will be needed to generate a net present value of $0?

b. The after-tax risk-free interest rate is 6 percent. What annual sales value will be needed to generate a net present value of $0 using a 6 percent discount rate?

12-5. Salt Lake Systems is a small company started by two recent college graduates to market a small-business inventory management system they developed and patented as a class project. The system requires a special hard-disk drive that plugs into a microcomputer.

Buy and Modify Alternative: With this alternative, Salt Lake Systems would buy standard hard-disk systems at $2,200 and then modify them at a cost of $900 each. Annual fixed cash outlays for the modification operation would be $50,000. Capital investment requirements will be $30,000 to modify.

Build Alternative: Under this alternative, Salt Lake Systems would construct the special hard-disk system from scratch. Component parts can be readily purchased, and the production process is not complex. The variable cost to build each special hard-disk system would be $2,000. Annual fixed cash outlays for the building alternative would be $100,000. Capital investment requirements will be $60,000 to build.

Salt Lake Systems plans to price the systems at $4,995 each because they have a patent and proprietary software. The partners estimate that they can complete 100 units a year, either building or modifying. Potential demand could be for thousands of units a year, but could also be only a fraction of capacity. The partners do not have enough information to estimate probabilities and cannot afford market research. They recognize that technology changes rapidly and, therefore, use a 3-year life for analysis. The cost of capital is 12 percent, and the partners are not subject to income tax. Use net present value break-even analysis to recommend a production method.

12-6. Upscale Home Fashions of Burlington pays fees to a delivery service that amount to an after tax cost of 2 percent of revenue. Sales have averaged approximately $1.5 million, but have been as low as $1 million and as high as $2 million in the past decade. Upscale could buy its own delivery truck for $30,000, after tax, eliminating the need for the delivery service. The truck would last 8 years, with a negligible salvage value. Salary for a driver and other operating costs would result in an after tax cash outlay of $20,000 a year. The company has a 10 percent cost of capital. Prepare a graphical sensitivity analysis, showing the relationship between net present value for the truck investment and sales for the store. Would you recommend acquisition of the truck?

12-7. For the delivery truck investment in problem 6, assume that expected sales are $1.5 million and the standard deviation of the probability distribution of sales is $300,000. Compute the expected net present value and standard deviation of net present value under the assumption that the cash flows are perfectly correlated.

12-8. Rework problem 7 on the assumption that cash flows are uncorrelated from year to year.

12-9. A rental property with a 20-year life can be purchased for $100,000. Net cash benefits per year have an expected value of $15,000 and a standard deviation of $5,000. At a 10 percent required return, compute the expected net present value and standard deviation of net present value under the assumption of

a. perfect correlation from year to year.

b. no correlation from year to year.

12-10. National Bank is considering a new loan product. Initial costs to design and introduce the product will be $200,000 (all numbers in this example are after tax). Managers are confident of achieving interest income of $1 million per year, but are not sure how much promotion will be needed to achieve that volume. They estimate promotion expense of $60,000 a year, with a standard deviation of $30,000. The initial market response will carry forward to future years, so perfect correlation is assumed. Managers are also uncertain about bad debt expense. The estimate is $50,000 a year, with a standard deviation of $20,000, and perfect correlation from year to year is assumed. Interest expense depends on interest rate movements and is also uncertain. The expected annual interest expense is $600,000, with a standard deviation of $100,000, and is treated as having no correlation from year to year. Other operating expenses will be $180,000 a year, and can be estimated with virtual certainty. The product will be evaluated over a 3-year time horizon because competitors will come in by that time and squeeze profit margins down to the point where the bank will just earn its 15 percent required return.

a. Find the expected net present value.

b. Find the standard deviation of present value for interest expense, bad debt expense, and promotion expense.

c. Assume independence between the three components analyzed in part b. Recognizing that the variance equals the sum of the variances, find the standard deviation of net present value.

12-11. An apartment house can be purchased for $200,000. Rent is expected to be $30,000 a year in the first year and is expected to grow at 5 percent a year. The standard deviation of cash flow is expected to be $3,000 in the first year and is also expected to grow at 5 percent a year. Rental income from year to year is expected to be perfectly correlated. Operating expenses are expected to be $8,000 a year, with a standard deviation of $2,000, and are expected to be uncorrelated from year to year. The salvage value after 10 years is estimated to be $300,000, with a standard deviation of $50,000. The various components of cash flow are uncorrelated, and the required return is 10 percent. The potential buyer pays no taxes.

a. Compute the expected net present value.

b. Compute the standard deviation of present value for each component of cash flow.

c. Assuming independence between components, the present values of components are independent variables. Recognizing that the variance of the sum of a series of independent variables equals the sum of the variances, find the standard deviation of net present value.

12-12. A capital investment requires a cash outlay of $60,000 and has a 3-year life. It provides cash inflows of $30,000 with a probability of .3 or $40,000 with a probability of .7. At a 10 percent required return, find the possible net present values and their probabilities, assuming

a. perfect correlation from year to year.

b. no correlation from year to year.

12-13. For problem 12, find the expected internal rate of return.

12-14. An investment costs $5,000, after tax considerations, and will generate cash flows of $1,000 a year over its life. The capital investment will last 8, 9, or 10 years, with probabilities of .4, .4, and .2 respectively. At a 10 percent required return, compute the expected net present value and standard deviation of net present value.

12-15. A capital investment requires an initial outlay of $1,000. In the first year, it will provide cash flows of $300 with a probability of .3, or $600 with a probability of .7. If cash flows in the first year are $600, they will be $700 or $800 in the second year, with a .5 probability of each outcome. If cash flows are $300 in the first year, they will be $300 in the second year. At a 10 percent required return, find each possible net present value and its associated probability. Is this investment attractive?

12-16. Cincinnati Express is a small regional airline. To open a new route, the airline must buy two commuter airplanes at an estimated cost of $3 million, after tax. Other start-up costs are estimated to be $500,000, after tax. Annual operating costs are expected to be $600,000 a year, after tax. Costs are largely fixed, and do not depend on revenue. As with many new routes into smaller towns, demand is uncertain until the service has actually been offered. Demand after the first year is expected to be very similar to that in the first year, though. A discrete approximation to the probability distribution for demand follows:

PROBABILITY	.10	.20	.40	.20	.10
Revenue (after tax)	700,000	900,000	1,200,000	1,500,000	2,000,000

If the route turns out to be unprofitable, the airplanes can be sold at the end of 1 year for an estimated market value of $2.5 million, after tax. The airplanes will last approximately 10 years, after which the estimated salvage value is $250,000, after tax. A 10-year horizon is used for decision making, and the company uses a 10 percent required return for decision making. Use decision tree analysis to evaluate this capital investment opportunity.

a. Would you recommend the capital investment for a small commuter airline that has only one other route, with that route being of similar size and marginally profitable?

b. Would you recommend the capital investment for a large commuter airline with dozens of profitable routes?

c. How would your recommendation be changed if any airline entering the route must continue the route for 10 years?

12-17. Harvey Publishing Company, a small publisher in Columbus, is considering a new book. Typesetting and related costs to prepare for production are $10,000. It will cost $2 per copy to produce the book. If additional copies are needed at a later time, the set-up cost will be $5,000 and the cost per copy will again be $2. The book will sell for $14 a copy. Royalties, commissions, shipping costs, and so on will be $4 a copy. If the book gets good reviews, it can be expected to sell 5,000 copies a year for 3 years. If it gets bad reviews, sales will be 2,000 copies in the first year, and will then cease. There is a .3 probability of a favorable review. Sally Harvey, president, faces a choice between ordering an immediate production run of 15,000 copies or a production run of 5,000 copies, followed by an additional production run at the end of the first year if the book is successful. All production runs must be in increments of 5,000 copies. Harvey uses a 10 percent required return for evaluating new investments. She will pay no taxes because of previous losses, and her capital is very limited. Use decision tree analysis to recommend a production schedule and decide whether to publish the book.

12-18. For the situation described in problem 17, some new information about demand has become available. If the book is successful in the first year, selling 5,000 copies, demand in the second and third years will be 5,000. If the book is unsuccessful in the first year, though, there is still a .2 probability of it catching on, with sales of 3,000 copies in the second year and 5,000 copies in the third year. Use decision tree analysis to develop a production plan.

12-19. Jane Engle, a new college graduate, wants to go into business and is considering a copy center in a small, new office park in San Jose. It will cost $100,000 after tax to open the business. Fixed costs are expected to be $50,000 a year, including her salary, and variable costs are expected to be 40 percent of revenue. Assume all costs are cash, for simplicity. She decided to limit the risk analysis to 10 years because changing technology could make this kind of business obsolete. She uses a 15 percent required return (the risk-free rate is 10 percent) and estimates that she will be in a 30 percent marginal tax bracket. Revenue is expected to be $90,000 a year. Model this business as a series of equations.

12-20. Jane Engle (problem 19) is uncertain about demand for the proposed copy center. She will be given the exclusive right to operate a copy center at the office park. If many small offices move in, demand will be large. But if a few large organizations take over the space, they will use their own facilities, and demand will be limited. She has estimated a probability distribution of revenues as follows:

PROBABILITY	.25	.50	.25
Annual Revenue	100,000	140,000	170,000

Use a Monte Carlo simulation with 10 iterations to analyze the problem. Instead of a random-number generator or roulette wheel, you may flip two coins for each iteration. If both come up tails, use revenue of $100,000. If both come up heads, use revenue of $170,000. If there is one head and one tail, use revenue of $140,000.

12-21. Using a computer and random-number generator, rework problem 20 using 100 iterations.

12-22. Please use the data from problem 8-5 to complete this problem. You have concluded that the two most influential variables on your NPV are changes in taste and preferences toward playing pool and the degree of competition. Before investing in this pool hall you would like to run several different scenarios to test the sensitivity of the NPV to these variables. You estimate that there are three different market responses, either early death after 2 years, a 5-year life, or a 7-year life. Salvage values for building and equipment (after taxes) would be $450,000 at the end of 2 years, $380,000 at the end of 5 years, and $250,000 at the end of 7 years. Competitive responses are very intense, normal, and weak. With a very intense competitive response the revenues per week would be only $3,500, with a normal competitive response the revenues would be $5,000 per week, and with a weak competitive response the revenues per week would be $6,500. All other numbers in the problem remain the same. Please complete the following table.

Net present value for nine scenarios:

	TWO-YEAR LIFE	FIVE-YEAR LIFE	SEVEN-YEAR LIFE
Intense competition			
Normal competition			
Weak competition			

CASE PROBLEM

Scandinavian Styles

Peter Nielsen and Jens Andersen moved to the United States as sales representatives for a Danish furniture manufacturer. Nielsen had the southeast territory and Andersen had the midwest territory, but they met several times a year and talked frequently on the phone to coordinate shipments. After several years of selling to retail stores that carried numerous styles, the two decided to start their own store specializing in Scandinavian furniture.

Nielsen and Andersen continued in their jobs for another year while they organized the business. They knew the demographic characteristics of Scandinavian furniture buyers from company studies and their own experience. Upper middle income and under 45 best described the group. Thus, they chose to locate in an upper-middle-income section of Springfield. Knowing that furniture was hardly a convenience good, and knowing they needed adequate display space, Nielsen and Andersen leased a 10,000-square-foot area in a small strip shopping center that had fallen on hard times due to the opening of a large shopping center several blocks away. The rent was low, and the space was adequate for their display needs. They thought they could generate customer traffic through advertising more effectively than by counting on an expensive location.

The major decisions of Nielsen and Andersen proved to be right. Despite a few mistakes and rocky periods, the business thrived. Within 2 years, business was suffering from severe space limitations. To control shipping costs, it was necessary to place large orders. Most of the furniture came "knocked down" and required final assembly. Thus, both storage and work space were needed. They handled the space needs temporarily by renting a small warehouse. This, however, was unsatisfactory as many customers wanted to take their purchases with them. A separate warehouse also created control problems. By the time they had been in business 5 years, the partners decided to build a new store, giving them adequate display, storage, and assembly space at one location. Again, the decision proved to be profitable.

Looking toward further growth, Nielsen and Andersen decided they would have to expand outside of the Springfield area. They decided on Oak Hill, a suburb in Andersen's old sales territory. The primary appeal of this location was that Andersen knew the area and market better than any other. Andersen would run the new store while Nielsen would stay in the old store. They decided to evaluate the expansion opportunity using a 10-year horizon; style changes or balance of payments problems could end their business.

A developer was in the process of building some store space that would be within the right rent range for a furniture store. Space could be had for $10 per square foot per year, and a 10-year lease was required. Nielsen and Andersen could cancel the lease at any time, but there would be a penalty of 20 percent of the remaining lease payments. The location looked good, but the question was how much space to rent.

Nielsen and Andersen agreed that 10,000 square feet was the optimal sales space. Andersen was in favor of taking 15,000 square feet of space so they would have 5,000 square feet for a storage and assembly area on site. Nielsen wanted to take a more conservative approach, using weekly drop-shipments from the Springfield location to deliver inventory to Oak Hill. The distance was over 500 miles, and this would add approximately 15 percent to the cost of the furniture, but risk would be reduced substantially, and the need for 5,000 square feet of space could be eliminated.

Andersen pointed out that if the store was successful, they would quite likely find themselves facing the necessity of buying their way out of the lease within 2 years to get warehouse and assembly space. An 8-year lease on 15,000 square feet would probably cost $12 a square foot by then. Nielsen was more concerned about buying out of a 15,000-square-foot lease after 1 year if the store was unsuccessful. Both partners agreed to study the alternatives some more over the weekend and to make a decision on Monday.

From their past experience and observations, Nielsen and Andersen believed the big risks in opening a store of this type occurred in the first year. They projected sales in the second year to be double those in the first year and predicted little growth beyond that. For purposes of analysis, the partners decided to concentrate on two cases with regard to first-year sales: weak and successful. Weak sales would be $250,000 the first year, and successful sales would be $600,000. The probabilities were estimated to be .7 for success and .3 for weak sales.

The primary up-front costs were promotion and miscellaneous expenses of $30,000 without the warehouse/assembly space and $50,000 with the warehouse/assembly space. These expenses would result in an immediate 28 percent tax savings. Inventory would cost $200,000 with the warehouse/assembly area and $100,000 without. It was estimated that the inventory could be liquidated at cost if or when the store was closed. There would be no accounts receivable because most customers used credit cards, and arrangements would be made with a finance company for those needing credit. Other current assets and current liabilities would also be negligible. Depreciation and noncash expenses would be minimal, so income and cash flow would be the same.

As a general guideline, Nielsen and Andersen estimated a cost of goods sold with on-site assembly at 60 percent of sales. Other variable costs would be 10 percent of sales. They estimated fixed costs other than rent of $4 a year for every square foot of space in either sales space or warehouse/assembly space. The partners faced 28 percent tax rates and used a 10 percent required return in their analysis.

Case Questions

1. Compute a net income break-even point for the smaller and larger facilities.
2. Find the sales level (after the first year) that will result in a net present value of $0. Remember that sales the first year will be half of those after the first year.
3. Prepare a decision tree analysis of the alternatives.
4. Prepare a graphical sensitivity analysis showing the relationship between sales level and net present value for each size alternative.
5. Should they lease space of 10,000 or 15,000 square feet? Why?

SELECTED REFERENCES

Aggarwal, Raj, and Luc A. Soenen. "Project Exit Value as a Measure of Flexibility and Risk Exposure." *Engineering Economist* 34 (Fall 1989): 39–54.

Arnold, Tom, and Richard L. Shockley, Jr. "Value Creation at Anheuser-Busch: A Real Options Example." *Journal of Applied Corporate Finance* 14 (Summer 2002): 52–61.

Bjerksund, Petter, and Steiner Ekern. "Managing Investment Opportunities under Price Uncertainty: From 'Last Chance' to 'Wait and See' Strategies." *Financial Management* 19 (Autumn 1990): 65–83.

Chiu, Chui-Yi, and Chan S. Park. "Fuzzy Cash Flow Analysis Using Present Worth Criterion." *Engineering Economist* 39 (Winter 1994): 113–138.

Eschenbach, Ted G., and Robert J. Gimpel. "Stochastic Sensitivity Analysis." *Engineering Economist* 35 (Summer 1990): 305–322.

Eschbenbach, Ted G., and Lisa S. McKeague. "Exposition on Using Graphs for Sensitivity Analysis." *Engineering Economist* 34 (Summer 1989): 315–333.

Gerchak, Yigal, and Thomas Åstebro. "Calculating the Expectation and Variance of the Present Value for a Random Profit Stream of Uncertain Duration." *The Engineering Economist* 45 #4 (2000): 339–349.

Hertz, David B. "Investment Policies That Pay Off." *Harvard Business Review* (January–February 1968): 96–108.

———."Risk Analysis in Capital Investment." *Harvard Business Review* (January–February 1964): 95–106.

Hurley, W. J. "On the Use of Martingales in Monte-Carlo Approaches to Multiperiod Parameter Uncertainty in Capital Investment Risk Analysis." *The Engineering Economist* 43 #2 (Winter 1998): 169–182.

Hurley, W. J., and L. D. Johnson. "Capital Investment under Uncertainty: Calculating the Present Value of the Depreciation Tax Shield When the Tax Rate Is Stochastic." *Engineering Economist* 41 (Spring 1996): 243–251.

Jones, P. C., W. J. Hopp, and J. L. Zydiak. "Capital Asset Valuation and Depreciation for Stochastically Deteriorating Equipment." *Engineering Economist* 38 (Fall 1992): 19–30.

Joy, O. Maurice, and Jerry O. Bradley, "A Note on Sensitivity Analysis of Rates of Return." *Journal of Finance* 28 (December 1973): 1255–1261.

Keeley, Robert, and Randolph Westerfield. "A Problem in Probability Distribution Techniques for Capital Budgeting." *Journal of Finance* 27 (June 1972): 703–709.

Kensinger, John W. "Adding the Value of Active Management into the Capital Budgeting Equation." *Midland Corporate Finance Journal* 5 (Spring 1987): 31–42.

Kulatilaka, N., and A. J. Marcus. "Project Valuation under Uncertainty: When Does DCF Fail?" *Journal of Applied Finance* 5 (1992): 92–100.

Lambert, R. "Executive Effort and Selection of Risky Projects." *The Rand Journal of Economics* 17 (Spring 1986): 77–86.

Markowitz, Harry M. "Investment for the Long Run: New Evidence for an Old Rule." *Journal of Finance* 31 (December 1976): 1273–1286.

Meimban, Julian J., III, John S. Morris, and Robert L. Govett. "The Evaluation of Wood-Fired Cogeneration Investments Using Monte-Carlo Simulation." *Engineering Economist* 37 (Winter 1992): 115–136.

Miller, Edward. "The Cutoff Benefit-Cost Ratio Should Exceed One." *The Engineering Economist* 46 #4 (2001): 312–319.

Murphy, K. "Corporate Performance and Managerial Remuneration: An Empirical Analysis." *Journal of Accounting and Economics* 7 (April 1985): 11–42.

Noble, Donald J. "Using Simulation as a Tool for Making Financial Decisions in an Uncertain Environment." *Industrial Engineering* 20 (January 1988): 44–48.

Quederni, Bechir N., and William G. Sullivan. "A Semi-Variance Model for Incorporating Risk into Capital Investment Analysis." *Engineering Economist* 36 (Winter 1991): 83–106.

Schnabel, Jacques A. "Uncertainty and the Abandonment Option." *Engineering Economist* 37 (Winter 1992): 172–177.

Schrieves, Ronald E., and John M. Wachowicz, Jr. "Proper Risk Resolution in Replacement Chain Analysis." *Engineering Economist* 34 (Winter 1989): 91–114.

Shashua, Leon, and Yaagov Goldschmidt. "Break-even Analysis under Inflation." *Engineering Economist* 32 (Winter 1987): 79–88.

Sick, Gordon A. "A Certainty-Equivalent Approach to Capital Budgeting." *Financial Management* 15 (Winter 1986): 23–32.

Thompson, Robert A., and Gerald J. Thuesen. "Application of Dynamic Criteria for Capital Budgeting Decisions." *Engineering Economist* 32 (Fall 1987): 59–87.

Trigerorgis, Lenos, and Scott P. Mason. "Valuing Managerial Flexibility." *Midland Corporate Finance Journal* 5 (Spring 1987): 14–21.

Tufekci, Suleyman, and D. B. Young. "Moments of the Present Worths of General Probabilistic Cash Flows under Random Timing." *Engineering Economist* 32 (Summer 1987): 303–336.

Wachowicz, John M., Jr., and Ronald E. Schrieves. "An Argument for 'Generalized' Mean-Coefficient of Variation Analysis." *Financial Management* 9 (Winter 1980): 51–58.

Weiss, Harry H. "An Accuracy Range System of Uncertain Appraisal." *Engineering Economist* 32 (September 1987): 197–216.

Whisler, William D. "Sensitivity Analysis of Rates of Return." *Journal of Finance* 31 (March 1976): 63–69.

Williams, Joseph T. "Trading and Valuing Depreciable Assets." *Journal of Financial Economics* (June 1985): 283–308.

Yoon, Kwangsun Paul. "Capital Investment Analysis Involving Estimate Error." *Engineering Economist* 35 (Fall 1990): 21–30.

CHAPTER 15

Arbitrage Pricing Theory, Option Pricing Theory, and Capital Budgeting

After completing this chapter you should be able to:

- Differentiate between the arbitrage pricing theory (APT) model and the capital asset pricing model (CAPM).
- Apply APT to calculate a risk-adjusted required return.
- List the four economic activity measures identified by Chen, Roll, and Ross as highly correlated with APT factors.
- Apply state-based arbitrage analysis to value a stream of cash flows.
- Define option terms.
- Identify embedded calls and puts when they exist in a capital project.
- Explain the role that options play in the selection of financing.
- Explain the role that stock options play in motivating managers to accept risk.
- Estimate the value of an option using the Black-Scholes pricing model.
- Know the variables that influence the value of an option and the relationship of each to the value of a call option.
- Describe several of the methods used by managers to manage exchange rate risk.

When Boeing Corporation started to work on the 7J7 jet design, the total investment was estimated at $3 billion, and the risks to the company were monumental. Shifting demand could leave the entire investment sitting high and dry. The risks of shifts were substantial because the development effort alone would require several years.

Management at Boeing was certainly interested in moving ahead while limiting its risk exposure. In addition, management did not want to undertake the investment unless its expected returns were sufficient to compensate stockholders for the risks involved. Arbitrage pricing models, discussed in the first part of this chapter, provide a way to evaluate expected benefits in relation to risk. Option pricing models, discussed in the second half of this chapter, are valuable tools for viewing and controlling risk in projects of this type. The $100 million Boeing spent on development over three years can be viewed as the purchase of an option giving the company an opportunity to make the full $3 billion investment if later conditions justified the action. The option approach allowed Boeing to move forward while limiting risk to an acceptable level.

Arbitrage pricing models and option pricing models use similar sets of assumptions to value different types of assets. Both models assume perfect markets in which there are no taxes, no transaction costs, and no restrictions on short sales. The two models apply these assumptions to different types of assets.

ARBITRAGE PRICING THEORY

Arbitrage is the process of increasing returns at no cost by taking advantage of inefficient price relationships. The classic example of an arbitrage opportunity involves a security trading at different prices on east coast and west coast exchanges. An arbitrage profit can be had by simultaneously buying in the low-price market and selling in the high-price market. It is, of course, necessary that there be no restrictions on trading so that it is possible to take advantage of the inefficient price relationship. An arbitrage opportunity also exists if one set of securities costs less than another set of securities that provides the same benefits in each possible state of nature; a short-sale[1] of the high-cost set and a purchase of the low-cost set are used in this case.

Investors taking advantage of arbitrage opportunities will quickly eliminate those opportunities. The high-priced set of assets will be bid down in price while the opposite will happen to the low-priced assets. Thus, countless investors seeking even the smallest arbitrage opportunity keep price and return relationships efficient. Arbitrage pricing theory is simply a theory of relationships among investment returns in a market in which arbitrage opportunities have been eliminated.

[1]A short-sale consists of borrowing a security and then selling that security. The short-seller repurchases the security at a later time and returns it to the owner. The short-seller's gain or loss depends on whether the security can be repurchased for less or more than the sale price. The short-seller must also pay the lender any dividends that would have been received.

TABLE 15-1 Price and Returns for Three Securities

Each security makes one payoff after a coin is flipped, as indicated. Market prices, it turns out, are not in equilibrium.

		PAYOFF	
SECURITY	PRICE	HEADS	TAILS
A	100.00	60.00	160.00
B	1.00	2.50	0
C	1.00	0	2.50

As a simple example of an arbitrage situation, consider three "securities," each of which will pay off after the flip of a single coin. The prices and payoffs are shown in Table 15-1.

An investor who is currently holding security A is searching for an arbitrage opportunity. The investor notes that twenty-four shares of security B will provide $60 if the coin comes up heads, and sixty-four shares of security C will provide $160 if the coin comes up tails. For $88, the investor can buy a combination of B and C that will exactly duplicate the returns from A. No rational investor would hold A in this situation. Investors attempting to sell A in order to purchase B and C will quickly bid the prices back into equilibrium.

One advantage of arbitrage pricing theory is that it does not rest on a set of complex and/or unrealistic assumptions about investor preferences. The general principle is based only on the assumptions that investors prefer more wealth to less wealth and that investors are risk-averse in a general way. However, market efficiency is assumed in that the absence of arbitrage profit opportunities is assumed. Furthermore, specific required return implications are based on assumptions about behavior of security returns, such as linear relationships between returns for individual investments and factors affecting returns for all investments. Finally, restrictions on the use of short-sale proceeds are assumed away, just as taxes and transaction costs are assumed away when constructing the mean-variance capital asset pricing model. Like the taxes and transaction costs, restrictions on the use of short-sale proceeds are part of the practical investment world. Since you sell short by borrowing shares, the lender of those shares typically requires a security deposit that uses up the short-sale proceeds. Only very large institutions may be able to avoid these restrictions on the use of short-sale proceeds. The ultimate tests of these models are not in the reality of assumptions, but in accuracy and usefulness. After exploring arbitrage pricing in some detail, we will turn to the questions of accuracy and usefulness.

The Standard Arbitrage Pricing Theory (APT)

There are many possible arbitrage pricing models, depending on things like assumptions about behavior of security returns. The arbitrage pricing model that has gained wide recognition is the linear model developed by Ross.[2] We follow convention in using the acronym APT to refer to the Ross model. The APT is based on the assumption of perfectly competitive, frictionless markets. The result of this assumption is that securities are priced so that there are no arbitrage profit opportunities. Furthermore, the APT is based on the assumptions that returns for assets are linearly related to certain overall factors and that the number of investments being considered is much larger than the number of factors. In other words, the APT is based on the assumption that the return for a particular asset during a particular period ($R_{s,t}$) is determined as follows:

$$R_{s,t} = E(R_s) + \beta_{s,1}F_{1,t} + \beta_{s,2}F_{2,t} + \ldots + \beta_{s,n}F_{n,t} + e_{s,t} \qquad \textbf{(15-1)}$$

where

$E(R_s)$ = expected return for asset s

$\beta_{s,n}$ = the sensitivity of return for asset s to factor n from a set of factors common to returns for all assets

$F_{n,t}$ = factor n of a set of factors common to returns for all assets, with each factor having an expected value of 0

$e_{s,t}$ = a random-noise term for security s, with an expected value of 0

Ross showed that if relationships described in Equation 15-1 hold, and arbitrage profit opportunities have been eliminated, then the expected return for an asset is:

$$E(R_s) = R_f + [E(R_1) - R_f]\,\beta_{s,1} + [E(R_2) - R_f]\,\beta_{s,2} + \ldots + [E(R_n) - R_f]\,\beta_{s,n} \qquad \textbf{(15-2)}$$

where

R_f = the risk-free interest rate

$E(R_n)$ = the expected return on a portfolio with unitary sensitivity[3] to factor n and zero sensitivity to all other factors

$\beta_{s,n}$ = the sensitivity of asset s to factor n

A formal derivation of Equation 15-2 is a bit tedious,[4] but a simple example can be used to illustrate why Equation 15-2 must hold in equilibrium. Assume that there are two factors, and three securities (a, b, and c) are to be combined in a portfolio. Information about the securities and unitary sensitivity portfolios follows.

[2]Stephen Ross, "The Arbitrage Theory of Capital Asset Pricing," *Journal of Economic Theory* (December 1976): 341–361.

[3]In a linear regression analysis between the factor and return for the portfolio, the beta would be 1.0.

[4]See Ross, "Arbitrage Theory," for a proof.

UNITARY SENSITIVITY PORTFOLIOS	SECURITY SENSITIVITIES		
$E(R_1) = .15$	$\beta_{a,1} = 1$	$\beta_{b,1} = 2$	$\beta_{c,1} = 1$
$E(R_2) = .20$	$\beta_{a,2} = 2$	$\beta_{b,2} = 1$	$\beta_{c,2} = 3$

Using Equation 15-2, and assuming a 10 percent risk-free rate, the equilibrium expected returns for these three securities are:

$$E(R_a) = .10 + 1(.15 - .10) + 2(.20 - .10) = .35$$

$$E(R_b) = .10 + 2(.15 - .10) + 1(.20 - .10) = .30$$

$$E(R_c) = .10 + 1(.15 - .10) + 3(.20 - .10) = .45$$

To demonstrate that the expected return determined with Equation 15-2 must be the expected return in equilibrium, we construct a portfolio with zero elasticity for both factor 1 and factor 2. This involves solving three simultaneous equations:

$$1W_a + 2W_b + 1W_c = 0$$

$$2W_a + 1W_b + 3W_c = 0$$

$$1W_a + 1W_b + 1W_c = 1$$

where W_a is the proportion of funds invested in security a, and so on. The first two equations require that portfolio sensitivity to factors 1 and 2 be zero, while the third equation requires that these three securities comprise the entire portfolio. Solving these simultaneous equations gives the solution $W_a = 5$, $W_b = -1$, and $W_c = -3$. Negative proportions for securities b and c imply short-sales of those assets.

The portfolio constructed with these proportions is risk free, because risk is captured through sensitivity to factors. Since the portfolio is risk free, it must provide the risk-free return. We see that this condition is satisfied:

$$E(R_p) = 5(.35) - 1(.30) - 3(.45) = \underline{\underline{.10}}$$

An increase or decrease in the expected return of any security that takes it away from the expected return specified in Equation 15-1 allows us to create a risk-free portfolio paying a return other than the risk-free rate. Suppose, for example, the expected return for security a is 40 percent. The expected return for the risk-free portfolio is therefore:

$$E(R_p) = 5(.40) - 1(.30) - 3(.45) = \underline{\underline{.35}}$$

A risk-free portfolio paying more or less than the risk-free return cannot exist in equilibrium,[5] so in equilibrium no security can have an expected return that violates Equation 15-2.

[5]Had the expected return for security a been less than the equilibrium required return, the portfolio would be risk free and would have a return below the risk-free rate. Short-selling of this portfolio would be a way to borrow below the risk-free rate.

If you are left with a nagging doubt about the possibility of some other, unimagined, equilibrium involving offsetting violations of Equation 15-2 by more than one security, see Ross's previously cited article for a formal derivation of Equation 15-2 as the only possible equilibrium position.

Equation 15-2 depends on the existence of unitary sensitivity portfolios, and people considering the APT for the first time are sometimes concerned about the existence of such portfolios in the real world. The creation of such portfolios is simply a simultaneous equations problem. For the previous example, the three securities can be combined to create unitary sensitivity portfolios for each factor. The unitary sensitivity portfolio for factor 1 is found by simultaneously solving the following set of equations:

$$1W_a + 2W_b + 1W_c = 1$$

$$2W_a + 1W_b + 3W_c = 0$$

$$1W_a + 1W_b + 1W_c = 1$$

Solving these simultaneous equations gives the portfolio with unitary sensitivity to factor 1, and no sensitivity to factor 2: $W_a = 3$, $W_b = 0$, and $W_c = -2$. A portfolio with unitary sensitivity to factor 2 can be created with equal ease. To create unitary sensitivity portfolios in practice, the only requirement is that there be one more nonredundant security than there are factors for which unitary sensitivity portfolios are needed. A security is nonredundant if its characteristics—betas with regard to all factors—cannot be duplicated by some combination of the other securities being considered.[6]

Like the CAPM, the APT provides a statement of the relationship between equilibrium expected return and sensitivity to certain factors affecting return. The APT is, therefore, an alternative to the CAPM for determining a risk-adjusted required return for capital investment analysis. Its relevance is the same as that of the CAPM in that they both provide information about the same variable: risk-adjusted required return. The choice between the two depends on accuracy and ease of use.

Note that if there is only one factor, and the portfolio with unitary sensitivity to that factor is the market portfolio, Equation 15-2 reduces to the CAPM formula for the relationship between beta for an investment and required return for that investment. The general form of the APT, though, makes no assumption about the number of factors, economic nature of the factors, or the portfolios with unitary sensitivity to those factors. In fact, the factors are generally constructed using the statistical tool of factor analysis[7] applied to returns for past

---

[6]A set of nonredundant assets can be constructed step-wise. Following the selection of any asset as the starting position, assets are added one at a time, with each potential new asset checked for redundancy through an attempt to replicate that asset's characteristics with some combination of assets already selected. Security c in the example would be redundant to a and b if there was a solution to the simultaneous equation problem:

$$1W_a + 2W_b = 1$$

$$2W_a + 1W_b = 3$$

$$W_a + W_b = 1$$

[7]See, for example, T. W. Anderson, *An Introduction to Multivariate Statistical Analysis,* 2nd ed. (New York: John Wiley and Sons, 1984).

periods. The objective of factor analysis is to explain variances in individual observations (security returns in our case) by statistically searching out a limited number of factors that explain a high percentage of variance. These factors may be thought of as indexes, in the same way we think of stock price indexes or consumer price indexes, because a single factor may capture a whole set of influences. A factor does not necessarily correlate with any single real economic variable, such as stock market returns or interest rates, although it is generally assumed that the factors represent real economic variables.[8]

To determine a risk-adjusted required return, the APT can be applied using securities that have been publicly traded over a historical period of sufficient length. The process is somewhat analogous to that using the CAPM with historical data, but more time consuming. First, a sample set of securities is selected. Then, returns are collected for each security in the sample for each of a number of historical holding periods. Factor analysis of the data is then performed using a commercially available computer program. The result is a set of factors that are common to returns for all securities.

Once the factor analysis is completed, the same sample set of securities, or a different sample set, is used to construct a unitary sensitivity portfolio for each factor. The first step in constructing these portfolios is to compute $\beta_{s,n}$s relating each security to each factor. The construction of these unitary sensitivity portfolios is a simultaneous equation problem, as previously illustrated, that can be solved using matrix algebra.

Once the unitary sensitivity portfolios are constructed, the difference between historical return for each portfolio and the historical risk-free return is used as the risk premium for that factor: $[E(R_n) - R_f]$. Alternately, expected return for each portfolio could be estimated from published forecasts of returns for the assets in the portfolio. This latter approach has been used for the market portfolio in mean-variance CAPM tests.

The $\beta_{s,n}$s for an investment that is being considered can be constructed using historical data or can be estimated by analysts who attempt to predict how the particular asset will respond to factors affecting each unitary sensitivity portfolio. If one is attempting to develop a risk-adjusted required return for a company, the historical $\beta_{s,n}$s may be used. If one is attempting to develop a risk-adjusted required return for a division, nonpublic company, or major capital investment, the pure play approach discussed in Chapter 14 can be used. One or more companies that are believed to have similar characteristics can be identified and their $\beta_{s,n}$s can be used as the estimated $\beta_{s,n}$s. State-based analysis can also be used. Return for each unitary sensitivity portfolio and return for the asset can be estimated in each state of nature, then the $\beta_{s,n}$s can be computed as was explained for a single beta in Chapter 14. Once the $\beta_{s,n}$s for the asset of interest are determined, the required return is then computed using Equation 15-2.

[8]The assumption that factors represent real economic variables is made strongly by Richard Roll and Stephen A. Ross in "A Critical Reexamination of the Empirical Evidence on the Arbitrage Pricing Theory: A Reply," *Journal of Finance* 39 (June 1984): 347–350.

The APT has potential accuracy advantages over the CAPM in that it is based on less restrictive assumptions about investor preferences. The APT also has the advantage of being a directly testable theory.

Tests of the APT

One of the key challenges with regard to the APT is the identification of factors and the economic surrogates for those factors that are necessary for many practical applications. Empirical research in this area consists of first carrying out factor analysis and then searching for economic surrogates for the factors. In a widely cited study, Chen, Roll, and Ross found four factors and found those factors to be highly correlated with the following economic variables:

1. Industrial production or the return on the market portfolio
2. Changes in the risk premium indicated by the difference between Aaa and Baa corporate bonds
3. The slope of the yield curve, represented by differences between yields to maturity on long-term and short-term government bonds
4. Unanticipated inflation[9]

Numerous other studies have been carried out with the objective of testing the theory and identifying economic counterparts of factors.[10] Fama and French, for example, found that firm size and book-to-market equity were primary explanatory variables, and possibly therefore surrogates for risk or sensitivity to one or more factors.[11] Unfortunately, the studies carried out to date have not resulted in a consensus on either the number of priced factors or their economic counterparts.

While there have been many tests of APT, they suffer from some of the same problems discussed with regard to the CAPM tests. Specifically, both sets of tests rely on historical returns and relationships as surrogates for expected returns and expected relationships. Substituting expectations for historical returns in tests would be more difficult for the APT than for the CAPM because sensitivities for multiple unitary sensitivity portfolios would be required.

The validity of most tests of the APT has been called into question for other reasons as well. Conway and Reinganum observed that empirical tests of the APT have used the same sample of securities to create factors and measure the relationship between return and factor sensitivity. Conway and Reinganum performed a cross-validation test in which the model was tested on a sample different

---

[9]Nai-Fu Chen, Richard W. Roll, and Stephen A. Ross, "Economic Forces and the Stock Market: Testing the APT and Alternative Asset Pricing Theories," UCLA Working Paper #20-83, December 1983.

[10]See, for example, Nai-Fu Chen, "Some Empirical Tests of the Theory of Arbitrage Pricing," *Journal of Finance* 38 (December 1983): 1393–1414; Richard Roll and Stephen Ross, "An Empirical Investigation of the Arbitrage Pricing Theory," *Journal of Finance* 35 (December 1980): 1073–1103; P. Dhrymes, Irwin Friend, and B. Gultekin, "A Critical Reexamination of the Empirical Evidence on the Arbitrage Pricing Theory," *Journal of Finance* 39 (June 1984): 323–346; and a reply to Dhrymes et al. by Roll and Ross in the same volume.

[11]Eugene F. Fama and Kenneth R. French, "The Cross-Section of Expected Stock Returns," *Journal of Finance* 47 (June 1992): 427–465.

from that used to identify factors.[12] They found only one factor that affected required return, which raises questions about earlier studies finding required returns to be affected by sensitivity to numerous factors. Using simulation, Kan and Zhang demonstrated that useless factors are often identified as useful.[13] Fama argued that if we do not know the set of priced factors in advance, it may be impossible to find them.[14]

The applicability of the APT is limited by difficulties in testing, identifying factors, and identifying economic surrogates for those factors. This is particularly true for capital budgeting. It will be difficult to estimate the sensitivity of a capital investment to a factor or a unitary sensitivity portfolio if the factors have not been clearly identified and given economic interpretations. A model in which required return is determined by sensitivity to undefined factors may be tough to sell to practicing managers.

The problems with the APT may be relieved through further research or the development of new methodology. If an understanding of the number of factors and their economic counterparts is developed, it will become easier to compute historical $\beta_{s,n}$s and to estimate $\beta_{s,n}$s for assets that do not have a history of holding period returns from public trading. A practitioner in the future may turn to *Value Line Investment Survey* and find listed below the market beta a series of betas relating securities to key economic variables. Empirical research may provide indications of the required returns as risk premiums for sensitivity to other economic variables. If information of this type becomes available through empirical research, the APT may provide superior estimates of value and required return while being nearly as easy to use as is the CAPM at present. In the meantime, state-based arbitrage analysis does have potential immediate, practical application.

State-Based Arbitrage Analysis of Capital Investments

Ross suggested a direct valuation of capital investments by finding a portfolio that would provide identical cash flows to the proposed capital investment in all conditions. The net present value is the cost of the asset subtracted from the cost of the portfolio of publicly traded securities that will replicate its cash flows.[15] To apply Ross's suggestion, Gehr demonstrated the use of a set of discrete states of nature that approximate the continual distribution of returns.[16] When managers at Sohio were considering the purchase of North Slope oil leases, for example, they could have used several economic growth scenarios along with two OPEC

---

[12]Delores A. Conway, and Marc R. Reinganum. "Capital Market Factor Structure: Identification through Cross Validation." University of Chicago Graduate School of Business Working Paper #183, July 1986.

[13]Raymond Kan and Chu Zhang, "Two-Pass Tests of Asset Pricing Models with Useless Factors," *Journal of Finance* 54 (February 1999): 203–235.

[14]Eugene F. Fama, "Determining the Number of Priced State Variables in the ICAPM," *Journal of Financial and Quantitative Analysis* 33 (June 1998): 217–231.

[15]Stephen A. Ross, "A Simple Approach to the Valuation of Risky Streams," *Journal of Business* (July 1979): 254–286.

[16]Adam K. Gehr, Jr., "Risk-Adjusted Capital Budgeting Using Arbitrage," *Financial Management* 10 (Winter 1981): 14–19.

cartel scenarios—success or collapse of the price control mechanism—to create a set of six discrete states for analysis. The discrete state approach is an extension of the approach used at the beginning of this chapter to value payoffs from a coin toss. The discrete state method avoids assumptions of linear relationships and may be easier to apply in some cases.

To apply the discrete state approach to a capital investment, m states of nature and m nonredundant alternate investments are identified. The investments can, for example, be publicly traded securities. Cash flow per dollar invested for each alternative investment in each state of nature is estimated. The portfolio that will duplicate the cash flow from the proposed capital investment in each state of nature is found by solving for the a_m in the simultaneous equation problem:

$$\begin{aligned} a_1r_{1,1} + a_2r_{1,2} + \ldots + a_mr_{1,m} &= CF_1 \\ a_1r_{2,1} + a_2r_{2,2} + \ldots + a_mr_{2,m} &= CF_2 \\ \vdots \qquad\qquad & \quad \vdots \\ a_1r_{m,1} + a_2r_{m,2} + \ldots + a_mr_{m,m} &= CF_m \end{aligned} \tag{15-3}$$

where $r_{i,m}$ is the estimated cash flow per dollar invested in asset m if state of nature i occurs, a_m is the amount invested in asset m, and CF_i is the expected cash flow from the candidate capital investment if state i occurs; each column represents an investment and each row represents a state of nature. Each equation requires that the portfolio provide the same cash flow as the capital investment in one state of nature. The sum of the a_js is the amount that must be invested in the alternate assets to duplicate the returns from the proposed capital investment. The cost of the proposed capital investment is subtracted from the cost of this portfolio to find the net present value of the capital investment.

Example: Assume Findlay Industries uses four states of nature in estimating annual cash flows from investments:

STATE	DESCRIPTION
1	Expanding economy and rising inflation
2	Expanding economy and decreasing inflation
3	Recession and decreasing inflation
4	Recession and increasing inflation

Those states include the primary factors that affect Findlay's success. Managers at Findlay perform risk analysis by determining each year's expected cash flow from a proposed capital investment in each state, rather than relying on a single estimate of annual cash flows. To apply arbitrage valuation, managers selected

TABLE 15-2 Capital Investment Information for Findlay Industries

This table contains expected annual cash flows from a capital investment in each state as well as year-end cash flow per dollar invested in each state for four common stock portfolios.

	CASH FLOW FROM CAPITAL INV.			YEAR-END IND. PORTFOLIO CASH FLOWS*			
STATE	YEAR 1	YEAR 2	YEAR 3	PORT. 1	PORT. 2	PORT. 3	PORT. 4
1	15,000	18,000	20,000	1.50	1.09	1.25	0.60
2	24,000	27,000	30,000	0.40	1.65	1.65	1.65
3	16,000	17,000	20,000	1.26	1.15	0.55	0.45
4	8,000	9,000	10,000	1.65	0.35	0.35	0.85

*Per $1 invested at the beginning of the year.

four industry common stock indexes to represent portfolios of common stock, and computed year-end cash flow in each state of nature per dollar invested in each portfolio at the beginning of the year (effectively assuming that the factors that affect returns on these broad-based industry portfolios are stable from year to year). Annual cash flows from a capital investment in each state, as well as year-end cash flow per dollar invested in each state, appear in Table 15-2.

Recall that the objective in arbitrage valuation is to find the amount that must be invested elsewhere to duplicate the cash flows from this capital investment. Let V_t be the total amount that must be invested in the alternate portfolios at the beginning of year t to duplicate cash flows from the proposed capital investment in each state at the end of year t. This amount can be found by solving Equations 15-3 once for each year. Taking year 3, for example, we would solve the following set of simultaneous equations:

$$1.50a_1 + 1.09a_2 + 1.25a_3 + 0.60a_4 = 20{,}000$$

$$0.40a_1 + 1.65a_2 + 1.65a_3 + 1.65a_4 = 30{,}000$$

$$1.26a_1 + 1.15a_2 + 0.55a_3 + 0.45a_4 = 20{,}000$$

$$1.65a_1 + 0.35a_2 + 0.35a_3 + 0.85a_4 = 10{,}000$$

The solution to this set of equations is a_1 = \$1,344, a_2 = \$14,653, a_3 = \$138, and a_4 = \$3,065. Therefore:

$$V_3 = \$1{,}344 + \$14{,}653 + \$138 + \$3{,}065 = \underline{\underline{\$19{,}200}}$$

The alternate portfolio will cost $19,200 at the beginning of year 3.

The amount that must be invested today in order to buy the alternate portfolio at the beginning of year t is then $V_t/(1 + R_f)^{t-1}$, where R_f is the risk-free interest rate. If the risk-free rate is 9 percent, the amount that must be invested elsewhere today in order to duplicate the capital investment's cash flows at the end of year 3 is:

$$19{,}200/1.09^2 = \underline{\underline{\$16{,}160}}$$

This process can then be repeated for the other 2 years to generate the amount that must be invested today to duplicate all future cash flows from the proposed investment. The net present value is the initial outlay for the proposed capital investment, subtracted from the amount that must be invested elsewhere to duplicate that investment's cash flows.

A problem with this approach is tedium. For a 30-year investment, it is necessary to solve the set of simultaneous equations 30 times, and the process must be repeated for each proposed capital investment. Fortunately, the process can be speeded up by finding the amount that must be invested at the start of a year to generate cash flow of $1 at the end of the year if state i occurs, and nothing if any other state occurs. Repeating this for each state gives us a set of factors to multiply directly against state-dependent cash flows to avoid repeated solutions of simultaneous equations. For example, the amount that must be invested at the start of a year to receive $1 at the end of the year if state 1 occurs, and nothing otherwise, is found by modifying the right-hand side of Equations 15-3 as follows:

$$1.50a_1 + 1.09a_2 + 1.25a_3 + 0.60a_4 = 1$$

$$0.40a_1 + 1.65a_2 + 1.65a_3 + 1.65a_4 = 0$$

$$1.26a_1 + 1.15a_2 + 0.55a_3 + 0.45a_4 = 0$$

$$1.65_1 + 0.35a_2 + 0.35a_3 + 0.85a_4 = 0$$

The solution to this set of equations is a_1 = $0.276580, a_2 = –$0.663653, a_3 = $1.462383, and a_4 = –$0.865780. Letting A_i be the amount that must be invested at the beginning of a year to generate $1 at the end of the year if state i occurs, and nothing otherwise:

$$A_1 = \$0.276580 - \$0.663653 + \$1.462383 - \$0.865780 = \$0.209530$$

This process is repeated for each of the other states by changing the row in which 1 appears on the right-hand side of Equations 15-3, to give us the set of factors:

$$A_1 = \$0.209530$$

$$A_2 = \$0.368550$$

$$A_3 = \$0.055874$$

$$A_4 = \$0.283564$$

These factors can now be multiplied directly against the capital investment's cash flows at the end of year t to provide the amount that must be invested elsewhere to duplicate those cash flows. The net present value becomes:

$$NPV = \sum_{t=1}^{n} (A_1CF_{t,1} + A_2CF_{t,2} + \ldots + A_mCF_{t,m})/(1 + R_f)^{t-1} - I_o \qquad \textbf{(15-4)}$$

where m is the number of states being used, $CF_{t,m}$ is cash flow from the capital investment in year t if state m occurs, and I_o is the initial outlay required. If Findlay is considering several hundred capital investments, the same A_ms can be used for all of the capital investments. It is only necessary to estimate cash flow for each investment each year in each state.

Findlay's capital investment costs $40,000, so the net present value is:

$$\begin{aligned} NPV = {} & (15{,}000 \times .209530 + 24{,}000 \times .368550 + 16{,}000 \times .055874 + 8{,}000 \times \\ & .283564) + (18{,}000 \times .209530 + 27{,}000 \times .386550 + 17{,}000 \times \\ & .055874 + 9{,}000 \times .283564)/1.09^1 + (20{,}000 \times .209530 + 30{,}000 \times \\ & .386550 + 20{,}000 \times .055874 + 10{,}000 \times .283564)/1.09^2 \\ & - 40{,}000 \\ = {} & \$7{,}113 \end{aligned}$$

The state-based arbitrage approach has several appealing features. Many risk analysis methods currently in use rely on identifying a set of scenarios and estimating return in each scenario. This approach is, therefore, an extension of familiar techniques. In addition, many managers are uncomfortable with the probability estimates necessary to go beyond scenario analysis and compute the expected values or standard deviations needed for some risk analysis methods. This approach avoids the problem of estimating probabilities. Some estimates of probabilities by the investing public are implied in the prices of the various securities, but these probabilities need not be discovered to perform an arbitrage valuation of a capital investment using the state approach. This approach is also free of the assumptions about linear relations to factors that are used in the APT. As with other arbitrage analysis forms, the state-based approach is free from assumptions about utility functions or degrees of risk aversion.

Arbitrage Pricing and Certainty Equivalents

The choice between certainty equivalents and risk-adjusted discount rates as practical capital budgeting tools has been debated for years. With risk-adjusted discount rates, expected cash flows are discounted to the present using a discount rate appropriate for the degree of risk involved. The use of risk-adjusted discount rates is usually based on the assumption of constant systematic risk, so that the same discount rate can be used for each future period, and this assumption is not always justified. Use of certainty equivalents avoids this problem. The year t **certainty equivalent** is the certain amount at the end of year t which, if discounted at the risk-free rate, is as desirable as the probability distribution of cash flows for year t. No assumptions about stability of risk for the proposed investment are needed to justify the certainty equivalents. Unfortunately, though, application of the certainty-equivalent approach has been hampered by the lack of a method for measuring the certainty equivalent.

Arbitrage pricing principles provide a way to measure certainty equivalents. In the Findlay Industries example, V_t was the amount that must be invested in the alternate portfolios at the *beginning* of year t to duplicate the year t cash flows from the proposed investment. The amount that must be invested today to duplicate those cash flows is therefore $V_t/(1 + R_f)^{t-1}$. The certainty equivalent for year t (CE_t) is the certain amount at the *end* of year t, which, when discounted to the present at the risk-free rate, is as attractive as the probability distribution of cash flows for the proposed investment at the end of year t. Therefore:

$$CE_t = V_t(1 + R_f)$$

and

$$NPV = \sum_{t=1}^{n} CE_t/(1 + R_f)^t - I_o$$

Arbitrage pricing models offer distinct advantages over the mean-variance capital asset pricing model in that they do not depend on restrictive assumptions and can easily handle multi-period cash flows involved in capital investment analysis. The primary disadvantages of the arbitrage pricing model, relative to the mean-variance capital asset pricing model, are related to questions that may be answered with additional empirical research. As the nature of the underlying factors becomes better understood, arbitrage pricing models may replace the mean-variance capital asset pricing model for much decision making.

OPTION PRICING MODELS (OPMS)

An **option** is a contract giving the holder the right to buy or sell an asset for a predetermined price. Interest in options was heightened in 1973 when the Chicago Board of Trade began organized trading in options on specified common stocks. Options have special characteristics that result in the need for special valuation tools. A widely recognized option pricing model was developed in that year by Black and Scholes.[17] It was soon recognized that common stock and debt share important characteristics with options.

OPMs are complementary to the mean-variance capital asset pricing model and arbitrage pricing models. The other two models focus on sensitivity to factors affecting returns on investments in general. OPMs focus on the role of total risk in valuing various claims against the stream of cash flows. Changes in nonsystematic risk often change the value of claims—debt and equity—even if they do not affect the overall value of the company. If capital budgeting is carried out with the objective of maximizing shareholder wealth, these changes in relative

[17]Fisher Black and Myron Scholes, "The Pricing of Options and Corporate Liabilities," *Journal of Political Economy* 81 (May–June 1973): 637–654.

values are important. Thus, OPMs provide useful insights for capital budgeting, financing of capital investments, and management compensation.

This section begins with some basic definitions. Then, a two-state OPM is used to develop the basic principles of option valuation. Following this, the more general Black-Scholes OPM is explained. Empirical evidence on the model is surveyed and application of the model to selection and financing of capital investments is covered.

Some Basic Terminology

To move along with minimum difficulty, it is helpful to provide a brief glossary of terminology at the outset.

Call option: an option to buy an asset.
Put option: an option to sell an asset.
Exercise of an option: the buying or selling of the asset as provided for in the option contract.
Exercise price (striking price): the price at which the asset can be bought or sold, as stated in the option contract.
Expiration date: the last day on which the option may be exercised. Most option contracts are not open-ended, and have a specific expiration date.
European option: an option that can be exercised only on the expiration date.
American option: an option that can be exercised at any time prior to its expiration date.
Writer: the person who sells an option contract to another, thereby granting the buyer an option to buy or sell the asset at the exercise price under the terms specified in the contract.

Options Illustrated

An options theoretician finds options everywhere. Many financial contracts are not called options, but have the major characteristics of options. Direct options and financial contracts that behave as options are discussed in the following paragraphs.

Publicly Traded Options. The options most widely recognized in the public press are options on common stocks. While options on common stocks have existed in limited supply for many years, public trading of these options began on the Chicago Board of Trade in 1973 and spread rapidly to other exchanges. In addition to providing a market for buying and selling, the Chicago Board of Trade standardized options in terms of exercise price and maturity. This greatly enhanced trading.

On October 5, IBM stock was trading for $43.75 a share. The prices of twelve different IBM options on that same day follow:

	STRIKE PRICE	CALL OPTION PRICES			PUT OPTION PRICES		
MATURITY:		OCT.	NOV.	JAN.	OCT.	NOV.	JAN.
	40	3 3/4	4 1/8	5	1/16	5/8	1 1/4
	45	5/16	1 1/4	2 1/4	1 5/8	2 7/16	3 1/2

We will focus on the January option with a $45 striking price. If IBM stock is selling for more than $45 on the January expiration date, the call option will be valuable because the holder can buy IBM stock below the prevailing market price; otherwise the option will be worthless. The price of the option today reflects investors' assessments of the likelihood of its having value on the expiration date. The January put option will be valuable on the expiration date if the price of IBM stock is less than $45; the put option allows the holder to sell stock above the prevailing market price in that case. Writers and buyers of options may be investors with different expectations, different risk-return utility functions, or different risks against which they want to hedge.

If you own IBM stock on October 5, and want to reduce risk, you can write a $45 January call option and receive $2.25. If the price of the stock falls or only increases moderately, you improve your income for the 3-month period by $2.25. The tradeoff is that if the stock is over $45, the option buyer will exercise the option and buy the stock from you for $45, thereby limiting your profits. The option buyer may be a speculator who hopes for a high return. If the price of IBM stock rises to $60 by expiration date, for example, the option buyer exercises the option by buying the stock for $45, and then immediately resells the stock for $60. The speculator's profit is the gain on the stock sale, minus the cost of the option: $15 – $2.25 = $12.75. The return on the original option investment is $12.75 ÷ $2.25 = 567 percent.

In addition to traded options, negotiated options are frequently used as well. A developer will often purchase an option on land, then work out detailed plans and secure financing. This arrangement limits the developer's risk exposure and capital requirements during the planning phase while also avoiding the risk that the land will not be available on acceptable terms after the planning is completed. The landowner is, of course, allowed to keep the amount paid for the option if the purchase is not completed. Furthermore, the landowner can probably get a higher price through the option arrangement than a developer would be willing to pay for a direct purchase.

Many options are not even formal contracts. Anheuser-Busch often expands into international markets with a modest investment such as a minority interest in an existing brewer. This gives the company experience in the new market. The experience often creates the opportunity to make much larger investments later.[18]

[18]Tom Arnold and Richard L. Shockley, Jr., "Value Creation at Anheuser-Busch: A Real Options Example," *Journal of Applied Corporate Finance* 14 (Summer 2002): 52–61.

Other Assets as Options

Assets such as corporate debt also have the characteristics of options. Capital structure and capital investment decisions can often be improved by taking advantage of the option characteristics of the assets. Many other contracts can be usefully analyzed as options.

Common stock. This is considered to be an option on the firm itself. If the firm is worth more than the amount owed when debt matures, the stockholders exercise their option to repay the debt and keep the residual value for themselves. If the firm is worth less than the amount of debt at maturity, the stockholders turn the firm over to the creditors. Companies like Wickes, LTV, and Continental Airlines have taken this latter course. These actions do not necessarily result in liquidation because the creditors may decide the firm is worth more as a going concern than it is worth in liquidation. Because common stock is effectively an option, options written on common stock are therefore options on options.

Debt. If common stockholders effectively hold an option, then creditors effectively purchased the firm and wrote an option in the form of common stock. Whirlpool's creditors, for example, put up $850 million of their own money and turned over control of the company to the stockholders who paid $1,350 million for their option to buy the company back from the creditors for $850 million. In an equilibrium market in which arbitrage profits are not possible, the value of the debt is the value of the firm, minus the value of the option in the form of common stock. Later in this chapter, we will use an option pricing model to determine the required interest rate on risky debt.

Contingent claims. Many investments and contracts call for payment if certain conditions occur. Even if these contracts are not strictly options, they can be valued as substitutes for options with the same payment characteristics. CEOs of publicly traded companies frequently receive stock options so that their wealth depends on the price of the stock exceeding the strike price of the option. Executives of companies that are not publicly traded frequently have compensation agreements that mimic stock options. They might, for example, receive a percent of income in excess of some target level. A manager's position in such a case may be perceived as paying a fixed amount plus a percent of profits if profit exceeds a satisfactory level, and zero otherwise—managers can be fired for unsatisfactory performance. The impact of a change in unsystematic risk on the value of the manager's contract may be entirely different from the impact on the value of the common stock. Later in this chapter, the use of an option pricing model to design a management compensation contract will be illustrated.

Capital investments. Many capital investments have option characteristics. Research programs and test-marketing of new products are classic examples of investments which create the opportunity to make additional, larger investments. Boeing's development efforts for the 7J7 airplane are an example. Rather than committing to a $3 billion production plan, the company committed to a $100 million, 3-year development program. This $100 million capital investment gave Boeing the option to acquire a $3 billion investment. As it turned out, management decided not to exercise the option, and did not go into production.

Graphical View of Options

Figure 15-1 graphically illustrates the nature of a call option. The area under the curve represents the entire probability distribution of values of the asset as of the option expiration date. The exercise price is the maximum that can be received by the person who owns the asset and wrote an option. The net amount received by the option buyer on the expiration date is the amount by which the value of the asset on that date exceeds the exercise price. Thus, a call option is simply the sale of part of the probability distribution of returns. Specifically, the shaded area to the right of the exercise price is the portion of the distribution that has been sold. Let P in Figure 15-1 be the exercise price of a put option. The holder of the IBM stock who writes a put option will be assured of receiving at least price P for the stock. Buying a put option, then, consists of paying someone to accept the risk of value being in some lower portion of the distribution.

A Two-State Option Pricing Model

A two-state option model is helpful in understanding the general principles of option valuation, and the implications of the OPM for capital budgeting and

FIGURE 15.1 Graphical Representation of an Option Contract
The area under the curve is the entire probability distribution of the asset's value on the option's expiration date. The shaded area is the portion of probability distribution of value that has been sold via the call option contract.

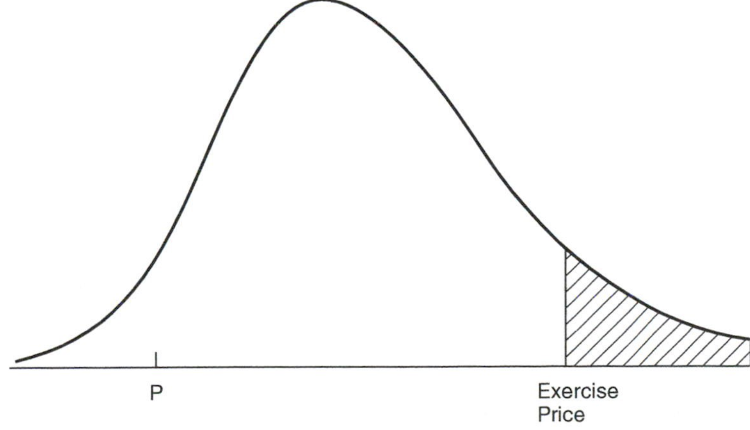

FIGURE 15.2 Stock Prices in a Simple Two-State Model
S_o is the present price of the stock. S_u and S_d are the two possible prices at the end of the single period.

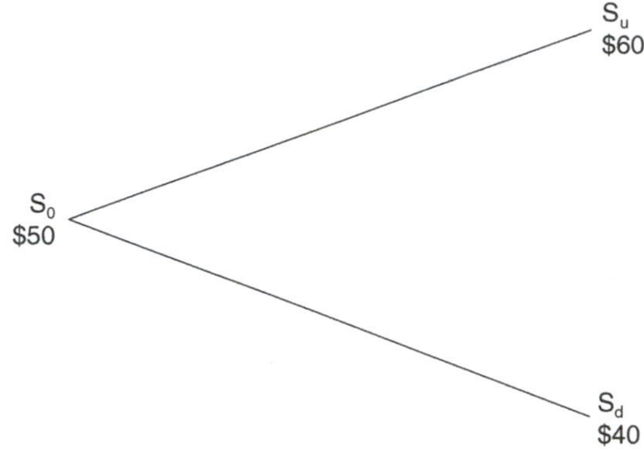

financing decisions.[19] This model assumes that there is only one period (however that period is defined) and there are only two possible values of the underlying asset at the end of that period—the option's expiration date. In addition, this model incorporates the assumptions inherent in some more general option pricing models:

1. The financial markets are frictionless, with no transaction costs and with information freely available to all.
2. There are no restrictions on short sales.
3. There are no dividends or other cash disbursements to the owners of the asset prior to the option's expiration date.
4. There are no opportunities for arbitrage profits; specifically, there are no opportunities to make risk-free investments earning above the risk-free rate.

To develop the price of a call option in a two-state world, we use a share of stock. The present price of the stock (S_o) is $50 a share. At the end of one period, the stock will have one of two values. The value if the stock goes up (S_u) is $60 and the value if the stock goes down (S_d) is $40. This situation is presented graphically in Figure 15-2.

Suppose a holder of one share of this stock decides to write (sell) call options against this stock. The stockholder writes q options and receives an amount of C per option. The options have an exercise price (E) of $45. If stock price S_d occurs, the option is worthless and the stockholder keeps stock worth $40. If stock price S_u occurs, the stockholder can sell the stock for $45 or buy back the

---

[19]The two-state model was developed by John C. Cox, Stephen A. Ross, and Mark Rubinstein, "Option Pricing: A Simplified Approach," *Journal of Financial Economics* 7 (September 1979): 229–263; and by Richard J. Rendleman, Jr., and Brit J. Bartter, "Two-State Option Pricing," *Journal of Finance* 34 (December 1979): 1093–1110.

FIGURE 15.3 Returns to an Option Writer in a Simple Two-State Model

The amount invested, after deducting the amount received for writing options, is shown on the left. The amount on the upper right is the amount received if the options are repurchased and the stock is sold for S_u. The amount on the lower right is the amount received for the stock with the options expiring unexercised.

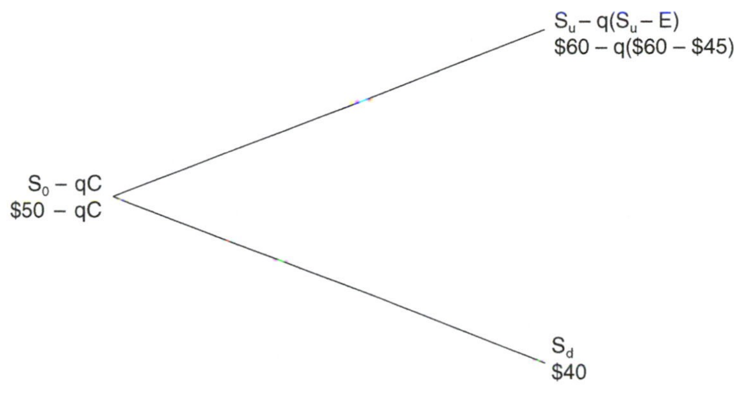

options. The options will then be worth (S_u – E) or $15 each. The stockholder's wealth will be the same whether she buys back the options or honors at least some of them by selling stock for $45. The initial investment and ending value amounts for the stockholder are summarized in Figure 15-3.

We want to find C, the market-clearing price of an option. To do this, we find the number of options the stockholder must write to create a risk-free investment. Specifically, we decide how many options the stockholder must write to receive the same amount whether S_u or S_d occurs. To do this, we first set wealth with S_u and S_d equal to each other:

$$S_u - q(S_u - E) = S_d$$

Then, we rearrange terms to solve for q:

$$q = (S_u - S_d)/(S_u - E) \qquad \textbf{(15-5)}$$

For the example, q = (60 – 40)/(60 – 45) = 1⅓; writing 1⅓ options will provide the same value in either state.

If the investment is to be risk free, and arbitrage profits are not possible, the risk free rate must be earned in either state. A risk-free return if S_d occurs means S_d must be greater than the initial net investment by the risk-free rate:

$$(S_o - qC)(1 + R_f) = S_d$$

Rearranging terms gives:

$$C = \frac{S_o - S_d/(1 + R_f)}{q}$$

Substituting in for the value of q, as determined in Equation 15-5, the equilibrium value of the call option is:[20]

$$C = [S_o - S_d/(1 + R_f)](S_u - E)/(S_u - S_d) \quad \textbf{(15-6)}$$

Applying this formula to the example, the value of a call option is:

$$C = [50 - 40/1.1](60 - 45)/(60 - 40) = \$10.227$$

The beginning and ending wealth positions are then:

$$\text{Beginning net investment} = 50 - (4/3)10.227 = \$36.36$$

$$\text{Value in the case of } S_u = 60 - (4/3)(60 - 45) = \$40$$

$$\text{Value in the case of } S_d = \$40$$

Thus, the stockholder earns a risk-free return of 10 percent in either case.

If the investment were risk free and did not earn a 10 percent return, the markets would not be in equilibrium and arbitrage opportunities would exist. An investor could earn infinite profits while accepting no risk by simply exploiting the arbitrage opportunity.[21]

Applying the same logic, the value of a put option is:[22]

$$P = [S_u/(1 + R_f) - S_o](E - S_d)/(S_u - S_d) \quad \textbf{(15-7)}$$

The simple two-state model can be used to identify the main factors that determine the value of an option. These factors can all be seen in Equations 15-6 and 15-7. The variables are the:

- starting price of the stock
- two possible ending prices of the stock
- risk-free rate
- exercise price of the option

For a more general model, the two ending stock prices are replaced with the variance of the stock's probability distribution of returns and time until expiration of the option.

---

[20]We can confirm that if the call option is priced as indicated, the risk-free rate is also earned if S_u occurs. But confirmation is unnecessary because the value of the call was derived under the requirement that the amount received be the same whether S_u or S_d occurred.

[21]If the option is overpriced, for example, an investor would buy all the stock that was available and write call options against the stock. The investor would be able to borrow at a risk-free rate to support the investment since the position would be riskless. The positions would be reversed if the call option was underpriced. Thus, the investor could earn virtually unlimited returns with virtually no capital.

[22]To develop the price of a put option, we use the same terminology as used in Figures 15-1 and 15-2, adding the term P to represent the value of a put option. Assuming $S_d < E < S_u$, the initial amount invested by someone who buys the asset and buys q put options is $S_o + qP$. The amount received at the end of the period is either S_u or $S_d + q(E - S_d)$. To earn the same return in either state, it is necessary that $S_u = S_d + q(E - S_d)$. To earn the risk-free rate, it is necessary that $S_u = (S_o + qP)(1 + R_f)$. Solving these two equations for P gives Equation 15-7.

The Black-Scholes Option Pricing Model

The Black-Scholes OPM allows valuation of an option when the underlying asset has a range of possible future values rather than just two possible values.[23] The Black-Scholes OPM uses the assumptions underlying the two-state model except that it substitutes a continuous distribution for a two-outcome discrete distribution of terminal asset values and allows the expiration date to be more than one period away. In addition to assuming frictionless markets, unrestricted short-selling, no cash payments on the underlying asset prior to option maturity, and no arbitrage profits, the Black-Scholes OPM requires the following additional assumptions:

1. The risk-free rate remains constant over time.
2. Assets are traded continuously.
3. Asset returns obey a stationary stochastic process over time[24] which results in asset return being lognormally distributed[25] for any finite period.

The Black-Scholes model focuses on European options, which can be exercised only at maturity; extensions of the model deal with American options and alternate patterns of price movement.[26] Black and Scholes employed the same general approach used to value options in the two-state model. They determined the conditions necessary for a risk-free investment to provide the risk-free return. Given the set of assumptions and the requirement that a risk-free combination of securities and options must provide the risk-free rate of return, they derived the value of an option as:

$$C = S_o N(d_1) - [E \div e^{R_f T}] N(d_2) \tag{15-8}$$

where

S_o is the current price of the stock

E is the exercise price of the option

R_f is the risk-free rate, continuously compounded

$N(d_i)$ is the value from the table of the normal distribution representing the probability of an outcome less than d_i

$d_1 = [\ln(S_o/E) + (R_f + .5\sigma_S^2)T]/(\sigma_S\sqrt{T})$

$d_2 = d_1 - (\sigma_S\sqrt{T})$

[23]Black and Scholes, "The Pricing of Options."

[24]A stationary stochastic returns process over time results in the mean and variance of the probability distribution of returns being the same for each period.

[25]In other words, the logarithms of the returns are normally distributed.

[26]See, for example, Robert Geske and Richard Roll, "On Valuing American Call Options with the Black-Scholes European Formula," *Journal of Finance* 39 (June 1984): 443–455; and Robert E. Whaley, "Valuation of American Futures Options: Theory and Empirical Tests," *Journal of Finance* 41 (March 1986): 127–150.

σ_S = standard deviation or the continuously compounded annual rate of return for the stock

T = time in years or fractions of years until the expiration date of the option

e = 2.71828 . . ., the base of the natural logarithm

Although a proof of the Black-Scholes option pricing model is exceedingly time consuming,[27] we can see the general characteristics by studying the components of Equation 15-8. For this purpose, it is helpful to adopt the perspective of a person who is choosing between an investment in the stock and purchase of the option. First, we note that the price of the option will increase with an increase in the price of the stock. This makes sense because a higher stock price means the option buyer saves more money by using the option to acquire a claim against future returns. Likewise, a higher interest rate increases the value of the option by increasing the advantage of spending only the cost of the option now and waiting to exercise the option if the stock price rises sufficiently. A higher variance of returns for the stock also increases the value of the option because a higher variance increases the probability that the ending stock price will be above the exercise price of the option. A higher variance also means a higher probability of a very low price, but that is the problem of the stockholder, not the option buyer. The value of an option also increases with an increase in the time until expiration. The longer the time until expiration, the greater the probability that the stock price will rise above the exercise price, and the greater the advantage of waiting to make the investment required to buy the stock. Finally, a lower exercise price makes an option more valuable for obvious reasons. The direction of relationship between each of these five factors and option price can be developed by armchair thought about options. Black and Scholes went the next step to develop the precise mathematical relationships between these five factors and option prices based on a specific set of assumptions about stock price movements.

Example: The stock of Howe Corporation is presently priced at $100 a share. A call option with 9 months until expiration and an exercise price of $120 is currently available. The risk-free interest rate is 10 percent a year, continuously compounded. Month-end prices for the previous 13 months appear in Table 15-3, along with the standard deviation of continuously compounded monthly returns. The value of the option is found as follows:

$$\text{Standard deviation of continuously compounded annual return} = .144\sqrt{12} = .50$$

[27]For the proof of this model see Black and Scholes "The Pricing of Options," or James R. Garven, "A Pedagogic Note on the Derivation of the Black-Scholes Option Pricing Formula," *Financial Review* 21 (May 1986): 337–344.

TABLE 15.3 Standard Deviation of Monthly Returns

Month-end prices for Howe Corporation stock are shown for thirteen months. The continuously compounded monthly return for month t is $\ln(\text{price}_t/\text{price}_{t-1})$.* The standard deviation of monthly returns is then the standard deviation of the numbers in column 3.

(1) MONTH	(2) MONTH-END PRICE	(3) CONTINUOUSLY COMPOUNDED MONTHLY RETURN
1	100	
2	120	0.18232
3	110	-0.08701
4	90	-0.20067
5	110	0.20067
6	120	0.08701
7	150	0.22314
8	120	-0.22314
9	120	0
10	130	0.08004
11	140	0.07411
12	130	-0.07411
13	120	-0.08004
Standard deviation		0.14420

*If dividends had been paid during month t, the holding period return would be $\ln[(\text{price}_t + \text{dividend}_t)/\text{price}_{t-1}]$. For the reasons for using the natural logarithm, see Equation 2-A-3 and the related discussion.

$$d_1 = [\ln(100/120) + (.1 + .5 \times .5^2).75]/\left(.5\sqrt{.75}\right) = -.03134$$

$$d_2 = -.03134 - \left(.5\sqrt{.75}\right) = -.4644$$

$$N(d_1) = .4875$$

$$N(d_2) = .3212$$

$$C = 100(.4875) - (120 \div e^{.10 \times .75}).3212 = \underline{\$12.99}$$

Empirical Evidence Concerning the Black-Scholes OPM

To test or apply the option pricing model, it is necessary to find values for each of the variables. The risk-free rate, the exercise price, and the time until expiration are known, and the beginning stock price is known for a publicly traded stock. The unknown variable is the variance. The variance can be estimated by studying the variance of holding period returns for the stock for past periods, just as the beta is routinely estimated from past holding period returns for the mean-variance capital asset pricing model.

Numerous tests of the Black-Scholes OPM have been conducted,[28] and some biases have been found in tests of the model. Black and Scholes, for example, found that the model underpriced options on low-variance stocks and overpriced options on high-variance stocks. These results were confirmed by other authors, although the bias with regard to in-the-money and out-of-the-money options appeared to have changed over time.

Biases in the model may arise from misspecification, difficulty in developing the variance measure, or some unknown cause. The Black-Scholes OPM is based on options that can only be exercised at maturity and is based on the assumption that the underlying asset generates no cash flows—that is, dividends prior to the expiration date. Some of the biases have been explained by using the Roll-Geske[29] dividend-adjusted model and some of the biases have been explained by using improved measures of variance. Securities priced out of equilibrium in an arbitrage context imply the opportunity for large profits, and nobody has been able to demonstrate superior profits by trading based on prices that are biased according to the Black-Scholes OPM.

Real Option Valuation

Many capital investments have the characteristics of options, and are referred to as **real options.** Suppose, for example, it would cost us \$2 million to begin production of a new product. If demand is high, we will generate cash flows with a present value of \$4 million. If demand is low, the project will generate cash flows with a present value of \$1 million. From past experience with other product introductions we know there is a .5 probability that the product will be successful. The expected NPV is therefore:

$$E(NPV) = .5 \times \$4{,}000{,}000 + .5 \times \$1{,}000{,}000 - \$2{,}000{,}000 = \$500{,}000$$

For a quick glance at the risks involved, note that there is a .5 probability of an outcome resulting in a negative NPV of \$1 million. We also have the opportunity to increase NPV and reduce risk by waiting 1 year to invest. During that year, we can conduct a \$100,000 research study that will tell us with certainty whether the project will be successful. If we determine that the project will be successful, we can then invest \$2 million to go into production. In options terminology, we are buying a call option. The various option value inputs are as follows:

---

[28]See, for example, Fisher Black and Myron Scholes, "The Valuation of Option Contracts and a Test of Market Efficiency," *Journal of Finance* 27 (May 1972): 399–418; Mark Rubinstein, "Nonparametric Tests of Alternative Option Pricing Models Using All Reported Trades and Quotes on the 30 Most Active CBOE Option Classes from August 23, 1976, through August 31, 1978," *Journal of Finance* 40 (June 1985): 455–480; W. Sterk, "Tests of Two Models for Valuing Call Options on Stocks with Dividends," *Journal of Finance* 37 (December 1982): 1229–1237; and Whaley, "Valuation of American Futures Options."

[29]Richard A. Roll, "An Analytic Valuation Formula for Unprotected American Call Options with Known Dividends," *Journal of Financial Economics* 5 (November 1977): 251–258, and Robert Geske, "A Note on the Analytical Valuation Formula for Unprotected American Call Options on Stocks with Known Dividends," *Journal of Financial Economics* 7 (December 1979): 375–380.

$$E = \$2{,}000{,}000$$

$$S_u = \$4{,}000{,}000$$

$$S_d = \$1{,}000{,}000$$

To apply options analysis to this investment, we must estimate S_o, the amount investors would pay today for these future benefits. We assume here that the values S_u and S_d do not have systematic risk so they can be discounted at the risk-free rate of 5 percent.

$$S_o = (.5 \times 4{,}000{,}000 + .5 \times 1{,}000{,}000)/1.05 = \$2{,}380{,}952$$

We assume that the $2 million exercise price, the future amount we must invest, is known. Using equation 15-6, the value of the call option is:

$$C = (2{,}380{,}952 - 1{,}000{,}000/1.05)(4{,}000{,}000 - 2{,}000{,}000)/(4{,}000{,}000 - 1{,}000{,}000) = \$952{,}381$$

The cost of the call option is the $100,000 research investment, so our NPV is $852,381. To see the relationship between option pricing and classic NPV, the NPV for this project with the investment expenditure is also $852,381 if we use the same risk assumptions made for the option-pricing model:

$$NPV = -100{,}000 + .5 \times (4{,}000{,}000 - 2{,}000{,}000)/1.05 = \$852{,}381$$

What if we were not certain about the future investment cost or the value of benefits in 1 year if the project is successful or unsuccessful? For classic NPV analysis, we would discount the expected value at a discount rate appropriate for its risk. For an option pricing approach, we would identify a certainty equivalent and discount it at the risk-free rate. Any difference in NPVs between the two methods would result from estimation error in determining certainty equivalents or risk-adjusted discount rates.

To apply the Black-Scholes option pricing model, we need a standard deviation of continuously compounded growth in value. With only two possible outcomes, expected return and standard deviation would be:

$$\text{Expected return} = .5 \times \ln(4{,}000{,}000/2{,}380{,}952) + .5 \times \ln(1{,}000{,}000/2{,}380{,}952) = -.17435$$

$$\sigma = \{.5[\ln(4{,}000{,}000/2{,}380{,}952) + .17435]^2 + .5[\ln(1{,}000{,}000/2{,}380{,}952) + .17435]^2\}^{.5} = .6931$$

Suppose, though, that these two possible outcomes are just samples from a lognormal distribution with a standard deviation of continuously compounded returns of .8400.

Using equation 15-8, and recognizing that T = 1 because we must make the production decision in 1 year, the value of the call option is found as follows (the risk-free rate with continuous compounding is ln(1.05) = .0488):

$$d_1 = [\ln(2{,}380{,}952/2{,}000{,}000) + (.0488 + .5 \times .8320^2)]/.8320 = .6842$$

$$d_2 = .6842 - .8320 = -.1478$$

$$N(d_1) = .7531$$

$$N(d_2) = .4413$$

$$C = 2{,}380{,}952 \times .7531 - [2{,}000{,}000/e^{.0488}].4413 = \$952{,}560$$

Subtracting the $100,000 research cost leaves a net present value of $852,560. The values are almost identical to those determined using the binomial model, but these identical results come from assuming a particular standard deviation of returns in the Black-Scholes model.

More important than the specific calculations is the general idea that the real option increased net present value and decreased risk. Investment in phases and purchase of additional information are essentially real option investments that both increase NPV and decrease risk. Managers have become increasingly aware of these opportunities and continually review capital budgeting plans with an eye toward real option opportunities.

Option Pricing Models and Financing of Capital Investments

To apply OPMs to selection and financing of capital investments, we should recognize that a company's capital investments are the assets underlying the various financial claims against the company: common stock, preferred stock, debt, warrants, convertible bonds, and so forth. All the claims against the company are combinations of the asset (the total stream of cash flows generated by the asset, to be more precise), riskfree debt, call options, and put options. It will be demonstrated for the two-state case, and can be shown for the continuous case as well, that the risky debt of the company could be made risk free by selling call options. Therefore, risky debt is effectively a combination of riskless debt and the purchase of call options. Stock is a call option giving the stockholders the right to reclaim the company from the creditors. Convertible bonds are combinations of bonds and call options. Warrants are pure call options.

The set of capital investments (the company itself) can be valued using present value analysis of cash flows, possibly applying the mean-variance capital asset pricing model or arbitrage theory to adjust for risk. The values of the individual claims can then be determined by breaking the claim down to components consisting of pure claims against the asset, risk-free debt, call options, and put options. If the objective in choosing and financing assets is to maximize shareholder wealth, it is necessary to consider both the impact of a capital investment on the total value of the company and the impact of the combined investment and financing decisions on the wealth of the shareholders. The use of the OPM in this context is illustrated in the following examples. The two-state model is used to simplify the illustrations, but the same conclusions could be reached with one of the continuous distribution OPMs.

Debt

One question when selecting assets is how those assets will affect the required returns on the various sources of capital. The mean-variance CAPM and arbitrage pricing theory were used to determine a required return for equity of an unleveraged company. Given a value of the total (unleveraged) company, the OPM can be used to determine the required interest rate on debt.

Suppose a company will be worth $1,950 if it is successful and $550 if it fails. The total (unleveraged) value of the company is currently $1,600. That value may simply be observed in the marketplace or it may have been determined by a method such as assigning probabilities to each of the possible outcomes and finding the present value of expected cash flows using the mean-variance capital asset pricing model to adjust for systematic risk. We do not need to know how the current value was determined though; we just need to know what it is.

The risk-free rate is 10 percent and the company wants to issue debt of $1,000. If the company issues debt, the creditors' position is the same as if they bought the company for $1,600 and sold an option to the stockholders for $600. The stockholders have the right to buy back the company if it is successful by paying off the debt. The exercise price of the option is the amount that must be paid to the creditors at the end of the period to eliminate their claims.

The call option price is the amount invested by the stockholders—the value of the company minus the amount of debt, or $600. The call price and other known factors are substituted into Equation 15-6, leaving only the exercise price unknown:

$$600 = [1{,}600 - 550/1.1](1{,}950 - E)/(1{,}950 - 550)$$

Solving for E gives $1,186. In other words, an equilibrium-priced debt contract will require the company to pay the creditors $1,186 if it is successful, and the creditors will receive $550 if the company fails. Since this is a one-period model, the interest rate on the debt is therefore $(1{,}186 - 1{,}000)/1{,}000 = 18.6$ percent for the period. Note that 18.6 percent is not the creditors' expected return, but the interest rate paid on the debt *if* the company does not default.

Stockholder Wealth and Risk Changes

OPMs are also useful for considering changes in risk. Suppose that after issuing the debt in the previous example, the company replaces one of its capital investments, changing its risk posture such that the value is $2,100 in the case of success and $400 in the case of failure. Suppose further that this change in risk posture increases systematic risk and therefore decreases the total value of the company to $1,550. The risk change decreases total value—the new asset has a negative net present value using normal capital budgeting methods. But the situation is different when viewed solely from the position of a stockholder.

Remembering that the stock is a call option, the value of the stock would increase to:

$$C = [1{,}550 - 400/1.1](2{,}100 - 1{,}186)/(2{,}100 - 400) = \$638$$

Since the total value of the company declined to \$1,550 and the value of the stockholders' claim increased to \$638, this implies that the value of the creditors' claim decreased to \$1,550 – \$638 = \$912.[30]

As another example, consider a company that has a current total value of \$1,000. The principal and interest due to the creditors at the end of one period is \$500. The risk-free rate is 10 percent and the standard deviation of continuously compounded return for the company for the period is 50 percent. The stock is a call option against the company and is valued as follows:

$$d_1 = [\ln(1{,}000/500) + (.1 + .5 \times .5^2)1] \,/\, (.5\sqrt{1}) = 1.8363$$

$$d_2 = 1.8363 - .5\sqrt{1} = 1.3363$$

$$N(d_1) = .9668$$

$$N(d_2) = .9093$$

$$C = 1{,}000(.9668) - (500 \div e^{\cdot 1}).9093 = \$555$$

The current value of the stock is therefore \$555 while the current value of the debt is then \$445. The coupon rate on the debt is then:

$$(500 - 445)/445 = 12.4\%$$

Suppose, now, the company changes its risk so that total value remains unchanged but the standard deviation of continuously compounded return increases to .60. Reworking the problem, the new value of C is \$565. The change in standard deviation, while not changing the value of the company, increases the value of the stock by \$10 and therefore decreases the value of the debt by \$10. The required yield to maturity on the debt increases to (500 – 435)/435 = 14.9 percent.

The increased risk of the company hurts the creditors because the amount they receive if the company is successful remains unchanged while the probability of default increases and the amount they receive in the case of default decreases. Since the debt is already outstanding, the creditors cannot demand a higher interest rate from the company as compensation for the extra risk. The stockholders are in the opposite position: the amount they receive in the case of default remains at \$0 while the amount they receive in the case of success increases. Thus, a capital investment may benefit the stockholders even if it decreases the value of the company. Restrictive covenants associated with bond

[30]If the risk had been nonsystematic, so that it did not affect the total value of the company, the value of the shareholders' claim would have increased sharply to \$665, and the value of the debt would have declined to \$935.

issues are designed to limit the ability of companies to transfer wealth for bondholders to stockholders by increasing risk.

Motivating Managers to Take Risks

The OPM can also be used to consider the motivation of managers to make capital investment and financing decisions. For the company in the two previous two-state examples, suppose the manager receives a salary of \$100 if the company is successful and \$0 if it fails; the manager is fired for failure. (The stated value of the company in the case of success is after paying the manager.) We start by looking at the beginning and possible ending values of the stockholders' claim in each case:

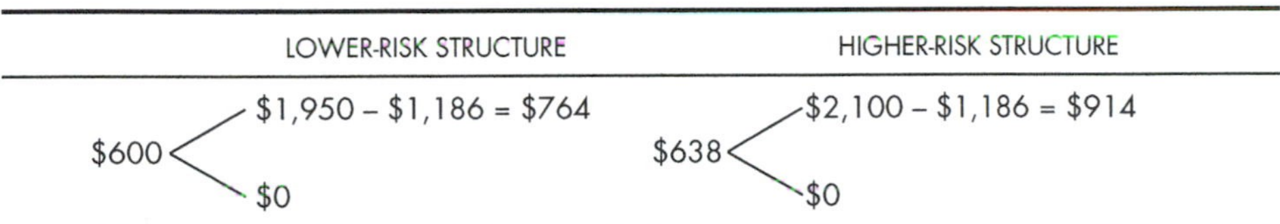

To determine if the manager would be happy with this change, we again look at the risk-free position. In this case, the manager can achieve a risk-free position through short-sales. With the low-risk structure, the manager could short-sell shares equal to 100/764 = 13 percent of the value of the company. The manager would receive .13 × 600 = \$78 immediately. In the case of success, the \$100 salary would be just sufficient to settle the short position. In the case of failure, short-sold stock would be worthless; the manager would receive no salary and would not have to spend money to cover the short position. Thus, the present value of the compensation package is \$78. Applying the same analysis to the high-risk situation, the present value of the compensation package is (100/914)638 = \$70. Even though the high-risk structure is better for shareholders, the manager is not likely to voluntarily make changes that will decrease the present value of the compensation package from \$78 to \$70.

To design a compensation package that will encourage the manager to choose the risk-return positions preferred by the shareholders, the present value of the compensation package must rise and fall with the present value of the shareholders' claim. With the low-risk structure, the present value of the combined owners' and manager's claims are \$600 + \$78 = \$678; in other words, the manager's claim is worth 78/678 = 11.5 percent of the combined owners' and manager's claims. If the fixed salary were replaced with ownership of 11.5 percent of the stock, the manager would still have a compensation package with a present value of \$78 with the low-risk structure, but the value would rise or fall with actions that caused the value of the stock to rise or fall. The manager would then be motivated to move to the high-risk structure preferred by the shareholders. The OPM illustrates the importance of designing contracts with managers so as to motivate them to make the choices preferred by shareholders.

As these examples illustrate, even nonsystematic risk can be important in that risk changes the relative values of claims against an income stream. Thus, nonsystematic risk and OPMs have important implications for capital budgeting, financing of capital investments, and the design of compensation arrangements. If these issues are not considered, management decisions will not lead to maximization of shareholder wealth.

The conclusions from OPM analysis may appear to negate the principles developed through the first fourteen and one-half chapters of this book. Prior to the OPM, value was affected only by systematic risk in the various models considered. The adjustments of required return for risk using asset pricing models did not take into consideration the role of risk in allocation of asset value among claimants. Management contracts that include stock options suggest that the implications of OPMs are widely used by companies in designing management contracts. The wide use of net present value and internal rate of return analysis by companies suggests that the ability to exploit existing creditors is not a major factor in most capital investment decision making. Restrictive bond covenants and the necessity of maintaining a good credit rating limit these opportunities. However, there are cases in which the position of one set of claimants relative to another is a key part of capital investment decision making, and option pricing models are important in these cases.

MANAGING EXCHANGE RATE RISK USING FUTURES, SWAPS, AND OPTIONS

Managing exchange rate risk is given a separate section in this chapter because it is an important part of international investment analysis. Fluctuations in exchange rates increase risk that can be decreased or eliminated with various hedging techniques.[31] Currency futures, swaps, and options are tools used to manage this risk. To truly understand the difference in these methods requires an understanding of the option instruments discussed previously in this chapter.

There are two types of exchange rate risk. **Translation** risk is the risk that reported income will fluctuate because of fluctuating exchange rates. Translation risk is a serious problem in a world in which accounting income matters, but it is only a risk of accounting numbers. **Transaction** risk is the risk that actual cash flows will fluctuate because of fluctuating exchange rates. Currency futures, swaps, and options are used to manage short-term transaction risk while balance sheet hedging is used to manage translation risk and longer-term transaction risk. Discussion of the first three methods of managing exchange rate risk follows. Balance sheet hedging is discussed in the financing section of the text.

---

[31]For a detailed argument for the use of hedging, see Gunter Dufey and S. L. Srinivasulu, "The Case for Corporate Management of Foreign Exchange Risk," *Financial Management* 12 (Winter 1983): 54–62.

Currency Futures

A currency future is simply a contract to exchange a specific amount of one currency for a specific amount of another currency at a designated future date. By agreeing to these conditions ahead of time, you can effectively eliminate exchange rate risk for a transaction.

Suppose, for example, you sign a contract to purchase a shipment of computer chips from Japan. Delivery and payment are to occur in 90 days, and you agree to pay 100 million yen. The spot exchange rate is 102.8 yen to the dollar, so you are agreeing to pay $972,763 at today's exchange rate. If the dollar falls in price to 95 yen by the end of 90 days though, the chips will cost you $1,052,632. This increase in price may completely wipe out your profits, but you can protect yourself with a futures contract. The 90-day forward rate is 102.5, so you can contract today to buy the 100 million yen in 90 days at a cost of $975,610. This reduces your risk by locking in the dollar cost of the chips.

Unfortunately, contracts are actively traded for only a half-dozen major currencies, and most contracts are for delivery 6 months or less in the future; a year is about the outer limit. Consequently, futures contracts cannot be used to hedge against the impacts of exchange rate fluctuations for capital investments generating cash flows over a period of 20 or 30 years.

Currency Swaps

A currency swap is a spot transaction in one direction offset by a futures contract in the opposite direction. We exchange one currency for another today, agreeing to reverse the transaction at a specified future date. The forward exchange rate is fixed, but may not be the same as the exchange rate for the spot transaction. Swaps may be used when futures contracts are not available. There are no listed futures contracts for the Indian rupee, for example, but a swap may be arranged. Swaps are sometimes made available by governments wishing to stabilize the currency.

Options

Futures contracts and swaps can be used to manage exchange rate risk when there is a known future need for a currency. Suppose, though, you are bidding to buy wool from Australians, with payment to be in Australian dollars. You must bid today, but it will be 2 months before you find out if your bid has been accepted. To avoid exchange rate risk, you can purchase Australian dollar currency options for the number of Australian dollars in the contract. If your offer is accepted, we have already locked in the U.S. dollar cost with the option contract. If your offer is rejected, you need not exercise the option (although you can resell the option at a profit if the Australian dollar has increased in value).

Like futures contracts, options are limited to a handful of leading currencies and have short lives; actively traded currency options do not extend beyond three months. They are available as both put and call options, though, so it is possible to lock in either a buying or a selling price of the foreign currency.

SUMMARY

This chapter focused on two approaches to valuation under risk: arbitrage pricing theory and option pricing models. Arbitrage pricing theory is an alternative to the mean-variance capital asset pricing model in that it is used to find the required return or value of a risky investment, based on systematic risk. Option pricing models focus on the values of claims against a risky investment, rather than just the investment itself. Option pricing models emphasize the importance of total risk in determining the values of the various claims against returns from investments.

Arbitrage pricing theory is not based on specific assumptions about utility functions of investors. Arbitrage pricing theory is based on the assumption of perfectly competitive, frictionless markets in which there are no restrictions on short sales, and there are therefore no arbitrage profit opportunities. The standard arbitrage pricing theory is based on the assumptions that returns for assets are related to certain overall factors in a linear form and that the number of investments being considered is much larger than the number of factors.

Arbitrage pricing theory can be used to determine required return as was done with the mean-variance CAPM, and it is possible to use arbitrage pricing models to directly value cash flows from a capital investment. Direct arbitrage valuation is based on finding the cost of a publicly traded portfolio that will duplicate the cash flows from the proposed capital investment. State-based arbitrage models are one alternative to the more widely recognized APT form for capital budgeting.

Option pricing models (OPMs) focus on the values of claims against an asset rather than the value of the asset itself. The option models consider the impact of systematic risk as well as nonsystematic risk, and they give insights with regard to how changes in risk change the values of the various claims against an income stream.

OPMs are based on the assumptions that there are no restrictions on short sales and that financial markets are frictionless, with information freely available to all. The Black-Scholes model for European options is based on the additional assumptions that options cannot be exercised until their expiration date and that there are no cash distributions to holders of the underlying asset prior to the option's expiration date. The Black-Scholes model is also based on the assumptions that the risk-free rate remains constant over time, assets are traded continuously, and asset returns obey a stationary stochastic process over time. Other extensions allow for the possibility of exercise before maturity.

OPMs are particularly useful for examining the values of claims against a company because all claims, whether debt, equity, or hybrid, are combinations of the underlying asset, risk-free debt, call options, and put options. OPMs can be used to determine the required interest rate on debt, to examine how a change in risk will change the relative values of the debt and equity claims against a company, and to determine the compensation contracts that will align the interests of managers and stockholders.

Exchange rate risk—translation risk and transaction risk—adds another dimension to risk analysis in that it increases uncertainty with regard to the number of dollars the company will finally end up with. We discussed three ways of managing exchange rate risk: (1) currency futures contracts, (2) swaps, and (3) options.

QUESTIONS

15-1. Compare the assumptions underlying arbitrage pricing theory with those underlying the mean-variance capital asset pricing model. Which set of assumptions seems more realistic to you? Why?

15-2. What conditions are necessary for the APT to reduce to the CAPM formula for the relationship between beta for an investment and required return for that investment?

15-3. Give examples of economic factors for which a higher expected return may be required as compensation for sensitivity.

15-4. Summarize the current state of empirical evidence with regard to arbitrage pricing theory.

15-5. What problems can arise in the application of discrete state arbitrage pricing theory to capital budgeting?

15-6. Define the following terms: (a) option, (b) call option, (c) put option, (d) European option, (e) American option, (f) exercise, (g) exercise price, (h) striking price, (i) exercise date.

15-7. Why is total risk important in option pricing models whereas only systematic risk is important in models such as the mean-variance capital asset pricing model?

15-8. Describe the characteristics of stocks and bonds in the context of option analysis.

15-9. What are the assumptions underlying the Black-Scholes option pricing model?

15-10. Summarize the empirical evidence with regard to the Black-Scholes option pricing model.

15-11. What are the general implications of option pricing theory for the design of management reward systems?

15-12. **(Applications)** Several years ago one of the big three automakers began marketing a diesel-powered minivan. The aftermarket for these vans turned out to be disastrous.

- **a.** In terms of options, what is the difference between the outright purchase of an asset like this minivan and the leasing of the minivan?
- **b.** In option terminology, what do you call the option at the end of the lease to turn the minivan over to the dealer?
- **c.** Would you consider this lease more like a European or an American option?
- **d.** With low market value after only a 3-year life, was leasing a good idea?

15-13. **(Ethical Considerations)** Recent television commercials have encouraged people to get out of low-earning savings accounts and into collateralized mortgage obligations (CMOs). The way CMOs work is a group of mortgages is pooled and usually the federal government guarantees it will return the principle and accrued interest should the original borrower default. The mortgage borrowers have the right to repay their mortgages if interest rates fall so that they can refinance at a lower interest rate. The risk with a CMO is that general interest rates will fall and borrowers will exercise this option.

a. Knowing what you know about options and the fact the borrower can and is likely to refinance when interest rates decline, why are these securities losing their popularity?

b. Would you market these 20-year securities to the elderly?

c. What are the ethical ramifications involved in selling these securities?

15-14. **(International)** Explain the difference between translation risk and transaction risk.

15-15. **(International)** Explain how the following are used to reduce exchange rate risk. What types of exchange rate risks are they typically used to reduce:

a. Currency futures?

b. Currency options?

c. Swaps?

15-16. **(International Ethical Considerations)** There is a school of thought which states that over a long period, gains in the currency market will be offset by losses in the currency market and that an unhedged position is just as profitable as a hedged position. Assume that shareholders are expecting to earn a higher rate of return for a given level of risk by purchasing stock in companies with significant international exposure. At the same time many of the managers at these companies are hedging this exposure at a significant cost with currency futures, swaps, and options. They do this to reduce the volatility on the balance sheet equity account because many bonuses are based on return on equity. Is there an ethical concern here? What is it and how can the situation be improved? If you were the manager, would you hedge your exposure?

PROBLEMS

15-1. A company evaluates its capital investments with regard to four factors. Information with regard to two capital investments and the four factors appears below. The risk-free rate is 6 percent. Find the required return for each capital investment.

FACTOR	EXPECTED RETURN FOR A UNITARY SENSITIVITY PORTFOLIO	FACTOR BETAS FOR THE CAPITAL INVESTMENTS A	B
GNP	10 percent	1.5	0.5
Bond Risk Premiums	8 percent	0.5	2.0
Yield Curve	7 percent	0.5	2.0
Inflation	7 percent	0.75	0.25

Compute the required returns for capital investments A and B.

15-2. Shown in the following table are betas for three securities with regard to each of two factors. Use this information to construct a unitary sensitivity portfolio with regard to each factor.

SECURITY:	A	B	C
Sensitivity to Factor 1	1.00	.50	0
Sensitivity to Factor 2	.50	.75	1.25
Expected return	.12	.10	.10

15-3. Compute the expected return for each unitary sensitivity portfolio in problem 2.

15-4. An investment has betas of 1.5 and –0.5 with regard to factors 1 and 2 respectively from problem 2. The risk-free rate is 6 percent. Based on the expected returns for unitary sensitivity portfolios computed in problem 3, what is the required return for this investment?

15-5. There are two possible states of nature. Cash flows per dollar invested for each of two securities in each state appear below, along with cash flow from a proposed capital investment. The capital investment costs $50,000. What is the net present value?

	SECURITY A	SECURITY B	CAPITAL INVESTMENT
State 1	.20	.30	$20,000
State 2	.50	.20	10,000

15-6. There are three possible states of nature. Cash flows per dollar invested for each of three securities in each state appear below, along with cash flows for a proposed capital investment. If the capital investment costs $50,000, what is the net present value?

	SECURITY A	SECURITY B	SECURITY C	CAPITAL INVESTMENT
State 1	.20	.30	.30	$20,000
State 2	.50	.20	.20	10,000
State 3	.10	.40	.60	12,000

15-7. Managers at Midwest Grain Exporters believe that their profitability depends on the productivity of the world economy, and world grain output. They decide to use four states of nature, including high and low levels of world economic growth and world grain output. They have identified four portfolios of alternate investments that are sensitive to these variables. The rate of return expected from each portfolio in each state is as follows. Determine the value, at the start of a year, of the portfolio that will provide $1 at the end of the year in each of the states, while providing nothing in the other states.

WORLD ECONOMIC GROWTH:	LOW		HIGH	
WORLD GRAIN PRODUCTION:	LOW	HIGH	LOW	HIGH
Portfolio 1	.10	.15	.16	.12
Portfolio 2	.12	.13	.14	.18
Portfolio 3	.15	.11	.13	.10
Portfolio 4	.09	.18	.11	.18

15-8. Managers at Midwest Grain Exporters (problem 7) are considering a new shipping facility. Cash flows each year will depend on the state of nature that occurs that year, as follows. At a 13 percent risk-free rate, what is the maximum price Midwest can afford to pay for the shipping facility?

WORLD ECON:	LOW		LOW	
WHEAT PROD: YEAR	LOW	HIGH	LOW	HIGH
1	$5,000	$1,000	$7,000	$4,000
2	$5,250	$1,050	$7,350	$4,200
3	$5,513	$1,103	$7,718	$4,410
4	$5,788	$1,158	$8,103	$4,631
5	$6,078	$1,216	$8,509	$4,862
6	$6,381	$1,276	$8,934	$5,105
7	$6,700	$1,340	$9,381	$5,360
8	$7,036	$1,407	$9,850	$5,628
9	$7,387	$1,477	10,342	$5,910
10	$7,757	$1,551	10,859	$6,205

15-9. A stock priced at \$20 a share will be worth either \$30 or \$10 at the end of one period. A call option has an exercise price of \$25 at the end of the period, which is also the expiration date. The risk-free rate is 6 percent.

a. A person could achieve a risk-free position by buying the stock and writing how many options?

b. What is the equilibrium price of a call option?

c. What would be the value of a put option with an exercise price of \$25?

15-10. A company is worth \$100,000. At the end of the period, the company will be worth either \$200,000 or \$30,000. The risk-free rate is 10 percent. How much can the company borrow based on a promise to repay \$60,000 if the company is successful, and to turn the company over to the creditors if it is unsuccessful?

15-11. A company is worth \$500,000. The company will be worth \$1 million at the end of one period if it is successful and \$100,000 if it fails. The risk-free rate is 10 percent. The company wants to borrow \$200,000 that will be repaid at the end of the period. What must be the effective interest rate?

15-12. A company is worth \$10 million now. The company will be worth \$20 million at the end of one period if it is successful and \$1 million otherwise. These values are before deducting the value of the manager's compensation. The manager receives \$100,000 if the company is successful, and \$0 otherwise. The company has debt with a face value of \$5 million. The \$5 million plus interest is due at the end of one period, and the risk-free rate is 8 percent. What is the equilibrium coupon interest rate on the debt?

15-13. For the company in problem 12, a change in risk structure leaves the beginning total value of the company unchanged, but changes the ending value to \$30 million if successful and \$500,000 otherwise. Would the shareholders prefer this change? Would the manager voluntarily change the company in this way?

15-14. For the company in problems 12 and 13, design a compensation program that would give the manager and shareholders identical attitudes toward risk.

15-15. The price of a company's stock is currently \$50. A call option with an exercise price of \$60 will expire in 6 months. The risk-free rate is 10 percent, and the standard deviation of the rate of the continuously compounded annual return for the stock is 50 percent. What is the value of the call option?

15-16. The stock of Manhattan Products Corporation is presently selling for \$50 a share. A call option with an exercise price of \$70 will expire in 6 months. The risk-free interest rate is 8 percent a year, compounded continuously. The standard deviation of the continuously compounded annual return for the stock is 60 percent. What is the value of the call option?

15-17. Month-end prices for Lawrence Corporation for thirteen recent months appear below. The company paid no dividends during that period, and the most recent price of the stock is $120. Options with 1 year until maturity and an exercise price of $140 are currently available. The risk-free rate is 10 percent a year, continuously compounded. What is the value of the call option?

MONTH	MONTH-END PRICE	MONTH	MONTH-END PRICE
1	120	8	140
2	110	9	100
3	130	10	120
4	120	11	110
5	130	12	100
6	150	13	120
7	160		

15-18. Norman Services has a total value of $1 million. The principle and interest owed to creditors at the end of one year is $600,000. The standard deviation of continuously compounded annual return for the company is .50. The risk-free rate is 10 percent continuously compounded. What are the market values of debt and equity? What is the contract (coupon) interest rate on the debt?

15-19. Suppose the standard deviation for Norman services (problem 18) decreased to .40 and the value of the company increased to $1,050,000. What would this do to the values of debt and equity? Would shareholders be in favor of this change?

15-20. We are preparing to sign an agreement to import clothing from France. The price is 100,000 francs and payment is due in 90 days. We have a contract to sell the goods for $18,000. The 90-day forward exchange rate is .1646. What will be our profit if we eliminate exchange rate risk with a forward exchange contract?

15-21. We have placed a bid for Canadian wheat for 1.2 million Canadian dollars. If our bid is accepted, we can resell the wheat for 1 million U.S. dollars. We will know if the bid has been accepted in 30 days. A 30-day option to buy Canadian dollars for 0.78 U.S. dollars each can be purchased for $0.0012 U.S. per Canadian dollar. What will be our profit if we buy options and the bid is accepted? What will be our loss if we buy options and the bid is rejected (assuming the options expire without being exercised)?

CASE PROBLEM

GRQ Properties

GRQ Properties was a small family partnership established for the purpose of investing in residential properties. The partnership started out by purchasing several single-family homes as rental properties. The partners studied the rental market carefully before investing, and chose houses in areas that turned out to have both strong rental demand and decent price appreciation. However, the partners discovered that identifying and keeping good tenants was difficult. Growth of the partnership was halted for several years until income stabilized and the managing partner, Joyce Green, learned more about dealing with tenants.

During this stabilization period, the tax law changed. The profitability of the partnership was satisfactory and relationships between the partners were harmonious, but the attractiveness of additional rental property purchases had declined because rents had not risen by enough to offset the new tax law changes.

Green, the managing partner, was eager to expand the business and began looking for other opportunities. She found a small one-office mortgage brokerage company for sale and proposed this to the partners as a new investment. The basic job of a mortgage broker of this type was to attract mortgage applicants and complete the mortgage application process. A mortgage banker actually made the loans, and then sold them to investors such as pension funds and savings and loans. The owner of the mortgage brokerage company wanted to retire, but was willing to work for several more years until Green learned the business. Green would quit her full-time job to manage the mortgage brokerage office. The business was for sale for $500,000.

Walter Ransom, one of the partners and a brother of Green, worked with Green to examine the investment proposal. The owner of the business provided audited financial statements to estimate the cash flow from the business, after deducting salaries, in each of four representative states of nature. These states included two rates of GNP growth and two levels of mortgage interest rates, as shown at the bottom of this page.

Ransom decided that an appropriate way to evaluate this business was to compare it with returns that could be earned elsewhere. He would be selling mutual fund shares to pay his part of the $500,000 cost, so he considered common stocks as the alternative. He estimated the annual return (cash flow per dollar invested) for four stock price indexes in each of the four states of nature by studying past performance of these indexes. He used the Standard and Poor's industrials, utilities, transportation, and financial indexes. His estimates of the returns for each index in each state are shown on the following page.

STATE	GNP GROWTH RATE	INTEREST RATE	ANNUAL CASH FLOW
I	0%	12%	–$100,000
II	0	6	100,000
III	5	12	100,000
IV	5	6	200,000

STATE	INDUSTRIALS	UTILITIES	TRANSPORTATION	FINANCIALS
I	.04	.06	.04	−.05
II	.15	.13	.15	.16
III	.03	.03	.04	.02
IV	.14	.09	.16	.12

Using this information Ransom felt that he should be able to make a decision about the desirability of the mortgage brokerage business investment. In the back of his mind, though, was the fact that harmonious family relations were at stake, in addition to his financial well-being.

Case Questions

1. Set up the simultaneous equation problem needed to find out how much must be invested in common stocks represented by these indexes to duplicate the cash flows from the mortgage brokerage business.
2. Solve the simultaneous equation problem (*Hint:* Excel can be used to solve these equations in only a couple of minutes).
3. Do you recommend investment in the proposed mortgage brokerage business?

SELECTED REFERENCES

Abuaf, Niso. "Foreign Exchange Options: The Leading Edge." *Midland Corporate Finance Journal* 5 (Summer 1987): 51–58.

Adler, Michael, and Bernard Dumas. "Exposure to Currency Risk: Definition and Measurement." *Financial Management* 13 (Summer 1984): 41–50.

Arnold, Tom, and Richard L. Shockley, Jr. "Value Creation at Anheuser-Busch: A Real Options Example." *Journal of Applied Corporate Finance* 14 (Summer 2002): 52–61.

Bakshi, Gurpid, Charles Cao, and Zhiwu Chen. "Empirical Performance of Alternative Option Pricing Models." *Journal of Finance* 52 (December 1997): 2003–2049.

Bansal, Ravi, David A. Hseih, and S. Viswanathan. "A New Approach to International Arbitrage Pricing." *Journal of Finance* 48 (December 1993): 1719–1747.

Black, Fisher, and John C. Cox. "Valuing Corporate Securities: Some Effects of Bond Indenture Provisions." *Journal of Finance* 31 (May 1976): 351–367.

Black, Fisher, and Myron Scholes. "The Pricing of Options and Corporate Liabilities." *Journal of Political Economy* 81 (May–June 1973): 637–654.

Bower, Dorothy H., Richard S. Bower, and Dennis E. Logue. "Arbitrage Pricing Theory and Utility Stock Returns." *Journal of Finance* 39 (September 1984): 1041–1054.

Burmeister, Edwin, and Marjory B. McElroy. "Joint Estimation of Factor Sensitivities and Risk Premia for the Arbitrage Pricing Theory." *Journal of Finance* 43 (July 1988): 721–735.

Chan, Louis K. C., Jason Karceski, and Josef Lakonishok. "The Risk and Return from Factors." *Journal of Financial and Quantitative Analysis* 33 (June 1998): 159–188.

Chang, Jack S. K., and Latha Shanker. "Option Pricing and the Arbitrage Pricing Theory." *Journal of Financial Research* 10 (Spring 1987): 1–16.

Chen, Nai-Fu. "Some Empirical Tests of the Theory of Arbitrage Pricing." *Journal of Finance* 38 (December 1983): 1393–1414.

Chen, Nai-Fu, Richard W. Roll, and Stephen A. Ross. "Economic Forces and the Stock Market: Testing the APT and Alternative Asset Pricing Theories." UCLA Working Paper #20–83, December 1983.

Childs, Paul D., Steven H. Ott, and Alexander J. Triantis. "Capital Budgeting for Interrelated Projects: A Real Options Approach." *Journal of Financial and Quantitative Analysis* 33 (September 1998): 305–334.

Chung, Kee H., and Charlie Charoenwong. "Investment Options, Assets in Place, and the Risk of Stocks." *Financial Management* 20 (Autumn 1991): 21–33.

Conway, Delores A., and Marc R. Reinganum. "Capital Market Factor Structure: Identification through Cross Validation." University of Chicago Graduate School of Business Working Paper #183, July 1986.

Cox, John C., Stephen A. Ross, and Mark Rubinstein. "Option Pricing: A Simplified Approach." *Journal of Financial Economics* 7 (September 1979): 229–263.

Dhrymes, P., Irwin Friend, and B. Gultekin. "A Critical Reexamination of the Empirical Evidence on the Arbitrage Pricing Theory." *Journal of Finance* 39 (June 1984): 323–346.

———. "New Tests of the APT and Their Implications." *The Journal of Finance* 40 (July 1985): 659–675.

Dixit, Avinash, and Robert Pindyck. "The Options Approach to Capital Investment." *Harvard Business Review* 73 (May–June 95): 105–126.

Downs, Thomas W., and Robert W. Ingram. "Beta, Size, Risk, and Return." *Journal of Financial Research* 23 (Fall 2000): 245–260.

Dufey, Gunter, and S. L. Srinivasulu. "The Case for Corporate Management of Foreign Exchange Risk." *Financial Management* 12 (Winter 1983): 54–62.

Dybvig, Philip H., and Stephen A. Ross. "Yes, the APT Is Testable." *Journal of Finance* 40 (September 1985): 1173–1188.

Erhardt, Michael C. "Arbitrage Pricing Models: The Sufficient Number of Factors and Equilibrium Conditions." *Journal of Financial Research* 10 (Summer 1987): 111–120.

Fama, Eugene F. "Determining the Number of Priced State Variables in the ICAPM." *Journal of Financial and Quantitative Analysis* 33 (June 1998): 217–231.

Fama, Eugene F., and Kenneth R. French. "The Cross-Section of Expected Stock Returns." *Journal of Finance* 47 (June 1992): 427–465.

Froot, Kenneth A. "A Framework for Risk Management." *Journal of Applied Corporate Finance* 7 (Fall 1994): 22–32.

Garven, James R. "A Pedagogic Note on the Derivation of the Black-Scholes Option Pricing Formula." *Financial Review* 21 (May 1986): 337–344.

Gehr, Adam K., Jr. "Risk-Adjusted Capital Budgeting Using Arbitrage." *Financial Management* 10 (Winter 1981): 14–19.

Geske, Robert. "A Note on the Analytical Valuation Formula for Unprotected American Call Options on Stocks with Known Dividends." *Journal of Financial Economics* 7 (December 1979): 375–380.

Geske, Robert, and Richard Roll. "On Valuing American Call Options with the Black-Scholes European Formula." *Journal of Finance* 39 (June 1984): 443–455.

Glen, Jack, and Philippe Jorion. "Currency Hedging for International Portfolios." *Journal of Finance* 48 (December 1993): 1865–1886.

Grenadier, Steven. "Option Exercise Games: An Application to the Equilibrium Investment Strategies of Firms." *The Review of Financial Studies* 15 (Summer 2002): 691–721.

Herath, Hemantha S. B., and Chas S. Park. "Economic Analysis of R&D Projects: An Options Approach." *The Engineering Economist* 44 # 1, (1999): 1–35.

Herath, Hemantha S. B., and Chas S. Park. "Multi-Stage Capital Investment Opportunities as Compound Real Options." *The Engineering Economist* 47 # 1 (2002): 1–27.

Hevert, Kathleen T. "Real Options Primer: A Practical Synthesis of Concepts and Valuation Approaches" *Journal of Applied Corporate Finance* 14 (Summer 2002): 25–40.

Huberman, Gur, Schmuel Kandel, and Robert Stambaugh. "Mimicking Portfolios and Exact Arbitrage Pricing." *Journal of Finance* 42 (March 1987): 1–9.

Ingersoll, J. E., and Stephen Ross. "Waiting to Invest: Investment and Uncertainty." *Journal of Business* (January 1992): 1–29.

Jacob, David P., Graham Lord, and James A Tilley. "A Generalized Framework for Pricing Contingent Cash Flows." *Financial Management* 16 (Autumn 1987): 5–14.

Jamshidian, F. "An Exact Bond Option Formula." *Journal of Finance* 44 (March 1989): 205–209.

Kan, Raymond, and Chu Zhang. "Two-Pass Tests of Asset Pricing Models with Useless Factors." *Journal of Finance* 54 (February 1999): 203–235.

Kaufold, Howaard, and Michael Smirlock. "Managing Corporate Exchange and Interest Rate Exposure." *Financial Management* 15 (Autumn 1986): 64–78.

Lee, Moon. "Valuing Finite-Maturity Investment Timing Options." *Financial Management* 26 (Summer 1997): 58–67.

Majd, Saman, and Robert S. Pindyck. "Time to Build, Option Value, and Investment Decisions." *Journal of Financial Economics* 18 (March 1987): 7–27.

Maloney, Peter J. "Managing Currency Exposure: The Case of Western Mining." *Journal of Applied Corporate Finance* 2 (Winter 1990): 29–34.

McCulloch, Robert, and Peter E. Rossi. "Posterior, Predictive, and Utility-Based Approaches to Testing the Arbitrage Pricing Theory." *Journal of Financial Economics* 28 (November–December 1990): 7–38.

McDonald, R., and D. Siegel. "The Value of Waiting to Invest." *Quarterly Journal of Economics* (November 1986): 707–727.

Miller, Edward. "A Problem in Textbook Arbitrage Pricing Theory Examples." *Financial Management* 18 (Summer 1989): 9–10.

Milne, Alistair, and A. Elizabeth Whalley. " 'Time to Build, Option Value and Investment Decisions': A Comment." *Journal of Financial Economics* 56 (May 2000): 325–332.

Moel, Alberto, and Peter Tufano. "When Are Real Options Exercised? An Empirical Study of Mine Closings." *The Review of Financial Studies* 15 (Spring 2002): 35–64.

Park, Chan S., and Hemantha S. B. Herath. "Exploiting Uncertainty—Investment Opportunities as Real Options: A New Way of Thinking in Engineering Economics." *The Engineering Economist* 45 #1 (2000): 1–36.

Pettway, Richard H., and Bradford D. Jordan. "APT vs. CAPM Estimates of the Return-Generating Function Parameters for Regulated Public Utilities." *Journal of Financial Research* 10 (Fall 1987): 227–238.

Phelan, Steven E. "Exposing the Illusion of Confidence in Financial Analysis." *Management Decision* 35 (January–February 1997): 163–169.

Reisman, Haim. "Reference Variables, Factor Structure, and Approximate Multibeta Representation." *Journal of Finance* 47 (September 1992): 1303–1314.

Rendleman, Richard J., Jr., and Brit J. Bartter. "Two-State Option Pricing." *Journal of Finance* 34 (December 1979): 1093–1110.

Roll, Richard A. "An Analytic Valuation Formula for Unprotected American Call Options with Known Dividends." *Journal of Financial Economics* 5 (November 1977): 251–258.

Roll, Richard, and Stephen A. Ross. "A Critical Reexamination of the Empirical Evidence on the Arbitrage Pricing Theory: A Reply." *Journal of Finance* 39 (June 1984): 347–350.

Ross, Stephen. "The Arbitrage Theory of Capital Asset Pricing." *Journal of Economic Theory* (December 1976): 341–361.

———. "An Empirical Investigation of the Arbitrage Pricing Theory." *Journal of Finance* 35 (December 1980): 1073–1103.

———. "A Simple Approach to the Valuation of Risky Streams." *Journal of Business* (July 1979): 254–286.

———. "Uses, Abuses, and Alternatives to the Net Present Value Rule." *Financial Management* 23 (Autumn 1994): 96–102.

Rubinstein, Mark. "Nonparametric Tests of Alternative Option Pricing Models Using All Reported Trades and Quotes on the 30 Most Active CBOE Option Classes from August 23, 1976, through August 31, 1978." *Journal of Finance* 40 (June 1985): 455–480.

Ryan, Harley E., Jr., and Roy A. Wiggins, III. "The Interactions Between R&D Investment Decisions and Compensation Policy." *Financial Management* 31 (Spring 2002): 5–29.

Shankin, Jay. "The Current State of the Arbitrage Pricing Theory." *Journal of Finance* 47 (September 1992): 1569–1574.

Siegel, Daniel R., James L. Smith, and James L. Paddock. "Valuing Offshore Oil Properties with Option Pricing Models." *Midland Corporate Finance Journal* 5 (Spring 1987): 22–30.

Sterk, W. "Tests of Two Models for Valuing Call Options on Stocks with Dividends." *Journal of Finance* 37 (December 1982): 1229–1237.

Stulz, R. M. "A Model of International Asset Pricing." *Journal of Financial Economics* 9 (December 1981): 383–406.

Stulz, René M. "Merton Miller and Modern Finance." *Financial Management* 29 (Winter 2000) 119–131.

Trigeorgis, L. "A Conceptual Options Framework for Capital Budgeting." *Advances in Futures and Options Research* 3 (1988): 145–167.

Whaley, Robert E. "Valuation of American Futures Options: Theory and Empirical Tests." *Journal of Finance* 41 (March 1986): 127–150.

CALLAWAY (A)

Union Electric (UE) joined the Nuclear Age in 1973 when it ordered two nuclear reactors from Westinghouse. The reactors, to be installed on a site in Callaway County, Missouri, were expected to cost a total of $1.05 billion, and were expected to produce a total of 2,300,000 kilowatts of electricity. UE derived 90 percent of its power from coal in 1973. The plan was to use 60 percent coal and 36 percent nuclear power by 1985.

The nuclear plant was expected to solve several problems. First, it would provide the additional capacity that was needed to meet projected demand. Second, it would avoid dependence on oil, which had become scarce and expensive in the wake of the OPEC oil embargo. Third, it would eliminate acid rain and other air pollution that was produced by coal-powered plants. Finally, nuclear power was expected to be a low-cost source of energy that would be important in developing the industrial base in UE's service area, which included substantial portions of Missouri and smaller areas of Illinois and Iowa.

An electric utility differs from the local 7-Eleven store in several important ways. First, the 7-Eleven store can get a new delivery of Pepsi in a few hours, but it takes years—often more than a decade—for a nuclear plant to add generating capacity. Second, the 7-Eleven store can tell its customers it is out of Pepsi, but the electric company must maintain adequate capacity to provide all the electricity wanted by all of its customers during the highest-demand hour of the year.[1] Finally, electricity is so important in industrialized economies that the entire welfare of a region is affected by its availability, as well as the cost of the electricity.

Peak-demand history and capacity for UE are shown in Table IV-1. Based on these data and other information, a 6.2 percent growth rate in demand was forecasted. This meant that the company would need to add approximately 4.2 million kilowatts of electrical capacity over the next 10 years. New coal-powered plants that were to come online were as follows.

Labadie, Mo.	1973	600,000 kW
Rush Island, Mo.	1976	600,000
Rush Island, Mo.	1977	600,000

Thus there was a need for an additional 2.4 million kilowatts of capacity. The 2.3 million kilowatts anticipated from the two Callaway units would provide the bulk of this need, although some additional capacity would still be required. Other capacity was also required to carry the company through until 1981, when the first Callaway unit would become operational. In addition, at least one antiquated plant would be shut down, again necessitating additional capacity.

[1]Generally between 1 P.M. and 3 P.M. on the hottest day in August.

TABLE IV-1 Demand and Capacity History For Union Electric

This table shows the actual peak-time demand and actual peak-time capacity of UE by year, taken from the company's annual reports.

YEAR	PEAK-TIME DEMAND	PEAK-TIME CAPABILITY
1963	2,891,000 kW	3,098,000 kW
1966	3,257,000	3,495,000
1967	3,438,000	3,840,000
1968	3,830,000	4,171,000
1969	4,078,000	4,611,000
1970	4,362,000	5,078,000
1971	4,503,000	5,682,000
1972	4,994,000	5,663,000

The economic justification for the Callaway plant was fairly simple in concept. Construction cost per kilowatt capacity was estimated to be $315 for a coal plant and $456 for a nuclear plant. Offsetting the higher construction cost was a major savings in fuel cost. A pound of "yellowcake" uranium fuel costing $7 could produce as much electricity as several tons of coal, and the price per ton of coal was higher than the price per pound of yellowcake. A ton of coal would produce approximately 2,000 kilowatts of electricity. We can work with an assumed hourly output of 4,380 hours per year for either plant.

Antinuclear groups objected to UE's plans on grounds of both safety and cost. First and foremost, an accident could cause thousands of deaths. In addition, it was necessary to find a way to store spent fuel for periods of up to 200,000 years. The economic benefits depended on relative construction costs, relative fuel costs, and electricity demand. Critics argued that earlier nuclear plants had incurred large cost overruns, and UE, having agreed to cost-plus contracts, could expect similar problems. Discovery of new uranium ore had begun to decline in the late 1960s, so the antinuclear groups argued that nuclear fuel costs could be expected to rise rapidly in the future as supplies became increasingly scarce. Finally, the most optimistic estimate called for the plant to be placed in service 8 years after the order was placed. Since construction of a nuclear plant required many more years than a coal plant, the economic viability of the whole project rested on an unproved ability to forecast long-term demand growth.

UE was able to point out that there had never been a serious nuclear accident, and nuclear reactors did not pollute the air or cause acid rain, as was the case with coal. The possibility of new pollution-control requirements made the cost of coal-powered plants unpredictable as well, and the price of coal in future periods was unknown. On the other hand, UE was able to lock in the cost of nuclear fuel by signing a 21-year fuel supply contract with Westinghouse. This was important because inflation was approximately 6 percent in 1973.

Charges to customers for construction in progress are an interesting aspect of public-utility rate setting. In setting rates, public utilities were allowed to include a fair return on invested capital. Invested capital included both operating plants and plants under construction. Thus UE was allowed to charge customers each year for a fair return on the amount that had already been spent on the nuclear plants, even though they were not yet producing electricity.

Case Questions

To focus on the areas of greatest interest, ignore taxes and assume that the primary objective is to produce electricity at the lowest possible cost. Also assume a 10 percent cost of capital. Assume that either plant will last 30 years and will have no salvage value, and assume a 3-year period to build a coal-powered plant and an 8-year period to build a nuclear plant.

1. Given the figures available in 1973, compare coal to nuclear fuel in terms of cost per kilowatt to the customer after the plant is completed. Assume that the price of coal is $7.20 per ton in 1973, and increases at a rate of 6 percent a year.
2. Given the figures available in 1973, compare coal to nuclear fuel considering both electricity cost after completion and amounts paid during construction.
3. Prepare a sensitivity analysis table for the proposed nuclear plants, considering variations in construction costs and fuel prices.
4. The general market prices of coal and yellowcake will depend on supply and demand for both fuels. Coal supplies are probably well known, but price will vary with demand. The supply of uranium is probably less certain, and the demand depends on the number of plants that are built. Thus the prices of both coal and yellowcake may vary. Furthermore, the cost of a coal-powered plant can vary, depending on changes in air pollution regulation. Discuss the diversification considerations affecting the decision from the point of view of (a) UE, (b) the customers, and (c) the stockholders.
5. Given the situation prevailing in 1973, would you recommend construction of the nuclear reactors?

CALLAWAY (B)

By the end of 1977, the nuclear power situation looked substantially different. In September 1975, Westinghouse announced unilateral cancellation of its nuclear contracts, accusing producers of price fixing. By 1976, the price of yellowcake was $42 a pound and still rising. UE's average coal cost was $15.04 in 1976 and $17.86 in 1977.

In November 1976, Missouri voters approved Proposition 1, which required that the cost of the new plant not be included in the rate base until the plant was in operation. This meant that the cumulative cost of funds over the construction period would be included in the asset base when the plant was placed in service.

Cost overruns were a concern in 1977. The cost estimate for the two Callaway units was raised to $1.8 billion in 1975. By 1977, the total construction cost estimate for Callaway was $2.385 billion, plus $262 million for an initial fuel charge in unit 1. Two specific reasons for cost overruns were changes in safety requirements and the addition of the cost of funds to the cost of the project rather than charging those costs to customers during construction. Nuclear plants being constructed by other utilities had often experienced cost overruns of 100 percent or more, and large numbers of orders had been canceled. Kay Dry, an antinuclear activist, asked, "Is even a reasonable ballpark estimate [of construction cost] possible?"

The starting dates had been delayed to 1982 for unit 1, partly because of Proposition 1. Demand for electricity had also slacked off, as shown in Table IV-2. This was at least partly the result of higher energy costs, but slower demand was also affected by a regional growth rate substantially below the growth rates in other parts of the country, such as the Southwest.

Safety issues were also causing increased concern. Indeed, changing policy on the part of the Nuclear Regulatory Commission was cited as one of the chief reasons for cost overruns. Since the construction contract was on a cost-plus basis, all cost increases were absorbed by UE.

In late 1977, calls for abandonment of the Callaway project were being made. Abandonment would mean stranding the investment of $224 million that had already been made, but it would avoid the additional $2.25 billion cost that was then being estimated for completion of the two projects. Abandonment would

TABLE IV-2 UE's Electricity Demand From 1973 Through 1977

YEAR	PEAK-TIME DEMAND	PEAK-TIME CAPABILITY
1973	5,138,000 kW	6,963,000 kW
1974	5,318,000	6,660,000
1975	5,363,000	6,474,000
1976	5,582,000	6,913,000
1977	5,837,000	6,891,000

also necessitate the construction of coal-powered plants, and the cost of coal-powered plants had nearly doubled because of pollution requirements.

Abandonment now would involve minimal shutdown costs because the generators had not yet been loaded with nuclear fuel. Closing down at the end of the plant's operating life could be expensive because of the radioactivity involved. Estimates of the closing costs ranged from 5 percent to 30 percent of initial construction cost.

Case Questions

1. How would each of the following be expected to affect UE's beta?
   a. A nuclear power plant involves increased fixed costs with the objective of reducing variable (fuel) costs.
   b. Construction costs are uncertain.
   c. Fuel costs are uncertain.
2. How should the risk of a nuclear accident be factored into the decision making?
3. What is the significance of the eventual spent-fuel storage problem?
4. Considering the situation at the end of 1977, would abandonment be in the interest of customers? stockholders?
5. Suppose that contract cancellation fees must be paid to contractors. How would these affect the decision making?

Financing Decisions and Required Return

PART FIVE

In the previous chapters the financing decisions were taken as given, and the focus was on the optimal use of money for capital investments. Financing and investment decisions are often intertwined, if for no other reason than that the cost of capital is affected by the company's financing decisions. In addition, the cost of capital may depend on which assets were selected. Financing decisions are analyzed directly in this part, and relationships between financing decisions and investment decisions are examined. Both the practice and theory of financing decisions are covered, and these topics are related to capital budgeting. Topics covered in this section include cost of capital, capital structure theory and practice, dividend policy, joint investment-financing decisions, leasing, and capital rationing.

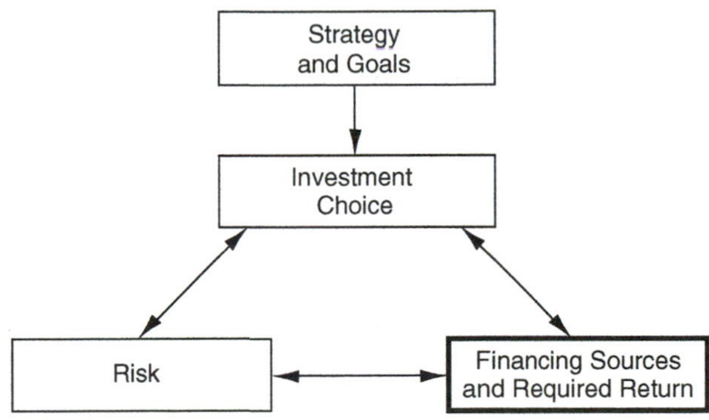

CHAPTER 16

Cost of Capital

After completing this chapter you should be able to:

- Explain to a classmate why a company must earn its cost of capital.
- Identify the typical sources of existing and additional capital.
- Calculate the after tax cost of existing debt and new debt.
- Compute the cost of existing and new preferred stock.
- Determine the cost of existing equity using the capital asset pricing model, the earnings yield model, and the dividend growth model.
- Calculate the cost of new equity using the earnings yield model and the dividend growth model.
- Discuss the advantages and disadvantages of the three possible weighting practices: book weights, market weights, and target weights.
- Analyze the liability side of an actual balance sheet to determine the market weights of each component in the capital structure.
- Describe the role that deferred taxes, accounts payable, accruals, short-term debt, leases, convertibles, and depreciation play in calculating the weights.
- Calculate the weighted average cost of capital for an actual corporation for increasing levels of investment.
- Utilize the weighted average cost of capital in judging potential capital projects and existing operations.
- Calculate the cost of capital for an international capital investment.

Opponents of nuclear power have traditionally focused their attention on safety, but some have turned their attention to the cost of capital. A nuclear power plant costs more to build than a coal- or oil-powered plant, but is expected to produce electricity at a lower operating cost per unit after construction. The pivotal question is whether the future savings justify the present cost.

The cost of capital has become a key consideration in the decision process. George Yarrow found that nuclear electricity was 29 percent less expensive than coal-produced energy at a 5 percent discount rate, but was more expensive than coal at a 10 percent discount rate.[1]

A company's **capital** structure is its mix of long-term financing sources, including debt, common stock, and preferred stock. The **cost of capital** is an average of the returns required by the various providers of capital to the business, weighted according to the proportion of capital coming from each source. The cost of capital links together many aspects of financial management because shareholder wealth is maximized through the process of arranging financing so as to minimize the cost of capital and choosing capital investments so as to maximize net present value, using the cost of capital as the required rate of return.[2]

In this chapter, the cost of capital concept is developed and procedures for estimating a company's cost of capital are explained. After learning the material in this chapter, you will be able to make a reasonable estimate of the cost of capital for an actual company. In the following chapters, the relationship between capital structure and the cost of capital is examined.

COST OF CAPITAL CONCEPT

The cost of capital is an **opportunity cost.** Money is a scarce resource, and when money is used for a capital investment, it is diverted from other productive uses. For a capital investment to be justified, the return on money used must be at least as great as the returns from alternate opportunities of equal risk. In most situations, money invested by a company must be raised from investors who could invest elsewhere. The cost of capital—the minimum acceptable rate of return—is the return that investors could earn in opportunities of equal risk. We will first apply this concept with a simple example in which the company raises money from only one source, and then develop the cost of capital when multiple sources of capital are used.

Pacific Corporation is a new company that is going to raise money only from creditors; it will have no equity. For simplicity, assume that Pacific pays no taxes. Investors who would consider loaning money to Pacific could invest their money at 10 percent in other loans of equal risk. Thus, they would be willing to loan

---

[1]"The 10% Solution," *The Economist* (July 6, 1988): 63.

[2]While the general objective is to minimize the cost of capital, strategic issues such as flexibility or the ability to withstand a price war may cause the wealth-maximizing capital structure to differ from that with the lowest average cost of funds.

money to Pacific only if they could expect a return of at least 10 percent. Managers at Pacific are considering an investment that will cost $1,000, will have a 1-year life, and will provide cash inflows of $1,150 at the end of the year. The amount the lenders would be willing to provide in exchange for a payment of $1,150 in 1 year is the present value (PV) of the $1,150:

$$PV = \$1{,}150/1.1 = \$1{,}045.45$$

In other words, Pacific could borrow $1,045.45 today in exchange for a promise to pay $1,150 in 1 year.[3] Suppose Pacific borrowed $1,045.45 and used $1,000 for the investment. The proceeds from the investment would be exactly enough to repay the loan, and the remaining $45.45 would be an immediate increase in wealth. Thus, the net present value of the investment is $45.45. The cost of capital is the return required to satisfy providers of funds, and the net present value is the amount of money investors would be willing to supply in exchange for the future cash flows from the investment, less the initial outlay.

The Weighted Average Cost of Capital Concept

In the previous example, capital was raised from only one source. However, capital is typically raised from a combination of sources in an effort to reduce the average required return. The **weighted average cost of capital** (WACC) is the rate of return that must be earned on assets in order to provide an expected return to all suppliers of funds equal to what they could expect from alternate investment opportunities of equal risk. This required return is an average of the required returns for the various sources, weighted according to the proportion of total capital raised from each source.

As an example, consider again Pacific's opportunity to invest $1,000 and receive $1,150 in 1 year. However, assume Pacific will be financed with a mix of debt and equity. Lenders require an 8 percent return while the equity holders require a 12 percent return. The equity holders require a higher return because they get paid from the money left after satisfying the creditors, so their investment is more risky. Suppose Pacific raises $1,000, with $750 from debt and $250 from equity. If we continue to assume no taxes, the return Pacific must earn to satisfy both groups is:

$$\frac{(\$750 \times .08) + (\$250 \times .12)}{\$1{,}000} = \frac{\$90}{\$1{,}000} = 9\%$$

The 9 percent required return is Pacific's weighted average cost of capital.

[3] The effective interest earned by the investors would be:

$$\frac{1{,}150 - 1{,}045.45}{1{,}045.45} = \frac{104.55}{1{,}045.45} = 10\%$$

A shorthand way to express the weighted average cost of capital is to use the formula:

$$WACC = \sum_{i=1}^{m} w_i k_i \tag{16-1}$$

where w_i is the proportion of capital coming from source i, k_i is the required rate of return for source i, and m is the number of different sources of capital used. Applying this formula to Pacific:

$$WACC = .75 \times .08 + .25 \times .12 = 9\%$$

The answer is the same as that obtained previously, but the computation is easier when there are numerous sources of capital.

The Marginal Cost of Capital Concept

In capital budgeting and cost of capital analysis, we follow the same principles used in most business analysis: we compare marginal benefits with marginal costs. The **marginal cost of capital** is the rate of return that must be earned on a new investment to satisfy investors. To illustrate the marginal cost of capital concept, suppose Pacific Corporation acquired the previously discussed $1,000 asset and the managers are now considering a new investment. The managers believe that the optimal capital structure consists of ¾ debt and ¼ equity. However, interest rates have risen so that Pacific must pay 9 percent interest on any new debt instead of the 8 percent rate being paid on existing debt. Equity holders can now expect a 16 percent return if they are to make new investments today in assets of equal risk to Pacific's stock. The marginal cost of capital is the weighted average cost of capital that must be earned on new investments:

$$WACC = .75 \times .09 + .25 \times .16 = 10.75\%$$

The old 9 percent WACC was the marginal cost of capital when the earlier investment was acquired. The marginal cost of capital increased because the general level of interest rates increased.

We should pause here to explain why the rate paid on the funds actually raised for a new capital investment may not be marginal cost of capital. Suppose managers at Pacific, which previously had $750 of debt and $250 of equity, decide to finance a new $1,000 investment entirely with debt. The higher debt ratio makes Pacific more risky, and therefore increases the required returns on both debt and equity; the required interest rate on debt jumps from 9 percent to 10 percent and the required return on equity jumps from 16 percent to 20 percent. The existing debt must be refinanced at the higher interest rate because debt covenants do not allow a debt to total assets ratio greater than .75. The amount that must be earned changes as follows:

New interest expense:	.10 × 1,750 =	$175
New required earnings for equity:	.20 × 250 =	$ 50
Total new required earnings		$225
Old interest expense:	.09 × 750 =	$ 67.50
Old required earnings for equity:	.16 × 250 =	40.00
Total old required earnings		$107.50
Increase in required earnings:	225 − 107.50 =	$117.50

The marginal cost of capital is the change in required earnings divided by the increase in total capital:

$$\text{WACC} = 117.50/1{,}000 = 11.75\%$$

Even though the interest rate paid on the new debt is only 10 percent, the marginal cost is 11.75 percent because the required return on other funds is increased by the addition of more debt. Use of the 10 percent direct borrowing cost as the cost of capital gives a false picture of the true costs from the change in financial structure.

We generally assume that the company is at its optimal debt-equity mix, and that any new capital will be raised in the same proportion as existing capital. If an increased ratio of debt to total capital would decrease the weighted average cost of capital because the company is not presently at the optimal mix, then the marginal cost of new debt might appear to be quite low. However, a new investment should not be justified by the benefits of moving to an optimal capital structure. The benefit from moving to an optimal capital structure can be had by raising more of one type of capital and using the proceeds to retire another, without making new investments.

The marginal cost of capital concept also applies if your company has funds on hand and is trying to decide whether to invest those funds or return them to the lenders and stockholders. Current market rates of return are still relevant in this situation. In the case of debt, for example, an alternative for old bonds with interest rates far below current interest rates is to buy back the old bonds at the low market price, effectively providing the company a yield to maturity[4] similar to current market interest rates. Thus, the benefit of having issued bonds when interest rates were lower can be fully realized without making a new capital investment.

Flotation costs may raise the cost of new capital a small amount above the cost of existing capital. Flotation costs are the costs associated with a new issue of debt or equity, such as the fees paid to investment bankers for handling the sale. Likewise, the administrative costs associated with buying back outstanding bonds may decrease the marginal required return necessary to justify continued use of those funds.

[4]The yield to maturity is the internal rate of return based on the current price and the stream of interest and principal payments.

COST OF CAPITAL COMPONENTS

Now that the general cost of capital principles has been developed, the next step is to determine the costs of the various components of capital so that these can be tied together in a single weighted average cost. Identification of the individual component costs is covered in this section.

Cost of Debt

If your company has no excess funds on hand and is considering new investments, the component cost of debt is the effective interest rate on new debt, adjusted for taxes. The interest rate on new debt can be estimated by talking to potential lenders and investment bankers. Alternately, the estimation can begin with observation of market interest rates on debt of similar risk such as bonds the rating agencies have assigned to the same risk class as your company's bonds. Another alternative is to use the effective interest rates earned by holders of the company's existing marketable debt.

IBM bonds maturing in 2013 pay annual interest of 7.5 percent of face value. The bonds were selling for $1,205 for every $1,000 of face value in early 2003. IBM must provide investors with a rate of return at least equal to the yield to maturity on the existing bonds if it is to sell new debt. The yield to maturity on the existing bonds can be found using the procedures discussed in Chapter 3 for finding the internal rate of return.[5] Applying the internal rate of return approach, and assuming year-end interest payments for simplicity, the yield to maturity on the IBM bond is 4.86 percent. This yield to maturity can be confirmed by noting that $\$1{,}205 = \$75\text{PVA1}_{10\text{yrs},4.86\%} + \$1{,}000/1.0486^{10}$. Investors would not be interested in buying new bonds of this company at this time unless they could expect a return of at least 4.86 percent.[6]

When a company issues new debt, there are often administrative costs, fees to investment bankers, and other flotation costs that can raise the effective interest cost. Suppose, for example, IBM issues new 10-year bonds promising annual interest of $48.60 on each $1,000 bond. Flotation costs are $25 per bond, so IBM will net only $975. The effective interest cost to IBM is the yield to maturity or internal rate of return at the $975 price. The yield to maturity at a $975 price is 5.19 percent. This can be confirmed by noting that $48.60\text{PVA1}_{10\text{yrs},5.19\%} + 1{,}000/1.0519^{10} = \$975$. Thus, the before tax cost of the new debt for IBM is 5.19 percent.

---

[5]An easily applied approximation formula can be used:

$$\begin{aligned}\text{YTM} &= [\text{Annual interest payment} + (\text{maturity value} - \text{market value})/n] \div [(\text{maturity value} + \text{market value})/2] \\ &= [75 + (1{,}000 - 1{,}205)/10] \div [(1{,}000 + 1{,}205)/2] = 4.94\%\end{aligned}$$

[6]Timing of tax payments may cause the required yield to maturity on new debt to be a bit different from the yield to maturity on existing debt. With IBM's 7.5 percent, 10-year bonds, the after tax yield to maturity (YTM*) for an investor in a 28 percent tax bracket is:

$$1{,}205 = 75(1 - .28)\text{PVA1}_{10\text{yrs},\text{YTM}^*} + [1{,}000 - (1{,}000 - 1{,}205).28]/(1 + \text{YTM}^*)^{10}$$

Solving with trial-and-error or other procedures, YTM* = 3.43 percent. For a new bond selling at par to provide the same after tax return, the interest rate must be .0343/(1 − .28) = 4.76%.

After Tax Cost of Debt

Interest expense and flotation costs are tax-deductible expenses in that they reduce taxable income. Thus, the after tax cost of existing debt (k_d) is approximately:

$$k_d = \text{YTM}\ (1 - \text{tax rate}) \qquad \textbf{(16-2)}$$

where YTM is the **yield to maturity** (effective interest rate) on existing debt. For a corporate tax rate of 35 percent and bonds with a yield to maturity of 4.86 percent, the cost of existing debt is approximately:[7]

$$k_d = .0486\ (1 - .35) = 3.16\%$$

To justify the use of funds on hand, the component cost of debt is 3.16 percent.

Flotation costs are also a tax-deductible expense, so the after tax cost of new debt (k_{nd}) is approximately:

$$k_{nd} = \text{YTM}_n\ (1 - \text{tax rate}) \qquad \textbf{(16-3)}$$

where YTM_n is the yield to maturity on the new debt, based on the net proceeds to the borrower. For a company with a 5.19 percent before-tax cost of new debt and a 35 percent marginal tax rate, the after-tax cost of new debt is approximately:[8]

$$k_{nd} = .0519\ (1 - .35) = 3.37\%$$

To justify borrowing more money, the component after tax cost of debt is 3.37 percent.[9]

---

[7]The exact after tax cost must take into consideration the timing of tax savings. For the 7.5 percent bond with 10 years until maturity, selling at $1205, the after tax cost to retire early is $1,205 + .35(1,000 – 1,205) = $1,133.25. The after tax annual interest payment avoided is $75(1 – .35) = $48.75, and the avoided principal payment in year 10 is $1,000. The discount rate that equates the avoided after tax future payments with the after tax outlay to retire the bond now is 3.29 percent. Management should not retire existing debt as long as a 3.29 percent component after tax cost of debt can be justified by investment opportunities.

[8]The timing of tax savings from flotation costs can affect the after tax cost of debt because flotation costs are paid up-front, but are amortized over the life of the bond for tax purposes. This raises the required return for IBM slightly:

Initial inflow = $1,000 – $25 = $975.00

Annual outflow = $48.60 – ($48.60 × .35) – ($25 ÷ 10).35 = $30.72

Cash outflow in year 10 to retire the bond = $1,000

The discount rate that equates these cash flows is 3.37 percent. In this case, the two approaches give differences so small that they are lost in the rounding.

[9]An alternative to adjusting the required return for flotation cost is to deduct the flotation cost as an initial cash outlay for the investment. The choice between the two approaches that assures wealth-maximizing decisions depends on the life of the company's competitive advantage, which is ultimately the source of a positive NPV. If funding is for longer than the life of the proposed capital investment, which is typically the case with equity financing, allocating all the flotation cost to the first use of those funds overstates the cost of funding for that project while understating the cost of funds for later projects. Suppose, for example, you are raising long-term funds for a 1-year investment, with the expectation of rolling over that 1-year investment indefinitely. By deducting flotation cost as a cash outflow, you are assigning all flotation costs to the first year. This may cause you to reject a series of profitable investments because the entire flotation cost for the series cannot be absorbed by the first use of funds. If you expect your competitive advantage to last for only the life of the initial investment, on the other hand, then flotation costs must be recovered over the life of that investment in order to make wealth-maximizing choices.

Cost of Preferred Stock

Preferred stock pays a fixed dividend and generally has no maturity date. The dividends are not, of course, contractual like the interest on debt. The main problems caused by a decision not to pay a preferred dividend are that the company's reputation is damaged, preferred stockholders may gain voting rights, and most preferred stock is cumulative, meaning that missed dividends must be made up before dividends can be paid to common stockholders. These problems are sufficient to keep most companies paying their preferred dividends unless they are in severe financial difficulty. The effective rate of return earned by a buyer of preferred stock is simply the dividend divided by the price. If your company has funds on hand and is facing the question of whether to invest in new projects or return money to investors, the component cost of existing preferred stock (k_p) is the return earned by an investor:

$$k_p = D_p/P_p \tag{16-4}$$

where D_p is the annual dividend per share for existing preferred stock and P_p is the price per share of existing preferred stock. This is the opportunity cost because one alternative use of available funds is the purchase of the preferred stock in the marketplace at the current price of P_p, thereby saving perpetual dividends of D_p. There is no adjustment for taxes because dividends do not result in a decrease in the company's income tax.

The effective cost to a company issuing new preferred stock is the dividend per year (D_{np}), divided by the amount the company can expect to net for a share after paying flotation costs (P_{np}). In other words, the cost of new preferred stock (k_{np}) is:

$$k_{np} = D_{np}/P_{np} \tag{16-5}$$

Example: Consolidated Edison's $5.00 preferred stock was selling for $83.01 a share in early 2003. The component cost of this preferred stock is:

$$k_p = 5.00/83.01 = 6.02\%$$

If Consolidated Edison has funds on hand, it can buy back the preferred stock in the marketplace for $83.01 a share. The $5.00 a year in dividends saved results in an opportunity cost of 6.02 percent. If Consolidated Edison needs to raise additional funds, however, the effective cost rises. In order to sell new $100 preferred stock at its par value of $100, a dividend of $6.02 per year would be required. If flotation costs for Consolidated Edison Motors will be 3 percent of new preferred stock issued, the net amount received per share will be $97. The component cost of new preferred is therefore:

$$k_{np} = 6.02/97 = 6.21\%$$

Cost of Common Stock

The principle of required return for common stock is the same as that for debt and preferred stock. The required return is an opportunity cost based on returns investors can expect from alternative investments of equal risk. For bonds and preferred stock, the current price was related to the promised series of payments in order to compute the rate of return expected by investors. However, there is no promised payment for common stockholders, and there is no direct way to observe the returns stockholders expect to earn on investments of equal risk. Thus, estimation procedures must be used.

In order to estimate the required return on common equity, it is necessary to know something about the nature of common stock itself. Common stock, like preferred stock, pays dividends. In the absence of stock repurchase, acquisition, or voluntary liquidation, the only thing shareholders will ever receive is dividends. A particular investor may receive money by selling stock to some other investor, but as a group investors receive nothing but dividends. The value of a share of stock, therefore, is the present value of the stream of future dividends. In other words:

$$P = \frac{D_1}{(1 + k_e)^1} + \frac{D_2}{(1 + k_e)^2} + \ldots \qquad (16\text{-}6)$$

where P is the price of the stock, D_t is the dividend at the end of the period t, and k_e is the required return on equity.

If the stream of future dividends were known, the discount rate that made the present value of dividends equal the stock's current price would be the investors' required return. However, future dividends are not known with certainty and in many cases are extremely difficult to predict. Various methods have been applied to overcome these problems and *estimate* the required return in different situations. The word *estimate* is emphasized because we cannot directly measure the shareholders' required return with certainty. The three most widely used estimation methods are the constant growth dividend valuation model, the earnings yield model, and the mean-variance capital asset pricing model. The appropriate method depends on the information available, and more than one method is often used as a check. The three most widely used methods are discussed here.

Constant Growth Dividend Valuation Model

In Chapter 3, we showed that if cash flows grow at a constant rate of g per period, Equation 16-6 may be reduced to:

$$P = D_1/(k_e - g) \qquad \textbf{(16-7)}$$

With a little rearrangement of terms, Equation 16-7 can be rewritten as:

$$k_e = (D_1/P) + g \qquad \textbf{(16-7a)}$$

As an example, suppose Davenport Corporation has just paid an annual dividend of \$3.50 per share, and dividends are expected to grow 4 percent a year. The dividends after one year (D_1) are therefore expected to be \$3.50 × 1.04 = \$3.64. If the stock has a current price of \$50 a share, this implies that the return expected by investors is:[10,11]

$$k_e = 3.64/50 + .04 = \underline{\underline{11.28\%}}$$

The dividend growth model analysis began with an observed price and last year's dividend, so the only item difficult to estimate is the dividend growth rate. If dividends have grown steadily in the past and there is reason to believe that pattern will continue, the historical growth rate can be used as g. Unfortunately, historical dividend growth is seldom that steady. In other cases, surveys of security analysts or published forecasts like those in *Value Line* are used to estimate g. Many public utilities survey hundreds of security analysts in preparation for rate hearings to determine analysts' estimates of dividend growth.

Another approach to estimating the dividend growth rate is based on the dividend payout ratio and the reinvestment rate. If dividends remain a constant percentage of earnings, the dividend growth rate will be:[12]

$$g = \text{return on reinvested equity} \times \text{retention rate}$$

For example, a company that retains 40 percent of earnings for reinvestment and is able to earn a return of 10 percent on the equity portion of funds reinvested in the company will have a dividend growth rate of:

$$g = .10 \times .40 = \underline{\underline{4.0\%}}$$

To apply this approach, it is necessary that the rate earned on additional equity investment in the company be known and steady, that earnings from existing investments be steady, and that the dividend payout ratio be constant. The growth rate can be estimated using Equation 16-7 only if these conditions are approximated.

There are many cases in which a company is not currently paying dividends, although dividends are expected at some future time. There are other cases in which dividends are being paid, but growth is erratic. Furthermore, there has been a trend toward paying out less in dividends and using free cash flow to buy

[10]Dividends are often paid quarterly rather than annually. Suppose, instead, that a quarterly dividend of \$0.85 has just been received and dividends are expected to grow at 1 percent a quarter. The return per quarter expected by investors is $(.85 \times 1.01)/50 + .01 = .02717$. The annual required return is then $(1.02717)^4 - 1 = 11.32\%$.

[11]If the required return is being computed 1/q of a period after the last dividend, rather than immediately after the last dividend, Equation 13-6 is rewritten $P = [D_1/(k_e - g)](1+ k_e)^{1/q}$. This equation can be solved for k by trial and error, as was done for the internal rate of return.

[12]*Proof:* Assuming that existing assets are invested at a constant rate of return, growth in earnings per share comes from reinvestment of earnings as follows:

$$EPS_{t+1} = EPS_t + \text{reinvestment rate} \times \text{retention rate} \times EPS_t$$

This equation can be rewritten $EPS_{t+1}/EPS_t - 1 = \text{reinvestment rate} \times \text{retention rate}$.

back stock instead. In these cases, it is necessary to turn to some other method to estimate the return required by common equity investors.

Earnings Yield Model

Managers sometimes use their company's earnings yield (earnings per share, price per share) as the required return on equity. The rationale for this measure is that the price per share is the amount that will be received from selling a new share and earnings per share are the amount that must be earned on the additional equity to avoid a dilution of earnings per share for the existing shareholders.

A problem with the earnings yield model is that it is based on accounting income rather than cash flow. Furthermore, it is based on earnings per share for a past period while the stock price reflects investors' expectations of future performance. For this reason, earnings yields based on early 2003 stock prices ranged from less than 2 percent for Chesapeake Energy to 100 percent for Price Communications. The earnings yield model is consistent with the cash flow approach used in the dividend growth model only if accounting earnings are the same as cash flow, and any retained earnings are reinvested at the required return on equity. If investors expect the company to have future investment opportunities with positive net present values, the earnings yield is not a good estimate of shareholders' required return.

Mean-Variance Capital Asset Pricing Model

The mean-variance capital asset pricing model approach differs from the cost of equity approaches previously discussed in that it focuses on market returns for investments of similar risk rather than investor response to a particular security. Thus, it can be used when earnings and dividends are unstable and when the stock is not publicly traded so there is no market price. As shown in Chapter 14, the mean-variance capital asset pricing model leads to the conclusion that the required return on equity is:

$$k_e = R_f + \beta_{s,m}(R_m - R_f) \tag{16-8}$$

where R_f is the current interest rate on risk-free investments; R_m is the expected return for investments in general, commonly referred to as expected return for the market portfolio; $\beta_{s,m}$ is the stock's beta (systematic risk) in relation to the market portfolio; and $R_m - R_f$ is therefore the risk premium for investments in general. The risk premium for a particular investment is then its beta multiplied by the general market risk premium.

Risk-free interest rates are widely published, with the interest rates on U.S. government bonds being commonly used as the risk-free rate. Betas for the stocks of publicly traded companies are computed using historical data and published in various investment advisory services such as *Value Line.* Alternately, betas can be computed directly from historical data as illustrated in Chapter 14. If the company's stock is not publicly traded so that there is no market price to use in computing holding period returns, betas for publicly traded companies believed to have similar risk characteristics can be used. Expected return for investments in general (R_m) is estimated from historical returns or surveys of investor expectations, as discussed in Chapter 14.

Example: The stock of Harley Davidson had a beta of 1.20, according to *Value Line.* The interest rate on long-term U.S. government bonds was 6 percent, and the estimated market risk premium was 5 percent. The required return for equity investors of Harley Davidson was therefore:

$$k_e = .06 + 1.20(.05) = \underline{\underline{12.00\%}}$$

By way of comparison, the required return under these conditions for a stock of average risk would be:

$$k_e = .06 + 1.00(.05) = \underline{\underline{11.00\%}}$$

While CAPM avoids the problems associated with earnings yield and dividend growth models, it comes with its own set of problems. Difficulties in estimating the required return for the market portfolio were discussed in Chapter 14. In addition, capital investment analysis creates problems in measurement of beta. Betas for your own company or comparable companies are usually estimated using monthly or annual holding period returns. These are not always close estimates of the betas of capital investments for which cash flow may occur many years in the future. One fact that leads to potential inaccuracy is that long-term government bonds, which are generally used as the risk-free rate for a capital investment, are themselves both risky and positively correlated with the market portfolio when returns are measured for short periods because their price fluctuates with changes in the general level of interest rates. One way around these problems is to compute the beta for a future cash flow by specifying states of nature, then estimating both returns for the market portfolio and cash flows from the project in each state of nature. This approach is, however, time consuming and therefore expensive.[13]

These various methods of estimating the cost of common equity exist primarily because it is impossible to observe directly the return investors are expecting from investments of similar risk. The choice of an appropriate measure in a particular situation depends primarily on the type of information that is available. In public utility rate cases, where cost of equity is critically important and decision making is done in public, the traditional method has been the dividend growth model, but the mean-variance capital asset pricing model and new methods such as the arbitrage pricing model have been used as well. With further research efforts, we will probably improve our ability to estimate the required return on equity, with or without direct observation of investor expectations.

[13]Lawrence Booth, "Estimating the Equity Risk Premium and Equity Costs: New Ways of Looking at Old Data," *Journal of Applied Corporate Finance* 12 (Spring 1999): 100–112; and Justin Pettit, "Corporate Capital Costs: A Practitioner's Guide," *Journal of Applied Corporate Finance* 12 (Spring 1999):113–120.

Cost of Existing Equity (Retained Earnings)

Once the return required by investors is determined, this return must be converted to a return required by the company to satisfy investors. The equity investors' required return is often used directly as the component cost of the equity portion of existing funds. Some authors, however, argue that there is an important tax issue involved. Equity funds on hand for investment often arise from retained earnings. If earnings are paid out in the form of dividends, many investors must pay taxes on the dividends, and therefore have less money to use or invest. If the earnings are reinvested internally instead of being paid out, the increase in earnings may cause the stock price to rise, and the gain would be taxed only when the stock was sold. Some authors suggest that the cost of existing equity funds is therefore the return required by shareholders, multiplied by (1 – the marginal tax rate of the average shareholder).

We estimated the required return of Harley Davidson shareholders to be 12 percent. If the average shareholder were in a 28 percent tax bracket, the opportunity cost of existing equity (k_e) using this approach would be:

$$k_e = .1200(1 - .28) = \underline{\underline{8.64\%}}$$

A problem with basing the opportunity cost of existing equity on the shareholders' tax rates is that tax rates vary among shareholders. Charitable endowment funds, pension funds, IRA accounts, and other personal pension accounts invest in common stock and pay no income tax. Stocks also are held by people in low marginal tax brackets, including retirees and young people who received stock as gifts. Therefore, taxes on dividend income are minimal or nonexistent for many shareholders. Furthermore, companies increasingly use retained earnings to buy back stock rather than paying dividends, thereby returning money to shareholders without the tax consequences of dividend payments. Consequently, most authors suggest the use of the equity investors' required return as the cost of existing equity capital, without adjustment for investors' tax rates.

Some authors use the term **cost of retained earnings** rather than cost of existing equity. One reason they use this terminology is that the existing equity choice facing a company is often between reinvesting this year's earnings and paying them out as dividends. However, companies without good investment opportunities can buy back common stock or even liquidate completely, so the term **existing equity** gives a more comprehensive view of the choices you face as a manager.

On the balance sheet, the common equity account is often broken into three categories: common stock, paid-in capital in excess of par, and retained earnings. These divisions exist for accounting purposes, but all common equity is money of the common stockholders being used in the company. Retained earnings do not have an opportunity cost different from the opportunity costs of shareholders' funds categorized in other common equity accounts.

Cost of New Equity

If your company has no funds available and must turn to outside sources, the return earned must be higher than that required by investors in order to cover flotation costs and still provide investors with their required return.

If all earnings are being paid out in the form of dividends, a commonly used formula for the cost of new common equity is:

$$K_{ne} = k_e/(1 - f) \quad \textbf{(16-9)}$$

where f is flotation cost as a percent of market price. Suppose, for example, Harley Davidson was going to sell new common stock and investors had a required return of 12 percent. If the stock was selling at $30 a share and the company would receive a net amount per share of only $27 from the sale of a new issue, the percentage flotation cost, f, would be 3/30 = .10 and the cost of new equity would be:

$$k_{ne} = .1200/(1 - .10) = \underline{\underline{13.33\%}}$$

If some earnings are being retained, resulting in anticipated dividend growth, the impact of flotation costs is decreased. This decrease occurs because the total amount of equity capital made available through the new issue includes both the money raised directly through the new issue and the retention of earnings on that money. The cost of new equity with dividend growth anticipated declines to:[14]

$$k_{ne} = D_1/[P(1 - f)] + g \quad \textbf{(16-10)}$$

Again taking Harley Davidson as an example, the annual dividend was $0.16 a share, and investors had a required return of 12 percent. If the stock price was $30, Equation 16-7a could be used to estimate an implied growth rate:

$$.1200 = 0.16(1 + g)/30 + g\text{; therefore } g = .1141$$

The estimated cost of new equity would therefore be:

$$k_{ne} = 0.16(1.1141)/[30(1 - .10)] + .1141 = \underline{\underline{12.07\%}}$$

---

[14]Each of these formulas for the cost of new equity depends on the assumption that cash inflows from the investment, other than the cash flows paid out as dividends, can be reinvested at k_{ne}. With Equation 16-9, this assumption is satisfied if the investment is a perpetuity. With Equation 16-10, this assumption is justified if a series of new investment opportunities paying k_{ne} is anticipated. To take another extreme position, assume the capital investment being financed has only a 1-year life, after which the funds must be invested at k_e. To justify selling new equity in this case, k_{ne} must equal $(1+ k_e)/(1 - f) - 1$ so that the flotation cost is completely recovered in the first year. Thus, the precise cost of new equity depends on the life of the investment being considered and investment opportunities available in the future.

WEIGHTS FOR THE WEIGHTED AVERAGE COST

To combine the previously determined component costs in a weighted average cost of capital, it is necessary to determine what percentage of total capital comes from each source. Assuming, for the moment, that the company is at what its managers consider to be its optimal capital structure (optimal mix of debt, equity, and other capital sources), the company will then continue to raise money in the same proportions. There will probably be small variations from these proportions because of economies of scale in raising money; if General Electric needs $100,000, the company will not raise that small amount with combination of debt and equity issues because the flotation costs would exceed the amount raised. However, small movements around the optimal capital structure need not be of concern for the purpose of our analysis.

Example: Tyler Corporation has no excess funds on hand. It maintains what management judges to be an optimal capital structure of 40 percent long-term debt, 10 percent preferred stock, and 50 percent common equity. The after tax costs of new funds in these three categories are 8 percent, 12 percent, and 15 percent, respectively. The proportion of the optimal capital structure represented by each source is multiplied by the cost of that source in determining a cost of capital. Using Equation 16-1, the weighted average cost of capital is therefore:

$$\text{WACC} = (.40 \times .08) + (.10 \times .12) + (.50 \times .15) = 11.9\%$$

The same computation is often set up in table form for convenience:

SOURCE	WEIGHT (PROPORTION)	COST	WEIGHTED COST
Debt	.40	.08	.032
Preferred Stock	.10	.12	.012
Common Stock	.50	.15	.075
Weighted average cost			.119

A choice must be made between weights (proportions) based on market values and weights based on the book values of capital sources. The conclusion that net present value measures the increase in shareholder wealth is based on the assumption that the capital structure remains unchanged; that is, the *value* of each component of capital remains a constant proportion of the total *value* of capital. The total value of capital, in turn, is the present value of future cash flows from the company's investments, and the value of each component of capital is then the present value of cash flows to that component. If markets are efficient, market values will equal present values of cash flows. Book values, on the other hand, represent historical cost. Therefore, market values appear to be a superior basis for developing weights.

Despite this conclusion, many companies use book value weights for what they view as practical considerations. Market weights change on an hourly basis as stock prices change, and managers like to fix their eyes on more stable targets. Book weights, although inconsistent with the theoretical justification for net present value, are stable.

The market values of stocks and bonds can generally be determined by reference to the financial press. For untraded bonds or for long-term debt not in the form of marketable securities, the market value can be estimated by finding the present value of remaining principal and interest payments, discounted at the yield to maturity for similar instruments that are publicly traded, possibly increasing the required interest somewhat to compensate investors for lack of marketability. Current maturities of long-term debt, which appear in the current liabilities section of the balance sheet, would generally be considered part of the debt capital used to finance fixed assets, as would the current portion of capital lease obligations.

The market value of common stock is the value of the common stockholders' total claims, which equals the number of shares outstanding, multiplied by the market price per share. The shareholders' claims are represented on the balance sheet by several separate accounts, including common stock, paid-in capital in excess of par, and retained earnings. The various common stock accounts do not, however, have separate values and costs in the cost of capital analysis. For untraded common stock, a value estimate can be made by such methods as computing the present value of the expected stream of future dividends at the required return on equity or referral to the price-earnings ratios of traded stocks of similar companies.

If a company is not at its optimal capital structure, but is in the process of working toward that target structure, then it makes sense to evaluate new projects with a cost of capital as it will be in the target capital structure. The target capital structure is used to determine the weights, and the costs of the various components are adjusted for estimates of what they will be when the optimal capital structure is realized.

MARGINAL COST OF CAPITAL SCHEDULE

As defined earlier in this chapter, the marginal cost of capital is the weighted average cost, assuming that new funds used for the investment will be in the same proportion as the company's existing capital structure. However, the marginal cost depends on whether internally generated funds are being used or capital is being raised from outside sources. If internally generated funds are adequate for all attractive investments, the marginal cost is the weighted average cost of existing funds. If funds must be raised externally, then flotation cost must be recognized in computing weighted average cost.

Example: Corvallis Corporation maintains a capital structure of 60 percent debt and 40 percent equity. The component costs of capital are as follows:

	DEBT	EQUITY
Cost of existing funds	6%	14%
Cost of new funds	7%	16%

The managers anticipate having \$50,000 of income available for reinvestment in the business over the next year. Depreciation, a noncash expense, of \$30,000 will be deducted in computing income, so the managers anticipate a total of \$80,000 in internally generated funds.

If Corvallis makes only \$30,000 of new capital investments, no new capital will be raised, and the marginal cost of capital will be the weighted average cost of existing funds:

$$WACC_1 = .6 \times .06 + .4 \times .14 = \underline{\underline{9.2\%}}$$

If only \$30,000 is invested, all income can be paid out as dividends, and the proportions of debt and equity in the capital structure will remain unchanged.

If the managers decide to invest more than \$30,000, the company will not retain all income. To maintain the optimal capital structure, though, the company must raise 60¢ of debt for each 40¢ of income retained. The total amount of additional capital the company can raise while using retained earnings for the equity portion is (where W_e is equity as a proportion of total funds):

$$\text{New retained earnings}/W_e = \$50{,}000/.4 = \underline{\underline{\$125{,}000}}$$

The weighted average cost in this range is based on the cost of *new* debt and *existing* equity:

$$WACC_2 = .6 \times .07 + .4 \times .14 = 9.8\%$$

Thus, the marginal cost of the first \$30,000 of investment capital is 9.2 percent, and the marginal cost of the next \$125,000 (\$75,000 of debt + \$50,000 of retained earnings) is 9.8 percent. Beyond this, both new debt and new equity must be raised, and the weighted average cost becomes:

$$WACC_3 = .6 \times .07 + .4 \times .16 = \underline{\underline{10.6\%}}$$

This schedule of costs can be plotted graphically as a marginal cost of capital schedule, which is illustrated in Figure 16-1. The marginal cost of capital schedule in Figure 16-1 is shown as stable at 10.6 percent for all amounts above \$155,000. It is possible that the cost would rise further if unusually large amounts of money were raised and this lead investors to perceive Corvallis as more risky because of its rapid growth.

An investment opportunity schedule for Corvallis is also shown in Figure 16-1. To simplify the discussion of investment opportunities, we assume for the moment that there are no mutually exclusive projects, and no multiple internal rate of return projects. We also assume that all projects are small. With these assumptions, all investments with internal rates of return above the weighted av-

FIGURE 16-1 Marginal Cost of Capital and Investment Opportunity Schedules
This figure shows a rising cost of capital schedule based on use of internal and external funds. The investment opportunity schedule represents the internal rates of return available on capital investments.

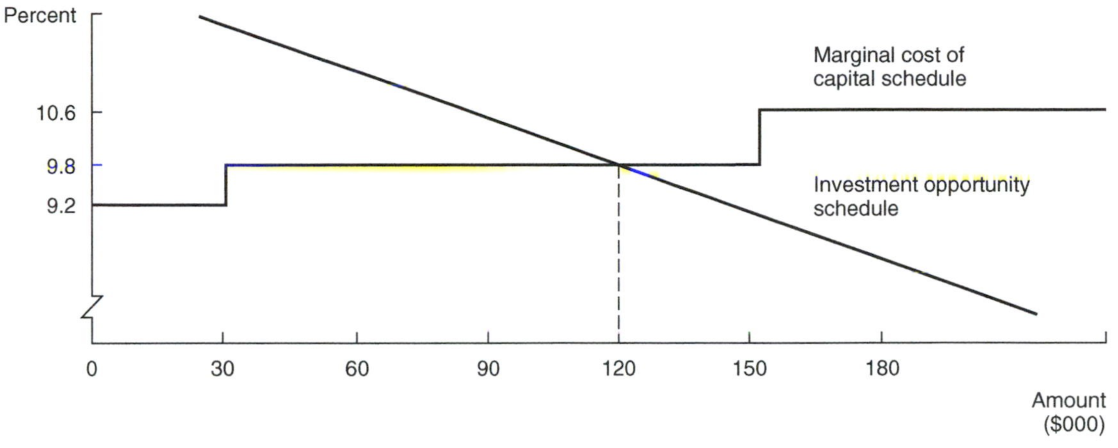

erage cost of capital will be accepted. We can therefore use the internal rate of return to define the investment opportunity schedule, as illustrated in Figure 16-1. The downward sloping investment opportunity curve reflects the fact that Corvallis has a few projects that will earn very high returns, but that as the company seeks to invest more and more, it must accept projects with ever-lower returns. It is important to note that the company invests up to the point where the marginal return on the next available project does not meet the cost of capital. If the company were to invest up to the point where the average return equaled the cost of capital, it would be accepting projects with returns below the marginal cost of capital and would thereby destroy the positive net present values created by its best projects.

In this case, the company has $120,000 of potential projects with internal rates of return above the 9.8 percent marginal cost of capital. Those projects will be accepted. Corvallis would finance the $120,000 by first using $30,000 of internally generated funds other than income. The remaining $90,000 can be funded with retained earnings of .4 × $90,000 = $ 36,000, and by issuing new debt in the amount of $54,000.

To provide an indication of the actual sizes of the steps in a marginal cost of capital schedule, Table 16-1 summarizes flotation costs as a percent of issue size. Because percentage issue costs decline as the size of the issue increases, the sizes of the steps will be inversely related to the size of the company.

TABLE 16-1 Flotation Costs as a Percent of Issue

This table shows flotation costs as a percent of issue, and therefore gives an indication of the sizes of steps in the weighted average cost of capital schedule. Total flotation costs include the underwriter's commission and other expenses, such as legal fees.

SIZE OF ISSUE (IN $ MILLIONS)	BONDS	PREFERRED STOCK	COMMON STOCK
0.0–0.5			23.7
0.6–0.9			20.9
1.0–1.9			16.9
2.0–4.9	6.2		12.4
5.0–9.9	3.2	2.6	8.1
10.0–19.9	1.9	1.8	5.9
20.0–49.9	1.4	1.7	4.6
50.0–99.9			4.2
100 and over	1.1	1.1	3.5

SOME ADDITIONAL ISSUES IN COST OF CAPITAL ANALYSIS

Deferred Taxes

Deferred taxes are often a substantial item on the liability side of the balance sheet, and may initially appear to be a cost-free source of funds with which to acquire new investments. Upon examination, however, it becomes clear that deferred taxes are *not* a source of investment capital. Deferred taxes appear on the balance sheet primarily because assets are being depreciated less rapidly for public reporting purposes than for tax purposes. These differences in depreciation cause income reported to the public to exceed income used by the Internal Revenue Service to determine the tax liability. The income tax expense on the income statement is the tax that would have been paid if publicly reported income was what the government taxed. The excess of the income tax expense on the income statement over the income tax actually paid to the government is treated as an addition to the deferred tax liability on the balance sheet. Deferred tax reflects the fact that if no new assets are acquired the income reported to the government will eventually be higher than the income reported to the public, and consequently, the income tax paid will be greater than the tax expense shown on the income statement.

For capital budgeting, we use projected cash flows, not income statement numbers. To forecast cash flows, we deduct taxes that will be paid, not the income tax expense on the public financial statements. Thus, the deferred tax, being nothing but a means of reconciling the financial statements with the actual cash flows, is not a source of cash with which to acquire capital investments.

Accounts Payable and Accrued Expenses

The logic applied to accounts payable, accrued expenses, and other spontaneous current liabilities is similar to that for deferred taxes. If the capital investment analysis is carried out on a cash flow basis, the payment of wages, material costs, and so on are recognized for capital investment analysis purposes when the payments are made, not when the liabilities are incurred. An account payable or an accrued expense is a forewarning that a cash payment is required, not a source of funds for making cash payments.

Short-term Debt

Short-term debt is a potential source of confusion and controversy in determining a cost of capital. Short-term borrowing may be used to meet temporary needs, such as a seasonal inventory buildup, or it may be used as permanent funding. In the latter case, the company finances part of its permanent needs with what is technically short-term debt, hoping thereby to reduce overall financing costs. Some companies, for example, borrow in the commercial paper market, with each individual issue of commercial paper maturing within 9 months and being repaid with the proceeds of a new issue. In other cases, companies may borrow from banks on a demand basis, but with the loans actually remaining outstanding for years even though they are technically callable on a moment's notice.

When short-term debt is used as permanent financing, it is clearly part of the company's permanent capital in substance, if not in form, and should be treated like other long-term debt in the cost of capital analysis. A decision to finance a long-term investment with short-term funds is a decision to speculate on interest rate movements. A long-term investment that is not profitable when financed with long-term sources of funds should not be justified by hopes of successful speculation on interest rate movements. After all, a manager with the exceedingly rare ability to forecast interest rates over the life of a capital investment can profit from that ability by trading in financial futures, without being distracted by capital investments. A simple and reasonable approach is to carry out capital budgeting assuming long-term investment will be financed from long-term sources of funds, and then make a separate decision about whether to speculate on interest rate movements.

When short-term borrowing is actually used for short-term needs, such as seasonal inventory buildups, the problem is a little more difficult. This financing is not part of the company's permanent capital, but the cost must be recognized somewhere in the analysis of a capital investment. One approach is to forecast the amount of short-term borrowing that will be used for a particular investment's seasonal working capital buildups, and compute net cash flow to capital after deducting cash flows to (or adding cash flows from) short-term creditors. This is appropriate if the short-term debt does not decrease the optimal amount of long-term debt in the capital structure.

A second possible approach to recognizing temporary short-term debt is to determine the average amount outstanding over the year and use that as an amount of debt, to be added to any long-term debt to arrive at total debt. This latter approach can be justified if the average amount of short-term debt directly decreases the optimal amount of long-term debt in the capital structure.

Leases

Leases are frequently used as an alternative to debt. Instead of signing a loan agreement calling for a fixed series of principal and interest payments, the company signs a lease agreement calling for a fixed series of lease payments over all or most of the asset's life. Accountants recognize the similarity of leasing and borrowing by classifying those leases that are close substitutes for borrowing as **financial leases,**[15] also called **capital leases,** and requiring the present values of the lease payments for those leases to appear as assets and long-term liabilities on the balance sheet. If a lease has the same economic consequences as debt, the present value of contractual lease payments should be treated as part of the long-term debt in cost of capital analysis as well. As a practical matter, the present value of lease payments appears on the balance sheet. As with debt, it is necessary to include the current portion of the lease obligation as well as the present value of payments on operating and capital leases that are due more than a year in the future.

The effective rate of return for a new lease contract can be found by computing an internal rate of return, with the lease payments being outflows and the avoided purchase price of the asset being a benefit. The effective rate of return is typically very close to that of the company's other long-term debt. For an existing lease, it is generally assumed that the required return (k_d) is the same as that for the long-term debt. The present value of the lease payments, discounted at the yield to maturity of existing debt, may be used as a substitute for the market value of the lease payments in determining weights for the weighted average cost of capital. Other aspects of lease analysis are discussed in Chapter 21.

Convertibles

Convertible bonds and convertible preferred stock can be exchanged for a specified number of shares of common stock at the option of the holder. These securities are effectively combinations of fixed-income securities and options. These securities, and their cost of capital implications, were examined using the option pricing models discussed in Chapter 15. A simpler approach is to estimate the market value of the convertible security without the conversion feature, then assume that the difference between market value and value as a nonconvertible security is an option investment.

---

[15]Financial leases are discussed in Chapter 21.

Example: Excel Corporation has sold 5-year 7 percent bonds, convertible to ten shares of common stock. The bonds are selling for $1,160, or $160 over their par value. The interest rate on bonds of this risk level is 8 percent, so the value as a nonconvertible bond is:

$$\$70PVA1_{5yrs,8\%} + \$1{,}000/1.08^5 = \underline{\underline{\$960}}$$

Thus, each bond represents a $960 pure debt instrument and ten options, each priced at ($1,160 – $960)/10 = $20. For computation of the weighted average cost of capital, the $960 is added to the market value of debt, at a before tax cost of 8 percent, and the $200 is added to the market value of a source of funding category called **options.**

The options have an exercise price of $100 each since an investor will have the choice of receiving the $1,000 bond value or ten shares of stock at maturity. Analysts estimate that there is a .7 probability that Excel's stock will be selling above $100 five years from now, and the expected value of the stock, *if it is selling above $100,* is $165. The implied expected payoff and expected return for each option is:

$$E(\text{Payoff}) = .7 \times (\$165 - \$100) = \$45.50$$

$$E(\text{Return}) = (45.50/20.00)^{1/5} - 1 = 17.87\%$$

Therefore, the capital components include an item called options, valued at $200 per bond, with a required return of 17.87 percent.

Depreciation-Generated Funds

A simple approximation to cash flow from operations is net income plus depreciation. Use of this form of cash flow approximation in forecasting benefits of capital investments often leads to controversy with regard to the role of depreciation and the cost of so-called depreciation-generated funds. If cash flows from operations exceed income, it is because assets have decreased or spontaneous liabilities have increased, and depreciation is just one of the ways in which the value of assets can decrease. Thus, there is nothing unique about depreciation-generated funds. It would be more appropriate to talk in general about "internally generated funds in excess of earnings," which can arise from decreases in assets or increases in spontaneous liabilities. These funds are simply existing funds available for reinvestment and have a cost equal to the weighted average cost of existing funds.

COSTS OF CAPITAL FOR INTERNATIONAL CAPITAL INVESTMENTS

A general principle of capital investment analysis is that the discount rate should reflect the marginal cost of capital, which is affected by characteristics of the company and may be affected by the characteristics of that particular project. International investments create different risks and may also create different investment opportunities. Both of these factors must be considered in the evaluation of international capital investments.

The cash flow from a foreign investment must be denominated in some currency, and the cost of capital should be denominated in the same currency. Chapter 14 provided guidelines for using the CAPM to compute the cost of equity for a foreign investment. We will assume here that the cost of equity has been determined in the manner suggested, and focus on developing the weighted average cost of capital.

In the simplest case, there is no difference in the cost of capital. Suppose, for example, that Barry Manufacturing wants to build an overseas factory to reduce production costs for its U.S. and global markets. It will fund the project in the United States, using the same mix of debt and equity it uses for its domestic projects. The systematic risk to Barry has to do with demand for its product in the U.S. and global markets, and is not different from the systematic risk of domestic production. There may be risks of government collapse and fluctuations in the value of Rutania's currency, but those are unsystematic risks and can be handled by adjusting expected cash flows for the probability of country collapse. Thus, the cost of capital in this international investment is the same as for domestic investment.

To add a complication, suppose Barry now decides to build a factory in another country for the purpose of selling in that country. The project will still be funded in the United States with the same mix of debt and equity used for domestic products. The cost of debt will not change in this case because Barry has sufficient reserves that its debt is very highly rated. The cost of equity will probably change, depending on the volatility of the target country, and can be computed using the methods discussed in Chapter 14. The cost of capital is then computed using the same weights and cost of debt used for domestic investments, but with a different cost of equity.

To add another complication, Barry will now finance the plant with a combination of equity raised in the United States. and debt raised in the target country. The reason for this borrowing is that the government of the target country will provide incentives in the form of cheap financing for a higher percentage of the cost of the plant than Barry would normally borrow. Since sales will be in the target country, the cost of equity must reflect that systematic risk, as discussed in Chapter 14. The cost of equity must also be adjusted for the higher beta that would result from a high debt to equity ratio. Like the cost of equity, the cost of debt must be converted to a dollar-denominated cost. The cost of capital weights then reflect the funding proportions for this project.

The equity residual method, discussed in more detail in Chapter 20, is an efficient way to handle projects with a mix of international funding. With the equity residual method, we compute the project's cash flow from and to the common stockholders. We would, for example, deduct the amount borrowed from the initial outlay to compute the equity investment. We would then deduct principal payments and after tax interest payments from annual cash flows to arrive at cash flows to stockholders. We would compute the present value of the equity cash flows at the cost of equity, which reflects the required return on equity for the project, as discussed in Chapter 14.[16]

Example: Barry manufacturing wishes to build a factory in Rutania, for the purpose of selling its products in Rutania. The factory will cost 38 million Rutanian Crowns, and the exchange ratio is currently 2 Crowns per dollar. The project will be funded with a 30-million Crown loan from the Rutanian government, financed at 3 percent interest and denominated in Crowns. Crown cash flow, after deducting debt repayment and after tax interest expense is 3 million Crowns a year for 5 years. The exchange rate has been stable, so the expected dollar annual cash flow is then $1,500,000 from an initial outlay of $4 million dollars. Using the methods explained in Chapter 14, Barry estimates the cost of equity for this international investment to be 18 percent. The equity residual NPV is then:

$$\$1{,}500{,}000\text{PVA1}_{5\text{yrs},18\%} - \$4{,}000{,}000 = \$690{,}756$$

A COMPREHENSIVE EXAMPLE

The balance sheet of Toys "R" Us is summarized in Table 16-2.[17] Deferred liabilities, such as deferred taxes, can be ignored because they reconcile reported income with cash flow and, thus, do not constitute sources of funds for capital

[16]For additional reading, see Thomas J. O'Brien, "The Global CAPM and a Firm's Cost of Capital in Different Currencies," *Journal of Applied Corporate Finance* 12 (Fall 1999): 73–79; Tom Keck, Erig Levengood, and Al Longfield, "Using Discounted Cash Flow Analysis in an International Setting: A Survey of Issues in Modeling the Cost of Capital," *Journal of Applied Corporate Finance* 11 (Fall 1998) 82–99; Ronald M. Schramm and Henry N. Wang, "Measuring the Cost of Capital in an International CAPM Framework," *Journal of Applied Corporate Finance* 12 (Fall 1999): 8–25; and Rene Stulz, "Globalization, Corporate Finance, and the Cost of Capital," *Journal of Applied Corporate Finance* 12 (Fall 1999): 63–72.

[17]Estimates in this example were prepared by the author from publicly available information and do not necessarily reflect estimates by Toys "R" Us management.

TABLE 16-2 Summary of the Balance Sheet of Toys "R" Us, Inc. (dollar figures are in millions)

Current liabilities	$1,588
Deferred taxes	176
Long-term debt	660
Obligation under capital leases*	10
Common stock, including excess over par value	345
Retained earnings	2,530
Translation adjustments	14
Total common stockholders' equity	2,889
Total liabilities and stockholders' equity	$5,323

*In this case the obligation under capital leases is such a very small source of funding that it is ignored. When it is material, it should be included both in the cost of funding and in the weighting as described earlier in the chapter.

investment. Likewise, the current liabilities can be ignored because an examination of the details of the financial report did not reveal any substantial amount of short-term borrowing that is effectively permanent. Only the costs of long-term debt, leases, and common equity are included in the weighted average cost of capital.

An examination of the footnotes reveals that the average maturity of the long-term debt is approximately 20 years and the average coupon interest rate on the long-term debt is approximately 8.22 percent.[18] The average yield to maturity on the company's bonds, found by checking the current financial press, was approximately 7.23 percent. At the then-prevailing 34 percent marginal tax rate, this implies an after tax cost of debt of:

$$k_d = .0723\,(1 - .34) = \underline{\underline{4.77\%}}$$

For a typical 20-year, 8.22 percent, \$1,000 bond paying interest annually (for simplicity) and providing a yield to maturity of 7.23 percent, the price will be the present value of the principal and interest payments, discounted at 7.23 percent: $\$82.20 PVA1_{20yrs,7.23\%} + \$1{,}000/1.0723^{20} = \underline{\$1{,}103}$.

In other words, the debt has a market value equal to 110.3 percent of its book value, or $1.103 \times \$660 = \underline{\$728 \text{ million}}$.

According to *Value Line Investment Services,* the beta of Toys "R" Us common stock was 1.35. The risk-free rate, represented by U.S. Treasury bonds, was approximately 6 percent. Using a market risk premium estimate of 5 percent,[19] the required return on equity can be estimated with the mean-variance capital asset pricing model to be:

$$k_e = .06 + 1.35(.05) = \underline{\underline{12.75\%}}$$

The market price per share of common stock was \$40. With 298 million shares outstanding, the total market value of the equity would therefore be $\$40 \times 298 \text{ million} = \underline{\$11{,}920 \text{ million}}$.

The weighted average cost of *existing* capital for Toys "R" Us would therefore be determined as follows:

SOURCE	MARKET VALUE	WEIGHT (PROPORTION)	REQUIRED RETURN	WEIGHTED COST
Debt	728	.0576	.0477	.0027
Equity	11,920	.9424	.1275	.1202
Weighted average cost of existing capital ($WACC_1$) =				.1229 or 12.29%

[18]It is becoming more common to disclose the fair market value of the outstanding long-term debt in the footnotes to the financial statements. If it is disclosed, you may not have to recalculate the market value if conditions have not changed since the balance sheet date.

[19]See Chapter 14 for a discussion of risk premiums.

If Toys "R" Us were to raise additional outside capital, the company would face flotation costs. If debt flotation costs are 2.25 percent, this raises the before tax cost of new debt to 7.45 percent, for an after tax cost of new debt of .0745(1 – .34) = 4.92 percent.

Assume that after flotation costs the cost for new equity is 13.48 percent. Toys "R" Us has never paid a dividend and is not expected to in the near future given the pool of projects available to management.

The Toys "R" Us statement of cash flows showed that $136 million in addition to income was generated from operations—primarily from decreases in asset values through depreciation. The required return for these $136 million of internally generated funds is the weighted average cost of existing capital: 12.29 percent. We assume a similar amount available in the upcoming year.

Toys "R" Us also had an income of $437 million, with nothing paid out in the form of dividends. If the same pattern continued over the next year, the company would have $437 million of retained earnings to reinvest. This equity would be matched with an amount of debt so that equity would remain 94.24 percent of total capital. The amount of new capital that can be supported using retained earnings as the equity portion is:

$$\text{Retained earnings} = .9424 \times \text{new capital}$$

$$\text{New capital} = \text{retained earnings}/.9424 = \$437/.9424 = \underline{\underline{\$464 \text{ million}}}$$

In this range, the required return on equity is the cost of existing equity, but the required return on debt is the cost of new debt. The weighted average cost of capital (WACC) for this $464 million is therefore:

$$\text{WACC}_2 = .0576 \times .0492 + .9424 \times .1275 = \underline{\underline{12.30\%}}$$

If the company wants to expand beyond this point, both debt and equity must be raised externally. The weighted average cost of capital then becomes:

$$\text{WACC}_3 = .0576 \times .0492 + .9424 \times .1348 = \underline{\underline{12.99\%}}$$

Summarizing, Toys "R" Us' marginal cost of capital schedule is as follows:

AMOUNT	FIRST $136 MILLION	NEXT $464 MILLION	ADDITIONAL CAPITAL
Cost	12.29%	12.30%	12.99%

Assume Toys "R" Us has the following investment opportunities available:[20]

[20] To justify a simple ranking according to internal rate of return, we again assume that each investment has only one internal rate of return and that there are no mutually exclusive investments.

INVESTMENT	A	B	C	D	E
Cost ($ millions)	300	150	125	20	200
Internal rate of return	14.25%	14.00%	12.75%	12.50%	12.40%

Figure 16-2 summarizes the marginal cost of capital schedule and investment opportunity schedule for Toys "R" Us. Given this hypothetical investment opportunity set, Toys "R" Us would maximize value for the shareholders by investing in projects A, B, C, and D. The marginal cost of capital that these projects must satisfy is therefore $WACC_2$ = 12.30 percent.

FIGURE 16.2 Marginal Cost of Capital and Hypothetical Investment Opportunity Schedule for Toys "R" Us

The cost of capital schedule is estimated from publicly available data, and the investment opportunity schedule is hypothetical. In this case, Toys "R" Us would invest $595 million. Additional investment would require acceptance of investments with negative net present values when evaluated at the marginal cost of capital.

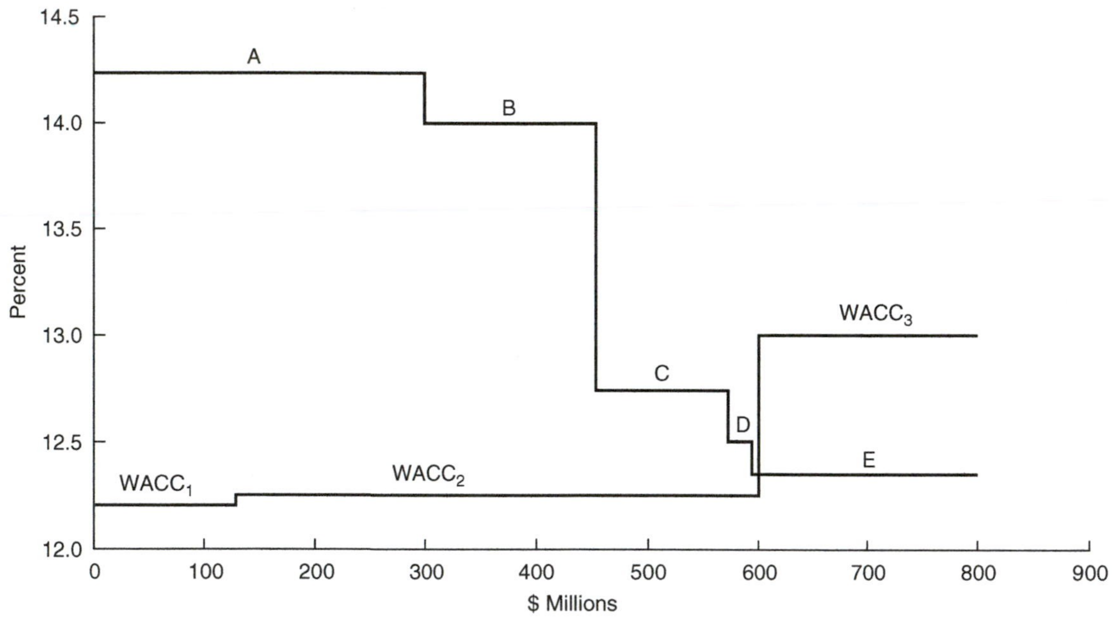

SUMMARY

The cost of capital is an **opportunity cost,** determined by the returns that could be expected by investors from other investments of equal risk. Since companies typically raise money through both debt and equity, the cost of capital is a weighted average of the costs of these various sources.

The **marginal cost of capital** is the cost of the next dollar invested: It is the change in after tax required payment to keep all providers of capital satisfied, divided by the change in total capital invested. Assuming that the company is at its target capital structure and that the target capital structure is measured in terms of the market value of each form of capital in proportion to the total, the marginal cost of capital is a weighted average of the costs of the various components used. If an investment has a positive net present value when evaluated at the marginal cost of capital, then that investment will increase the wealth of the shareholders.

In order to determine the marginal cost of each component of capital, one must determine if that component is available from internal sources or must be raised externally. The cost of existing debt is generally the yield to maturity on existing bonds, adjusted for the tax deductibility of interest. Once the component costs of capital have been determined, a marginal cost of capital curve can be constructed. The marginal cost in each range is the weighted average cost of the funds, either external or internal, that would be used in that range. Assuming the company is at its optimal or target mix, the proportions used in the weighted average cost of capital analysis should be the market value of each capital component, as a percent of the total market value of capital.

A capital investment is attractive if the net present value is positive at the marginal cost of capital for the funds that must be raised if that investment is to be accepted.

QUESTIONS

16-1. For what purposes is the cost of capital used?

16-2. Explain the meanings of the expressions (a) weighted average cost of capital, (b) marginal cost of capital.

16-3. What do we mean when we say the cost of capital is an opportunity cost?

16-4. Why do companies raise funds from a combination of sources?

16-5. Why is the effective interest rate on debt multiplied by (1 – tax rate) when similar adjustments are not made to the required return on preferred stock and common stock?

16-6. Why are several formulas often used to estimate the cost of common equity instead of *the* right formula?

16-7. Why are market value weights used instead of book value weights in computing a weighted average cost of capital?

16-8. Why would a company face a marginal cost of capital schedule instead of a single weighted average cost of capital?

16-9. How should the following be treated in the estimation of the cost of capital? (a) deferred taxes, (b) accounts payable, (c) accrued expenses, (d) short-term debt, (e) depreciation-generated funds.

PROBLEMS

16-1. Midwest Electric's bonds will mature in 20 years. The coupon interest rate on the bonds is 7 percent, paid at the end of each year. The bonds have maturity values of $1,000 each and are currently selling at a market price of $744.59. What is the yield to maturity? (Solve by finding the internal rate of return.) If the company's marginal tax rate is 35 percent, what is the after tax cost of existing debt?

16-2. Midwest Electric's preferred stock has a par value of $100 a share and a market price of $80 a share. Dividends per year are $10. What is the cost of existing preferred stock?

16-3. In order to sell new $100 par-value preferred stock at a price of $100, Midwest Electric must pay a dividend that will provide a dividend yield equal to the cost of preferred stock determined in problem 2. Flotation costs would be $5 a share. What is the cost of new preferred stock?

16-4. Midwest Electric is expected to pay a dividend of $5 per share over the next year, and the stock is currently selling for $50 a share. If dividends are expected to grow at 5 percent a year, what is the cost of existing common stock?

16-5. Flotation costs for a new issue of common stock in problem 4 would be $3 a share. What is the cost of new equity for Midwest Electric?

16-6. The 10-year bonds of Indiana International have a yield to maturity of 9.186 percent. The company can sell new 10-year bonds to provide this same interest rate, but flotation costs will be 5 percent of issue price. The company has a 35 percent marginal tax rate. What is the after tax cost of existing debt and new debt?

16-7. Michigan Corporation is expected to have earnings per share of $10 over the next year. Dividends are expected to be kept at 60 percent of earnings, and retained earnings are expected to be reinvested at a 14 percent rate of return. The price of the stock is presently $40. What is the anticipated growth rate of dividends, and what is the cost of existing equity? (**Hint:** remember that g = return on reinvested equity × retention rate.)

16-8. American Services Corporation's common stock has a beta of 1.30. The interest rate on U.S. Treasury bonds is 8 percent, and the interest rate on U.S. Treasury bills is 6 percent. Assuming an average market risk premium of 5 percent, use the mean-variance capital asset pricing model to estimate the cost of existing common equity for American.

16-9. American Service Corporation's common stock (see problem 8) has a price of $20 a share, and dividends are expected to be $2 a share for the next year. What is the implied growth rate of dividends? If flotation costs would be $2 a share, what is the cost of new equity?

16-10. CalMark is a privately held company, so there is no information about beta available. However, a company in the same business with a debt to equity ratio the same as that of CalMark is publicly traded and has a beta of 1.2. If the risk-free rate is 9 percent, and the average market risk premium is 5 percent, what is the estimated cost of existing equity for CalMark?

16-11. Annual dividends for Adams Mills are shown below. The price of Adams Mills' stock was around $14 at the end of 1994, and earnings per share for 1994 were $1.28. The risk-free rate was 7 percent and, according to *Value Line,* the beta was .90. Estimate the cost of equity using the dividend growth model, the earnings yield model, and the mean-variance capital asset pricing model (assume a 5 percent market risk premium). Why are the answers not the same for each method of computation? Which cost of equity estimate should the company use?

Year	1993	1994	1995	1996	1997	1998	1999	2000	2001	2002	2003
Dividend	.00	.10	.10	.10	.10	.10	.10	.12	.15	.17	.21

16-12. Return on market value of equity for Adams Mills (problem 11) was 9.14 percent. The dividends were 16.4 percent of income. What is the implied dividend growth rate? Given a 2003 dividend of $0.21 and a 2003 year-end price of $14, what is the cost of equity?

16-13. Contal Corporation has equity with a market value of $1 million, debt with a market value of $2 million, and a financial lease calling for payments of $100,000 a year for 10 years. The cost of equity is 15 percent, the interest rate on debt is 10 percent, and the tax rate is 35 percent, so the after tax cost of debt is 6.5 percent. The lease is of similar risk to the debt, so the value of the lease payments can be found by discounting them at the interest rate on the debt. What is the weighted average cost of capital?

16-14. Several recent college graduates are planning to open a computer service business. Each person must invest $20,000 to provide the necessary equity capital. Kirsten Maull is considering joining the group and wants to determine what would be a reasonable opportunity cost for equity invested in this way. All such businesses are small, so there are no publicly traded companies to use for comparison. Ms. Maull talked to an accounting professor who was considered an expert on small business valuation, and he indicated that a typical small service business would sell for about five times earnings. She looked at the stock market to consider alternatives. Smaller companies being traded on the over-the-counter stock market had price-earnings ratios averaging about six. The higher-risk companies traded on the organized exchanges had betas of 2.0 and above. Ms. Maull guessed that this investment would be of similar risk to investment in a stock with a beta of 2.0. The risk-free rate at the time was 8 percent, and Ms. Maull believed, from her finance studies, that the market risk premium was about 5 percent. What required return should Ms. Maull use in evaluating the business opportunity being considered?

16-15. Texal Corporation has $4 million of long-term debt, $1 million of preferred stock, and $5 million of common stock on its balance sheet. The market value of the debt is 80 percent of book value, the market value of preferred stock is 70 percent of book value, and the market value of common stock is 130 percent of book value. The after tax costs of existing debt, existing preferred stock, and existing common stock are 6 percent, 9 percent, and 15 percent, respectively. What is the marginal cost of existing capital?

16-16. Carolina Corporation has a capital structure consisting of 60 percent debt and 40 percent equity. The cost of existing equity is 14 percent and the cost of new equity is 16 percent. The cost of existing debt is 7 percent and the cost of new debt is 8 percent. Over the next year, net income is expected to be $1 million and management will not consider dividends of less that $400,000. Funds from operations other than income are expected to be $300,000. Prepare a marginal cost of capital schedule for Carolina Corporation.

16-17. A major private university is considering new insulated windows for one of its buildings. The risk-free rate is 8 percent, and the university can borrow for 10 percent a year. The benefit from the windows depends on energy prices. Oil-exploring companies also depend on energy prices, and have betas of 1.3. The average risk premium for common stock investments is 5 percent. The university could use endowment fund money currently invested in common stock. What is the appropriate required return for this investment?

16-18. KanAg Corporation has a marginal cost of capital schedule as follows:

	WEIGHTED AVERAGE COST
First $1 million	12%
Second $2 million	13%
Amounts above $3 million	15%

The company is considering the following assets:

			NET PRESENT VALUE AT WACC OF		
ASSET	COST	IRR	12%	13%	15%
A	$1,000,000	17%	$400,000	$350,000	$250,000
B	900,000	16	200,000	190,000	150,000
C	600,000	15	200,000	180,000	0
D	500,000	14	100,000	60,000	–50,000
E	500,000	13.8	150,000	80,000	–70,000
F	500,000	13.5	80,000	30,000	–100,000

In which asset should the company invest?

16-19. The balance sheet of Wisconsin Dairy Products, in millions of dollars, is shown below.

Current assets	$100	Current liabilities	$ 50
Fixed assets	400	Long-term debt	200
		Deferred taxes	50
		Common stock	100
		Retained earnings	100
Total assets	$500	T L & NW	$500

The debt consists of 20-year, 8 percent, $1,000 bonds, presently selling at $701.25. Flotation costs on new bonds would raise the effective before tax interest cost to 0.5 percent above the yield to maturity on existing debt. The company has 10 million shares of common stock outstanding, with a market price of $30 a share. The stock has a beta of 1.5. The risk-free rate is 10 percent and the average market risk premium is 5 percent. Flotation costs would raise the effective cost of new equity by 1 percent over the cost of existing equity. Over the next year, which is the company's capital investment planning period, the company expects to have $20 million of internally generated funds in addition to net income of $30 million. At least half of the net income must be paid out in dividends. The company faces a 35 percent marginal tax rate. Prepare a marginal cost of capital schedule.

16-20. **(Applications)** Coca-Cola states in its 1992 annual report: "Over the last five years, Economic Profit has increased at an annual compound rate of 27 percent, resulting in Economic Value Added of $952 million." If economic profit is calculated by subtracting the dollar cost of capital (percent times capital in use) from the net operating income after taxes, discuss ways management can increase the economic profit.

16-21. **(Application)** The following information was taken from the Chrysler and Ford 1992 annual reports (some pooling of accounts was necessary; amounts in millions as of 12-31-92):

	CHRYSLER	FORD
Accounts Payable	$ 5,798	$ 26,813
Short-Term Debt and Current Portion of Long-Term Debt	2,117	35,242
Accrued Liabilities	4,090	9,983
Long-Term Debt	13,434	63,262
Accrued Pension or Post-retirement Obligations	4,187	15,714
Common Equity	7,538	14,752
Other Pooled Accounts (not considered capital by the writers)	3,489	14,779
Total Liabilities and Equities	$40,653	$180,545

a. Using book values, what is the value of total capital for Chrysler and Ford?

b. Assume that all the book values above are approximate market values, with the exception of common equity, which is selling for $52 per share for Chrysler, with 295,892,000 shares outstanding, and for $58 per share for Ford, with 486,500,000 shares outstanding. Please recompute the total capital for Chrysler and Ford.

c. In 1992 Ford reduced its Common Equity account by $7.54 billion to reflect its existing obligation for post-retirement benefits other than pensions. Chrysler decided to delay recognition of its $4.7 billion obligation until 1993. In 1993 Chrysler will reduce equity by the estimated after tax cost of $4.7 billion by reporting a large loss on the income statement in the same manner that Ford reported a large loss in 1992. What impact does this have on the weights in percentage terms used for debt and equity in calculating the cost of capital?

d. Given your answer to the previous question, is it better to use market values or book values when calculating the weightings for debt and equity in the capital structure?

16-22. **(Ethical considerations)** It is fashionable today to report an "Economic Profit" amount to your shareholders in the annual report when management is discussing performance. Assume that economic profit is reported income plus interest (capital × WACC). Assume that you had been given the task to calculate the "economic profit" for McDonald's 1992 annual report and were presented with the following information:

	AT BOOK	AT MARKET
Long-Term Debt	3,446,000,000	3,646,000,000
Preferred Stock	680,000,000	751,000,000
Common Equity	6,635,000,000	17,706,000,000
After Tax Cost of Debt		.6%
Cost of Preferred Stock		.7%
Cost of Common Stock (using the dividend growth model)		.11%
Cost of Common Stock (using the earnings yield model)		.5%
Cost of Common Stock (using the capital asset pricing model)		.12%
After Tax Income plus Interest Expense		.$1,205,000,000

a. If you use book values and the dividend growth model, what is McDonald's economic profit or loss?

b. If you use market values and the dividend growth model, what is McDonald's economic profit or loss?

c. What additional method will show the greatest economic profit?

d. Calculate and justify what you believe is the fairest representation of McDonald's 1992 economic profit or loss.

CASE PROBLEM

Wal-Mart Cost of Capital

Wal-Mart, with $55 billion in sales in 1992, is the world's largest retailer.[21] It operates nearly 2,000 Wal-Mart discount stores in the United States, approximately 200 Sam's Clubs membership-warehouse stores, and a specialty distribution segment that serves 30,000 convenience stores and independent grocers. Discount stores' sales accounted for 73 percent of 1992 sales. Membership club sales were the second-largest area, accounting for 22 percent of 1992 sales. The remaining 5 percent of Wal-Mart's sales were accounted for by McLane & Western convenience store and independent grocer supply division. Thus, Wal-Mart was one of the companies that had resisted the trend toward diversifying into everything from aardvarks to zymometers.

Concentration did not mean lack of growth, however. New capital expenditures in 1992 alone were $3.5 billion, plus an associated investment in working capital of $1.8 billion. If Wal-Mart was to make optimal capital investment decisions, it was clear that an accurate estimate of the cost of capital was needed.

Wal-Mart presently had 2.3 billion shares of common stock outstanding. The stock had a beta of 1.3 and was selling at $30 a share in 1992. The yield to maturity on U.S. Treasury bonds was 6.5 percent, and Treasury bills were selling to yield 3 percent in 1993. Based on dividends to date, dividends per share during the year 1993 were expected to be $.12. Historical dividends per share and earnings per share were as shown at the bottom of this page.

Wal-Mart's balance sheet, of January 31, 1993, summarizes the company's financial structure (Table 16-3). Most of the company's debt was not actively traded. However, the company disclosed in a note to the financial statements that long-term debt with a book value of $3.073 had a fair market value of $3.357 billion. Assuming the average stated rate on outstanding securities was 7.5 percent, the yield to maturity would be 6.87 percent. It was assumed that other long-term debt would sell at a similar yield to maturity if the debt were publicly sold.

Wal-Mart was a heavy user of commercial paper with an average daily balance outstanding for 1992 of $1.184 billion. The weighted average before tax interest rate on this paper was 3.5 percent.

Wal-Mart has $1.818 billion in capital lease obligations on the balance sheet. In the footnote there is a historical 8 to 14 percent imputed discount rate used in calculating this obligation. Given the overall decline in interest rates, the lower end of the range, or 8 percent, is probably the better estimate of what future leases will

YEAR	1982	1983	1984	1985	1986	1987	1988	1989	1990	1991	1992
Dividends	.01	.01	.01	.02	.02	.03	.04	.06	.07	.09	.11
Earnings	.06	.09	.12	.15	.20	.28	.37	.48	.57	.70	.87

[21]This analysis, along with necessary estimates, was prepared by the author and does not represent the views of managers at Wal-Mart.

TABLE 16-3 Wal-Mart Balance Sheet

Amounts stated are in millions of dollars, and the date of the balance sheet is January 31, 1993.

ASSETS	
Current assets	$10,197
Property, plant, and equipment	9,794
Other assets	574
TOTAL ASSETS	$20,565
LIABILITIES AND EQUITIES	
Current liabilities:	
Accounts payable	$ 3,873
Commercial paper	1,588
Accrued expenses and taxes	1,233
Long-term debt maturing within 1 year	13
Capital lease obligations due within 1 year	46
Long-term liabilities:	
Long-term debt	3,073
Capital lease obligations	1,772
Deferred income taxes	207
Shareholder equity:	
Common stock	230
Capital in excess of par	527
Reinvested earnings	8,003
TOTAL LIABILITIES AND STOCKHOLDERS' EQUITY	$20,565

cost. Details of the long-term capitalized lease obligations and additional operating lease obligations are as follows:

YEAR	AGGREGATE MINIMUM LEASE PAYMENTS DUE (IN $ MILLIONS)
1993	$ 486
1994	476
1995	470
1996	475
1997	464
Thereafter	5,316

The "thereafter" amount is assumed to be due at $443 million per year for the next 12 years from 1998 to 2009. The market rate of interest to be used to find the market value of these lease obligations is assumed to be 8 percent.

There were no shares of preferred stock outstanding. Wal-Mart had a 37 percent combined federal and state marginal tax rate in 1992.

Case Questions

1. Estimate the market value of each component of the capital structure.
2. Estimate the required return for each component of the capital structure.
3. Estimate the weighted average cost of capital for Wal-Mart.
4. In which area of your analysis is there the greatest potential for error? Why? Is there anything that could be done to improve estimates in this area?

SELECTED REFERENCES

Adler, Michael. "The Cost of Capital and Valuation of a Two-Country Firm." *Journal of Finance* 29 (March 1974): 119–132.

Arditti, Fred D. "The Weighted Average Cost of Capital: Some Questions on Its Definition, Interpretation, and Use." *Journal of Finance* 28 (December 1973): 1001–1007.

Booth, Lawrence. "Estimating the Equity Risk Premium and Equity Costs: New Ways of Looking at Old Data." *Journal of Applied Corporate Finance* 12 (Spring 1999): 100–112.

Booth, Lawrence. "A New Model for Estimating Risk Premiums (Along with Some Evidence of Their Decline): *Journal of Applied Corporate Finance* 11 (Spring 1998): 109–120.

Brennan, Joseph F., and Paul R. Moul. "Does the Constant Growth Discounted Cash Flow Model Portray Reality?" *Public Utilities Fortnightly* 121 (January 21, 1988): 24–29.

Brigham, Eugene F., and Louis C. Gapenski. "Flotation Cost Adjustments." *Financial Practice and Education* 1 (Fall/Winter 1991): 29–34.

Brown, Robert J., and Mukund S. Kulkarni. "Duration and the Risk Adjustment of Discount Rates for Capital Budgeting." *Engineering Economist* 38 (Summer 1993): 299–307.

Conine, Thomas E., Jr., and Maurry Tamarkin. "Divisional Cost of Capital Estimation: Adjustment for Leverage." *Financial Management* 14 (Spring 1985): 54–58.

Constantinides, G. "Warrant Exercise and Bond Conversion in Competitive Markets." *Journal of Financial Economics* (September 1984): 371–398.

Dangerfield, Byron, Lawrence H. Merk, and C. R. Narayanaswamy. "Estimation of the Cost of Equity: Current Practices and Future Trends in the Electric Utility Industry." *The Engineering Economist* 44 #4, (1999): 377–387.

Diamond, Douglas W., and Robert E. Verrecchia. "Disclosure, Liquidity, and the Cost of Capital." *Journal of Finance* 46 (September 1991): 1325–1359.

"Division Hurdle Rates and the Cost of Capital." *Financial Management* 18 (Spring 1989): 18–25.

Dumas, Bernard, and Bruno Solnik. "The World Price of Foreign Exchange Risk." *Journal of Finance* 50 (June 1995): 445–479.

Fama, Eugene F., and Kenneth R. French. "Business Conditions and Expected Returns on Stocks and Bonds." *Journal of Financial Economics* 25 (November 1989): 23–49.

Fama, Eugene F., and Kenneth R. French. "The Corporate Cost of Capital and the Return on Corporate Investment. *Journal of Finance* 54 (December 1999): 1939–1967.

Frankel, Jeffrey A. "The Japanese Cost of Finance: A Survey." *Financial Management* 20 (Spring 1991): 95–127.

Fuller, Russell J., and Halbert S. Kerr. "Estimating the Divisional Cost of Capital: An Analysis of the Pure-Play Technique." *Journal of Finance* 36 (December 1981): 997–1009.

Gallinger, George W., and Glenn V. Henderson, Jr. "Public Utility Cost of Capital Models: An Examination of Assumptions." *Engineering Economist* 34 (Spring 1989): 177–184.

Gup, Benton E., and Samuel W. Norwood III. "Divisional Cost of Capital: A Practical Approach." *Financial Management* 11 (Spring 1982): 20–24.

Harris, Robert S., and Felicia C. Marston. "Estimating Shareholder Risk Premia Using Analysts' Growth Forecasts." *Financial Management* 21 (Summer 1992): 63–70.

Harris, Robert S., Thomas J. O'Brien, and Doug Wakeman. "Divisional Cost-of-Capital Estimation for Multi-Industry Firms." *Financial Management* 8 (Summer 1979): 74–84.

Howe, Keith M., and James H. Patterson. "Capital Investment Decisions under Economies of Scale in Flotation Cost." *Financial Management* 14 (Autumn 1985): 61–69.

Hubbard, Carl M. "Flotation Costs in Capital Budgeting: A Note on the Tax Effect." *Financial Management* 13 (Summer 1984): 38–40.

Hubbard, Jeff, and Roni Michaely. "Do Investors Ignore Dividend Taxation? A Reexamination of the Citizens Utilities Case." *Journal of Financial and Qualitative Analysis* 32 (March 1997): 117–135.

Jakque, Andrea S., and Gabriel Hawawini. "Myths and Realities of the Global Capital Market: Lessons and Myths for Financial Managers." *Journal of Applied Corporate Finance* 6 (Fall 1993): 81–90.

Keck, Tom, Eric Levengood, and Al Longfield. "Using Discounted Cash Flow Analysis in an International Setting: A Survey of Issues in Modeling the Cost of Capital." *Journal of Applied Corporate Finance* 11 (Fall 1998): 82–99.

Kester, W. Carl, and Timothy A. Luehrman. "What Makes You Think U.S. Capital Is So Expensive?" *Journal of Applied Corporate Finance* 5 (Summer 1992): 29–41.

Lee, Inmoo, Scott Lochhead, Jay Ritter, and Quanshui Zhao. "The Costs of Raising Capital." *Journal of Financial Research* 19 (Spring 1996): 59–74.

Linke, Charles M., and J. Kenton Zumwalt. "Estimation Biases in Discounted Cash Flow Analysis of Equity Capital Cost in Rate Regulation." *Financial Management* 13 (Autumn 1984): 15–21.

O'Brien, Thomas J. "The Global CAPM and a Firm's Cost of Capital in Different Currencies." *Journal of Applied Corporate Finance* 12 (Fall 1999): 73–79.

Pástor, Ľuboš, and Robert F. Stambaugh. "Costs of Equity Capital and Model Mispricing." *Journal of Finance* 54 (February 1999): 67–121.

Pettit, Justin. "Corporate Capital Costs: A Practitioner's Guide," *Journal of Applied Corporate Finance* 12 (Spring 1999): 113–120.

Reeb, David M., Sattar A. Mansi, and John M. Allee. "Firm Internationalization and the Cost of Debt Financing: Evidence from Non-Provisional Publicly Traded Debt." *Journal of Financial and Quantitative Analysis* 36 (September 2001): 395–414.

Riener, Kenneth D. "A Pedagogic Note on the Cost of Capital with Personal Taxes and Risky Debt." *Financial Review* 20 (May 1985): 229–235.

Schramm, Ronald, and Henry Wang. "Measuring the Cost of Capital in an International CAPM Framework." *Journal of Applied Corporate Finance* 12 (Fall 1999): 63–72.

Stein, Jeremy C. "Internal Capital Markets and the Competition for Corporate Resources." *Journal of Finance* 52 (March 1997): 111–133.

Stulz, René M. "Globalization, Corporate Finance, and the Cost of Capital." *Journal of Applied Corporation Finance* 12 (Fall 1999): 8–25.

Taggart, Robert A., Jr. "Allocating Capital among a Firm's Divisions: Hurdle Rates vs. Budgets." *Journal of Financial Research* 10 (Fall 1987): 177–189.

———. "Consistent Valuation and Cost of Capital Expressions with Corporate and Personal Taxes." *Financial Management* 20 (Autumn 1991): 8–20.

CHAPTER 20

Interactions between Investment and Financing Decisions

After completing this chapter you should be able to:

- Explain to a friend the separation principle in regard to wealth created from investing in positive net present value projects versus wealth transferred or created from changing the capital structure (or financing mix).
- Differentiate between projects that transfer wealth from one financing source to another, ones that create wealth, and ones that do both.
- Describe how certain projects can change the overall risk of the firm in such a way that the optimal mix of debt and equity may change and the cost of debt and/or equity may change.
- Recognize projects that have special financing attached to them and which should be considered when evaluating their acceptability.
- Calculate an Arditti-Levy net present value that adjusts for a change in the financing mix.
- Compute a Myers adjusted net present value.
- Determine an equity residual net present value.
- Recognize situations that may have an investment and financing interaction.

The state of Massachusetts wanted to attract new business to a state that was losing its traditional industrial base. Under the leadership of governor and presidential aspirant Michael Dukakis, the state provided $500 million of low-interest financing for companies willing to expand in Massachusetts.

For reasons discussed in the following paragraphs, we generally operate under the assumption that capital budgeting decisions can be separated from capital structure decisions. This assumption does not hold, though, if you are choosing between factory sites in Connecticut and sites in Massachusetts. The interest savings from the choice of a Massachusetts site must be factored into the decision. Similar circumstances occur when lease options are available or when manufacturers offer incentive financing. Decision making when financing and investment decisions interact are covered in this chapter.

THE SEPARATION PRINCIPLE

The **separation principle** is one of the traditional bases for capital budgeting. The separation principle states that the attractiveness of a capital investment is independent of how that particular investment is financed. A review of the reasons for the separation principle creates the foundation for dealing with exceptions. The separation principle gained prominence in capital budgeting as a response to erroneous attempts to make undesirable investments look desirable by tying them to debt financing. Suppose, for example, Pitt Corporation, a company with $1 million of capital, is financed with 40 percent debt and 60 percent equity. The after tax costs of debt and equity are 15 percent and 8 percent, respectively, so the weighted average cost of capital is:

$$\text{WACC} = .6(.15) + .4(.08) = 12.2\%$$

A manager at Pitt is trying to justify a proposed $200,000 capital investment, but the investment has an internal rate of return of only 12.1 percent. The manager tries to justify the investment by saying that the project can be financed entirely with debt.

To see the fallacy of this justification and the importance of the separation principle, consider what happens if Pitt invests in this project. Assume the company was previously at its optimal capital structure, that the cost of equity will rise to 16 percent with the increased leverage, and the cost of debt will rise to 9 percent. The weighted average cost of capital after the new asset is acquired with all-debt financing will be:

$$\text{WACC} = .5(.16) + .5(.09) = 12.5\%$$

To find the marginal cost of capital if the investment is financed exclusively with debt, recognize that Pitt must earn an after tax return of 12.5 percent on $1,200,000 of assets, whereas the previous requirement was that it earn 12.2 percent on $1,000,000 of assets. Thus, the required after tax benefit increases by:

$$\text{Increase in required benefit} = .125(\$1{,}200{,}000) - .122(\$1{,}000{,}000) = \$28{,}000$$

This means that the marginal cost of capital is $28,000/$200,000 = 14%.

If your company is at its optimal capital structure, it minimizes its marginal cost of capital for a new project by financing with the existing mix. If your company is not at its optimal capital structure, you need not make a capital investment to get to the optimal structure. You can gain the benefit of moving to the optimal capital structure by issuing one type of security and buying back the other. Thus, the company will maximize the wealth of the shareholders by applying the separation principle. The shareholder wealth-maximizing company will create the capital structure that minimizes the weighted average cost of capital, then choose investments with internal rates of return above that weighted average cost of capital.

Because of flotation costs and economies of scale, in securities issues, a company may move around the optimal capital structure, issuing debt one time it needs money and issuing equity the next time. The separation principle still holds in these cases because any movement away from the optimal capital structure is purely temporary and only for the purpose of minimizing transaction costs. You would not maximize value by selecting 9 percent return projects one month because it was the month you were issuing debt, knowing you would be turning down 14 percent return investments the next month because you would be issuing equity that month.

Exceptions to the Separation Principle

The separation principle is an important response to what can otherwise be erroneous decisions. But, like most simple rules, it does not always hold. An investment may transfer wealth from creditors to stockholders, or vice versa, and that wealth transfer must be considered in capital budgeting. Alternately, the capital investment may change the risk characteristics of the firm, and change the optimal debt ratio. Some investments also create the opportunity for special financing such as industrial revenue bonds, and those benefits must be recognized. This chapter focuses on exceptions to the separation principle.

WEALTH TRANSFERS AND CAPITAL INVESTMENT DECISIONS

Litzenberger documented wealth transfer effects in his study of the Unocal and Phillips Petroleum restructurings.[1] To see how a wealth transfer might occur, assume that the Pitt Corporation from the previous example has \$400,000 of long-term debt and \$600,000 of equity outstanding. The company can issue \$200,000 of new debt without refinancing the old debt. The increased debt ratio makes old debt more risky—the required return increases and the price falls—but Pitt need not pay the higher required return because the interest rate is already contractually set. The existing creditors simply lose wealth. The necessary after tax benefit before the expansion was:

$$.15(\$600{,}000) + .08(\$400{,}000) = \$122{,}000$$

[1]Robert H. Litzenberger, "Some Observations on Capital Structure and the Impact of Recent Recapitalizations on Share Prices," *Journal of Financial and Quantitative Analysis* 21 (March 1986): 59–71.

The necessary after tax benefit after financing a new $200,000 asset entirely with debt is:

$$.16(\$600{,}000) + .08(\$400{,}000) + .09(\$200{,}000) = \$146{,}000$$

The marginal cost of capital for a $200,000 investment is therefore:

$$\text{Marginal Cost of Capital} = (\$146{,}000 - \$122{,}000) \div \$200{,}000 = 12.0\%$$

With wealth transfer from creditors to shareholders, the marginal cost of capital is 12 percent, below the weighted average cost of capital at the optimal capital structure. Thus, the wealth transfer effect may make an otherwise undesirable capital investment attractive. If it was necessary to pay the higher interest rate to all creditors, the all-debt financing would result in a 14 percent marginal cost of capital, well above the 12.2 percent cost at the optimal capital structure.

Other considerations often negate the wealth transfer effect. First, one must be cautious in assigning the benefit of wealth transfer to a particular investment by decreasing the marginal cost of capital for that investment. If you can issue debt and buy back equity, the same wealth transfer can be achieved independent of investment decisions. Even if wealth transfer can be achieved only through acquisition of assets, the benefit will generally be available regardless of which asset is acquired. Consequently, the marginal cost of capital based on wealth transfer must generally be applied to all proposed investments in choosing the appropriate investments. The wealth transfer effect generally results in a cost of capital schedule such as that in Figure 20-1 rather than a lower cost of capital for a specific investment. Furthermore, the stepped cost of capital curve illustrated in Figure 20-1 occurs only if it is not possible to issue additional debt to buy back equity.

FIGURE 20-1 Cost of Capital Schedule with Wealth Transfer

This shows a lower cost of capital up to some amount of money that results from a wealth transfer action, with the marginal cost of capital being above the old costs of capital beyond that amount.

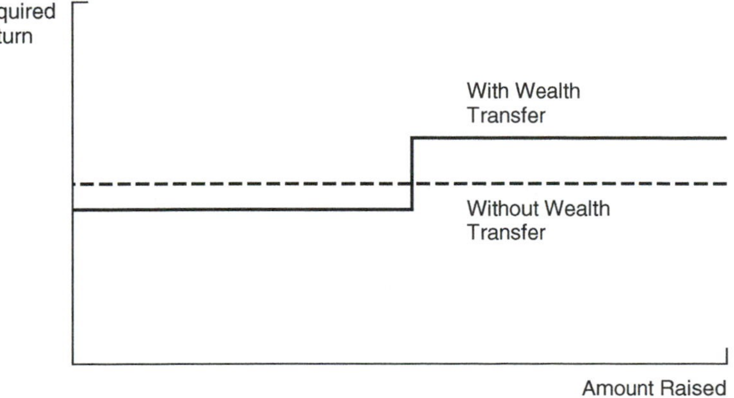

The wealth transfer benefit would accrue to a particular investment only if there was some characteristic of that investment that meant that it alone could be used to capture the wealth transfer benefit. This could be the case if, for example, one particular investment created the opportunity for secured financing.

Second, restrictive covenants associated with debt issues are specifically designed to limit these wealth transfers. If the old debt has restrictive covenants limiting total debt to 40 percent of capital, Pitt must retire the old debt and replace it with new debt costing 9 percent after tax. This eliminates the opportunity for wealth transfer and means that the marginal cost of capital is minimized by staying at the old debt ratio.

Future financing needs are an important consideration in wealth transfer situations. When the old debt matures, you must either issue higher interest rate debt or change the capital structure to minimize the cost of capital again. Asset acquisition in future periods also results in increased needs for financing. The past manipulations may affect the reputation of your company and affect the future cost of funds. Thus, availability of funds and the future weighted average cost of capital must be considered in the analysis.

Example: For the previous example, assume that Pitt Corporation's existing assets will generate a perpetuity of $122,000. The proposed new asset will generate an after tax cash flow of $83,413 at the end of each year for 3 years. The debt with an 8 percent after tax interest rate must be repaid over the first 2 years. If Pitt takes advantage of the wealth transfer opportunity now, its reputation will be affected. Investors will believe the company intends to finance with one-half debt even if it temporarily lowers the debt ratio. Therefore, the required interest rate on new debt will be 9 percent after tax, and the required return on equity will be 16 percent, even if the company lowers its debt ratio. As a result, the optimal capital structure in the future is half debt after Pitt has once moved to that position. The present values of all future cash flows are shown in Table 20-1 for both the all-debt financing of the expansion and financing of the expansion using 40 percent debt.

In examining the present values in Table 20-1, note that discount rates change from period to period with the changed leverage alternative. Applying present value principles for changing interest rates that were developed in Chapter 3, the present values are:

$$\text{Year 1 flow: } \frac{204{,}413}{1.121} = \$182{,}348$$

$$\text{Year 2 flow: } \frac{204{,}413}{1.121 \times 1.121} = \$162{,}666$$

$$\text{Year 3 flow: } \frac{204{,}413}{1.121 \times 1.121 \times 1.125} = \$144{,}594$$

At the start of year 4, Pitt will have an annuity of $122,000 a year forever. With the changed leverage, the value of that annuity, as of the end of year 3 or the start of year 4, is $122,000 ÷ .125 = $976,000. With changed leverage, the value of that annuity, as of now, is:

TABLE 20-1 Present Value with and without a Capital Structure Shift

This table shows the present value of all future cash flows for Pitt Corporation with and without an attempt by managers to transfer wealth from existing creditors by increasing the debt ratio.

YEAR:	1	2	3	4
CASH FLOWS				
Existing assets	$122,000	$122,000	$122,000	$122,000
New asset	83,413	83,413	83,413	—
Total cash flow	$205,413	$205,413	$205,413	$122,000
UNCHANGED LEVERAGE				
Required return	12.2%	12.2%	12.2%	12.2%
Total cash flow	$205,413	$205,413	$205,413	$122,000
Present value	$183,078	$163,171	$145,428	$707,981
Total present value = $1,199,658				
CHANGED LEVERAGE				
Required return	12.1%	12.1%	12.5%	12.5%
Present value	$183,242	$163,462	$145,300	$690,377
Total present value = $1,182,380				

$$\text{Present value of annuity} = \frac{976{,}000}{1.121 \times 1.121 \times 1.125} = \$690{,}377$$

For the particular example in Table 20-1, the higher cost of capital later offsets the benefit of a lower initial cost of capital. Wealth was transferred away from existing creditors, but the wealth transfer was not sufficient to offset the longer-term detrimental effects of the leverage change. Likewise, the proposed capital investment is not attractive because it was attractive only if the marginal cost of capital could be brought below 12.1 percent.

If Pitt were able to refinance at the end of year 3 and return to a 12.2 percent cost of capital, a different picture would emerge. Likewise, existing debt with very long maturity would increase the attractiveness of the change in capital structure. On the other hand, a need for additional funds for other new investments would further decrease the attractiveness of the capital structure change if it was not possible to return to the old capital structure later.

Information Asymmetry and Wealth Transfer

Wealth transfer can also occur because investor expectations differ from those of management. Suppose, for example, that Garden Corporation has annual income of $100 and has 100 shares of stock, so the earnings per share are $1.00. Income is distributed as dividends, and investors expect this level of income to continue indefinitely. Investors require a 20 percent return, so the price of a share of stock is $5.00.

Management at Garden Corporation knows that investors are wrong. Earnings and dividends will double next year with no new investment, and will stay at that same level forever. Once investors see the new earnings, the price of the stock will double to $10.

Garden Corporation also has a new investment opportunity requiring $100 of new equity, and promising perpetual income and dividends of $30 a year. With a 20 percent required return, the investment obviously has a positive net present value. The investment must be made now, and investors do not know that the new investment will provide superior returns, so twenty additional shares of stock must be sold at $5.00 a share. After earnings from existing assets double, the earnings per share and anticipated stock price will be as follows:

$$\text{Earnings per share} = \$230 \div 120 = \$1.92$$

$$\text{Anticipated stock price} = \$1.92 \div .20 = \$9.60$$

Because investors are uninformed, and the current stock price is unchanged by the investment, the stock price a year later is depressed. Wealth is created by the new investment, but that wealth and more is transferred from old to new stockholders.[2] This analysis would suggest that an otherwise profitable investment should be forgone. Before carrying this point too far, it is important to note that managers frequently overestimate their prospects.[3]

INVESTMENTS THAT CHANGE THE RISK CHARACTERISTICS OF THE FIRM

In Chapters 14 and 15 we focused on how systematic risk and other sensitivities to overall market conditions affect required return for an individual capital investment. Now that capital structure principles have been developed, we can combine concepts from portfolio theory and capital structure theory to also consider the impact of nonsystematic risk on required return for an individual capital investment. This section begins with investments that change the optimal mix of debt and equity, but do not change the component costs of either of these sources of capital. The analysis is then extended to consider investments that change both component costs and optimal mix.

---

[2]The problem that arises when investors do not correctly recognize future investment opportunities is developed further in John C. Woods and Maury R. Tandall, "The Net Present Value of Future Investment Opportunities: Its Impact on Shareholder Wealth and Implications for Capital Budgeting Theory," *Financial Management* 18 (Summer 1989): 85–92.

[3]For additional related reading, see David I. Levine, "Do Corporate Executives Have Rational Expectations?" *Journal of Business* 66 (April 1993): 271–293; and Robert Parrino and Michael S. Weisbach, "Measuring Investment Distortions Arising from Stockholder-Bondholder Conflicts," *Journal of Financial Economics* 53 (July 1999): 3–42.

Investments that Change the Optimal Debt Ratio

Recall from Chapter 13 that the variance of returns for a portfolio depends on the variances of the assets in that portfolio, and on their covariances. If the correlation between two assets is less than perfect, combining those two assets may result in a portfolio with less variance than either of the assets considered alone. This benefit of diversification is not closely related to systematic risk, which is sensitivity to one or more overall market conditions. Thus, two investments may have identical betas, and still result in a portfolio with less variance than that possessed by either investment independently. Portfolio effects were measured in terms of returns in Chapter 13, but can also be measured in terms of cash flows.

Recall from Chapter 17 that the optimal amount of debt is affected by the risk of not being able to take advantage of tax savings from interest and by the risk of bankruptcy. These risks can be reduced, and the optimal debt ratio increased, by increasing the stability of income and cash flow. Therefore, an investment that has a low correlation with the company's existing assets can increase the optimal debt ratio even if systematic risk is not affected.

In the simplest case of changing debt capacity, the component costs remain unchanged, but the optimal debt ratio increases due to low or negative correlation between cash flows for the investment and cash flows for the company's existing assets. In this case, the marginal cost of capital (MCC) for the investment is based on the increase in the total optimal amount of debt if the investment is accepted:

$$\text{MCC} = \frac{k_d \times \text{Increased debt} + k_e \times \text{Increased equity}}{\text{Total investment required}} \qquad \textbf{(20-1)}$$

where k_d and k_e are respectively the after tax costs of debt and equity.

Example: Pitt Corporation in the previous examples had a capital structure consisting of \$400,000 of debt and \$600,000 of equity before expansion, and this was believed to be optimal for the existing asset base. The after tax costs were 8 percent and 15 percent respectively. Pitt was considering a new \$200,000 capital investment. Suppose that this investment would improve stability of cash flow and profit, so the optimal debt ratio with this new investment would be 0.45. This means that:

$$\text{new debt} = .45(\$1{,}200{,}000) - .40(\$1{,}000{,}000) = \$140{,}000$$

and new equity will therefore be \$200,000 – \$140,000 = \$60,000.

In other words, the marginal financing for the investment will be 70 percent debt and 30 percent equity. Assuming the component costs do not change, the required return for this investment is

$$\text{MCC} = .7(.08) + .3(.15) = \underline{\underline{10.1\%}}$$

Investments That Change the Optimal Debt Ratio and Component Costs

An investment that changes the company's optimal debt ratio will probably change the component costs of funds as well. In this case, the marginal cost of capital is again the guideline. In the absence of an opportunity to transfer wealth from creditors to shareholders, the marginal cost of the increase in debt as a result of adding a new asset is:

$$\text{Marginal cost of debt} = \frac{k_{dn}\text{Debt}_n - K_{do}\text{Debt}_o}{\text{Debt}_n - \text{Debt}_o} \qquad \textbf{(20-2)}$$

where k_{do} and k_{dn} are respectively the costs of debt at the old and new optimal debt ratios. Debt_o and Debt_n are the optimal amounts of debt before and after acquisition of the asset.

The marginal cost of equity is defined in a similar manner:

$$\text{Marginal cost of equity} = \frac{k_{en}\text{Equity}_n - K_{eo}\text{Equity}_o}{\text{Equity}_n - \text{Equity}_o} \qquad \textbf{(20-3)}$$

where k_{eo} and k_{en} are respectively the costs of equity before and after acquisition of the new asset. Equity_o and Equity_n are the optimal amounts of equity before and after acquisition of the new asset.

Example: For Pitt Corporation in the previous examples, assume again that there is no opportunity to transfer wealth from existing creditors to stockholders, or vice versa. Assume again that the proposed new asset will increase the optimal debt ratio from .40 to .45. With acquisition and optimal financing of the new asset, the after tax cost of debt will decrease to 7.9 percent and the cost of equity will increase to 15.2 percent. The marginal costs of debt and equity are therefore:

$$\text{Marginal cost of debt} = \frac{.079 \times 540,000 - .08 \times 400,000}{540,000 - 400,000} = 7.614\%$$

$$\text{Marginal cost of equity} = \frac{.152 \times 660,000 - .15 \times 600,000}{660,000 - 600,000} = 17.200\%$$

Since the \$200,000 increase in assets results in an increase of \$140,000 in the optimal amount of debt, the debt ratio for the investment is .7, and the marginal cost of capital for the investment is:

$$\text{MCC} = .7 \times .07614 + .3 \times .1720 = 10.490\%$$

You can find the same marginal cost of capital without finding component costs. First, find the required earnings (after tax but before interest) with and without the new asset. Then, express the required earnings as a percent of the increases in assets:

$$\text{MCC} = \frac{(.079 \times 540{,}000 + .152 \times 660{,}000) - (.08 \times 400{,}000 + .15 \times 600{,}000)}{1{,}200{,}000 - 1{,}000{,}000}$$

$$= 10.490\%$$

In looking at the marginal cost of capital in this way, it is important to stress again the difference between an asset that changes the optimal amount of debt and the decision to finance an asset in a certain way even if the asset does not change the optimal amount of debt. The company might actually finance one asset entirely with debt, recognizing economies of scale in raising money and realizing that it will move back to its optimal debt ratio by issuing equity to finance another project next month. This type of incremental financing does not change the marginal cost of capital for the investment.

The difficulty in applying the marginal cost of capital concept with changing debt capacity should not be trivialized. Estimation of investor response to both a new asset and a new financing mix is hardly a trivial process. As discussed in Chapter 17, though, there are methods available for making estimates. Making decisions based on the best estimates available is better than simply ignoring the possible impact of a new asset on the company's optimal capital structure and component costs of capital.[4]

Investments That Change Debt Maturity

The maturity of debt, and therefore its cost, is another consideration. Optimal debt maturity is often linked directly to the maturity, risk, and liquidity of assets. A common approach to choosing debt maturity is to match the payment series for the debt to the anticipated life and annual cash flows of the project being funded. Thus, the component costs of debt may be different for an asset with a 1-year life and another asset with a 10-year life.

Asset liquidity clouds the maturity picture because liquidity essentially gives the company an option to sell the asset if conditions change. Lenders may be unwilling to make long-term loans because the company can restructure its assets after the loan is made. Lenders may also be unwilling to make short-term loans because cash flows from the asset are not sufficient to repay at an early maturity. The company may be required to rely on equity financing unless it agrees to restrictive covenants limiting its ability to sell assets without lender permission. [5]

---

[4]For additional work on the marginal cost of capital for an investment with changes in the optimal capital structure, see Thomas E. Conine, Jr., "Debt Capacity and the Capital Budgeting Decision: Comment," *Financial Management* 9 (Spring 1980): 20–22; Hayne E. Leland, "Agency Costs, Risk Management, and Capital Structure," *Journal of Finance* 53 (August 1998): 1213–1243; John D. Martin and David F. Scott, Jr., "Debt Capacity and the Capital Budgeting Decision," *Financial Management* 5 (Summer 1976): 7–14; John D. Martin and David F. Scott, Jr., "Debt Capacity and the Capital Budgeting Decision: A Revisitation," *Financial Management* 9 (Spring 1980): 23–26; Erwan Morellec, "Asset Liquidity, Capital Structure, and Secured Debt," *Journal of Financial Economics* 61 (August 2001): 172–206; Stewart C. Myers, "Interactions of Corporate Financing and Investment Decisions—Implications for Capital Budgeting," *Journal of Finance* 29 (March 1974): 1–25; S. Ghon Rhee and Franklin L. McCarthy, "Corporate Debt Capacity and Capital Budgeting Analysis," *Financial Management* 11 (Summer 1982): 42–50.

[5]For further reading on maturity issues, see Erwan Morellec, "Asset Liquidity, Capital Structure, and Secured Debt," *Journal of Financial Economics* 61 (August 2001): 172–206; and Frederick C. Scherr and Heather M. Hulbert, "The Debt Maturity Structure of Small Firms," *Financial Management* 30 (Spring 2001): 85–111.

SPECIAL FINANCING OPPORTUNITIES AND CAPITAL INVESTMENT EVALUATION

Some investments generate special financing opportunities that would not be available if the asset were not acquired. Low interest rate incentive financing for the purchase of automobiles is the most visible example. Use of industrial revenue bonds to provide low-interest loans, such as the $1 billion provided to businesses by the state of New Jersey, is another example. Likewise the bonds sold by various cities to help baseball teams finance stadiums provide low-cost financing for investments made at a specific location. Real estate investors often find that the type and availability of financing depend on the particular property being acquired. Leases are another example of special financing, and those are discussed in Chapter 21. Hellman and Puri observed that venture capital, one type of special financing, is available to the innovators in Silicon Valley, but not the followers. This is but another example of how good strategic positioning can also result in more favorable terms on financing.[6]

Special financing can be recognized through adjustment to the weighted average cost of capital, but proper specification of the weighted average cost of capital is difficult because the amount and maturity of the financing may not coincide with the optimal financing mix for the investment. Calculations can be simplified and risk of error reduced if the net present value of the project is first computed as if special financing were not available. Then, the net advantage of the special financing (NAF) is added to the net present value to give an adjusted net present value. This approach is particularly easy to use if the investment's risk is the same as the average risk of the company or a division for which the weighted average cost of capital has already been determined.

The net advantage of financing is the present value of the difference between the after tax principal and interest payments for special financing and what would be required for regular financing with the same maturity. We assume special debt financing since that is the type generally observed. The formula for the net advantage of special financing (NAF) is:

$$\text{NAF} = \text{Amount of special financing} - \left[\sum_{t=1}^{n} \frac{P_t + Int_t(1 - T_c)}{(1 + k_d)^t}\right] \quad \textbf{(20-4)}$$

where P_t and Int_t are the principal and interest payments on the special financing. T_c is the corporate tax rate and k_d is the cost of the corporation's regular debt.[7]

Example: Philadelphia Corporation has a weighted average cost of capital of 12 percent. The corporate tax rate is 35 percent and the company can borrow at

---

[6]Thomas Hellman and Manju Puri, "The Interaction Between Product Market and Financing Strategy: The Role of Venture Capital," *The Review of Financial Studies* 13 (Winter 2000): 959–984.

[7]The amount of special financing is used in the formula instead of the present value of principal and interest payments on regular debt because the present value of after tax principal and interest payments on regular debt, discounted at the after tax cost of debt, always equals the amount borrowed.

an interest cost of 10 percent. The company is considering a new plant that would cost \$8 million and would generate year-end cash flows of \$1 million after tax but before considering interest. The plant would have the same average risk as the company's other assets and would have a 20-year life. The net present value is therefore:

$$NPV = \$1{,}000{,}000PVA1_{20yrs,12\%} - \$8{,}000{,}000 = -\$530{,}556$$

The investment is, therefore, unattractive.

However, the community is willing to provide a \$6 million loan with a 6 percent interest rate and the entire principal due in 10 years. The net advantage of the special financing is \$6 million, minus the present value of the principal payment and after tax interest payments, discounted at the after tax cost of the company's regular debt:

$$\begin{aligned} NAF = {} & \$6{,}000{,}000 - \$6{,}000{,}000 \times .06 \times (1 - .35)PVA1_{10yrs,6.5\%} \\ & - \$6{,}000{,}000/1.065^{10} \\ = {} & \underline{\underline{\$1{,}121{,}458}} \end{aligned}$$

The net present value with special financing (NPVF) is then:

$$NPVF = NPV + NAF = -\$530{,}556 + \$1{,}121{,}458 = \underline{\underline{\$590{,}902}}$$

The special financing achieves the community's objective. The capital investment is unattractive without special financing, but becomes attractive with special financing. The investment will increase shareholder wealth.

SOME ALTERNATE METHODS FOR DEALING WITH FINANCING MIX

While the net present value has been espoused throughout this book, alternatives, such as the internal rate of return and payback, also were included because they are used in practice. Likewise, there are several formulations of the net present value that recognize the impact of leverage. Each of these is used in practice, and is therefore worthy of note.[8]

Standard Net Present Value

The alternate methods should be compared to the standard net present value method, which uses a weighted average cost of capital to discount future cash

[8]For a more detailed discussion of these alternate approaches, see Donald R. Chambers, Robert S. Harris, and John J. Pringle, "Treatment of Financing Mix in Analyzing Investment Opportunities," *Financial Management* 11 (Summer 1982): 24–41.

flows. To put everything in comparable terms, the net present value method using the weighted average cost of capital—the method used throughout this book—is:[9]

$$NPV(WACC) = \sum_{t=1}^{n} \frac{EBIT_t(1 - T_c) + Dep_t}{(1 + k_o)^t} - I_o \qquad \textbf{(20-5)}$$

where $EBIT_t$ is earnings before interest and tax in period t, Dep_t is depreciation in period t, T_c is the corporate tax rate, and I_o is the initial investment. Depreciation is added because it was deducted in arriving at EBIT even though it was not a cash expense. The marginal cost of capital applicable to the investment, k_o, is based on the weighted average cost of capital concept. This will be the weighted average cost of capital for the firm unless the investment changes the optimal debt ratio or the component costs. In these cases, the marginal cost of capital will be determined as explained earlier in this chapter.

It should be noted that k_o incorporates both the risk of the investment and the financing mix. It is generally assumed that k_o remains constant over the life of the investment, although this assumption is not required. For k_o to remain constant, it is generally necessary that the debt ratio and risk remain constant over the life of the investment.

Arditti-Levy Net Present Value

An alternate to the standard net present value has been supported by Arditti and Levy.[10] This approach is often used by public utilities; Southwestern Bell Telephone company used this method, for example. The Arditti-Levy net present value formula, NPV(AL) is:

$$NPV(AL) = \sum_{t=1}^{n} \frac{(EBIT_t - Int_t)(1 - T_c) + Dep_t + Int_t}{(1 + k_{AL})^t} - I_o \qquad \textbf{(20-6)}$$

where $k_{AL} = wk_d/(1 - T_c) + (1 - w)k_e$. In this equation, $k_d/(1 - T_c)$ is the before tax marginal cost of debt for the investment. Int_t is the increase in interest expense as a result of the investment, and k_e is the marginal cost of equity for the project.

The difference between the Arditti-Levy method and the standard weighted average cost of capital approach is that the tax saving from interest is recognized in the numerator rather than the denominator. The Arditti-Levy method gives the same net present value as the standard net present value if the debt is held at a constant percent of value throughout the asset's life.

---

[9]To simplify the discussion, we abstract from other cash flows, such as change in net working capital.

[10]Fred D. Arditti and Haim Levy, "The Weighted Average Cost of Capital as a Cutoff Rate: A Critical Examination of the Classical Textbook Weighted Average," *Financial Management* 6 (Fall 1977): 24–34.

Public utility commissions, which set prices, aim for net present values of zero, based on the Arditti-Levy method. After the commissions estimate k_{AL}, they set rates so that their estimate of k_{AL} can be achieved. The regulated utilities then evaluate investments using k_{AL} and Equation 20-6.

Adjusted Present Value

The adjusted present value method was developed by Myers to consider interactions between investment and financing decisions.[11] The formula for the adjusted present value is:

$$APV = \sum_{t=1}^{n} \frac{EBIT_t(1 - T_c) + Dep_t}{(1 + k_u)^t} - I_o + \sum_{t=1}^{n} \frac{T_c Int_t}{(1 + R_d)^t} \tag{20-7}$$

where k_u is the required return appropriate for an unleveraged investment, and R_d is the interest rate on the corporation's debt:

$$R_d(1 - T_c) = k_d$$

With a little manipulation, it can be seen that the cash flows discounted in the adjusted present value are the same as those discounted in the Arditti-Levy approach. The difference is that one required return is used for the interest tax shield and another is used for other cash flows. The adjusted present value is different from the standard net present value and the Arditti-Levy net present value, except under special conditions. The adjusted present value avoids the necessity of assuming that debt remains a constant percent of value. Unfortunately, it requires estimation of the debt ratio for each future period to estimate interest expense in future periods. This may be difficult because interest expense is not limited to debt specifically used to finance the investment, but depends on the investment's contribution to the corporation's debt capacity each period. The model also appears to be based on an implied assumption that debt results in tax shields, but that there are no other costs or benefits associated with debt. In other words, agency costs and bankruptcy costs are assumed to be unaffected by debt. The adjusted present value would increase with all increases in the ratio of debt to total assets.

A modified version of the adjusted present value is used in Chapter 21 for lease analysis.

Equity Residual Net Present Value

The equity residual method treats financing alternatives by focusing entirely on the cash flows to equity holders. The formula for the equity residual net present value, NPV(ER), is:

[11] Myers, "Interactions of Corporate Financing and Investment Decisions."

$$\text{NPV(ER)} = \sum_{t=1}^{n} \frac{(\text{EBIT}_t - \text{Int}_t)(1 - T_c) + \text{Dep}_t + (B_t - B_{t-1})}{(1 + k_e)^t} - (I_o - B_o) \quad \textbf{(20-8)}$$

where B_t is the amount of debt supported by the investment at time t, and B_o is the initial amount of debt used to finance the investment.

The equity residual method has intuitive appeal in that it focuses on the cash flows to shareholders. The equity residual net present value is the same as the standard net present value if debt is a constant percent of value throughout the asset's life. Like the adjusted present value, the equity residual net present value provides a method for dealing with changes in capital structure over the life of an asset. It also provides a method of dealing with differences in contribution to debt capacity between assets.

The equity residual method is particularly popular with financial institutions. They view borrowed money as their basic raw material rather than a component of a capital structure. Also, regulations set equity capital requirements that vary by type of asset held. Consequently, bank managers are turning from a return on total assets focus to a return on equity focus.[12] Of course, use of the equity residual method does not change the general principles with regard to the marginal amount of debt and equity assigned to a particular project. The equity residual method should not be used as a justification for the type of erroneous analysis that was illustrated at the beginning of this chapter.[13]

Example: Fullerton Corporation is considering a new $1 million automated cutter. For simplicity, assume the cutter will last for only 2 years and will have no salvage value. Depreciation will be $500,000 a year. The cutter will generate earnings before interest and tax of $150,000 a year. Fullerton maintains debt equal to 75 percent of value, using the present value of future cash flows to represent value. Fullerton can borrow at 12 percent, and the required return on equity is 15 percent. The tax rate is 35 percent, and the weighted average cost of capital is therefore:

$$\text{WACC} = .75(.12)(1 - .35) + .25(.15) = \underline{\underline{.0960}}$$

The annual cash flow and standard net present value is (numbers are expressed in thousands):

$$\text{Annual cash flow} = \$150(1 - .35) + \$500 = \underline{\underline{\$597.50}}$$

$$\text{NPV(WACC)} = \frac{\$597.50}{1.096} + \frac{\$597.50}{1.096^2} - 1{,}000 = \underline{\underline{\$42.58}}$$

To find the Arditti-Levy net present value, we need to know the amount of debt outstanding each period. Fullerton's policy is to have debt equal 75 percent

[12]Kenneth A. Froot and Jeremy C. Stein, "A New Approach to Capital Budgeting for Financial Institutions," *Journal of Applied Corporate Finance* 11 (Summer 1998): 59–69.

[13]For another approach, see Richard S. Ruback, "Capital Cash Flows: A Simple Approach to Valuing Risky Cash Flows." *Financial Management* 31 (Summer 2002): 85–103.

TABLE 20-2 Debt Schedule for Fullerton Corporation

This table shows the debt and interest payments each period, based on the assumption that Fullerton maintains debt equal to 75 percent of the present value of future cash flows. (Dollar amounts are in thousands.)

YEAR:	0	1	2
Cash flow	−1,000.00	597.50	597.50
Present value of remaining cash flows (k_o = 9.6%)	1,042.58	545.16	0
Debt at end of period	781.94	408.87	0
Interest (12% of debt at the end of previous period)	93.83	49.06	

of the value of remaining cash flows. The resulting debt schedule is in Table 20-2. The discount rate and Arditti-Levy net present value are then:

$$k_{AL} = .75(.12) + .25(.15) = .1275$$

$$NPV(AL) = \frac{(150 - 93.83)(1 - .35) + 500 + 93.83}{1.1275} + \frac{(150 - 49.06)(1 - .35) + 500 + 49.06}{1.1275^2} - 1,000$$

$$= \underline{\$42.58}$$

To find the adjusted present value, it is necessary to have a cost of capital for an unleveraged firm. Assume that cost of capital would be 12.7787 percent. The adjusted present value is then:

$$APV = \frac{150(1 - .35) + 500}{1.127787} + \frac{150(1 - .35) + 500}{1.127787^2} + \frac{.35(93.83)}{1.12} + \frac{.35(49.06)}{1.12^2} - 1,000$$

$$= \underline{\$42.58}$$

The equity residual net present value is then found as follows:

$$NPV(ER) = \frac{(150 - 93.83)(1 - .35) + 500 + (408.87 - 781.94)}{1.15} + \frac{(150 - 49.06)(1 - .35) + 500 + (0 - 408.87)}{1.15^2} - (1,000 - 781.94)$$

$$= \underline{\$42.58}$$

These examples stress the importance of assumptions underlying capital budgeting. The justification for the standard net present value method is based on the assumptions that risk and optimal capital structure are not affected by the investment under consideration and remain constant in future periods. To justify the standard net present value, we further assume that debt remains a constant percentage of the remaining *value* of cash flow throughout the life of the assets. If these assumptions hold, the standard net present value equals the Arditti-Levy net present value and the equity residual net present value. However, the adjusted present value is consistent with the standard net present value only with an additional assumption about the relationship between the leveraged and unleveraged cost of capital. When the assumptions needed to justify the net present value are not met, it is necessary to consider the interactions between the investment and financing decisions of the firm in capital budgeting.

SUMMARY

The separation principle states that the selection of capital investments is independent of the selection of financing methods. There are sound reasons for this principle, as a general guideline, but there are situations in which an investment affects the optimal debt ratio and/or the component costs of capital. In those cases, the financing implications of the investment must be considered in the capital budgeting process.

Wealth transfer situations are one case in which the separation principle does not hold. Some capital investments can transfer wealth from creditors to stockholders. A classic example is a project that increases total risk, thereby decreasing the value of existing debt. These investments can be analyzed using a marginal cost of capital analysis that recognizes the benefit of not having to pay a higher interest rate on existing debt. The immediate wealth increase benefits must, however, be weighed against a possible higher weighted average cost of capital in future periods when new financing is needed, and the firm is perceived as more risky. Furthermore, wealth transfers raise serious ethical concerns if they are based on deception of any type.

Investments that change the optimal debt ratio without changing the component costs of capital are a special type of consideration. An investment can increase the optimal debt ratio by having less variability of earnings and cash flows, or by having low correlation with the other assets of the firm. In these cases, the marginal cost of capital for the investment depends on the optimal amounts of debt and equity that will be added as a result of the investment.

In many cases, both the optimal debt ratio and the component costs of capital are changed by the acceptance of the project. The marginal cost of capital in these cases is the total increase in earnings after tax, but before interest, necessary to service the debt and equity financing that will be used to finance the investment and move the company to its new optimal capital structure, as a percent of the amount of investment.

Instead of using a marginal cost of capital approach based on the weighted average costs to deal with interactions between investment and financing decisions, some companies choose other methods. The Arditti-Levy method focuses on cash flows, including interest tax shield, and finds the present value with a discount rate based on the required return on equity and before tax cost of debt. The adjusted present value approach discounts earnings after tax and before interest at the appropriate discount rate for an unleveraged firm, and then discounts interest tax shields at the interest rate for debt. The equity residual method identifies cash flows after principal and interest payment, and then finds the present value using the marginal cost of equity as the discount rate. The standard net present value, Arditti-Levy net present value, and the equity residual net present value are identical if debt is held at a constant proportion of value and cost of capital is estimated using as weights the amount of each component as a percent of value. Managers have found each of the methods to be useful in particular situations.

QUESTIONS

20-1. What is the separation principle?

20-2. Why has the separation principle been important in capital budgeting?

20-3. What are the main exceptions to the separation principle?

20-4. Explain how a change in capital structure might transfer wealth from creditors to stockholders.

20-5. Explain how a capital budgeting decision might transfer wealth from creditors to stockholders.

20-6. As a business manager, what is your ethical responsibility when you have an opportunity to transfer wealth from creditors to stockholders?

20-7. What are the characteristics of an investment that would cause it to increase the firm's optimal debt ratio?

20-8. Why might special low-cost financing be available for a specific investment but not available for other investments being considered by the firm?

20-9. What are the advantages and disadvantages of the adjusted present value in comparison to the standard net present value as a capital budgeting tool?

20-10. What are the advantages and disadvantages of the equity residual net present value in comparison to the standard net present value as a capital budgeting tool?

20-11. What are the conditions necessary for the net present values to be identical using the standard net present value, the Arditti-Levy net present value, and the equity residual net present value?

PROBLEMS

(For simplicity, assume year-end cash flows.)

20-1. San Diego Corporation has debt of $1 million and equity of $1 million. The after tax costs of debt and equity are 6 percent and 14 percent respectively. A proposed $200,000 capital investment has an internal rate of return of 9 percent. The project proponent has suggested that the investment is attractive as long as it is financed entirely with debt. An increase in the debt ratio would increase the after tax cost of all debt to 7 percent and would increase the cost of equity to 14.25 percent. What is the marginal cost of capital if the investment is financed entirely with debt? Should the company invest in the new asset?

20-2. For San Diego Corporation (problem 1), assume that the existing debt has a very long maturity, so the higher interest cost applies only to the new debt. The company does not anticipate expansion beyond this $200,000 investment.

a. Will the change in the debt ratio increase shareholder wealth?

b. Should San Diego Corporation invest in this asset if it is the only way the debt ratio can be increased?

c. Should San Diego Corporation invest in this asset if an alternative is to increase the debt ratio by issuing debt and buying back common stock?

20-3. Palo Alto Corporation has existing assets that will generate a perpetuity of $200,000 a year. The company has $1 million of debt and $1 million of equity outstanding. The after tax costs are 7 percent and 14 percent respectively. The company is considering a new capital investment that will cost $200,000 and will generate cash flows of $20,000 a year in perpetuity. The company can finance the asset entirely with debt, but this will raise the after tax costs of debt and equity to 8 percent and 14.25 percent, respectively.

a. Is the investment attractive if existing debt is a perpetuity, with the interest rate already determined by contract?

b. Is the investment attractive if existing debt must then be refinanced at an after tax cost of 8 percent, in order to issue the new debt?

20-4. Davis Corporation is financed with $1 million of debt and $1 million of equity. The interest rate on debt is 10 percent, and the required return on equity is 16 percent. The tax rate is 40 percent.

a. What is the weighted average cost of capital?

b. Suppose Davis adds $100,000 of debt. As a result of this change in capital structure, the required interest rate on debt rises to 11 percent, and the required return on equity increases to 17 percent. The higher interest rate must be paid on all existing debt as well as new debt. What is the marginal cost of this additional $100,000 of debt?

20-5. For Davis Corporation (problem 4), assume that existing debt is a perpetuity, and it will therefore be necessary to pay the higher interest rate only on new debt. What is the marginal cost of the additional $100,000 of debt?

20-6. The existing assets of San Francisco Corporation generate cash flows of $100,000 a year, with a standard deviation of $50,000. A proposed capital investment will generate cash flows of $40,000 a year, with a standard deviation of $10,000. Cash flows from the new investment are uncorrelated with those from existing investments. Cash flow to service debt is 10 percent of the amount of debt outstanding. Cash flows are normally distributed and San Francisco Corporation defines its debt capacity as the amount of debt it can carry and have not more than a 5 percent probability of having inadequate cash flow to service debt. What is the contribution of the new investment to the company's optimal amount of debt?

20-7. Los Angeles Corporation has a capital structure consisting of $500,000 of debt and $500,000 of equity. The after tax costs of debt and equity are 8 percent and 12 percent respectively. A new $200,000 capital investment will increase the optimal debt ratio to 0.55, with no change in component costs. What is the marginal cost of capital for this investment?

20-8. Riverside Corporation has a capital structure consisting of $1 million of debt and $1 million of equity. After tax costs of debt and equity are 7 percent and 15 percent respectively. A proposed $1 million capital investment will increase the optimal debt ratio to .6, with component costs of debt and equity increasing to 7.1 percent and 15.2 percent respectively. There is no opportunity to transfer wealth from existing creditors to stockholders. What is the marginal cost of capital for this new investment?

20-9. Lodi Corporation has a weighted average cost of capital of 10 percent. The company is considering a new facility near Bakersfield. The facility will cost $10 million and will generate after tax cash flows of $2 million a year for 7 years. The local government is willing to provide a $3 million, 5-year balloon payment loan with an after tax interest rate of 5 percent paid annually and the entire principal paid at maturity. The after tax cost of debt for Lodi Corporation is otherwise 7 percent. Is the investment attractive

a. without the special financing?

b. with the special financing?

20-10. The city of Berkeley wants to encourage the location of a research center in the community. The center will create high-paying jobs and will not generate pollution. The center is a nonprofit organization and therefore does not pay taxes. Another community has offered to provide a $10 million, 20-year 5 percent loan, to be repaid in equal annual installments of $802,426. Otherwise, the center would have to pay interest of 8 percent on its financing. Instead of offering low-cost financing, Berkeley may offer free land. How much must the land be worth for the value of Berkeley's incentive package to be the same as that of the competing city?

20-11. A $1 million investment will generate earnings before interest and tax of $110,000 a year for its 5-year life. Depreciation will be $200,000 a year, and the company's tax rate is 40 percent. The company maintains a capital structure of one-half debt and one-half equity. The interest rate on debt is 10 percent and the required return on equity is 14 percent. The company will repay debt so that debt remains at 50 percent of the present value of remaining cash flows. Compute the standard net present value.

20-12. For the investment in problem 11, compute the Arditti-Levy net present value.

20-13. For the investment in problem 11, compute the equity residual net present value.

20-14. For the investment in problem 11, the discount rate for an unleveraged investment is 12 percent. Compute the adjusted present value.

20-15. Valley Public Service, a regulated utility, has a marginal tax rate of 40 percent. The company is financed with 40 percent debt and 60 percent equity. The interest rate on debt is 10 percent and the cost of equity is 14 percent. The company needs to expand to meet customer demand. The expansion will require a capital investment of $50 million. The asset life is 10 years. For simplicity, assume 10-year straight-line depreciation with a full year's depreciation in the first year of operation. The debt portion of financing will be repaid in ten equal annual installments, so that debt always equals 40 percent of the present value of remaining payments. Operating expenses other than interest and depreciation will be $15 million a year. The public service commission wants to set a rate that will generate enough revenue to provide a net present value of $0. How much revenue is needed if revenue will be the same each year?

20-16. Sunset Bank, one of the major banks on the West Coast, is considering a new loan product. The cost of equity is 16 percent, and the bank does not believe the product will change the cost of equity. Initial development costs will be $1 million, but these are tax-deductible expenses. It is estimated that an average loan balance of $50 million will be generated, and the product will have a life of 5 years. Approximately 95 percent of the loan portfolio will be financed with debt, costing 8 percent, and the rest will be financed with equity. The average interest rate on the loans will be 14 percent, and operating costs will be 3 percent of loan balance. Use the equity residual net present value to determine if the loan product is desirable.

20-17. Sunset Bank (problem 16) is also considering a new automatic teller machine (ATM) network. The ATMs will be financed with one-half debt and one-half equity. The debt will carry an interest rate of 10 percent and will be repaid in 8 equal annual installments. The total cost of the system will be $5 million, and the depreciation life will be 7 years, using depreciation rates explained in Chapter 8. Operating costs other than depreciation will be $1 million a year and the system will generate additional fee revenue of $2 million a year over its anticipated 8-year life. Use the equity residual net present value method to determine if the asset is attractive.

20-18. **(Applications)** The following list of events took place in the 1990s:

a. Goodyear Tire and Rubber Co. sold its Scottsboro, Alabama, polyester tire cord and fabric plant to Akzo for $105 million. The proceeds were to be used to reduce Goodyear's $3.7 billion debt.

b. MCI board authorized the repurchase of as many as 15 million shares of the 262 million shares outstanding. The repurchased shares will be used for its employee benefit program.

c. Wal-Mart agreed to buy a number of Pace Wholesale stores from K-Mart. This move decreased K-Mart's warehouse club exposure and increased the number of warehouse clubs owned by Wal-Mart to approximately 200.

d. Mercedes Benz chose Alabama as the site for its new auto plant after huge tax concessions and up-front incentives were given by the state.

e. Reynolds Metal was negotiating the sale of its Eskimo Pie Corp. to Nestlé USA. Reynolds would use the proceeds to invest in its other businesses. Required for each event:

  I. State whether you believe wealth was created, shifted, or both created and shifted between the financing sources for each firm. (Make whatever assumptions are necessary.)

  II. List the parties to whom wealth accrued and the parties from whom wealth was lost for each firm.

  III. Discuss the shifting of risk, if any, between the parties in each firm.

20-19. **(Ethical considerations)** In the late 1980s Kolhberg, Kravis, Roberts and Company took RJR Nabisco private for approximately $23 billion in debt. Prior to this RJR Nabisco was approximately a $10 billion company with $2 billion in long-term debt. Several pension plans and insurance companies held a sizable portion of the long-term debt prior to the leveraged buyout. After the buyout many of these debt-holders sued to try and recover what was reported in the press as a $200 million loss in market value for the existing bonds. Because there were no put options (giving the debt-holder the right to sell the debt to the corporation) attached to the existing debt, all of this debt remained outstanding after the leveraged buyout.

a. In terms of risk and required rate of return, why did the market value of the outstanding debt decrease with the announcement of the leveraged buyout?

b. In terms of wealth, was wealth created or transferred with this leveraged buyout? Explain.

c. Please comment on the ethical responsibilities of management in relation to the debt-holders and stockholders in this situation.

CASE PROBLEM

Black Shoe Company

The shoe industry is labor intensive, and shipping costs are modest, so the shoe industry in the United States has been severely hurt by foreign competition. Shoe manufacturing in the United States had been concentrated in large factories in Northern industrial cities, and labor costs were at least several times those available in countries such as Taiwan. Abandoned shoe factories became symbols of the rust belt: a northern tier dotted by the hulks of dying industries.

Black Shoe Company was one of the leading shoe companies in the United States. It produced and distributed a wide range of shoes for both men and women, priced in the middle and upper-middle ranges. Black had been forced to follow the national trend in relying increasingly on overseas production. Black had followed this policy with some regret, because management had a strong preference for manufacturing in the United States. Nevertheless, overseas sources seemed to be necessary for survival. Black built several overseas factories and contracted with other overseas manufacturers to build shoes of its design.

Despite success with overseas sources, management was interested in finding a way to keep at least some manufacturing in the United States. National pride, advertising advantages, and protection from fluctuating exchange rates were their primary motives. Automation was one way to reduce labor costs, but opportunities for increased automation were limited by constant changes in style. Thus, lower labor costs appeared to be essential if any manufacturing was to be kept in the United States.

A strategy task force was put together to work on ways to manufacture in the United States, and the Clear Spring, Missouri, proposal resulted. The fundamental strategy was to build small factories in rural areas where wages were low and unemployment was high. It was envisioned that one large factory would be replaced by ten small, rural factories employing approximately 400 people each. The Clear Spring proposal was the prototype for this strategy.

Clear Spring was a town of 2,500 in the Ozark region of southern Missouri. With surrounding towns and rural populations included, 12,000 people lived within a 12-mile radius of Clear Spring. The primary industries in the area were forestry and agriculture, and both were marginal. The hillsides were too steep for farming, while the soil in the valleys was thin and stony. Forestry consisted of harvesting naturally growing trees for low-grade lumber use such as railroad ties, pallets, and firewood. Railroad construction had slowed dramatically, plastic pallets were replacing wood for many uses, and it was uneconomical to truck firewood to major cities such as St. Louis.

By official estimates there were 4,800 people in the Clear Spring area labor force, with 10 percent of those unemployed. The potential labor pool for the factory was much higher than 480 though. Many of the employed worked poor farms, held seasonal jobs in lumbering, or drove 60 miles to jobs in Cape Girardeau. Furthermore, as many as 1,200 women who were not considered part of the workforce, because they had not applied for jobs recently, would be happy to work if good job opportunities were available. When American Hat opened a small factory 30 miles away at Honesty, they had been flooded with applications.

The proposed factory would consist of an 80,000-square-foot, one-story building. Land would cost $40,000 and the building would cost $1,600,000. Most of the equipment would be transferred from a large factory that had been shut down because it could not compete with foreign producers. Installation of existing equipment and purchase of a small amount of new equipment would cost approximately $600,000. The expenditure would be capitalized and depreciated over 7 years for tax purposes, although the equipment would last 10 years. If all-new equipment was used instead, the cost would be $1,800,000, and the new equipment would last for 20 years, although it would be depreciated over 7 years. The equipment would be placed in service January 1, and Black had a 34 percent tax rate. Net working capital requirements would be no greater, and possibly a little less, than those required to have the shoes produced overseas under contract. Design and start-up costs, which would not be capitalized, were estimated to be $300,000, but those costs would be cut in half if additional small factories were built.

It was estimated that the factory would produce 1.4 million pairs of shoes a year. Labor costs would be $5.7 million a year; materials would cost $4.3 million a year. Utilities, insurance, and other miscellaneous expenses, excluding depreciation, would cost $1.1 million a year. Black could purchase the same shoes under contract with a Taiwanese firm for $8.64 a pair, including shipping. However, the price could rise or fall sharply with a change in exchange rates. Through its distribution system, Black could sell the shoes at a wholesale price averaging $10.44, while incurring sales costs of 10 percent of sale price. Headquarters overhead was allocated to the divisions at 5 percent of sales.

Black Shoe's financial structure consisted of 30 percent debt and 70 percent equity. The yield to maturity on long-term U.S. government bonds was 8.13 percent, and Black's common stock had a beta of 1.1. The yield to maturity on Black's existing bonds was 9.76 percent. The mayor of Clear Spring had offered to donate the land and sell industrial revenue bonds to cover the $1,600,000 cost of the building. The industrial revenue bonds would carry an interest rate of 7.32 percent, and would be repaid in installments of $80,000 a year for 20 years.

Case Questions

1. How should the industrial revenue bonds be treated in the analysis?
2. Compute the net present value of the Clear Spring plant.
3. Discuss the risks involved with building the factory and not building the factory.
4. Should Black build the Clear Spring factory? Why or why not?

SELECTED REFERENCES

Arditti, Fred D., and Haim Levy. "The Weighted Average Cost of Capital as a Cutoff Rate: A Critical Examination of the Classical Textbook Weighted Average." *Financial Management* 6 (Fall 1977): 24–34.

Bergman, Yaacov Z., and Jeffrey L. Callen. "Opportunistic Underinvestment in Debt Renegotiation and Capital Structure." *Journal of Financial Economics* 29 (March 1991): 137–171.

Berkovitch, Elazar, and M. P. Narayanan. "Timing of Investment and Financing Decisions in Imperfectly Competitive Financial Markets." *Journal of Business* 66 (April 1993): 219–248.

Bohl, Alan, and Frederic H. Murphy. "The Effect of the Mix of Equity and Debt on the Selection of Projects." *Engineering Economist* 37 (Fall 1991): 61–74.

Brigham, Eugene F., and T. Craig Tapley. "Financial Leverage and Use of the Net Present Value Investment Criterion: A Reexamination." *Financial Management* 14 (Summer 1985): 48–52.

Chambers, Donald R., Robert S. Harris, and John J. Pringle. "Treatment of Financing Mix in Analyzing Investment Opportunities." *Financial Management* 11 (Summer 1982): 24–41.

Cooper, Ian, and Julian R. Franks. "The Interactions of Financing and Investment Decisions When the Firm Has Unused Tax Credits." *Journal of Finance* 38 (May 1983): 571–583.

Fries, Steven, Marcus Miller, and William Perraudin. "Debt in Industry Equilibrium." *Review of Financial Studies* 10 (Spring 1997): 39–67.

Froot, Kenneth A., and Jeremy C. Stein. "A New Approach to Capital Budgeting for Financial Institutions." *Journal of Applied Corporate Finance* 11 (Summer 1998): 59–69.

Golbe, Devra L., and Barry Schachter. "The Net Present Value Rule and an Algorithm for Maintaining a Constant Debt-Equity Ratio." *Financial Management* 14 (Summer 1985): 53–58.

Greenfield, Robert L., Maury R. Randall, and John C. Woods. "Financial Leverage and Use of the Net Present Value Investment Criterion." *Financial Management* 12 (Autumn 1983): 40–44.

Hellman, Thomas, and Manju Puri. "The Interaction Between Product Market and Financing Strategy: The Role of Venture Capital." *Review of Financial Studies* 13 (Winter 2000): 959–984.

Kamath, Ravindra R. "Long-Term Financing Decisions: Views and Practices of Financial Managers of NYSE Firms." *Financial Review* 32 (May 1997): 331–356.

Kensinger, John W., and John D. Martin. "Project Financing: Raising Money the Old-Fashioned Way." *Journal of Applied Corporate Finance* 1 (Fall 1988): 69–81.

Laber, Gene. "Bond Covenants and Forgone Opportunities: The Case of Burlington Northern Railroad Company." *Financial Management* 21 (Summer 1992): 71–77.

Leland, Hayne E. "Agency Costs, Risk Management, and Capital Structure." *Journal of Finance* 53 (August 1998): 1213–1243.

Levine, David I. "Do Corporate Executives Have Rational Expectations?" *Journal of Business* 66 (April 1993): 271–293.

Litzenberger, Robert H. "Some Observations on Capital Structure and the Impact of Recent Recapitalizations on Share Prices." *Journal of Financial and Quantitative Analysis* 21 (March 1986): 59–71.

Morellec, Erwan. "Asset Liquidity, Capital Structure, and Secured Debt." *Journal of Financial Economics* 61 (August 2001): 172–206.

Myers, Stewart C. "Interactions of Corporate Finance and Investment Decisions—Implications for Capital Budgeting." *Journal of Finance* 29 (March 1974): 1–25. Also, see comment and reply in *Journal of Finance* 32 (March 1977): 211–220.

Parrino, Robert, and Michael S. Weisbach. "Measuring Investment Distortions Arising from Stockholder-Bondholder Conflicts." *Journal of Financial Economics* 53 (July 1999): 3–42.

Ravid, S. Abraham. "On Interactions of Production and Financial Decisions." *Financial Management* 17 (Autumn 1988): 87–99.

Rhee, S. Ghon, and Franklin L. McCarthy. "Corporate Debt Capacity and Capital Budgeting Analysis." *Financial Management* 11 (Summer 1982): 42–50.

Ruback, Richard S. "Capital Cash Flows: A Simple Approach to Valuing Risky Cash Flows." *Financial Management* 31 (Summer 2002) 85–103.

Scherr, Frederick C., and Heather M. Hulbert. "The Debt Maturity Structure of Small Firms." *Financial Management* 30 (Spring 2001): 85–111.

Shimpi, Prakash A., and Swiss Re. "Integrating Risk Management and Capital Management." *Journal of Applied Corporate Finance* 14 (Winter 2002): 27–40.

Taggart, Robert A., Jr. "Capital Budgeting and the Financing Decision: An Exposition." *Financial Management* 6 (Summer 1977): 59–64.

Woods, John C., and Maury R. Tandall. "The Net Present Value of Future Investment Opportunities: Its Impact on Shareholder Wealth and Implications for Capital Budgeting Theory." *Financial Management* 18 (Summer 1989): 85–92.

CHAPTER 21

Lease Analysis

After completing this chapter you should be able to:

- Differentiate between the lessee and the lessor.
- Discuss the differences between an operating lease, a financial lease, a leveraged lease, and a sale and leaseback.
- List and explain eight reasons for leasing.
- Know who receives the tax benefits (depreciation expense) from the leased asset.
- Calculate and compare the net present value of purchasing an asset with the net present value of leasing an asset.
- Recognize a situation where an otherwise negative net present value project may become positive with lease financing.
- Identify the appropriate interest rate to use when discounting the cash flows from a leased asset.
- Adjust your analysis when comparing the performance of a leased asset with the performance of a purchased asset.
- Describe the different financial disclosures necessary for a capital lease versus an operating lease.
- List the conditions that separate a capital lease from an operating lease.
- Identify and discuss some of the factors or reasons for the popularity of leasing in practice.

Steven F. Udvar-Hazy and Louis L. Gonda met in college and, being airplane buffs, decided to start a commuter airline. The airline, funded with $100,000 of capital from their Hungarian immigrant families, failed. As part of their effort to dispose of the airplanes, the two friends leased a DC-8 to Aeromexico. One lease lead to another and the business was transformed into International Lease Finance Corp. (ILC). Although no longer owning an airline, the two friends are among the world's leading owners of airplanes.

In 1988, ILC placed the largest airplane purchase order in history. They ordered $5 billion worth of airplanes from Boeing and Airbus Industries. All of the airplanes were to be leased to airlines, reflecting the airlines' growing reliance on leasing as a method for acquiring airplanes.[1] The airlines are not alone. Leasing has grown in popularity as a means of acquiring a wide variety of assets, including automobiles, computers, offices, and factories.

A **lease** is a contract by which the owner of property gives someone else the right to use that property for a specified time period in exchange for specified payments. In this chapter, we focus on the choice between leasing and purchasing as a means of acquiring the use of an asset. Present value of cash flows and financial statement impact are considered, along with other factors that bear on the choice between leasing and owning. Based on this analysis, the impact of a lease alternative on the desirability of a capital investment is considered. The analysis of a capital investment also is considered for situations in which the asset cannot be purchased, and the only alternative is leasing.

OVERVIEW OF LEASES

The two parties to a lease are the lessor and the lessee; if you rent an apartment, the landlord is the **lessor** and you are the **lessee.** An overview of types of assets leased, types of lessors and lessees, and types of lease contracts is provided in the following paragraphs.

Types of Assets Leased

Leasing first became popular in connection with real estate: land and buildings. Those of us who have lived in apartments or rented houses have been lessees. In recent decades, leasing has expanded to serve as a method of acquiring a broad variety of assets. Motor vehicle leasing is a well-established industry, and leasing of equipment ranging from computers to factory machinery and total factories has also become popular. Leasing was originally limited to assets that could be transferred to other users if the lessee defaulted, but leasing of user-specific assets has become increasingly popular.

GTE Corporation provides us with an example of the growing use of leases as a means of acquiring an ever-increasing range of assets. When GTE wanted to place its $248 million Spacenet 3 satellite transponder in orbit, it arranged for a

[1]"An Order of Wings to Go," *Business Week* (May 30,1988): 32.

group of investors to buy the transponder, and then signed an agreement to lease the transponder from the investors. This particular transaction fell through when the rocket carrying the satellite malfunctioned and was destroyed shortly after takeoff in Kourou, French Guiana.[2] While the enthusiasm of the insurance companies may have suffered, enthusiasm for leasing was not dampened. Leasing is being used to acquire an ever-growing variety of assets. It is possible to go into business today by leasing a building, leasing the production machinery, leasing the office furniture, and leasing the motor vehicles needed to transport products. Several companies are even offering to lease employees.

Lessees include individuals, businesses, nonprofit organizations, and governments. Individuals regularly lease homes, automobiles, computers, and even furniture. Land, buildings, and equipment are leased by businesses, nonprofit organizations, and governments.

Lessors are divided into two broad groups: those interested in selling a product and those interested only in providing financing. Computer companies, for example, view the lease as a way to persuade customers to acquire a product they may be unwilling to buy. Banks, commercial finance companies, leasing companies, and wealthy individuals, on the other hand, purchase assets and lease those assets to others as an alternative to lending money or investing in stock. As real estate limited partnerships decreased in popularity after tax reform, leasing limited partnerships such as Atel Cash Distribution Fund and Phoenix Leasing Capital Assurance Fund grew. Investment bankers often aid in packaging complex lease transactions.

There are four widely used lease arrangements: operating leases, financial leases, leveraged leases, and sale and leaseback. These are discussed in the following paragraphs.

Operating Lease

An operating lease, also called a **service lease** or **service contract,** commits the lessor to provide and maintain the asset. These leases, which date back to at least the leasing of Model T Fords in 1918, gained popularity in the computer business. People were unfamiliar with computers, and the operating lease assured them that the manufacturer was committed not just to delivering and setting up the equipment, but also to assuring its continued serviceability. Operating leases are widely used for computers and other office equipment, and for motor vehicles. Portland General Electric signed an operating lease contract to sell its Boardman power plant while continuing to use the electricity generated there.

Operating leases often do not run for the life of the asset. Automobile leases, for example, are often for a period less than half of the average life of an automobile. Furthermore, many operating leases include a provision allowing the lessee to cancel the agreement before the end of the lease, normally with a cancellation penalty. Thus, the lessor is generally at risk with regard to the terminal

[2]This example and numerous other examples cited in this chapter come from "Top 10 Lease Transactions of '85 Total $4.1 Billion," *Pension and Investment Age* (April 14, 1986): 31+; and M. Douglas Dunn and Bernard C. Topper, Jr., "Terms and Conditions for Electric Utility Success with Leveraged Leases," *Public Utilities Fortnightly* 119 (April 16, 1987): 14–23.

value of the asset at the end of the lease period. TRAC (Terminal Rental Adjustment Clause) leases, often used for motor vehicle financing, transfer terminal value risk to the lessee by requiring the lessee to guarantee a specified market value of the asset at the end of the lease.[3]

Financial Lease

A financial lease, also called a **capital lease,** is purely a method of financing. The lessor neither maintains the equipment nor otherwise assures its serviceability. Furthermore, a financial lease is often for all or most of the service life of the asset so that the lessor has minimal risk with regard to the later value of the asset, unless the lessee defaults. The lessor in a financial lease is, therefore, in a position similar to that of a secured creditor.

In a typical financial lease arrangement, the lessee selects the asset and negotiates the price. The lessee also negotiates independently with a bank, commercial finance company, or leasing company that will serve as lessor. The lessor buys the asset and simultaneously leases the asset to the lessee. Typically, the asset moves from the manufacturer to the lessee, with the lessor taking title but not physical possession. From the perspective of both the lessor and lessee, the lease is simply an alternative to a loan.

Leveraged Lease

A leveraged lease is a lease in which the lessor uses borrowed money to acquire the asset to be leased. As an example of a leveraged lease, consider a steam and electric plant leased by PSE Corporation. GE Credit became the owner (and lessor) of the $233 million plant by putting up $80 million. The remainder was provided in the form of loans by a group of banks. This lease also qualifies as a financial lease as long as PSE remains responsible for maintenance and operation. Lease payments from the lessee go to a trustee, who uses the bulk of the payments to pay the lenders. The lessor, as owner of record, gets the benefits of depreciation tax savings and investment tax credits, if any. The lessor may be a bank, leasing company, wealthy individual, or limited partnership. The lender may be a life insurance company, charitable trust, or other investor in a low tax bracket. In some cases, such as El Paso Electric's lease for its Palo Verde Nuclear plant, a public bond issue is used for the debt portion of the financing. The leveraged lease allows assignment of cash flows and tax benefits among parties according to their particular tax situations, and, therefore, reduces the cost of the lease.

The tax law with regard to leveraged leases has been tightened somewhat in recent years. The lessor must now expect to make a profit independent of tax considerations in order for the tax deductions to be allowed.

---

[3]Many automobile leases that sound too good to be true are based on the lessee guaranteeing a high market value at the end of the lease. Tax law penalizes terminal rental adjustment clauses in leases for assets other than motor vehicles and trailers.

Sale and Leaseback

With a sale and leaseback arrangement, the owner of an asset contracts to sell the asset and to lease it from the buyer, typically under a financial lease arrangement. Thus, the financial lease is an alternative to borrowing against an asset already owned. The sale and leaseback is a way to raise money based on an asset while continuing to use the asset. An example is Tuscon Electric's sale of its Springerville generating plant for $850 million, while simultaneously agreeing to lease the plant back from the new owner. To keep terminology straight, a **direct lease** involves leasing an asset not previously owned by the lessee while a sale and leaseback involves leasing an asset that was previously owned by the lessee.

REASONS FOR LEASING

The growth in leasing must be attributed to real or perceived advantages of leasing over other methods of financing the acquisition of an asset. Some of the major reasons generally given for leasing are discussed in the following paragraphs.

Increased Availability of Financing. In the event of default, a lessor can often reclaim the leased asset faster and easier than would be the case for a secured lender. Therefore, lessors are often willing to provide assets through a lease when the company's credit rating would not be strong enough to induce a creditor to make money available. The creditor compensates for risk by financing only part of the cost of the asset, while leases often provide close to 100 percent financing.[4] Furthermore, the lessor is also often willing to arrange for lease payments over the entire life of the asset, while creditors will want to protect themselves by requiring that the loan be completely repaid well before the end of the asset's life. Because of the increased protection of the lessor, an organization that needs an asset can often arrange a lease faster than a loan, and with divulgence of less information.

Leasing is also used when restrictive covenants limiting additional borrowing have been accepted as part of past financings. Since a lease is not technically a loan, a lease can sometimes be used when additional borrowing is not allowed. CBI Corporation listed debt covenants as one of the reasons it was seeking off-balance-sheet financing when it arranged an operating lease for its air exchange plant, according to its treasurer, Buell T. Adams. This opportunity has been decreased because many loan agreements now include covenants limiting leases as well as additional borrowing.

Shift of Ownership Risk. The purchaser of an asset faces uncertainty with regard to serviceability, obsolescence, and residual value of the asset at the end of its use life. Leases can be a tool for decreasing or shifting those risks. When an asset is purchased, there is an agency-type problem in that the buyer must often rely on the seller's word and reputation with regard to asset quality. While there

[4]Business Aircraft Finance is one company that provides 100 percent financing ["To Finance or Lease," *Business Monthly* (August 1987): 72+].

may be a warranty, the burden of enforcing the warranty falls on the buyer. With an operating lease, the lessor promises not just the asset, but the service. The lessee has the option of ceasing lease payments if the asset is not serviceable. While there is the potential for a lawsuit when payments are stopped, the burden of enforcing the contract is shifted to the lessor. Thus, the operating lease is a method of assuring quality.

Obsolescence risk is not eliminated by the lease, but a lease is often a method of transferring that risk. Many leases give the lessee the option to cancel before the end of the lease, normally with some cancellation penalty. A cancellation option transfers the risk of obsolescence to the lessor. Likewise, the lessor is generally the party at risk with regard to the residual value of the asset at the end of the lease. Needless to say, these risks are still borne by someone, and the lease will be priced so that the lessor is compensated for risk bearing. As with other insurance, though, the lessee may feel that the reduction of risk is worth the cost incurred.

Flexibility. Flexibility is another advantage of leasing. Particularly with a cancellation provision,[5] the lessee can respond quickly to changing market conditions. A St. Louis marketer of photocopy machines advertises a cancellation clause in its lease that can be used if the customer's needs change. This is probably a more appealing scenario to the customers than the search for a buyer for a used copying machine.

Tax Advantages. Depreciation tax savings are of little use to nonprofit organizations and companies not making profits. Furthermore, the tax reform act of 1986 limits the amount of income that can be sheltered from taxes through the use of accelerated depreciation. A lease transfers depreciation tax benefits to the lessor. If the lessor is in a better position to use these benefits, the lease may be less expensive than the purchase. General Electric Credit received an immediate $35 million of tax benefits in 1985 from its position as lessor of PSE's electric and steam generating plant.[6] In other cases, a lease for less than the tax depreciation life of the asset effectively allows a more rapid write-off for tax purposes than would be possible with a purchase. Graham et al. found direct evidence that leasing is more popular among company's paying lower effective tax rates.[7]

Accounting Benefits. When assets and debt are placed on the company's books, the debt to equity ratio increases, and ratios measuring the efficiency of asset usage decline.[8] In addition, the combined interest and depreciation expenses cause income to decline. Accounting rules discussed later in this chapter require a financial lease to be treated on the accounting statements as if the asset were purchased. An operating lease, on the other hand, results in no

[5]See Thomas E. Copeland and J. Fred Weston, "A Note on the Evaluation of Cancelable Operating Leases," *Financial Management* 11 (Summer 1982): 60–67.

[6]Immediate tax benefits were decreased by the Tax Reform Act of 1986, but tax benefits still exist.

[7] John R. Graham, Michael L. Lemmon, and James S. Schallheim, "Debt, Leases, Taxes, and the Endogeneity of Corporate Tax Status," *Journal of Finance* 53 (February 1998): 131–162.

[8]These ratios include sales to total assets (turnover) and sales to fixed assets.

change to the balance sheet and may result in lower reported expenses than would occur if the asset were purchased. When CBI Corporation of Oak Brook, Illinois, sold an $18 million air-separation plant to GATX Corporation, it simultaneously signed a 15-year operating lease contract. As a result, CBI moved $18 million of assets off its balance sheet, freed up $18 million of cash to expand or repay debt, and still maintained use of the plant. A sale and leaseback may also generate one-time accounting income, such as the $79 million gain recognized by Oglethorpe Power Corporation through a sale and leaseback of its Sherer coal-fired Unit 2. The financial statement impacts of leases are covered later in this chapter.

Circumvent Decision Process. The purchase of an asset often requires a lengthy capital expenditure approval process. In some cases, though, acquisition of an asset through a lease is not subjected to the same decision process. Thus, a manager may be able to acquire an asset quickly through a lease when a request to purchase would be time consuming, and the response to the request would be uncertain. Circumvention of the company's decision process will not generally contribute to shareholder wealth maximization, but leases are sometimes used for this purpose anyway.

Reimbursement. Some organizations, such as hospitals, are reimbursed based on expenses incurred. When assets are leased, the lease payments are allowed as expenses. When assets are purchased, depreciation is allowed as an expense. If a cost of money is not also allowed with the purchase, reimbursement will generally be greater with a lease.[9] Electric utilities sometimes use leases to delay rate increases by smoothing cost recovery evenly across an asset's life.

Lower Cost. Other things aside, a lease will be attractive if the present value of the net cash outflows to lease is less than the present value of the net cash outflows to buy. The net result of many of the considerations previously discussed may be that the lease is a lower-cost alternative to the purchase. To the extent a lease results in less cash outflow than a loan, it also decreases the probability of default and bankruptcy.

TAXES AND LEASING

In general, the lessor receives the tax benefits of ownership. The lessor reports the lease payment as income and reports the depreciation on the asset as an expense in computing taxable income. The lessee reports the lease payment as an expense in computing taxable income.

The main tax complication is with regard to the question of whether a contract is really a lease, or an installment sale masquerading as a lease. If the Internal Revenue Service is successful in upholding its opinion that a particular

---

[9]See Rodney Roenfeldt and Jerome S. Osteryoung, "Lease-Cost Measurement of Hospital Equipment," *Financial Management* 8 (Spring 1979); 24–35.

contract is really an installment sale, the lease payments are treated as principal and interest payments on a loan while the lessee is treated as the owner of the asset for tax purposes.

To decide if a contract is a genuine lease, the fundamental question is *who bears the risks of ownership?* The IRS *may* decide to challenge a lease contract if *some* of the following guidelines are violated:

1. The term of the lease must not exceed 30 years.
2. The remaining useful life of the asset after the end of the lease must be at least 20 percent of the original estimated useful life, and the asset must be potentially useful to others besides the lessee.
3. The lease payments must provide the lessor a reasonable rate of return apart from tax benefits.
4. The lease should not include a bargain option to buy the asset or renew the lease.
5. The lease should not have early payments that are substantially higher than later payments.
6. The lease agreement should not limit the lessee's right to issue debt or equity.

CASH FLOW ANALYSIS FOR LEASE VS. BUY DECISIONS

The choice between leasing and purchasing often boils down to a pure cost question: Is the present value of the net cash outflows to lease greater or less than the present value of the net cash outflows to purchase?

The cost to lease an asset is generally the present value of the after tax lease payments. For a lease covering n periods, the general formula for the cost is:[10]

$$\text{Cost to lease} = \sum_{t=0}^{n} \frac{(1-T)L_t}{(1+k_d)^t} \tag{21-1}$$

where T is the tax rate, L_t is the lease payment in period t, and k_d is the company's after tax cost of debt.

The cash flows to lease are clear, at least in principle, but the reasons for using the after tax cost of debt as the discount rate may need a bit of clarification. The appropriate discount rate for present value calculations in general is the rate of return available on alternatives of equal risk. The stream of payments

[10]This formula assumes that tax benefits occur at the same time as lease payments. Frequently, lease payments are at the beginning of each year, while the tax reduction is spread over the year. In these cases, the present value of the lease payments and tax savings should be computed separately so that the timing of each can be accurately recognized.

for a lease is a set of contractual, fixed payments,[11] generally substituted for a set of fixed payments on debt. Therefore, the lease payments are as certain as the payments on debt; either type of payment will be made unless the company defaults. Likewise, the tax savings are as likely to occur as the tax savings that would result from interest expense on debt. Consequently, the after tax lease payments are as risky as the after tax debt payments they supplant, and should be discounted at the after tax cost of debt to compare lease with purchase.

Example: Kellnor Corporation needs a new computer system. The computer system can be leased for $21,000 at the *beginning* of each year for 7 years. Kellnor's marginal income tax rate is 35 percent, and the company can borrow money at an interest rate of 12.31 percent. The after tax cost of debt is, therefore, .1231 (1 − .35) = 8 percent. Assuming tax savings occur at approximately the same time as lease payments, the cost of leasing is determined by finding the after tax lease payment and then multiplying by the present value of $1 at the beginning of each year for 7 years:[12]

$$\text{Cost of leasing} = \$21{,}000(1 - .35)5.6229 = \$76{,}753$$

The cost to buy an asset is generally the present value of the after tax cash flows to purchase:[13]

$$\text{Cost to buy} = I_o + \sum_{t=0}^{n} \frac{(1-T)OC_t - T \times Dep_t}{(1+k_d)^t} - \frac{\text{Net terminal value}}{(1+k_o)^n} \quad \textbf{(21-2)}$$

where I_o is the initial outlay; OC_t is expected operating cost in period t that will be borne by the user if the asset is purchased, but not if it is leased; net terminal value is the terminal value of the asset, less any tax or other expense associated with the sale; and k_o is the company's weighted average cost of capital.

For the analysis of the purchase decision, the discount rates are again based on risk. Depreciation tax savings are generally felt to be low-risk cash flows, and the general practice is to use the after tax cost of debt, effectively assuming these flows have a degree of predictability similar to debt payments and their associated tax savings.

Readers are occasionally concerned about discounting depreciation tax savings at the after tax cost of debt when these same cash flows were discounted at the weighted average cost of capital in the original capital budgeting analysis. When net cash flows are being analyzed, a discount rate for average risk can be used, but when cash flow components are being analyzed individually, as is done

[11]For variable lease payments, see Stewart D. Hodges, "The Valuation of Variable Rate Leases," *Financial Management* 14 (Spring 1985): 68–74.

[12]The present value factor for $1 at the *beginning* of each year for 7 years is $(1.08)PVA1_{7\text{years},8\%} = 5.6229$.

[13]This formula again assumes that tax savings occur at the same time as expenses. If this is not the case, operating costs and resulting tax savings should be found separately to recognize the actual timing of these flows.

in lease analysis, discount rates appropriate for those particular components should be used.[14,15]

If operating costs are highly predictable, they are discounted at the after tax cost of debt, as illustrated in Equation 21-2. Many operating costs associated with fixed assets are certain or have only nonsystematic risk and should, therefore, be discounted at the after tax cost of debt. Uncertain operating costs require another discount rate, though. As pointed out in Appendix 14-A, an operating cost that is positively correlated with the company's cash inflows is discounted at a discount rate higher than the cost of debt, and vice versa. If operating costs tend to increase proportionally with the company's other cash flows, as would frequently be the case when operating costs depend on the level of activity, the weighted average cost would be the appropriate discount rate for operating costs.

The net terminal value is usually an uncertain amount,[16] and the general practice is to assume it has a risk similar to the average risk of the other cash flows of the company. The weighted average cost of capital is, therefore, used as the discount rate. The required return can be adjusted using methods described in Chapters 14 and 15 if it is believed that the systematic risk associated with net terminal value is greater or less than the systematic risk for the company as a whole, or option pricing models can be applied.[17]

In computing the cost of owning, the present value of the after tax principal and interest payments on a loan that is displaced by the lease is sometimes substituted for the cost of the asset itself. But the present value of the after tax payments on a loan (principal payments, plus interest payments, minus tax savings from interest payments), discounted at the after tax cost of debt, equals the amount borrowed. This relationship holds as a matter of definition because the after tax cost of debt is the internal rate of return relating after tax principal and interest payments with net loan proceeds.[18] Therefore, substituting the present value of the loan payments results in considerably more calculation and the same cost of buying.

A common error in comparing lease with purchase is to recognize the original cost, as is done in Equation 21-2, and also add the present value of interest payments on a loan. Because I_o equals the cost and also equals the present value of after tax principal and interest payments, adding the present value of interest payments again is clearly a case of double counting.

---

[14]See Appendix 14-A for a demonstration of the consistency between discounting total cash flows for average risk and discounting components at rates appropriate for those components.

[15]Despite these assurances, we must take seriously the concerns of practitioners like Roger L. Carson, who expresses concern about using multiple discount rates in practical settings. Roger L. Carson, "Leasing, Asset Lines, and Uncertainty: A Practitioner's Comments," *Financial Management* 16 (Summer 1987): 13–16.

[16]Salvage value and other lease-related cash flows are affected by inflation as well as other uncertainties. For a discussion of the role of inflation in lease analysis, see Shalom Hochman and Ramon Rabinovitch, "Financial Leasing under Inflation," *Financial Management* 13 (Spring 1984): 17–26.

[17]Wayne Y. Lee, John D. Martin, and Andrew J. Senchak, Jr., "The Case for Using Options to Evaluate Salvage Values in Financial Leases," *Financial Management* 11 (Autumn 1982): 33–41.

[18]The skeptical reader can confirm this for any loan amount, any interest rate, any payment sequence, and any tax rate desired.

TABLE 21-1 Cost of Buying Calculation

The cost of buying calculation is illustrated for a $100,000 asset with a 5-year tax life and 7-year useful life. Contractual maintenance expense of $6,000 a year can be avoided with a lease. The after tax cost of debt is 8 percent and the weighted average cost of capital is 12 percent. The net salvage value at the end of 7 years is $20,000.

YEAR:	0	1	2–5	6	7
Purchase	100,000				
Maintenance		6,000	6,000	6,000	
		× (1 − .35)	× (1 − .35)	× (1 − .35)	
After tax maintenance		3,900	3,900	3,900	
Depreciation[a]		10,000	20,000	10,000	
		× .35	× .35	× .35	
Depreciation tax savings		3,500	7,000	3,500	
Net salvage value					20,000
Net cash outflow	100,000	400	−3,100	400	−20,000
Present value factor[b]	1.0000	.9259	3.0668	.6302	.4523
Present value	100,000	370	−9,507	252	−9,046
Cost of Owning = $82,069					

[a]Current tax law requires depreciation during acquisition year to be based on the assumption the asset was acquired at midyear.

[b]Note that the discount rate is 12 percent for the salvage value and 8 percent for all other cash flows.

Example: Kellnor Corporation, in the previous example, can purchase a computer system for $100,000, with the system to be placed in service on January 1. The system will have a 5-year tax life and a 7-year use life. At the end of 7 years, the system will have a salvage value, net of taxes and removal costs, of $20,000. If Kellnor purchases the system, it must provide maintenance that would otherwise be provided by the lessor. The maintenance cost is $6,000 at the end of each year for 6 years, with a fixed-price maintenance contract. Kellnor will use straight-line depreciation. The after tax cost of debt is 8 percent and the weighted average cost of capital is 12 percent.[19] The cost of buying is the present value of all the cash flows associated with owning. The cost of buying is computed in Table 21-1.

The cost of buying the computer system was $82,069 while the cost of leasing was $76,753. Therefore, leasing would be preferred.

The net advantage of leasing over owning (NAL) can be found by subtracting the cost of leasing from the cost of owning. Subtracting Equation 21-1 from Equation 21-2 gives the NAL:[20]

[19]Assume for simplicity that taxes also occur at year end.

[20]For a detailed analysis of lease valuation, see John J. McConnel and James S. Schallheim, "Valuation of Asset Leasing Contracts," *Journal of Financial Economics* 12 (August 1983): 237–261.

$$NAL = I_o + \sum_{t=0}^{n} \frac{(1 - T)OC_t - T \times Dep_t}{(1 + k_d)^t} - \frac{\text{Net terminal value}}{(1 + K_o)^n} - \sum_{t=0}^{n} \frac{(1 - T)L_t}{(1 + k_d)^t} \tag{21-3}$$

Example: For the previously considered computer system, the net advantage of leasing is:

$$NAL = \$82{,}069 - \$76{,}753 = \$5{,}316$$

Since the net advantage of leasing is positive in this case, leasing would be preferred over owning, other things being equal.

The Lessor's Perspective

If we reverse the signs for all of the cash flows in Equation 21-3, we have the cash flows from the perspective of the lessor. The lessor buys the asset, collects lease payments, pays agreed-to operating costs, receives the depreciation tax benefits, receives the terminal value, and pays for the use of funds. Therefore, changing the sign of the NAL gives the net present value that will be realized by the lessor, other things being equal. For the previously considered computer system, the NAL is $5,316 so the lessor's NPV is –$5,316.

Does this mean leasing is a zero-sum game in which one party's gain is another party's loss? If that were the case, it would be difficult to explain the popularity of leasing. The zero-sum game exists only if expected cash flows to the lessor are the reverse of expected cash flows to the lessee, risk is the same for both parties, and the cost of funds is the same for both parties. There are numerous reasons this equivalence may not hold in practice.

From the time of Adam Smith, we have known that specialization increases productivity. Different lenders specialize in different types of loans for example. Lessors specialize in not only providing the funding, but also accepting the risks of ownership. Thus, they may have lower costs of funds, less risk, and different expected ownership costs than would be true for the company wishing to use the equipment. Many of the advantages of leasing discussed in this chapter are not automatically disadvantages to a lessor just because they are advantages to a lessee. Commercial airliner leasing is one such example. Many commercial carriers have bad credit ratings and may not have enough income to take advantage of the depreciation tax savings. Because it specializes, an airliner leasing company has the ability to quickly reclaim an airplane and lease it to someone else if the original lessee airline gets in trouble. As a result, its borrowing costs are lower than those of the airline, and its loss in case of default is less than that of a typical secured lender. Specialization allows everyone to win.

LEASING AND CAPITAL INVESTMENT DECISIONS

In the previous examples, the choice was between leasing and buying; we assumed that the asset would be acquired one way or the other. There are, however, situations in which lease terms may be attractive enough to turn the net present value of an investment from negative to positive. The capital budgeting implications of attractive leasing terms are treated in the following paragraphs.

The net present value if the asset is leased is simply the net present value if the asset is purchased, plus the net advantage of leasing. Suppose, for example, the net present value of the investment analyzed in Table 21-1 was –$3,000, determined by the normal capital budgeting methods described in Chapter 5. The investment proposal would be rejected. But the net advantage of leasing is $5,316, so the net present value with leasing is –$3,000 + $5,316 = $2,316.

CAPITAL BUDGETING WHEN AN ASSET CAN ONLY BE LEASED

Some capital investments are assets that cannot be purchased. Many retail locations, for example, are only available on a lease basis, and departments in retail stores are being leased with increased frequency. If a retail store in leased space at one location is being compared to a store in purchased space at another location, a meaningful method of comparison must be developed.

Companies will sometimes deduct the lease payments from the benefits to arrive at net cash flows, and then discount the net cash flows at the weighted average cost of capital or the cost of equity. This, though, is equivalent to discounting the lease payment as well as the project cash flows at the weighted average cost of capital or cost of equity rather than the after tax cost of debt. As illustrated in the next example, this form of analysis is biased in favor of the leased asset.

If the lease payment is purely a financing cost, we can discount the after tax lease payment at the after tax cost of debt, and discount all other cash flows at the weighted average cost of capital. More typically though, the lease payment includes compensation for various costs and benefits: the use of money, operating expenses, and depreciation tax savings, to name a few. If the lease payments replace fixed costs, the cash flows left after deducting the lease payments may be more risky than the net cash flows from ownership. An alternative that will generally categorize the risk from various cash flows correctly is to estimate the cost of the asset if it could be purchased, and use that cost in the analysis.

Example: Oceanside Corporation can lease an asset for $75,000 at the end of each year for the asset's 10-year life. The asset will generate earnings before depreciation and tax of $100,000 a year, and all cash flows occur at year-end. The company has a 35 percent tax rate, pays a 10 percent interest rate on debt, and has a 12 percent weighted average cost of capital. The asset cannot be purchased, but it is estimated that an asset of this type would be worth approximately

$500,000 if it could be purchased. Assuming depreciation of $50,000 a year, annual cash flows to purchase and to lease are as follows:

	BUY	LEASE
Earnings before depreciation and tax	$100,000	$100,000
– Depreciation	50,000	0
– Lease payment	0	75,000
Earnings before tax	$ 50,000	$ 25,000
Tax	17,500	8,750
Net income	$ 32,500	$ 16,250
+ Depreciation	50,000	0
= Cash flow	$ 82,500	$ 16,250

Using the first approach, the investment is attractive because the net present value is positive:[21]

$$\$16{,}250 PVA1_{10yrs,12\%} = \underline{\underline{\$91,816}}$$

Discounting lease payments at the after tax cost of debt, the net present value is substantially lower:

$$100{,}000(1-.35)PVA1_{10yrs,12\%} - 75{,}000(1-.35)PVA1_{10yrs,6.5\%} = \underline{\underline{\$16{,}809}}$$

Using the estimated purchase price, the net present value to purchase is:

$$NPV_{purchase} = 82{,}500PVA1_{10yrs,12\%} - 500{,}000 = -\$33{,}857$$

and the net advantage of leasing is:

$$\begin{aligned} NAL &= 500{,}000 - .35 \times 50{,}000 \times PVA1_{10yrs,6.5\%} - (1 - .35)75{,}000PVA1_{10yrs,6.5\%} \\ &= \underline{\underline{\$23{,}740}} \end{aligned}$$

The net present value with the leasing option is:

$$NPV = -\$33{,}857 + 23{,}740 = \underline{\underline{-\$10{,}117}}$$

The net present value in this example ranged from plus $91,816 to minus $10,117. This range occurred despite the fact that the same *net* annual cash flow of $16,250 was used in each analysis. The only thing that changed was the discount rate being applied to each component of cash flow. Obviously, the discount rate

[21]Discounting the $16,250 at the cost of equity might seem to be appropriate, but it is not. A lease that provides 100 percent financing will have a positive NPV at any discount rate as long as the *expected* cash flows after deducting the lease payments are positive. Thus, there is no effective way to adjust for risk through the choice of a discount rate when the net cash flow is the cash flow after deducting lease payments.

choice is critical for the analysis, and the discount rate depends on the risk of each component of cash flow when evaluating an asset that can only be leased. Correctly assessing the risks of those cash flows is, therefore, critical.

FINANCIAL STATEMENT IMPACTS OF LEASES

While the main focus of the analysis is on cash flows, it is unrealistic to ignore financial or capital statement impacts of capital investments. Management reward systems are often based on reported income, and financial statements are the information available to lenders and stockholders. Although it seems unlikely that sophisticated investors would be fooled, many managers seem to place a value on "window dressing" which is the name applied to activities designed purely to improve the appearance of the financial statements. Financial statement impacts are examined in the following paragraphs.

Accountants recognize two types of leases: operating leases and financial leases. The treatment of a lease on the financial statements depends on which type of lease it is. Accountants classify a lease as a financial lease if it meets one of the following tests, and as an operating lease otherwise:

1. The lease transfers ownership of the property to the lessee at the end of the lease term.
2. The lease contains a *bargain* purchase option.
3. The lease term is 75 percent or more of the estimated economic life of the leased property.
4. At the beginning of the lease term, the present value of the minimum lease payment equals or exceeds 90 percent of the fair market value of the asset. The minimum lease payment is the smallest possible lease payment if the lease payments depend on some future events; for a fixed-cost lease, the contractual lease payment is the minimum lease payment.

If a lease is considered an operating lease, the lease payment is treated as an expense on the income statement and the balance sheet is not affected.

Accountants consider a financial lease to be a close substitute for acquisition of the asset through an installment loan. The accountants attempt to show financial leases on the financial statements as if they were purchases. An asset equal to the present value of the lease payments is placed on the balance sheet and offset by a loan on the liability side equal to the present value of all future lease payments. The lease payments are then treated as principal and interest payments on a loan. The lease payment does not appear as an expense on the income statement, but interest on the implied loan and depreciation on the implied asset do appear on the income statement. The treatment of a lease on the financial statements can substantially affect the company's reported profitability.

Example: San Diego Industries is required to install new pollution-control equipment. The equipment will be acquired on January 1, 1999. The equipment will have a 10-year life for accounting purposes and a 5-year life for tax purposes. The equipment can be bought for $200,000, and financed with a 10 percent installment loan; payments would be \$32,549 at the end of each year for 10 years. Alternately, the asset could be acquired through a lease, with payments of \$32,549 at the end of each year for 10 years.

If the lease is considered an operating lease, San Diego will show a lease expense of \$32,549 on the income statement, and the balance sheet will be unaffected. If the lease is considered a financial or capital lease, the accountants will first find the present value of the lease payments, discounted at the company's 10 percent borrowing cost:

$$\text{Present value of lease payments} = 32{,}549\text{PVA1}_{10\text{yrs},10\%} = \$200{,}000$$

This \$200,000 is the implied asset value.

With the financial lease, the income statement will not reflect a lease payment, but will show depreciation on the implied asset and interest on the implied loan. Straight-line depreciation is often used for accounting purposes, so the depreciation will be \$200,000 ÷ 10 = \$20,000 and interest for 1988 will be another .10 × \$200,000 = \$20,000. Even though the series of payments for all three methods of acquisition are the same, the financial lease or purchase would result in \$40,000 of expenses on the income statement, while the operating lease would result in only \$32,549 of expenses.

Turning to the balance sheet at the end of 1999, the operating lease would not have any impact. The purchased asset, though, would have a book value of \$200,000, minus one year's accounting depreciation, or \$180,000. Thus, total assets would increase by \$180,000. The same thing would be true for the financial lease. Assuming no changes in other assets and no changes in equity, reported debt would also be \$180,000 greater at the end of 1999 with either the purchase or financial lease.

The financial statements for San Diego Industries appear in Table 21-2. The first column is the actual 1998 statement. The second column is the pro forma 1999 financial statement with an operating lease. The third column is the pro forma 1999 financial statement with a purchase or financial lease. Since the pollution-control equipment generates no revenue, profitability goes down regardless of the method of acquisition. But the impact of a financial lease or purchase is substantially worse than the impact of an operating lease. The profit margin on sales, return on assets, return on equity, and debt to total assets ratios are all lower with the financial lease or purchase than with the operating lease.

It should be noted that the net advantage of leasing is –\$11,031 in this situation, indicating that the purchase is preferred over the lease[22] on a present value basis. But managers may not choose to purchase. Concern over what is reported may override concern about the actual cash flows generated, and lead to the choice of the operating lease if that alternative is available.

---

[22]The net advantage of leasing was found using Equation 21-3. Note that the after tax cost of debt is 6.5 percent and accelerated tax depreciation for a 5-year asset is used to find the NAL:

$$\text{Dep}_1 = .2 \times 200{,}000 = \$40{,}000,\ \text{Dep}_2 = .4 \times 160{,}000 = \$64{,}000,\ \text{and so on:}$$

$$\text{NAL} = 200{,}000 - .35(40{,}000)/1.065 - .35(64{,}000)/1.065^2 - .35(38{,}400)/1.065^3 - .35(23{,}040)/1.065^4 - .35(23{,}040)/1.065^5 - .35(11{,}520)/1.065^6 - (1 - .35)32{,}549\text{PVA1}_{10\text{yrs},6.5\%} = -\$11{,}031$$

TABLE 21-2 Financial Statement Impacts of Purchase, Operating Lease, and Financial Lease for San Diego Industries

This table illustrates the impacts of three methods of acquiring an asset that can be purchased for $200,000, with installment loan financing, or acquired through lease payments with a present value of $200,000.

		PRO FORMA 1999	
	1998	OPERATING LEASE	PURCHASE OR FINANCIAL LEASE
Sales	$1,000,000	$1,000,000	$1,000,000
Cost of goods sold	600,000	600,000	600,000
Admin. Expense	140,000	140,000	140,000
Depreciation	60,000	60,000	80,000
Lease payments	0	32,549	0
Interest expense	40,000	40,000	60,000
Earnings before tax	160,000	127,451	120,000
Tax (35%)	56,000	44,608	42,000
Net income	$ 104,000	$ 82,843	$ 78,000
Total assets	$1,000,000	$1,000,000	$1,180,000
Debt	$ 400,000	$ 400,000	$ 580,000
Equity	600,000	600,000	600,000
Total liabilities and equity	$1,000,000	$1,000,000	$1,180,000
Profit margin (net income/sales)	10.4%	8.3%	7.8%
Return on assets (net income/total assets)	10.4%	8.3%	6.6%
Return on equity (net income/equity)	17.3%	13.8%	13.0%
Debt to total assets	.40	.40	.49

The objective of accountants in the treatment of financial leases is to accurately report the economic nature of the contract, and to discourage decision making aimed at distorting the information reported through financial statements. Further changes in accounting rules would be needed to remove the financial statement advantages of an operating lease over a financial lease.

CURRENT LEASING PRACTICE

Several surveys of leasing practice have been conducted, and several studies have been aimed at finding out why some companies use leases more than others. With regard to decision techniques, evaluation of after tax lease payments using an after tax cost of debt, as discussed in this chapter, is common practice.[23] Ang and Peterson found that companies that used substantial amounts of borrowing also used substantial amounts of leasing,[24] which is consistent with the explanation that leases are used to extend debt capacity. In contrast, Graham et al. found a negative relationship between operating leases and tax rates while debt was positively correlated with tax rates, supporting the idea that leases are a substitute for debt for low tax rate firms.[25] Sharpe and Nguyen found that leases are more common with lower-rated, cash-poor firms, the types of companies that tend to have high borrowing costs.[26] Krishnan and Moyer found evidence that companies are more likely to lease if the likelihood of bankruptcy and the associated costs of bankruptcy are high in the industry.[27] Mehran et al. found that companies with high CEO ownership were more likely to lease, possibly to reduce risk.[28]

Smith and Wakeman found that, as would be expected, the tax rates of lessors and lessees were important factors in determining who acted as lessors and lessees. Smith and Wakeman also observed eight factors which appeared to make the decision to lease more likely:

1. The value of the asset is less sensitive to use and maintenance decisions. This decreases the agency problems associated with the contract.
2. The asset is not specialized to the firm. An asset that can be used by others generates fewer risks for the lessor.
3. The expected period of use is short relative to the useful life of the asset. The lessor is often in a better position to find a new user than is the lessee.
4. Corporate bond contracts contain specific financial policy covenants. As explained earlier, a lease can sometimes be used to acquire an asset when additional borrowing is not allowed.
5. Management compensation contracts contain provisions specifying payoffs as a function of the return on invested capital. In these cases, leases reduce the asset base on paper while still giving the company the same assets to use in generating income.
6. The firm is closely held so that risk reduction is important. Leases transfer risks such as obsolescence risk and nonperformance risk to people or organizations who may be able to diversify away those risks.
7. The lessor has market power. In some cases, lessors make assets available only on a lease basis. This way, they can control how the assets are used. Only lessors with market power can do this, because competition would otherwise force them to offer sale contracts as well.

---

[23]T. J. O'Brien and B. H. Nunnally, Jr., "A 1982 Survey of Corporate Leasing Analysis," *Financial Management* 12 (Summer 1983): 30–39.

[24]James Ang and Pamela Peterson, "The Leasing Puzzle," *Journal of Finance* 39 (September 1984): 1055–1065.

[25]Graham et al., op cite.

[26]Steven A. Sharpe and Hien H. Nguyen, "Capital Market Imperfections and the Incentive to Lease," *Journal of Financial Economics* 39 (December 1995): 271–294.

[27]V. Sivarama Krishnan and R. Charles Moyer, "Bankruptcy Costs and the Financial Leasing Decision," *Financial Management* 23 (Summer 1994): 31–42.

[28]Hamid Mehran, Robert A. Taggart, and David Yermack, "CEO Ownership, Leasing, and Debt Financing," *Financial Management* 28 (Summer 1999): 5–14.

8. The lessor has a competitive advantage in asset disposal. If the lessor is also the manufacturer or dealer, for example, the lessor can capitalize on a network of sales contacts to sell or re-lease an asset when another user would have difficulty finding a buyer.[29]

The factors that seem to affect the leasing decision in practice are consistent with the general reasons for leasing cited earlier in this chapter and also are consistent with the principles of lease analysis developed in this chapter.

SUMMARY

A lease is a contract by which the owner of property gives someone else the right to use that property for a specified amount of time in exchange for specified payments. In a lease contract, the owner is called the **lessor** and the party who has the use of the asset in exchange for payments is called the **lessee.** An operating lease, also called a **service lease** or **service contract,** commits the lessor to provide and maintain the asset. A **financial lease** is purely a method of financing. The lessor neither maintains the equipment nor otherwise assures its serviceability. A **leveraged lease** is a lease in which the lessor uses borrowed money to acquire the asset to be leased. With a **sale and leaseback** arrangement the owner of an asset contracts to sell the asset and to lease it from the buyer, typically under a financial lease arrangement.

Reasons for Leasing. The primary reasons generally cited for leasing are (1) increased availability of financing, (2) shift of ownership risk, (3) flexibility, (4) tax advantages, (5) accounting benefits, (6) opportunity to circumvent the capital investment decision process, (7) reimbursement formulas, and (8) lower cost.

Cash Flow Analysis of Lease vs. Buy Decisions. A lease can be compared to a purchase based on the present value of the cash flows to lease and the present value of the cash flows to own. The net advantage of leasing is the difference between the present value of cash flows to own and cash flows to lease.

Leasing and Capital Budgeting. The sum of the net present value of a purchased asset and the net advantage of leasing is the net present value if the asset is leased. An asset that has a negative net present value if purchased is still attractive if the net advantage of leasing is larger than the amount of negative net present value.

Financial Statement Impacts of Leases. If accountants classify a lease as an operating lease, the lessee shows the lease expense on the income statement, and the balance sheet is not affected. If the accountants classify a lease as a financial lease, an asset with a value equal to the present value of the lease payments is implied, and the lease payments are treated as payments on an installment loan for the implied asset. The lease payment is replaced on the income

[29]Clifford W. Smith, Jr., and L. MacDonald Wakeman, "Determinants of Corporate Leasing Policy," *Journal of Finance* 40 (July 1985): 896–910.

statement by implied interest expense and implied depreciation. The implied asset and implied debt are placed on the balance sheet. An operating lease often looks better on the financial statements than a purchase or a financial lease.

QUESTIONS

21-1. Define the terms (a) lease, (b) lessor, (c) lessee, (d) financial lease, (e) operating lease, (f) leveraged lease, and (g) sale and leaseback.

21-2. What types of assets can be leased?

21-3. What types of organizations act as lessors? as lessees?

21-4. What are the main advantages of leasing that may cause companies to choose that method of acquiring assets?

21-5. What are the conditions that may cause the Internal Revenue Service to treat a lease as if it were a purchase?

21-6. What happens if the Internal Revenue Service treats a lease as if it were a purchase?

21-7. What conditions may make it possible for a lessor to offer a lease that would yield a smaller present value of cash costs than a purchase?

21-8. What conditions cause accountants to consider a lease to be a financial or capital lease?

21-9. How does the accounting treatment of a financial lease differ from that of an operating lease?

21-10. Why is the depreciation tax shield discounted at the after tax cost of debt in computing the net advantage of leasing when it was discounted at the weighted average cost of capital in other capital budgeting analysis?

PROBLEMS

21-1. Booth Corporation is considering a minicomputer that can be leased for $2,000 a year for 5 years. The company's marginal tax rate is 35 percent and the yield to maturity on the company's debt is 9.23 percent. Compute the cost to lease if lease payments and associated tax savings are at the

a. beginning of each year.

b. end of each year.

21-2. For the asset in problem 1, lease payments are at the beginning of each year, and tax payments are spread over the year. Assume, for simplicity, that tax payments occur at midyear. Compute the cost of leasing.

21-3. A dental X-ray machine can be leased for $1,000 at the beginning of each month for 4 years. The dental clinic's borrowing rate is 10.769 percent and the tax rate is 35 percent. For simplicity, treat both the lease payments and the associated tax savings as if they arrived at year-end. What is the cost to lease?

21-4. A $30,000, 12.308 percent loan will be paid off in 3 years. At the end of each year, a $10,000 principal payment will be made, plus an interest payment of 12.308 percent of the amount owed at the beginning of the year. The borrower faces a 35 percent marginal tax rate.

a. Ignoring taxes, find the present value of the principal and interest payments, discounted at the interest rate on the debt.

b. Find the present value of the after tax principal and interest payments, discounted at the after tax cost of debt.

21-5. Hodges Corporation is considering a new asset that can be purchased for \$100,000. Maintenance costs will be \$5,000 a year for the asset's 8-year actual life, and are highly predictable. The asset will be depreciated over an 8-year life for tax purposes, using depreciation of \$12,500 a year (for simplicity). The asset will be placed in service on January 1. The asset will have no salvage value. Assume all cash flows other than the initial purchase are year-end, the tax rate is 34 percent, and the after tax cost of debt is 6 percent. What is the cost to buy?

21-6. Ann Arbor salvage needs a new compactor that can be purchased for \$100,000. The asset will last for 10 years, but has a tax life of 5 years. Operating costs, excluding depreciation, will be \$20,000 a year. The asset will be placed in service January 1 and depreciated using the straight-line method. The estimated salvage value, before tax, is \$10,000. The tax rate is 34 percent, the after tax cost of debt is 6 percent, and the weighted average cost of capital is 12 percent. Assume the operating costs are highly predictable and that all cash flows occur at year-end. What is the cost to own?

21-7. For the asset in problem 6, assume the operating costs are highly correlated with (have the same beta as) the company's net cash flows. Find the cost to own.

21-8. Las Cruces Printing is considering a new press. The press can be purchased on January 1 for \$24,000. The press has an 8-year actual life and a 5-year tax life. Depreciation will be straight line, and the estimated salvage value is \$6,000, before tax. Operating expenses will be \$2,000 a year, and are not correlated with any other activity. Instead of purchasing, the company can lease the asset for \$5,250 at the *beginning* of each year for 8 years. Operating costs will be paid by the lessor. Assume all cash flows except the lease payments and initial purchase price occur at year-end. The tax rate is 34 percent, the weighted average cost of capital is 12 percent, and the after tax cost of debt is 6 percent. Should the company lease or buy?

21-9. For the press in problem 8, what is the minimum salvage value for the purchase to be preferred over the lease?

21-10. For the press in problem 8, what is the maximum acceptable lease payment if the lease is to be preferred over the purchase?

21-11. You want a new status automobile for personal use. Neither depreciation nor interest payments will be tax deductible. You can buy the automobile for \$23,450, with a \$5,000 down payment and a 12 percent, 40-month loan. The monthly payments will be \$561.91. Alternately, you can lease the automobile with only a \$500 refundable security deposit and lease payments of \$499 at the beginning of each month for 40 months. Using a 12 percent annual required return to evaluate the salvage value, what must the car be worth at the end of 40 months for the purchase to be more attractive than the lease?

21-12. Lansing Electric is considering a new automatic test unit. The asset can be purchased on January 1 for $45,000. The asset has a 6-year actual life, a 5-year tax life, and no anticipated salvage value. Depreciation will be $9,000 a year (for simplicity) if the asset is acquired. The asset will generate earnings before tax of $6,600 a year. The company has a 35 percent tax rate, a 10 percent weighted average cost of capital, and a 6 percent after tax cost of debt. Assume benefits and taxes occur at year-end.

a. Is this an attractive investment?

b. The asset can also be leased for $7,500 at the beginning of each year for 6 years. What should the company do?

21-13. Milwaukee Supply is considering asset A, which can be leased for $30,000 at the beginning of each year for 10 years and would be placed in service on January 1. The lease is a financial lease arrangement, not providing for any maintenance. This asset will generate earnings before lease payments and taxes of $45,000 a year for 10 years. The company has a 34 percent tax rate. The company has a 10 percent before tax cost of debt and a 10 percent weighted average cost of capital. Although the asset is not available for purchase, it is estimated that an asset of this type would sell for approximately $215,000, would have a 5-year tax life, and would have no salvage value. Should it be leased?

21-14. Asset A in problem 13 is mutually exclusive with regard to asset B. Asset B can only be purchased—for $215,000. Asset B will generate earnings before depreciation and tax of $50,000 a year for its 10-year life. The asset will be placed in service on January 1, and straight-line depreciation will be used for a 5-year tax life. The asset is not expected to have a salvage value. Should the company choose asset A, asset B, or neither asset?

21-15. Rochester Human Services Association needs a new blood-storage unit. A blood-storage unit can be purchased for $100,000. The asset has a 5-year tax life and a 6-year actual life. The asset will be placed in service on January 1 and is expected to have no salvage value. Both the association and the potential lessor can borrow at 10 percent. The lessor is in a 40 percent tax bracket and the association pays no income tax. The lessor will also provide maintenance services worth $5,000 a year. What is the maximum lease payment the association would be willing to make, and what is the minimum lease payment the lessor would be willing to accept?

21-16. Athens Technology can purchase a needed asset for $100,000 or lease it for $30,000 at the end of each year for 5 years. The lease would be considered an operating lease and the asset would have a 5-year life for accounting purposes. The company would finance the purchase with a 10 percent loan, and has a 34 percent tax rate. Show the impact of the purchase and the lease on accounting income for the first year.

21-17. The balance sheet for Athens Technology follows. Show how the balance sheet would look immediately after acquiring the asset in the previous problem

a. through a purchase.

b. through an operating lease.

Current assets	$200,000	Current liabilities	$100,000
Fixed assets	400,000	Long-term debt	200,000
Total assets	$600,000	Owners' equity	300,000
		Total liab. & o. e.	$600,000

21-18. A lease calls for payments of $20,000 at the beginning of each year for 5 years. The lease is considered a financial lease by the accountants. The company pays a 10 percent interest rate on debt. What is the implied asset value and the implied first-year interest? What are the total first-year implied interest and depreciation expenses? What would be the total first-year expense if the lease were considered an operating lease?

21-19. A needed asset can be purchased by Jackson Bearing Service on January 1 for $50,000, and placed in service on January 1. The asset has a 6-year actual life and a 5-year tax life. The company's tax rate is 35 percent. The after tax cost of debt is 6 percent, the before tax cost of debt is 9.23 percent, and the weighted average cost of capital is 10 percent. Alternately, the asset can be leased for $10,700 at the beginning of each year for 6 years. The asset is expected to have a $10,000 salvage value. Consider both the cash flows and the financial statement impacts. Should the company purchase or lease the asset?

21-20. **(Applications)** The Limited, Inc., is a specialty retailer with nearly $7 billion in sales in 1992. They operate The Limited, Lerner, Lane Bryant, Victoria's Secret, Structure, Bath & Body Works, and several specialty stores under different names. In total they had 4,425 stores at the end of 1992. In the 1992 annual report they reported no capitalized lease obligations. In the footnotes to the same annual report they reported minimum rent commitments under noncancelable leases of:

1993	$ 527,000,000
1994	524,600,000
1995	508,300,000
1996	490,800,000
1997	466,800,000
Thereafter	$2,636,000,000

The Limited, Inc., had the following capital structure disclosed in the balance sheet:

Long-Term Debt	$ 541,639,000
Stockholders' Equity (at book value)	2,267,617,000

They had 362,648,000 shares outstanding with a market price of $23 each. Their beta was 1.5 and the cost of existing equity using the CAPM was 15 percent. The before tax cost of debt was approximately 7.5 percent with an after tax cost of 4.6 percent.

a. Assuming the $2,636,000,000 labeled "thereafter" equals $439,000,000 per year for the next 5 years (1998 to 2002) and $441,000,000 in the sixth year (2003), what is the present value of the lease commitments for The Limited?

b. Calculate the weighted average cost of capital without the lease commitments and then with the lease commitments.

c. For a project that involves the opening of a new store by signing a lease for the store, which discount rate is more appropriate?

21-21. **(Ethical considerations)** Within the last 5 years, the practice of leasing people has become more and more popular in practice. Under the typical agreement, an employment agency hires the individuals and takes care of the payroll duties and the required labor reporting. As the client businesses need additional staff, the individuals are contacted by the employment agency and told where to report for work. Some of these workers are hired by the client business if the demand is expected to continue and the leased worker is "working out" in the job. When demand is not sufficient to maintain the leased person, the business notifies the employment agency, and the person is either reassigned, furloughed, or terminated.

a. In a purely financial sense, leasing people has some of the same benefits and disadvantages as leasing any other asset. From the corporate perspective, what are the benefits and disadvantages of leasing employees?

b. Ethically, who assumes most of the risk under the set-up described above? Given that managers should have the best information concerning the employment needs of the organization and a fiduciary responsibility to the shareholders and other parties, comment on the ethical issues surrounding the leasing of employees. Describe the situations in which you feel leasing people is acceptable and where you feel it is unacceptable.

c. Do you expect this practice to increase or decrease in popularity in the future? Why?

CASE PROBLEM

National Petrochemical

National Petrochemical was a producer of various chemicals, primarily based on petroleum. Security analysts had been critical of National for several reasons. First and foremost, return on equity was low and declining. National had a profit margin on sales similar to the rest of the industry, but National had a lower total asset turnover ratio and used less financial leverage than the industry. While asset turnover and profit margin had improved slightly in the past year, operating costs had increased faster than sales and total asset turnover had declined. None of these trends seemed healthy. National's operating results for 1993 and 1994 are shown in Table 21-3.

TABLE 21-3 Financial Statements for National Petrochemical

All dollar amounts are in thousands. 1993 statements are actual and 1994 statements are forecast, based on results for the first three quarters.

YEAR:	1993	1994
Sales	$561,225	$572,250
Cost of goods sold	470,675	477,925
Gross profit	90,550	94,325
Operating costs	44,875	46,750
Net operating income	45,675	47,575
Interest expense	11,850	11,325
Earnings before tax	33,825	36,250
Income tax	14,771	16,947
Net income	$ 19,054	$ 19,303
Current assets	$199,575	$203,225
Fixed assets	186,925	224,825
Other assets	86,050	76,925
Total assets	$472,550	$504,975
Current liabilities	$104,000	$131,500
Long-term debt	76,350	68,350
Other liabilities	43,175	56,725
Common equity	249,025	248,400
Total liab. & net worth	$472,550	$504,975

For comparison, average ratios for a sample of six similar companies were as follows:

RATIO	1993 COMPETITOR AVERAGES
Sales/total assets	1.3
Net income/sales	4.00%
Net income/total assets	5.20%
Debt/total assets	50.53%
Return on equity	11.34%

Profitability problems were on the mind of the controller, Irene Watson, when she began to analyze two proposals for a new telephone system for the company's headquarters. There was no question about the need for a new system, but the choices available would affect the company's financial position differently. The impact of a communication system was small compared to something like a new factory. But Watson knew that performance would be improved by doing a lot of small things right, not by one or two dramatic actions. She was, therefore, determined to make a communication system decision that would move the company in the right direction.

One system consisted of a central telephone switch located on National's premises. This switch would cost $4,832,000, including installation. A parts inventory would cost $223,680 and would have no salvage value. Maintenance was estimated at $343,267 a year. The system would be placed in service for tax purposes on December 31, 1994, and would have a depreciation life of

7 years. However, National's lease on its headquarters building only had 5 years to run, and it was not anticipated that the system would have any salvage value if National moved at the end of 5 years. The system would be financed with a 5-year term loan requiring equal annual payments. Space, insurance, and electricity costs would be approximately $110,000 a year.

The regional telephone company had proposed an alternate system, using the telephone company's local switching office. That system would require service contract payments of $1,800,000 a year. Payments would be made at the beginning of each month.

National had a weighted average cost of capital of 13 percent and a borrowing rate of 10 percent. Including state and local taxes, National expected to have a 40 percent marginal tax rate in 1994 and later years although the historical average rate was higher for reasons not relevant to this case.

Case Questions

1. Compute the present value of the cash flows to own over a 5-year period.
2. Compute the present value of the cash flows for 5 years with the telephone company service contract.
3. Assume the 1995 financial statement is the same as the pro forma 1994 statement, except for tax rates, and the impact of the new telephone system.
   a. Show the financial statement impacts of the purchase.
   b. Show the financial statement impacts of the service contract.
4. Should National purchase the equipment or enter into a service contract?

SELECTED REFERENCES

Ang, James S., and Pamela P. Peterson. "The Leasing Puzzle." *Journal of Finance* 39 (September 1984): 1055–1065.

Bayless, Mark E., and J. David Diltz. "Capital Leasing and Corporate Borrowing." *Engineering Economist* 32 (Summer 1987): 281–302.

———. "An Empirical Study of Debt Displacement Effects of Leasing." *Financial Management* 15 (Winter 1986): 53–60.

Bierman, Harold, Jr. "Buy Versus Lease with an Alternative Minimum Tax." *Financial Management* 17 (Winter 1988): 87–91.

Carson, Roger L. "Leasing, Asset Lines, and Uncertainty: A Practitioner's Comments." *Financial Management* 16 (Summer 1987): 13–16.

Copeland, Thomas E., and Fred J. Weston. "A Note on the Evaluation of Cancelable Operating Leases." *Financial Management* 11 (Summer 1982): 60–67.

Crawford, Peggy J., Charles P. Harper, and John J. McConnel. "Further Evidence on the Terms of Financial Leases." *Financial Management* 10 (Autumn 1981): 7–14.

Dunn, M. Douglas, and Bernard C. Topper, Jr. "Terms and Conditions for Electric Utility Success with Leveraged Leases." *Public Utilities Fortnightly* 119 (April 16, 1987): 14–23.

Franks, Julian R., and Stewart D. Hodges. "Lease Valuation When Taxable Earnings Are a Scarce Resource." *Journal of Finance* 42 (September 1987): 987–1007.

Graham, John R., Michael L. Lemmon, and James S. Schallheim. "Debt, Leases, Taxes, and the Endogeneity of Corporate Tax Status." *Journal of Finance* 53 (February 1998): 131–162.

Grimlund, Richard A., and Robert Capettini. "A Note on the Evaluation of Cancelable Operating Leases." *Financial Management* 11 (Summer 1982): 68–72.

Hartman, Joseph C., and Jack R. Lohman. "Multiple Options in Parallel Replacement Analysis: Buy, Lease, or Rebuild." *Engineering Economist* 42 (Spring 1997): 223–248.

Heaton, Hal. "Corporate Taxation and Leasing." *Journal of Financial and Quantitative Analysis* 21 (September 1986): 351–359.

Hochman, Shalom, and Ramon Rabinovitch. "Financial Leasing under Inflation." *Financial Management* 13 (Spring 1984): 17–26.

Hodges, Stewart D. "The Valuation of Variable Rate Leases." *Financial Management* 14 (Spring 1985): 68–74.

Krishnan, V. Sivarama, and R. Charles Moyer. "Bankruptcy Costs and the Financial Leasing Decision." *Financial Management* 23 (Summer 1994): 31–42.

Lease, Ronald C., John J. McConnell, and James S. Schallheim. "Realized Returns and the Default and Prepayment Experience of Financial Leasing Contracts." *Financial Management* 9 (Summer 1980): 11–20.

Lee, Wayne Y., John D. Martin, and Andrew J. Senchak, Jr. "The Case for Using Options to Evaluate Salvage Values in Financial Leases." *Financial Management* 11 (Autumn 1982): 33–41.

Levy, Haim, and Marshall Sarnat. "Leasing, Borrowing, and Financial Risk." *Financial Management* 8 (Winter 1979): 47–54.

Mehran, Hamid, Robert A. Taggart, and David Yermack. "CEO Ownership, Leasing, and Debt Financing." *Financial Management* 28 (Summer 1999): 5–14.

Mukherjee, Tarun K. "A Survey of Corporate Leasing Analysis." *Financial Management* 20 (Autumn 1991): 96–107.

Roenfeldt, Rodney L., and Jerome S. Osteryoung. "Analysis of Financial Leases." *Financial Management* 2 (Spring 1973): 74–87.

———. "Lease-Cost Measurement of Hospital Equipment." *Financial Management* 8 (Spring 1979): 24–35.

Schall, Laurence D. "Analytical Issues in Lease vs. Purchase Decisions." *Financial Management* 16 (Summer 1987): 17–20.

Sharpe, Steven A., and Hien H. Nguyen. "Capital Market Imperfections and the Incentive to Lease." *Journal of Financial Economics* 39 (December 1995): 271–294.

Smith, Bruce D. "Accelerated Debt Repayment in Leverage Leases." *Financial Management* 11 (Summer 1982): 73–80.

Smith, Clifford W., Jr., and L. MacDonald Wakeman. "Determinants of Corporate Leasing Policy." *Journal of Finance* 40 (July 1985): 895–910.

Steele, Anthony. "Difference Equation Solutions to the Valuation of Lease Contracts." *Journal of Financial and Quantitative Analysis* 19 (September 1984): 311–328.

Weingartner, H. Martin. "Leasing, Asset Lives, and Uncertainty: Guides to Decision Making." *Financial Management* 16 (Summer 1987): 5–12. Also see "Rejoinder" on pages 21–23.

CHAPTER 22

Capital Rationing

After completing this chapter you should be able to:

- Explain how the capital markets may influence a firm to ration capital.
- Criticize and/or justify a management policy limiting the amount of capital to be invested in a specific time period.
- Differentiate between single-period capital rationing and multiple-period capital rationing.
- Describe how some companies use the internal rate of return to ration capital and the conditions necessary for a wealth-maximizing decision when ranking with the internal rate of return.
- Calculate the profitability index and understand what this measures.
- Select between mutually exclusive investments within a capital rationing framework.
- List resources, other than cash, that can be the limiting or rationed resource in deciding among mutually exclusive investments.
- Prepare a presentation to an executive committee detailing why your firm should ration capital.

In January 1988, William H. Sullivan, Jr., found himself in imminent danger of losing his New England Patriots football team, while his son Charles was in imminent danger of losing the stadium. The junior Sullivan bought the Patriots' stadium in 1981 and then invested heavily in a new electronic scoreboard and luxury boxes. He also invested in a harness racing track and a deal to license products associated with a Michael Jackson tour. He was saddled with $40 million of debt on a stadium for which he had paid only $5 million. In the meantime, the senior Sullivan invested heavily in players and gave an option to acquire the team in order to secure debt financing. He then tried to sell stock to buy back the option, but investors were not interested. By early 1988, the creditors were preparing to exercise their option, and Charles Sullivan was in default on $20 million of debt.[1]

The Sullivans' problems illustrate the difficulties that can follow uncontrolled expansion. If the expansion appears to be uncontrolled or unprofitable, the investing public declines to furnish equity under terms that managers will accept. Expansion is then financed with debt, at increasingly higher interest rates and with increasingly onerous conditions attached. It may be argued that the Sullivans' underlying problem was that they made capital investments that did not have positive net present values. However, unprofitable investments are more likely to occur when expansion is uncontrolled. One way to control expansion and avoid problems of this type is to use capital rationing. Capital rationing occurs when the total capital budget is limited, forcing rejection of some capital investments that have positive net present values.

Survey results suggest that most companies operate under capital rationing at least part of the time,[2] so a reasonable basis for decision making under capital rationing is needed. The goal of maximizing wealth is still the main capital budgeting criterion when we face capital rationing, but future investment opportunities and future availability of funds must be considered in selecting investments to achieve that goal.

Capital rationing differs from the mutually exclusive investment decisions discussed in Chapter 7. Mutually exclusive investments are generally competing methods of achieving the same goal or competing uses of a scarce resource other than money. When two investments are mutually exclusive, there are often physical reasons why both cannot be chosen. Competitors under capital rationing are competing uses of the same scarce money.

This chapter begins with a discussion of why capital rationing occurs. Then, a general model for capital budgeting under capital rationing is developed. Next, a usable approach is developed under some reasonable simplifying assumptions. Finally, we will consider the joint problems of capital rationing and mutually exclusive investments.

REASONS FOR CAPITAL RATIONING

The numerous explanations for capital rationing that have been cited fall into one of two broad categories: management policy and capital market conditions.

---

[1] *Business Week* (January 25, 1988): 40.

[2] Larry J. Gitman and J. R. Forrester, Jr., "A Survey of Capital Expenditure Techniques Used by Major U.S. Firms," *Financial Management* 6 (Fall 1977): 66–71; J. W. Petty, D. F. Scott, and M. M. Bird, "The Capital Expenditure Decision-Making Process of Large Corporations," *Engineering Economist* 20 (Spring 1975): 159–172; and Marc Ross, "Capital Budgeting Practices of Twelve Large Manufacturers," *Financial Management* 15 (Winter 1986): 15–22.

Capital Market—Imposed Rationing

Rationing never occurs in theoretical perfect markets because companies can always raise money if they have attractive investments. But information limits and transaction-related costs can lead to capital rationing in real markets. Capital markets impose capital rationing when investors and lenders absolutely refuse to provide capital beyond some specific amount. Market-imposed rationing also occurs when the marginal cost of capital rises vertically as more capital is sought. Both types of rationing can be dealt with using the same model because absolute refusal to furnish more funds is an extreme case of a vertically rising marginal cost of capital.

Figure 22-1 illustrates market-imposed capital rationing. Up to amount A, the company's marginal cost of capital is 10 percent. Above amount A, the cost rises to 12 percent. **Friction costs** are one common reason for a rising cost of capital schedule. The cumulative amount represented by A may be provided from internally generated funds, for example, while amounts beyond A must be raised externally. The cost of internally generated capital is the return that could be earned outside the firm if the funds were returned to shareholders and lenders, *minus* taxes and other friction costs that would be incurred if funds were returned to investors. The cost above A would then be the return that could be earned outside the firm by shareholders and lenders, *plus* flotation costs associated with raising new capital. The estimation of these costs was treated in Chapter 16.

FIGURE 22-1 Investment Opportunity and Cost of Capital Schedule
Amount A can be raised internally at a 10 percent cost of capital. If the company wants to raise additional funds, the cost will rise to 12 percent because of flotation costs. The highest-return investment opportunity available to the company is 15 percent, and to invest an amount greater than A, the company must accept investments with returns below 11 percent.

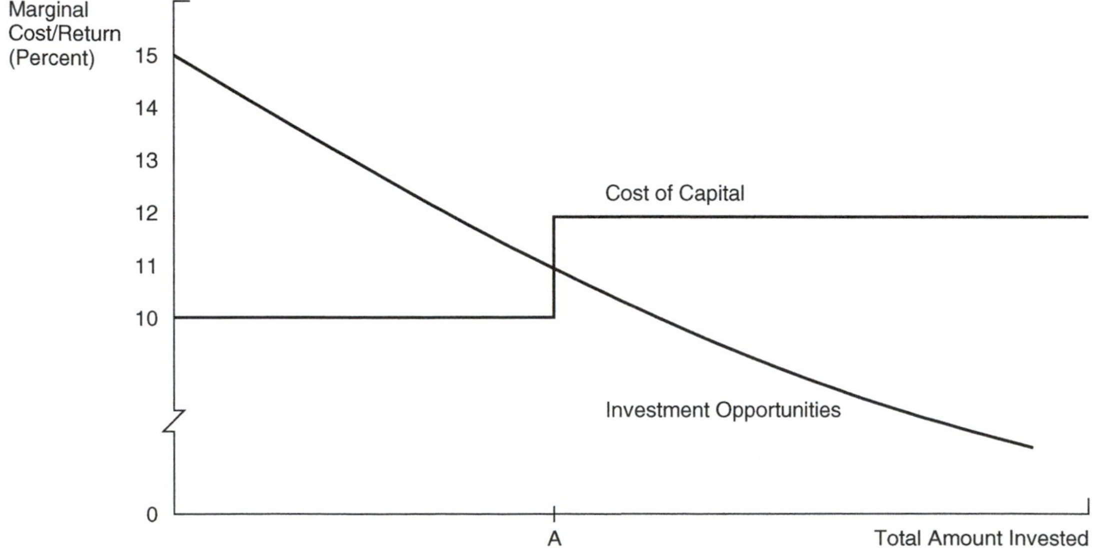

In Figure 22-1, 12 percent and 10 percent are sometimes referred to as the "borrowing" and "lending" rates. The company has available amount A. The company can "lend" some of that money at 10 percent by buying back its own securities or buying similar securities. If the company wants to "borrow" by raising additional funds, it must pay 12 percent. For a large company with publicly traded stock, the jump at A may be as small as a fraction of 1 percent. A small, privately held company wanting to sell its stock to the public for the first time may experience flotation costs in excess of 30 percent of the market value of the new capital. Companies of this type will experience substantial vertical segments of their marginal cost of capital schedules.

In Figure 22-1, the investment opportunity schedule represents the investments being considered by the company.[3] (For simplicity, assume investments precede benefits and each investment has only one internal rate of return.) The company could earn a 15 percent return on the last dollar invested if it invested only small amounts. If the company invested amount A, though, it would earn a return of 11 percent on the last investment. Beyond amount A, the company would be raising money at a cost of 12 percent to invest in assets earning less than 11 percent. Given this set of investment opportunities, the company will maximize wealth by investing amount A and rejecting some investments providing returns above 10 percent.

Even if the marginal cost of capital schedule has vertical segments, capital rationing may not occur. Capital rationing occurs only if the investment opportunity schedule intersects a vertical segment of the cost of capital schedule. A sufficient shift of the investment opportunity schedule to either the left or the right in Figure 22-1 would move this company out of capital rationing. This can explain why companies report capital rationing in some years and not in others.

The greater the increase in the marginal cost of capital at quantity A, the greater the likelihood of market-imposed capital rationing. If the marginal cost of capital rose to infinity at A—an absolute refusal to supply more than amount A to the company—there would be a high probability of market-imposed capital rationing occurring. Absolute refusal could occur because of problems like information asymmetry. Suppose, for example, that potential investors are much less optimistic than management about investment opportunities. Suppose, for example, that potential investors believe that proposed new capital investments will force the company into bankruptcy. Since lenders do not expect to receive either principal or interest payments, there is no level of promised interest payment that will compensate them for their risk. Whited suggests that information asymmetry may be a particularly important source of capital restraint for distressed companies.[4]

---

[3]In practice the curve is not smooth, but consists of steps because of lumpiness; many investments must be taken in their entirety or not at all. Lumpiness is a potential problem for the projects near the intersection with the cost of capital schedule. Because of lumpiness, it may be necessary to carry over some money from one year to the next in short-term investments. Lumpiness is not an important problem for large firms considering making hundreds or thousands of capital investments every year. Methods of expanding the analysis to deal with lumpiness where this is a problem are taken up later.

[4]Toni M. Whited, "Debt, Liquidity Constraints, and Corporate Investment: Evidence from Panel Data," *Journal of Finance* 47 (September 1992): 1425–1460.

Some prefer to define capital rationing as the absolute refusal of investors to provide funds at any price.[5] The reason for using a broader definition of capital rationing here is that the decision problems are similar whether investors absolutely refuse to provide more money or the marginal cost of capital schedule is vertical at its intersection with the investment opportunity schedule. In either case, the company will reject investments that have positive net present values when evaluated using the marginal cost of capital for the last dollar used.

Capital Rationing as Management Policy

Capital rationing as management policy occurs when managers set an upper limit on the total amount of capital investment for a period, even if additional funds could be raised and investments with positive net present values are being rejected. An example of capital rationing by managers would be a decision to limit investment to an amount less than A in Figure 22-1.

Capital rationing may be used as a method of management control. If all investments with positive net present values are accepted in a large organization, this leaves the choices of both rate and direction of growth in the hands of managers well down in the organization; there will be no strategy.

Capital rationing is one way to implement strategy and avoid uncontrolled growth. Top executives can set a total capital budget amount for the year, which defines the target rate of asset growth. Then, the capital budget can be allocated among divisions based on strategic decisions about areas of growth. Additional rounds of allocation may take place within divisions in a similar manner. Finally, the individual capital investment proposals in each responsibility area compete for the capital budget allocated to that area, assuming the supply of attractive proposals is adequate. With this approach, top executives know the direction of growth, amount of growth, and amount of new money they must raise. While rejecting positive net present value investments may seem like an expensive way to implement controls, managers often find this approach more workable than any known alternatives.[6] In a survey of major corporations, Klammer, Koch, and Wilner found that 72 percent of the responding companies start with a predetermined capital budget amount rather than funding all positive net present value investments.[7]

Closely related to management control is the problem of risk control. The faster a company grows, the greater the portion of its business that is untested,

---

[5]Brigham and Gapenski, for example, define capital rationing as occurring when the "size of the [capital] budget is less than the investment called for by the NPV (or IRR) criterion." [Eugene F. Brigham and Louis C. Gapenski, *Intermediate Financial Management* (Hinsdale, Ill.: Dryden Press, 1985), 404.] A in Figure 22-1 is the amount called for by the net present value criterion, given the cost of capital and investment opportunity schedules, so the problem illustrated in that figure would not meet Brigham and Gapenski's definition of capital rationing. Bierman and Smidt, on the other hand, identify differences between "lending" and "borrowing" rates as one of the causes of capital rationing. [Harold Bierman, Jr., and Seymour Smidt, *The Capital Budgeting Decision,* 7th ed. (New York: Macmillan Company, 1988), 191–196.

[6]For additional discussion of these problems, see Robert H. Litzenberger and O. Maurice Joy, "Decentralized Capital Budgeting Decisions and Shareholder Wealth Maximization," *Journal of Finance* 30 (September 1975): 993–1002.

[7]Thomas Klammer, Bruce Koch, and Neil Wilner, "Capital Budgeting Practices—A Survey of Corporate Use," University of North Texas, mimeo, 1988.

the greater the number of people who are not well known, and so on. Thus, rapid growth and risk often go hand in hand. It was rapid growth, especially the purchase of MGM's library of classic films for $1.5 billion on the heels of several other expansionary ventures, that forced Ted Turner to give up part of his control of his TBS broadcasting empire in order to secure an equity infusion when things did not work out as well as expected.

Because of problems like those encountered by Turner, rapid growth and management comfort are often in opposition. Wright suggested that some top managers are uncomfortable with a range of responsibility that increases too rapidly and, therefore, use capital rationing as a tool for limiting growth.[8]

Managers also use capital rationing because they are unhappy with the conditions under which additional funds would be furnished from outside sources. Myers's pecking order hypothesis suggests that managers prefer debt over equity, and will only resort to equity when they cannot borrow more.[9] An extension of this view may be an unwillingness to invest beyond amounts that can be funded with internally generated funds and new debt. There is usually not a clear point at which debt becomes absolutely unattainable. More typically, the restrictions imposed by lenders may become increasingly unacceptable as the debt level rises. Managers may be willing to limit the company's growth and give up some wealth rather than accept outside interference.

Management-imposed capital rationing may be used as a surrogate method for dealing with other scarce resources, such as a shortage of middle managers. More wealth would probably be created by seeking to maximize net present value subject to a constraint on the number of middle-level managers used, but a constraint on total capital may be simpler to implement.

Some managers use capital rationing with the anticipation that competition for limited funds will separate good investments from bad. A manager may, for example, be tempted to use overly optimistic projections to get a pet project approved. If acceptance of one investment means rejection of another, though, assumptions and forecasts will be vigorously challenged. This may discourage managers from making overly optimistic projections as well as flushing out such exaggeration when it does occur. This motivation for capital rationing is supported by a study showing a tendency for capital investment proposals to be overly optimistic.[10,11] Some top managers also believe that subordinates are kept on their toes by competition for capital investment dollars.

Difficulty in estimating the cost of capital is another reason for using capital rationing. As discussed earlier in this text, decades of research have failed to result in ways to precisely measure the cost of capital in practice. On the other

---

[8]F. K. Wright, "Project Evaluation and the Managerial Limit," *Journal of Business* (April 1964): 179–185.

[9]Stewart C. Myers, "The Capital Structure Puzzle," *Journal of Finance* 39 (July 1984): 575–592.

[10]Meir Statman and Tyzoon T. Tyebjee, "Optimistic Capital Budget Forecasts," *Financial Management* 14 (Autumn 1985): 27–33.

[11]A closely related bias results from estimation error in the face of imperfect information. Given a large number of possible capital investments with actual NPVs that are slightly negative, measurement error will cause the estimated NPVs for some projects to be positive, and only those projects will be proposed to top management. See Edward Miller, "The Cutoff Benefit-Cost Ratio Should Exceed One." *Engineering Economist* 46 #4 (2001): 312–319.

hand, Jagannathan and Meier have shown that when capital rationing is used, the optimal decision is relatively robust with regard to the cost of capital estimate.[12]

Given all the reasons for using capital rationing, it is not surprising that capital rationing is frequently observed in practice.

A MODEL FOR CAPITAL RATIONING

Regardless of whether capital rationing is chosen by managers or imposed by capital markets, the company has a fixed amount of capital available for some period, referred to as the **capital rationing period.** The appropriate objective for a wealth-maximizing firm working with a fixed pool of capital is to use that fixed pool of capital to maximize future wealth over the time that capital is available for use. To maximize wealth in the face of capital rationing, we can, therefore, decide to maximize wealth as of the end of the capital rationing period. We will illustrate the application of this principle with single-period capital rationing, and then move to a more general model.

Single-period Capital Rationing

Single-period capital rationing occurs when capital rationing is not expected to occur after the initial period. In this situation, we can reasonably assume that any funds not invested in the proposed set of investments will be invested elsewhere at the company's cost of capital. As illustrated next, wealth will be maximized if the company simply acts to *allocate scarce capital so as to maximize net present value.*

Example: GNW Corporation has $1,000 available to invest and has two investments available. GNW is experiencing single-period capital rationing and has a 10 percent cost of capital. GNW wants to maximize wealth as of the end of the single capital rationing period. The cash flows for the proposed investments are as follows (I_o is the initial outlay and CF_t is cash flow at the end of year t):

INV.	I_O	CF_1	CF_2	CF_3
A	700	300	200	500
B	500	400	200	100

GNW can choose only one of these investments with its budget constraint, and unused funds will be invested at the 10 percent cost of capital. The company's wealth as of the end of the first period is the cash it has on hand at the end of the first period, plus the present value of cash flows to be received later. Year-end wealth for each investment alternative follows.

[12]Ravi Jagannathan and Iwan Meier, "Do We Need CAPM for Capital Budgeting?" *Financial Management* 31 (Winter 2002): 55–77.

$$A: (\$1{,}000 - \$700)(1 + .10) + \$300 + \$200/(1 + .10) + \$500/(1 + .10)^2 = \underline{\underline{\$1{,}225.04}}$$

$$B: (\$1{,}000 - \$500)(1 + .10) + \$400 + \$200/(1 + .10) + \$100/(1 + .10)^2 = \underline{\underline{\$1{,}214.46}}$$

If neither A nor B is chosen, the $1,000 would be invested at 10 percent and the company would have $1,100 at the end of the year. Therefore, investment A will *increase* wealth at the end of the rationing period by $1,225.04 – $1,100.00 = $125.04, and B will increase wealth at the same time by $114.46; A is preferred. The net present value is the present value of the amount by which the terminal wealth is increased:

$$NPV_A = \$125.04/(1 + .10) = \$113.67$$

$$NPV_B = \$114.46/(1 + .10) = \$104.05$$

Note that the net present value computed in this way for the single-period rationing case is identical to the traditionally computed net present value:

$$NPV_A = \$300/1.1 + \$200/1.1^2 + \$500/1.1^3 - \$700 = \underline{\underline{\$113.67}}$$

$$NPV_B = \$400/1.1 + \$200/1.1^2 + \$100/1.1^3 - \$500 = \underline{\underline{\$104.05}}$$

Thus, allocation of scarce capital so as to maximize net present value will maximize wealth in the face of single-period capital rationing.

Multi-period Capital Rationing

Multi-period capital rationing is more complicated because it is necessary to estimate investment opportunity rates in future periods. Recall that the objective is to use the fixed pool of money available for the capital rationing period to maximize wealth as of the end of the rationing period. Going back to GNW, assume that capital rationing will last for 2 years. Any funds not used at the beginning can be invested for the 2-year period at a 20 percent annual return. Funds available at the end of year 1 can be invested at 15 percent for the remaining year of capital rationing.

If GNW chooses neither investment A nor B, the amount it will have at the end of the 2-year rationing period is $\$1{,}000(1 + .20)^2 = \$1{,}440$. If GNW invests only in project A, $300 will still be invested for 2 years at 20 percent. Wealth at the end of the capital rationing period will be:

$$300(1 + .20)^2 + 300(1 + .15) + 200 + 500/(1 + .10) = \underline{\underline{\$1{,}431.55}}$$

The investment in project A will, therefore, *decrease* terminal wealth by $1,440.00 – $1,431.55 = $8.45.

This method of analysis can be summarized graphically as follows:

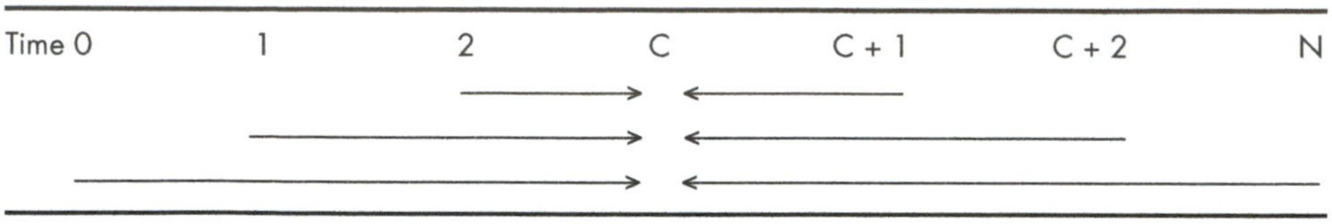

Time 0	1	2	C	C + 1	C + 2	N
		——→	←——			
	————	——→	←————	———		
———	———	——→	←———	———	———	

The process can also be reduced to a formula for the increase in wealth as of the end of the capital rationing period:

$$TW_c = \sum_{t=1}^{c} CF_t(1 + R_t)^{c-t} + \sum_{t=c+1}^{n} CF_t/(1 + k)^{t-c} - I_0(I + R_0)^t \qquad \textbf{(22-1)}$$

where

TW_c = contribution to wealth as of the end of the capital rationing period

c = the number of periods capital rationing will occur

n = the number of years until the end of the investment's life

R_t = the rate of return at which funds available at time t can be reinvested until the end of the capital rationing period

k = the cost of capital

Returning to GNW, the terminal wealth contribution of investments A and B are:

$$A: TW_c = 300(1 + .15) + 200 + 500/(1 + .10) - 700(1 + .20)^2 = \underline{\underline{-\$8.45}}$$

$$B: TW_c = 400(1 + .15) + 200 + 100/(1 + .10) - 500(1 + .20)^2 = \underline{\underline{\$30.91}}$$

Note that A was preferred with single-period capital rationing, but A is unattractive and B is preferred with this capital rationing scenario.

Although terminal wealth maximization leads to the optimal choice, managers often prefer to talk about net present value impact. The net present value impact is simply the present value of the terminal wealth increase. The net present value of terminal wealth (NPV_{TW})[13] is found by dividing Equation 22-1 by $(1 + k)^c$:

[13]We assumed that money available at time t could be reinvested until the end of the capital rationing period at rate R_t. If funds available at the end of period t can be invested for only one period at rate R_t, then Equation 19-2 must be rewritten as:

$$NPV_{TW} = \frac{\sum_{t=1}^{c} CF_t(1 + R_t)(1 + R_{t+1})\cdots(1 + R_{c-1})}{(1 + k)^c} + \sum_{t=c+1}^{n} CF_t/(1 + k)^t - \frac{I_0(1 + R_t)(1 + R_{t+1})\cdots(1 + R_{c-1})}{(1 + k)^c}$$

Applying this formula to GNW's investment A:

$$NPV_{TW} = \frac{300(1 + .15) + 200}{(1 + .10)^2} + \frac{500}{(1 + .10)^3} - \frac{700(1 + .20)(1 + .10)}{(1 + .10)^2} = \$27.72$$

$$NPV_{TW} = \frac{\sum_{t=1}^{n} CF_t(1+R_t)^{c-t}}{(1+k)^c} + \sum_{t=c+1}^{n} CF_t/(1+k)^t - \frac{I_o(1+R_o)^c}{(1+k)^c} \qquad \textbf{(22-2)}$$

For GNW's investment alternatives, the net present value impacts are:

$$A:\ NPV_{TW} = \frac{300(1+.15)+200}{(1+.10)^2} + \frac{500}{(1+.10)^3} - \frac{700(1+.20)^2}{(1+.10)^2} = \underline{\underline{-\$6.99}}$$

$$B:\ NPV_{TW} = \frac{400(1+.15)+200}{(1+.10)^2} + \frac{100}{(1+.10)^3} - \frac{500(1+.20)^2}{(1+.10)^2} = \underline{\underline{\$25.54}}$$

The example was simplified by assuming that an unlimited amount could be invested at a 20 percent return in the first year. Often, though, the company faces an investment opportunity schedule such as that in Figure 22-1, so that the marginal rate of return declines as the amount of new investment increases. The example was also simplified by assuming that the cost of capital was the same in each future period; the company may face a different cost of capital in each future period. These complications make it necessary to jointly select the set of present and future investments. Given the necessary forecasts of future cash flows and investment opportunities, this can be done using mathematical programming procedures explained in Chapter 24. Unfortunately, the analysis is further complicated if investment opportunities in future periods are unknown.

If you do not know how to forecast investment opportunities 10 years from now, and are discouraged at the thought of developing a complex mathematical programming model, take heart. Equation 22-2 can be simplified and a complex multi-period joint solution can be avoided if you are willing to make the following simplifying assumptions:

1. Capital rationing will continue as long as the lives of the investments currently being considered.[14]
2. The marginal cost of capital, k, will be the same for each period.
3. The reinvestment opportunity rate, R, will be the same for each period.
4. Lumpiness is not a significant problem. Lumpiness refers to the fact that certain assets and sources of funds can be acquired only in units of some minimum size. Ford cannot, for example, build an efficient $100,000 automobile factory or raise $7,000 by selling new equity to the public.

With this set of assumptions, Equation 22-2 simplifies to:

$$NPV_{TW} = \left[\sum_{t=1}^{n} CF_t/(1+R)^t\right]\left[(1+R)^c/(1+k)^c\right] - I_o(1+R)^c/(1+k)^c \qquad \textbf{(22-3)}$$

[14]Alternately, as will be seen, a simple solution is available if capital rationing is only expected to last for one period.

The term $(1 + R)^c/(1 + k)^c$ is a multiplier that will be the same for all investments. Therefore, we can factor out that multiplier and choose investments so as to maximize:

$$NPV_R = \sum_{t=1}^{n} CF_t/(1 + R)^t - I_o \qquad \textbf{(22-4)}$$

where NPV_R is the net present value computed with the internal reinvestment opportunity rate rather than the cost of capital. Note that like the original net present value, NPV_R measures the increase in wealth given the set of assumptions used to derive NPV_R.

Looking at Figure 22-1, the assumptions to justify use of Equation 22-4 could be fulfilled by assuming that conditions in the future will be the same as now: the cost of capital, k, will be 10 percent and the reinvestment opportunity rate, R, will be the rate at the intersection of the two schedules: 11 percent.

With these simplifying assumptions, optimal investment selection under capital rationing is again a problem of choosing the set of investments that will maximize net present value. The only difference is that the reinvestment opportunity rate is used instead of the cost of capital as the discount rate. Many companies use this simplified assumption approach because they believe future cost of capital and investment opportunity schedules are too uncertain to justify the use of mathematical programming techniques. Furthermore, investment decisions are decentralized and spread through the year so that a joint decision is not feasible.

Example: Oakland Corporation anticipates having $1 million of internally generated funds available this year, at a 10 percent cost of capital. Oakland is privately owned at present and raising additional capital would require turning to outside markets. Investment bankers indicate that the markets are not currently receptive to new issues, so the marginal cost of externally generated capital would be 15 percent. Management decides that a conservative assumption of a 12 percent reinvestment rate should be used for planning since large amounts can be invested at that rate. The company has the investment opportunities listed in Table 22-1.

If Oakland Corporation expects capital rationing to continue in future years, it will choose investments so as to maximize net present value with a 12 percent discount rate, subject to a constraint of no more than $1 million being invested this year. The combination A, B, D provides the maximum possible net present value using a 12 percent discount rate: $137,000.

THE INTERNAL RATE OF RETURN AND CAPITAL RATIONING

Some companies use the internal rate of return as a selection method under capital rationing. The internal rate of return ranking will lead to selection of the wealth-maximizing set of investments if lumpiness is not a problem; capital rationing will continue as long as the lives of investments currently being consid-

TABLE 22-1 Investment Opportunity Schedule for Oakland Corporation

The capital investments described in this table represent the investment opportunities currently available to Oakland Corporation. The company has $1 million to invest.

OPPORTUNITY	COST	LIFE	IRR	NPV(10%)	NPV(12%)
A	$ 500,000	5 years	20%	$134,000	$103,000
B	400,000	5 years	15	52,000	30,000
C	100,000	3 years	14	7,000	3,000
D	100,000	10 years	13	13,000	4,000
E	100,000	20 years	12.5	17,000	3,000
F	1,000,000	10 years	12	87,000	0
G	2,000,000	20 years	10	0	-245,000

ered; all proposed investments have the same risk; and the reinvestment rate, R, meets the following conditions:

1. R will be the same each period.
2. R will exceed the marginal cost of capital for the last dollar used.
3. R is the return on the highest-return opportunity that would be rejected with an internal rate of return ranking.

Using Table 22-1, an internal rate of return ranking would lead to selection of investments A, B, and C. The highest-return rejected project would be D, with an internal rate of return of 13 percent. Choice of A, B, and C would maximize wealth if the investment opportunity rate in future periods was 13 percent, because these are the only investments with positive net present values at a 13 percent discount rate.[15] Therefore, given these assumptions, the internal rate of return ranking leads to the same choice as NPV_R.

Choosing investments according to internal rate of return ranking will also maximize wealth if the cash inflows from each project can be reinvested for the planning horizon at a rate equal to the internal rate of return for that project.[16] This is, however, a somewhat questionable assumption. Would it not make more sense, for example, to assume that marginal cash inflows can be reinvested at the internal rate of return of the lowest-return project being accepted, or the highest-return project being rejected?

Multiple Internal Rates of Return and Capital Rationing

Dorfman has shown that when a company is facing capital rationing and an investment has more than one internal rate of return, the highest internal rate of

[15]We know from Chapter 6 that an investment with an internal rate of return above the discount rate has a positive net present value, and vice versa.

[16]Robert Dorfman, "The Meaning of Internal Rates of Return," *Journal of Finance* 36 (December 1981): 1011–1021.

return is the rate at which a starting capital base will grow if all cash flows from the project are invested in projects with the same internal rate of return.[17] If this assumption about the reinvestment opportunity rate does not seem reasonable, the problem can be avoided by choosing according to net present value using the assumed reinvestment opportunity rate.

THE PROFITABILITY INDEX AND CAPITAL RATIONING

The profitability index (previously defined in Chapter 6) is sometimes suggested as a method of selecting investments under capital rationing. However, a study of Table 22-1 will make it clear that a profitability index ranking using the cost of capital will *not* lead to the optimal decision. On the other hand, a profitability index ranking using the 12 percent opportunity rate expected for future periods will lead to the wealth-maximizing choice in the absence of lumpiness.[18] As an example of why lumpiness causes problems, suppose a company with $100,000 to allocate has the following investment opportunities, each of which must be taken in its entirety or not at all:

INVESTMENT	COST	NPV	PROFITABILITY INDEX
H	$ 10,000	$ 5,000	1.5
I	100,000	20,000	1.2

A profitability index ranking would lead to the choice of H and the rejection of I; this choice would not maximize wealth.[19] An initial ranking by profitability index followed by checking of projects near the cut-off point is usually sufficient to pick up these problems and make the necessary adjustments. In summary, the profitability index using the reinvestment rate is not an alternative to Equation 22-4, but a way to apply Equation 22-4.

[17]Robert Dorfman, Op. cit.

[18]For this purpose, the profitability index should be computed using only the initial cash outlay in the denominator, not the present value of all capital outlays for the investment as is sometimes done in other settings. The reason for this measurement method is that we are trying to find the set of investments that leads to the maximum attainable wealth creation, given the constraint on initial capital.

[19]If leftover funds are invested at the weighted average cost of capital, the $90,000 left over after investment in asset H creates additional net present value of $0.

SELECTION AMONG MUTUALLY EXCLUSIVE INVESTMENTS UNDER CAPITAL RATIONING

A general model for choice among mutually exclusive investments under capital rationing requires the use of mathematical programming, illustrated in Chapter 24. However, the forecasting problems associated with these models can often be avoided by using the assumptions of constant values of R and k in future periods if some simplifying conditions exist.

One simplifying condition is *the company has enough capital this period to accept all investments with returns above R,* the future investment opportunity rate. In this case, the most desirable of the mutually exclusive investments is the one that maximizes net present value over the life of the scarce resource, using R to compute the net present value as was done in Equation 22-4. If the lives of mutually exclusive investments differ, and the constraining resource can be reused, the equivalent annuity is used. The only change from use of the equivalent annuity in the absence of capital rationing is that R is used instead of k in the computations.

If there is not enough capital to accept all non–mutually exclusive investments with returns above R this period, the choices become a bit more complex. The analysis is still based on the net present value over the constraining resource's life for each possible use of the resource. In this case, though, it is necessary to consider any possible paths of usage that involve a less capital-intensive use of the resource in the beginning, followed by a more capital-intensive use later. It is also necessary to consider the possibility of not using the scarce resource at all. The total set of investments, including one of the mutually exclusive investments, is chosen so as to maximize total net present value.

Example: Basin Corporation operates under capital rationing and has $10,000 to invest this year. The assumed investment opportunity rate in future years is 12 percent. Basin is considering the three capital investment proposals summarized below. Investments A and B are mutually exclusive because they use the same scarce resource: a dock. The dock can be reused indefinitely, but it is not possible to add a second dock. It is possible to acquire more than 1 unit of C.

INVESTMENT	COST	LIFE	NPV_R	EQUIVALENT ANNUITY
A	$ 5,000	5 years	$ 767.64	$212.95
B	10,000	10 years	1,300.45	230.16
C	5,000	5 years	600.00	166.45

The alternatives available and their net present values are summarized in Table 22-2. If delayed use of the scarce resource is feasible, the best alternative is to acquire 2 units of C now and acquire B in 1 year. If delayed use is not feasible, the best alternative is to acquire A and C now, and then replace A with B in 5 years.

TABLE 22-2 Analysis of Capital Investment Alternatives for Basin Corporation

The five alternatives and their net present values are summarized. Investments A and B are mutually exclusive.

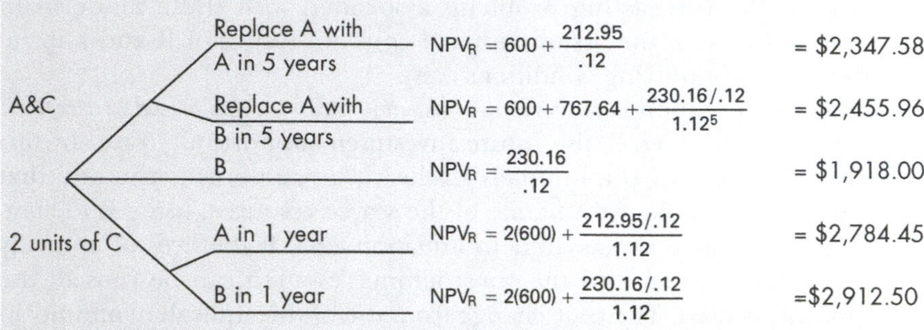

SUMMARY

Capital rationing occurs when a company limits the total capital budget, thereby forcing it to choose between capital investments with positive net present values. Capital rationing may be imposed by the capital markets or may be the result of management decisions.

Capital market–imposed rationing may be the result of (1) friction costs or other problems resulting in vertical segments in the cost of capital schedule or (2) absolute inability to raise additional capital.

Managers may use capital rationing as a means of controlling the amount and direction of growth. Capital rationing also is viewed as a way to control risk. Managers may use capital rationing as a surrogate method for dealing with other scarce resources such as management time. Managers may use capital rationing because they are unhappy with control problems or other unfavorable aspects of new funds acquisition. Capital rationing also forces competition for scarce resources, and may result in better investment proposals working their way through the decision process.

A general wealth-maximizing solution under capital rationing requires the identification of the set of investments that maximizes terminal wealth, given the investment opportunities this period and every other period. Since the returns on marginal cash flows in future periods generally depend on the amount of cash flow in those periods, a complex joint selection problem is involved, and mathematical programming is generally required.

Fortunately, selection according to the net present value using the reinvestment opportunity rate as the discount rate leads to wealth maximization under reasonable simplifying assumptions. The profitability index and internal rate of return rankings, if properly applied, can lead to rankings that maximize value under capital rationing by leading to the choice of the same set of investments that would be chosen using the net present value criterion directly.

After a wide variety of capital investment selection problems have been considered, the conclusion is that a properly computed net present value is the superior criterion when the various criteria give conflicting rankings. It has also been demonstrated that when internal rate of return and net present value signals conflict under capital rationing, the net present value signals are correct.

QUESTIONS

22-1. What is meant by the expression **capital rationing?**

22-2. Why would managers voluntarily ration capital?

22-3. What conditions could lead to capital market–imposed capital rationing?

22-4. What is the capital budgeting objective when capital rationing is experienced?

22-5. What simplifying assumptions are necessary for the optimal investment set under capital rationing to be the set that maximizes net present value, using the investment opportunity rate as the required return? Are these assumptions reasonable enough to use in practical decision making?

22-6. If capital rationing is not expected to occur after selection from the current set of proposed projects in the current period, what is the appropriate method for capital investment selection?

22-7. Under what conditions will an internal rate of return ranking give the optimal set of capital investments under capital rationing?

22-8. If the internal rate of return is being used in a capital rationing situation, which internal rate of return is the appropriate one when there is more than one internal rate of return?

22-9. Discuss the usefulness of the profitability index in a capital rationing situation.

22-10. What assumption is necessary to use Equation 22-4 when both capital rationing and mutual exclusiveness problems are encountered?

PROBLEMS

22-1. Athens Product Company has $1 million of internally generated funds available, at a required return of 10 percent. To raise additional external funds, friction costs would increase the required return to 14 percent. The company has available the following investments:

INVESTMENT	AMOUNT	IRR
A	$500,000	20%
B	500,000	15
C	500,000	12
D	500,000	10

a. Will the company experience capital rationing?
b. How much will the company invest?

22-2. Bowling Green Corporation has $1 million of internally generated funds available to invest. The required return on these funds is 12 percent, and friction costs will increase the required return on new capital to 16 percent. The company has the investment opportunities shown below.

INVESTMENT	AMOUNT	IRR
A	$500,000	20%
B	500,000	18
C	500,000	19
D	500,000	15

a. Will the company experience capital rationing?
b. How much will the company invest?

22-3. Cleveland Consolidated is expecting capital rationing to last for the next 3 years. The company's cost of capital is 10 percent, and that cost of capital is expected to continue indefinitely. Cash flows available prior to year 3 are expected to earn a rate of return of 20 percent a year until the end of capital rationing. A proposed capital investment costs $100,000 and is expected to generate cash flows of $30,000 at the end of each year for 6 years. Is the investment attractive? Why?

22-4. For Cleveland Consolidated (problem 3), a mutually exclusive investment to the investment in the previous problem has a cost of $100,000 and generates cash flows of $50,000 at the end of each year for 3 years. Which investment is preferred? Why?

22-5. Akron Transportation Service is operating under capital rationing, and expects to be in a capital rationing environment for 3 years. The cost of capital is 10 percent. A $100,000 capital investment will provide cash flows of $30,000 at the end of each year for 5 years. Funds not used immediately can be invested until the end of the capital rationing period at a 20 percent annual return. Funds available at the end of the first year can be invested at 18 percent until the end of the rationing period, and funds available at the end of the second year can be invested for 1 year at 15 percent. Is that capital investment attractive? Why?

22-6. Oxford Supply has $1 million available to invest this period. The cost of capital is 10 percent, and is expected to remain at 10 percent in future periods. The company faces capital rationing and will not be able to raise additional funds. The capital rationing is expected to last for 2 years. Funds available at year 1 can be invested to earn 20 percent for the remaining year. Any idle funds not invested in capital investments now can be invested in temporary money market securities at an 8.3 percent return for 1 year. The company is considering one investment. The investment will require an initial outlay of $1,000,000. This investment will provide cash flows of $400,000 after 1 year and $800,000 after 2 years. Is the investment attractive?

22-7. Toledo Electrosensor has $1 million available to invest this year. The company is experiencing capital rationing and expects to experience capital rationing for 2 years. The weighted average cost of capital is 10 percent and is expected to remain at 10 percent. Funds not used for capital investment this year can be temporarily invested to earn the cost of capital for a 1-year period. Funds available at the end of 1 year can be invested to earn 15 percent return for the following year. Initial outlays and year-end cash inflows for investments being considered by Toledo Electrosensor are summarized as follows:

INVESTMENT\YEAR	0	1	2
A	-500,000	300,000	350,000
B	-500,000	200,000	550,000
C	-1,000,000	300,000	1,140,000

Which investment(s) should the company choose?

22-8. For Toledo Electrosensor in the previous problem, suppose that cash flows available at the end of 1 year could be invested at a return of 25 percent for the following year. Which investment(s) should be chosen in this case?

22-9. Cincinnati Technology is facing capital rationing. The company has $1,000 of cash on hand for investment this year and is expecting an additional $1,000 from existing operations at the end of 1 year. At the end of 2 years, capital rationing will no longer be a problem. Initial outlays and year-end cash inflows from projects available now and at the end of 1 year follow.

INVESTMENT\YEAR	0	1	2	3
A		-1,000	1,200	
B	-500	0	1,000	
C		-1,000	1,300	
D		-2,000	1,200	1,500

The company's cost of capital is 10 percent. If part of the $1,000 currently available is not used, it can be invested for a year at a 6 percent risk-free interest rate. Select the optimal set of investments.

22-10. Marietta Stoneware is operating under capital rationing, and that situation is expected to continue for 5 years. The cost of capital is presently 10 percent and is not expected to change. The investment opportunity rate is 20 percent and is not expected to change for the next 5 years. A proposed capital investment costs $1 million and will provide cash flows of $300,000 at the end of each year for 5 years. Is the investment attractive? Why?

22-11. Lexington Linotype has $1 million to invest and is operating under capital rationing. The cost of capital and investment opportunity rate are 10 percent and 25 percent, respectively; neither is expected to change over the next 5 years. Initial outlays and year-end cash flows for three investment alternatives follow. Which investments, if any, should Lexington Linotype select? Why?

INVESTMENT\ YEAR	0	1	2	3	4	5
A	-500,000	100,000	100,000	200,000	200,000	400,000
B	-500,000	200,000	200,000	100,000	100,000	100,000
C	-1,000,000	300,000	300,000	300,000	300,000	300,000

22-12. Louisville Foods is operating under single-period capital rationing. The company, which has $100,000 to invest and has a 10 percent cost of capital, is considering two $100,000 investments. The first investment provides cash flows of $20,000 at the end of each year for 10 years. The second investment provides cash flows of $30,000 at the end of each year for 5 years. Which investment should be chosen? Why?

22-13. Boone Corporation faces capital rationing and is considering the following mutually exclusive investments either of which will require an outlay of $500,000. The cost of capital is 10 percent.

INVESTMENT	NPV(10%)	NPV(20%)	IRR
A	$100,000	$50,000	25%
B	150,000	10,000	21

a. Which investment should be chosen if the capital rationing is expected to occur only in the current period?

b. Which investment should be chosen if the capital rationing is expected to continue, and the reinvestment opportunity rate is 20 percent?

22-14. For the capital investments in problem 13, which capital investment should be chosen if the proceeds from either capital investment can be reinvested at the same rate of return as was earned by that investment?

22-15. Hazard Corporation is operating under capital rationing and expects to be in that condition indefinitely. Year-end cash flows for two mutually exclusive investments follow. The scarce resource can be reused for a similar investment at the end of the life of either asset. The cost of capital is 10 percent, and the investment opportunity rate is 15 percent. Which investment should be chosen?

INVESTMENT\YEAR	0	1	2	3	4
A	−1,000	400	400	400	400
B	−500	275	275	275	

22-16. A company facing capital rationing is considering the following capital investments:

INVESTMENT	COST ($ THOUSANDS)	IRR	NPV(10%)	NPV(12%)	NPV(20%)
A	500	15.24%	$69	$41	($51)
B	300	22.11	98	79	14
C	200	14.98	28	16	(23)
D	100	15.00	13	8	(11)
E	100	17.28	11	7	(3)
F	100	12.47	14	2	(28)
G	100	11.84	9	(1)	(30)

The company has $1 million available from internal sources, and a return of 10 percent is required on these funds to satisfy investors. The company could raise up to $1 million more externally, but the cost would be 20 percent.

a. Management believes that the internal rate of return on the highest IRR project that is rejected represents the reinvestment rate that will be available in future periods. Which investments should be selected?

b. Management wants to use a more conservative reinvestment rate assumption: 12 percent. Which investments should be selected?

22-17. For the set of investments in problem 16, assume the company has $1.1 million of internal funds available. Which investments would be chosen with each of the following management decisions?

a. Management believes that the internal rate of return on the highest IRR project that is rejected represents the reinvestment rate that will be available in future periods.

b. Based on a study of investments available today, management decides to base decisions on a more conservative reinvestment rate assumption: 12 percent.

c. Management decides to base the decision on an even more conservative reinvestment rate assumption: 10 percent.

22-18. Investments C and D in problem 16 are mutually exclusive. Investment C has a life of 6 years and investment D has a life of 4 years. The company assumes a 12 percent reinvestment opportunity rate in future years. If the company has $1 million to invest this period, which investments should be chosen under each of the following assumptions?

a. The scarce resource cannot be reused, and it must be used this period or not at all.

b. The scarce resource cannot be reused, but its use can be delayed until next year.

c. The scarce resource can be reused, it is possible to switch from investment type D to investment type C at the expiration of D, and the resource must be used in the current period or not at all.

d. Conditions described in (c) hold, except that the use of the resource can be delayed until next year.

22-19. **(Applications)** In late 1993, Boston Chicken, Inc., a fast-food restaurant specializing in meals of rotisserie roasted chicken, fresh vegetables, salads, and other side dishes, made an initial public offering of 1,900,000 shares or 11 percent of the company at an offer price of $20 a share. By the end of the first day of trading the stock price had reached $48. It was one of the hottest offerings in that year.

At the time of the offering Boston Chicken owned and operated 28 stores in Boston, Detroit, New York, Denver, Philadelphia, and Toledo. They had 147 stores operating under various franchise agreements and 612 stores committed to franchise agreements. Management believed that "rapid penetration in areas of dominant influence" was critical to the company.

Franchising can be considered a useful strategy to alleviate many of the constrained or rationed resources discussed in this chapter. Boston Chicken could have chosen to slow the expansion of its outlets. Instead, it opted for franchise agreements that require, on average, a franchise fee of $35,000 per store and 5 percent of gross revenue. The existing stores averaged $850,000 in sales in 1993 and this is assumed to continue with the new stores.

Use the following assumptions in answering the questions below:

- All expansion is in the form of franchised outlets.
- New stores open at a rate of 200 stores per year and this number grows at a rate of 10 percent per year until 4,000 stores are opened. (This is approximately how many Taco Bells there were at the end of 1992.)
- Cash expenses consume 91 percent of the "5 percent of revenue" so 9 percent of the fee will be cash profit.
- There is a 15 percent cost of equity with an all-equity financed firm.

a. Using the assumptions above, calculate the net present value of Boston Chicken, Inc.

b. What is 11 percent of the company worth? Why do you think the price differs from the $91,200,000 value set by the market at the end of the first day ($\$48 \times 1{,}900{,}000$ shares)?

c. Discuss the reasons you believe franchising was used by the management of Boston Chicken, Inc.

22-20. **(Ethical considerations)** You are the newly promoted Director of Strategic and Financial Planning. Part of your new job is to recommend a capital budgeting dollar level for the following year. You have put together the following list of investments along with the probability of success for each. In the past you have observed that most of the managers that have been promoted have a string of successes to their credit and no failures. The net present value of each of the investments in the list is high enough to give each a positive expected net present value. Your preliminary listing is as follows:

	COST	PROBABILITY OF SUCCESS
Replacement of current equipment	1,000,000	100%
Expansion of existing products in existing markets	500,000	75%
Introduction of new product into new markets	500,000	30%
Introduction of existing products into new markets	500,000	50%
Automation of existing plant & delivery processes	500,000	85%

a. At what level would you recommend cutting off capital investment for the coming year, given the investment listing above? What is the personal ethical dilemma here?

b. What personal or corporate limiting factors might cause you to change your decision toward capital rationing or toward accepting all of the investments?

c. If marketing is the only limiting factor and the investments all have an equal expected net present value, which investments would you recommend and in which order?

CASE PROBLEM

Heritage Corporation

Harold Gray started Heritage Corporation as a one-man carpentry shop in Lansing, Michigan, in 1892, and gradually expanded to eighty employees by the time of his retirement in 1928. Gray maintained a conservative growth pattern, rarely using debt and never turning to outside sources of equity. As a result, he handed a debt-free company to his son, John, on what turned out to be the eve of the Great Depression.

The depression was an extremely difficult time for the furniture business, although fine furniture was not hit as hard as the lower-priced lines. Many furniture companies that had grown more rapidly, with high debt and high fixed costs, went bankrupt. John credited the survival of Heritage to business skill, low fixed costs, and no debt.

John retired in 1954, turning the business over to his son, Fred, who joined other furniture companies in moving to North Carolina in 1958. This move had been under consideration since the early 1950s because labor costs in Lansing were high and the supply of prime Michigan hardwood was declining. In the following years, the firm benefited from the Baby Boom and a growing number of affluent

TABLE 22-3 Pro Forma Financial Statements for Heritage Corporation

Sales	$432,731	Current assets	$122,437
Net operating income	30,499	Fixed assets	239,439
Interest expense	2,816	Total assets	$361,876
Earnings before tax	27,683		
Income tax	8,392	Current liabilities	$ 64,138
Net income	$ 19,291	Long-term debt	44,865
		Deferred taxes	13,596
– Dividends	5,000	Common stock	239,277
+ Depreciation	15,485	Total liabilities & net worth	$361,876
+ Deferred tax increase	1,677		
= Cash flow	$ 31,453		

Americans. Fred took advantage of this position to maintain a sound growth policy through the 1960s and 1970s. By the time of his retirement in 1980, Heritage had become one of the major producers of fine furniture. Furthermore, this position had been obtained without selling outside equity and with the addition of very little debt. Because Heritage was privately owned, there was no clamor for dividends, and Fred had been able to pour nearly 90 percent of earnings back into the business. The primary debt of the company was in the form of industrial revenue bonds provided by communities as incentives for factory expansion.

Fred's retirement marked the end of an era. There was no family member to take over the business, so the reins passed to Lynn Shelby, who had come up through the marketing side of the business. The influence of the family was hardly lost in this transition. The stock was held entirely by family members, who comprised the board of directors. The family members wanted to continue the tradition of maintaining little or no debt and funding equity growth through retained earnings, but the family also wanted some dividend income. Specifically, they wanted a total dividend payment of $5 million a year. Based on the company's pro forma financial statements (Table 22-3), it appeared that $31,453,000 would be available for investment over the next year. The remaining problem was the choice of specific capital investments.

PROPOSED CAPITAL INVESTMENTS

Management was considering six capital investment proposals. (All dollar amounts and rates of return for these projects are after tax.)

1. Invest $6.4 million in an efficiency improvement program at the Greenhill

plant. The efficiency program was expected to generate after tax cash flows of $1,364,000 at the end of each year for 10 years.

2. Buy a small, specialty furniture company for $23.6 million. The company would complement Heritage's existing products, and marketing could be handled by Heritage's existing sales organization. Cash flow was expected to be $2.58 million at the end of the first year, and was expected to grow at 3 percent a year thereafter.
3. Build a new mill at Bernwood. The project would require 2 years for completion. Outlays of $5.2 million would be required immediately and another $5.8 million would be required in 1 year. Operation would begin in year 3. Cash flows would then be $2.8 million at the end of each year for 10 years, with an estimated terminal value of $5 million, after tax.
4. Invest $3 million in a new design and development center. Operating costs for the center would then be $460,000 at the end of each year. While improved designs were expected, there was no identifiable cash flow benefit.
5. Purchase tracts of young hardwood for $400 an acre. Maintenance costs would be $12 an acre, payable at the end of each year, for 15 years. The hardwood could be harvested and sold to produce cash flow of $3,100 an acre. Immediately after harvest, the land would have a value of $200 an acre. At least 200,000 acres of young hardwood were available, in plots of almost every possible size. Timberland is easily bought and sold at any state of maturity to provide the owners the same rate of return regardless of how long it is held.
6. Invest in 1-year U.S. government securities yielding 7.1 percent after tax, or buy 5-year U.S. government securities yielding 8.9 percent after tax.

Due to uncertainty in the business, Heritage generally used a 10-year planning horizon for evaluating new investments. However, exceptions were made in certain cases, such as purchase of timber stands. It was impossible to evaluate these investments unless a longer life was considered. Heritage had a weighted average cost of capital of approximately 13 percent.

Shelby knew that nothing could be done about the board's capital rationing policy immediately, but saw modification of this policy as an important objective. Shelby decided to work under the assumption that it would take 5 years to persuade the board to change its policy. Capital rationing would be eliminated if the policy was changed, although the cost of capital was not expected to change significantly.

Case Questions

1. What combination of investments will maximize shareholder wealth?
2. What combination of investments would maximize shareholder wealth if no investments earning more than the weighted average cost of capital would be available after the initial investment decision?
3. Assume existing investment opportunities other than the acquisition can be postponed until the end of the 5-year rationing period, but no other investments with returns above the weighted average cost of capital will be available. Identify the investment choices and timing that will maximize shareholder wealth.

SELECTED REFERENCES

Barbarosoglu Güulay, and David Pinhas. "Capital Rationing in the Public Sector Using the Analytical Hierarchy Process." *Engineering Economist* 40 (Summer 1995): 315–341.

Borun, Victor M., and Susan L. Malley. "Total Flotation Costs for Electric Utility Company Equity Issues." *Public Utilities Fortnightly* 117 (February 20, 1986): 33–39.

Burton, R. M., and W. W. Damon. "On the Existence of a Cost of Capital under Pure Capital Rationing." *Journal of Finance* 29 (September 1974): 1165–1173.

Dorfman, Robert. "The Meaning of Internal Rates of Return." *The Journal of Finance* 36 (December 1981): 1011–1021.

Forsyth, J. D., and D. J. Laughhunn. "Rationing Capital in a Telephone Company." *Financial Management* 3 (Autumn 1974): 36–43.

Gahlon, James M., and Roger D. Stover. "Debt Capacity and the Capital Budgeting Decision: A Caveat." *Financial Management* 8 (Winter 1979): 55–59.

Gitman, Larry J., and J. R. Forrester, Jr. "A Survey of Capital Expenditure Techniques Used by Major U.S. Firms." *Financial Management* 6 (Fall 1977): 66–71.

Jagannathan, Ravi, and Iwan Meier. "Do We Need CAPM for Capital Budgeting?" *Financial Management* 31 (Winter 2002): 55–77.

Kira, Dennis, Martin Kusy, and Ian Rakita. "The Effect of Project Risk on Capital Rationing under Uncertainty." *The Engineering Economist* 45 #1 (2000): 37–55.

Klammer, Thomas, Bruce Koch, and Neil Wilner. "Capital Budgeting Practices—A Survey of Corporate Use." University of North Texas, mimeo, 1988.

Litzenberger, Robert H., and O. Maurice Joy. "Decentralized Capital Budgeting Decisions and Shareholder Wealth Maximization." *Journal of Finance* 30 (September 1975): 993–1002.

Martin, John D., and David F. Scott, Jr. "Debt Capacity and the Capital Budgeting Decision." *Financial Management* 5 (Summer 1976): 7–14.

———. "Debt Capacity and the Capital Budgeting Decision: A Revisitation." *Financial Management* 9 (Spring 1980): 23–26.

Myers, Stewart C. "The Capital Structure Puzzle." *Journal of Finance* 39 (July 1984): 575–592.

Petty, J. W., D. F. Scott, and M. M. Bird. "The Capital Expenditure Decision-Making Process of Large Corporations." *Engineering Economist* 20 (Spring 1975): 159–172.

Rhee, S. Ghon, and Franklin L. McCarthy. "Corporate Debt Capacity and Capital Budgeting Analysis." *Financial Management* 11 (Summer 1982): 42–50.

Ross, Marc. "Capital Budgeting Practices of Twelve Large Manufacturers." *Financial Management* 15 (Winter 1986): 15–22.

Statman, Meir, and Tyzoon T. Tyebjee. "Optimistic Capital Budget Forecasts." *Financial Management* 14 (Autumn 1985): 27–33.

Wei, Chiu-Chi, Chie-Bein Chen, and Chih-Hung Tsai. "An Efficient Approach to Prioritize Projects under Budget Constraints." *The Engineering Economist* 44 # 3 (1999): 261–275.

Weingartner, H. Martin. "Capital Rationing: Authors in Search of a Plot." *Journal of Finance* 32 (December 1977): 1403–1431.

Whited, Toni M. "Debt, Liquidity Constraints, and Corporate Investment: Evidence from Panel Data." *Journal of Finance* 47 (September 1992): 1425–1460.

Wright, F. K. "Project Evaluation and the Managerial Limit." *Journal of Business* (April 1964): 179–185.

IBM

International Business Machines, commonly referred to as IBM or Big Blue, was one of the great long-term success stories in American business. The company was formed in 1911 as Computing-Tabulating-Recording Company and went on to become the country's dominant producer of information handling equipment, including computers and office typewriters. After seven decades in business, the company was still growing at over 15 percent a year.

IBM's stock had been an extremely profitable investment over the years. However, there were still critics who suggested that wealth could be increased more rapidly by a more aggressive approach to capital structure and dividend policy. This debate was particularly relevant in 1984 as competition was heating up in the rapidly expanding microcomputer market and IBM was considering its first acquisition in 20 years.

IBM's financial statements for years prior to 1984 appear in Table V-1. These are supplemented by a 10-year history of stock-related information in Table V-2. Table V-3 includes a detailed breakdown of long-term debt. Most notable are an extremely conservative balance sheet and a declining dividend payout ratio. It is hard to compare a company like IBM to any peer group, but the average large competitor maintained a debt ratio of approximately 54 percent and a dividend payout ratio of approximately 41 percent. Times interest earned ratios of leading competitors were less than half that of IBM.

The critics of IBM focused on three facts:

1. The company held almost $5 billion in marketable securities, accounting for 13 percent of total assets. With short-term interest rates under 9 percent, it was argued that this money should be invested in the company, paid out in the form of dividends, or used to repurchase common stock.
2. The debt ratio was far below the industry average, despite IBM being the industry leader. It was argued that IBM should be able to carry more debt than other companies in the industry and, therefore, was not at its optimal capital structure. This meant higher taxes and less advantage of leverage for the stockholders.
3. The declining dividend payout ratio was criticized in light of the falling debt ratio and the growing balance of marketable securities. As shown in Table V-2, most companies had increased their payout ratios over the 10-year period, while IBM's payout ratio had declined. Likewise, price-earnings ratios had increased for other companies and decreased for IBM during the period. Money was available to pay dividends, and failure to increase dividends may have signaled shareholders that declines in earnings growth were coming, resulting in lower price-earnings ratios than had occurred in the early 1970s.

TABLE V-1 IBM Financial Statements (in $ millions)

	1980	1981	1982	1983
Sales	$10,919	$12,901	$16,815	$23,274
Rentals	$10,869	10,839	11,121	9,230
Services	4,425	5,330	6,428	7,676
Total revenue	$26,213	$29,070	$34,364	$40,180
Cost of sales	4,238	5,162	6,682	9,748
Cost of rentals	3,841	4,041	3,959	3,141
Cost of services	2,187	2,534	3,047	3,506
Selling & admin.	8,094	8,383	9,286	10,614
Research & devel.	2,287	2,451	3,042	3,582
Interest expense	273	407	454	390
Other income	430	368	328	741
Inc. before tax	5,723	6,460	8,222	9,940
Income tax	2,326	2,850	3,813	4,455
Net income	$ 3,397	$ 3,610	$ 4,409	$ 5,485
Cash dividends	2,008	2,023	2,053	2,251
Cash		$ 454	$ 405	$ 616
Marketable sec.		1,575	2,895	4,920
Notes & accts rec.		4,382	4,976	5,735
Other accts rec.		410	457	645
Inventory		2,803	3,492	4,381
Prepaid exp.		685	789	973
Total CA		10,309	13,014	17,270
Rental machines		9,252	9,117	6,812
Plant & equip.		7,545	8,446	9,330
Other assets		2,001	1,964	3,831
Total assets	$26,381	$29,107	$32,541	$37,243
Tax liabilities		$ 2,412	$ 2,584	$ 3,220
Loans payable		773	529	532
Wages payable		1,556	1,959	2,450
Other current liab.		2,585	3,137	3,305
Total CL		7,326	8,209	9,507
Deferred inv. tax cr.		252	323	713
Pension plan reserves		1,184	1,198	1,130
Long-term debt	2,099	2,669	2,851	2,674
Stockholders equity	16,578	17,676	19,960	23,219
TL & NW	$26,381	$29,107	$32,541	$37,243

TABLE V-2 Stock History of IBM and the S&P 500

	1974	1975	1976	1977	1978	1979	1980	1981	1982	1983
IBM*										
EPS	3.12	3.34	3.99	4.58	5.32	5.16	6.10	5.63	7.39	9.04
DPS	1.39	1.63	2.00	2.50	2.88	3.44	3.44	3.44	3.44	3.71
Payout	0.45	0.49	0.50	0.55	0.54	0.67	0.56	0.61	0.47	0.41
PE ratio	16.5	15.3	16.6	14.5	12.7	13.9	10.4	10.3	9.4	12.7
S&P 500 AVERAGES										
PE ratio	8.6	10.9	11.2	9.3	8.3	7.4	7.9	8.4	8.6	12.5
Payout	0.39	0.47	0.42	0.43	0.44	0.41	0.42	0.43	0.50	0.55

*IBM information taken from *Value Line.*

TABLE V-3 Details of IBM's Long-Term Debt (in $ millions)

9.5% notes, due 1986	$ 500
% sinking fund notes, due 1985–2003	500
10.80% notes, due 1984–1986	240
12.9% notes, due 1984–1992	678
11.6% notes, due 1984–1992	249
Foreign-denominated notes	755
Total	2,922
Current maturities	248
Total long-term debt	$2,674

IBM had 610,724,261 shares of common stock outstanding at the beginning of 1984, with a market price of $120 a share. The beta for IBM was close to 1.0, and IBM's bonds were rated Aaa. Interest rates were as follows in early 1984.

3-month Treasury bills	8.93%
Aaa corporate bonds	12.20%
Long-term U.S. government bonds	11.67%
Baa corporate bonds	13.65%

The computer marketplace was in the midst of two revolutions in 1984. One revolution started with the introduction of PCs. By 1984, IBM was winning the battle to set the industry standards. It was becoming increasingly clear that competitors would be forced to follow the operating standards set by IBM. Unfortunately, though, competitors were doing this entirely too well. Low-priced clones were a formidable source of competition and were squeezing profit margins.

Finding a way to set standards while maintaining market share and profitability in this important area would be a major challenge.

At the other end of the market, a bitter battle was shaping up for the automated office. The automated office would have an information processing system with a telecommunications system at its center. Both voice communications and communications among computers are handled through this same nerve system. AT&T, the leader in telecommunications systems, had expanded into computer lines and was prepared to offer a complete integrated system. IBM had the advantage in computers, but had yet to develop a telecommunications system to use in offering an integrated package. An acquisition of another company to gain a strong position in telecommunications could easily cost $1 billion.

Case Questions

1. What are the possible reasons for holding almost $5 billion in marketable securities? Should the level of marketable securities be changed?
2. Does IBM have excess debt capacity? In answering this question, consider stability of cash flow in relation to debt repayment obligations as well as cash reserves, access to capital markets, and IBM's competitive position in the industry.
3. Plot IBM's earnings per share and dividends per share on a graph. Identify the dividend policy followed as well as any possible change in dividend policy. What would be the possible reasons for changes in dividend policy?
4. Compute the weighted average cost of capital for IBM, given its 1983 capital structure.
5. Recommend a policy with regard to capital structure, dividends, and marketable securities.

APPENDIX A

Mathematical Tables

TABLE A-1 Future Value of a Single Payment of \$1 = $(1 + k)^n$

Periods (n)	Percent (k) 1%	2%	3%	4%	5%	6%	7%	8%	9%	10%	12%	14%	15%	18%	20%	25%
1	1.0100	1.0200	1.0300	1.0400	1.0500	1.0600	1.0700	1.0800	1.0900	1.1000	1.1200	1.1400	1.1500	1.1800	1.2000	1.2500
2	1.0201	1.0404	1.0609	1.0816	1.1025	1.1236	1.1449	1.1664	1.1881	1.2100	1.2544	1.2996	1.3225	1.3924	1.4400	1.5625
3	1.0303	1.0612	1.0927	1.1249	1.1576	1.1910	1.2250	1.2597	1.2950	1.3310	1.4049	1.4815	1.5209	1.6430	1.7280	1.9531
4	1.0406	1.0824	1.1255	1.1699	1.2155	1.2625	1.3108	1.3605	1.4116	1.4641	1.5735	1.6890	1.7490	1.9388	2.0736	2.4414
5	1.0510	1.1041	1.1593	1.2167	1.2763	1.3382	1.4026	1.4693	1.5386	1.6105	1.7623	1.9254	2.0114	2.2878	2.4883	3.0518
6	1.0615	1.1262	1.1941	1.2653	1.3401	1.4185	1.5007	1.5869	1.6771	1.7716	1.9738	2.1950	2.3131	2.6996	2.9860	3.8147
7	1.0721	1.1487	1.2299	1.3159	1.4071	1.5036	1.6058	1.7138	1.8280	1.9487	2.2107	2.5023	2.6600	3.1855	3.5832	4.7684
8	1.0829	1.1717	1.2668	1.3686	1.4775	1.5938	1.7182	1.8509	1.9926	2.1436	2.4760	2.8526	3.0590	3.7589	4.2998	5.9605
9	1.0937	1.1951	1.3048	1.4233	1.5513	1.6895	1.8385	1.9990	2.1719	2.3579	2.7731	3.2519	3.5179	4.4355	5.1598	7.4506
10	1.1046	1.2190	1.3439	1.4802	1.6289	1.7908	1.9672	2.1589	2.3674	2.5937	3.1058	3.7072	4.0456	5.2338	6.1917	9.3132
11	1.1157	1.2434	1.3842	1.5395	1.7103	1.8983	2.1049	2.3316	2.5804	2.8531	3.4785	4.2262	4.6524	6.1759	7.4301	11.642
12	1.1268	1.2682	1.4258	1.6010	1.7959	2.0122	2.2522	2.5182	2.8127	3.1384	3.8960	4.8179	5.3503	7.2876	8.9161	14.552
13	1.1381	1.2936	1.4685	1.6651	1.8856	2.1329	2.4098	2.7196	3.0658	3.4523	4.3635	5.4924	6.1528	8.5994	10.699	18.190
14	1.1495	1.3195	1.5126	1.7317	1.9799	2.2609	2.5785	2.9372	3.3417	3.7975	4.8871	6.2613	7.0757	10.147	12.839	22.737
15	1.1610	1.3459	1.5580	1.8009	2.0789	2.3966	2.7590	3.1722	3.6425	4.1772	5.4736	7.1379	8.1371	11.974	15.407	28.422
16	1.1726	1.3728	1.6047	1.8730	2.1829	2.5404	2.9522	3.4259	3.9703	4.5950	6.1304	8.1372	9.3576	14.129	18.488	35.527
17	1.1843	1.4002	1.6528	1.9479	2.2920	2.6928	3.1588	3.7000	4.3276	5.0545	6.8660	9.2765	10.761	16.672	22.186	44.409
18	1.1961	1.4282	1.7024	2.0258	2.4066	2.8543	3.3799	3.9960	4.7171	5.5599	7.6900	10.575	12.375	19.673	26.623	55.511
19	1.2081	1.4568	1.7535	2.1068	2.5270	3.0256	3.6165	4.3157	5.1417	6.1159	8.6128	12.056	14.232	23.214	31.948	69.389
20	1.2202	1.4859	1.8061	2.1911	2.6533	3.2071	3.8697	4.6610	5.6044	6.7275	9.6463	13.743	16.367	27.393	38.338	86.736
21	1.2324	1.5157	1.8603	2.2788	2.7860	3.3996	4.1406	5.0338	6.1088	7.4002	10.804	15.668	18.822	32.324	46.005	108.42
22	1.2447	1.5460	1.9161	2.3699	2.9253	3.6035	4.4304	5.4365	6.6586	8.1403	12.100	17.861	21.645	38.142	52.206	135.53
23	1.2572	1.5769	1.9736	2.4647	3.0715	3.8197	4.7405	5.8715	7.2579	8.9543	13.552	20.362	24.891	45.008	66.247	169.41
24	1.2697	1.6084	2.0328	2.5633	3.2251	4.0489	5.0724	6.3412	7.9111	9.8497	15.179	23.212	28.625	53.109	79.497	211.76
25	1.2824	1.6406	2.0938	2.6658	3.3864	4.2919	5.4274	6.8485	8.6231	10.835	17.000	26.462	32.919	62.669	95.396	264.70
30	1.3478	1.8114	2.4273	3.2434	4.3219	5.7435	7.6123	10.063	13.268	17.449	29.960	50.950	66.212	143.37	237.38	807.79
35	1.4166	1.9999	2.8139	3.9461	5.5160	7.6861	10.677	14.785	20.414	28.102	52.800	98.100	133.18	328.00	590.67	2465.2
40	1.4889	2.2080	3.2620	4.8010	7.0400	10.286	14.974	21.725	31.409	45.259	93.051	188.88	267.86	750.38	1469.8	7523.2
45	1.5648	2.4379	3.7816	5.8412	8.9850	13.765	21.002	31.920	48.327	72.890	163.99	363.68	538.77	1716.7	3657.3	22958
50	1.6446	2.6916	4.3839	7.1067	11.467	18.420	29.457	46.902	74.358	117.39	289.00	700.23	1083.7	3927.4	9100.4	70064

TABLE A-2 Present Value of a Single Payment of $1 = $\frac{1}{(1+k)^n}$

n/k	1%	2%	3%	4%	5%	6%	7%	8%	9%	10%	12%	14%	15%	18%	20%	25%
1	0.9901	0.9804	0.9709	0.9615	0.9524	0.9434	0.9346	0.9259	0.9174	0.9091	0.8929	0.8772	0.8696	0.8475	0.8333	0.8000
2	0.9803	0.9612	0.9426	0.9246	0.9070	0.8900	0.8734	0.8573	0.8417	0.8264	0.7972	0.7695	0.7561	0.7182	0.6944	0.6400
3	0.9706	0.9423	0.9151	0.8890	0.8638	0.8396	0.8163	0.7938	0.7722	0.7513	0.7118	0.6750	0.6575	0.6086	0.5787	0.5120
4	0.9610	0.9238	0.8885	0.8548	0.8227	0.7921	0.7629	0.7350	0.7084	0.6830	0.6335	0.5921	0.5718	0.5158	0.4823	0.4096
5	0.9515	0.9057	0.8626	0.8219	0.7835	0.7473	0.7130	0.6806	0.6499	0.6209	0.5674	0.5194	0.4972	0.4371	0.4019	0.3277
6	0.9420	0.8880	0.8375	0.7903	0.7462	0.7050	0.6663	0.6302	0.5963	0.5645	0.5066	0.4556	0.4323	0.3704	0.3349	0.2621
7	0.9327	0.8706	0.8131	0.7599	0.7107	0.6651	0.6227	0.5835	0.5470	0.5132	0.4523	0.3996	0.3759	0.3139	0.2791	0.2097
8	0.9235	0.8535	0.7894	0.7307	0.6768	0.6274	0.5820	0.5403	0.5019	0.4665	0.4039	0.3506	0.3269	0.2660	0.2326	0.1678
9	0.9143	0.8368	0.7664	0.7026	0.6446	0.5919	0.5439	0.5002	0.4604	0.4241	0.3606	0.3075	0.2843	0.2255	0.1938	0.1342
10	0.9053	0.8203	0.7441	0.6756	0.6139	0.5584	0.5083	0.4632	0.4224	0.3855	0.3220	0.2697	0.2472	0.1911	0.1615	0.1074
11	0.8963	0.8043	0.7224	0.6496	0.5847	0.5268	0.4751	0.4289	0.3875	0.3505	0.2875	0.2366	0.2149	0.1619	0.1346	0.0859
12	0.8874	0.7885	0.7014	0.6246	0.5568	0.4970	0.4440	0.3971	0.3555	0.3186	0.2567	0.2076	0.1869	0.1372	0.1122	0.0687
13	0.8787	0.7730	0.6810	0.6006	0.5303	0.4688	0.4150	0.3677	0.3262	0.2897	0.2292	0.1821	0.1625	0.1163	0.0935	0.0550
14	0.8700	0.7579	0.6611	0.5775	0.5051	0.4423	0.3878	0.3405	0.2992	0.2633	0.2046	0.1597	0.1413	0.0985	0.0779	0.0440
15	0.8613	0.7430	0.6419	0.5553	0.4810	0.4173	0.3624	0.3152	0.2745	0.2394	0.1827	0.1401	0.1229	0.0835	0.0649	0.0352
16	0.8528	0.7284	0.6232	0.5339	0.4581	0.3936	0.3387	0.2919	0.2519	0.2176	0.1631	0.1229	0.1069	0.0708	0.0541	0.0281
17	0.8444	0.7142	0.6050	0.5134	0.4363	0.3714	0.3166	0.2703	0.2311	0.1978	0.1456	0.1078	0.0929	0.0600	0.0451	0.0225
18	0.8360	0.7002	0.5874	0.4936	0.4155	0.3503	0.2959	0.2502	0.2120	0.1799	0.1300	0.0946	0.0808	0.0508	0.0376	0.0180
19	0.8277	0.6864	0.5703	0.4746	0.3957	0.3305	0.2765	0.2317	0.1945	0.1635	0.1161	0.0829	0.0703	0.0431	0.0313	0.0144
20	0.8195	0.6730	0.5537	0.4564	0.3769	0.3118	0.2584	0.2145	0.1784	0.1486	0.1037	0.0728	0.0611	0.0365	0.0261	0.0115
21	0.8114	0.6598	0.5375	0.4388	0.3589	0.2942	0.2415	0.1987	0.1637	0.1351	0.0926	0.0638	0.0531	0.0309	0.0217	0.0092
22	0.8034	0.6468	0.5219	0.4220	0.3418	0.2775	0.2257	0.1839	0.1502	0.1228	0.0826	0.0560	0.0462	0.0262	0.0181	0.0074
23	0.7954	0.6342	0.5067	0.4057	0.3256	0.2618	0.2109	0.1703	0.1378	0.1117	0.0738	0.0491	0.0402	0.0222	0.0151	0.0059
24	0.7876	0.6217	0.4919	0.3901	0.3101	0.2470	0.1971	0.1577	0.1264	0.1015	0.0659	0.0431	0.0349	0.0188	0.0126	0.0047
25	0.7798	0.6095	0.4776	0.3751	0.2953	0.2330	0.1842	0.1460	0.1160	0.0923	0.0588	0.0378	0.0304	0.0160	0.0105	0.0038
30	0.7419	0.5521	0.4120	0.3083	0.2314	0.1741	0.1314	0.0994	0.0754	0.0573	0.0334	0.0196	0.0151	0.0070	0.0042	0.0012
35	0.7059	0.5000	0.3554	0.2534	0.1813	0.1301	0.0937	0.0676	0.0490	0.0356	0.0189	0.0102	0.0075	0.0030	0.0017	0.0004
40	0.6717	0.4529	0.3066	0.2083	0.1420	0.0972	0.0668	0.0460	0.0318	0.0221	0.0107	0.0053	0.0037	0.0013	0.0007	0.0001
45	0.6391	0.4102	0.2644	0.1712	0.1113	0.0727	0.0476	0.0313	0.0207	0.0137	0.0061	0.0027	0.0019	0.0006	0.0003	0.0000
50	0.6080	0.3715	0.2281	0.1407	0.0872	0.0543	0.0339	0.0213	0.0134	0.0085	0.0035	0.0014	0.0009	0.0003	0.0001	0.0000

TABLE A-3 Future Value of an Annuity of $1 = $\frac{(1+k)^n - 1}{k}$

n/k	1%	2%	3%	4%	5%	6%	7%	8%	9%	10%	12%	14%	15%	18%	20%	25%
1	1.0000	1.0000	1.0000	1.0000	1.0000	1.0000	1.0000	1.0000	1.0000	1.0000	1.0000	1.0000	1.0000	1.0000	1.0000	1.0000
2	2.0100	2.0200	2.0300	2.0400	2.0500	2.0600	2.0700	2.0800	2.0900	2.1000	2.1200	2.1400	2.1500	2.1800	2.2000	2.2500
3	3.0301	3.0604	3.0909	3.1216	3.1525	3.1836	3.2149	3.2464	3.2781	3.3100	3.3744	3.4396	3.4725	3.5724	3.6400	3.8125
4	4.0604	4.1216	4.1836	4.2465	4.3101	4.3746	4.4399	4.5061	4.5731	4.6410	4.7793	4.9211	4.9934	5.2154	5.3680	5.7656
5	5.1010	5.2040	5.3091	5.4163	5.5256	5.6371	5.7507	5.8666	5.9847	6.1051	6.3528	6.6101	6.7424	7.1542	7.4416	8.2070
6	6.1520	6.3081	6.4684	6.6330	6.8019	6.9753	7.1533	7.3359	7.5233	7.7156	8.1152	8.5355	8.7537	9.4420	9.9299	11.259
7	7.2135	7.4343	7.6625	7.8983	8.1420	8.3938	8.6540	8.9228	9.2004	9.4872	10.089	10.730	11.067	12.142	12.916	15.073
8	8.2857	8.5830	8.8923	9.2142	9.5491	9.8975	10.260	10.637	11.028	11.436	12.300	13.233	13.727	15.327	16.499	19.842
9	9.3685	9.7546	10.159	10.583	11.027	11.491	11.978	12.488	13.021	13.579	14.776	16.085	16.786	19.086	20.799	25.802
10	10.462	10.950	11.464	12.006	12.578	13.181	13.816	14.487	15.193	15.937	17.549	19.337	20.304	23.521	25.959	33.253
11	11.567	12.169	12.808	13.486	14.207	14.972	15.784	16.645	17.560	18.531	20.655	23.045	24.349	28.755	32.150	42.566
12	12.683	13.412	14.192	15.026	15.917	16.870	17.888	18.977	20.141	21.384	24.133	27.271	29.002	34.931	39.581	54.208
13	13.809	14.680	15.618	16.627	17.713	18.882	20.141	21.495	22.953	24.523	28.029	32.089	34.352	42.219	48.497	68.760
14	14.947	15.974	17.086	18.292	19.599	21.015	22.550	24.215	26.019	27.975	32.393	37.581	40.505	50.818	59.196	86.949
15	16.097	17.293	18.599	20.024	21.579	23.276	25.129	27.152	29.361	31.772	37.280	43.842	47.850	60.965	72.035	109.68
16	17.258	18.639	20.157	21.825	23.657	25.673	27.888	30.324	33.003	35.950	42.753	50.980	55.717	72.939	87.442	138.10
17	18.430	20.012	21.762	23.698	25.840	28.213	30.840	33.750	36.974	40.545	48.884	59.118	65.075	87.068	105.93	173.63
18	19.615	21.412	23.414	25.645	28.132	30.906	33.999	37.450	41.301	45.599	55.750	68.394	75.836	103.74	128.11	218.04
19	20.811	22.841	25.117	27.671	30.539	33.760	37.379	41.446	46.018	51.159	63.440	78.969	88.212	123.41	154.73	273.55
20	22.019	24.397	26.870	29.778	33.066	36.786	40.995	45.762	51.160	52.275	72.052	91.025	102.44	146.62	186.68	342.94
21	23.239	25.783	28.676	31.969	35.719	39.993	44.865	50.423	56.765	64.002	81.699	104.76	118.81	174.02	225.02	429.68
22	24.472	27.299	30.537	34.248	38.505	43.392	49.006	55.457	62.873	71.403	92.503	120.43	137.63	206.34	271.03	538.10
23	25.716	28.845	32.453	36.618	41.430	46.996	53.436	60.893	69.532	79.543	104.60	138.29	159.27	244.48	326.23	673.62
24	26.973	30.422	34.426	39.083	44.502	50.816	58.177	66.765	76.790	88.497	118.15	158.65	184.16	288.49	392.48	843.03
25	28.243	32.030	36.459	41.646	47.727	54.865	63.249	73.106	84.701	98.347	133.33	181.87	212.79	342.60	471.98	1054.7
30	34.785	40.568	47.575	56.085	66.439	79.058	94.461	113.28	136.31	164.49	241.33	356.79	434.75	790.95	1181.8	3227.1
35	41.660	49.994	60.462	73.652	90.320	111.43	138.24	172.32	215.71	271.02	431.66	693.57	881.17	1816.7	2948.3	9856.8
40	48.886	60.402	75.401	95.026	120.80	154.76	199.64	259.06	337.88	442.59	767.09	1342.0	1779.1	4163.2	7343.8	30088
45	56.481	71.893	92.720	121.03	159.70	212.74	285.75	386.51	525.86	718.90	1358.2	2590.6	3585.1	9531.5	18281	91831
50	64.463	84.579	112.80	152.67	209.35	290.34	406.53	573.77	815.08	1163.9	2400.0	4994.5	7217.7	21813	45497	280255

TABLE A-4 Present Value of an Annuity of \$1 = $\frac{1 - 1/(1+k)^n}{k}$

n/k	1%	2%	3%	4%	5%	6%	7%	8%	9%	10%	12%	14%	15%	18%	20%	25%
1	0.9901	0.9804	0.9709	0.9615	0.9524	0.9434	0.9346	0.9259	0.9174	0.9091	0.8929	0.8772	0.8696	0.8475	0.8333	0.8000
2	1.9704	1.9416	1.9135	1.8861	1.8594	1.8334	1.8080	1.7833	1.7591	1.7355	1.6901	1.6467	1.6257	1.5656	1.5278	1.4400
3	2.9410	2.8839	2.8286	2.7751	2.7232	2.6730	2.6243	2.5771	2.5313	2.4869	2.4018	2.3216	2.2832	2.1743	2.1065	1.9520
4	3.9020	3.8077	3.7171	3.6299	3.5460	3.4651	3.3872	3.3121	3.2397	3.1699	3.0373	2.9137	2.8550	2.6901	2.5887	2.3616
5	4.8534	4.7135	4.5797	4.4518	4.3295	4.2124	4.1002	3.9927	3.8897	3.7908	3.6048	3.4331	3.3522	3.1272	2.9906	2.6893
6	5.7955	5.6014	5.4172	5.2421	5.0757	4.9173	4.7665	4.6229	4.4859	4.3553	4.1114	3.8887	3.7845	3.4976	3.3255	2.9514
7	6.7282	6.4720	6.2303	6.0021	5.7864	5.5824	5.3893	5.2064	5.0330	4.8684	4.5638	4.2883	4.1604	3.8115	3.6046	3.1611
8	7.6517	7.3255	7.0197	6.7327	6.4632	6.2098	5.9713	5.7466	5.5348	5.3349	4.9676	4.6389	4.4873	4.0776	3.8372	3.3289
9	8.5660	8.1622	7.7861	7.4353	7.1078	6.8017	6.5152	6.2469	5.9952	5.7590	5.3282	4.9464	4.7716	4.3030	4.0310	3.4631
10	9.4713	8.9826	8.5302	8.1109	7.7217	7.3601	7.0236	6.7101	6.4177	6.1446	5.6502	5.2161	5.0188	4.4941	4.1925	3.5705
11	10.368	9.7868	9.2526	8.7605	8.3064	7.8869	7.4987	7.1390	6.8052	6.4951	5.9377	5.4527	5.2337	4.6560	4.3271	3.6564
12	11.255	10.575	9.9540	9.3851	8.8633	8.3838	7.9427	7.5361	7.1607	6.8137	6.1944	5.6603	5.4206	4.7932	4.4392	3.7251
13	12.134	11.348	10.635	9.9856	9.3936	8.8527	8.3577	7.9038	7.4869	7.1034	6.4235	5.8424	5.5831	4.9095	4.5327	3.7801
14	13.004	12.106	11.296	10.563	9.8986	9.2950	8.7455	8.2442	7.7862	7.3667	6.6282	6.0021	5.7245	5.0081	4.6106	3.8241
15	13.865	12.849	11.938	11.118	10.380	9.7122	9.1079	8.5595	8.0607	7.6061	6.8109	6.1422	5.8474	5.0916	4.6755	3.8593
16	14.718	13.578	12.561	11.652	10.838	10.106	9.4466	8.8514	8.3126	7.8237	6.9740	6.2651	5.9542	5.1624	4.7296	3.8874
17	15.562	14.292	13.166	12.166	11.274	10.477	9.7632	9.1216	8.5436	8.0216	7.1196	6.3729	6.0472	5.2223	4.7746	3.9099
18	16.398	14.992	13.754	12.659	11.690	10.828	10.059	9.3719	8.7556	8.2014	7.2497	6.4674	6.1280	5.2732	4.8122	3.9279
19	17.226	15.678	14.324	13.134	12.085	11.158	10.336	9.6036	8.9501	8.3649	7.3658	6.5504	6.1982	5.3162	4.8435	3.9424
20	18.046	16.351	14.877	13.590	12.462	11.470	10.594	9.8181	9.1285	8.5136	7.4694	6.6231	6.2593	5.3527	4.8696	3.9539
21	18.857	17.011	15.415	14.029	12.821	11.764	10.836	10.017	9.2922	8.6487	7.5620	6.6870	6.3125	5.3837	4.8913	3.9631
22	19.660	17.658	15.937	14.451	13.163	12.042	11.061	10.201	9.4424	8.7715	7.6446	6.7429	6.3587	5.4099	4.9094	3.9705
23	20.456	18.292	16.444	14.857	13.489	12.303	11.272	10.371	9.5802	8.8832	7.7184	6.7921	6.3988	5.4321	4.9245	3.9764
24	21.243	18.914	16.936	15.247	13.799	12.550	11.469	10.529	9.7066	8.9847	7.7843	6.8351	6.4338	5.4509	4.9371	3.9811
25	22.023	19.523	17.413	15.622	14.094	12.783	11.654	10.675	9.8226	9.0770	7.8431	6.8729	6.4641	5.4669	4.9476	3.9849
30	25.808	22.396	19.600	17.292	15.372	13.765	12.409	11.258	10.274	9.4269	8.0552	7.0027	6.5660	5.5168	4.9789	3.9950
35	29.409	24.999	21.487	18.665	16.374	14.498	12.948	11.655	10.567	9.6442	8.1755	7.0700	6.6166	5.5386	4.9915	3.9984
40	32.835	27.355	23.115	19.793	17.159	15.046	13.332	11.925	10.757	9.7791	8.2438	7.1050	6.6418	5.5482	4.9966	3.9995
45	36.095	29.490	24.519	20.720	17.774	15.456	13.606	12.108	10.881	9.8628	8.2825	7.1232	6.6543	5.5523	4.9986	3.9998
50	39.196	31.424	25.730	21.482	18.256	15.762	13.801	12.233	10.962	9.9148	8.3045	7.1327	6.6605	5.5541	4.9995	3.9999

TABLE A-5 Continuous Compounding Future Value of a Single Payment of $1 = $e^{k'n}$

n/k'	1%	2%	3%	4%	5%	6%	7%	8%	9%	10%	12%	14%	15%	18%	20%	25%
1	1.0101	1.0202	1.0305	1.0408	1.0513	1.0618	1.0725	1.0833	1.0942	1.1052	1.1275	1.1503	1.1618	1.1972	1.2214	1.2840
2	1.0202	1.0408	1.0618	1.0833	1.1052	1.1275	1.1503	1.1735	1.1972	1.2214	1.2712	1.3231	1.3499	1.4333	1.4918	1.6487
3	1.0305	1.0618	1.0942	1.1275	1.1618	1.1972	1.2337	1.2712	1.3100	1.3499	1.4333	1.5220	1.5683	1.7160	1.8221	2.1170
4	1.0408	1.0833	1.1275	1.1735	1.2214	1.2712	1.3231	1.3771	1.4333	1.4918	1.6161	1.7507	1.8221	2.0544	2.2255	2.7183
5	1.0513	1.1052	1.1618	1.2214	1.2840	1.3499	1.4191	1.4918	1.5683	1.6487	1.8221	2.0138	2.1170	2.4596	2.7183	3.4903
6	1.0618	1.1275	1.1972	1.2712	1.3499	1.4333	1.5220	1.6161	1.7160	1.8221	2.0544	2.3164	2.4596	2.9447	3.3201	4.4817
7	1.0725	1.1503	1.2337	1.3231	1.4191	1.5220	1.6323	1.7507	1.8775	2.0138	2.3164	2.6645	2.8577	3.5254	4.0552	5.7546
8	1.0833	1.1735	1.2712	1.3771	1.4918	1.6161	1.7507	1.8965	2.0544	2.2255	2.6117	3.0649	3.3201	4.2207	4.9530	7.3891
9	1.0942	1.1972	1.3100	1.4333	1.5683	1.7160	1.8776	2.0544	2.2479	2.4596	2.9447	3.5254	3.8574	5.0531	6.0496	9.4877
10	1.1052	1.2214	1.3499	1.4918	1.6487	1.8221	2.0138	2.2255	2.4596	2.7183	3.3201	4.0552	4.4817	6.0496	7.3891	12.182
11	1.1163	1.2461	1.3910	1.5527	1.7333	1.9348	2.1598	2.4109	2.6912	3.0042	3.7434	4.6646	5.2070	7.2427	9.0250	15.643
12	1.1275	1.2712	1.4333	1.6161	1.8221	2.0544	2.3164	2.6117	2.9447	3.3201	4.2207	5.3656	6.0496	8.6711	11.023	20.086
13	1.1388	1.2969	1.4770	1.6820	1.9155	2.1815	2.4843	2.8292	3.2220	3.6693	4.7588	6.1719	7.0287	10.381	13.464	25.790
14	1.1503	1.3231	1.5220	1.7507	2.0138	2.3164	2.6645	3.0649	3.5254	4.0552	5.3656	7.0993	8.1662	12.429	16.445	33.115
15	1.1618	1.3499	1.5683	1.8221	2.1170	2.4596	2.8577	3.3201	3.8574	4.4817	6.0496	8.1662	9.4877	14.880	20.086	45.251
16	1.1735	1.3771	1.6161	1.8965	2.2255	2.6117	3.0649	3.5966	4.2207	4.9530	6.8210	9.3933	11.023	17.814	24.533	54.598
17	1.1853	1.4049	1.6653	1.9739	2.3396	2.7732	3.2871	3.8962	4.6182	5.4739	7.6906	10.805	12.807	21.328	29.964	70.105
18	1.1972	1.4333	1.7160	2.0544	2.4596	2.9447	3.5254	4.2207	5.0531	6.0496	8.6711	12.429	14.880	25.534	36.598	90.017
19	1.2092	1.4623	1.7683	2.1383	2.5857	3.1268	3.7810	4.5722	5.5290	6.6859	9.7767	14.296	17.288	30.569	44.701	115.58
20	1.2214	1.4918	1.8221	2.2255	2.7183	3.3201	4.0552	4.9530	6.0496	7.3891	11.023	16.445	20.086	36.598	54.598	148.41
21	1.2337	1.5220	1.8776	2.3164	2.8577	3.5254	4.3492	5.3656	6.6194	8.1662	12.429	18.916	23.336	43.816	66.686	190.57
22	1.2461	1.5527	1.9348	2.4109	3.0042	3.7434	4.6646	5.8124	7.2427	9.0250	14.013	21.758	27.113	52.457	81.451	244.69
23	1.2586	1.5841	1.9937	2.5093	3.1582	3.9749	5.0028	6.2965	7.9248	9.9742	15.800	25.028	31.500	62.803	99.484	314.19
24	1.2712	1.6161	2.0544	2.6117	3.3201	4.2207	5.3656	6.8210	8.6711	11.023	17.814	28.789	36.598	75.189	121.51	403.43
25	1.2840	1.6487	2.1170	2.7183	3.4903	4.4817	5.7546	7.3891	9.4877	12.182	20.086	33.115	42.521	90.017	148.41	518.01
30	1.3499	1.8221	2.4596	3.3201	4.4817	6.0496	8.1662	11.023	14.880	20.086	36.598	66.686	90.017	221.4	403.4	1808.0
35	1.4191	2.0138	2.8577	4.0552	5.7546	8.1662	11.588	16.445	23.336	33.115	66.686	134.29	190.57	544.57	1096.6	6310.7
40	1.4918	2.2255	3.3201	4.9530	7.3891	11.023	16.445	24.533	36.598	54.598	121.51	270.43	403.43	1339.4	2981.0	22026
45	1.5683	2.4596	3.8574	6.0496	9.4877	14.880	23.336	36.598	57.397	90.017	221.41	544.57	854.06	3294.5	8103.1	76880
50	1.6487	2.7183	4.4817	7.3891	12.182	20.086	33.115	54.598	90.017	148.41	403.43	1096.6	1808.0	8103.1	22026	268337

APPENDIX B

The Standard Normal Distribution

z	.00	.01	.02	.03	.04	.05	.06	.07	.08	.09
0.0	.0000	.0040	.0080	.0120	.0160	.0199	.0239	.0279	.0319	.0359
0.1	.0398	.0438	.0478	.0517	.0557	.0596	.0636	.0675	.0714	.0753
0.2	.0793	.0832	.0871	.0910	.0948	.0987	.1026	.1064	.1103	.1141
0.3	.1179	.1217	.1255	.1293	.1331	.1398	.1406	.1443	.1480	.1517
0.4	.1554	.1591	.1628	.1664	.1700	.1736	.1772	.1808	.1844	.1879
0.5	.1915	.1950	.1985	.2019	.2054	.2088	.2123	.2157	.2190	.2224
0.6	.2257	.2291	.2324	.2357	.2389	.2422	.2454	.2486	.2517	.2549
0.7	.2580	.2611	.2642	.2673	.2704	.2734	.2764	.2794	.2823	.2852
0.8	.2881	.2910	.2939	.2967	.2995	.3023	.3051	.3078	.3106	.3133
0.9	.3159	.3186	.3212	.3238	.3264	.3289	.3315	.3340	.3365	.3389
1.0	.3413	.3438	.3461	.3485	.3508	.3531	.3554	.3577	.3599	.3621
1.1	.3643	.3665	.3686	.3708	.3729	.3749	.3770	.3790	.3810	.3830
1.2	.3849	.3869	.3888	.3907	.3925	.3944	.3962	.3980	.3997	.4015
1.3	.4032	.4049	.4066	.4082	.4099	.4115	.4131	.4147	.4162	.4177
1.4	.4192	.4207	.4222	.4236	.4251	.4265	.4279	.4292	.4306	.4319
1.5	.4332	.4345	.4357	.4370	.4382	.4394	.4406	.4418	.4429	.4441
1.6	.4452	.4463	.4474	.4484	.4495	.4505	.4515	.4525	.4535	.4545
1.7	.4554	.4564	.4573	.4582	.4591	.4599	.4608	.4616	.4625	.4633
1.8	.4641	.4649	.4656	.4664	.4671	.4678	.4686	.4693	.4699	.4706
1.9	.4713	.4719	.4726	.4732	.4738	.4744	.4750	.4756	.4761	.4767
2.0	.4772	.4778	.4783	.4788	.4793	.4798	.4803	.4808	.4812	.4817
2.1	.4821	.4826	.4830	.4834	.4838	.4842	.4846	.4850	.4854	.4857
2.2	.4861	.4864	.4868	.4871	.4875	.4878	.4881	.4884	.4887	.4890
2.3	.4893	.4896	.4898	.4901	.4904	.4906	.4909	.4911	.4913	.4916
2.4	.4918	.4920	.4922	.4925	.4927	.4929	.4931	.4932	.4934	.4936
2.5	.4938	.4940	.4941	.4943	.4945	.4946	.4948	.4949	.4951	.4952
2.6	.4953	.4955	.4956	.4957	.4959	.4960	.4961	.4962	.4963	.4964
2.7	.4965	.4966	.4967	.4968	.4969	.4970	.4971	.4972	.4973	.4974
2.8	.4974	.4975	.4976	.4977	.4977	.4978	.4979	.4979	.4980	.4981
2.9	.4981	.4982	.4982	.4983	.4984	.4984	.4985	.4985	.4986	.4986
3.0	.4987	.4987	.4987	.4988	.4988	.4989	.4989	.4989	.4990	.4990

Name Index

Subject Index